DEVELOPMENT ASSISTANCE POLICIES AND THE PERFORMANCE OF AID AGENCIES

This book combines in one volume studies of the major trends and structural changes of financial flows and development assistance policies, and the approaches, techniques of project appraisal and strategies of aid agencies as well as problems of project implementation based on the agencies' direct experience in the field. It covers the basic elements of three major aspects of aid: international finance, project appraisal and implementation, and economic development.

The Introduction (Chapter 1) sets out the problems to be faced, summarises the purpose and major findings of the book and makes recommendations on how the objectives of international development strategy can be met.

Part I (Chapters 2–10) discusses the performance of financial flows, development assistance policies and aid agencies in OECD/DAC member countries, with case-studies of the USA, the UK, West Germany, Japan, the Netherlands, Sweden and the EEC.

Part II (Chapters 11–25) covers the work of OPEC development funds, regional development banks and the World Bank Group, with case-studies of the Kuwait, Abu Dhabi, Saudi and Arab Funds, the Arab Bank for Economic Development in Africa, the Islamic Development Bank, the OPEC Fund for International Development, the African, Asian, Caribbean and Inter-American Development Banks, the International Bank for Reconstruction and Development, the International Development Association and the International Finance Corporation.

There are two Appendixes: Appendix I is a comparative synopsis of twenty-eight aid agencies according to standard classification while Appendix II summarises the international development strategy formulated during the second and third UN development decades (the 1970s and 1980s), including the North–South dialogue, the New International Economic Order, the Brandt Commission, World Bank development reports and the OECD research project on facing the future.

Dr Hassan M. Selim is Adviser General of the Abu Dhabi Fund for Arab Economic Development. A graduate of Cairo University, he gained scholarships from the Ford Foundation and the Egyptian Government and obtained his MA and then in 1969 his PhD (economics) at the University of Colorado, Boulder, USA. Formerly Senior

Expert at the Institute of National Planning, Cairo, he has taught at the American University in Cairo and at the University of Nebraska and has also worked at the Economic Growth Centre at Yale University. He has been Director of the Research Department and Assistant Director General of Operations of the Abu Dhabi Fund for Arab Economic Development. An active member of several international associations, he has published many articles in English and Arabic.

Development Assistance Policies and the Performance of Aid Agencies

Studies in the Performance of DAC, OPEC, the Regional Development Banks and the World Bank Group

HASSAN M. SELIM, Ph.D.

Adviser General
Abu Dhabi Fund for
Arab Economic Development

St. Martin's Press   New York

© Dr. Hassan M. Selim 1983

All rights reserved. For information, write:
St. Martin's Press, Inc., 175 Fifth Avenue, New York, NY 10010
Printed in Hong Kong
First published in the United States of America in 1983

ISBN 0-312-19669-5

Library of Congress Cataloging in Publication Data

Selim, Hassan M.
   Development assistance policies and the performance of AID agencies.

   Bibliography: p.
   Includes index.
    1. Economic assistance.   2. Economic assistance—Evaluation.   I. Title.
HC60. S417 1983   338.91   82-21550
ISBN 0-312-19669-5

To my wife Faika
and my children,
Monna and Tarek Selim

Contents

List of Charts	xii
List of Tables	xiii
List of Appendix Tables	xix
Preface	xx
List of Abbreviations	xxiv

1 INTRODUCTION
Setting out the Problem	1
Purpose of the Book	2
Summary of the Main Findings	3
Profile of the Study	4
Towards Meeting the Objectives of International Development Strategy	24

PART I The Performance of Financial Flows, Development Assistance Policies and Aid Agencies in OECD/DAC Member Countries

2 THE PERFORMANCE OF THE DEVELOPMENT ASSISTANCE COMMITTEE
	31
The Establishment of the Development Assistance Committee	31
Official Development Assistance	32
DAC Contributions to Multilateral Institutions	34
Private Flows	35

3 THE UNITED STATES OF AMERICA
	39
The Performance of US Official Development Assistance	39
US Private Flows Relative to Total Flows	40
US Development Assistance Policy	42
The Development Assistance Programme of the Agency for International Development	46

vii

The Security Supporting Assistance Programme	48
The Public Law 480 Programme	49
The Experience of AID in Project Evaluations	52

4 THE UNITED KINGDOM 55
The Performance of UK Official Development Assistance	55
UK Private Flows	59
The UK Development Assistance Policy	61
Administration of UK Financial Flows	65
The Overseas Development Administration	65
The Commonwealth Development Corporation	69

5 FRANCE 80
The Performance of French Official Development Assistance	80
French Private Flows at Market Terms	82
French Development Assistance Policy	85
Administration of French Financial Flows	88
The Experience of Caisse Centrale de Coopération Economique	88

6 WEST GERMANY 97
The Performance of West German Official Development Assistance	97
Private Flows	99
West Germany's Development Assistance Policy	101
Administration of West German Financial Flows	104
The Deutsche Entwicklungsgesellschaft	104
Kreditanstalt für Wiederaufbau	109

7 JAPAN 118
The Performance of Japan's Official Development Assistance	118
Japan's Private Flows	118
Japanese Development Assistance Policy	122
Administration of Japan's Financial Flows	124
The Overseas Economic Co-operation Fund	124
The Export-Import Bank of Japan	127
Japan International Co-operation Agency	131

8 THE NETHERLANDS ... 138
   The Performance of Dutch Official Development Assistance ... 138
   Dutch Private Flows ... 140
   Dutch Development Assistance Policy ... 142
   Administration of the Netherlands Aid Programme ... 146
      The Netherlands Investment Bank for Developing Countries ... 148
      The Netherlands Finance Company for Developing Countries ... 149

9 SWEDEN ... 157
   The Performance of Swedish Official Development Assistance ... 157
   Swedish Private Flows ... 159
   Swedish Development Assistance Policy ... 161
   Administration of the Swedish Aid Programme ... 163
      The Swedish International Development Authority ... 163

10 THE COMMISSION OF THE EUROPEAN ECONOMIC COMMUNITY ... 173
   The Performance of EEC Official Development Assistance ... 173
   Development Assistance Policy of the EEC under the Lomé Conventions ... 175
   Aid Administered by the EEC ... 180
      The European Development Fund ... 180
      The European Investment Bank ... 185

PART II The Performance of OPEC Development Funds, Regional Development Banks and the World Bank Group

11 THE PERFORMANCE OF THE ORGANISATION OF THE PETROLEUM EXPORTING COUNTRIES ... 199

12 THE KUWAIT FUND FOR ARAB ECONOMIC DEVELOPMENT ... 211

13 THE ABU DHABI FUND FOR ARAB ECONOMIC DEVELOPMENT ... 217

Contents

14　THE SAUDI FUND FOR DEVELOPMENT　225

15　THE ARAB FUND FOR ECONOMIC AND SOCIAL DEVELOPMENT　234

16　THE ARAB BANK FOR ECONOMIC DEVELOPMENT IN AFRICA　246

17　THE ISLAMIC DEVELOPMENT BANK　257

18　THE OPEC FUND FOR INTERNATIONAL DEVELOPMENT　268

19　THE AFRICAN DEVELOPMENT BANK　276

20　THE ASIAN DEVELOPMENT BANK　287

21　THE CARIBBEAN DEVELOPMENT BANK　303

22　THE INTER-AMERICAN DEVELOPMENT BANK　317

23　THE INTERNATIONAL BANK FOR RECONSTRUCTION AND DEVELOPMENT　339

24　THE INTERNATIONAL DEVELOPMENT ASSOCIATION　359

25　THE INTERNATIONAL FINANCE CORPORATION　380

APPENDIX I　A PROFILE SUMMARY OF SELECTED AID AGENCIES　403
　DAC Development Agencies　403
　OPEC Development Agencies　430
　Multinational Arab/OPEC Development Agencies　436
　Regional Development Banks　444
　The World Bank Group　460

APPENDIX II　A SURVEY OF INTERNATIONAL DEVELOPMENT STRATEGY　472
　The UN Second Development Decade　472

Preparation for the Third UN Development Decade	473
The North–South Dialogue	475
The New International Economic Order	476
The Brandt Commission	478
The World Development Reports	480
The OECD Research Project on Facing the Future	483
The Role of Agriculture	484
The Club du Sahel	486
Least Developed Countries	487
Notes	492
References	512
Questionnaire Sheet	520
Index	523

List of Charts

The following charts illustrate the flow of financial resources to developing countries and multilateral agencies by type

1 Total DAC countries (1970–80)	33
2 USA (1970–80)	41
3 UK (1970–80)	56
4 France (1970–80)	81
5 West Germany (1970–80)	98
6 Japan (1970–80)	119
7 The Netherlands (1970–80)	139
8 Sweden (1970–80)	158
9 EEC (1973–80)	174

List of Tables

Table 2.1	DAC contributions to multilateral institutions as a percentage of total ODA (1961–80)	35
Table 2.2	Contributions of individual DAC members in multilateral institutions as a percentage of ODA (1970, 1975, 1980)	36
Table 2.3	Country share of DAC members in private flows (1979, 1980)	37
Table 3.1	ODA, private flows as a percentage to US total resource flows and total DAC countries (1970–80)	42
Table 3.2	Development assistance programmes by function proposed for FY1980	48
Table 3.3	Major distribution of security supporting assistance programme proposed for FY1980	49
Table 3.4	PL 480 Title II proposed FY1980 by region	51
Table 4.1	The share of private flows at market terms to total resource flows and its major components in UK 1970–80	60
Table 4.2	CDC distribution by region of group capital invested and outstanding commitment (1977–80)	71
Table 4.3	CDC functional classification of group capital committed and invested in continuing projects 1978–80	72
Table 5.1	Percentage share of French total official flows to total resource flows (1970–80)	82
Table 5.2	The share of French private flows at market terms in relation to total resource flows and its major components (1970–80)	83
Table 5.3	Caisse Centrale commitments (1974–80)	90
Table 5.4	Breakdown by sector of Caisse Centrale's operations (1979–80)	91
Table 5.5	Geographical distribution of Caisse Centrale financing (1974–80)	92

List of Tables

Table 6.1	Components of West Germany's private flows (1970–80)	100
Table 6.2	DEG's commitments during 1978–80 and total commitments by continent up to 31 December 1980	106
Table 6.3	KfW's cumulative commitments of loans and grants as of 31 December 1980 by region	110
Table 6.4	KfW's cumulative technical co-operation commitments as of 31 December 1980 by region	111
Table 7.1	Japan's total official flows, total private flows as a percentage of total resource flows 1970–80	120
Table 7.2	Percentage distribution of the components of private flows at market terms in Japan (1970–80)	121
Table 7.3	OECF commitments by sector in volume and percentages (end of September 1978, end of February 1981)	126
Table 7.4	OECF's regional distribution at the end of February 1981 compared with the end of September 1978	127
Table 7.5	Export-Import Bank of Japan, financial situation (FY1977–FY1980)	128
Table 7.6	Credit commitments by area (FY1977–FY1980)	130
Table 7.7	Overseas direct loan commitments by area provided by the Export-Import Bank of Japan (FY1977–FY1980)	132
Table 7.8	Participants in training programme by region (1977–79)	134
Table 8.1	Dutch total official flows, private flows at market terms as percentages of total resource flows (1970–80)	140
Table 8.2	Percentage components of Dutch private flows at market terms (1970–80)	141
Table 8.3	Loans and grants provided by the Netherlands Investment Bank for developing countries (1974–80)	149
Table 8.4	Loans and grants contracted in 1979 by the Netherlands Investment Bank for target developing countries	150
Table 8.5	FMO geographical distribution commitments during 1978–80	152
Table 9.1	Swedish official flows, private flows at market	

List of Tables

	terms as a percentage of total Swedish resource flows (1970–80)	159
Table 9.2	Major components of Swedish private flows as a percentage of total private flows (1970–80)	160
Table 9.3	Aid through SIDA to developing countries 1978/79	168
Table 9.4	Geographical distribution of SIDA commitments and disbursements in 1978/79 and 1979/80	168
Table 10.1	Capital structure and borrowing of the European Investment Bank	186
Table 10.2	Finance provided by EIB from 1985 to 1980	188
Table 10.3	EIB financing provided within the Community in 1980 and from 1958 to 1980. Breakdown by economic policy of objectives	189
Table 10.4	EIB financing provided outside the Community in 1980 and cumulative up to 1980	191
Table 11.1	Current account for industrial, oil-exporting and non-oil developing Countries (1975–80)	201
Table 11.2	Net oil imports by non-OPEC developing countries – 1978/79	202
Table 11.3	OPEC ODA net disbursements in US$m and as percentages of GNP (1973–80)	205
Table 11.4	Loans and grants by Arab OPEC development institutions in 1980	210
Table 12.1	Sectoral and geographical distribution of fund loans (1.1.1962–30.6.1980)	213
Table 13.1	Geographical distribution of the fund's loans 1974–80	219
Table 14.1	Loans extended by Saudi Fund by country and region 1978–80	228
Table 14.2	Project cycle identified in six Arab Funds	231
Table 15.1	Subscribed shares of the capital of AFESD by country	235
Table 15.2	Summary of the financial position of AFESD (1974–80)	236
Table 15.3	AFESD cumulative loans by country and their percentages (1974–80)	239
Table 16.1	Original subscription to ABEDA by Arab member countries	247
Table 16.2	Capital subscription by Arab member countries to ABEDA and their voting powers	248

List of Tables

Table 16.3	Summary of ABEDA's operations 1975–80	249
Table 16.4	ABEDA's geographical distribution of commitments between Eastern and Western African countries 1975–80	250
Table 16.5	ABEDA's sectoral distribution of commitments 1975–80	251
Table 17.1	Islamic Development Bank's member countries subscription and voting power	258
Table 17.2	IsDB's operations over five years (1976–80)	260
Table 17.3	The cumulative sectoral distribution of IsDB's project financing (1976–80)	261
Table 17.4	Status of authorised disbursement of the bank (1976–80)	262
Table 18.1	Initial contributions of OPEC members to the OPEC Fund	269
Table 18.2	OPEC Fund commitments and disbursements, as of 31 December 1980	271
Table 18.3	OPEC Fund loan commitments to LLDCs and MSAs, as of 31 December 1980	274
Table 18.4	OPEC Fund's cumulative project lending operations as of the end of 1980	274
Table 18.5	OPEC Fund: technical assistance projects, as of 31 December 1980	275
Table 19.1	AfDB cumulative loan approvals by sector 1977–80	280
Table 19.2	Initial subscription of non-regional states	283
Table 20.1	Subscriptions to the capital stock and voting power of the Asian Development Bank as of 31 December 1980	289
Table 20.2	AsDB's cumulative loan approvals by country and by source of funds 1967–80	292
Table 20.3	AsDB's cumulative technical assistance by country 1967–80	293
Table 21.1	CDB's total resources, 1980 and 1979	306
Table 21.2	Approvals of loans, contingent loans, equity and grants (net) by country and by fund 1970–80	308
Table 22.1	Subscription to authorised capital stock of the bank and contribution quotas for the Fund for Special Operations	320
Table 22.2	Development of total resources of the bank 1961–80	321

Table 22.3	IDB's distribution of cumulative loans by sector (1961–80)	322
Table 22.4	IDB's cumulative lending by country 1961–80	324
Table 22.5	Development of the bank's authorised annual loans by origin 1961–80	326
Table 22.6	IDB complementary financing operations as of 30 June 1979	328
Table 22.7	Regional and non-regional members of IDB and their voting power 31 December 1980	331
Table 23.1	IBRD original subscriptions	341
Table 23.2	IBRD's subscribed capital, new borrowing and net income 1971–80	343
Table 23.3	IBRD Gross Commitments in US$m (1950–60)	344
Table 23.4	IBRD, geographical distribution by region (1962–70)	346
Table 23.5	The distribution of the bank's lending by sector (1978–81)	347
Table 23.6	IBRD loan commitments and disbursements (1971–81)	348
Table 23.7	IBRD lending by region (1971–81)	348
Table 23.8	World Bank Group: working plan 1981–85	355
Table 24.1	IDA initial subscriptions	361
Table 24.2	The development of IDA replenishments	362
Table 24.3	IDA credits by economic sector (1964–70)	365
Table 24.4	IDA geographical distribution by region (1962–70)	366
Table 24.5	IDA credits and disbursements (1971–81)	367
Table 24.6	IDA trends in lending by sector in US$m and percentages (1978–81)	368
Table 24.7	IDA lending by region (1971–81)	369
Table 24.8	IDA Part I member countries and corresponding members in the World Bank voting power 30 June 1980	371
Table 24.9	IDA lending by sector (1978–80)	376
Table 24.10	Per cent drawings on commitments to IDA 6 (1981–90)	377
Table 24.11	Commitments to IDA and GDP of contributors in IDA 5 and IDA 6 1978–80, 1981–83	378
Table 25.1	Subscriptions to capital stock of the International Finance Corporation	383
Table 25.2	IFC's resources and income (1976–81)	385

Table 25.3	IFC total commitments and portfolio (cumulative) during the period 1961–70	386
Table 25.4	IFC commitments by type of business cumulative totals (1957–71)	387
Table 25.5	Geographical distribution of IFC's investment to developing countries	388
Table 25.6	IFC's operations – 1975–81	393
Table 25.7	IFC's 'Indicative' operational programme for FY1979–83	399
Table 25.8	'Indicative' regional distribution of IFC investments (FY1973–77, FY1979–83)	401

List of Appendix Tables

The following tables summarise the flow of financial resources to developing countries and multilateral agencies by type

2.1	Total DAC countries (1970–80)	38
3.1	USA (1970–80)	54
4.1	UK (1970–80)	79
5.1	France (1970–80)	96
6.1	West Germany (1970–80)	117
7.1	Japan (1970–80)	137
8.1	The Netherlands (1970–80)	156
9.1	Sweden (1970–80)	172
10.1	EEC (1973–80)	195

Preface

The original idea of this book goes back to September 1971 at the time when I was participating, with an award granted by the Institute of National Planning in Cairo, in a six-month training programme sponsored by the United Nations Industrial Development Organisation (UNIDO) at its headquarters in Vienna. This involved, among other things, an Inter-regional Training Seminar in Investment Promotion Techniques, which gave me an opportunity for field trips to industrial and financial organisations in Vienna, Warsaw and London. In addition, in order to fulfil the requirements of this programme, I undertook research at the UNIDO HQ, on the basis of visits to development organisations in Paris and London, and published a document, *External Sources of Financing Economic Development*,[1] in which a thorough study of the experience of a group of selected developed market economies, the USA, the UK, West Germany and France, in contrast with that of the centrally planned economies of the USSR, Poland and Hungary, as well as of the World Bank Group (IBRD, IDA and IFC), was undertaken with a view to identifying the major trends, geographical distribution and structural changes of financial flows as well as the administration and policies guiding the transfer of capital and know-how to developing countries during the decade of the 1960s. The coverage of the study was based on the fact that these countries and organisations were the most prominent sources of finance to developing countries and the main supporters of development assistance efforts at that time. As the subject is one of great interest to an economist from a developing economy, although this study partially satisfied my concern in the areas dealt with, a number of issues and a lot of questions remained unanswered and were kept until the opportunity arose for further work on the subject.

During my work in the Abu Dhabi Fund (ADFAED), which I joined in 1973, the old interest was again revived, especially as it related to my main responsibilities and duties in the Fund. Accordingly, a proposed extension of the study was sought and as a result visits were arranged to three important organisations – Caisse Central de Coopération Economique (CCCE) in Paris, Kreditanstalt für Wiederaufbau (KfW) in Frankfurt and the Commonwealth Development Corporation (CDC) in London – to exchange views and obtain information on the activities, performance and trends of those organisations with particular emphasis on project appraisal. As an outcome, a report *Financing and Project Appraisal in Developing Countries* was written.[2] Additional visits were also arranged to other organisations and prominent international banks: OECD HQ and the OECD Development Centre in Paris; the Dresdner Bank and Deutsch Bundesbank in Frankfurt; Barclays International, the Chartered Bank, Lloyds Bank and National and Grindlays Bank as well as the Economist Intelligence Unit in London. In occupying technical posts in ADFAED, being Assistant Director General for Operations and Director of Research, I have gained practical experience of wider scope in the fields of project appraisal, international finance and development through my participation as a member/head of missions to countries in Africa, Asia and the Middle East. During my long years of work with ADFAED, I have also had the opportunity to represent the fund at a number of conferences and seminars arranged by UNCTAD, FAO, the Society for International Development (SID) and World Bank consultative groups as well as at meetings held informally between OPEC and DAC and joint meetings of Arab Funds and other symposia. These formal and informal discussions have, no doubt, roused old ideas and stimulated my desire to combine observations with facts in research dealing with the more intricate subject of international financial flows, emphasising the approaches, techniques and strategies of donors. Effectively, the work on this book started in January 1980. Progress made was governed by the other duties and responsibilities which I have since been entrusted with as Adviser General to ADFAED. In gathering information about the performance of aid agencies covered in this book, questionnaires were sent to the twenty-eight agencies, followed by consultations with some of them. In addition, reference was made primarily to Annual Reports and other documents published by these agencies and a number of correspondents were helpful. Other material was gathered through reference to regular reports, books and other published materials. One of the basic features of this study is its comprehensiveness in nature and methodology. It combines in one volume the major trends and structural changes of financial flows and development assistance policies, and the approaches, techniques of project appraisal and strategies of aid agencies as well as problems of project implementation based on their field experience. It deals in a comparative manner with the basic elements of three major aspects of aid: international finance, project appraisal and implementation, and economic development. I am aware that the scope of the book is overambitious. However, the unsatisfactory state of international development strategy in not achieving its objectives is serious and deserves much comprehensive work.

The book is in two parts, containing twenty-five chapters and two appendixes. The Introduction (Chapter 1) sets out the problem facing the world, summarises the purpose, profile and main findings of this study and makes recommendations on how the objectives of international development strategy can be met. Part I (Chapters 2–10) deals with the performance of financial flows, development assistance policies and aid agencies in OECD/DAC member countries – case-studies of the USA, the UK, France, West Germany, Japan, the Netherlands, Sweden and the EEC. Part II (Chapters 11–25) deals with the performance of OPEC development funds, regional development banks and the World Bank Group. Studies on OPEC Funds cover the Kuwait, Abu Dhabi, Saudi and Arab Funds, the Arab Bank for Economic Development in Africa, the Islamic Development Bank and the OPEC Fund for International Development. Studies on regional development banks cover the African, Asian, Caribbean and Inter-American Development Banks; while the World Bank Group studies cover the International Bank for Reconstruction and Development, the International Development Association and the International Finance Corporation. There are two Appendixes: Appendix I is a comparative synopsis of twenty-eight aid agencies according to standard classification while Appendix II covers the subject of international development strategy formulated for the second and third UN development decades (the 1970s and 1980s) as well as the North–South dialogue, the New International Economic Order, the Brandt Commission, the World Bank's development reports, the OECD research project on facing the future and others.

I am deeply indebted to ADFAED for its generous financial support to this research project throughout the whole period. I owe a debt to Dr Hassan Abbas Zaki, former Director General of ADFAED and presently a member of its Board of Directors and the Economic Adviser to the President of the UAE for his encouragement, suggestions and valuable comments throughout my work on this project. His contribution to the design of the questionnaire sheet and his support at the early stages were more than helpful. I also wish to express my gratitude and appreciation to Mr Nasser Al-Nowais, Director General of

ADFAED, for his support and continuous co-operation and encouragement without which this study would not have been completed.

To Mr Peter Hellyer, Adviser, Foreign Language Broadcasting, Ministry of Information and Culture, Abu Dhabi, who has checked the original manuscript, I wish to extend my thanks and appreciation. Also, my thanks and appreciation are due to the Fund's Library staff, especially to Mrs Arwa Shabeebi and Mr Yousef Al-Awad, for their co-operation and efficient services, and to Miss Maha Shawwa for drawing the charts. I am much in debt to my secretary Mrs Belmira D'Souza and my former secretary Mrs J. L. McQuid for their excellent work in typing and retyping this large volume of tedious work. Mrs Harriette D'sa also helped in typing Appendix I and Miss Juliet M. Izzat typed two chapters in the text.

Also most helpful were the fruitful information and official documents obtained through Mr John G. Wilcox in the US Embassy, Mr James W. Watt in the UK Embassy and Mr H. H. Driesser, of the Royal Netherlands Embassy in Abu Dhabi. During my visits to the development agencies, I have received every assistance and co-operation, for which I am most grateful. Thanks are also due to Mr J. Bartsch, Head of the Non-DAC Section of OECD; to Mr Comohiko Kobayashi (Director) and Dr (Mrs) Traute Scharf in the Development Centre of OECD in Paris: to Mr John Leech, CDC in London; to M. Roland Billecart, Director General, M. Michel Penet and M. Pené Mallorga of CCCE in Paris; to Mr Assessor Rudolf, Mr Jürgen R. Trede and Mr Karl A. Kern of KfW in Frankfurt; to Lord Kindersley, Mr M. Williams, Mr J. K. Wright and Mr P. H. Charters of the Overseas Development Administration in London; to Mr Robert Wook, Director of the Overseas Development Institute in London; and to many others whose co-operation is highly appreciated.

Last, but not least, to my wife Dr Faika El-Refaie and my children Monna and Tarek, I owe much for their patience, understanding and moral support.

I wish to emphasise that opinions expressed in this book do not necessarily represent either those of the Abu Dhabi Fund or of other agencies referred to in this book and are in no way binding to them. Any errors that remain are my sole responsibility.

Abu Dhabi
United Arab Emirates   HASSAN M. SELIM

List of Abbreviations

AAAID	Arab Authority for Agricultural Investment and Development
ABEDA	Arab Bank for Economic Development in Africa (French abbreviation BADEA)
ACP	African, Caribbean and Pacific
ADFAED	Abu Dhabi Fund for Arab Economic Development
AfDB	African Development Bank
AfDF	African Development Fund
AFESD	Arab Fund for Economic and Social Development
AID	Agency for International Development
AMF	Arab Monetary Fund
AsDB	Asian Development Bank
BIS	Bank for International Settlements
CBA	Cost-benefit Analysis
CCCE	Caisse Central de Coopération Economique
CDB	Caribbean Development Bank
CDC	Commonwealth Development Corporation
CGIAR	Consultative Group on International Agricultural Research
CIEC	Conference on International Economic Co-operation
DAC	Development Assistance Committee
DAG	Development Assistance Group
DEG	Deutsche Entwicklungsgesellshaft – German Development Company
DFI	Development Finance Institutions
DIE	Développement industriel a l'étranger
DMCs	Developing Member Countries
DOM	Départements d'Outre-Mer
ECA	Economic Commission for Africa
ECAFE	Economic Commission for Asia and the Far East
EEC	European Economic Community
EDF	European Development Fund
EIB	European Investment Bank

List of Abbreviations

EKN	Swedish Export Credits Guarantee Board
ESCAP	Economic and Social Commission for Asia and the Pacific
FAC	Fund for Aid and Co-operation
FAO	Food and Agricultural Organisation
FCO	Foreign and Commonwealth Office
FMO	Nederlandse Financierings-Maatschappij Voor Ontwikkelingslanden (Netherlands Finance Company for Developing Countries)
FSO	Fund for Special Operations
GATE	German Appropriate Technology Exchange
GNP	Gross National Product
IBRD	International Bank for Reconstruction and Development
IC	Intra-regional Capital
IDA	International Development Association
IDB	Inter-American Development Bank
IFAD	International Fund for Agriculture Development
IFC	International Finance Corporation
ILO	International Labour Organisation
IMF	International Monetary Fund
IsDB	Islamic Development Bank
JERTO	Japan External Trade Organisation
JICA	Japan International Co-operation Agency
JOCV	Japan Overseas Co-operation Volunteers
KFAED	Kuwait Fund for Arab Economic Development
KfW	Kreditanstalt für Wiederaufbau
LIBOR	London Inter-bank Offered Rate
LLDCs	Least Developed Countries
MAMC	Managa Agricultural Management Centre
MSACs	Most Seriously Affected Countries
NTF	Nigerian Trust Fund
OAPEC	Organisation of Arab Petroleum Exporting Countries
OAU	Organisation for African Unity
OC	Ordinary Capital
OCR	Ordinary Capital Resources
OCT	Overseas Countries and Territories
ODA	Official Development Assistance
ODM	Overseas Development Ministry
OECD	Organisation for Economic Co-operation and Development

List of Abbreviations

OECF	Overseas Economic Co-operation Fund
OEEC	Organisation for European Economic Co-operation
OLADE	Latin American Energy Organisation
OOF	Other Official Flows
OPEC	Organisation of Petroleum Exporting Countries
OPIC	Overseas Private Investment Corporation
PCRs	Project Completion Reports
PEO	Post-evaluation Office
PPARs	Project Performance Audit Reports
RNR	Renewable Natural Resource
SAAFA	Special Arab Aid Fund for Africa
SAREC	Swedish Agency for Research Co-operation
SF	Special Funds
SFD	Saudi Fund for Development
SIDA	Swedish International Development Authority
TOM	Territoires d'Outre-Mer
UFINEX	Union pour le Financement et l'Expansion du Commerce International
UNCTAD	United Nations Conference on Trade and Development
UNDP	United Nations Development Programme
UNICEF	United Nations Children's Fund
UNIDO	United Nations Industrial Development Organisation
UNRWA	United Nations Relief and Works Agency
WFP	World Food Programme

1 Introduction

SETTING OUT THE PROBLEM

Attacking absolute poverty within the context of international development strategy is a key issue that should be given more important world concern. Despite growing world concern since the Second World War for narrowing the gap between rich and poor nations, the experience of the world community in fighting poverty has been disappointing. The community of nations is faced with such wide-ranging problems as instability in the global monetary system, wild fluctuations in commodity markets, large-scale international transfer payments, several years of drought afflicting most continents, the virtual loss of the world's foodgrain reserves, deteriorating economic prospects in the poor regions, a worldwide recession in trade, unemployment and persistent inflation. The United Nations Seventh Special Session in September 1975 recognised that the international order would only be stable if it was seen by its members to be fundamentally just. It thus concluded that the achievement of this broad objective could best be furthered by compromises and mutual accommodation. Co-operation, rather than confrontation, has since characterised the numerous negotiations aimed at bringing about a more equitable world system. Though a workable agreement has not been reached on a strategy for longer term international development co-operation, there is a process under way to reform the old international order.

An agreement which recognises the unique situation of the poorest countries remains a key objective. On the other hand, the principal international, regional and national aid agencies concerned with problems of world poverty have not been able to reach agreement on attacking absolute poverty or on how to meet the objectives of the international development strategy. A report has been submitted to the Club of Rome, entitled *Reshaping the International Order*,[1] which represents the result of two years of teamwork by a group of experts in international co-operation, recruited from both developing and developed countries. In essence it is an independent contribution to the discussion of the New International Economic Order as adopted by the United Nations General Assembly in its Sixth and Seventh Special Sessions (1974 and 1975) and of ways to attain the international order as recommended by the group. The key argument runs as follows. As a consequence of technological and ecological developments the interdependence of all parts of the globe has increased to the point where the welfare of humanity as a whole – including even future generations – must be taken as the goal of the order to be established and the policies to be followed. The developments include those in arms and industrial technology, population growth and environmental pressure. The only acceptable goal is the welfare of all and as an integral part of it the welfare of the poor masses in the developing countries. High priorities amongst those to be set are those of a higher production of food in developing regions, and a better income for the poorest people. The policies of developed countries and of transnational corporations should be guided by these top priorities of the Third World, as well as by their own goals. In the long run – ten to twenty years – the interests of the developing and the developed world run parallel.[2]

The problem is how to bring back some order into this great disorder in the aftermath of the Second World War. We had the Marshall Plan for Europe but what we really need now is a Marshall Plan to abolish poverty or a Marshall Plan for Africa, Asia and Latin America. The new era of global interdependence poses new challenges not only for the industrialised nations but also for the developing nations. The international community should reach specific agreements to provide the necessary additional assistance and transfer of financial resources from rich to poor countries in programmes which meet basic needs, in collaboration with a vigorous effort by the poorest nations themselves. This would give reality to the prospect that key development objectives can be achieved in the low-income, low-growth regions of the world.

PURPOSE OF THE BOOK

The purpose of this book is to evaluate aid performance to meet international development strategy. For this purpose, an investigation of the performance of the financial flows to developing countries and multilateral institutions of selected donors of the Development Assistance Committee's members (the USA, the UK, France, West

Germany, Japan, the Netherlands, Sweden and the Commission of the European Economic Community (EEC)), covers the composition of their Official Development Assistance (ODA) and private flows at market terms, their development assistance policies, and the performance of their aid agencies. Reviews of OPEC member countries' aid performance by evaluating their aid agencies (national and multinationals), an evaluation of the performance of Regional Development Banks and the World Bank Group in their efforts towards developing countries in general and least developed ones in particular are also included in this study. The study of aid agencies covered twenty-eight cases based upon questionnaire sheets, consultations, correspondence, documents and Annual Reports. It covered almost standard classification of these institutions. This classification took the following form: establishment and financial resources; scope of activities; terms and conditions; management and organisational structure; approaches and techniques applied; strategy for financing and technical assistance; problems of project implementation; and remarks from field experience. An evaluation of the performance of these aid agencies, based upon comprehensive coverage of their operations, is also discussed. Finally, measures and proposals to strengthen the performance of aid agencies in transferring financial resources and technical assistance to developing countries in general and least developed ones in particular are the outcome of this study.

SUMMARY OF THE MAIN FINDINGS

DAC Member Countries

The performance of DAC (Development Assistance Committee) countries combined in the transfer of financial resources to developing countries falls far short of the 0.7 per cent target for Official Development Assistance (ODA). Although all DAC countries accepted the UN development strategy, only Scandinavian countries and the Netherlands have recently attached importance to the need to meet the target of 0.7 per cent of their GNP. ODA of DAC countries is heavily influenced by a few large donors, the United States, France, West Germany, Japan and the United Kingdom being the five big donors. However, although these five countries have increased their assistance in the 1970s compared to the 1960s, their share of the total ODA provided by DAC members has declined drastically. There was a steadily growing

DEVELOPMENT ASSISTANCE POLIC[Y]

DAC

Official Development Assistance (ODA): bilateral and multilateral
Private flows: Direct investments, Export credits and others
Development assistance policies
Aid agencies

1. USA	Agency for international Dev. (AID) (1)
2. UK	Overseas Dev. (2) Administration Commonwealth (3) Dev. Corp. (CDC)
3. France	Caisse Central (4) de Coopération Economique (CCCE)
4. FRG	German Dev. (5) Company (DEG) Kreditanstalt (6) für Wiederanfban (KfW)
5. Japan	Overseas Econ. (7) Co-opr. Fund (OECF) Export Import (8) Bank of Japan Japan Int. Co-opr. (9) Agency (JICA)
6. Netherlands	Netherlands (10) Invest. Bank Netherlands (11) Fin. Com. (FMO)
7. Sweden	Swedish Int. Dev. (12) Authority (SIDA)
8. Commission of the European Eco. Community	European Dev. (13) Fund (EDF) European Invest. (14) Bank (EIB)

OPEC DEV. FUNDS

National Arab/OPEC Development Funds
1. Kuwait Fund (KFAED)
2. Abu Dhabi Fund (ADFAED)
3. Saudi Fund (SADF)

Multinational Arab/OPEC Development Agencies
4. Arab Fund (AFESD)
5. Arab Bank (BADEA)
6. Islamic Dev. Bank (IsDB)
7. OPEC Fund for Int. Dev.

1. Establishment & fin. resources

4. Management & organisational structure

7. Strategy & future strategy for financing & technical assistance

1. Middle-income developing countries

4. Project aid

Evaluation of Aid

ERFORMANCE OF AID AGENCIES

REGIONAL DEV. BANKS	WORLD BANK GROUP
frican Dev. Bank (AfDB) (22) sian Dev. Bank (AsDB) (23) aribbean Dev. Bank (CDB) (24) ter-American Dev. Bk. DB) (25)	1. International Bank for Reconstruction & Dev. (IBRD) (26) 2. International Development Association (IDA) (27) 3. International Finance Corporation (IFC) (28)

cope of activities	3. Terms and conditions
pproaches taken	6. Techniques applied
roblems of implementation follow up	9. Remarks from field experience

east developed countries	3. Programme aid
conomic and social sectors	6. Aid evaluation by institution

meet the international development strategy

trend towards contributions of all DAC members to multilateral institutions in the 1970s compared with the 1960s. This expansion in the multilateral share in ODA was largely accounted for by the substantial IDA replenishments and by the rapid expansion of the regional development banks. Private flows at market terms have shown a rapid increase over the 1970s as a whole compared to the 1960s. Five countries (USA, UK, West Germany, Switzerland and France) dominated these flows.

The United States

The United States is the largest DAC donor in absolute terms of ODA, but has tended increasingly over the years to lag behind other DAC countries in terms of percentage of its GNP. The share of US ODA to total DAC/ODA declined during the 1970s, while its share in private flows to total DAC private flows showed no major trend during the same period, with average private flows higher than ODA flows.

The US foreign aid programme has gone through many substantive changes as well as several changes in name. A new approach for the US foreign aid policy during the 1970s was prepared which recommended a new focus for US programmes with fresh emphasis on multilateral organisations, and a new institutional framework. The development policy towards developing countries was assigned to support US economic objectives and at the same time to strengthen the US overall relations with developing countries. This policy emphasised the tremendous importance of participation in the international development banks, which was considered to be the most controversial part of the US programme.

The Agency for International Development (AID), which was established in 1961 under the Foreign Assistance Act to extend development loans repayable in dollars and tied to US commodities and services, grants and technical assistance for emergencies and certain contributions to international development organisations, confirmed the need for complete and periodic coverage for most of its activities to measure progress and to make project management more effective.

The United Kingdom

The United Kingdom experienced a declining share of its contributions in ODA during the 1970s compared with the 1960s, as a result of the growing share of other DAC members and an increase in its private flows. As in the case of the USA, the UK has never reached the UNCTAD target of 0.7 per cent of ODA/GNP, but the performance of the UK in this respect was better than that of the USA. UK contributions to multilateral institutions increased during the second half of the 1970s due mainly to the capital subscription payments of IDA and other regional banks.

The British Government has never had a very clear-cut policy towards private investment in developing countries. Bilateral aid has remained tied to the procurement of British goods and services. However, a limited amount of this aid could be untied where appropriate, for example to meet local costs associated with aid projects, and in particular cases some third-country procurement could be permitted.

The Overseas Development Administration, a semi-autonomous unit within the Foreign and Commonwealth Office, extending soft loans mainly to developing commonwealth countries in the form of projects and aid programmes, has concentrated its aid on individual projects and in most countries it has not provided a sufficient number of projects in any one sector to justify the sectoral approach.

The Commonwealth Development Corporation (CDC), a public corporation established by Act of Parliament in 1948 which operates on broadly commercial lines by offering investments in development projects in developing countries in which it is empowered to operate, has experienced project cost escalations and financial control problems.

France

France is the second biggest donor among DAC countries in ODA, but its share for the 1970s was almost constant. Its share of total official bilateral flow to its total resource flows declined as a result of the growing importance of its private flows at market terms, especially during the latter part of the 1970s, accompanied by an increase of its contributions to multilateral institutions.

France has a concept of priority areas for development policy. Historical reasons were behind the well-established foreign aid policy in African (including North Africa) French-speaking countries for expanding the markets for French products. Official development assistance policy in France is based upon this concept of priority. On the other hand, French financial flows at market terms are based upon the mode of private investors and the conditions of the financial markets. The French authorities have attached great importance to technical and cultural co-operation in education, agricultural and industrial technology, but at the same time made grants for capital and infrastructure projects. The trend towards an increase in the multilateral contributions has become more marked in the course of commitments in this area. Nearly half of the French bilateral aid is directed to the least developed countries and to the most seriously affected countries combined. A large proportion of bilateral assistance is accounted for by technical co-operation related mainly to food aid in the Sahel, Asia and North African countries.

Caisse Centrale de Coopération Economique (CCCE), a public corporation with an independent legal personality, operating on a project basis with an emphasis on project-type production of mainly agricultural and industrial projects, extending long-term loans as the main principal form of its activities, has experienced problems related to the quality of technical leadership in rural development, to the standing and competence of industry, to the strict management of public utility companies, and to the balanced operations of public utility services.

West Germany

West Germany took third place after the USA and France during the 1970s. Its share of total DAC/ODA was higher than the share of the UK. Like the other big donors, its contributions to multilateral institutions have grown as a share of ODA and are expected to grow still further in the near future. Moreover, as with other big donors, private flows at market terms increased in both volume and percentage during the second half of the 1970s. As in the case of the USA and UK, West Germany has never reached the UNCTAD target of 0.7 per cent of ODA/GNP.

The development assistance policy of Western Germany implies in particular that bilateral ODA is to be increasingly concentrated on the very poor countries and on rural development and food production. Differentiation of financial terms has been introduced, and new forms of co-operation proposed, including technical assistance against payment, triangular arrangements with OPEC countries, and an increasing share of multilateral assistance. As part of the reallocation of assistance to the poor countries, greater focus is being put on African countries. Measures to promote agriculture and rural development have increased in importance in the West German aid programme. The Federal Government has also decided to convert the development credits promised to the least developed countries into grants if the country concerned so requests, though reserving the right to examine and negotiate the cases individually, in keeping with a resolution of March 1978 of the Trade and Development Board (UNCTAD).

The Deutsche Entwicklungsgesllschaft (DEG), or German Development Company was set up by the Federal German Government in 1962 for the purpose of encouraging and supporting private investment activities in developing countries. It concentrates its activities on the establishment or expansion of small and medium-sized enterprises in the form of joint ventures in the mining, industrial, agricultural and tourism sectors. Its experience has shown that circumstances are increasingly against more investment by the German raw materials industry in producer countries, particularly in Third World countries rich in raw materials – for example, a smaller metal content of new deposits, less favourable sites and increased infrastructure costs, longer running-in periods of projects, and higher capital and political risks.

Kreditanstalt für Wiederaufban (KfW), is a West German corporation under public law. Its purposes are granting loans for projects serving the reconstruction or promotion of the West German economy, granting loans in connection with export transactions of domestic enterprises, issuing guarantees, and granting loans for financing projects in developing countries. KfW's field experience has shown that many capital-aid projects involve investment costs per job far exceeding the average figures, especially in the case of infrastructure projects. It has also shown that some developing countries lack a correct assessment of project appraisal.

Japan

Japan has been the fourth largest donor of ODA after the United States, France and West Germany. Its ODA has increased substantially since 1973 with the percentage distribution between bilateral official development assistance and the contribution to multilateral institutions almost constant. Japanese private flows at market terms had increased approximately ten times by the end of the 1970s compared with 1970 as a result of an increasingly wide range of incentive measures.

As a resource-poor country, Japan believes that her economic growth can be maintained only when relations with developing countries are harmonious, secure and friendly. From this viewpoint, Japan believes that close relations with these countries must be strengthened. A new economic and Social Seven-year Plan in Japan, FY1979–FY1985, indicated an active role to expand ODA, and to promote private sector co-operation on a comprehensive scale so as to complement ODA. Loan terms are based mainly on the recipient country's economic situation with consideration being given to its relations with Japan in political, economic and other fields. Under the plan, the Japanese Government intends to more than double its aid in a five-year period through an increase in ODA.

The Overseas Economic Co-operation Fund (OECF) of Japan was established in 1961 for the purpose of promoting overseas economic co-operation. It is considered as Japan's principal organ for extending ODA to developing countries. Its field experience has shown that loans' performance is hampered by delays at project sites, cost overrun, low disbursement, delayed projects and fall in commodity disbursement.

The Export-Import Bank of Japan (EXIM Bank) was established in 1950 as an independent governmental financial institution designed to supplement and encourage commercial banks in financing exports, imports and overseas investments in the field of trade between Japan and foreign countries. Although the bank's operating rules do not restrict it to one particular currency, the bank funds itself primarily in yen and all export suppliers' credits are denominated in yen.

The Japan International Co-operation Agency (JICA) was established in 1974, under the Japan International Co-operation Agency Law, as an executive organ of Japan's international co-operation services for the socio-economic progress of developing countries. Its experience has shown that because different types of surveys are needed at successive stages of projects, the completion of one project could require three or four surveys. Since the utmost precision is required for the preparation of a detailed project design these surveys are usually costly and time-consuming; reflecting the way money is being misspent.

The Netherlands

The Netherlands' net financial flows of ODA increased steadily during the 1970s, ranking it as the sixth donor in absolute terms of ODA since 1978, when it overtook Canada, and it is estimated that the Netherlands will maintain its position among DAC members for the next few years. The performance of the Dutch ODA as a percentage of its GNP is similar to the performance of Sweden where both have exceeded the 0.7 per cent target of UNCTAD during the second half of the 1970s. In general, the bulk of Dutch ODA is mainly in the form of bilateral official development assistance, while contributions to multilateral institutions represent on the average about one-third of the Dutch ODA Programme in the 1970s. The Netherlands is a source of substantial flows of private capital to developing countries due to the long-standing economic and commercial interests of Dutch multinational companies in developing countries. During the 1970s, with few exceptions, the share of Dutch private flows was slightly higher than its share of official flows.

Dutch development assistance policy is generally directed towards the realisation of the objectives laid down in the strategy for development by the United Nations, and the implementation of the recommendations worked out by the Development Assistance Committee of the OECD. The Netherlands has adopted a policy of concentrating aid in a few 'main target' countries to enhance the effects of both financial and technical aid. The funds for activities in non-target countries are made available under the budget item 'Direct aid to the poorest nations or groups', and may be injected either bilaterally or multilaterally.

The Netherlands Investment Bank for Developing countries acts as the agent of the government in the matter of aid. Its function lies within the framework of bilateral development aid provided by the Government. The bank's field experience generally indicates that the present shortage of food in developing countries demands an intensification of efforts to increase agricultural production which requires, among other things, simultaneous implementation of a coherent package of measures aimed at eliminating the factors that stand in the way of higher production and better distribution of food.

The Netherlands Finance Company for Developing Countries (FMO) was formed in 1970 by co-operation between Dutch private business and industry and the State of the Netherlands for the purpose of stimulating economic and social progress in developing countries by promoting local business and industry. From field experience the company's problems of implementation are related mainly to the increased number of projects that reached the stage of implementation which resulted in a heavier work load for the projects' management and delays in their completion.

Sweden

During the 1970s Swedish ODA grew in a consistently sustained manner. Since 1975, Sweden has become the eighth donor among the seventeen DAC member countries after the big five, the Netherlands and Canada. In terms of ODA/GNP, Sweden has fulfilled and exceeded the 0.7 per cent target since 1975. Swedish total resource flows to developing countries and multilateral institutions are mainly official flows. With the exception of 1971, Swedish bilateral official development assistance was higher than its contributions to multilateral institutions during the 1970s. The main feature of Swedish private investment in developing countries is that it is mainly directed to countries other than those receiving substantial official assistance from Sweden, whereas investment guarantees are restricted to countries receiving Swedish assistance.

Swedish policy for overall co-operation with developing countries emphasises the importance of an active and co-ordinated effort, based on mutual interest. Solidarity with the poor of the Third World provides a sufficient motive for a large-scale Swedish assistance programme, which was the view endorsed by the Riksdag in 1962, and confirmed by the Commission for the Review of Swedish International Development Co-operation. The goals of Swedish assistance policy are based upon the criteria that Swedish efforts should contribute to growth of resources, economic and social equalisation, economic and political independence, and democratic social development. The financial terms of Swedish ODA are among the most concessional in the DAC member countries. In 1978, Sweden decided to write off all outstanding debt from ODA loans extended to the least developed and most seriously affected countries.

The Swedish International Development Authority (SIDA) was established in 1965 as a Central Government Agency for the preparation and implementation of Swedish programmes for bilateral development co-operation. SIDA comments from field experience stress the importance of improvement of on-going projects, better awareness of the importance of good project preparation and goal analysis, and awareness of some of the risks in projects aiming at economic development, such as widened income gaps.

The European Economic Community

The flow of financial resources to developing countries and multilateral institutions by the Commission of the European Economic Community (EEC) is only in the form of official flows. Bilateral official development assistance by the EEC constitutes the major component of ODA while contributions to multilateral institutions, which started in 1974, represented on the average about 13 per cent during the second half of the 1970s. Grants and grant-like contributions represent the major part of the bilateral official development assistance, and food aid grants represent almost the whole contribution by the EEC to multilateral institutions.

The European Community's policy towards the Third Word combines two approaches: special contractual agreements on a regional basis, and action at world level. The Community has concluded a wide range of regional agreements: the Lomé Agreements, the agreements with the Maghreb countries and with Mashreq countries. These kinds of regional agreements combine all types of financial, technical and commercial action, written into international treaties ratified by the Parliaments. On the other hand, the Community's global policy for co-operation with the Third World, taking account of the growing interdependence between North and South, needs greater financial resources. Financial aid by itself is only one aspect of the problem. Developing countries must be able to guarantee their export earnings against violent fluctuations, they need to have the best possible access to the industrialised world's markets, to acquire industrial technology and know-how easily and cheaply. Thus the Community's co-operation policy with developing countries can be recognised as being of only marginal importance as long as it consists only of financial aid.

The first European Development Fund (EDF) was established in 1959 as an implementing convention of the Treaty of Rome governing the special relations between the EEC and dependent overseas countries and territories. The fund's financed operations are devised and implemented jointly by the donors and recipients of the Community's funds. The European Investment Bank (EIB) was created as a non-profit independent public institution by the Treaty of Rome, which came into force on 1 January 1958, establishing the European Economic Community. The bank's basic function is to contribute, on a non-profit-making basis, to the balanced development of the Community. Since 1963, the bank has assisted in implementing the Community's policy of economic and financial co-operation with an increasing number of developing countries. Problems of implementation from the experience of these two institutions are identical. These problems are mainly related to different information received by different donors from recipient developing countries. Thus co-financing and co-ordination among different donors financing the same project in the same country are of great importance. The experience of these two institutions has also shown that former French African colonies received the highest share of the Community's financing due to their historical background, and before Britain joined the European Common Market.

OPEC Development Funds

The pattern of relationship between the OPEC and the non-OPEC developing countries is in the field of finance. OPEC member countries, in response to the increase in oil revenues, individually and collectively, created national, regional and multilateral funds for the purpose of channelling financial resources to other Third World countries. Such financial flows have been channelled either directly to individual developing countries or indirectly through international organisations. The objectives of these financial flows are either to alleviate balance of payments adjustment problems or to provide development finance for particular projects. If OPEC aid is to be judged by the standard target proclaimed by the UN, and more recently by the Brandt Commission, of the level of ODA to reach 0.7 per cent of the GNP of the donor country, then the major OPEC donors have far exceeded that level since 1974. However, as in the case of DAC member countries, the volume of OPEC aid is still far below the financial needs of the developing countries. Non-concessional flows from OPEC member countries have been heavily influenced by the predominant position occupied by the IMF oil facility, particularly during 1974 and 1975.

The various OPEC aid organisations have relatively little experience in extending development assistance to developing countries, compared to that of development aid organisations in the industrialised countries, and those of international organisations. OPEC organisations can be divided into two types. First are the national funds, including the Kuwait Fund for Arab Economic Development (KFAED), the Abu Dhabi Fund for Arab Economic Development (ADFAED), the Saudi Fund for Development (SFD), the Iraqi Fund for External Development, the Libyan Bank for Foreign Assistance, and the Venezuelan Fund. The second type is multilateral in nature, including the Arab Fund for Economic and Social Development (AFESD), the Islamic Development Bank (IsDB), the Arab Bank for Economic Development in Africa (ABEDA), the Arab Monetary Fund (AMF), the Arab Authority for Agricultural Investment and Development (AAAID), and the OPEC Fund for International Development. All members of these organisations are themselves developing countries, with most of them still dependent mainly on their oil revenues to finance their economic development.

The relations between these OPEC aid organisations and the developing countries are concerned primarily with the provision of financial aid for development, given mainly in the form of finance for development projects and technical assistance. With the exception of the Kuwait Fund for Arab Economic Development, founded in 1961, the Arab Fund for Economic and Social Development launched in 1971, and the Abu Dhabi Fund for Arab Economic Development, established in the same year, all other funds and agencies were established after the increases in oil prices during 1973–74, with the specific objective of directing surplus oil revenues either directly or indirectly through regional and international organisations to the Third World. Most aid provided by these organisations has been directed towards the least developed countries (LLDCs).

The Kuwait Fund

The Kuwait Fund for Arab Economic Development was established as a public corporation with an independent legal personality to assist Arab States in developing their economies by providing project loans and technical assistance for the implementation of their development programmes. Since 1974 KFAED has extended its mandate to provide foreign assistance to all developing countries in the world. Problems of implementation from the fund's own experience are mainly related to delays in ratification, appointments of consultants, issue of tenders, analysis of bids, submission of withdrawal applications, and progress reports.

The Abu Dhabi Fund

The Abu Dhabi Fund for Arab Economic Development was created as a general corporation with an independent legal personality for the purpose of extending loans, technical assistance and equity participation to Arab States. Since 1974, the scope of the fund's activities has enlarged to include African and Asian developing countries as well. The fund's problems of implementation of projects are probably the same as in the case of the Kuwait Fund. Moreover, ADFAED's field experience with developing countries is mainly related to problems of priority areas, implementation and decision-making. I therefore recommend the creation of effective machinery for joint project implementation and follow-up between all OPEC funds.

The Saudi Fund

The Saudi Fund for Development was established in 1974 for the purpose of providing financing for development projects in Arab, Islamic and friendly developing countries by the provision of concessionary loans. The fund's problems of implementation are similar to those of KFAED and ADFAED. However, SFD's particular problems are related to the selection of foreign consultants and their preference, agreements between host governments and contractors. The fund also believes that contractors are considered to be unfair as they take advantage of the position of the developing countries. As SFD does not follow a strategy for financing or provide technical assistance, and as its activities are related mainly to the transportation sector, it is recommended that if the fund were to follow a programme of lending for this sector as a key sector for development with its good impact upon foreign trade among least developed countries, it could then gain great experience in feasibility studies of projects related to this sector, playing a leading role, and hence providing technical assistance in this field.

The Arab Fund

The Arab Fund for Economic and Social Development was established as an Arab regional financial institution with an independent legal personality for the purpose of financing development and social projects in Arab countries. AFESD participates in technical assistance projects, particularly in human resources and exploitation of natural resources in the least developed Arab countries; it also encourages the investment of public and private capital in the Arab economy. It shares with other Arab/OPEC funds the common problems of implementation; however, as a co-ordinator among other Arab funds, it has a difficult task, especially with relation to the procedure for the withdrawal of loans and procedures for implementation. The performance of AFESD revealed that it has a still larger role to play in fostering Arab regional projects in different sectors and in different Arab countries, as well as in Arab joint co-ordination policies, foreign aid policies and financial policies. It should become more active in playing a pioneer role for suggesting an Arab aid development strategy and in establishing an Arab machinery for follow-up and implementation of development financing. In addition, the fund has not yet proved to be active in the field of Arab social development, an important area that will be of great importance in the years to come.

The Arab Bank in Africa

The Arab Bank for Economic Development in Africa was established in 1973 as an independent regional financial institution, financed by member countries of the Arab League for the purpose of participating in the economic development of non-Arab African countries, the provision of Arab capital in African developments, and providing technical assistance for Africa. Problems of implementation from ABEDA's own experience are related to the lack of local currencies, delay in disbursements, bad management, lack of direct communication, problems of productivity of labour, lack of stability in economic systems in some countries, rise of total costs of projects during implementation, fluctuations in the value of foreign currencies, and problems with contractors and consultants as well as different estimates of total costs and components for a project submitted to different donors. The bank also faces chronic problems in the case of least developed African countries, namely the Sahel countries. A strategy for Arab aid organisations in Sahel countries presented by the bank is based upon basic alternatives with emphasis upon mining and road projects. It is also based upon an integrated approach for development assistance to these countries. Any sort of strategy for Sahel countries should be primarily based upon solving the chronic problems facing these countries, mainly in irrigation, water supplies and dams as well as human resource development. From its performance, the bank is active in these fields but to implement this new strategy, it is diverting its activities towards different aspects of development which are not considered to be top priority for a strategy to be implemented in Sahel countries.

The Islamic Development Bank

The Islamic Development Bank (IsDB) was established in 1975 as an international financial institution to foster the economic development and social progress of member countries and Muslim communities individually as well as jointly in accordance with the principles of the Sharaih (Muslim code of law). The activities of the IsDB include project financing and technical assistance, equity participation, leasing, profit-sharing and foreign trade financing. The bank's experiences in the problems of project implementation and follow-up are generally similar to the problems of other aid organisations, especially those problems related to the LLDCs. IsDB experience revealed that inadequate co-ordination in the various stages of project management is the major cause of cost overruns. The bank's performance indicates that it has made a promising start towards achieving its objectives, and should continue to progress towards those goals, provided that more financial resources are committed, when it should make greater efforts in the fields of technical assistance and investment promotion.

The OPEC Fund

The OPEC Fund for International Development was established by virtue of an agreement signed by all OPEC member countries in 1976 for the purpose of reinforcing financial co-operation between OPEC member countries and other developing countries by providing financial support on appropriate terms to assist them in their economic and social development efforts. The fund operates in all developing countries, other than OPEC member countries, with special emphasis on assisting least developed countries. It extends three types of loans: balance of payments support loans, programme loans, and project loans. The fund also, in co-operation with international agencies, provides technical assistance grants. The administration of the fund loans has generally been left to an appropriate co-financing agency. More recently, however, amendments to the agreement establishing the fund included a clause enabling the fund to appraise and administer its own projects. The fund plans gradually to strengthen its appraising capacity, especially in the energy sector.

OPEC Funds' Strategy

The OPEC funds have different strategies that are evident from their choice of projects. Recently, however, they have tended to concentrate on aid to the LLDCs, especially through the financing of infrastructural and agricultural projects. It is now time that a clear and well-defined strategy should be drawn up for these OPEC development institutions to ensure that aid continues to be extended to the developing countries of the Third World. Such aid can help in the restoration of political and economic stability and can enable them to develop and progress. In the future such aid can lead to co-operation between the OPEC donors and the recipients in the field of investment. It is also important that the LLDCs should receive priority in the provision of concessionary assistance. OPEC development funds should also finance projects that will contribute to the promotion of international trade among developing countries (including OPEC countries themselves), as well as paying special attention in the future to public service projects, which are of great importance for any development programme. There is always a need for further co-ordination between the various OPEC development institutions, so that together they can finance big projects that will consequently have major effects on the recipient countries. This can best be achieved through the drawing up of a general strategy for OPEC aid agencies.

Regional Development Banks

The African Development Bank

The African Development Bank (AfDB), like the Asian, Caribbean and Inter-American Banks, was shaped largely by the historical circumstances which led to its creation. However, the bank is unique among the regional banks in that throughout its early history, it was a purely regional institution without financial support from outside. It was established in 1964 for the purpose of contributing to the economic development and social progress of its regional members both individually and jointly. AfDB finances investment projects and programmes in its regional members, promotes investment in Africa of public and private capital in projects or programmes, and provides technical assistance. Problems of implementation from the bank's own experience are mainly related to meeting the obligations from the host governments necessary for completing projects on schedule as well as delays in the receipt of progress reports. The performance of AfDB revealed that the bank has no guidelines for project appraisal techniques and this was a handicap for its standard of performance. Such guidelines should be adopted before, and not after, an invitation is extended to non-regional states to participate in its membership. If the bank intends to emphasise its African character, it ought to be aware of African techniques and procedures.

The Asian Development Bank

The Asian Development Bank (AsDB) started operations in 1966 as an international regional development finance institution owned by its member governments. In size it falls between the Inter-American Development Bank and the African and Caribbean Development Banks. The purpose of the bank is for lending funds and providing technical assistance to developing member countries in the region of Asia and the Far East, including the South Pacific, and for promoting investment and generally fostering economic growth in the region. Lending operations of AsDB are mainly based on two kinds of loans – ordinary loans to the somewhat better-off developing member countries, and concessional loans to its poorest member countries. Technical assistance grants are financed mainly from the Technical Assistance Special Fund of the bank. Problems of implementation from the bank's own experience are related to the fact that some of its borrowers have not had much experience in procedures followed by international financial institutions. There are also problems arising from the fact that certain countries are situated beyond easy physical access and project implementation in these countries is somewhat slower than in others. As AsDB's future strategy will place more emphasis on small and least developed member countries, the performance of the bank reveals that it will face considerable problems of implementation. The bank clearly has to provide more technical assistance for these countries to avoid such problems. However, the availability of funds needed to solve these problems in the greater part of the world will remain an open question. The aim of the bank can only be to help each developing member country to find its own solutions. The solution of the Asian drama of poverty is far beyond the capacity of such institutions as AsDB, but the more strength and power it has, the more effective will be the impact of its operations.

The Caribbean Development Bank

The Caribbean Development Bank (CDB) was established as a regional development organisation in 1970 to contribute to the harmonious economic growth and development of the member countries of the Caribbean region and to promote economic co-operation and integration among them with special regard to the needs of the less developed members of the region. Projects financed by the bank from both ordinary capital and special funds resources cover a wide range of development activities. CDB also provides technical assistance to the borrowing member states, particularly the LLDCs. Problems of implementation from the bank's own experience are mainly related to frequent delays in implementation, due largely to the lack of expertise in the borrowing countries, and legal and administrative hold-ups in decisions to satisfy conditions of precedent. The performance of CDB indicates that it has many problems to overcome in the 1980s so long as its member countries are facing serious economic problems. The bank should, however, be able to ease these problems gradually over the decade, if it chooses to adopt for itself a leading role in economic co-operation and integration among its member states. As with the other two regional banks (AfDB and AsDB), the problem of CDB's limited financial resources will be a severe handicap, and it should therefore raise its capital substantially by further expanding its membership to non-regional countries and organisations, while keeping its Caribbean character.

The Inter-American Development Bank

The Inter-American Development Bank (IDB) was established in 1959 as a regional development organisation to contribute to the acceleration of the process of economic and social development of the regional developing member countries, both individually and collectively. The bank's scope of activities covers the area of the western hemisphere in the Latin American and Caribbean regions. The projects that the bank is financing cover all major sectors. The bank's complementary financing programme is a mechanism designed to increase the flow of private capital for Latin American development. IDB has realised that, in providing development loans, it cannot substitute its management or its technical capabilities for those of the borrowers, and has instead designed systems to obtain the same degree of assurance regarding each project as if the bank were managing or carrying out the work itself. The performance of the bank indicates that it has followed a concrete pattern of lending policy. Its strategy for financing and its future prospects regarding extending more aid to its least developed member countries are, however, questionable. Its social programme of lending is another aspect to which the bank has to give more attention in the near future. IDB should develop a character markedly different from that of its first two decades to cope with the new environment and changes that have taken place in recent years. As the establishment of the bank has coincided with the period of greatest activity in the formation of groups of countries in the process of integration, it should be more active as a form in which significant aspects of its activities are developed so that it can participate more effectively in the process of Latin American economic integration.

World Bank Group

The International Bank for Reconstruction and Development

The International Bank for Reconstruction and Development (IBRD) was established in 1944 and commenced operations in 1946 for the purpose of assisting in the reconstruction and development of territories of members by facilitating the investment of capital for productive purposes, and encouragement of the development of productive facilities and resources in less developed countries. The bank operates in all economic sectors and provides technical assistance as an integral part of its operations. Its operations cover Africa, Asia, Europe, the Middle East, Latin America and the Caribbean. IBRD's general policy for financing is directed towards increased emphasis on investments that can improve the productivity and well-being of the mass of poor people in developing countries. As for its general policy for technical assistance, emphasis is given to the need to enhance the economic development of member countries, in general, with additional direct technical assistance to some countries in the Middle East, Latin America and Africa as an important part of the bank's financial projects. Problems of project implementation from the bank's own experience are related to physical implementation and construction, costs and financial matters, and operational issues. Political problems as such and other exogenous factors are behind some other problems. These problems are brought to the attention of borrowers and corrective action is recommended. The performance of the bank has shown that it has done much for developing countries in the 1970s. However, it could have done more had it adjusted its activities more rapidly to more constructive directions. IBRD must be ready to face the challenging problems of development in the 1980s, and without increasing its financial resources substantially it will be handicapped in solving the serious financial problems that will face its developing member countries. This requires a structural change in its Articles of Agreement and membership and its voting power. As the bank has already increased its capital, its status should be amended to change its 1:1 gearing ratio to a 2:1 ratio as recommended by the Brandt Commission, which would enable it to raise its borrowing capacity. In addition, the need for more World Bank co-financing with the private sector is going to be a major issue for IBRD in the 1980s, seeking more ways in which additional funds can be obtained from the private sector through co-financing and co-operation between the private sector and the bank. Unless these three big issues (membership and voting power, gearing ratio, and co-financing with the private sector) are adopted in the 1980s, the World Bank will be unable to meet its obligations as a world development institution.

The International Development Association

The International Development Association (IDA) was established in 1960 as a soft-loan affiliate of the World Bank to promote economic development, increase productivity and raise standards of living in the less developed areas of the world included within its membership by providing finance to meet their important developmental requirements on terms which are more flexible and bear less heavily on the balance of payments than those of conventional loans, thereby furthering the developmental objectives of IBRD and supplementing its activities. IDA assistance is concentrated on the very poor countries; its strategy in the 1970s attempted to overcome the difficulties of directing the benefits of development projects primarily toward the 'target group' of the rural population. IDA strategy for the 1980s is based upon the needs of the poorest countries for greatly expanded external assistance on concessionary terms; its Sixth Replenishment has taken into account the international development strategy for the 1980s to fulfil these needs. Problems of project implementation of the association's own experience are mainly related to the problem of monitoring and analysis of delays in implementation. There are uniform standards that can be applied in judging whether a project should have been completed faster than was actually the case. Most measurement is done against earlier expectations which might have been unrealistic. Identification of the problems along with the experience gained in prior projects in various countries and sectors have resulted in better prepared projects executed on a more timely basis. The critical issue arising from IDA's performance is the fact that if its resources remain inadequate, many high-priority development projects will have to be shelved and millions of people will be left out of the development process, with their search for productive work and a better life delayed. Foreign sources of finance capable of providing loans on terms as favourable as those of IDA are few. Thus IDA effectiveness depends upon the willingness of the governments of the rich countries to contribute more resources for IDA's replenishments, but on a politically neutral basis. The worst aspects of absolute poverty in poor countries include not only low income, but also malnutrition, a high rate of child mortality, disease and ignorance; all can be helped by human development programmes, an area to which IDA needs to give greater attention in the coming years.

The International Finance Corporation

The International Finance Corporation (IFC) was established in 1956 as an affiliate of the World Bank to encourage the flow of domestic and foreign capital into productive investments in developing countries. The corporation supplements the economic development efforts of the

IBRD and IDA by providing capital in any form; long-term loans, equity subscriptions, or a combination of both. An increasing proportion of the corporation's investments was planned to be directed to natural resource development, particularly energy resources. Its future financing strategy will be directed to the least developed regions and within countries into the least developed parts. Technical assistance is provided to its member countries, mainly in the financial institutions on the basis of resource availability. Problems of implementation from the corporation's own experience are related mainly to project definition and preparation, although the corporation provides extensive assistance to project sponsors. Implementation responsibility remains in the hands of the project sponsor, and although the corporation takes equity in firms, it does not participate in active management of these firms. The performance of IFC indicates that it should give great attention in the near future to policies for project identification, definition, appraisal and follow-up and implementation, that is policies related to the project cycle based upon concrete guidelines for project appraisal, taking into consideration all the management problems that it has faced in the field. In addition, it should carry out an international investment strategy by devising new methods to allow its member countries to assess and compare various opportunities across national borders, taking into consideration the different political, economic and market contexts as well as the respective accounting methods that should be used. This would obviously add a new dimension to IFC's activities.

TOWARDS MEETING THE OBJECTIVES OF INTERNATIONAL DEVELOPMENT STRATEGY

The present study has proved that the current situation of the transfer of financial resources to developing countries, the development assistance policies, and the performance of aid institutions of DAC, OPEC, the regional development banks and the World Bank Group have not been able to attack absolute poverty or to meet the objectives of international development strategy. The international community should reach specific agreements to provide the necessary additional assistance and the transfer of financial resources from rich to poor countries in programmes that meet the basic needs, in collaboration with vigorous efforts by the poorest nations themselves, and further action in co-financing and a development strategy to face the future of global interdependence.

The basic problem facing global interdependence is seen in the widening gap between the haves' and the have nots, and although the first and second decades of development designated by the UN Conference on Trade and Development have elapsed, both decades have failed to achieve satisfactory results. The situation was worse in the least developed countries where limited resources, drought, population growth, balance of payments difficulties, and a burden of heavy debt have eroded any hope for real development. The drama of poverty and the reshaping of the international economic order are two faces of the same coin, namely helping the poorest countries to help themselves through self-reliance and being partners in development. We must hope for future co-operation against international confrontation and world disaster. Some countries have succeeded in alleviating the burden of poverty by abolishing all foreign debt: Sweden and other Scandinavian countries are good examples. Other countries have increased their amount of ODA as the Netherlands did, while some others shifted aid funds for the benefit of LLDCs as West Germany did. These countries should encourage others, who have not yet shared in solving the burden of poverty, to co-operate in future co-financing on their terms.

A long-standing feature of international resource transfers is that the amounts received by developing countries vary widely from country to country, even between countries with broadly similar needs, due mainly to political factors and self-economic interests of the donor countries. Lower-income countries, considered as a group of the least developed among developing countries, have attracted a disproportionately small share of such resources in relation to their population and needs. These countries, with few exceptions, are located mainly in two areas: 'Sub-Sahara Africa' and 'Southern Asia', as the two most depressed regions of the world. Concessionary assistance must be concentrated on these two large poorest regions. This geographical redistribution of concessionary assistance has to take account of the absorptive capacities of these countries and a selective action which has an effective impact on the poorest groups and therefore on sectors such as agriculture and infrastructure – the adoption of the 'Basic Needs' criteria.

The enlargement of developing countries' markets through the creation of common markets, preferential trading blocks and similar arrangements is a necessary condition for self-sustained growth and the transformation of these economies to cope with the 'New International Economic Order'. In this regard, the approach of fostering ODA and investments through a more active role of co-financing between DAC, OPEC, the regional banks, the World Bank Group and international commercial banks could be adopted as a future strategy to be realised in a consistent manner. International multilateral lending organisations could be useful channels through which global co-financing 'Aid Programmes' could be adopted. This could ideally be co-ordinated with other bilateral aid programmes.

OPEC countries should be viewed as developing countries as their oil is prone to depletion and they do not possess any other natural resources and are still in the early stages of development. However, these countries have now made their mark in the field of development assistance as new partners showing a promising willingness. Their role is rapidly growing with a good impact on the development efforts of the recipient countries and international organisations. OPEC aid agencies have developed common appraisal and loan-withdrawal procedures and have been able to co-finance jointly among themselves. They choose a lead agency which negotiates with the recipient country on behalf of all participants. DAC members as a group have never developed such a close relationship, but Denmark, Finland, Norway and Sweden carried out joint projects in the early years of their bilateral aid programmes. However, the importance of joint Nordic projects diminished as the Nordic countries acquired greater experience in their bilateral activities. Developing countries have a preference for joint financing under a strong lead agency as it requires united funds and a similar approach to project assistance. By contrast, DAC member countries in general prefer to participate in parallel financing since it requires no departure from their own individual procedures, criteria and preference, and permits the tying of aid and the imposition of related restrictions on procurements. Co-financing could be encouraged and made more efficient by early and more frequent exchange of information on a regular institutionalised basis. For that purpose a pooled information system for co-financed projects could be strengthened under the leading role of the World Bank. OPEC member countries and their aid agencies could combine their efforts more actively under a new established OPEC Development Assistance Committee similar to the OECD Development Assistance Committee.

The adoption of measures to improve project implementation and disbursements is an important and practical issue. Approaches and techniques of project appraisal should be directly related and oriented to the recipient country based upon economic and social criteria rather than commercial ones. It is not only the volume of aid commitments but rather the quality of aid performance and the validity of sound projects that badly need to be disbursed and implemented faster. Problems of project management in the recipient countries should be solved by intensive programmes for technical assistance carried out jointly by aid agencies. Trilateral co-operation based upon comparative advantages and the cost of natural resources in developing countries, the transfer of adapted technology, and capital funds from aid agencies represent the best approach for solving the problems of project implementation and follow-up.

Development aid institutions could play a much greater role by mobilising capital funds through international capital markets. The World Bank and other multilateral development lending institutions, such as IDB and AsDB, have already made arrangements for expanded co-financing with private banks. These are welcome developments which should be pursued actively. This requires an agreement to raise substantially the financial resources of these institutions and amendments of their Articles of Agreement to make their scope of activities more effective and promising in meeting the objectives of international development strategy.

Part I

The Performance of Financial Flows, Development Assistance Policies
and Aid Agencies in OECD/DAC Member Countries

Case-studies

1 USA
2 UK
3 France
4 West Germany
5 Japan
6 Netherlands
7 Sweden
8 Commission of the European Community

2 The Performance of the Development Assistance Committee

THE ESTABLISHMENT OF THE DEVELOPMENT ASSISTANCE COMMITTEE

The history of DAC goes back to 1959. In the course of considering which changes should be made in the Organisation for European Economic Co-operation (OEEC), brought into existence a decade earlier to facilitate the European recovery programme, it was agreed that a Development Assistance Group (DAG) should be established to act as a forum for the discussion of common problems between the growing number of western countries which supplied, or could begin to supply, aid to developing countries. The establishment of the DAG furthered the American objective of encouraging European countries, and especially West Germany, to take on a growing share of the defence and aid burden. The DAG came into existence even before the OEEC was transformed in 1961 into the OECD. Once the latter was established the DAG was transformed into the DAC and made an integral part of the new structure, although membership of the two organisations was not identical.[1] Members of the OECD are Australia, Austria, Belgium, Canada, Denmark, Finland, France, West Germany, Greece, Iceland, Ireland, Italy, Japan, Luxembourg, New Zealand, the Netherlands, Norway, Portugal, Spain, Sweden, Switzerland, Turkey, the UK and the USA. Participating in the work of the Development Assistance Committee are Australia, Austria, Belgium, Canada, Denmark, Finland, France, West Germany, Italy, Japan, the Netherlands, New Zealand, Norway, Sweden, Switzerland, the UK, USA and the EEC. Greece, Iceland, Ireland, Luxembourg, Portugal, Spain and Turkey are members of OECD but not of DAC, while the Commission of the European Communities is a member of DAC but not of OECD. The chief official handling aid and development matters is the Director of the Development Assistance Committee, who has under him three divisions – the Economic Development Division, the Aid Review Division and the Financial Policy Division – and a statistical unit.

DAC member countries are considered to be the major source of information on the total flow of financial resources from the developed market economies. The flow covered by the reports of DAC in general and for each member country has been classified as follows:

I Official Development Assistance (ODA), comprising:
  (a) bilateral ODA;
  (b) contributions to multilateral institutions.
II Other Official Flows (OOF), comprising:
  (a) bilateral OOF;
  (b) multilateral institutions.
III Grants by private voluntary agencies.
IV Private flows at market terms:
  (1) direct investment;
  (2) bilateral portfolio investment and other;
  (3) multilateral portfolio investment;
  (4) private export credits.

OFFICIAL DEVELOPMENT ASSISTANCE

Official Development Assistance provided by DAC members combined reached US $14,696 m in 1977, US $19,882 m in 1978, US $22,375 m in 1979 and US $26,776 m in 1980. These figures can be compared with US $13,585 m in 1975, US $6832 m in 1970, and US $4628 m in 1960. The rate of growth of ODA during the 1970s was higher than during the 1960s. Contrary to these figures in $ nominal prices, ODA as a percentage of Gross National Product declined in the 1970s compared with the 1960s. The ratio reached 0.35 per cent in 1978 and 1979, 0.37 per cent in 1980 compared with 0.45 per cent in 1965 and 0.51 per cent in 1960. The ratios show considerable differences between DAC individual countries, with Scandinavian countries and the Netherlands recently showing a better performance – Appendix 2.1 and Chart 1 show the performance of DAC countries in providing financial flows to developing countries and multilateral agencies during 1970–80.

The performance of DAC countries combined falls far short of the 0.7 per cent target for ODA. Although all DAC countries accepted the UN

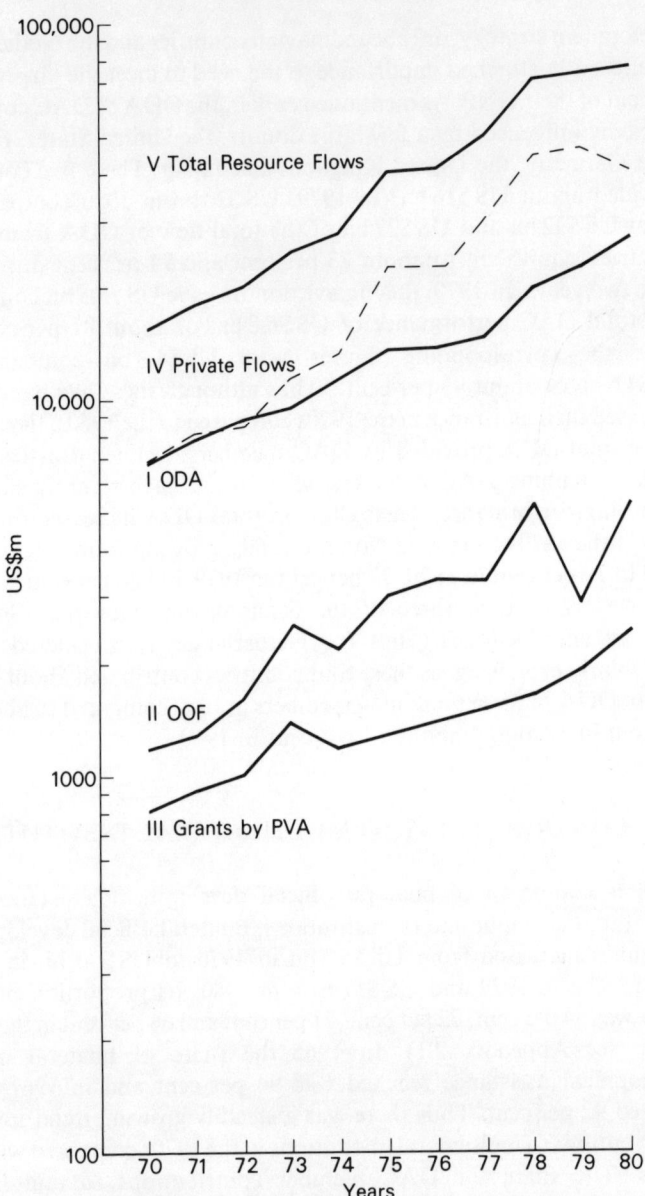

CHART 1 Flow of financial resources to developing countries and multilateral agencies by type: total DAC countries 1970–80

Source: Appendix 2.1

development strategy, only Scandinavian countries and the Netherlands have recently attached importance to the need to meet the target of 0.7 per cent of their GNP. As mentioned earlier, the ODA of DAC countries is heavily influenced by a few large donors, the United States, France, West Germany, the United Kingdom and Japan. These five countries provided about US $16 bn[2] in 1979, US $20 bn in 1980 compared to about US $22 bn and US $27 bn of the total flow of ODA from DAC countries, equivalent to about 73 per cent and 74 per cent during the same two years. In 1970, the big five donors gave US $5.5 bn compared to a total DAC performance of US $6.8 bn, or about 81 per cent. In 1960, the corresponding figures were US $4.3 bn compared to US $4.6 bn or about 93 per cent.[3] Thus although these five big donors increased their assistance in the 1970s compared to the 1960s, their share of the total ODA provided by DAC members declined drastically.

The remaining DAC members, as a group, have recently shown a promising performance. Their share in total ODA increased dramatically in the 1970s compared with the 1960s, growing from 7 per cent in 1960 to 19 per cent in 1970, 27 per cent in 1979 and 26 per cent in 1980. The performance of three of the Scandinavian countries (Sweden, Norway and Denmark) and the Netherlands, is considered to be particularly promising, as these four countries contributed about 51 per cent of ODA of these remaining members in 1980 compared to about 30 per cent in 1970 and about 17 per cent in 1960.

DAC CONTRIBUTIONS TO MULTILATERAL INSTITUTIONS

ODA is composed of bilateral official development assistance and contributions to multilateral institutions. Bilateral official development assistance increased from US $5.7 bn in 1970 to US $9.8 bn in 1975, US $15.9 bn in 1979 and US $17.6 bn in 1980. Its proportion of total ODA was 84 per cent, 72 per cent, 71 per cent and 66 per cent in the same years (see Appendix 2.1). In 1965 the share of bilateral official development assistance reached was 94 per cent and in 1961–63 it reached 92 per cent. Thus there was a steadily growing trend towards contributions to multilateral institutions in the 1970s compared with the 1960s. The share for DAC member contributions to multilateral institutions is shown in Table 2.1. The Pearson target that these contributions should reach at least 20 per cent of ODA by 1975[4] has been met. The expansion in the multilateral share in the 1970s was largely accounted for by the substantial IDA replenishments and by the

TABLE 2.1 DAC Contributions to Multilateral Institutions as a Percentage of Total ODA (1961–80)

Years	$m	Percentage of ODA
1961–63	467	8
1965	348	6
1970	1124	16
1975	3770	28
1977	4612	31
1978	6759	34
1979	6461	29
1980	9135	34

Sources: OECD, *Development Co-operation*, Reviews, 1971–81.

rapid expansion of the regional development banks. Table 2.2 shows the contributions of individual DAC members in multilateral institutions.

From Table 2.2, it is clear that by 1975 all DAC member countries, except Australia, France and the EEC, had exceeded the 20 per cent Pearson target, and by 1980, Austria, France and the EEC were exceptions. The contributions of individual DAC members in 1980 continued to reflect wide disparities, Austria with 15 per cent and France with 17 per cent contributing the smallest shares. Italy, on the other hand, contributed 89 per cent, and the Scandinavian countries' contributions were as follows: Finland 43 per cent, Norway 43 per cent, Denmark 46 per cent and Sweden 27 per cent. Canada gave 38 per cent, Japan 41 per cent, West Germany 35 per cent and the US 39 per cent. These countries far exceeded the Pearson target and their shares were higher than the average of the total DAC countries, which reached 34 per cent in 1980. The rest of the DAC member countries, although exceeding the Pearson target, were below the average.

PRIVATE FLOWS

Private flows at market terms have shown a rapid increase over the 1970s as a whole compared to the 1960s. Private flows increased from US$6.9bn in 1970 to US$22bn in 1975 and US$47bn in 1979,

TABLE 2.2 Contributions of Individual DAC Members in Multilateral Institutions as a Percentage of ODA (1970, 1975, 1980)

Country	1970	1975	1980
Australia	6	14	27
Austria	60	23	15
Belgium	23	33	24
Canada	23	30	38
Denmark	37	46	46
Finland	—	43	43
France	11	14	17
Germany, FR	22	31	35
Italy	57	68	89
Japan	19	26	41
Netherlands	21	40	26
New Zealand	—	24	28
Norway	60	44	43
Sweden	46	34	27
Switzerland	39	32	31
UK	11	34	30
USA	13	27	39
EEC	—	15	19
Total DAC countries	16	28	34

Sources: For contributions in US$: OECD, *Development Co-operation*, Reviews, 1974–81.

compared with US $3 bn in 1960, US $4 bn in 1965 and US $6 bn in 1969. The share of private flows in total financial flows to developing countries and multilateral agencies by DAC members reached about 64 per cent in 1979 compared with about 44 per cent in 1970 and about 39 per cent in 1960. During the 1960s private flows at market terms were dominated by five countries: USA (35%), France (14%), the Federal Republic of Germany (12%) UK (11%) and Italy (9%). These five countries contributed about 80 per cent of the total DAC private flows.[5] From 1973 Switzerland came into the picture, replacing Italy in the big five in DAC private flows. In 1979 the shares of these five countries in total private flows were as follows: USA (26%), UK (19%), Federal Republic of Germany (7%), Switzerland (11%) and France (11%). These five countries contributed together about 74 per cent of total DAC private flows.[6] By 1980, total private flows of DAC member countries declined to reach about US $42.6 bn, due mainly to a sharp decline (about two-thirds) in US private flows from US $12.00 bn in 1979 to only US $4.3 bn in 1980. The big five countries in total private flows took their place as follows: UK (26%), France (16%), West Germany (14%), US (10%) and Switzerland (10%). However, there has been a change in the importance of some of these countries in their performance in private flows (notably USA): these five member countries as a group in 1979 together contributed about 76 per cent of total DAC private flows. Table 2.3 shows the individual shares of DAC members in private flows in 1979 and 1980.

TABLE 2.3 Country Share of DAC Members in Private Flows (1979, 1980)

Country	Share of country members 1979 %	1980 %
Australia	0.3	0.4
Austria	0.3	0.2
Belgium	3.4	5.1
Canada	2.4	2.4
Denmark	0.3	0.4
Finland	0.2	0.2
France	10.8	16.6
Germany, Federal Republic	7.3	14.8
Italy	7.0	6.9
Japan	10.0	4.8
Netherlands	1.0	1.5
New Zealand	0.003	0.1
Norway	0.6	0.8
Sweden	0.6	2.1
Switzerland	11.1	5.9
UK	19.1	27.3
USA	25.6	10.6
Total DAC countries	100	100

Source: OECD, *Development Co-operation*, Reviews 1980, 1981.

APPENDIX 2.1 The Flow of Financial Resources to Developing Countries and Multilateral Agencies by Type, Total DAC Countries (1970–1980)

US$m

Disbursements Net disbursements	1970[a]	1971[a]	1972	1973	1974	1975	1976	1977	1978	1979	1980
I Official Development Assistance (a+b)	6,831.6	7,759.3	8,671.5	9,378.0	11,316.8	13,585.1	13,665.4	14,695.7	19,881.8	22,375.4	26,775.7
(a) Bilateral ODA	5,707.4	6,420.9	6,766.5	7,109.6	8,257.1	9,815.3	9,504.6	10,083.7	13,122.6	15,913.8	17,640.8
(b) Contributions to multilateral institutions	1,124.2	1,338.6	1,905.0	2,268.2	3,059.6	3,769.6	4,160.9	4,611.9	6,759.2	6,461.4	9,134.9
II Other Official Flows, (a+b)	1,152.3	1,271.1	1,581.5	2,462.9	2,183.1	3,023.6	3,305.3	3,319.1	5,214.3	2,656.3	5,279.8
(a) Bilateral OOF	879.7	1,003.3	1,207.3	2,073.2	2,198.9	2,944.6	3,186.1	3,192.4	5,057.6	2,900.0	5,386.3
(b) Multilateral institutions	272.6	267.2	374.2	389.7	−15.8	79.0	119.1	126.7	156.7	(−243.8)	(−106.5)
Subtotal (I+II): Total official flows	7,983.9	9,030.4	10,253.0	11,840.9	13,499.9	16,608.7	16,970.7	18,014.8	25,096.1	25,031.5	32,055.5
III Grants by private voluntary agencies	858.3	912.8	1,035.9	1,364.5	1,217.3	1,341.8	1,354.5	1,488.8	1,663.2	1,946.3	2,370.9
IV Private flows at market terms (1–4)	6,870.6	8,068.2	8,618.8	11,449.5	13,266.0	22,427.6	22,417.0	29,987.9	44,611.3	46,965.4	40,634.9
(1) Direct investment	3,528.7	3,706.8	4,443.4	6,710.6	7,060.1	10,493.8	7,823.9	8,791.7	11,439.4	13,491.2	8,896.2
(2) Bilateral portfolio invest and other	726.0	759.7	2,078.8	3,285.7	3,794.6	5,238.8	6,072.5	10,453.8	21,256.4	21,951.5	17,702.3
(3) Multilateral portfolio investment	474.2	770.5	667.3	257.5	−69.5	2,552.9	3,096.8	2,642.3	2,228.5	2,099.5	1,468.8
(4) Private export credits	2,141.7	2,831.3	1,412.0	1,195.7	2,480.8	4,141.9	5,423.8	8,100.0	9,686.8	9,423.2	12,567.7
V Total resource flows (I–IV)	15,713.1	18,011.3	19,907.8	24,655.2	27,983.2	40,378.1	40,742.2	49,491.7	71,370.6	73,943.3	75,061.3
ODA as % of GNP	0.34	0.35	0.33	0.30	0.33	0.35	0.33	0.31	0.35	0.35	0.37
Total resource flows as % of GNP	0.77	0.80	0.76	0.79	0.81	1.05	0.98	1.05	1.26	1.14	1.04

[a] Totals for New Zealand are excluded since detailed components are not available
Sources: OECD, *Development Co-operation,* Reviews 1974–81.

3 The United States of America

THE PERFORMANCE OF US OFFICIAL DEVELOPMENT ASSISTANCE

The United States is the largest DAC donor in official development assistance, but tended increasingly over the period 1960–80 to lag behind other DAC countries in terms of percentage of its GNP. The declining trend of US ODA/GNP started in the early years of the 1960s when the ratio declined from 0.53 in 1960 to 0.49 in 1965 and the declining trend continued drastically as it reached 0.31 in 1970, 0.26 in 1975 and 0.20 in 1979. However, the ratio increased to 0.27 in 1980, but the projection of US ODA/GNP in the first half of the 1980s is a declining trend according to the *World Development Report* 1981 of the World Bank.

Net flows of ODA reached an average of US $3.33bn during 1960–69[1]. However, while there was an increase in the amount of ODA provided by the US in the 1970s on the average, there was a decline in 1973, 1977 and 1979 (see Appendix 3.1). US contributions to multilateral institutions grew rapidly in the 1970s compared with the 1960s, while the share relative to bilateral official development assistance reached 63 per cent in 1980 compared with 36 per cent in 1975, 15 per cent in 1970 and 2 per cent in 1965.[2] This growing trend of US contribution to multilateral institutions was marked by increased aid to regional development banks and institutions. US bilateral other official flows increased from US $168.0m in 1970 to US $1112.0m in 1980. The bulk of this flow was mainly from official export credits (including funds in support of private export credits) which reached US $815.0m in 1980 compared with US $168m in 1970 and US $56.6m in 1965. Equities and other bilateral assets reached US $297.0m in 1980 compared with only US $6.0m in 1973. Grants by private voluntary agencies reached US $1301.0m in 1980 compared with US $598.0m in 1970. The ratio of grants by private voluntary agencies to total official flows increased from 19 per cent in 1970 to 23 per cent in 1973 then it declined to 16 per cent by 1980 (see Appendix 3.1 and Chart 2).

US PRIVATE FLOWS RELATIVE TO TOTAL FLOWS

US private flows to developing countries totalled US $12,008.0m in 1979 compared with US $2394.7m in 1970 and US $1859.0m in 1965, a continuous growth from 1970 to 1974. By 1975 US private flows had increased considerably to reach a level of US $11,799.0m but then they declined to about half this level in 1976. Direct investment constituted the most important part of US private flows as it reached about 67 per cent in 1979, 61 per cent in 1975, 73 per cent in 1970 and 68 per cent in 1965.[3] US private flows represented an average of about 51 per cent of the total US flows during the period 1970–79 compared with 29 per cent during 1966–68.[4] By the year 1980, US private flows declined drastically to reach US $4,301.0m, due to a sharp decline in export credits and negative balance of multilateral portfolio investment. Table 3.1 shows a comparison of US ODA and US private flows with US total resources flows and total DAC countries.

The following observations can be made from Table 3.1:

(1) US ODA as a percentage of total US flows declined during the period 1970–75, started to increase until 1978 then declined in 1979 with an average of 37 per cent during the period 1970–79.
(2) US private flows as a percentage of total US flows increased during the period 1970–75, started to decline until 1978, then increased in 1979 with an average of 51 per cent during the period 1970–79.
(3) The share of US ODA to total DAC ODA declined (with one exception in 1976) during the period 1970–79, with an average of 33 per cent.
(4) The share of US private flows to total DAC private flows reached an average of 33 per cent during the period 1970–79, with no clear trend.
(5) The share of US total flows to total DAC flows has shown a declining trend (with the exception of 1974, 1975, and 1979), with an average of 33 per cent.
(6) The year 1980 witnessed a shift in the composition of US financial flows in favour of ODA, accompanied by a declining share of US in total DAC financial flows.

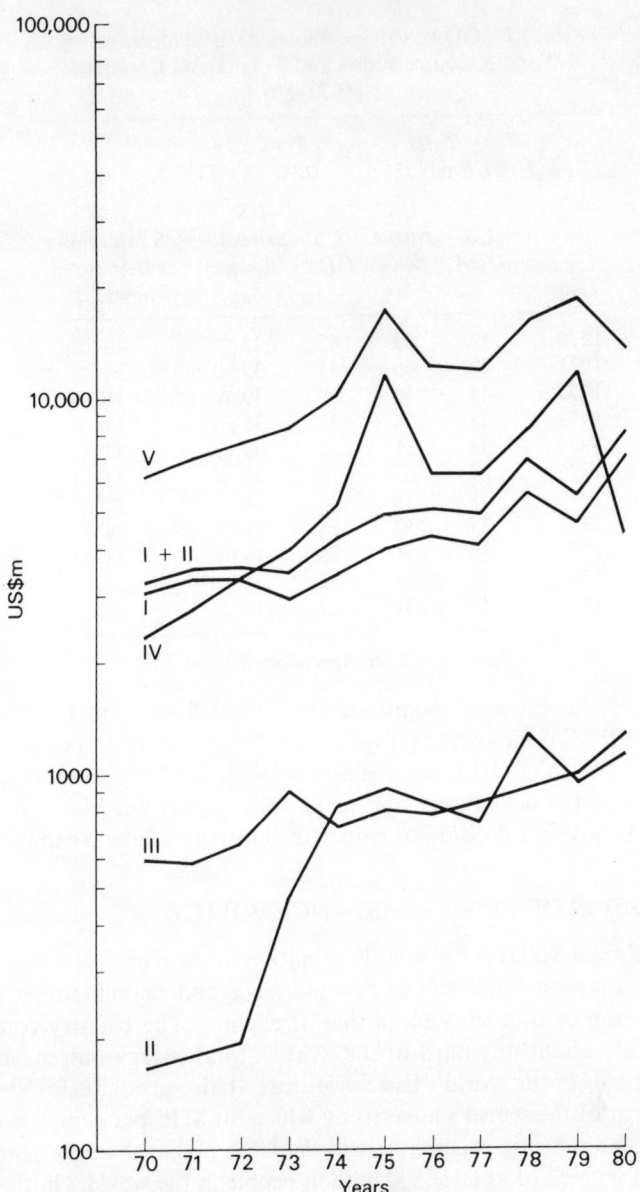

CHART 2 The flow of financial resources to developing countries and multilateral agencies by type: USA 1970–80

Source: Appendix 3.1

TABLE 3.1 ODA, Private Flows as a percentage of US Total Resource Flows and Total DAC Countries (1970–80)

Years	Total US flows %		Total DAC %		US total flows to DAC total flows %
	US ODA %	US private flows %	US ODA %	US private flows %	
1970	49	39	45	35	40
1971	48	40	43	35	38
1972	44	44	39	39	38
1973	36	48	32	35	34
1974	33	51	30	40	37
1975	29	67	29	53	43
1976	35	52	32	29	30
1977	35	52	28	21	24
1978	35	51	28	19	23
1979	25	64	21	26	25
1980	52	31	27	10	18

Source: Original data from Appendixes 2.1 and 3.1.

From the above observations the United States was therefore the largest DAC donor with average private flows, during the period (1970–79), higher than ODA. United States ODA/GNP may be expected to decline in the near future and its performance is uncertain, given the administration's decision to reduce the growth of federal expenditures.

US DEVELOPMENT ASSISTANCE POLICY

The United States is the wealthiest nation in the world. It is one of the world's largest importers of raw materials and manufactured goods, importing considerably more than it exports. The country consumes annually about one-third of the world's total energy output and just under half of the world's basic resources. It also accounts for about 65 per cent of the world's advertising which, at $115 per capita per year, makes advertising expenditures in the USA higher than the yearly per capita income of at least 800 million people in the world. On the other hand, the United States is the largest of the very few food-surplus countries in the world, and it supplies almost half of the world's food exports.[5]

Over the years since the Marshall Plan, the US foreign aid programme has gone through many substantive changes as well as several changes in name. In the 1950s foreign aid was justified primarily as a national security measure, needed to strengthen allies and to build up low-income countries so that they would be less vulnerable to communist invasion or takeover.[6] In the 1960s, the trend was more toward strengthening a number of countries against internal subversion, but there was also a trend toward development as a goal in itself. There were seen to be economic, social, and political components of development – all leading toward the target of self-sustaining growth. There were countries which, with the help of foreign aid, did reach this target – notable cases being Greece, Taiwan, Brazil and Mexico.[7] A new approach for US foreign aid policy during the 1970s was proposed, of which the following is a summary.[8]

In 1968 the Congress of the United States expressed a desire for changing the entire US foreign aid policy, calling on the President to undertake reappraisal of US foreign assistance programmes and to submit recommendations to Congress on appropriate reforms. In a report to the President of the United States, the task force on international development recommended a new focus for US programmes with emphasis on multilateral organisations, and a new institutional framework consisting of:

(1) *A US International Development Bank*: responsible for making capital and related technical assistance loans in selected countries and for selected programmes of special interest to the US.
(2) *A US International Development Institute*: to seek new breakthroughs in the application of science and technology to resources and processes critical to the developing nations.
(3) *The Overseas Private Investment Corporation (OPIC)*: as authorised by Congress, to mobilise and facilitate the participation of US private capital and business skills in international development.
(4) *A US International Development Council*: to ensure that international development receives greater emphasis in US trade, investment, financial, agricultural, and export-promotion policies. It would also be responsible for making sure that US assistance policies are effectively directed toward long-term development purposes and are co-ordinated with the work of international organisations.

On 15 September 1970, the President of the United States proposed a major transformation in the foreign assistance programme, based upon the recommendations of the Task Force on International Development. In his message to Congress, the President spelt out the major changes in the world which required new responses. Moreover, he proposed that the United States should redirect its policies which bore on development to ensure that they reinforced the new approach outlined in his message. In this connection the President proposed the following:

(1) The United States should move promptly toward initiation of a system of tariff preferences for the exports of manufactured products of the lower income countries in the market of all of the industrialised countries.
(2) An elimination of those tying restrictions on procurement which hinder US investment guarantee programmes in their support of US private investment in the lower income countries.
(3) All donor countries should take steps to end the requirement that foreign aid be used to purchase goods and services produced in the nation providing the aid.

On 21 April 1971 the President sent new assistance legislations to Congress. In his message on reorganisation of United States foreign assistance programmes, he proposed two bills – the International Security Assistance Act and the International Development and Humanitarian Assistance Act – and announced a number of administrative actions which he intended to take:

(1) To create a United States International Development Corporation and a United States International Development Institute to replace AID.
(2) To provide adequate funding for these new programmes to support essential United States foreign policy objectives in the years ahead.
(3) To place greater reliance on international institutions and encourage them to play an increasing leadership role in the world development process.

Moreover, the President indicated that the new bilateral assistance programme must achieve several objectives:

(1) Clearly identify United States aid objectives: security assistance, development assistance and humanitarian assistance.

(2) In the area of development assistance, work within a framework set by the international institutions.

The proposed foreign aid bill was defeated in the Senate, but different proposals offered by the senators helped to clarify the direction of US foreign aid policy in the future. In recognition of these different historical and economic patterns, Congress passed a new Foreign Assistance Act in 1973 which adopted a quite different focus. In a special report to Congress in 1975, AID described the terms of the new directions. Earlier development strategies assumed that economic growth would soon trickle down to the poor masses. In fact, while the large mass of the poor in some countries benefited from development to some degree, many of the very poorest were either no better, or even worse off, than a decade earlier. Recognition of these trends and their serious implications had led to a shift in US development assistance strategy.[9] The US stake in a new development strategy oriented toward meeting basic human needs was discussed by administrative officials, members of Congress, and representatives of labour, farmers, business and the public. As chief spokesmen for the administration view on foreign aid,[10] John J. Gilligan, Administrator of AID and C. Fred Bergsten, Assistant Secretary of the Treasury for International Affairs, emphasised the mutual economic interests of the US and the developing countries, and took note of the dramatic change in this relationship over the last twenty years. Most Americans, Gilligan noted, did not know that they depended on the developing world for many critical resources including oil, tin, aluminium and copper, to name only a few, and that the US needed the developing world not only for these raw materials, but also as markets for US products. US exports to developing countries were greater than to Europe or Japan, having tripled over the last five years to almost $30bn, and they translated into millions of jobs for Americans. Moreover, almost half of US direct investment overseas was in the Third World. These facts, said Governor Gilligan, indicated that the US stake in the economic and social progress of the poor countries could not be discussed apart from US national security and well-being. As Gilligan indicated: 'We simply cannot afford to allow global problems of hunger, physical degradation and poverty to block the way of progress in economic and social development'.[11]

The policies of the Carter Administration towards developing countries were designed to support US economic objectives and at the same time to strengthen US overall relations with Third and Fourth World countries. Mr Bergsten outlined some of the specifics of the US programme that could be summarised as follows:

(1) Dynamic non-inflationary growth should be assured in the US itself.
(2) Stability of the international monetary system was essential for all nations.
(3) The most open possible trading arrangements were very much in the interests of the US.
(4) It was also in the economic interest of the US to negotiate international commodity agreements, to stabilise prices, and to support the establishment of buffer stocks.
(5) Foreign investment was an area in which the US and the developing countries had common interests.

Of the many elements in the US aid package, Mr Bergsten emphasised the tremendous importance of participation in the international development banks, which currently appeared to be the most controversial part of the US programme. He insisted that the advantages to the US of channelling an important share of its aid through the banks outweighed the inherent disadvantages of the US being unable to control them.[12] Members of the Senate and House had expressed their concern for meeting the basic needs of the poorest majority in developing countries as well as for the international economic policies of the US as they related to the developing world, concerns which were little understood but were of growing importance to the US.

The United States appears to have an important new opportunity to work with other nations in applying science and technology to development problems. To meet their requirements for technology, the developing countries appear to be seeking a strategy of building their own capabilities for research and development, and expanding collaboration among themselves and with the developed countries.[13] US initiatives can help to realise this strategy and its research and development community should stand ready to respond.

THE DEVELOPMENT ASSISTANCE PROGRAMME OF THE AGENCY FOR INTERNATIONAL DEVELOPMENT

The Agency for International Development, established in 1961 under the Foreign Assistance Act as amended, is a public institution, acting as an agency for the US government's foreign economic aid activities. The

Act provides that the aid programme be administered by an officer to be appointed by the President in a unit within the State Department. The Act also prescribes the amounts authorised to be spent in the first year of the new programme and the conditions attached thereto. The President delegated the spending authority given to him by Congress to the Secretary of State who in turn delegated it to the Administrator of AID. The latter, however, continues to be appointed directly by the President and, although the Secretary of State reserves the right to exercise the powers himself, the Administrator is in fact allowed to operate with a high degree of independence.[14] On 15 September 1970 the President sent a message to Congress proposing basic changes in the administration of development assistance.

The changes included:

(i) separation of US military aid from US development assistance in the basic legislation;
(ii) changes of development aid gradually from bilateral to multilateral administration;
(iii) separation of development loans from technical assistance.

There was some feeling in favour of supporting the separation of legislation for military aid from that for development aid.[15]

AID is the principal US government agency responsible for extending development loans repayable in dollars and tied to US commodities and services. It is the largest single source of dollar-repayment in US financial flows. It also supports assistance which takes the form of grants and technical assistance for emergencies and certain contributions to international development organisations.[16] The development assistance programme of AID consists of integrated project assistance, in the form of either loans or grants, in the sectors of food and nutrition (including agricultural production and rural development), health and population, education and human resources development. The primary objective of the development assistance programme is to assist developing countries in pursuing basic human-needs-oriented development strategies giving particular attention also to the role of women and private voluntary organisations. AID requested $2051.7m for the development assistance programme for the fiscal year 1980 compared with the $1830.6m programme in the fiscal year 1979 – Table 3.2 shows the proposed distribution of the 1980 development assistance programmes.

The Functional Development Assistance and Sahel programmes which include agriculture, rural development and nutrition, population,

TABLE 3.2 Development Assistance Programmes by Function Proposed for FY1980 (US$m and percentage of total)

Type of programme	US$m	%
Food and nutrition	715.4	40.7
International organisations and programmes	277.2	15.8
Population planning	216.3	12.3
Health	146.6	8.3
Selected development activities	136.1	7.8
Education and human resources	119.5	6.8
Sahel development programme	105.0	6.0
International disaster assistance	25.0	1.4
American schools and hospitals abroad	15.0	0.9
Total proposed[a]	1756.1	

[a] Excluding operating expenses and Foreign Service Retirement Fund. Including these two items the total is $2051.7m.
Source: Original data: Agency for International Development, *Congressional Presentation, Fiscal Year 1980*, Main Volume, Department of State, AID, Washington DC, 1 February 1979.

health, education and human resources and related development activities were set at $1438.9m in FY1980. The distribution of these programmes by region indicates a concentration on Asia ($507.9m or 35 per cent) and Latin America ($230.3m or 16 per cent). African aid is proposed at $217.0m (15 per cent), the Sahel Development Programme $105.0m (7 per cent), the Middle East only $57.6m (4 per cent). Inter-regional aid is proposed at $321.1m or 22 per cent of these programmes.

THE SECURITY SUPPORTING ASSISTANCE PROGRAMME

The security supporting assistance programme is designed to promote economic or political stability in areas of special foreign policy interests. Economic assistance under this programme can take the form of budget support, programme assistance, cash grants or capital projects, and may be extended on a loan or a grant basis. Congress has directed that assistance under this programme be used, where possible, to promote development efforts to aid the poor and conform with the aims of the development assistance programme. The security supporting assistance programme proposed $1995.1m for FY1980 compared with $1921.2m in FY1979. It was proposed that 86 per cent of the total security supporting assistance be allocated to the Middle East. Proposed levels for Israel and Egypt were the same as appropriated in FY1979. Security supporting assistance funds also relieve economic dislocations resulting from the struggle for majority rule in Southern Africa, and provide support to Turkey in its efforts to stabilise its economy. The administration's requests for UN forces in Cyprus, Spain, the Sinai Support Mission and the Philippines were covered in the Security Assistance Presentation of the Departments of State and Defence. Table 3.3 shows the major distribution of the security supporting assistance programme proposed for FY1980.

TABLE 3.3 Major Distribution of Security Supporting Assistance Programme Proposed for FY1980 (US $m and percentage)

Allocations	US $m	%
Israel	785.0	39.3
Egypt	750.0	37.6
Rest of Middle East excluding Jordan, Syria	192.0	9.6
Africa	100.0	5.0
Jordan	60.0	3.0
Syria	60.0	3.0
Security supporting assistance administered by the State Dept.	48.1	2.4
Total proposed	1995.1	

Source: Original data, Agency for International Development, *Congressional Presentation, Fiscal Year 1980*, Main Volume, Dept. of State, AID, Washington DC, 1 February 1979.

THE PUBLIC LAW 480 PROGRAMME

The Public Law 480 Programme (PL 480) provides agricultural commodity assistance, primary food aid. The programme has undergone several modifications from 1954 when the Agricultural Trade Development and Assistance Act (better known as Public Law 480) was enacted. The programme comprised three categories:

Title I: provided for sale of local currencies;
Title II: provided for disposals as emergency relief;
Title III: provided for disposals through voluntary relief agencies.

Of these, Title I was the most important – in terms both of dollar magnitude and of implications for trade and development. In 1959 Title IV was introduced to provide long-term credit for dollar purchases of surplus agricultural commodities for domestic consumption. The recipient country – under Title IV – pays in dollars and in reasonable annual amounts of periods not to exceed 20 years. In 1966 a legislation – The Food for Peace Act – was provided for two categories:

Title I: sales for dollar credits and local currencies;
Title II: donations.

Sales for local currencies were the largest single category of the programme during the early 1960s, whereas sales for dollar credits (corresponding to Title IV from 1959–66) constituted only a small fraction but increased in importance after 1965 until they reached 48 per cent compared with 3 per cent in 1962. Sales for local currencies reached a level of 52 per cent in 1968 compared with 97 per cent in 1962. Donations were of two kinds: direct donations to recipient governments which included economic development grants, child programmes, emergency relief; and donations to international organisations which included grants to UN Programmes (UNRWA and UNICEF) and to the World Food Programme.[17]

Recently, the classification of the PL 480 – Food for Peace Programme was provided under three main categories:

Title I: authorises concessional sales of US farm products to developing countries. These sales are repayable in dollars at low interest rates over a period of up to 40 years.
Title II: provides food donations to meet famine and other urgent relief requirements, to combat malnutrition especially among children, and to promote economic and community development, mainly through food for work projects.
Title III: provides food for development programmes (but funded under Title I) to offer a substantial incentive for low-income countries to undertake additional development programmes to improve the quality of life for poor people, particularly in rural areas. Multiyear supply commitments

of up to five years assure countries that they have priority access to PL 480 food. Local currencies generated through sales of Food for Peace commodities, which are used to support agreed-upon development efforts, may be created against dollars which would otherwise have to be repaid to the United States.

For FY1980, a Title I Programme of $785m was proposed on the basis of seasonal average prices projected by the US Department of Agriculture. It proposed to finance shipment of 5.1 million tons of food compared with an estimated 4.9 million tons in FY1979. Legislation requires that at least 75 per cent of the volume of Title I food aid be initially allocated to countries with per capita incomes at or below the poverty criteria of the International Development Association (IDA) – $580 per year. Eligibility for Food for Development (Title III) programmes is also limited to this group of countries.[18]

A Title II Programme of $536m, including $184m for ocean transportation costs, was proposed. This should finance shipments of the grain equivalent of 1.6 million tons, including a minimum of 1.3 million tons through voluntary agencies and the World Food Programme (WFP). Through the AID-funded 'Title II Outreach Project' $9.4m is being provided to US private voluntary organisations over the period FY1978–81 to help meet their logistical support costs for establishing or expanding feeding programmes for needy people in rural areas – particularly in African countries which cannot afford to finance such costs. An illustrative breakdown of the FY1980 programme by region is shown in Table 3.4.

TABLE 3.4 PL 480 Title II Proposed FY1980 by Region (US $000s)

Region	1978	1979	1980
Near East	50,170	49,200	45,252
Latin America	42,100	58,263	46,165
Africa	85,411	62,367	63,625
Asia	150,097	148,736	160,995
Total	327,778	318,566	316,037

Source: *Agency for International Development, Congressional Presentation*, Fiscal Year 1980, Main volume, Dept. of State, AID, Washington, DC, 1 February 1979.

It should be indicated that the machinery to co-ordinate the above three programmes – development assistance programme of AID, security supporting assistance programme and PL 480 programme – and to integrate them into overall relations with the developing countries has been through the Development Co-ordination Committee, chaired by the Administrator of AID, which was created in 1973 and has been given wide responsibilities.

THE EXPERIENCE OF AID IN PROJECT EVALUATIONS

AID missions and bureaux evaluate each of their operational non-capital assistance projects annually. In addition, missions and headquarters perform a number of special evaluations of projects, subsector and sector country programmes, and assistance problems and techniques. A Central Office of Programme Methods and Evaluation has the functions of innovation, co-ordination and support. For non-capital project assistance, there is a procedural link between the design, implementation and evaluation stages. A structured summary of a project's objectives including internal and external casual linkages, constraints and measurement indicators, is used as the basis for planning and approving a non-capital project, to oversee implementation and to clarify and re-examine the original design as a necessary prelude to evaluation. The decision that annual evaluations would be required for technical assistance and certain projects was made in AID headquarters with agreement by each of the regional bureaux. The experience confirms the need for complete and periodic coverage for most AID activities, to measure progress and to re-assess relevance. AID policy is to encourage the recipient country to assume the leadership in planning, managing and evaluating development projects and programmes which are financially assisted by AID. A manual and work sheets are provided: the 'Project Evaluation Guidelines' and 'Project Evaluation Workbook' respectively. AID has found that the effective management of project-level assistance requires a system of complete and periodic coverage with simplified but rigorous evaluation. The cost:benefit ratio is made most favourable by the use of knowledgeable project management staff as evaluators. This eliminates briefing and familiarisation costs, assures direct feedback, and integrates the planning, implementation and evaluation functions. Evaluation aims simultaneously at a set of purposes: modifying the design of unsatisfactory activities, improving implementation, devising new alternatives to assure success and greater efficiency, drawing on past experience to improve planning and implementation, determining new policy orientations, etc. Changes have been made in some overall programming policies and aid criteria as a result of special evaluations and sometimes from lessons learned from regular project evaluations.[19]

The evaluation of Food for Peace Grant Programmes (aimed to review Title II of PL 480) used to occur as part of the budget process in countries where special studies about the nutritional or developmental impact were undertaken. In 1971, AID decided to undertake a worldwide evaluation of the programme. A detailed questionnaire was developed that asked 'whether best obtainable results are being achieved with the Title II foods, and if not, why not, and what changes should be made to improve performance'. The areas for study included such subjects as: examination of AID policies and priorities, implications of dependence on donated commodities, economic impact of work projects, programme administration, host governments' interests and attitudes, and the relationship of programmes to national goals. The completed study contained a number of policy and operational recommendations that have been to a larger extent reflected in guidance issued by AID headquarters on future programming. Recommendations included such matters as placing increased emphasis on nutrition education along with food distribution, encouraging host countries to prepare food and nutrition plans, and giving priority to recipients in special target groups especially pre-school children and breast-feeding mothers. There were suggestions on improved systems of data handling. Another condition was that food-for-work projects were generally making a significant impact on economic and human development in the recipient countries and should receive more emphasis.[20]

APPENDIX 3.1 The Flow of Financial Resources to Developing Countries and Multilateral Agencies by Type
(1970–80)
Country: USA

Disbursements Net disbursements	1970	1971	1972	1973	1974	1975	1976	1977	1978	1979	US$m 1980
I Official Development Assistance (a+b)	3,050.0	3,324.0	3,349.0	2,968.0	3,439.0	4,007.0	4,334.0	4,159.0	5,663.5	4,684.0	7,138.0
(a) Bilateral ODA	2,657.0	2,893.0	2,724.0	2,337.0	2,557.0	2,941.0	2,838.0	2,897.0	3,474.0	4,076.0	4,366.0
(b) Contributions to multilateral institutions	393.0	431.0	625.0	631.0	882.0	1,066.0	1,496.0	1,262.0	2,189.5	608.0	2,772.0
II Other Official Flows (a+b)	168.0	180.0	196.0	477.0	823.0	920.0	822.0	752.0	1,288.0	953.0	1,112.0
(a) Bilateral OOF	168.0	180.0	196.0	477.0	823.0	920.0	822.0	752.0	1,228.0	953.0	1,112.0
(b) Multilateral institutions	—	—	—	—	—	—	—	—	0.0	0.0	0.0
Subtotal (I+II): Total official flows	3,218.0	3,504.0	3,545.0	3,445.0	4,262.0	4,927.0	5,156.0	4,911.0	6,951.5	5,637.0	8,250.0
III Grants by private voluntary agencies	598.0	599.0	669.0	905.0	735.0	804.0	789.0	840.0	924.0	1,029.0	1,301.0
IV Private flows at market terms (1–4)	2,394.7	2,785.0	3,360.0	3,996.0	5,273.0	11,799.0	6,399.0	6,159.0	8,287.0	12,008.0	4,301.0
(1) Direct investment	1,742.0	2,010.0	1,976.0	2,887.0	3,788.0	7,241.0	3,119.0	4,866.0	5,619.0	7,986.0	3,367.0
(2) Bilateral portfolio investment and other	198.0	263.0	947.7	969.4	1,103.4	3,231.0	2,160.0	−263.7	3,391.7	4,146.0	1,125.1
(3) Multilateral portfolio investment	372.0	322.0	102.0	−135.0	−59.0	2,405.5	1,296.0	892.0	−568.0	−290.0	−1,092.0
(4) Private export credits	82.7	190.0	334.3	274.0	440.6	290.5	−176.5	664.7	−155.7	165.6	900.6
V Total resource flows (1–IV)	6,210.7	6,888.0	7,574.0	8,346.0	10,270.0	17,530.0	12,344.0	11,910.0	16,162.5	18,674.0	13,852.0
ODA as % of GNP	0.31	0.32	0.29	0.23	0.24	0.26	0.25	0.22	0.27	0.20	0.27
Total resource flows as % of GNP	0.63	0.65	0.65	0.79	0.73	1.15	0.72	0.63	0.77	0.79	0.53

Sources: OECD, *Development Co-operation*, Reviews 1974–81.

4 The United Kingdom

THE PERFORMANCE OF UK OFFICIAL DEVELOPMENT ASSISTANCE

The United Kingdom is one of the five largest contributors among DAC members. Its share in total DAC/ODA was about 7 per cent in 1980 compared with 13 per cent for West Germany, 12 per cent for Japan, 15 per cent for France and 27 per cent for the United States in the same year. During the 1970s this share was almost constant compared with the 1960s. In 1960, the UK was the third biggest donor of ODA after the USA (58 per cent) and France (18 per cent). This declining share of the UK contribution in ODA during the 1970s was a result of the growing share of other DAC members and an increase in UK private flows. The United Kingdom is also considered to be one of the oldest donors, with growing relationships with many of the developing countries. UK ODA reached US $1780.9m in 1980 compared with US $2066.8m in 1979, and US $834.8m in 1976: see Appendix 4.1 and Chart 3. This compares with an average of US $443.8m in 1967–69 and US $407m in 1960.[1]

As in the case of the United States, the United Kingdom has never reached the UNCTAD target of 0.7 per cent of ODA/GNP. However, the performance of the UK in this respect was better than that of the USA: ODA/GNP reached 0.34 per cent in 1980 and 0.52 per cent in 1979 compared with 0.27 and 0.20 per cent for the USA. In 1970 the ratio reached 0.36 per cent for the UK compared with 0.31 for the USA. In 1960 the ratio was 0.56 per cent for the UK compared with 0.53 for the USA – see Appendixes 3.1 and 4.1. While United Kingdom ODA/GNP dropped sharply in 1980 by 15 per cent, its lowest ratio since 1973, this reflects, to a large extent, the fact that the UK did not deposit any promissory notes to IDA before the end of the calendar year 1980, and also that drawings by some of its major recipients were slower than anticipated. While an increase in the UK ODA/GNP ratio can be expected in 1981 (0.48 per cent according to the World Development Report of 1981), future ODA volume prospects will be affected by the

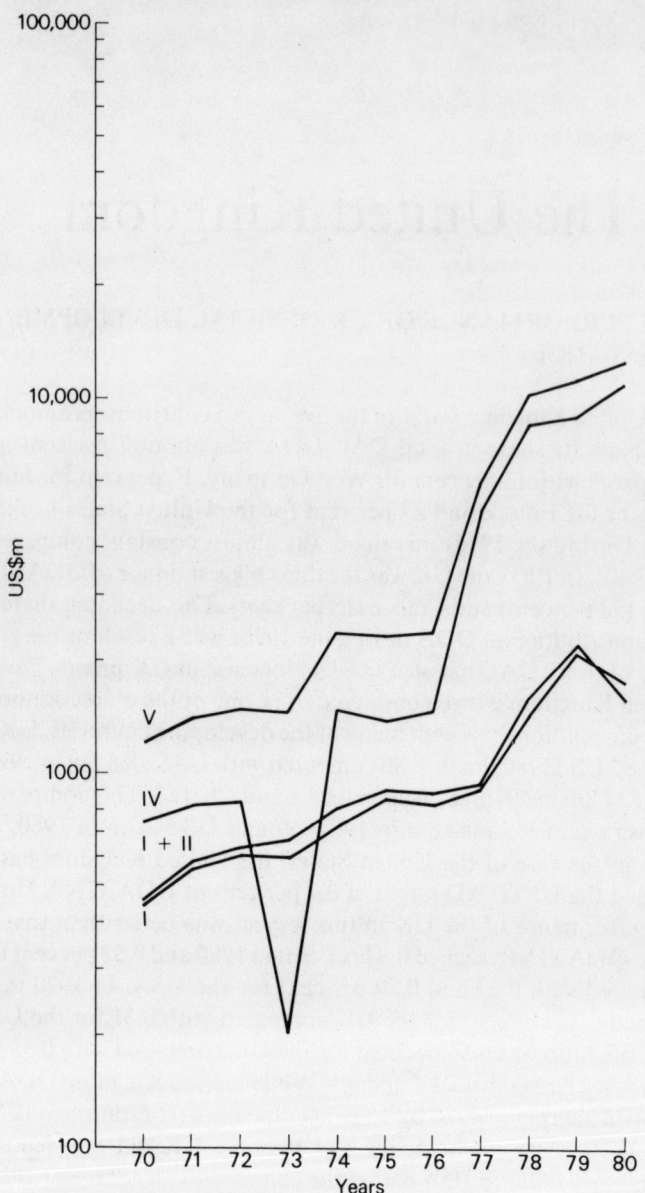

CHART 3 Flow of financial resources to developing countries and multilateral agencies by type: UK 1970–80

Source: Appendix 4.1

British Government's policy of overall public expenditure restrictions. According to the most recent White Paper on Public Expenditure published by the British Government on 10 March 1981, the aid budget is to be cut by 15 per cent in real terms during the period 1980/81 – 1983/84.[2]

UK bilateral development assistance reached US $1255.1m in 1980 (70 per cent of ODA) compared with US $399.0m in 1970 (89 per cent of ODA). UK contributions to multilateral institutions therefore increased during the second half of the 1970s, reaching US $903.2m in 1979 compared with US $358.7m in 1977, US $160.8m in 1973 and only US $47.9m in 1970. The substantial increase of UK contributions to multilateral institutions which occurred in 1978 was mainly due to capital subscription payments, IDA alone received US $315.8m.[3] Other official flows totalled US $134.7m in 1979 in the form of bilateral OOF compared to only US $23.0m in 1977 and US $6.5m in 1970. Total official flows by the UK reached US $2201.5m in 1979 compared with US $937.1m in 1977 and US $453.4m in 1970. By 1980, total official flows by the UK had declined to reach US $1617.3m due to domestic decline in contributions to multilateral institutions, mainly to IDA – see Appendix 4.1.

UK official flows may be divided in the following ways:[4]

(i) grants and loans to independent countries, to assist development or to support their budgets or balance of payments;
(ii) grants and loans to British dependencies under the Colonial Development and Welfare Acts to assist development and social welfare or to support local budgets;
(iii) projects initiated by international organisations, as well as regular subscriptions and replenishments.

The whole of the UK's official flows are financed directly from the current budget, mainly through an annual provision by Parliament on the basis of estimates of expenditure presented to it. During the 1960s, most of the UK development aid went to Commonwealth countries, of which about 75 per cent was in the form of bilateral aid. For example, in 1968 the total bilateral official aid to Commonwealth countries amounted to US $403m, of which US $96m was for India, US $26m for Kenya, and US $16m for Malta. Distribution within the Commonwealth countries was characterised, however, by a very heavy concentration on the smaller countries in proportion to their population size. About 10 per cent of the UK total official flows was in bilateral aid to non-

Commonwealth countries, and about 15 per cent was through multilateral agencies, most of which also eventually reached Commonwealth countries.[5] Technical assistance started to play a more important part in the UK's foreign aid policy, increasing from 23 per cent of gross bilateral ODA in 1970 to 34 per cent in 1973. Repayment terms softened during this period (1970–73), as the share of grants in total commitments increased from 49.5 to 61.5 per cent, while the grant element of loans improved from 63.4 to 66.6 per cent. The grant element of ODA as a whole rose from 81.5 to 87.1 per cent during the period 1970–73. The UK was therefore in compliance with the general provisions of the DAC's Recommendations on Terms of Aid during these years.

Bilateral financial assistance was, in principle, tied to procurement in the United Kingdom. In the case of dependencies and Caribbean and African countries, a limited amount of procurement in third countries was permitted.[6] The United Kingdom first announced its intention of directing more aid to the poorer countries in 1975, and all governmental aid to poorer countries since then has been in the form of grants. The bilateral programme in 1977 was divided almost equally between project aid, programme aid and technical co-operation. Projects were directed towards all sectors (with a recent preference for rural development) while programme aid consisted mostly of the provision of maintenance equipment in connection with previous projects. About two-thirds of bilateral aid in 1977 was still extended to members of the Commonwealth, while in the same year, 56 per cent of bilateral ODA went to low-income countries and 21 per cent to LLDCs.[7] In 1978, 90 per cent of United Kingdom ODA (including all government aid to low-income and least developed countries) was in the form of grants, and the grant element of ODA commitments was 92 per cent. In July 1978, the Government of the United Kingdom announced that it proposed to take steps to remove the burden of the repayment of past aid loans, or to adopt equivalent measures for seventeen of the poorest developing countries. Bilateral ODA was extended to some 130 countries, with an emphasis on poorer recipients in Africa and South Asia. Major recipients in 1978, in order of importance, were India, Bangladesh, Kenya, Malawi, Pakistan, Jamaica and Zambia, the first five of which had per capita incomes of less than $400. About a third of the bilateral programme was in the form of technical co-operation, with the remainder being divided almost equally between project and non-project aid.[8] An important change took place in 1979 in the relationship of the former Ministry of Overseas Development with the Foreign and Commonwealth Office (FCO). The Government decided on taking office that the then Ministry of Overseas Development should be converted into an Overseas Development Administration within the FCO. Responsibility for overseas development was delegated by the Secretary of State to a Minister of State who has the additional title of Minister for Overseas Development. Following this change, the organisation of responsibility within the FCO for aid policy and for policy on North–South relations has been rationalised.[9]

Grants by private voluntary agencies in the UK reached US $57.3m in 1979 compared with US $36.6m in 1970. The amount during the period 1971–79 was almost stationary in cash terms but its share of total resource flows declined from about 3 per cent in 1970 to about 0.5 per cent in 1979. By 1980, grants by private voluntary agencies increased to reach US $104.7m, with a slight increase of its share in total UK resource flows as it reached 0.8 per cent – see Appendix 4.1.

UK PRIVATE FLOWS

UK private flows at market terms to developing countries increased sharply in the three years of 1977 and 1978–80. With the exception of 1973 (when private flows were only 14 per cent of total resource flows), private flows to developing countries were higher than the official flows during the period 1970–80. They reached US $11,073.1m (87 per cent of total resource flows) in 1980 compared with US $4942.1m (83 per cent) in 1977, US $1508.8m (64 per cent) in 1974, and US $740.6m (60 per cent) in 1960 – see Appendix 4.1. In 1965, UK private flows to developing countries reached US $547.1m (53 per cent of the total resource flows).[10] Direct investment and export credits during the first half of the 1970s constituted the larger portion of private flows. However, their importance declined during the second half of the 1970s and the main bulk of the increase of UK private flows was mainly attributed to bilateral portfolio investment which reached 78 per cent in 1977 and 71 per cent in 1979 of the private flows during these years. During 1980, the share of private export credit more than doubled to reach 26 per cent while the share of bilateral portfolio investment declined to 65 per cent, accompanied by a sharp decline in direct investment from 17 per cent in 1979 to only 9 per cent in 1980. Table 4.1 shows the share of UK private flows to total flows, and their major components.

The UK has made important direct investments in developing countries in all the major sectors: oil, mining, manufacturing, agricul-

TABLE 4.1 The Share of Private Flows at Market Terms to Total Resource Flows and their Major Components in UK
1970–80
(Percentages)

Year	Private flows to total resource flows %	Direct investment to private flows %	Private export credits to private flows %	Bilateral portfolio Investment and other to private flows %
1970	60	43	59	(−2)
1971	57	40	72	(−11)
1972	56	42	64	(−6)
1973	14	39	55	(−2)
1974	64	46	23	31
1975	60	57	30	14
1976	62	64	28	8
1977	83	12	10	78
1978	84	18	11	72
1979	80	17	12	71
1980	87	9	26	65

Source: Original data from Appendix 4.1.

ture, commerce and banking. Oil investments were spread very widely over the developing countries, whereas investments in other sectors were more concentrated in Commonwealth countries.[11] The government pursues an active policy to stimulate additional private flows to developing countries and the changing composition of the private flows is very noticeable. Private export credits during the period 1970–73 were much higher than direct investment, but since 1974 the volume of direct investment has been much higher than the private export credits – see Appendix 4.1. The flow of portfolio investment from the London capital market, which used to be of major importance, was relatively slight. Since March 1974, the exchange control regulations, which formerly applied only to the non-sterling area, have been extended to the overseas sterling area (except the Republic of Ireland) and have become, for practical purposes, uniform for all developing countries.[12] The overseas investment insurance scheme, which came into operation in July 1972, was administered by the Export Credits Guarantee Department (ECGD). The scheme was available for new investments which satisfy exchange control requirements. The likely effect of the project on the economy of the host country is taken into account in assessing the risks attached to the investment. The UK fiscal system does not contain any measures designed to favour direct investment in developing countries; however, some of the UK's double taxation agreements contain matching credit provisions in respect of pioneer industry tax reliefs offered to investors by developing countries. The UK has double tax relief agreements with more than sixty countries, including most Commonwealth countries, and gives unilateral double tax relief in other cases while a direct investor in an overseas company is taxed in the UK only on dividends received from overseas. Under the importation system of corporation tax introduced with effect from April 1973, a company pays corporation tax at a single rate on all its profits whether distributed or undistributed. The Overseas Investment and Export Guarantees Act 1972 provided for a scheme of financial support for pre-investment studies by UK private investors in developing countries.[13]

THE UNITED KINGDOM DEVELOPMENT ASSISTANCE POLICY

The Minister of Overseas Development of the UK, in a speech on 24 September 1969 at the Vienna Institute for Development, outlined his (Labour) government's development assistance policy in developing countries as follows:

> If you ask me whether Britain is doing enough in the fight against world poverty the answer must be an emphatic 'no'. Britain is not doing enough, neither are any of the other donor nations. We all could do more, and should do more. Specifically, we would aim to reach an aid performance of 1 per cent of our gross national product within the next few years.[14]

The British Government has never had a very clear-cut policy towards private investment in developing countries in particular. The introduction of Corporation Tax by a Labour Government in 1965 was partially intended to make all forms of direct overseas investment less profitable relative to domestic investment with a consequent decline in the flow of direct private investment from Britain to all developing countries. The tax has been retained by subsequent Conservative administrations. The Reddaway Report proposed that investment in developing countries should have most favoured treatment, suggesting that the Bank of England should take this into account when vetting individual projects as well as putting the selection procedure on a more comprehensive and permanent basis. The Ministry of Overseas Development has, however, had its hands tied ever since it was set up in 1964, due to the continuing precariousness of the British economy. The Minister of Overseas Development, in a statement to the House of Commons in November 1969, announced that the government had decided that from 1971/72 all economic aid would be consolidated into one official aid programme. Thus the 1 per cent UNCTAD II target which included private as well as official flows depended upon the level of private flows, which was difficult to predict. If the level of private flows were high, these, together with the increases announced in official aid up to 1973/74, could result in the UK reaching the 1 per cent target. In April 1971, the Overseas Development Administration announced a number of measures decided on by the government to encourage UK private investment in developing countries. The most important measure was the introduction of a scheme for ensuring new direct investment from Britain against non-commercial risks of war, expropriation and restrictions on remittances. The scheme applied to all overseas countries and encouraged British investment primarily in developing countries. It was administered by the Export Credits Guarantee Department, effectively from 1972.[15]

The UK published a medium-term plan in January 1975 which implied a 3 per cent annual increase in aid appropriations in constant prices. However, because of the economic situation in the UK, the level of aid remained stagnant. There was a slight improvement in the financial terms of the UK loans in 1974 but the overall grant element of bilateral commitments declined slightly from 87.1 per cent in 1973 to 86.3 per cent in 1974. This was due to a 65 per cent increase in loan commitment during that year. The trend was reversed in 1975 following the decision taken by the Labour Government in June 1975 that its government-to-government aid to the 'poorest countries' – up to $200 per capita GNP – should normally be extended on grant terms. The UK proposed that all donations should normally be extended on grant terms and that all donors should extend at least 60 per cent of their aid to the poorest countries. The UK also announced its intention of directing more aid to the relief of poverty in rural areas. A Rural Development Department was set up in the Overseas Development Ministry in 1975 to co-ordinate policy in this sector, and to co-operate in the preparation of comprehensive rural development projects.[16] The UK aid budgets for both 1977/78 and 1978/79 were affected by the government cuts announced in December 1976 (£50m for 1977/78 and £50m for 1978/79). The UK in 1976 intensified its policy of concentrating bilateral aid on the poorest countries, and gross disbursements to countries with per capita GNP of less than $200 amounted to about 60 per cent of the total. Some 90 per cent of bilateral aid continued to be extended to Commonwealth countries.[17] Although the UK's bilateral aid policy concentrated on rural development and the poorest groups, a significant proportion (especially for non-project aid) in 1978 was going toward the industrial, communications and heavy power sectors. New initiatives were taken in 1978 by the Ministry of Overseas Development to develop alternative sources of energy which would be relevant to the needs of developing countries. An energy adviser was appointed and three working groups were set up to deal respectively with solar energy, wind, wave, tidal energy and water power, and biomass.[18]

During 1978 British development strategy remained as described in the 1975 White Paper—'More Help for the Poorest'. The Conservative Government elected on 3 May 1979 initiated a review of the size and composition of the aid programme as part of a general review of public expenditure and has already implemented a reorganisation of the administration of the aid programme. The Secretary of State for Foreign and Commonwealth Affairs became fully responsible for overseas development and the Ministry of Overseas Development has again become part of the Foreign and Commonwealth Office, as the Overseas Development Administration. The minister in charge was a Minister of State for Foreign and Commonwealth Affairs as well as Minister for Overseas Development, although the Overseas Development Administration remained self-contained for administrative purposes. The focus on poverty, particularly on rural development, contained in the 1975 White Paper, has created problems for the UK, as for other donors. Nevertheless, by 1978 the UK had had some success in implementing this strategy. In general, bilateral aid remained tied to the procurement of British goods and services. However, a limited amount of this aid could be untied, where appropriate, for example to meet local costs associated with aid projects, and in particular cases some third country procurement could be permitted. Loan commitments could, if the recipient wished, be untied for procurement in the poorest developing countries. The UK policy on local costs continued to accord with the 'Guidelines on Local Financing' adopted by the DAC in 1977. For certain kinds of projects, particularly many of those intended directly to help the poorest, UK participation necessarily involved providing a local cost component. The requirement of middle-income developing countries for external sources of finance was recognised and a number of measures were implemented by the UK to encourage a flow of resources to those countries through private flows at market terms. In addition, the UK continued to give ODA support to some middle-income countries, usually under arrangements co-ordinated by the IMF and related to serious trading and economic difficulties. Such aid was in the form either of short-term programme aid or of debt rescheduling while the UK also agreed projects with a number of other multilateral and bilateral donors including the IBRD, France and West Germany. While there are advantages to be gained from co-financing, experience has shown that it is likely to make more demands upon staff resources than similar bilateral projects. The UK participated in a number of consortia and donor co-ordinating groups including those for India, Indonesia, Bangladesh, Sri Lanka, Nepal and the Caribbean and favoured the organised co-ordination of aid where this was undertaken in full partnership with the recipients. The Overseas Development Administration played a co-ordinating and advisory role in full paid technical co-operation arrangements but generally was operationally involved only in agriculture. In other sectors, the UK ministries concerned normally dealt directly with overseas governments while the British Council was responsible for paid technical co-operation in education and training. The Select Committee on Overseas Development examined government policy and actions across the spectrum of overseas development; it did not confine itself solely to aid matters. As a House of Commons Select Committee it was able to take written and oral evidence from experts outside government, such as voluntary organisations and private sector interests, in addition to evidence from the Overseas Development Administration and other government departments. The Select Committee's authority automatically terminates on the dissolution of Parliament and the decision on whether or not they are re-established rests with the new Parliament.[19]

In 1981 the British Government[20] announced new aid initiatives to help the poorest countries within existing resources as follows:

(1) £1.5m to be earmarked over the next three years to assist a number of African countries to strengthen their national agricultural research system.
(2) £4m in 1983/84 to strengthen institutional support in the field of water supply.
(3) £1.5m to step up support for population programmes.
(4) £2m for energy resource planning.

The British Government advocated that high priority should be given to stimulating food production and improving food supplies in developing countries, and that this action should be concentrated on the poorest countries. The gross official aid programme in 1981/82 was over £1000m; about two-thirds of the British bilateral aid programme went (in 1980/81) to the poorest countries which find it more difficult to gain from trade or private investment. The United Kingdom and other EEC member states aim to allocate 0.15 per cent of GNP as aid to LLDCs. On the other hand, the British Government believes that it is important to encourage private lending and direct investment to developing countries. However, direct investment depends on the policies adopted by developing countries and on creating confidence between host governments and investing firms, and the size of the British financial flows to developing countries depends on the strength of its domestic economy.

ADMINISTRATION OF UK FINANCIAL FLOWS

The Overseas Development Administration

The Management of the British Aid Programme

The British aid programme in 1980 was managed by the Overseas Development Administration, a semi-autonomous unit within the Foreign and Commonwealth Office. One of the junior ministers under the Secretary of State for Foreign and Commonwealth Affairs has the title of Minister for Overseas Development and enjoys a high degree of delegated authority on aid matters. The delegation is informal, all powers legally belonging not to the Minister for Overseas Development but to the Foreign Secretary. During the Labour Governments of 1964–70 and 1974–79, the Overseas Development Administration was given higher status as the Ministry of Overseas Development. The organisational structure for foreign aid in the United Kingdom changed several times during the 1960s. At the beginning there was no separate Department of State responsible for foreign aid. The Foreign Office handled aid to foreign countries, the Commonwealth Relations Office to independent Commonwealth countries, and the Colonial Office aid to colonies. In 1961, the Department of Technical Co-operation (DTC), was set up to take over all technical assistance functions from the political ministries. The DTC was given its own junior minister and operated as an administrative agency carrying out policy laid down by the major ministers. When the Labour Party came to power in 1964, a Ministry of Overseas Development (ODM) was established.[21] The ODM took over the functions of DTC and was also made responsible for all capital aid. Budgetary aid to the remaining colonies continued to be administered by the Colonial Office, which was subsequently merged into the Commonwealth Relations Office and later amalgamated with the Foreign Office, while Britain's relations with the World Bank continued to be primarily a Treasury responsibility. With these exceptions, ODM managed the whole British aid programme. Its first Minister (Mrs Barbara Castle) was a member of the Cabinet, and this was widely taken as a sign that development assistance was to be given a new priority.[22] The Treasury maintained a close watch over those of the ODM's activities which had financial or balance of payments implications, and its administration costs were financed directly from the budget, like those of other government departments. The financial terms of ODM aid to individual countries were related to their economic circumstances with special attention to their per capita incomes and balance of payments. Countries with low per capita incomes, which formed the bulk of the recipients of UK aid, usually received interest-free loans. Capital assistance to Asia, Latin American countries and Turkey was, however, generally wholly tied to procurement from the UK.[23]

The Ministry of Overseas Development (ODM) was unfortunate in being placed in charge of a succession of five ministers during the period 1964-70. The second minister was, like the first, a member of the Cabinet; but from August 1966 the Minister of Overseas Development did not have a seat in the cabinet. When the Conservative Government took office in June 1970, it carried out a review of the structure of government. As part of the changes, the Ministry of Overseas Development was transferred into the Foreign and Commonwealth Office under the title of Overseas Development Administration.[24] It is hard to tell whether the merger enabled or contributed to a reorientation of criteria; every government has different priorities, and even if the geographical distribution of aid seems to have become more heavily influenced by political and commercial objectives, a reorientation of this sort could easily be effected without any change in the formal status of the ODM.[25] The downgrading of overseas aid in political terms represented by the consistent Conservative policy of subordinating its minister to the Foreign Office, without a Cabinet seat, represented different priorities in Labour and Conservative thinking. Without an independent voice, the department handling overseas aid was less able to participate effectively in internal government discussions on financial priorities.

Project Appraisal in Developing Countries

The Ministry of Overseas Development prepared *A Guide to the Economic Appraisal of Projects in Developing Countries*,[26] the purpose of which was to provide a practical basis for the economic appraisal of projects financed by the public sector and for securing private sector projects subject to public sector approval. The methodology developed in the guide was based largely on the analytical framework of the OECD manual of *Industrial Project Appraisal in Developing Countries*, Volume II (Social Cost-Benefit Analysis) by I. M. D. Little and J. A. Mirrlees, published by the OECD Development Centre in 1969. The analytical framework underlying the OECD Manual had been extended beyond the industrial sector and designed particularly for use in developing economies. The basic assumption underlying the methodology as developed in the *Guide* is that a government's objective when making public investment decisions is the greatest possible increase in the standard of living of the population over a period of time, or, more formally, the optimisation of income flows over a period of time. The guide emphasised three basic concepts:

(1) *The use of international prices and not local domestic prices* as in less developed countries prices of goods and services prevailing in local markets often provide a much less reliable guide to their costs as far as the national economy is concerned. Problems are caused by relative prices failing to reflect social opportunity costs when the possibilities of international trade are taken into account. The general principle adopted to deal with this is to value inputs and outputs at international border prices excluding the effects of such factors as tariffs, subsidies and excise taxes. The application of this concept involves a judgment as to the appropriate boundary between traded and non-traded goods, and an important consideration is the nature of the foreign trade regime in operation in any particular country and the likelihood of its changing over time.

(2) *The use of a shadow wage rate for all labour inputs*; to the extent that the opportunity cost of labour, in the sense of output foregone elsewhere, is used as a basis for costing labour when

making investment decisions, and income will probably be redistributed in favour of low-income workers more effectively than if market wage rates were used in appraising investments. The central authorities may wish to reflect the distributional issues, if they wish to discriminate between classes of beneficiaries in their project selection.

(3) *The use in all calculations of a single rate of discount*, chosen to measure the marginal social return on public investment, as any investment project involves a stream of costs and benefits through time. The discount rate or the Accounting Rate of Interest (ARI) shows how the costs and benefits of a project in any one year are to be valued in relation to those of any other year. Costs and benefits for each year of the project's life can then be added and the difference between the sum of the costs and benefits is the Net Present Value (NPV). The choice of discount rate is of critical importance and the ARI selected for economic appraisals of projects should be the marginal social rate of return on investment.

It should be indicated that the use of the *Guide* involves value judgements in dealing with many of the questions arising from project choice which are ultimately the responsibility of the central authorities. The economic planning staff of the Ministry of Overseas Development in 1978 prepared a folder of two volumes on *Appraising Investment Proposals*.[27] The folder was addressed to geographical division economists and contained a collection of articles and notes on a wide diversity of projects and proposals for expenditure of public funds. The purpose was to explain some of the problems to economists and others so as to assist in more effective appraisal. The folder was not concerned with project appraisal methodology, which was covered in the *Guide to Project Appraisal*. The articles in the folder covered a wide scope of different projects in different sectors like buildings, computers, co-operatives, credit institutions, dairy projects, dams, desalination, educational television, energy, ground-water drilling, hospitals, housing, irrigation studies, etc. The projects presented were based on the best information available for creating new aspects and alterations but the monetary values presented were out of date.

The Overseas Development Administration also prepared a series of 'Project Data Handbooks',[28] covering different projects and based upon their experience in different sectors in developing countries. The handbooks deal with existing projects and their contributions to economic and social development in different developing countries as case-studies for specific sectors. They cover the problems of the sector, factors for progress, schemes, developmental priorities, and essential requirements of the sector in order of importance as recommendations for projects under consideration. These studies did not follow the general framework of the *Guide to the Economic Appraisal of Projects in Developing Countries*, but they were considered to be of great importance as post-evaluation studies based upon field experience. The Overseas Development Administration has also produced several 'Sector Appraisal Manuals' covering different sectors.[29] The articles in the manuals have been written by the members of the geographical division of the economic planning staff. They are concerned with understanding policy operations, appraising institutions and understanding specific investment proposals. However, despite the fact that these manuals are considered to be of great importance, their use is limited due to the fact that they are not related to the *Guide for Project Appraisal*. Also, the Overseas Development Administration has not devoted much attention to sectoral evaluation except in recent years. The main reason for this is that it had concentrated its aid on individual projects and in most countries had not provided a sufficient number of projects in any one sector to justify the sectoral approach. Another argument against the manuals is that on the technical assistance side the statistics have not been organised and there are few data on how technical assistance was distributed between sectors.[30]

The Commonwealth Development Corporation[31]

Establishment and Financial Resources

The Commonwealth Development Corporation (CDC) is a public corporation originally established by Act of Parliament in 1948 as the Colonial Development Corporation to assist the economic development of the then British-dependent territories. It is a statutory organisation which is required to break even, taking one year with another. The CDC's objective is to invest its funds in countries in which it is empowered to operate in development projects which not only help to increase the wealth of the countries, but also yield a reasonable return on the money invested. It is empowered to undertake – either alone or in association with others – projects for the promotion or expansion of economic development enterprises covering basic development, primary production and processing and industry and commerce. It does not have power to undertake projects of a social nature such as schools and hospitals, government buildings or other buildings or works for the public service. The CDC operates on broadly commercial lines and it does not make grants, but offers investment in the development of resources. The International Finance, Trade and Aid Act, 1977 increased CDC's long- and medium-term borrowing powers to £500m and left unchanged its power to borrow up to £10m on short term. Of the £500m, up to £480m may be borrowed from UK Exchequer funds. The minister may, by order made with the consent of the Treasury, increase the long- and medium-term borrowing powers to £570m of which not more than £550m come from Exchequer funds. The CDC's activities now principally cover the developing countries of the Commonwealth, but ministerial approval has also been obtained for operations in the following non-Commonwealth countries: Costa Rica, Ecuador, Honduras, Indonesia, the Philippines, Thailand, Ethiopia, Rwanda, Sudan, Zaire, Cameroon, the Ivory Coast, Liberia and Tunisia. Table 4.2 shows the CDC distribution by region of group capital invested and oustanding commitments.

In these countries, CDC finances productive and viable projects capable of servicing the capital invested out of their revenues, of the following kinds:

(1) *Infrastructure projects*: power, water, transport (economic infrastructure only).
(2) *Productive projects*: agriculture, forestry, fisheries, livestock, industry, minerals, tourism.
(3) *Others*: development finance companies, housing finance, land development.

Participation

The bulk of CDS's investment is in long-term and medium-term loans. CDC does not normally make short-term loans. About 13 per cent of the total portfolio is in equity holdings. CDC's investments are not tied to UK procurement or British sponsors. UK suppliers are, however, expected to have full opportunity to tender. The sponsor is usually required to be responsible for overrun costs and end finance, but CDC, as an investor, takes account of future financial requirements, especially for expansion. Table 4.3 shows the functional classification of group capital committed and invested in continuing projects.

TABLE 4.2 CDC Distribution by Region of Group Capital Invested and Outstanding Commitments (1977–80) (£m)

	Caribbean	East Asia[a] and Pacific Islands	East Africa	Central Africa	Southern Africa	West Africa	Other areas	Total
1977								
Invested	52	68	41	52	30	18	2	261
Outstanding commitment	5	15	16	15	14	7	—	73
1978								
Invested	51	70	45	57	35	16	1	275
Outstanding commitment	4	27	24	18	15	16	—	104
1979								
Invested	50	82	54	64	42	20	1	313
Outstanding commitment	12	19	30	15	16	44	—	136
1980								
Invested	48	90	68	71	46	24	3	350
Outstanding commitment	15	50	37	19	6	38	—	165

[a] In 1980, East Asia Invested £61m and Pacific Islands Invested £29m. East Asia outstanding commitment £33m, and Pacific Islands outstanding commitment £17m.

Sources: CDC *Annual Reports*, 1977, 1978, 1979 and information received from CDC.

TABLE 4.3 CDC Functional Classification of Group Capital Committed and Invested in Continuing Projects 1978–80

	1978				1979				1980			
	Committed £000s	%	Employed £000s	%	Committed £000s	%	Employed £000s	%	Committed £000s	%	Employed £000s	%
Basic development												
Power and water	81,418	21.5	72,888	26.5	92,044	20.5	75,774	24.2	119,692	23.2	82,452	23.5
Housing finance	56,294	14.8	46,655	17.0	58,623	13.0	50,362	16.1	53,873	10.4	51,218	14.6
Transport	5,020	1.3	5,020	1.8	4,468	1.0	4,468	1.4	4,034	0.8	4,034	1.2
Total basic development	142,732	37.6	124,563	45.3	155,135	34.5	103,604	41.7	177,599	34.4	137,704	39.3
Primary production and processing												
Renewable natural resources	159,873	42.2	97,812	35.6	206,517	46.0	118,237	37.8	223,899	43.4	104,791	40.1
Minerals	172		172		7,672	1.7	2,172	0.7	7,462	1.4	3,662	1.1
Total primary production and processing	160,045	42.2	97,984	35.6	214,189	47.7	120,409	38.5	231,361	44.8	144,453	41.2
Industry and commerce												
Development companies	34,864	9.2	30,639	11.1	41,424	9.2	35,478	11.3	50,241	9.7	40,985	11.7
Industry	35,153	9.3	15,737	5.7	32,519	7.2	20,588	6.6	50,902	9.9	21,556	6.1
Hotels	6,564	1.7	6,179	2.3	6,064	1.4	6,064	1.9	6,073	1.2	6,073	1.7
Total industry and commerce	76,581	20.2	52,555	19.1	80,007	17.8	62,130	19.8	107,216	20.8	68,614	19.5
Total	379,358	100	275,102	100	449,331	100	313,143	100	516,176	100	350,771	100

Sources: CDC, *Annual Reports,* 1978, 1979, 1980.

CDC Technical Assistance

CDC has a number of specialist departments, especially for agriculture, which provide management and technical services linked to CDC's investment operations. Other departments provide specialist and technical services and advice on engineering, housing, taxation, marketing, law, etc. CDC is also able to provide personnel recruitment services and purchase of equipment and stores. The experience available within CDC has led to co-operation with public development finance corporations and others, especially in the agricultural sector. Most developing countries lack trained managers, particularly in agriculture, and this led CDC to set up the Mananga Agricultural Management Centre (MAMC) in Swaziland in 1973. This centre does not teach agriculture as such but offers three-month courses in management and financial administration for students drawn from all over the world who are concerned with the management of large agricultural enterprises.

Whilst CDC does not have finance available for experimental agriculture or research, except in so far as it undertakes agronomy and crop production work on its many projects, it has staked a certain amount of risk money on pilot projects and crop trials. In a number of cases, where such efforts have been successful, significant areas of land have been opened, money has been attracted from other organisations and sometimes crops new to the area have been introduced. An example of such projects is The Savannah Sugar Company Ltd in Nigeria where a four-year pilot sugar project has led to the development, jointly with the Federal Government, of 12,500 ha of sugar-cane under irrigation, of which 5500 ha will be worked by 1100 cane farmers. Construction of a mill capable of producing 100,00 tonnes of sugar per annum is already complete.

Over the years, CDC's management and technical capacity has enabled it more generally to play a valuable pioneering role in, for instance:

(i) developing the formula of nucleus estate and smallholder schemes which are by now a recognised instrument for large-scale agricultural development of benefit to the widest section of the rural population;
(ii) the introduction of new crops such as cocoa to Sabah where now it is fast becoming Malaysia's third major export crop;
(iii) laying the foundations for a forest industry in Swaziland and Fiji long before these became of interest to commercial partners;

(iv) developing the concept of local development finance companies to serve the smaller industrial project normally outside the grasp of foreign institutions;
(v) sponsoring the growth of housing finance institutions which bring the benefit of lower and middle-income home ownership as well as the formation of private savings.

CDC has made considerable contributions to the financial well-being of thousands of people and helped in the economic development of many countries. The development of cash crops has introduced people to the reality of a life above subsistence level. The construction of irrigation projects, such as the Swaziland Irrigation Scheme, has provided employment, training and the potential for a much higher standard of farming and living and the capacity to earn much-needed foreign exchange. In a number of cases CDC's support has been vital to the development and efficiency of local statutory boards, for example the Kenya Tea Development Authority, the Kasungu Flue-cured Tobacco Authority and the Tobacco Board of Zambia.

CDC currently manages some 35 projects (agriculture, housing finance, land development, development finance companies, etc.) as well as providing hotel management through its associated company, Hallway Hotels Overseas Limited. It has also seconded staff members to certain projects whose management needed strengthening. CDC has also been responsible for setting up local development finance companies, usually in partnership with the host government and bilateral agencies from other European countries. The function of these development companies is to provide finance for industrial and commercial and, in some cases, agricultural and property developments of a size smaller than can be handled by CDC centrally. Where the contribution sought from CDC to a project is too small in relation to CDC's investigation and supervision costs, it will, in appropriate circumstances, refer the sponsors to the manager of the local company concerned.

CDC Term Loans

The terms of every CDC loan and equity investment are subject to separate negotiation, loan rates of interest and repayment conditions depending, inter alia, on the nature of the project, the purpose for which the loan is required, the period and the value of the security to be given. It should be noted that CDC is predominantly a provider of medium- and long-term development money. It normally charges a fee as consideration for its commitment to provide funds on which sponsors of projects have a right of call over a period of time. This fee is charged at a rate per cent per annum and is normally calculated, as from the date of CDC's commitment, on the undrawn balance. CDC reserves the right to ask for a fee for its service in investigating a project and negotiating the provision of procurement of finance. The amount of the fee will not necessarily be related to the amount of finance so provided or procured, but will be designed to cover at least part of CDC's costs. It also requires reimbursement in respect of all legal costs and expenses properly incurred by it in connection with the preparation and execution of all formal documents relating to CDC's agreement to participate in or procure finance for any project.

Concessionary Assistance. Loan terms for renewable natural resource (RNR) projects (agriculture, etc.) are more favourable than for more commercial projects.

Interest Rate. For RNR projects the interest rate is around $7\frac{1}{2}$ per cent (so long as no private party profits from the concessionary terms). For other projects it is generally in line with the rates of local development banks and international agencies but determined in the light of the needs of the project.

Repayment Period. For RNR projects the repayment is usually up to 20 years, less for industrial or more commercial ones. For housing finance it is up to 25 years.

Grace Period. This is determined in the light of the project's cash flow.

Guarantee. Commercial security is usually considered an adequate guarantee but government guarantees are required where the government is a partner or the project's viability in some other way depends on government policy, for example through marketing controls.

Insurance. The project's assets are required to be fully insured.

CDC Management and Administration

CDC operates through a decentralised structure with regional offices (Caribbean, Asia, Pacific Islands, East and Central, Southern and West Africa) and a number of country representatives. Regional Controllers are overseas members of the Executive Management Board in London, headed by CDC's General Manager. Investment and policy guidelines are made by the CDC Board whose members are appointed by the Minister for Overseas Development but include no civil servants. Regional Controllers and their staff are concerned directly with the operation of projects and are on the Board of project companies.

Marketing Studies

CDC's Marketing Department provides information on marketing prospects for commodities and export potential of specific products. It also undertakes the marketing of certain products if so requested by the project. The project sponsor is usually required to submit evidence of the domestic and/or export market for his products.

Approaches Taken and Techniques Applied

Approaches to CDC should usually be to the Regional Controller or have his support. To qualify for consideration by the Corporation a project must:

  (i) be within CDC's statutory terms of reference;
 (ii) have good development value for the territory concerned, and the approval of the territorial government;
(iii) be shown to have good prospects of commercial viability;
(iv) have management of high calibre, either provided or procured by its sponsors.

The Investigations Department appraises projects in consultation with other specialist departments. Financial analysis of projects is usually followed by an economic cost-benefit analysis to determine the development value to the host country. CDC's Engineering Department scrutinises proposals to ensure that the technology is not more sophisticated than can be operated by the local labour or maintained by local mechanical services, as well as being in balance with other parts of the project. Second-hand machinery is particularly carefully inspected.

CDC Strategy for Financing and Technical Assistance

The strategy is for gradual expansion in countries where CDC is already operational and into new developing countries. Priority is given primarily to RNR projects but also to public utilities and industry. Tourism and the provision of housing finance presently occupy a low priority.

CDC's approach to housing, at least in Africa, is centred on the African Development Bank's proposal for a finance Corporation to be known as SHELTER-AFRIQUE. The object of this corporation will be to raise a substantial volume of funds to be channelled into approved lower and middle-income housing schemes undertaken by existing housing institutions in Africa. It will also assist governments of countries which do not as yet have such institutions to set them up on sound lines. AfDB has found growing support both within and outside Africa since SHELTER-AFRIQUE offers a major contribution to a sector of paramount social significance to all African governments and their peoples. It also offers an opportunity to see funds disbursed and put to work immediately through a network of existing and proven institutions; and the support and experience of institutions like CDC and the Caisse Centrale de Coopération Economique which have substantial amounts of their own capital invested in these and similar institutions and operations.

In general CDC will place the emphasis on operations concerned with the improvement of agricultural production and rural incomes, especially in the poorer countries, though not to the exclusion of other productive and soundly based enterprises with good development value. Technical assistance efforts need to be linked to the prospect of CDC investment. A subject yet to be explored is the extent to which technical assistance could be provided to an agency in one country which was prepared to make investments jointly with CDC in another. CDC attaches the greatest importance to closer collaboration and co-financing with Arab and OPEC aid funds. It considers that its capacity for project identification, development and management, as well as its long experience in project financing, are bases for a useful partnership with others.

Problems of Implementation and Remarks from Field Experience

These usually centre around cost escalations and financial control. Regional Office supervision and Head Office monitoring are designed to deal with such aspects. CDC projects taken as a whole have performed reasonably well, even in times of economic uncertainty and recession, although some projects experience difficult trading conditions when price levels for their products fall sharply. Projects which export their products make a significant contribution to host countries' balance of payments. CDC attaches the utmost importance to sound management and the first concern of CDC and its partners is to secure this.

It is recognised that finance and technical assistance alone do not provide the whole solution to the development problems facing the Third World. The developing countries, and particularly the least developed of them, need help from effective and experienced management so as to ensure that projects are carried out as planned and within approved budgets and timetables and that scarce development resources are used to the best advantage. The most important resource of developing countries is their people, that is why CDC-managed projects give priority to training nationals of host countries for management, professional and technical posts up to top levels. CDC has found that one of the quickest ways of equipping nationals for posts of responsibility in projects in which it invests is through involvement in the management of the project. The corporation provides staff for some 60 projects of which some 35 have appointed CDC as corporate managers, thereby securing not only its training techniques but also all the back-up services which it provides through its regional and territorial offices overseas and from its London headquarters.

APPENDIX 4.1 The Flow of Financial Resources to Developing Countries and Multilateral Agencies by Type (1970–80)
Country: UK

Disbursements Net disbursements	1970	1971	1972	1973	1974	1975	1976	1977	1978	1979	US$m 1980
I Official Development Assistance (a+b)	446.9	561.8	608.7	602.9	729.8	863.2	834.8	914.1	1,472.4	2,066.8	1,780.9
(a) Bilateral ODA	399.0	487.8	480.9	442.1	509.2	566.3	580.8	555.4	852.5	1,163.6	1,255.1
(b) Contributions to multilateral institutions	47.9	74.0	127.8	160.8	220.6	296.9	254.0	358.7	619.9	903.2	525.8
II Other Official Flows (a+b)	6.5	12.0	9.2	61.4	80.4	30.8	31.4	23.0	109.2	134.7	−163.6
(a) Bilateral OOF	6.5	12.0	9.2	61.4	80.4	30.8	31.4	23.0	109.2	134.7	−163.6
(b) Multilateral Institutions											0.0
Subtotal (I+II): Total official flows	453.4	573.8	617.9	664.3	810.2	894.0	886.2	937.1	1,581.6	2,201.5	1,617.3
III Grants by private voluntary agencies	33.6	46.2	50.0	56.4	56.1	53.3	47.0	50.0	50.2	57.3	104.7
IV Private flows at market terms (1–4)	740.6	811.8	833.2	208.4	1,508.8	1,406.0	1,494.5	(4,942.1)	8,711.5	8,960.3	11,073.1
(1) Direct investment	321.6	321.2	350.3	80.5	694.7	796.5	953.9	(610.9)	1,535.5	1,505.8	1,046.8
(2) Bilateral portfolio investment and other	−17.4	−92.5	−52.5	−4.7	460.8	194.0	122.8	3,859.6	6,231.6	6,393.6	7,203.5
(3) Multilateral portfolio investment	(−)	—	(−)	18.0	—	—	—	—	0.0	0.0	0.0
(4) Private export credits	436.4	583.1	535.4	114.6	353.2	415.5	417.8	(471.6)	944.3	1,060.9	2,822.8
V Total resource flows (I–IV)	1,227.6	1,431.8	1,501.1	1,472.7	2,375.1	2,353.3	2,407.7	5,929.2	10,343.3	11,219.1	12,795.0
ODA as % of GNP	0.36	0.40	0.38	0.34	0.37	0.37	0.38	0.37	0.48	0.52	0.34
Total resource flows as % of GNP	1.02	0.96	0.92	0.82	1.23	1.02	1.08	2.42	3.35	2.83	2.43

Sources: OECD *Development Co-operation*, Reviews 1974–1981.

5 France

THE PERFORMANCE OF FRENCH OFFICIAL DEVELOPMENT ASSISTANCE

France is the second biggest donor among DAC countries, making a national effort to transfer official development assistance to developing countries and multilateral agencies. Its share in total DAC/ODA reached 15 per cent in 1980 but its share for the 1970s was almost constant. At the beginning of the 1960s, French ODA reached 18 per cent of total DAC/ODA; it reached US $4052.7m in 1980 compared with US $2090.9m in 1975 and US $971.0m in 1970 (see Appendix 5.1) that is compared with an average of US $878.0m during 1967–69.[1] France's performance in providing ODA in the 1960s was in some years higher than the projected target of 0.7 per cent of UNCTAD II, and the country was the best amongst the big five donors during the 1970s. In 1980, France increased both bilateral and multilateral disbursements and its ODA progressed as a share of GNP from 0.59 per cent in 1979 to 0.62 per cent in 1980 – see Appendix 5.1 and Chart 4. According to the World Development Report of 1981, the French ODA/GNP ratio is going to be constant up to 1983, then a slight increase will occur in 1984 and 1985.

French bilateral official development assistance reached US $3351.3m (83 per cent of ODA) in 1980 compared with US $1788.7m (86 per cent of ODA) in 1975 and US $868.1m (89 per cent of ODA) in 1970. Contributions to multilateral institutions increased from US $102.9m in 1970 to US $302.2m in 1975 and to US $701.3m in 1980. This leads us to indicate that France has therefore maintained a steadily declining ratio of bilateral official development assistance to ODA during the 1970s. Other official flows (OOF) were mainly in bilateral terms which increased from US $28.0m in 1970 to US $333.7m in 1975 and to US $691.1m in 1980. French total official flows (ODA + OOF) reached US $4743.8m (41 per cent of total resource flows) in 1980 compared with US $2424.6m (62 per cent) in 1975 and US $999.0m (54 per cent) in 1970.

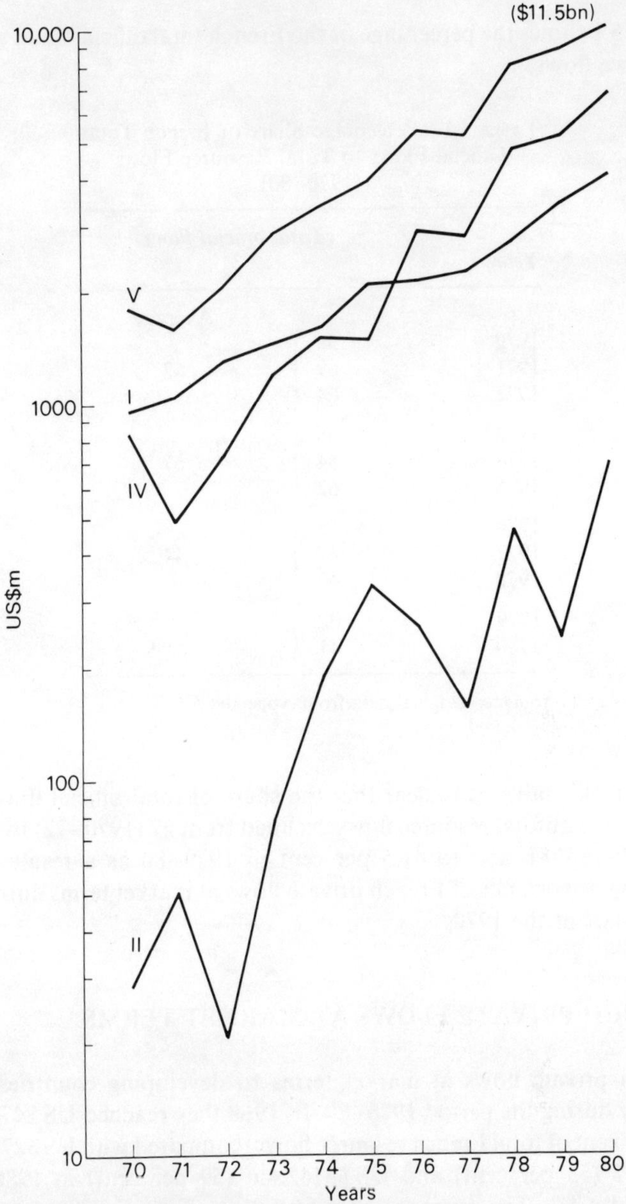

CHART 4 Flow of financial resources to developing countries and multilateral agencies by type: France 1970–80

Source: Appendix 5.1

Table 5.1 shows the percentage of the French total official flows to total resource flows.

TABLE 5.1 Percentage Share of French Total Official Flows to Total Resource Flows (1970–80)

Years	Total official flows %	Average
1970	54	
1971	69	62
1972	64	
1973	56	
1974	54	57
1975	62	
1976	45	
1977	47	44
1978	40	
1979	42	
1980	41	41.5

Source: Original data from Appendix 5.1.

From this table, it is clear that the share of total official flows as a percentage of total resource flows declined from 62 (1970–72) to 44 per cent (1976–78), and to 41.5 per cent in 1979–80 as a result of the growing importance of French private flows at market terms during the latter part of the 1970s.

FRENCH PRIVATE FLOWS AT MARKET TERMS

French private flows at market terms to developing countries grew rapidly during the period 1976–80. In 1968 they reached US $4741.1m (60 per cent of total French resource flows) compared with US $2770.8m in 1977 (53 per cent) and US $6742.4m (59 per cent) in 1980 – see Appendix 5.1. The average share of private flows during the period 1976–80 reached 57 per cent compared with 43 per cent during 1973–75 and 37 per cent during 1970–72. During the first three years of the 1970s direct investment and private export credits provided the main volume of total private flows, but after this period direct investment declined as a share of total private flows until it reached 9 per cent in 1978 and 13 per cent in 1980, compared with 28 per cent in 1970 and 35 per cent in 1971. Private export credits showed no clear trend and its share in total private flows fluctuated yearly within a range of 64 per cent in 1977 and 36 per cent in 1979 with the exception of the two years of 1973 and 1974 when it reached 29 and 17 per cent respectively. Bilateral portfolio investment and other grew during the period 1973–80 with one exception in 1977 when it reached 26 per cent. This indicates that both private export credits and bilateral portfolio investment and other played an important role in French total private flows during the second half of the 1970s as direct investment has declined sharply during the last five years. Table 5.2 shows the share of French private flows to total resource flows and its components.

TABLE 5.2 The Share of French Private Flows at Market Terms in Relation to Total Resource Flows and its Major Components
1970–80
(percentages)

Years	Private flows to total resource flows %	Direct investment to private flows %	Private export credits to private flows %	Bilateral portfolio Investment and other to private flows %
1970	45	28	37	35
1971	30	35	45	16
1972	35	31	37	31
1973	44	23	29	48
1974	46	15	17	67
1975	38	18	37	45
1976	55	8	51	40
1977	53	10	64	26
1978	60	9	42	49
1979	58	13	36	45
1980	59	13	39	46

Source: Original data from Appendix 5.1.

The substantial increase in the private sector flows in 1978 was attributed to an increase of 186 per cent in banking sector transactions directed towards a number of middle- or higher income countries (comprising essentially Algeria, the Bahamas, Bahrain, Brazil, the

Netherlands, Antilles, Mexico and Nigeria). There was also a substantial increase of 43 per cent in direct investment, especially in Spain and Argentina.[2] The legal and administrative treatment of French direct investment in the developing countries is different for franc area countries[3] and other developing countries. French residents were free to invest in the franc area without prior authorisation up to 1967, while exports of long-term capital to developing countries outside the franc area required official authorisation. The attitude of the French authorities towards investment abroad progressively became very liberal. In 1967, the regulations were even further relaxed and direct investment in countries outside the franc area became virtually free (subject only to notification to the Ministry of Finance which, however, has the authority to reject the transaction). Guaranteed convertibility of currency is one of the most powerful incentives to private investment, and the structure of the franc area provides effective encouragement. The currencies issued by the Central Bank of the Central African States (Cameroon, Central African Republic of Chad, Congo and Gabon) and by the Central Bank of the West African States (Benin, Ivory Coast, Niger, Senegal, Togo and Upper Volta) were defined in terms of the French franc and guaranteed by the French Treasury. As for conditions for eligibility, the operation must be of definite benefit to the French economy appraised on the basis of the direct and indirect effects shown by an analysis through time of the investment programme submitted.[4] Official financial support of private investments comprises:

(1) The Caisse Centrale de Coopération Economique (CCCE);
(2) The Fund for Aid and Co-operation (FAC);
(3) Union pour le financement et l'expansion du commerce international (UFINEX);
(4) Development industriel a l'etranger (DIE).

Fiscal measures related to tax incentives to investment in developing countries fall into five groups:

(1) Countries with which there are no tax conventions: direct application of French tax laws.
(2) A group comprising Guinea, Vietnam, Cambodia, and Laos. French regulations traditionally apply to these countries a system of fiscal neutrality.
(3) A group comprising the French overseas territories, the African States and Madagascar, Algeria and Tunisia. These states are

linked to France by bilateral tax conventions designed to eliminate double taxation.
(4) Conventions of a special type are already in force (this is the case with Israel, India, Lebanon, Pakistan, Brazil, Iran, Singapore, Malaysia and the Philippines) or being negotiated, with certain developing countries outside the franc area.
(5) The French authorities have made special tax arrangements to encourage private investment in the French Overseas Departments.

As an incentive to encourage the setting-up of establishments which are of definite benefit to the French economy, the state has introduced, by stages, under the Ministry for Economic Affairs and Finance, a system of official guarantees against political risks which may affect invested capital.[5]

FRENCH DEVELOPMENT ASSISTANCE POLICY

France has a concept of priority areas for development policy. Historical reasons were behind the well-established foreign aid policy in African (including North Africa) French-speaking countries for expanding the markets for French products. Official development assistance policy in France is based upon this concept of priority. On the other hand, French private flows at market terms are based upon the mode of private investors and the conditions of the financial markets. As regards the application of aid, it is the heavy concentration of funds in the technical assistance sector, particularly the educational-cultural field, which distinguishes France from other donors and this feature can only be ascribed to France's well-known determination to promote its language and culture as widely as possible. The French government believes that the human factor is paramount in the accelerated economic development of developing countries. This accelerated development is conditioned by human as well as financial investments. As a result, France provided over 40 per cent of all technical co-operation personnel supplied by DAC member countries during the period 1962–68. The French authorities attached great importance to technical and cultural co-operation in education, agriculture and industrial technology, but at the same time made grants for capital and infrastructure projects. For example, in 1968 they accounted for $190m of which the main recipients were African States and Malagasy (38 per cent), the Overseas Departments (21 per cent), Algeria (13 per cent) and the overseas territories (11 per cent). The share of industry in the total grants amounted to 27 per cent. Loans for capital projects in the franc area were on a small scale whereas loans to countries outside the area showed a tendency to rise. The reason was that the French government regarded the franc area countries as not rich enough to charge heavy interest and amortisation payments.[6]

In 1973, French aid to the Overseas Departments and Territories represented 38 per cent of ODA. The grant element of the official aid programme, which had been rising steadily since 1971, was estimated at 91 per cent in 1973 (86 per cent in 1972). After excluding from ODA those loans which no longer met the norms laid down by the 1972 Recommendation, the grant element of loans was estimated at 45 per cent in 1973 compared with 32 per cent in 1972. The procurement restrictions attached to France's official aid varied with the recipient countries. For countries outside the franc area, all loans were tied to purchases in France, but derogation was granted where French industry was unable to provide the necessary goods.[7]

The financial terms of French aid, which had improved in 1973, hardened a little in 1974, and in spite of some improvements for the poorest countries, which received a larger proportion of grants, the terms given to countries not among the traditional recipients of French aid remained relatively hard. A special effort was made on behalf of the Sahel countries. Additional contributions for the countries most seriously affected by the increase of the price of oil amounted to $51m in 1974 and commitments under this heading increased further in 1975.[8] The overseas departments and territories' share of total aid disbursements rose slightly in 1975, from 38 to 39 per cent, and aid to LLDCs accounted for 9 per cent of total bilateral commitments, the same percentage as in 1974. The trend towards an increase in the multilateral contributions became more marked in the course of commitments in this area with participation in the African Development Fund announced in May 1976, membership of the Inter-American Development Bank (July 1976), participation in IFAD ($25m), the decision to provide 50 per cent of the capital of the African Solidarity Fund, amounting to Ffr100m in 1976, and the maintaining of France's relative share in the Fifth Replenishment of IDA. Bilateral aid to the LLDCs and to the MSAs represented 10 and 30 per cent of bilateral ODA respectively in 1976, that is 0.05 and 0.14 per cent of French GNP.[9] In 1977, the share of French aid to the overseas departments and territories, which had increased steadily up until 1976, levelled off at 51 per cent of bilateral ODA, compared with 30 per cent for states coming under the responsibility of the Ministry for Co-operation, 10 per cent for the Maghreb and 9 per cent for other countries. As a percentage of GNP, French aid to the LLDCs remained slightly higher in 1977 (0.04 per cent) than the DAC average (0.03 per cent). France has continued to be well ahead of all other DAC countries in the volume of technical assistance provided. The bulk was directed towards the education sector, and France was also very active in the field of research, particularly in the agricultural sector.[10] No major change in French development policy seems likely in the short term. Its main new component seems to be the decision to double the French contribution to UNDP by 1981. It should also be noted that the government has reaffirmed its intention to reach the 0.7 per cent target. In 1978, the geographical breakdown of French bilateral aid showed a slight decrease from 52 to 50 per cent in the proportion granted to the Départements and Territoires d'Outre-mer (DOM and TOM); the share going to States coming under the responsibility of the Ministry for Co-operation (30 per cent) and to the Maghreb (10 per cent) remained unchanged, while the proportion of bilateral aid granted to other countries increased. French aid policy continued to be directed primarily to education and, to a lesser extent, to health and the development of public services. A large proportion of bilateral assistance (60 per cent in 1978) was accounted for by technical co-operation. The biggest increase in 1978 related to food aid which more than doubled, directed to a growing number of recipient countries, mainly in the Sahel, Asia and North Africa.[11]

French ODA in 1979 increased appreciably due to the rise in multilateral contributions, and in particular in contributions to the European Development Fund and to the regional banks and funds. The new category of loans on especially soft terms, introduced by the Caisse Centrale de Coopération Economique in 1978 and designed to benefit the poorest countries or those in exceptional difficulty, made its first appearance in 1979. Bilateral aid continued to be given to a very large extent (60 per cent) in the form of technical assistance. The geographical distribution of French bilateral aid in 1979 was fairly stable, with almost half the flows directed towards DOM and TOM, 29 per cent to states coming within the sphere of the Ministry for Co-operation, and 8 per cent to the Maghreb countries, while the share of the rest of the world (13 per cent) continued to rise steadily. In addition, a 'concerted plan of action for the development of Africa' (CADA) was launched at the end of 1979 to co-ordinate the aid of a member of donor countries in this region.[12] Bilateral assistance from France to LLDCs amounted to $395m in 1980, equivalent to 0.06 per cent of GNP. During the 1981

United Nations Conference on the Least Developed Countries, France stated that it would be increasing its assistance to those countries to the level of 0.10 per cent of GNP in 1981; rising to 0.15 per cent in 1985.[13]

ADMINISTRATION OF FRENCH FINANCIAL FLOWS

There are five principal sources responsible for different aid operations:[14]

  (i) The Ministry for Co-operation;
 (ii) The Directorate-General for Cultural, Scientific and Technical Relations;
(iii) The Central Fund for Economic Co-operation (CCCE);
(iv) The Treasury;
 (v) The Ministry of State for the Overseas Departments and Territories.

The functions of the agencies are distinguished principally by the countries they cover. DOM/TOM are the responsibility of the Ministry of State for the Overseas Departments and Territories, but the specialist ministries and the CCCE also provide aid there. The French-speaking countries South of Sahara (EAM) receive both financial and technical assistance from the Ministry for Co-operation and loans from the CCCE. Since 1975 CCCE has been entitled to extend its operations outside French-speaking areas in Africa. In other countries loans and grants are primarily the responsibility of the Ministry of the Economy and the Treasury while technical assistance falls to the Directorate-General. In addition, the specialist ministries, principally the Ministry of Education, play a large part in providing technical assistance within their respective fields; this is a more important role in the case of France than in that of other donors because of the large share of the French programme which goes in technical assistance.

THE EXPERIENCE OF CAISSE CENTRALE DE CO-OPÉRATION ECONOMIQUE[15]

Establishment and Financial Resources

Caisse Centrale de Coopération Économique is a public corporation of independent legal personality with a capital of Ffr200m since 1978 (as a development bank). Its capacity for financing is Ffr1bn and the nature of its resources, which come mainly from long-term borrowing (by issuing bonds) does not enable it to make grants and limits its action to financing by way of loans and, to a minor degree, by taking holdings. CCCE has no regional programme for financing in advance. It operates on a project basis, with an emphasis on 'project-type' productive projects, mainly agricultural and industrial, and long-term loans remain its principal method of aid. It is also incidentally charged with the administration of aid which is not provided out of its own funds. It is the executive agent of the Fund of Aid and Co-operation in Tropical Africa, of the Ministry of Foreign Affairs Technical Assistance Programme in Algeria and various countries outside the franc area, and of government loans from Treasury funds to various countries, including those of North Africa. But its main activity remains the carrying out of banking operations on its own capital resources, its reserve funds, Treasury loans, resources obtained through its bond issues, and the excess of expected repayments over its own outstanding obligations. It extends these credit facilities in individual cases for specific projects after examination of their financial, economic and social effects and of their contribution to the country's economic development.

Caisse Centrale can provide technical assistance for short or longer periods and mainly for finance and management. It provides assistance to countries on request, either by sending staff members on field missions or on specific assignments, or by participating in the training of professional personnel. Some staff members on assignment still serve in specialised institutions, particularly in credit institutions, but some also serve in the capacity of technical advisers to government services. There is a growing tendency to provide experts in management and finances inside the projects themselves or in the structures in charge of bringing them into operation.

Scope of Activities

Loans at preferential interest rates which are known as 'first window' loans and account for the bulk of the CCCE's activities, rose from Ffr373m in 1974 to Ffr1200m in 1979. They amounted to about Ffr1500m in 1980, so that since 1974 they have multiplied in value by 4 in current francs and by about 2.4 in real terms, taking account of the increase in French export prices. Loans from the 'second window', which offer favourable repayment periods, but interest rates which can be borne only by the more advanced countries or in the case of particularly profitable ventures, totalled about Ffr1095m in 1980 compared with Ffr400m in 1979. The overall pattern is one of relative stability in the total volume of commitments since 1977, but the main feature is a very clear improvement in the distribution of lending between the two 'windows', with the proportion of 'first window' commitments rising from 52 per cent in 1976 to 75 per cent in 1979 and declining to 58 per cent in 1980. Table 5.3 shows the CCCE's commitments during 1974–80.

TABLE 5.3 Caisse Centrale Commitments (1974–80) (Ffrm)

	1974	1975	1976	1977	1978	1979	1980
Loans							
'First window'	372.5	482.6	650.9	800.4	965.6	1200.4	1499.5
'Second window'	—	170.0	613.6	521.0	521.0	399.5	1094.5
Shareholdings	2.3	2.4	7.8	17.9	6.5	2.6	7.0
Total	374.8	655.0	1272.3	1339.3	1493.1	1602.5	2601.0

Sources: Caisse Centrale de Coopération Economique, *Annual Report*, 1979.
Caisse Centrale De Coopération Economique, *Aperçu des Opérations dans les Pays d'Afrique et de l'Ocean Indien en 1980*.

The sectoral distribution has shown that the Caisse Centrale in 1980 allocated 63 per cent of its finance to directly productive activities compared with 65 per cent in 1979 and 71 per cent in 1978. Moreover, the sectors concerned, especially rural production, were those in which the initiation and formulation of projects posed the greatest problems. By introducing new procedures for very long-term and very low-interest loans which are more attuned to the poverty of rural regions, the Caisse Centrale has been able to increase the proportion of its financing allocated to rural development. In 1980 the funds allocated to the development of industry and tourism totalled Ffr860m compared with Ffr485m in 1979, slightly less than the amount for rural development (Ffr559m). The programmes in the electricity sector in 1979 were on a more modest scale than before but increased substantially in 1980. An expansion of tourism and more business hotels in Africa are urgently needed. The figures for the financing of public infrastructure were exceptionally high in 1979 and 1980. In the financing of investments for railways and telecommunications, purchases of equipment were often combined with schemes aimed at improving management through training and advisory services for staff and raising the standard of maintenance.

CCCE has taken part in raising finance for very large projects, notably in conjunction with Arab funds and banks with which it continues to maintain very close relations. In 1979, however, the programmes selected were generally medium-sized, so that the Caisse Centrale was able to provide a higher proportion of the finance required than is normally the case. Table 5.4 shows the sectoral distribution of CCCE's operations.

TABLE 5.4 Breakdown by Sector of Caisse Centrale's Operations (1979–80)

	1980 (Ffrm)	%	1979 (Ffrm)	%	1978 %	Average for 1976 to 1980 %
Rural development	782.3	30.1	559.1	34.9	23.9	30.0
Mining	108.3	4.2	140.8	8.8	11.8	7.5
Industry, small business	205.5	7.9	145.1	9.1	20.1	10.9
Electricity	463.1	17.7	99.5	6.2	12.6	17.8
Tourism	83.1	3.2	99.5	6.2	2.5	3.0
Total for productive sectors	1642.3	63.1	1044.0	65.1	70.9	69.2
Railways	59.0	2.3	184.2	11.5	8.5	7.0
Roads, seaports, airports	481.3	18.5	122.1	7.6	8.5	9.5
Telecommunications	210.9	8.1	156.5	9.8	8.1	8.0
Urban infrastructure	106.6	4.1	43.0	2.7	0.2	2.5
Total for public infrastructure	857.8	33.0	505.8	31.6	25.3	27.0
Total for financial operations	100.9	3.9	52.7	3.3	3.8	3.8
Overall total	2601.0	100.0	1602.5	100.0	100.0	100.0

Sources: Caisse Centrale de Coopération Economique, *Annual Report, 1979*.
Caisse Centrale de Coopération Economique, *Aperçu des Opérations dans les Pays d'Afrique et de l'Ocean Indien en 1980*.

Despite the reduction in CCCE's role in the overseas departments, its total financing on its own account was 5 per cent up in 1978, at Ffr1880m compared with Ffr1790m in 1977 and Ffr1810m in 1976. In 1979 it increased to reach Ffr1970m. Various factors entered into the stabilisation of financing over the period 1977–79, which followed upon very sharp increases in 1975 and 1976. In the African and Indian Ocean countries there was a substantial increase in conventional low-interest loans (+23 per cent in 1977, +21 per cent in 1978) and a levelling-off of 'second window' loans granted at market rates (−15 per cent in 1977, stable in 1978). In the overseas departments there was a steady reduction in commitments, the corollary of the reform in the distribution of long-term credit (−34 per cent in 1977, −29 per cent in 1978). Table 5.5

TABLE 5.5 Geographical Distribution of CCCE Financing (1974–80)

Year	Total commitments (Ffrm)	African and Indian Ocean countries (Ffrm)	%	Overseas Territories (Ffrm)	%	Overseas departments (Ffrm)	%
1974	817	392	48	163	20	262	32
1975	1105	655	59.3	200	18.1	250	22.6
1976	1810	1272	70.3	215[a]	11.9	323	17.8
1977	1790	1339	74.8	237	13.2	214	12.0
1978	1880	1493	79.4	235	12.5	152	8.1
1979	1970	1630	81.3	235	12.0	133[b]	6.8
1980	3143	2601	82.8	351	11.2	191	6.1

[a] Five territories.
[b] Through its subsidiary Socredom.
Sources: Caisse Centrale, *Annual Reports* 1978, 1979, 1980.

shows the geographical distribution of CCCE financing during 1974–80.

Total financing in foreign countries and the overseas territories, where the Caisse Centrale has retained its full role, has risen from Ffr555m in 1974 to Ffr1487m in 1976, Ffr1728m in 1978, Ffr1838m in 1979, and Ffr2952m in 1980. Funds for the countries in Africa and the Indian Ocean, which accounted for less than half of the total in 1974, amounted to 81 per cent in 1979, confirming that the Caisse Centrale is destined to play an increasingly important role in aid for the Third World.

The Terms and Conditions of Caisse Centrale

Interest rate: first window: 3.5–7 per cent, 1979 average rate 5.8 per cent but since then especially favourable conditions can be applied for poorest countries (1.5 per cent for the first 10 years, 2 per cent afterwards);
Second window: market rate 14.75 per cent (since October 1980).
Repayment period: in general 10–20 years.
Grace period: up to 10 years. Government guarantee is always required.
No insurance.
There is no restriction on the use of its funds to finance local expenditure on the execution of the projects.

Management and Administration

CCCE is subject to ministerial supervision jointly exercised by the Ministry of Finance (Treasury) and the minister responsible for the country under consideration. The latter is either the Minister for Co-operation, in the case of African countries and Madagascar, the Minister for Foreign Affairs in the case of other countries, or the Minister for the Départements et Territoires d'Outre-mer. The Caisse Centrale has a managing director appointed to a supervising board (Conseil de Surveillance). The Chairman of the Board is designated by the Minister of Finance. Any loan or equity investment by CCCE is subject to approval of the Board which can itself, for smaller loans, delegate part of its power either to a Loan Committee, the members of which are chosen among the members of the Board, or even to the managing director for loans that are smaller still. The total staff of the Caisse Centrale is about 1000 (in 1980), of which about 650 are 'permanent' staff members enjoying a career status; other staff members, about 360, usually nationals of the country in which they are serving, are under special contracts.

The operations of CCCE are carried out under three main departments:

(1) *Development Department* for appraisal missions, supervision, follow-up of projects.
(2) *Foreign Financing Department* (for foreign countries) studies, loan negotiations and disbursements.
(3) *Department for French Overseas Departments and Territories* The CCCE maintains overseas agencies.

As from 1 March 1981, the organisational structure of CCCE, based on geographical distribution, is as follows: Western Africa, Central Africa and Eastern and Indian Ocean. For each department there are two units – economic and financial, and technical.

Approaches and Techniques Applied

Marketing studies are carried out by a small unit and are related mainly to economic studies. In the various sectors of investment (public utilities, electricity, mining and industry, agriculture and housing), CCCE makes a choice among the applications it receives in the light of its available resources, the value of the projects to the applicant countries, and the rules imposed upon it by its role as a Development Bank. It takes no initiative in launching projects; it can only deal with applications submitted or approved by states or their national institutions. On the other hand, any development project with reasonable financial prospects is eligible for financing by CCCE. Applications are studied by both the local agency and the Paris Foreign Financing Department, with the technical support of the experts of the Development Department. If the dossier is accepted, it is then submitted to the Board for a decision.

Marketing studies and trends of prices of raw materials are used as a basis for feasibility studies. The interest shown in a project is essentially estimated from its economic or financial profitability.

Strategy for Financing and Technical Assistance

This is to concentrate upon solving the crop problem (the food problem) and to raise productivity in the agricultural sector. For that purpose, the future strategy of financing of CCCE will be related to:

(1) Development of crop projects, either for export or for local consumption.
(2) Financing infrastructure projects related to agriculture or energy, like dam projects, land reclamation, irrigation projects, transportation, etc.
(3) Financing educational projects. For some time CCCE has agreed to finance specialised professional training in order to help implement a project or secure its maintenance. It has for example started providing loans for professional training in Cameroon, the Ivory Coast, Senegal, Seychelles and Niger.

CCCE is intending to draw its future strategy for financing on the basis of 30 per cent for infrastructural projects sector and 70 per cent for the productive projects sector. As for other financing, technical assistance provided by CCCE will be mainly related to solving the problems of management, finance and education and promoting development banks in countries in need of that type of assistance, with more emphasis in rural areas for extending lines of credit by development banks. The Caisse Centrale has a good experience in this field in different countries.

Problems of Implementation and Remarks from Field Experience

The experience of project implementation and follow-up of the Caisse Central (especially in Africa) has brought out some problems which are common to most of the sectors in which it acts. These problems are related to the quality of technical leadership in rural development, to the standing and competence of promoters in industry, to the strict management of public utility companies which it supports, and to the balanced operation of public utility services, and are all different aspects of the same problem, namely, the need to ensure, in the interest of the beneficiary states themselves, the effectiveness of the aid granted. CCCE has been organised to cope with these problems. This is done by a team of professionals located in Regional Offices and from Headquarters. Recently, CCCE has also set up a unit for post-evaluation of projects. The staff have indicated that developing countries, and the most underdeveloped, should help the aid agencies in proceeding accurately along the stages of project appraisal. Co-operation between both sides is a must. On one hand, the recipient country should do everything possible to facilitate the appraisal stages, and on the other hand, the aid agency should make the process easier and less complicated. Appraisal project by project should be the theme of technical, financial and economic studies. In this respect, depending too much on mathematics or modelling techniques appears to be an unsound basis. The social contribution of each project, in employment, urbanisation, the problems of rural areas, income distribution, etc. has proved from the field experience of CCCE the main contribution towards development. In this respect CCCE considers itself to be and should be a banker for development and not a banker for profit. Moreover, the experience of CCCE in the field has proved that financial aid cannot contribute towards solving development problems unless it is combined with the existence of technical executives and teams competent to make proper use of it.

APPENDIX 5.1 The Flow of Financial Resources to Developing Countries and Multilateral Agencies by Type (1970–80)
Country: France

Disbursements Net disbursements	1970	1971	1972	1973	1974	1975	1976	1977	1978	1979	US$m 1980
I Official Development Assistance (a+b)	971.0	1,075.3	1,320.3	1,488.4	1,615.6	2,090.9	2,145.5	2,266.8	2,705.3	3,370.0	4,052.7
(a) Bilateral ODA	868.1	946.6	1,128.9	1,294.3	1,389.4	1,788.7	1,845.5	1,916.9	2,350.6	2,786.0	3,351.3
(b) Contributions to multi-lateral institutions	102.9	128.7	191.5	194.1	226.2	302.2	299.9	349.9	354.7	583.9	701.3
II Other Official Flows (a+b)	28.0	50.2	21.6	77.4	190.3	333.7	257.6	157.7	462.9	237.6	691.1
(a) Bilateral OOF	28.0	50.2	21.6	77.4	190.3	333.7	257.6	157.7	462.9	237.6	691.1
(b) Multilateral institutions	—	—	—	—	—	—	—	—	—	—	0.0
Subtotal (I+II): Total official flows	999.0	1,125.5	1,341.9	1,565.8	1,805.9	2,424.6	2,403.1	2,424.5	3,168.2	3,607.6	4,743.8
III Grants by private voluntary agencies	6.3	7.2	7.9	10.0	12.5	15.2	15.1	16.3	19.9	23.5	35.7
IV Private flows at market terms (1–4)	829.3	490.8	732.2	1,224.3	1,544.7	1,502.1	2,897.7	2,770.8	4,741.1	5,053.5	6,742.4
(1) Direct investment	235.1	(170.4)	230.6	287.1	239.4	274.2	245.5	264.7	413.4	681.2	899.5
(2) Bilateral portfolio investment and other	290.5	80.4	230.6	583.0	1,037.6	676.4	1,163.4	720.8	2,334.5	2,289.3	3,096.6
(3) Multilateral portfolio investment	—	18.0	—	—	—	—	—	—	0.0	282.3	109.8
(4) Private export credits	303.7	222.0	271.0	354.2	267.7	551.5	1,488.8	1,785.2	1,993.2	1,800.7	2,636.6
V Total resource flows (I–IV)	1,834.6	1,623.5	2,082.1	2,800.1	3,363.1	3,941.9	5,315.9	5,211.6	7,929.2	8,684.6	11,521.8
ODA as % of GNP	0.66	0.66	0.67	0.57	0.59	0.62	0.62	0.60	0.57	0.59	0.62
Total resource flows as % of GNP	1.24	1.00	1.06	1.09	1.22	1.17	1.53	1.37	1.68	1.52	1.77

Sources: OECD, *Development Co-operation*, Reviews 1974–81.

6 West Germany

THE PERFORMANCE OF WEST GERMAN OFFICIAL DEVELOPMENT ASSISTANCE

The Federal Republic of Germany (West Germany) is one of the five largest contributors among DAC members. Its share of total ODA provided by DAC members reached 13 per cent in 1980 compared with 12 per cent in 1975, 9 per cent in 1970 and 5 per cent in 1960. West Germany took third place (in 1980) following the USA and France. Its share of total DAC/ODA was higher than the share of the UK and Japan and it is estimated that West Germany will maintain its position for the coming few years.

ODA provided by West Germany reached US$3517.4m in 1980 compared with US$1688.8m in 1975 and US$599.0m in 1970. Bilateral ODA reached US$2274.3m (65 per cent of ODA) in 1980 compared with US$1160.9m (69 per cent of ODA) in 1975 and US$466.1m (78 per cent of ODA) in 1970 – see Appendix 6.1 and Chart 5. This indicates (as with the other big donors) that the contributions to multilateral institutions have grown as a share of ODA and are expected to grow still further in the near future. Contributions to multilateral institutions reached US$1243.1m in 1980 compared with US$527.9m in 1975, and US$132.9m in 1970. Other official flows, mostly bilateral, increased rapidly during 1970–73, to reach US$229.2m in 1973 compared with only US$132.1m in 1970, but declined drastically during the period 1974–77 to reach only US$61.0m in 1977 compared with US$96m in 1974. It then increased sharply during 1978 to reach US$221.8m, then declined in 1979 to reach US$111.7m but sharply increased in 1980 to reach US$630.0m. Total official flows (ODA + OOF) in general reached US$4147.4m (39 per cent of total flows) in 1980 compared with US$1697.9m (34 per cent) in 1975, and US$731.1m (49 per cent) in 1970. This indicates, as with other big donors, that private flows at market terms increased in both volume and percentages during the second half of the 1970s – see Appendix 6.1. During the second half of the 1960s the

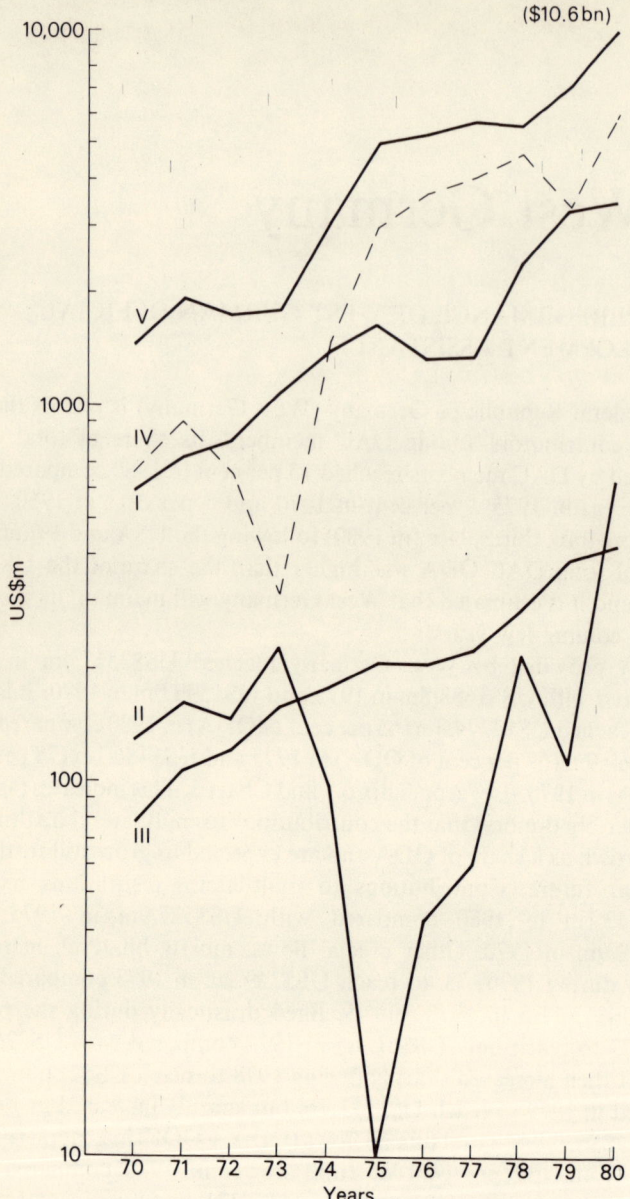

Chart 5 Flow of financial resources to developing countries and multilateral agencies by type: West Germany 1970–80

Source: Appendix 6.1

expansion of total financial flows from West Germany was almost entirely in private flows at market terms which increased very sharply from US$297m in 1966 to US$1502m in 1969. The development of private capital flows during this period reflected both the great importance of the private development efforts and the liquidity of the economy providing advantages in interest rates and the desirability of the Deutsche Mark as a strong currency in relation to other international issues or currencies as well as certain institutional and policy changes.[1]

As in the case of the USA, UK and Japan, West Germany has never reached the UNCTAD target of 0.7 per cent of ODA/GNP. After a decline in West Germany's ODA disbursements in 1976 and 1977, with ODA falling in 1977 to its lowest GNP ratio, there was a recovery in 1978 and medium-term policy, as adopted by the cabinet in July 1979,[2] pointed to a rising ODA/GNP share over the following years. According to the new plan, the budget of the Ministry of Economic Cooperation adopted an annual increase of 12.5 per cent each until 1983, and its growth rate would be at least double that of the overall budget. Thus the ODA/GNP ratio reached 0.44 per cent in 1979 and 0.43 per cent in 1980 and it is estimated (according to the *World Development Report 1981*) that it will reach 0.45 per cent in 1983, the last year of the medium-term plan.

PRIVATE FLOWS

West Germany's private flows at market terms to developing countries have grown very rapidly since 1974, after a decline during the period 1971–73 – see Appendix 6.1. Table 6.1 shows the development of the percentages of the components of West Germany's private flows.

It is hard to indicate a major trend for any of the components of West Germany's private flows. The year 1973 showed a sharp increase in direct investment which has been compensated for by a negative flow of bilateral portfolio investment and private export credits. During 1977–78, the share of direct investment was almost constant while bilateral portfolio investment declined. During the same period, multilateral portfolio investment declined while private export credits sharply increased. The largest individual categories in 1978 were credits from domestic banks followed by private export credits, direct investment and multilateral portfolio investment. During 1979, multilateral portfolio investment increased to reach 27 per cent of the total private flows while bilateral portfolio investment declined to 23 per cent and during

TABLE 6.1 Components of FRG's Private Flows 1970–80 (percentages)

Year	Direct investment %	Bilateral portfolio investment and other %	Multilateral portfolio investment %	Private export credit %
1970	47	16	9	28
1971	39	3	13	45
1972	89	(−12)	32	(−9)
1973	247	(−87)	38	(−98)
1974	48	19	(−2)	35
1975	27	29	12	33
1976	21	31	25	23
1977	21	53	22	4
1978	22	34	17	27
1979	24	23	27	26
1980	26	28	23	23

Source: Original data from Appendix 6.1.

1980 shares of both direct investment and bilateral investment slightly increased while the shares of multilateral portfolio investment and private export credits slightly declined. West Germany has one of the most comprehensive systems of incentives for private investment in developing countries. This reflects both the importance which the government attributes to private development efforts and the serious obstacles which had to be overcome in post-war years to encourage an increase in the outflow of private investment to developing countries. By the end of 1976, the government had concluded bilateral agreements with 48 developing countries for the protection and promotion of West Germany's direct investment. The purpose of these agreements was to give investors a guarantee based upon international law and providing for arbitration, that their capital investment will be subject to equitable, fair and non-discriminatory treatment. The agreements were intended to protect investors from such actions as discriminatory administrative measures (withholding of import licences, impeding access to raw materials, discriminatory taxation of social payments, etc.), and expropriation without compensation. A system of guarantees against political risk for private direct investments abroad was established in 1960 and subsequently improved several times, being exclusively confined to investments in developing countries. The West German Government has also sought to stimulate private investment by providing special tax incentives for investment in developing countries within the framework of the Law on Tax Measures for Foreign Investment by German Industry, and the Foreign Taxation Act, as well as by favourable tax treatment of investment income from developing countries, especially within the framework of double taxation agreements. The government has encouraged the setting up of investment advisory services within the framework of several existing official institutions in order to help small and medium-sized firms, in particular, to set up branch establishments in developing countries. The most important institution of this kind is the Federal Agency for Foreign Trade Information in Cologne which was supported and supervised by the Ministries of Economic and Foreign Affairs. Contacts between West Germany's industry and business partners from developing countries were also established occasionally by the German Foundation for International Development (DSE) in Berlin.[3]

WEST GERMANY'S DEVELOPMENT ASSISTANCE POLICY

In 1971 new points of emphasis for development policy were set by UNCTAD III and at the United Nations Conference on Environment in Stockholm. The results were taken into account when work was started on the review and continuation of the Development Policy Concept of the German Federal Government, first adopted on 11 February 1971. It has since been supplemented by basic statements concerning a European development policy, the protection of the environment and the utilisation of mineral resources. Moreover, the original statements on trade and monetary policy and on the instruments of West German development policy have been revised in the light of the experience gained. The German Federal Government believed that the changes that have been made would help to attain the goals of the concept in due course and would make efficient use of a larger volume of resources for development.[14] The Development Policy Concept of 1975 implied in particular that bilateral ODA should be increasingly concentrated on the very poor countries and on rural development and food production. Since 1976 differentiation of financial terms was introduced, and new forms of co-operation were proposed, including technical assistance against payment, and triangular arrangements with OPEC countries, and the share of multilateral assistance was around 30 per cent of total ODA.[5] West Germany's geographic distribution of bilateral ODA is, in principle, worldwide, but the government has stated in a number of policy documents its intention of concentrating an increasing proportion on LLDCs, MSAs and, generally, the poorest developing countries. In 1977, LLDCs received 22 per cent of total bilateral ODA net disbursements and MSAs 41 per cent. As part of the reallocation of assistance to the poorer countries, greater focus has been given to African countries, which accounted for 42 per cent of total bilateral aid in 1977. Measures to promote agriculture and rural development have increased in importance in the West German aid programme and as part of the effort to intensify technological and scientific co-operation with developing countries, a new department – the German Appropriate Technology Exchange (GATE) – was set up in 1978 at the German Agency for Technical Co-operation (GTZ) to build up a technological question and answer service accessible to all interested public and private bodies and to act as a link with other comparable international and national institutions.[6] The Cabinet of the Federal Republic in May 1979 adopted a seventeen-point policy statement on co-operation with developing countries aiming at supplementing the development Policy Concept of the Federal Republic of Germany of 1975 to meet the changed requirements in the overall development policy situation. An increasing emphasis is to be given to co-operation with developing countries in the energy field and to measures designed to combat absolute poverty (basic-need concept). New guidelines have also been prepared for co-operation with the more advanced developing countries.[7]

The bilateral co-operation between West Germany and individual developing countries covers a wide range of projects and programmes implemented jointly by the governments involved. The West German Government committed itself to the task of contributing to the advancement of developing countries over twenty years ago, and its policy vis-à-vis the developing countries, which is closely linked to policies in other fields, contributes to the reduction of tensions and to peace. West Germany respects the developing countries' decisions as to the course they wish to take, but the prerequisite for co-operation is that the developing countries desire it and are willing to make contributions of their own. Multilateral co-operation represents a considerable portion of the FRG's contributions in the Third World, channelled via international development organisations. Participation in the European Community's development programme is also a top priority, and West Germany's contribution to the European Development Fund reached approximately 26 per cent in 1979. The value that the Federal Government places on multilateral co-operation in development is shown by the more than DM850m it allocated for this purpose in 1978, which is approximately a quarter of its total contributions to developing countries. The Federal Government has also decided to convert the development credits promised to the LLDCs into grants if the country concerned so requests, though reserving the right to examine and negotiate the cases individually, in keeping with a resolution of March 1978 of the Trade and Development Board (UNCTAD). Since 1978, in order to ease the debt situation of the developing countries, the Federal Government has provided grants specifically for development projects in the LLDCs. The Federal Government orientated its co-operation in development according to the decisions of the European Community and the principles adopted by OECD and the United Nations, it also intensified private co-operation of industry with the developing countries.

West Germany's contribution to projects and programmes with the developing countries consists of either long-term, low-interest credits or grants. There are two determining factors: the nature of the project and the economic situation of the country involved. In all cases the purpose of the project is carefully examined, and the way the contributions are used is clearly monitored. As was agreed at the 1978 Geneva Conference, the LLDCs receive grants for all development projects while other countries receive credits for investment projects, commodity aid and loans to development banks, with terms and conditions of these credits determined by the economic capacity of the recipient countries. The most favourable terms, similar to those of the IDA (0.75 per cent interest; 50-year term, including 10 years free from repayments), are granted to the countries most seriously affected (MSAs) by the raw materials crisis. Certain comparatively more advanced developing countries are granted less easy terms: 4.5 per cent interest; 20-year term, including 5 years free from repayments. The conditions for the remaining developing countries are: 2 per cent interest; a term of up to 30 years, including 10 years free from repayments.[8] The new West German *Policy Paper on Co-operation with Developing Countries*[9] adopted by the cabinet in July 1980, included a large emphasis on aid intended to fight absolute poverty, on rural development and on the strengthening of the planning, management and implementation capacity of the very poor countries. It also included increased co-operation with developing countries in the energy field and the protection of natural resources (such as reafforestation). As regards geographic priorities, the Policy Paper recommended an intensified co-operation with poorer developing countries, particularly in the poverty belts of Africa and Asia, and a further concentration of aid on the least-developed countries.

ADMINISTRATION OF WEST GERMAN FINANCIAL FLOWS

The Deutsche Entwicklungsgesellschaft – The German Development Company

Establishment and Objectives

The German Development Company (DEG) was set up by the Federal German Government in 1962 for the purpose of encouraging and supporting private investment activities in developing countries. The company invests in private enterprises in developing countries by participating in their equity capital, granting loans and advising enterprises interested in investments in developing countries and it endeavours to bring together prospective investment partners in a joint venture.[10] The DEG definition of its purpose and functions was influenced by the pattern of the International Finance Corporation (IFC) and the Commonwealth Development Corporation (CDC). It is a non-profit-making institution, but operates on normal business principles to the extent that this is compatible with its general objectives. The Federal Government does not interfere with the selection of the individual projects, but provides the initial capital and is represented on the board of directors. The DEG concentrates its activities on the establishment or expansion of small and medium-sized enterprises in the form of joint ventures in the industrial, agricultural and tourist sectors. The company does not normally provide more than half of the total finance required, and projects must eventually be capable of self-financing. In special cases the DEG may participate in state-owned or state-controlled enterprises if they follow normal business principles. DEG's financial resources consist of its own funds, trust funds and funds raised in the German capital market. DEG share capital (31 December 1980) was DM1.0bn, general reserves DM156.0m, and trust funds (loans from the Federal Republic of Germany and other trust funds) DM96.6m.[11]

Scope of Activities

Since 1962 the DEG has provided help for a limited period to West German investors in the Third World in establishing themselves. Once the equity stake has been sold and/or the loan with equity features repaid, the DEG's funds become available again for new investment. At the end of 1970, the commitments by DEG were 104 projects of which 46 were in preparation. The distribution of the project commitments in 1970 was 36 projects in Africa, 32 in Latin America, 19 in Asia and 17 in Europe with a total share of DM218m.[12] At the end of 1978, DEG'S commitments since 1962 had been made in respect of a total of 233 enterprises, of which 185 were still using DEG funds. By economic sectors, new business in 1978 was dominated by commitments in the service sector (49 per cent) and in manufacturing (41 per cent). By region the focus, in 1978, was on Africa, and particularly on the poorest developing countries. Projects in 13 African developing countries received commitments totalling DM58.3m (52 per cent of new commitments). Among these were eight countries from the LLDCs and the MSAs: Cameroon, Egypt, the Ivory Coast, Kenya, Malawi, Niger, Rwanda and Tanzania. These countries accounted for 56 per cent of new commitments in African developing countries. Projects in eight Asian developing countries received commitments totalling DM34.4m (31 per cent of all new commitments); those in three developing countries in Central and South America attracted commitments totalling DM13m (11 per cent of all new commitments). Commitments in four Southern European developing countries (Greece, Portugal, Spain, Yugoslavia) ran to DM6.5m (6 per cent of all new commitments). Of the DEG's overall commitments at the end of 1978 (DM551m), Africa accounted for 52 per cent (1977: 50 per cent); Asia's share was 23 per cent (1977: 24 per cent); Central and South America fell back slightly to 16 per cent (1977: 17 per cent). The position of the Southern European developing countries remained unchanged, with 9 per cent of commitments. Of the 62 developing countries to which funds were committed 24 belong to the group of LLDCs and MSAs. In 1979, DEG new commitments reached DM107.5m, a decline of about 4 per cent relative to 1978. Africa received about 55 per cent compared with 52 per cent in 1978, while Asia had 17 per cent compared with 31 per cent, Central and South America 7 per cent compared with 11 and Europe 20 per cent compared with 6 per cent. 1980 showed a change in DEG distribution as Asia received 58 per cent of total commitments, Africa 22, Central and South America 11, and Europe 9 per cent. Total commitment up to 31 December 1980 reached DM724.7m compared with DM621m as of the end of 1979, an increase of about 17 per cent. Table 6.2 shows the DEG's commitments during 1978–80 and total commitments by continent up to 31 December 1980.

Of these cumulative commitments, LLDCs and MSACs received DM210.1m (29%), newly industrialising countries DM220.0m (30%)

TABLE 6.2 DEG's Commitments during 1978–80 and total Commitments by Continent up to 31 December 1980 (DMm)

Continent	1978 Commitments	%	1979 Commitments	%	1980 Commitments	%	Cumulative up to 31 December 1980	%
Africa	58.2	52	59.6	55	28	22	347.7	48
Asia and Oceania	34.4	31	18.6	17	75	58	196.9	27
Central and S. America	13.0	11	7.3	7	14	11	103.6	14
Europe	6.5	6	22.0	20	12	9	76.5	11
Total	112.2	100	107.5	100	129.0	100	724.7	100

Source: DEG, Annual Reports, 1978, 1979, 1980.

and remaining developing countries (including supra-regional projects) DM294.6m (41%). The sectoral pattern of total DEG commitments was 25% for development banks, 20% for raw materials and producer goods, 19% for capital goods, 12% for consumer goods, 9% for mining, 5% for agriculture, 5% for food, drink and tobacco, and 5% for other services.[13]

Terms and Conditions

DEG commitments are normally comprised of an equity participation and a loan. The form and amount of the financial contribution depend on the financial needs of the project company and the commitment of the German partner. The terms are to be tailored to the specific needs of the project. For equity investment, the term is generally limited in time, usually twelve years but at least eight. As for loans with equity features, the term is usually from eight to fifteen years with a grace period of usually two years, but not more than five. Rates of interest are adjusted to market rates for comparable loans, taking into account refinancing as well as foreign exchange provisions and taxation in the country of investment. In general, DEG charges 1.5 per cent of its commitments (capital participation and/or loan with equity features) as a contribution to the appraisal costs and advisory services rendered in connection with the project.[14]

Approaches and Techniques Applied

Once a common concept for co-operation and partnership has been developed, DEG appraises the project in West Germany and in the country of investment. This appraisal is based on the documentation provided by the West German technical partner. DEG expects sufficiently detailed information, covering especially the following points:

(i) West German, local and other partners;
(ii) product range, manufacturing techniques and know-how;
(iii) supply markets and procurement of raw materials;
(iv) market;
(v) location;
(vi) machinery;
(vii) manpower requirements;
(viii) management;
(ix) costs, earnings, profit;

(x) financial needs and cover;
(xi) form and amount of DEG's financial assistance.

As a result of the appraisal, forecasts are prepared. They include projections on production, financial structure, costs and earnings as well as on the liquidity of the project company for at least five years of operation. The results of the forecasts are cleared with the partner and they are considered as target figures for the project company. With its computer programmes, DEG calculates alternative plans and the results are offered to its partners against cost contributions.[15]

Strategy for Financing and Technical Assistance

DEG's general strategy[16] is to assist the founding of new enterprises on a partnership basis by German firms in developing countries by providing capital and know-how. DEG has become an important partner to the German raw materials supply industry, particularly as regards investment to safeguard raw materials supplies. Following the progress through the Lomé II agreement which covers a number of products for which the EEC relies on Africa, supplying raw materials to the countries of the European community, including West Germany, is of the first order of importance. DEG's strategy is based upon the belief that in the long run, industrial co-operation cannot be left to raw-material-rich and -poor developing countries alone to overcome the growing income differential between them. Even if the raw-material-rich Third World countries transfer part of their extra income to the poorer developing countries, the current balance will still be in structural imbalance. Thus, there is a need for long-term measures to provide opportunities to intensify tripartite co-operation between the industrial countries and the raw material-rich and -poor countries.

Problems of Implementation and Remarks from Field Experience

DEG has emphasised obstacles to investment in raw materials in developing countries as circumstances have been increasingly against more investment by the German raw materials industry in producer countries, particularly in Third World countries rich in raw materials.[17] Other obstacles to investment have been the smaller metal content of new deposits, less favourable sites and thus increased infrastructure costs, longer running in periods for projects, higher capital and political risks. The field experience of DEG in this regard reveals that investment in the extraction and primary processing sectors is stagnating and expenditure on exploration is declining. Promotion measures have been taken both at the national and the international levels. Efforts are under way to protect stocks of particularly sensitive raw materials by offering the option of Bundesbank refinancing. There is also the Federal Government's range of guarantees to cover mining investments in the Third World against political risks, and, in addition, to cover untied lending on raw material projects against part of the economic risk. The DEG, with KfW and local development banks, are available as financially strong partners particularly suited to this task. On the international level there has been progress through the implementation of the Lomé II agreement.

Kreditanstalt für Wiederaufbau[18]

Establishment and Financial Resources

The Kreditanstalt für Wideraufbau (KfW) is a corporation under public law. It has its seat at Frankfurt (Main) and no branch offices. The capital of the corporation amounts to DM1bn, with the Federal Republic providing DM800m, and the Lander (the individual states) DM200m. For the purpose of procuring the necessary funds the corporation may issue bearer bonds, and take loans from the Federal Government, from the Deutsche Bundesbank and from foreign countries. The short-term liabilities of the corporation must not exceed 10 per cent of the medium and long-term liabilities. The bonds issued by the corporation in domestic currency are suitable for the investment of funds belonging to minors.

Scope of Activities

KfW's functions and activities are as follows:

(1) Granting loans for projects serving for the reconstruction or promotion of the West German economy.
(2) Granting loans in connection with export transactions of domestic enterprises.
(3) Issuing guarantees.
(4) Granting loans for financing projects in other countries which are worthy of promotion, in particular within the scope of development assistance.

KfW has no limitation by region and provides assistance to all developing countries (more than 80 countries). It participates in almost all kinds of projects, especially those related to agricultural and educational developments with social implications. KfW provides soft loans and technical assistance to developing countries with no tied conditions. Capital aid loans as well as the non-returnable financial contribution extended within the framework of technical assistance are granted and handled by KfW on behalf of the Federal Government on the basis of a procedure established in co-ordination with the Federal Government and defined for capital aid among other things in the *Guidelines for Bilateral German Capital Aid*, with the procedure varying depending on the different categories of objectives. Capital aid is granted almost exclusively in the form of loans, but in exceptional cases may also be non-returnable contributions to finance in particular social infrastructural projects in the LLDCs.

Lending to developing countries is one of KfW's main tasks. In this respect, capital aid, financing means of which are appropriated from budget funds, plays a dominant role beside the export credits and other financial loans. Some two-thirds of total commitments to developing countries regularly account for this sort of credit to help finance those projects which improve the living conditions of large population groups in developing countries. Table 6.3 shows KfW's cumulative commitments of loans and grants by region.

TABLE 6.3 KfW's Cumulative Commitments of Loans and Grants as of 31 December 1980 by region (DMm)

Region	Loans	Grants	Loans and grants
Asia	15,381.5	567.4	15,948.9
Africa	7,719.3	933.8	8,653.1
America	2,582.2	11.8	2,594.0
Europe	5,810.1	—	5,810.1
Total	31,493.1	1,513.0	33,006.1

Source: Kreditanstalt für Wiederaufbau (KfW), *Annual Report* 1980.

Technical Assistance

KfW provides technical assistance by financing feasibility studies for the preparation of capital aid projects, supporting technical, economic or financial measures related to the project. Technical assistance is extended for training, research and consultation purposes, serving primarily to finance interconnected measures supplementing a project. Table 6.4 shows KfW's cumulative technical co-operation commitments by region.

TABLE 6.4 KfW's Cumulative Technical Co-operation Commitments as of 31 December 1980 by Region (DMm)

Region	Technical assistance (Grants)
Asia	69.0
Africa	158.9
America	12.1
Europe	0.8
Total	240.8

Source: Kreditanstalt für Wiederaufbau Annual Report 1980.

Terms and Conditions

The proposal for the terms and conditions of the loan states the loan term, the period free from redemption (grace period), and the interest rate. The proposal distinguishes between transfer conditions – governing the relationship between Kreditanstalt and the borrower – and channelling conditions agreed upon between the borrower and the project/programme sponsor. Since 1972, the transfer conditions have been largely standardised and, since 1976, they have been graded as follows:

(1) Loans to countries which the United Nations recognise as being particularly needy – LLDCs and MSAs – are granted at an interest rate of 0.75 per cent for a 50-year term (including a 10-year grace period).
(2) Loans to developing countries at an intermediate stage in development bear interest at a rate of 2 per cent and are granted for 30-year terms including a 10-year grace period.

(3) Loans to countries at an advanced stage in development or having high foreign exchange proceeds of their own are granted at an interest rate of 4.5 per cent for a 20-year term including a 5-year grace period.

According to KfW terms and conditions all private projects should be guaranteed by the governments concerned.

Management and Administration

Members of the Board of Management are appointed upon recommendation of the Legal and Administrative Committee by the Board of Directors for a maximum of five years; they may be reappointed or their terms of office may be extended up to five years in each case. This requires another resolution by the Board of Directors which may be passed no sooner than one year prior to the termination of the current term of office. The Board of Directors may revoke the appointment of a member of the Board of Management if there is a serious reason for the action. The Board of Management (Article 6 of the Law) conducts the business and administers the assets of the corporation in conformity with the law, the by-laws, and any rules for the Board of Management that the Board of Directors may issue. The Board of Management is responsible to the Board of Directors for duly performing its duties and for carrying out all resolutions of the Board of Directors. At regular intervals, at least every three months, the Board of Management reports in writing to the Board of Directors on the course of business and the financial position of the corporation. On occasions of importance, furthermore, the Board of Management reports in writing to the Chairman or the Deputy Chairman of the Board of Directors; in urgent cases reporting may be oral, to be followed by a report in writing without undue delay. The report must conform to the principles of conscientious and true accounting.

Marketing Studies

Marketing studies should be included in all the feasibility studies. KfW finances marketing studies as part of technical assistance.

Approaches Taken

The application is a precondition of the granting of German capital aid. It is intended to make sure that public funds are used exclusively in those sectors considered by the developing country to have priority. No special form is required for the loan application which is to describe the measure (project, programme, commodity aid) to be financed as well as its costs and the loan amount applied for. The government of the developing country addresses its application to the Government of the Federal Republic of Germany, usually through the West German embassy. The application is then handled by the Federal Ministry for Economic Co-operation (MEC) competent for development assistance. The requested capital aid loan is granted on the basis of a government agreement. Under this agreement, the government of West Germany enables the government of the developing country – or any other borrower to be selected by both parties – to obtain loans up to a certain amount from KfW, usually for projects that are already defined in broad outlines, if an appraisal carried out by KfW proves the projects to be worthy of promotion. Moreover, the government agreement lays down the basic conditions concerning the agreements to be concluded with Kreditanstalt.

Techniques applied

All standard techniques of appraisal are applied. The technical appraisal depends on the type and the special features of the project. It covers the technical conception, that is design, execution and operation of the project, and determines whether the project has been duly planned in accordance with sound engineering principles and whether, with regard to the technology involved, it is tailored to the country's requirements; in this connection, the capital and labour intensity involved in the technical solution and the latter's operation are also of importance. In the course of the technical appraisal of the project, alternative solutions are also examined to find out whether less expensive solutions might not answer the purpose just as well. A technical combination at previous or subsequent stages of production, the effects on the environment and the conditions necessary to ensure the plant's operation such as the availability of labour as well as supply and sales prospects and the kind and extent of the consulting services envisaged for the project execution and the management, are further points to be studied within the framework of the appraisal. Finally, information about the planning, contract awarding and delivery, about the construction, setting-up and operation of the plants, as well as a detailed time-schedule for the execution of the project is also examined.

The financial project analysis is focused on profitability and liquidity aspects. Depending on the type of project, detailed calculations are necessary in this connection (calculation of the internal rate of return, of the capital expenditure and the financial requirements, profit and loss account, balance-sheet and cash-flow forecasts). When analysing the economic and socio-economic effects of the project, a cost-benefit analysis is made, if possible, by which the project's effects on economic growth are measured. In addition, the following aspects are taken into account: creation of additional jobs, diversification of the production structure, effects of the project on the balance of payments, on the national budget, on the distribution of income and property, and other macroeconomic aspects including the basic socio-economic requirements: education, health, housing, and social security. Distinction is also made between the following types of investment studies: the investment opportunity study; the pre-feasibility study; and the feasibility study. All these studies pursue the above-mentioned general line, they differ, however, as far as their specific objectives are concerned.

It is the objective of the investment opportunity study to make a first selection from all existing investment possibilities. Therefore, it has to give a very detailed analysis of the overall situation of the country concerned in order to establish priorities according to which the further screening of the projects will be effected. The second part of the study consists of a general, but quantitative analysis of the different investment possibilities.

The pre-feasibility study, as a second stage of the screening procedure, is based on the priorities already established and contains a more detailed analysis of the investment projects previously selected. The feasibility study, finally, is concerned with a precise, detailed scrutiny of those projects, the execution of which appears recommendable on the grounds of the preceding analyses.

Strategy for Financing and Technical Assistance

Considering that roughly 80 per cent of the destitute population in developing countries live in rural areas and that the majority of these countries, even if imports are taken into account, sometimes have substantial food deficits, the key role of agricultural and, generally speaking, rural development for the overcoming of mass proverty and underemployment becomes apparent. The task is to support the underemployed in rural areas, the small-holders, tenant farmers and landless workers, in such a way as to raise productivity, to maintain and expand employment facilities and to exploit better the soil available.

Such a promotion of agriculture must be supplemented by the development of small crafts and trades in rural areas and in suburban areas. To accomplish this the possibilities of employing seasonally idle labour reserves in community development programmes can to a large extent also be utilised for improving rural infrastructure. A development strategy such as this may bring about more economic growth than a strategy mainly based on industrial development; but it can only be successful if the developing countries resolutely see to this task themselves.

KfW has given examples of how to operate agricultural projects and programmes of capital aid in order to achieve broader effects with a given volume of investment capital. These considerations were based, among other things, on many years' systematic recordings of data on credit programmes for the promotion of commercial and agricultural small enterprises in developing countries. Attempts to work out development policies which better account for the employment problem encounter various practical difficulties. This also applies to the contribution which – multilateral as well as bilateral – governmental development assistance can make to this end. The churches, charitable institutions and foundations have less difficulty in orientating development programmes towards the requirements of poor population groups in developing countries by motivating the population to help themselves. West German capital aid projects have shown that there are limits to a marked shift in emphasis for the benefit of an employment-orientated development policy, particularly for a donor of bilateral aid like West Germany.

Technical assistance of the kind necessary to make up completely for the bottlenecks mentioned could often be given more efficiently and at less cost by other more advanced developing countries. This better reflects the basic idea of help to help oneself than if the industrial countries tried to close the gap by a massive presence. In the sense of a tripartite co-operation, then the industrial countries could give financial assistance for those projects.

For future industrial co-operation with developing countries it seems increasingly appropriate to stretch the cheap but scarce capital aid funds by commercial loan funds. If so, the terms and conditions of the financing at large would have to correspond both to the development level of the individual country and to the relevant kind of project. In more advanced countries, mixed forms of capital aid loans and export financing seem suitable for commercial projects. The share of capital aid in financing can then be smaller; the developing country has developed more and the project is more commercial. In this way, the terms and conditions of total financing can be adapted to the efficiency of the recipient country and the scope of capital aid can be extended.

Problems of Implementation and Remarks from Field Experience

According to the experience gained in the field of West German capital aid, many capital aid projects involve investment costs per job exceeding by far the average figures. This naturally applies to infrastructure projects which, although tending to improve the employment situation in their initial stage, normally do not give reason to expect any substantial effects on employment when put into operation. Projects of material infrastructure, such as of roads or energy supply, are to provide for income and employment for instance in agriculture, industry or small crafts and trades, which is why investment in these sectors should have a particularly favourable effect on employment; but in the case of the industrial projects which were financed from West German capital aid direct, the costs of investment per work place only very rarely were below DM100,000, in the large majority of cases more or less noticeably above this amount. The possibilities of implementing adapted technological procedures, which are examined each time before a project is financed from capital aid, in this field have been found to be very limited.

Some developing countries lack a correct assessment of project evaluation. The real benefit of the project is a benefit for themselves and a good exercise for the country itself in the field of development appraisal. These countries should try to understand the need for project appraisal in depth within a reasonable time and not be satisfied with a 'quick chat'; they should wait more patiently for the correct implementation of project execution for the benefit of their countries. The issue that should be stressed in this field is the need to recognise the mutual benefits between lenders and recipients. On the lending side, public opinion wants to be sure that 'tax money', deducted from their income to finance projects in developing countries, is used effectively and projects which are financed are sound and meet the criteria of mutual benefit; a political issue, but one that cannot be ignored.

APPENDIX 6.1 The Flow of Financial Resources to Developing Countries and Multilateral Agencies by Type (1970–80)

Country: Federal Republic of Germany

Disbursements Net disbursements	1970	1971	1972	1973	1974	1975	1976	1977	1978	1979	US$m 1980
I Official Development Assistance (a+b)	599.0	734.2	808.3	1,102.0	1,433.4	1,688.8	1,384.0	1,386.0	2,418.7	3,350.1	3,517.4
(a) Bilateral ODA	466.1	529.6	601.5	791.4	1,015.0	1,160.9	1,044.1	1,028.1	1,560.7	2,160.9	2,274.3
(b) Contributions to multilateral institutions	132.9	204.7	206.8	310.6	418.4	527.9	339.9	357.9	857.7	1,189.2	1,243.1
II Other Official Flows (a+b)	132.1	164.2	148.5	229.2	96.0	9.1	43.0	61.0	221.8	111.7	630.0
(a) Bilateral OOF	79.6	144.4	115.9	223.6	94.5	−12.3	15.4	57.8	217.4	110.0	633.0
(b) Multilateral institutions	52.5	19.8	32.6	5.6	1.5	21.4	27.6	3.2	4.4	1.7	−3.0
Subtotal (I+II): Total official flows	731.1	898.4	956.8	1,331.2	1,529.4	1,697.9	1,427.0	1,447.0	2,640.2	3,461.8	4,147.4
III Grants by private voluntary agencies	77.8	108.3	123.6	157.2	177.4	205.1	204.6	225.0	284.0	389.4	420.7
IV Private flows at market terms (1–4)	678.2	908.5	675.8	318.3	1,469.3	3,058.8	3,682.2	4,081.6	4,707.8	3,437.4	6,015.8
(1) Direct investment	317.5	358.1	601.2	786.6	701.3	815.9	765.4	846.0	1,025.1	817.7	1,578.9
(2) Bilateral portfolio investment and other	110.4	24.5	−83.2	−277.7	281.1	884.1	1,137.8	2,161.2	1,578.7	794.3	1,692.0
(3) Multilateral portfolio investment	63.1	116.0	219.4	121.4	−29.3	353.2	930.4	901.4	816.1	928.0	1,355.9
(4) Private export credits	187.2	409.9	−61.6	−312.0	516.2	1,005.6	848.6	173.0	1,287.9	897.4	1,389.1
V Total resource flows (I–IV)	1,487.1	1,915.2	1,756.2	1,806.7	3,176.1	4,961.7	5,313.8	5,753.6	7,632.0	7,288.6	10,584.0
ODA as % of GNP	0.32	0.34	0.31	0.32	0.37	0.40	0.31	0.27	0.38	0.44	0.43
Total resource flows as % of GNP	0.79	0.88	0.68	0.52	0.83	1.19	1.19	1.12	1.19	0.96	1.28

Sources: OECD, Development Co-operation, Reviews 1974–1981.

7 Japan

THE PERFORMANCE OF JAPAN'S OFFICIAL DEVELOPMENT ASSISTANCE

Japan has been the fourth largest donor of ODA after the USA, France and West Germany. Japan's share in total DAC/ODA flows reached 6.7 per cent in 1970, 8.4 per cent in 1975 and 12.3 per cent in 1980, compared with 4.2 per cent in 1965 and 2.3 per cent in 1960. ODA as a percentage of GNP in Japan reached 0.32 per cent in 1980 compared with 0.23 per cent in both 1975 and 1970 – see Appendix 7.1 and Chart 6. Further increase in ODA in Japan is expected on the basis of the Japanese Government's declared intention to extend during the years 1981–85 at least double the amount of ODA disbursed during the previous five years, while endeavouring to increase the ODA/GNP ratio.[1]

Japan's ODA to developing countries and multilateral agencies reached $3303.7m in 1980 compared with $1147.7m in 1975 and $458.0m in 1970. Since 1973, it has increased substantially compared with the first three years of the 1970s – see Appendix 7.1. Japan's bilateral official development assistance reached $1960.8m (59 per cent of ODA) in 1980 compared with $850.4m (74 per cent) in 1975 and $371.5m (81 per cent) in 1970. Thus Japan's ODA contribution to multilateral institutions has grown rapidly during the second half of the 1970s. Japan's OOF increased from $693.6m in 1970 to $1369.4m in 1975 and to $1478.0m in 1980. With the exception of the years 1974, 1978, 1979 and 1980. OOF were larger than ODA and most of these flows were mainly conducted as bilateral flows. Japan's total official flows (ODA + OOF) increased from $1151.6m in 1970 to $2517.1m in 1975 and $4781.7m in 1980. Table 7.1 shows the share of Japan's total official flows compared with private flows.

JAPAN'S PRIVATE FLOWS

The Japanese Government has encouraged private investment in developing countries with an increasingly wide range of incentive

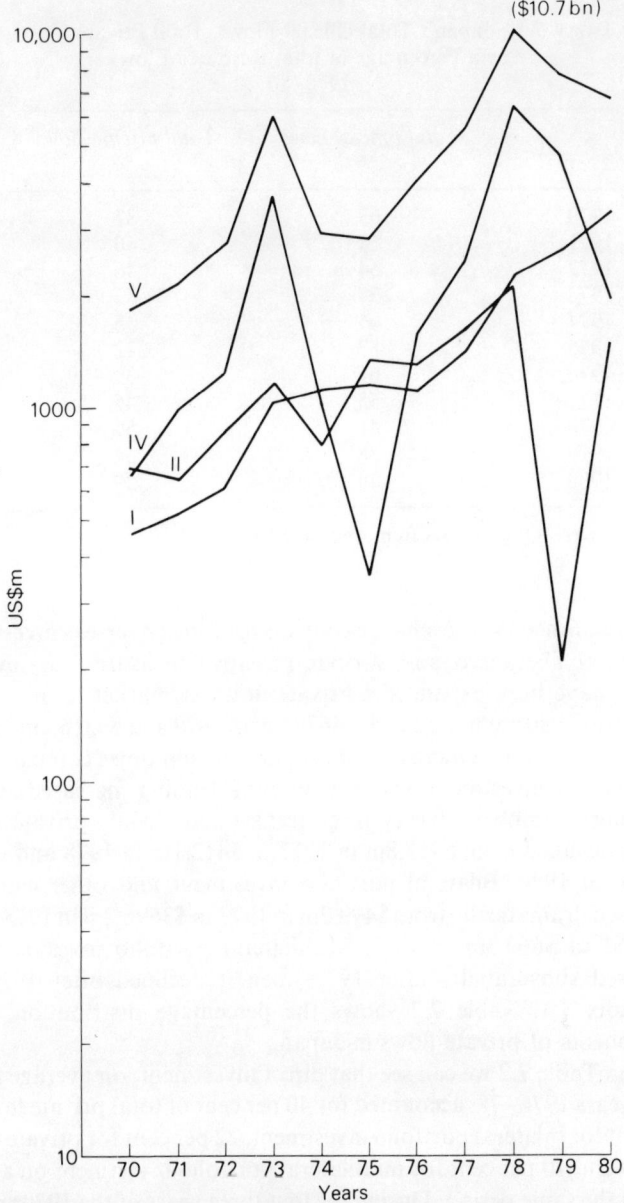

CHART 6 Flow of financial resources to developing countries and multilateral agencies by type: Japan 1970–80

Source: Appendix 7.1

TABLE 7.1 Japan's Total Official Flows, Total Private Flows, as a Percentage of total Resource Flows 1970–80

Years	Total official flows %	Total private flows %
1970	63	37
1971	54	46
1972	54	46
1973	37	62
1974	65	35
1975	87	12
1976	61	39
1977	55	45
1978	41	59
1979	38	62
1980	70	29

Source: Original data from Appendix 7.1.

measures. Since 1971, exchange controls for direct overseas investments have been liberalised and various incentive measures for investing abroad have been expanded.[2] Private flows at market terms reached $1957m in 1980 compared with $4689.0m in 1979 and $6316.7m in 1978, by which time it had increased approximately ten times compared with 1970. Direct investment and private bank lending increased sharply, reflecting a number of very large transactions, while private export credits declined from $913.8m in 1977 to $412.1m in 1978 and to only $73.7m in 1980. Bilateral portfolio investment and other categories increased dramatically from $499.2m in 1977 to $3696.2m in 1978 then it declined to $660.3m in 1980. Multilateral portfolio investment also increased substantially after 1977, then it declined after 1979 – see Appendix 7.1. Table 7.2 shows the percentage distribution of the components of private flows in Japan.

From Table 7.2 we can see that direct investment, on average for the three years 1976–78, accounted for 40 per cent of total private flows, 28 per cent for bilateral portfolio investment, 22 per cent for private export credits and 10 per cent for multilateral portfolio investment on average during the same period. During the first three years of the 1970s private export credits reached an average of 41 per cent, direct investment 26 per cent, bilateral portfolio investment 22 per cent and multilateral portfolio

TABLE 7.2 Percentage Distribution of the Components of Private Flows at Market Terms in Japan 1970–80
(as percentages of total private flows)

Years	Direct investment %	Bilateral portfolio investment and other %	Multilateral portfolio investment %	Private export credits %
1970	39	0.5	3	58
1971	23	14	13	51
1972	16	51	17	15
1973	36	49	4	12
1974	68	16	1.5	14
1975	63	1	2	23
1976	70	6	3	21
1977	29	20	13	37
1978	21	59	14	7
1979	15	58	14	14
1980	46	34	16	38

Source: Original data from Appendix 7.1.

investment 11 per cent. Thus direct investment increased much faster than private export credit during the period 1976–78, due to a sharp increase in commercial bank lending. By 1980 both the shares of direct investment and private export credit had increased while the share of bilateral portfolio investment had markedly declined.

Fiscal incentives have been adopted in Japan to encourage investment in developing countries and since the early 1960s a number of fiscal measures have been taken to prevent the export of private capital to developing countries from being placed at a disadvantage, and to harmonise the legislation governing domestic and overseas investment. One of the basic rules has been the granting of equal treatment to domestic and foreign investment while double taxation agreements and agreements to extend tax credits have been concluded by Japan with various countries. Potential Japanese investors can apply for information on investment possibilities to the Export-Import Bank of Japan, and the Overseas Economic Co-operation Fund (OECF), as well as to the Japan External Trade Organisation (JETRO) and the Institute of Developing Economies.[3]

JAPANESE DEVELOPMENT ASSISTANCE POLICY

Since her Constitution excludes war as a means of solving international disputes, Japan's foreign policy consists basically of making tremendous efforts to strengthen peace. Underdeveloped 100 years ago, Japan has become a developed country as a result of the efforts on the part of both the government and the people, as manifested in the government's leadership, the promotion of education, the diligence of the people and the quick assimilation of modern technology. Therefore Japan, with her own experience of development, is in a position to contribute positively to that of the developing countries. Moreover, economic co-operation is of great significance to the long-term development of the Japanese economy, and this concept, one of the main pillars of Japan's foreign policy, compels Japan to strive to ease the North–South problem through economic co-operation. Japan's technical co-operation with other countries started with her participation in the Colombo Plan in 1954, only two years after the signing of the San Francisco Peace Treaty. In 1955, reparation payments to Burma started (total: $200m), followed by similar payments to the Philippines in 1956 (total: $550m) and to Indonesia in 1958 (total: $223m). Government loans (so-called 'Yen Credit') which constitute the main part of Japan's current aid programme, started in 1958 with the first yen credit of $50m to India.[4] The purpose of Japan's economic co-operation with the developing countries is to facilitate their self-help efforts and promote their economic and social development, to enhance the welfare of the people as a result of such development, and thus to stabilise the people's livelihood. It is Japan's belief that its powerful economy, the world's second largest today, should be utilised to make the necessary efforts toward achieving the developing countries' welfare. Secondly, resource-poor Japan believes, at the same time, that her economic growth can be maintained only when relations with the developing countries are harmonious, secure and friendly. From this point of view, Japan believes that close relations with these countries must be strengthened. ODA is the most important form of economic co-operation, defined as providing funds or technology under the following conditions:

(1) They are offered by the government or its agencies.
(2) The main purpose is to contribute to economic development and welfare improvement in the developing countries.
(3) The offer must not place an extra burden on the recipient country and the grant element is more than 25 per cent.

Debt relief is defined as follows:

(1) Where the commercial debt of a developing country to a private Japanese company cannot be paid due to the deterioration of its international balance of payments, the Japanese Government refinances the debt through the central government of the recipient country.
(2) When loans from the Japanese Government cannot be repaid by the recipient country, the Japanese Government reschedules the maturity.

In 1978, Japan's total amount of such debt relief stood at $8.1m (¥1.7bn). Loan terms are based mainly on the recipient country's economic situation with consideration being given to its relations with Japan in political, economic and other fields. The loans are made on a case-to-case basis, and it is important to note that the terms of loans have been gradually softened not merely with respect to interest rates, but also to maturity and grace periods.[5] As the mutually interdependent relationships between Japan and the developing countries become closer, economic co-operation – which assists the self-help efforts of developing countries towards economic and social development – is growing in importance. On this basis, the New Economic and Social Seven-year Plan in Japan, FY1979–FY1985,[6] indicated the aim actively to expand ODA and to promote private sector co-operation on a comprehensive scale so as to complement ODA. For the expansion of economic co-operation, the Plan indicated:

(1) In view of the fact that 'the development of human resources' is the very foundation of 'nation-building', greater emphasis is to be placed on co-operation for 'the development of human resources' in Japan's future aid policies.
(2) To meet the diverse demands of developing countries, financial co-operation should be expanded and promoted and, in order to contribute to 'the development of human resources' in developing countries, technical co-operation should be expanded.
(3) To bring about a greater understanding of the situation in developing countries and their true needs, training of human resources and promotion of and exchanges in scientific research and culture are sought in a wide range of fields. In conjunction with this, efforts should also be made to gain a broad national understanding of the current state of Japan's economic co-operation.

Under the Plan, the Japanese Government intends to more than double its aid in the five-year period through an increase in ODA, recognising the important role of economic co-operation for the resolution of North–South problems. In order to improve the quality of aid, the government also intends to promote further grants, technical assistance and the trend towards untied assistance.

ADMINISTRATION OF JAPAN'S FINANCIAL FLOWS

The Ministry of Foreign Affairs is responsible for negotiations with foreign governments on economic co-operation. The Ministry consults with other ministries concerned where necessary, especially the Ministry of Finance, the Ministry of International Trade and Industry, and the Economic Planning Agency for government loans. As for the most important matters pertaining to economic co-operation, the cabinet is the highest decision-making organ of the government, which has a number of individual economic co-operation agencies.[7] The following are Japan's three main agencies for government-level co-operation.

The Overseas Economic Co-operation Fund[8]

Establishment and Financial Resources

The OECF was established on 16 March 1961, in accordance with The Overseas Economic Co-operation Fund Law of 27 December 1960, and started its operations on the same date. As of the end of FY1978 (31 March 1979), the fund was capitalised at ¥603,244m. It was established for the purpose of promoting overseas economic co-operation in order to contribute to the industrial development and economic stability of South East Asia and other overseas developing regions; in particular, it engaged in activities necessary to provide a smooth supply of funds in cases where it was difficult to obtain the funds necessary for such development and stability from the Export-Import Bank of Japan and ordinary financial institutions. Since July 1975, overlapping in the scope of lending activities of the OECF and the Export-Import Bank of Japan (Japan's two principal organs for the provision of economic co-operation with developing countries) has been eliminated. All loans to the government or governmental agencies of developing countries are provided by OECF in cases where the grant element of the relevant lending terms and conditions is 25 per cent or more. Loans to Japanese corporations are, in principle, provided by the Export-Import Bank of Japan. OECF may, however, finance projects in the field of agriculture, forestry, fisheries and mining (limited to prospecting), pre-investment studies and experimental projects which are deemed to be conducive to the economic development of the recipient countries, when it is difficult for the Export-Import Bank of Japan to make the loan. Thus the OECF has been playing an important role as Japan's principal organ for extending ODA to developing countries. In 1966, OECF began to lend development funds directly to foreign governments.

The financial needs of OECF are met primarily by an annual appropriation from the General Account of the government, borrowing from the Trust Fund Bureau, which administers funds accumulating from Post Office Savings and Post Office Insurance premiums, and the OECF's own funds, including interest on and repaid principal of loans. For several years after the commencement of its operations, OECF was entirely dependent on appropriations from the government for the supply of funds needed for its operations. In June 1966, it was authorised to borrow from the Trust Fund Bureau, in view of the expansion of its lending activities through the commencement of making loans to foreign governments. Since 1966, the volume of government appropriations and borrowings from the Trust Fund Bureau has increased considerably, reflecting an upsurge in the volume of loans and investment. As of the end of September 1978, OECF's capital amounted to ¥598,244m and the outstanding balance of borrowings from the Trust Fund Bureau amounted to ¥432,838m.

Scope of Activities

OECF undertakes the following activities:

(1) Extending loans to governments and governmental agencies of developing countries.
(2) Extending loans to Japanese corporations.
(3) Investing in Japanese corporations and contributing to such international arrangements as 'buffer stocks' maintained under various international commodity agreements.

As of the end of February 1981, OECF total commitments reached ¥29,681bn compared with ¥1889bn at the end of September 1978. Disbursements were ¥18,891bn compared with ¥1154bn, and the outstanding balance of loans and investments (funds disbursed and not yet repaid) reached ¥16,765bn compared with ¥1034bn during the same period. This gives us an indication of the rapidly growing activities of the fund from the third quarter of 1978 to the end of FY1980 (April 1980–1 March 1981). The distribution of OECF commitments by sector as of the end of February 1981 has not shown structural changes relative to its distribution at the end of September 1978. Table 7.3 shows the sectoral distribution of OECF.

TABLE 7.3 OECF Commitments by Sector in Volume and percentages (end February 1981 compared with end September 1978)

Sector	End of September 1978 Amount (¥bn)	%	End of February 1981 Amount (¥bn)	%
Electric power	389	21	6,463	21.8
Transportation	373	20	6,837	23.0
Telecommunications	111	6	1,623	5.5
Irrigation and flood control	53	3	1,031	3.5
Agriculture, forestry and fisheries	120	6	1,749	5.9
Manufacturing and mining	349	18	4,928	16.6
Social services	40	2	1,154	3.9
Development loan through banking system	14	1	269	0.9
Commodity loans	420	22	5,506	18.6
Others	20	1	122	0.4
Total	1889	100.00	29,681	100.00

Sources: OECF, *Annual Report* 1979 and information received from OECF.

Terms and Conditions of Loans

Of all loans extended by OECF, the softest loan bears an interest of 1.75 per cent per annum with a 30-year maturity, including a 10-year grace period. The hardest bears 5.75 per cent interest and matures in 15 years, including a 5-year grace period. Interest rates and repayment terms have varied according to the situation of the country and the nature of the project involved. Since 1975, there has been an increased provision of untied loans, in terms of number and volume. In 1977, of a total of 71 loans, 66 were untied (of which 60 were for the LLDC categories) accounting for 87 per cent of all loans to foreign governments in terms of loan commitments. Loan commitments to Japanese corporations in 1977 had an average interest rate of 4.94 per cent and matured in an average 9 years and 3 months.

Strategy for Financing and Technical Assistance

The experience of OECF has shown that it is tending to extend its activities to other sectors to meet the requirements of developing countries. For example, in 1977, OECF made its first loan commitments for the educational sector, and commitments for the medical sector followed thereafter. As for the regional distribution, close historical, geographical, cultural and economic ties with the rest of Asia have led to Japan playing an important role in the economic and social development of the region. For this reason, OECF lending to the Asian region accounted for about 80 per cent of cumulative loan commitments as of the end of September, 1978, and the same as of the end of February 1981. Since 1977, however, there has been a trend toward geographical diversion in OECF's lending to foreign governments. Table 7.4 shows OECF regional distribution by region.

TABLE 7.4 OECF's Regional Distribution at the end of February 1981 compared with the end of September 1978

Region	End of September 1978 (¥bn)	%	End of February 1981 (¥bn)	%
Asia	1,511	80	23,745	80.0
Middle East	30	1.6	762	2.6
Africa	219	11.5	3,172	10.7
Central and South America	107	5.6	1,732	5.8
Oceania	9	0.5	132	0.4
Others	13	0.7	137	0.5
Total	1,889	100.0	29,681	100.0

Sources: OECF, *Annual Report* 1979 and information received from OECF.

The Export-Import Bank of Japan[9]

Establishment and Financial Resources

The bank was established in December 1950 under the name of the Export Bank of Japan, and was renamed the Export-Import Bank of Japan in April 1952. It is an independent governmental financial institution designed to supplement or encourage commercial banks in financing exports, imports and overseas investments for the purpose of facilitating economic interchange mainly in the field of trade between Japan and foreign countries. With the rapid expansion of the Japanese economy and trade in the 1950s and 1960s, the bank expanded the scope of its operations to include loans to domestic corporations and direct loans to foreign governments or corporations, refinancing and guaranteeing of obligations. Its operational funds consist of paid-up capital, borrowings and internal resources.

Capital: capital is wholly subscribed and paid by the government from its Industrial Investment Special Account.

Borrowings: the bank is authorised to borrow from the government's Trust Funds. It may also borrow from foreign financial institutions and foreign capital markets.

Internal resources: loan repayments, reserve funds, etc.,

Financial situation of the bank: Table 7.5 shows the highlights of the financial situation of the bank as at 31 March 1978, 1979, 1980 and 1981.

TABLE 7.5 Export-Import Bank of Japan Financial Situation (FY 1977–FY 1980) (¥bn)

	FY1977	*FY1978*	*FY1979*	*FY1980*
For the year				
Credit commitments	902.3	1173.6	839.4	926.1
Disbursements	937.8	1344.4	864.5	826.7
Guarantees	13.0	18.8	10.7	2.7
At the year's end				
Total assets	4383.6	4964.2	5150.7	n.a.
Loans outstanding	4188.6	4788.4	4986.3	5101.7
Guarantees outstanding	74.1	82.1	62.7	42.6
Capital	880.3	905.3	925.3	937.3

Sources: The Export-Import Bank of Japan, *Annual Report* FY1979 year ended 31 March 1980; *Annual Report* 1978, year ended 31 March 1979; for FY1980, information received from the Export-Import Bank of Japan.

Scope of Activities

The bank's activities are classified into the following types of programme, through which it contributes not only to Japanese economy but also to the development of developing nations.

(1) Loans to domestic corporations:
   (i) export supplier's credit: provision of funds to Japanese exporters to enable them to extend supplier's credit for the export of heavy machinery and equipment including ships, aircraft and rolling stock, and their parts and accessories;
   (ii) technical service credit: provision of funds to Japanese firms for the export of technical services;
   (iii) import credit: provision to Japanese importers of funds required for the import of goods and equipment which are essential to the Japanese economy;
   (iv) overseas investment credit: provision to Japanese firms of the funds necessary for their investment in undertakings abroad or for their capital participation in foreign companies and corporations.
(2) Direct loans to foreign governments and corporations.
   Buyers' credit bank-to-bank loans are extended to foreign governments, their agencies, foreign local public authorities or foreign corporations (buyers' credit), and to foreign financial institutions (bank-to-bank loans) for the import of equipment and technical services from Japan. Governmental loans are extended on the basis of government-to-government exchanges of Notes.

In addition to the above types of programme, the bank is authorised to provide refinancing loans to foreign governments or banks under special circumstances to enable them to repay their existing debts to Japan. The bank makes loans when it is difficult for commercial banks and other private financial institutions to provide funds on ordinary terms, and the repayment is considered assured. Commercial banks also make loans jointly with the Export-Import Bank in the case of export supplier's credit, technical service credit and import credit.

The experience of the bank's credit commitments by area has shown that commitments made for financial arrangements related to North America increased from 4 per cent in 1977 to 31 per cent in 1978 and declined to 9 per cent in 1979 and 4 per cent in 1980. The increase in 1978 was a result of the expansion of the urgent import scheme which led to a sharp rise in imports of uranium concentrate and aircraft and the procurement of enrichment services for uranium. Commitments for the African region rose on a value basis in 1978 and accounted for 17 per cent of the total due to a number of major buyers' credit arrangements and urgent imports of ships registered in African nations. In 1979 it declined in value terms but accounted for 18 per cent of the total commitments and 9 per cent in 1980. The share of commitments to Europe declined from 26 to 13 per cent due to the drop in export suppliers' credits for ship financing and the decline in bank loans to Eastern Europe. In 1979 it increased to reach 22 per cent and reached 20 per cent in 1980. The decline in export suppliers' credits for the Middle East (West Asia) led to a drop in the regional share from 21 per cent in 1977 to 8 per cent in 1978 and 4 per cent in both 1979 and 1980. Table 7.6 shows the development of the bank's credit commitments by area.

TABLE 7.6 Credit Commitments by Area
(FY1977–FY1980)
(¥bn)

	FY1977 Amount	%	FY1978 Amount	%	FY1979 Amount	%	FY1980 Amount	%
East Asia	84.7	9	75.1	6	81.3	10	299.6	32
Southeast Asia	81.1	9	113.5	10	88.1	10	130.5	14
West Asia	189.0	21	99.2	8	32.8	4	34.6	4
North America	37.8	4	358.5	31	74.0	9	38.3	4
Latin America	89.5	10	137.5	12	166.0	20	72.2	8
Europe	236.2	26	152.4	13	184.3	22	186.9	20
Africa	159.1	18	196.2	17	153.7	18	87.5	9
Oceania	24.8	3	37.3	3	59.2	7	76.6	8
International organisations	—	—	4.0	0	—	—	—	—
Total	902.3	100	1173.6	100	839.4	100	926.1	100

Note 1: Includes amount under foreign currency lending plans.
2: West Asia includes the Middle East.
3: Figures are not necessarily equal to the total due to rounding in the process of calculation.
Sources: Export-Import Bank of Japan, *Annual Report*, fiscal 1979 year ended 31 March 1980 and *Annual Report*, Fiscal 1978 year ended 31 March 1979, and information received from the Export-Import Bank of Japan.

Commitments of the Export-Import Bank in direct loans to foreign governments and corporations amounted to ¥58.8bn in 1979 and ¥140.8bn in FY1978, a decline of about 33 per cent from the level of FY1977. Buyers' credits bank-to-bank loans have become an increasingly important means of financing the exports of industrial plants in recent years. Reflecting the loss of competitiveness due to the appreciation of the yen and the absence of major new projects during the year, the total amount of commitments for buyers' credits and bank-to-bank loans showed a decline from FY1977 of about 36 per cent, to ¥132.7bn and a decline of about 56 per cent, to ¥58.5bn, in FY1979. In FY1980, commitments for overseas direct loans (buyers' credits and bank-to-bank loans) to East Asia reached 50 per cent, Europe 30 per cent, Southeast Asia 9 per cent and Latin America 9 per cent. Among overseas

Japan

direct loans, no commitment was made for government loan during fiscal years 1979 and 1980. The FY1980 has shown high commitments to East Asia as a separate region for the first time. Table 7.7 shows the development of overseas direct loan commitments by area.

Strategy for Financing and Technical Assistance

Bank strategy is based upon the following:

(1) Participating actively in helping to solve the world's increasingly serious energy problem through development of oil resources as well as alternatives to oil as a source of energy, including LNG, nuclear power and coal.
(2) Exporting technology to respond to the requests of the developing nations.
(3) Contributing to the promotion of imports entering Japan, for the restoration of a balanced pattern of trade.
(4) Participating actively in international conferences and sponsoring them where appropriate.

Japan International Co-operation Agency

Establishment and Financial Resources

JICA was established in August 1974, under the Japan International Co-operation Agency Law (Law No. 62, 1974) as an executive organ of Japan's international co-operation services for the socio-economic progress of developing countries. The agency carries out its international co-operation under the supervision of the Ministry of Foreign Affairs, its supervising authority, as well as of the Ministry of Agriculture, Forestry and Fisheries and the Ministry of International Trade and Industry, as regards matters in their respective fields.[10] The funds required by JICA for carrying out its technical co-operation activities are budgeted by the Japanese Government under its ODA programme.

Scope of Activities

The activities of the agency fall under the following major categories:

  (i) government-sponsored technical co-operation;
 (ii) grant-aid co-operation promotion programme;

TABLE 7.7 Overseas Direct Loan Commitments by Area Provided by the Export-Import Bank of Japan FY1977–FY1980
(¥bn)

	FY1977			FY1978			FY1979			FY1980		
	Buyers' credits and bank-to-bank loans	Total	%	Buyers' credits and bank-to-bank loans	Total	%	Buyers' credits and bank-to-bank loans	Total	%	Buyers' credits and bank-to-bank loans	Total	%
East Asia	—	—	—	—	—	—	—	—	—	143.9	143.9	50
Southeast Asia	2.2	4.2	2	—	2.1	1	10.6	10.6	18	27.1	27.1	9
West Asia	9	9	5	—	—	—	—	—	—	—	—	—
Latin America	21.0	21.0	10	28.4	28.4	20	10.7	10.7	18	24.5	24.5	9
Europe	114.2	114.2	55	42.7	42.7	30	7.5	7.5	13	85.8	85.8	30
Africa	59.8	59.8	29	57.6	63.7	45	30.1	30.1	51	4.4	4.4	2
Oceania	—	—	—	—	—	—	—	—	—	0.1	0.1	0
Int. organisations	—	—	—	4.0	4.0	3	—	—	—	—	—	—
Total	207.0	209.0	100	132.7	140.8	100	58.8	58.8	100	285.7	285.7	100

Note: West Asia includes the Middle East.
The difference between total and buyers' credits and bank-to-bank loans represents the governmental loans for FY1977–FY1978.
Sources: Export-Import Bank of Japan, *Annual Report 1978*, year ended 31 March 1979; *Annual Report 1979*, year ended 31 March 1980; for FY1980, information received from the Export-Import Bank of Japan.

(iii) dispatch of Japan Overseas Co-operation Volunteers (JOCV);
(iv) development co-operation programme (investment and financing of development projects);
(v) emigration services;
(vi) training and recruiting of qualified Japanese experts for technical co-operation.

JICA's share in the total expense for technical co-operation by the government in FY1979 was 66 per cent.[11]

Training Programme

There are two types of training courses conducted in Japan for overseas participants. One comprises group training courses organised according to what JICA regards as the greatest common needs of the developing countries. The other comprises individual training courses in response to specific requirements of a region or a country. Training in Japan is offered at the Uchihara International Agricultural Tranining Centre and the Kanagawa International Fisheries Training Centre, both operated by JICA, and at other appropriate institutions with the co-operation of research and experiment stations of the government, local public bodies, universities, private enterprises, etc. JICA operates international training centres, in addition to those mentioned, in Tokyo, Hachioji, Osaka, Nagaya and Kobe. Table 7.8 shows participants in training programme by region.

The number of participants in JICA training programmes by region in 1980 was as follows.[12]

Asia	2413
Africa	444
Latin America	883
Oceania	61
Europe	59
Others	1
Total	3861

Development Survey Programme

JICA conducts development surveys as part of Japan's government-sponsored technical co-operation. The bases and purposes of the surveys vary widely, according to the nature or objectives of each

TABLE 7.8 Participants in Training Programmes by Region (1977–1979)

Region	1977		1978		1979	
	No. of participants	Total participants %	No. of participants	Total participants %	No. of participants	Total participants %
Asia	1472	55.0	1618	56.8	1757	56.2
Latin America	512	19.1	529	18.6	633	20.3
Middle East	458	17.2	457	16.0	486	15.6
Africa	181	6.8	201	7.0	206	6.6
Others	50	1.9	45	1.6	42	1.3
Total	2673	100	2850	100	3124	100

Source: Japan International Co-operation Agency, *Annual Reports*, 1978, 1979, 1980.

individual project for which co-operation is requested by the recipient country. Specifically, the development surveys can be classified as follows.

Firstly, the types known as 'reconnaisance survey', 'preliminary survey' and 'basic survey', which are carried out to prepare the master plan of the project and to chart its course, or to pass judgement as to whether it is desirable to proceed to the next stage of survey, that is the feasibility study.

Second, the 'feasibility studies', conducted to map out the facilities' construction plan and the implementation plan for the project, and to provide comments and recommendations on the project feasibility from economic, financial and technical viewpoints. Feasibility studies require a longer period to prepare than any other development surveys.

Third, the 'Surveys for detailed design', aimed at providing various data, detailed designs, specifications, etc. required for construction work involved in the project. These surveys are for obtaining various data (including final drawings and specifications) needed to implement a planned project. Since the utmost precision is required for the preparation of a detailed project design and related work, these surveys are usually costly and time-consuming. There has been growing demand for Japan's co-operation in such surveys.

In 1979, development surveys were conducted for 253 projects. A total of 253 survey teams were dispatched and 2327 experts were assigned overseas. By regions, 1322 (54.3%) experts were sent to Asia; 363 (13.5%) to Latin America; 338 (11.7%) to the Middle East; 258 (11.3%) to Africa; 46 (1.6%) to others. By country, 335 (17.3%) experts were sent to Indonesia; 237 (9.8%) to Thailand; 244 (9.7%) to the Philippines; 152 (5.5%) to Malaysia; 103 (4.9%) to Egypt. By sector, 375 (16.1%) experts were for agriculture; 242 (10.4%) for economic planning and the administrative field.[13]

Development Co-operation Programme

Co-operation in social development, agriculture and forestry, and mining and manufacturing was inaugurated in August 1974, when JICA was established, as a new area of Japan's international co-operation activities, not previously undertaken by the agency's predecessors, the Overseas Technical Co-operation Agency and the Japan Emigration Service. Co-operation in these new fields of development is designed to achieve two specific objectives not adequately fulfilled under the former co-operation system due to the lack of close linkage between government-sponsored and private-sponsored co-operation, and of integration of technical and financial co-operation.

Under the new system, JICA aims at broadening its overseas co-operation activities in the developing countries in the following ways:

(1) Qualitative and quantitative improvement of Japan's international co-operation.
(2) Diversification of co-operation fields by promoting assistance in:
   (i) development projects in industry, natural resources and foreign trade;
   (ii) infrastructural improvement for agriculture and welfare;
   (iii) social development, covering education, medical care, etc.

The prime objective is to ensure a combination by the agency of technical co-operation with a smooth supply of soft loans which, for reasons of risk, profitability or technical difficulties involved in the projects, are difficult to obtain from the Export-Import Bank of Japan or the Overseas Economic Co-operation Fund. In 1977, loan agreements concluded for financial co-operation amounted to a total of ¥2899m (16 projects). By sector ¥2290m (15 projects) was appropriated for agricultural and forestry development and Y609m (1 project) for mining and manufacturing development.

Basic surveys were carried out for nine agriculture and forestry projects and five projects for mining and manufacturing industries. Technical guidance for a related programme was provided for fifteen participants accepted from Thailand in the agricultural sector. Also, seven experts were dispatched to Indonesia, Paraguay and Malaysia for technical assistance in the agriculture, forestry and social development sectors.[14] During FY1978, JICA offered Y5,833m for seven projects for expansion of the related facilities and ¥1154m for six experimental projects. The loans totalled Y6987m for 13 projects. On the expenditure basis, loans for the expansion of facilities reached ¥2633m and those for experimental projects ¥808m, totalling ¥3471m.[15] During FY1979, JICA consented to give ¥840m for three projects for expansion of the related facilities and ¥4843m for five experimental projects. The loans totalled ¥5684m for eight projects. On the contract basis, loans for the expansion of facilities reached ¥1114m and those for experimental projects ¥4690m, totalling ¥5804m.[16]

APPENDIX 7.1 The Flow of Financial Resources to Developing Countries and Multilateral Agencies by Type (1970–80)
Country: Japan

Disbursements Net disbursements	1970	1971	1972	1973	1974	1975	1976	1977	1978	1979	US$m 1980
I Official Development Assistance (a + b)	458.0	510.7	611.1	1,011.0	1,126.2	1,147.7	1,104.9	1,424.4	2,215.4	2,637.5	3,303.7
(a) Bilateral ODA	371.5	432.0	477.8	765.2	880.4	850.4	753.0	899.2	1,531.0	1,921.2	1,960.8
(b) Contributions to multi-lateral institutions	86.5	78.7	133.3	245.8	245.8	297.3	352.0	525.2	684.4	716.3	1,342.9
II Other Official Flows (a + b)	693.6	651.1	856.4	1,178.9	788.9	1,369.4	1,333.4	1,622.6	2,152.6	210.1	1,478.0
(a) Bilateral OOF[a]	492.6	408.0	531.0	823.8	806.8	1,354.5	1,247.8	1,499.0	1,990.2	440.4	1,589.9
(b) Multilateral institutions	201.0	243.1	325.4	355.1	−17.9	14.9	85.6	123.6	162.4	(−230.2)	−111.9
Subtotal (I+II): Total official flows	1,151.6	1,161.8	1,467.5	2,189.9	1,915.1	2,517.1	2,438.3	3,047.0	4,368.0	2,847.6	4,781.7
III Grants by private voluntary agencies	2.9	3.1	5.6	6.8	8.7	10.0	16.2	18.3	18.9	19.0	26.4
IV Private flows at market terms (1–4)	669.4	975.6	1,252.3	3,647.5	1,038.5	352.4	1,548.1	2,469.6	6,316.7	4,689.0	1,957.8
(1) Direct investment	261.5	222.4	204.0	1,301.1	705.4	222.7	1,084.2	724.4	1,318.3	690.6	906.0
(2) Bilateral portfolio investment and other	3.5	133.8	640.3	1,771.0	169.4	4.0	99.9	499.2	3,696.2	2,715.2	660.3
(3) Multilateral portfolio investment	17.5	125.4	217.4	135.3	15.1	6.9	45.0	332.2	890.1	640.7	317.8
(4) Private export credits	386.9	494.0	190.6	440.1	148.7	82.7	319.0	913.8	412.1	642.5	73.7
V Total resource flows (I+IV)	1,824.0	2,140.5	2,725.4	5,844.2	2,962.3	2,879.6	4,002.6	5,534.9	10,703.5	7,555.6	6,765.9
ODA as % of GNP	0.23	0.23	0.21	0.25	0.25	0.23	0.20	0.21	0.23	0.26	0.32
Total resource flows as % of GNP	0.92	0.95	0.93	1.44	0.65	0.59	0.72	0.81	1.09	0.75	0.65

[a] Official funds in support of private export credits amounted to $231.6m in 1975 (−$95.8m) in 1974 included in II(a) above.

Sources: OECD Development Co-operation, Reviews 1974–1981.

8 The Netherlands

THE PERFORMANCE OF DUTCH OFFICIAL DEVELOPMENT ASSISTANCE

The Dutch net flows of ODA increased steadily during the 1970s and Dutch ODA represented about 6 per cent of the total DAC flows in 1980, ranking the Netherlands as the sixth donor in absolute terms of ODA. This trend is in contrast to the position of the Dutch aid programme during the 1960s, when it represented only 0.75 per cent in 1960 and 1.19 per cent in 1965 of the total of DAC member flows. Since 1978, the Netherlands has replaced Canada as the sixth largest donor amongst the DAC members. In quantitative terms Dutch ODA reached $1577.2m in 1980 compared with $604.0m in 1975, and $196.4m in 1970. The performance of Dutch ODA during the 1970s was thus steadily growing, with a sustainable rate of growth – see Appendix 8.1 and Chart 7. The performance of Dutch ODA as a percentage of its GNP is similar to the performance of both Sweden and Norway. Netherlands' ODA reached a record level of 0.99 per cent of GNP in 1980 (the best performance among DAC member countries in that year) compared with 0.75 per cent in 1975 and 0.61 per cent in 1970. In view of the continued high level of budgetary resources devoted to ODA, the Netherlands' net disbursements may be expected to remain in the vicinity of 1 per cent of GNP.

The bulk of Dutch ODA is mainly in the form of bilateral official development assistance, while contributions to multilateral institutions represent on the average about one-third of the Dutch ODA programme. The two components of the Dutch ODA programme steadily increased during the 1970s with the exception of 1972 when contributions to multilateral institutions reached more than 50 per cent of ODA. Bilateral official development assistance was much higher than contributions to multilateral institutions during 1977–80. Other official flows are minor in significance and are included in bilateral other official flows. The Dutch total official flows in general reached $1606.9m in 1980

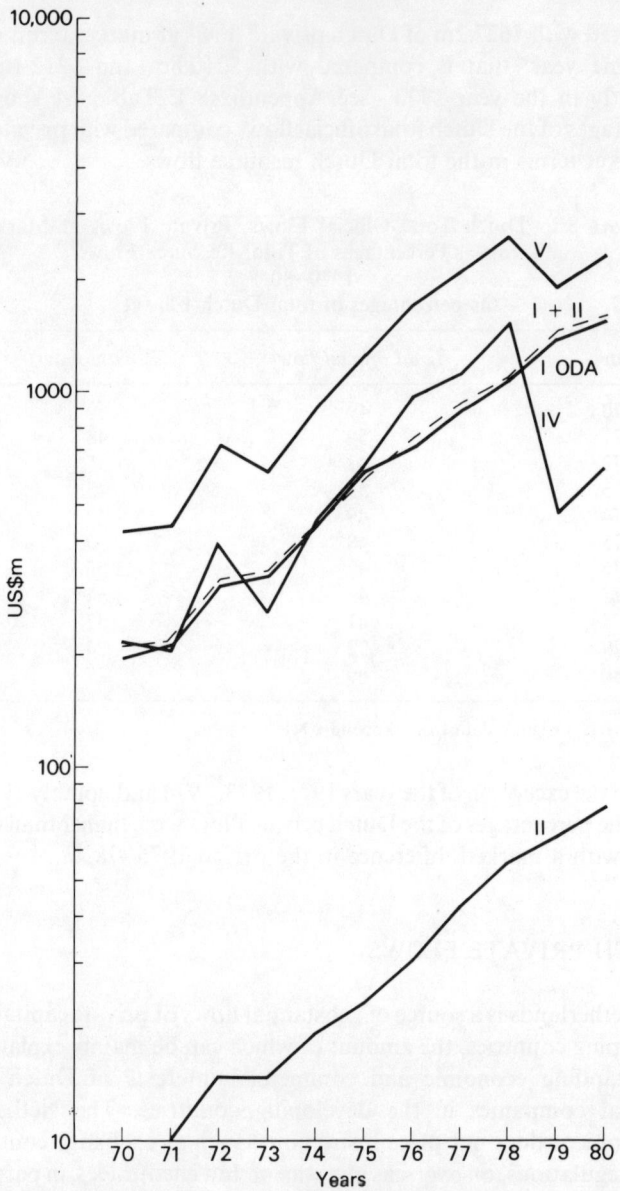

CHART 7 Flow of financial resources to developing countries and multilateral agencies by type: The Netherlands 1970–80

Source: Appendix 8.1

compared with $627.2m of Dutch private flows at market terms during the same year, that is compared with $210.8m and $212.1m subsequently in the year 1970 – see Appendix 8.1. Table 8.1 shows the percentages of the Dutch total official flows compared with private flows at market terms in the total Dutch resource flows.

TABLE 8.1 Dutch Total Official Flows, Private Flows at Market Terms as Percentages of Total Resource Flows 1970–80
(as percentages of total Dutch Flows)

Year	Total official flows	Private flows
1970	49	50
1971	50	48
1972	43	55
1973	55	43
1974	49	49
1975	48	50
1976	42	56
1977	43	54
1978	41	57
1979	72	24
1980	69	27

Source: Original data from Appendix 8.1.

With the exception of the years 1971, 1973, 1974 and notably 1979 and 1980, the percentages of the Dutch private flows were higher than official flows, with a marked difference in the period 1976–78.

DUTCH PRIVATE FLOWS

The Netherlands is a source of substantial flows of private capital to the developing countries, the amount of which can be mainly explained by long-standing economic and commercial interests of Dutch multinational companies in the developing countries. The Netherlands Government does not place restrictions, such as exchange controls or other regulations, on overseas investment, but encourages, in particular, private investment by small and medium-sized Dutch firms in developing countries.[1]

Dutch private flows at market terms increased from $212.1m in 1970 to $628.9m in 1975. In 1978 they reached the highest level of $1542.6m then declined to reach only $477.2m in 1979 and $627.2m in 1980 – see Appendix 8.1. The two main components of Dutch private flows during 1970–78 were direct investment and bilateral portfolio investment. The former increased from $183.2m in 1970 to $241.7m in 1974, while the latter increased from $26.7m to $151.4m during the same period. Since 1975, bilateral portfolio investment has increased more rapidly than direct investment, to reach $344.2m in 1975, $560.9m in 1977 and $917.5m in 1978, then it declined to $150.9m in 1979 and $125.2m in 1980. In comparison, direct investment reached $228.5m, $485.7m and $443.5m, then declined to $167.4m and $135.2m during the same years. Private export credits reached $357.6m in 1980 compared with $169.9m in 1979, $56.0m in 1975 and only $2.4m in 1970 – see Appendix 8.1. Table 8.2 shows the percentage components of Dutch private flows at market terms.

TABLE 8.2 Percentage Components of Dutch Private Flows at Market Terms 1970–80

Year	Direct investment %	Bilateral portfolio investment and other %	Multilateral portfolio investment %	Private export credits %
1970	86	13	(−0.1)	1.1
1971	62	22	13	2.5
1972	81	1.5	(−0.1)	17
1973	34	21	28	17
1974	54	34	0.04	12
1975	36	55	0.03	9
1976	25	48	17	10
1977	43	50	(−0.04)	7
1978	29	59	(−0.3)	12
1979	35	32	(−2.3)	36
1980	22	20	1.5	57

Source: Original data from Appendix 8.1.

The Netherlands has concluded bilateral agreements with several developing countries which, among other things, provided for the protection of private investment. Agreements of this nature have been concluded with Tunisia, the Ivory Coast, Cameroon, Senegal, Indonesia, Sudan, Kenya, Tanzania, Uganda, Malaysia, Morocco, the Republic of Korea, Yugoslavia and Egypt. Although bilateral agreements have a positive influence on the amount of bilateral portfolio investment, one cannot say in general that these bilateral agreements were the main reasons for the expansion of these investments. Moreover, an investment guarantee scheme was passed by the Dutch Parliament in 1969 and provided for state reinsurance of non-commercial risk policies contracted between investors and certain Dutch banks or insurance companies designated by the Ministry of Finance. Bilateral tax agreements have also been concluded with developing countries. In situations not covered by bilateral tax conventions, Dutch tax law does not in general make any distinction in the treatment of income from investment in developing and developed countries.[2]

DUTCH DEVELOPMENT ASSISTANCE POLICY

Dutch development assistance policy in general is directed as far as possible towards the realisation of the objectives laid down in the UN strategy for development, and the implementation of the recommendations worked out by the Development Assistance Committee of the OECD. The fundamental features of Dutch policy on bilateral co-operation with developing countries are based upon:

(1) The concentration of co-operation on a certain number of 'main target' countries.
(2) The programming of aid over a period of four years, on the basis of the allocations established for the target countries.
(3) The assumption that the developing country itself is responsible for fixing priorities in respect of the expenditure of the funds made available and the organisation and implementation of projects.

The Netherlands has for years adopted a policy of concentrating aid in a few countries. A 1968 policy document set out the reasons: the Dutch Government has found that concentration tends to enhance the effects of both financial and technical aid, because it enables the donor to become familiar with the receiving countries' administration and customs, and to gain an understanding of the nature and scope of its needs. Concentration also makes for effective and enduring co-operation between the administrations of both donor and receiving countries, and between donor countries themselves.[3]

The Netherlands exceeded the 0.7 per cent of GNP target for ODA for the sixth consecutive year in 1980. The financial terms of ODA softened in 1978, the grant element of total ODA increasing from 91 to 93 per cent, and the Netherlands continued to be in full compliance with the DAC Terms of Recommendation. In 1978, the Netherlands cancelled all ODA debts owed by four LLDCs (Bangladesh, Sudan, Tanzania and Upper Volta). Loans are partially untied in favour of procurement in the developing countries. The Netherlands bilateral ODA is directed primarily to the poorer population groups in the target countries, in particular the rural poor. The highly flexible 'direct aid' programme provides another means of tackling the immediate problem of poverty through either bilateral or multilateral channels. Programmes carried out jointly with voluntary agencies are stressing similar goals.[4]

Promoting a more equitable distribution of wealth and encouraging self-reliance are the two major aims of Netherlands policy on development co-operation. This applies to both the macro and the micro level. With regard to the macro level, it was stated in the explanatory memorandum to the 1974 Budget that this necessarily leads to an integrated approach: development aid, plus trade policy, plus economic structural policy, plus foreign policy, all supported by a domestic welfare policy, and linked together to achieve one and the same set of goals. The choice of these goals requires an integrated approach at micro level too, that is within development aid itself. The number of development aid instruments used in the context of Netherlands development co-operation has increased over the years. They include multilateral and bilateral aid, project and programme aid, financial aid and technical assistance. The increase in the Netherlands budget for development aid also makes it possible to offer more bilateral aid to non-target countries than in the past, both on an *ad hoc* basis and within the special programme for the relief of direct want. Implementation of the bilateral development policy requires that the Netherlands be sufficiently acquainted with the recipient country to determine that the aid offered will be as useful as possible a contribution to the development of the recipient country. In order that the funds set aside for target countries be put to optimum use, the Netherlands believes it is necessary that a continuous dialogue with each of these countries be maintained, desirable in connection with the identification, preparation, appraisal, implementation, follow-up and evaluation of development co-operation activities, but naturally also to help to decide on what activities the available funds will be spent. Points which may be raised during such discussions are: the debt burden, trade restrictions, raw material prices, restructuring, the new economic order and associated problems. The disbursement consultations are usually held once a year, after they have been prepared in collaboration with the developing country concerned.

The funds for activities in non-target countries are made available under the budget item 'Direct aid to the poorest nations or groups' and may be injected either bilaterally or multilaterally, whichever is the more suitable. This type of aid involves:

(1) Aid to countries and groups in acute emergencies (such as refugee aid and disaster relief).
(2) Aid to developing countries with a common specific problem such as drought, migration, reconstruction following a recent war/or recent independence, and to the MSA countries.
(3) Assistance to isolated activities designed to produce direct results for the benefit of the poorest population groups and the more neglected regions in a particular developing country in the relatively short term.

Thus studies, research, the institutional structuring of government machinery and other long-term activities of a more 'preparatory' nature are excluded. All developing countries are eligible for assistance at this latter level in which the assumed effect of an activity on the position of the poorest groups is of paramount importance in the final appraisal, rather than the social and political structure of the country in which the activity will be carried out. In view of the nature of the funds available for this purpose no institutionalised disbursement consultations are held with these developing countries.[5]

As the Netherlands Government considers that the stimulation of capital flows to developing countries is clearly in the interests of both developed and developing countries, its development co-operation policy may be summed up as follows:[6]

(1) The Netherlands will continue to urge the largest donor countries to increase their ODA efforts in order to approach the generally accepted target of 0.7 per cent of GNP. In its discussions with like-minded countries, the Netherlands will take the initiative towards setting an aid target in excess of 0.7 per cent.
(2) The non-ODA component of the Dutch aid programme will be reduced and a larger proportion of the total ODA flows will go to the poorest countries. In the appropriate international forums, the Netherlands will call for measures with the same aim.
(3) The Netherlands will continue to make financial contributions

to the World Bank and to regional banks to ensure an adequate growth in real terms of their activities, taking into account the capacity for implementing, the lending policy of the institutions concerned and the absorptive capacity of the recipient countries.
(4) The Netherlands is in favour of institutionalised co-operation between OECD and OPEC countries in the financing of projects in developing countries.
(5) The Netherlands will take initiatives in the World Bank and the regional development banks to increase opportunities involving co-financing with commercial banks. Talks will be started with banks in the Netherlands on stimulating the participation of private capital from the Netherlands in co-financing activities.
(6) The government will create an extra facility with the aim of guaranteeing export credits within wider margins than under the present facility, in cases where the destination and nature of the transaction can be regarded as highly desirable from the point of view of development co-operation.
(7) As part of its policy of promoting mutual trade between developing countries, the Netherlands will participate in discussions on the establishment of an International Export Credit Guarantee Facility.
(8) Together with the commercial banking system, the Government will investigate the extent to which banks in the Netherlands can undertake activities to make credit more readily available to small farmers and small-scale industry in developing countries, and the official measures required to stimulate this.
(9) The Netherlands will co-operate in improvements of an institutional nature which will help to widen markets. The government will pay close attention to developments in this area, including the proposals for an International Loan Insurance Fund.
(10) In participating in the work of the Board of Governors of the IMF, the Netherlands will continue to take a positive attitude on parallel financing and on the recommendations that have been drawn up on conditionality. The latter means that elements other than simply the short-term balance-of-payments situation, such as development aspects, may be considered as criteria for IMF support.
(11) The Netherlands will co-operate within the IMF and the Bank for International Settlements (BIS) in working towards achieving an improvement in the flow of information to and from

commercial banks concerning the situation and economic management in developing countries.

The Explanatory Memorandum relating to the 1979 Budget stated that a number of modifications would be made to policy, the purpose of which would be to speed up the realisation of the programme and increase its effectiveness. These modifications were further elaborated and refined and measures of an organisational nature were also taken to improve the implementation of the proposed changes. The decision made to include the present direct aid to poorest countries in the Budget was based on the fact that there was a need for an aid instrument that could be used rapidly and flexibly to relieve emergency situations that were not satisfactorily covered by normal forms of aid. In addition, there was the need for a policy instrument to give additional emphasis to essential components of development policy. Examples of the major components of policy are:

(i) making structural improvements to the position of developing countries (self-reliance);
(ii) combating poverty;
(iii) meeting basic needs;
(iv) promoting human rights.

With regard to the disbursement of funds, the selection of aid activities is on the basis of specific criteria derived from these essential policy components, while the form of the aid and the channel used are selected in such a way as to achieve the aim of the activity as rapidly and as effectively as possible. In addition consideration has also been given to secondary conditions relating to the effectiveness of implementation. A comparison of the criteria governing aid with the practice leads to the conclusion that flexibility could be improved, partly because the funds are being increasingly allocated in advance among the various channels. The existing organisational structure of the Directorate-General for International Co-operation tends to favour such an approach.[7]

ADMINISTRATION OF THE NETHERLANDS AID PROGRAMME

The Netherlands aid programme is managed by the Directorate-General for International Co-operation which forms part of the Ministry of Foreign Affairs but enjoys a high degree of autonomy and has its own minister. Besides the Directorate-General for International

Co-operation, the Ministry of Foreign Affairs has two other policy directorates, for European co-operation and for general political affairs. The Directorate-General also handles relations with international organisations dealing with political affairs.

The Ministries of Economic Affairs and of Finance have an important voice in the determination of general principles for aid but, once the principles are established, much less influence on allocations and application. The Directorate-General is anxious to limit the aid work performed directly by government departments and to delegate to separate organisations such work as is not of a policy character. The Netherlands Investment Bank for Developing Countries is the executive agency for bilateral financial aid and a number of other autonomous or semi-autonomous bodies handle such functions as investment guarantees, co-operation with private capital, and the encouragement of exports by developing countries to the Netherlands.[8]

In 1979, the Ministers of Foreign Affairs and Development Co-operation decided to reorganise the Directorate-General of International Co-operation along the following lines:[9]

(1) Bilateral technical and financial assistance to Africa, Asia and Latin America is to be organised by three separate departments in order to ensure an integrated approach.
(2) A separate department is to be established to deal with aid in co-operation with non-governmental organisations, universities and international educational establishments, and to deal also with research.
(3) A civil service steering committee has been given responsibility for overall guidance of the reorganisation process. The committee is assisted by an external organisation adviser specialising in processes of change.
(4) It has been decided to set up a separate unit to co-ordinate direct aid to the poorest countries and groups and to place the unit under the immediate authority of the Deputy Director General for bilateral co-operation.
(5) A sector unit is to be formally established within the Directorate General of International Co-operation with the job of collecting information on and mobilising as efficiently as possible the knowledge and experience available in the most important development sectors such as agriculture, industry, health and housing. Such expertise is required to improve the effectiveness of development co-operation.

The Netherlands Investment Bank for Developing Countries[10]

The Function of the Bank

The function of the bank lies within the framework of the bilateral development aid provided by the government and it acts as the agent of the government in the matter of aid. The government determines which countries shall receive aid, the conditions on which this shall be provided and the purpose for which it shall be used. The bank, at the request of the government, then provides loans and pays grants to the selected countries, or to bodies nominated by them, and makes payments to suppliers of goods and/or services as well as taking steps to ensure that the funds are used for the purposes agreed between the Netherlands Government and the receiving country. The role of the bank may thus be described as one of a trustee with somewhat extended powers.

Loans and Grants from the Bank

The bank provides loans in its own name and with a guarantee from the government. The resources to finance these are obtained, also under government guarantee, by issuing loans in the public and private sectors of the capital market. In principle, the loans are partially untied, so that the proceeds may be used in the Netherlands or in developing countries, including the recipient country. The terms of the loans furnished by the bank, which vary according to the degree of development of the country concerned, are as follows:

(i) 3.75 per cent interest, 30-year life including an 8-year period of grace;

(ii) 2.5 per cent interest, 30-year life including an 8-year period of grace;

(iii) 0.75 per cent interest, 50-year life including a 10-year period of grace.

The terms stated in (ii) are known as the DAC conditions, since they were laid down by the Development Assistance Committee of the Paris-based OECD. Those stated in (iii) are known as the IDA conditions, since they are employed by the International Development Association. The LLDCs receive aid solely in the form of grants. The others, who are assisted wholly or partly with loans, are divided into three groups for the purpose of interest which, as stated above, ranges from 0.75 to 3.75 per cent. The loans are partially untied under an agreement between a number of member states of the DAC. Grants are in principle subject to the provision that they will be spent on goods or services of Dutch origin. Table 8.3 summarises the total facilities provided by the bank.

TABLE 8.3 Loans and Grants provided by the Netherlands Investment Bank for Developing Countries 1974–80 (Gldm)

Year	Loans		Grants		Total	
	Number of countries	Amount	Number of countries	Amount	Number of countries[c]	Amount
1974	9	357	—	—	9	357
1975	14	305	10	142	18	447
1976	16	861	11	114	19	975
1977	19	739	15	341	23	1080
1978	14	637	12	403	23	1040
1979	17[a]	670	14[b]	490	28	1060
1980	20	910	11	453	24	1363

[a] Involving 24 contracts.
[b] Involving 25 contracts.
[c] As some countries received both loans and grants, this total is less than the sum of the countries in the preceding columns.
Source: The Netherlands Investment Bank for Developing Countries, *Annual Reports* 1977, 1978, 1979, 1980.

The countries which receive bilateral project and programme aid from the Netherlands are referred to as target countries. A breakdown of the loans and grants for these countries in 1979 is shown in Table 8.4.

In 1980 the Netherlands Government concentrated its development aid on the following target countries: Bangladesh, Pakistan, Sri Lanka, India, Indonesia, Upper Volta, Tanzania, Yemen Arab Republic, Kenya, Sudan, Egypt, Zambia and Colombia. Loans and grants contracted by the bank for target developing countries in 1980 reached Gld824m (Gld493m for loans for six countries and Gld331m for grants for ten countries), where some countries have received both loans and grants.[11]

The Netherlands Finance Company for Developing Countries[12]

Establishment and Financial Resources

The Nederlandse Financierings Maatschappij voor Ontwikkelingslanden NV (Netherlands Finance Company for Developing

TABLE 8.4 Loans and Grants Contracted in 1979 by the Netherlands Investment Bank for Target Developing Countries (Gldm)

Target country	Loans contracted	Grants contracted	Total
Bangladesh	—	71	71
Colombia	12	—	12
Cuba	—	—	—
Egypt	18	10	28
India	164	61	225
Indonesia	110	—	110
Jamaica	—	—	—
Kenya[a]	—	15	15
North Yemen	24	9	33
Pakistan	40	20	60
Peru[a]	43	—	43
Sri Lanka	28	13	41
Sudan[a]	—	25	25
Tanzania[a]	—	71	71
Tunisia	—	—	—
Upper Volta	—	28	28
Zambia	5	5	10
Total	444	328	772

[a] These target countries also received emergency aid not relating to specific projects in 1979. This was provided within the framework of direct aid to the poorest countries and groups.

Source: The Netherlands Investment Bank for Developing Countries, *Annual Report*, 1979.

Countries – FMO) was formed in 1970. It arose from co-operation between Dutch private business and industry and the State of the Netherlands. The latter holds 51 per cent of the share capital – 49 per cent is owned by more than 140 Dutch shareholders, mainly industrial firms and banks, and also the Trade Union Federations. The funds for investment are obtained from state guaranteed borrowings on the Dutch capital market and from state contributions in the form of interest-free loans and interest subsidies. FMO's aim is to stimulate economic and social progress in developing countries by promoting local business and industry. The emphasis is on productive activities capable of contributing significantly to that development and which are at the same time economically viable. FMO co-operates with Dutch firms that are involved in enterprises in developing countries either as joint financiers, suppliers or contractors of goods, or as providers of know-how and management. Co-operation with Dutch firms is not a prerequisite, however, nor is it written into the objects of the company. There is also no obligation to spend in the Netherlands the funds which FMO invests in a project.

The FMO is a company with limited liability: the paid-up share capital amounted (in 1978) to Gld5.2m (approximately $2m). In addition, the government provides the FMO with working capital by extending loans or grants, or by guaranteeing FMO loans raised on the capital market.

Scope of Activities

FMO provides finance and technical assistance, by making contributions to feasibility studies, and also by acting as an intermediary in establishing contacts and actively supervising the management of the projects and development banks in which it is involved. It is among the few financial institutions that are able to contribute to the equity of firms in developing countries by participating in their share capital. In view of the objects of FMO, it is intended when the time is ripe to sell such share capital interests to buyers in the countries where the enterprises are established. Most of the finance made available by FMO, however, is in the form of loans. In exceptional cases the provision of grants is not entirely ruled out. To meet the special needs of enterprises in developing countries for management skills, technical know-how and experience, FMO assists in the provision and financing of specialists' services, training facilities and management. FMO's total financial interest in a project as a rule amounts to at least Gld250,000 and at the most Gld10m, and more than 10 per cent and less than 50 per cent of the total finance for the project. Large and very large projects or enterprises generally have other channels open to them for raising finance and acquiring know-how. Table 8.5 shows FMO geographical distribution commitments and number of projects.

Terms and Conditions

Geographically FMO's area of operations covers in principle all developing countries. Some preference is shown for the poorest countries and the poorest regions in developing countries. For practical reasons, and for reasons that have to do with the Dutch Government's

TABLE 8.5 FMO Geographical Distribution Commitments during 1978–80

Country	Amount outstanding			Number of projects		
	1980 (Gldm)	1979 (Gldm)	1978 (Gldm)	1980	1979	1978
Bangladesh	1.250	—	—	1	—	—
Botswana	1.681	1.824	—	1	1	—
Upper Volta	1.665	1.535	—	1	1	—
Brazil	8.552	4.422	4.422	1	1	1
Ecuador	0.497	0.497	0.497	1	1	1
Egypt	2.600	—	—	1	—	—
Gabon	4.322	4.322	—	1	1	—
Ghana	3.986	3.986	3.752	2	2	2
India	1.343	1.449	1.054	1	1	1
Indonesia	37.580	31.197	28.965	10	9	9
Ivory Coast	10.058	9.964	6.102	2	2	1
Jamaica	3.835	—	—	1	—	—
Cameroon	3.669	3.889	3.889	2	2	2
Congo	7.606	7.036	7.039	1	1	1
Lesotho	2.250	1.500	1.500	1	1	1
Liberia	7.900	8.300	8.300	2	2	2
Malawi	2.250	2.250	—	1	1	—
Malta	4.502	4.502	4.002	1	1	1
Nigeria	8.773	8.773	8.773	2	2	2
Pakistan	3.600	—	—	1	—	—
Senegal	2.199	2.199	2.199	1	1	1
Sierra Leone	2.734	2.711	1.888	3	3	2
Sudan	1.824	1.824	—	1	1	—
Sri Lanka	8.232	4.537	0.436	4	2	1
Tanzania	8.590	2.160	2.160	4	2	2
Tunesia	8.205	10.012	11.505	9	10	11
Total	149.703	118.514	96.483	56	48	41

Source: Information received from FMO.

policy on development co-operation, there are some countries where FMO may not be prepared to undertake activities.

FMO is mainly concerned with the industrial (manufacturing) and agricultural sectors. This does not imply the exclusion of enterprises in other sectors, though it does mean that projects in these sectors will receive less priority. As regards the financial sector, however, it should be added that FMO attaches great value to the function that development banks fulfil in developing countries. Participations in these banks therefore play a very significant part in FMO's activities seen as a whole.

Interest Rate. The interest charged generally corresponds to that payable on similar loans in the country where the financed enterprise is established. Depending on the envisaged profitability the interest payable may be fixed at a lower rate for part of the period of the loan. Rates for loans for highly profitable projects are 1 to 2 per cent above market rates (a premium regarded as normal to cover the costs of the company and enable it to make a small profit). When the profitability of a project is lower, loans on more favourable terms are obtainable and funds are not tied to the purchase of Dutch equipment. FMO charges a commission on the total amount that may be borrowed under the loan agreement. The commission is payable in a lump sum and is deductible by FMO from the first disbursement.

Repayment Period. Loans are granted as a rule for periods varying from 5-15 years, depending on the nature of the financed activities. In appropriate cases a period may be agreed during which no redemption payments are due.

Security Required. In consultation with other financiers and in compliance with the provisions of local legislation, FMO requires security in the form of collateral on appropriate assets.

Management of the Company

The company's affairs are directed by a management under a Supervisory Board. Finance or services provided by FMO require the approval of a Projects Committee which, like the Supervisory Board, is composed of representatives of the state and of the private sector. As a rule FMO claims the right to appoint a director to the Board of firms which it finances.

Approaches Taken and Techniques Applied

If it appears from an initial verbal or written approach that FMO may be willing to provide joint finance for an enterprise, the next step is for the party taking the initiative to submit a written application accompanied by a completed short questionnaire, which will have been sent to him upon the initial approach. The projects financed by the FMO are expected to contribute to the economic development of the beneficiary countries and should be economicaly viable. The criteria on which FMO bases its decision to finance an enterprise or to provide or finance technical assistance imply in the first place that FMO examines whether a project belongs to its field of operations, and whether it can provide the services requested or needed. Next it looks at the extent to which implementation of the project would contribute towards the desired social and economic development, in which respect it is largely guided both by the Dutch Government's policy on development co-operation and by the development aspirations of the authorities in the countries themselves. Essentially this amounts to devoting attention to the envisaged effects of combating poverty, creating employment, providing training and transferring know-how, promoting a good working climate with reasonable terms of employment and social security provisions, the use of local raw materials, the influence on the balance of payments, the encouragement of self-reliance, effects on the environment and the impact on existing socio-cultural patterns. At the same time FMO examines whether the proposed productive activities have a sufficiently sound economic basis. This involves first and foremost looking at the reputation and quality of the partners and of the management. It also includes scrutinising the proposed ownership structure, the planned organisation, the financial structure, the expected return on investment, the projected cash flow, the quality and quantity of available manpower and raw materials, the prospects for sales volume and selling prices, and the technical production facilities.

Problems of Implementation and Remarks from Field Experience

The increase in the number of projects that have reached the stage of implementation has resulted in a heavier work load for the project management department, whose professional staff have had to be enlarged to cope with it. On the basis of the written report required from the enterprises that the company finances – a requirement which in general is properly complied with – and by visiting the projects on the spot, FMO endeavours to keep as well informed as possible on the progress being made. To enable them to identify potential problems at an early stage, these visits are not confined to projects that are in more or less serious difficulties. With a view to efficiency the itineraries are organised in such a way that several projects can be visited en route or in a region during one journey. In exercising project management function FMO is confronted with the special difficulties which investing in developing countries entail. Compared with the significant challenges of business enterprise in the West, special efforts are usually required from the local entrepreneur in developing countries. The company has learned from experience that many unexpected obstacles are encountered, including delays in the implementation of projects. It therefore takes much patience and time before local enterprises acquire an established position. Encouragement of the often scarce entrepreneureal talent and business initiative and their function as a catalyst of social and economic progress in developing countries is therefore a task that deserves special attention.

Some enterprises, although producing products of good quality, were faced with marketing problems. In this context it should be noted that firms in developing countries find it difficult as a rule to operate on export markets. Cheap imports often make it difficult for them to sell their products locally, added to which is the fact that buyers on the local market tend to prefer goods of inferior quality to the more expensive quality products. Generally speaking, it takes a few years for people to change from price-conscious to quality-conscious buyers, and during that time the company's projects are confronted with selling difficulties. In such cases FMO tries in its project management to ensure that the projects it finances do not find themselves in competition with other local enterprises producing cheap products of inferior quality. Enterprises producing quality products must endeavour to maintain their sales by means of marketing support measures and the input of special know-how. Another problem the company faces from time to time concerns difficulties between the partners in joint ventures financed by FMO. As a result of setbacks experienced in the initial phase of a project and later, the partners may have differences of opinion that sometimes constitute a serious threat to the continued existence of the project. In such cases FMO endeavours to play a conciliatory role. Since the alteration of the Act relating to FMO in 1977 FMO has been able to help in solving other problems arising from imperfections in such areas as the organisation and management of enterprises that it finances by recruiting experts and making them available to projects entirely or partly at its own expense.

APPENDIX 8.1 The Flow of Financial Resources to Developing Countries and Multilateral Agencies by Type (1970–80)
Country: Netherlands

Disbursements Net disbursements	1970	1971	1972	1973	1974	1975	1976	1977	1978	1979	US$m 1980
I Official Development Assistance (a + b)	196.4	216.1	306.7	322.1	436.0	604.0	719.9	899.6	1,073.5	1,403.6	1,577.2
(a) Bilateral ODA	154.6	152.3	192.9	230.0	302.6	365.1	496.2	643.6	789.2	962.0	1,174.4
(b) Contributions to multilateral institutions	41.8	63.8	113.8	92.1	133.4	238.8	223.7	256.0	284.3	441.6	402.8
II Other Official Flows (a + b)	14.4	2.8	5.3	14.7	8.4	1.5	3.9	2.2	20.1	2.2	29.7
(a) Bilateral OOF	14.4	2.8	5.3	14.7	8.4	1.5	3.9	2.2	20.1	2.2	29.7
(b) Multilateral institutions	—	—	—	—	—	—	—	—	—	—	0.0
Subtotal (I + II): Total official flows	210.8	218.9	312.0	336.8	444.4	602.5	723.8	901.8	1,093.6	1,405.8	1,606.9
III Grants by private voluntary agencies	5.2	10.0	15.0	15.0	19.5	23.5	30.4	42.7	55.5	65.3	78.7
IV Private flows at market terms (1–4)	212.1	208.8	394.5	260.2	445.1	628.9	972.3	1,128.8	1,542.6	477.2	627.2
(1) Direct investment	183.2	130.2	321.3	88.5	241.7	228.5	244.7	485.7	443.5	167.4	135.3
(2) Bilateral portfolio investment and other	26.7	46.9	5.9	55.6	151.4	344.2	463.5	560.9	917.5	150.9	125.2
(3) Multilateral portfolio investment	−0.2	26.4	−0.5	72.1	0.2	0.2	165.8	−0.4	−5.1	−11.0	9.1
(4) Private export credits	2.4	5.3	67.8	44.0	51.8	56.0	98.3	82.6	186.7	169.9	357.6
V Total resource flows (I–IV)	428.1	437.7	721.5	612.1	909.0	1,254.9	1,726.5	2,073.3	2,691.7	1,948.2	2,312.8
ODA as % of GNP	0.61	0.58	0.67	0.54	0.63	0.75	0.82	0.85	0.82	0.93	0.99
Total resource flows as % of GNP	1.34	1.18	1.59	1.03	1.31	1.55	1.96	1.96	2.06	1.29	1.46

Sources: OECD, *Development Co-operation*, Reviews 1974–81.

9 Sweden

THE PERFORMANCE OF SWEDISH OFFICIAL DEVELOPMENT ASSISTANCE

During the 1970s Swedish ODA grew in a consistently sustained manner. Since 1975 Sweden has been the eighth largest donor, in absolute terms, among the 17 DAC member countries following the USA, France, West Germany, Japan, the UK, the Netherlands and Canada. Its share in total ODA/DAC donors was 3.45 per cent in 1980 compared with 4.17 per cent in 1975 and 1.71 per cent in 1970, compared with only 0.15 per cent in 1960 and 0.65 per cent in 1965. In quantitative terms, Swedish ODA reached $923.1m in 1980 compared with $956.1m in 1979, $566.0m in 1975 and $117.0m in 1970. In terms of ODA/GNP, Sweden has fulfilled and exceeded the 0.7 per cent target since 1974, as it reached 0.76 per cent in 1980 compared with 0.94 per cent in 1979, 0.82 per cent in 1975 and 0.38 per cent in 1970 – see Appendix 9.1 and Chart 8.

The sharp drop in Sweden's ODA/GNP ratio in 1980 compared with 1979 was mainly due to the fact that the IDA VI agreement did not become effective during 1980 as originally foreseen, so that Sweden was not in a position to deposit any notes with IDA, in addition to some slowdown in the disbursement of bilateral aid. An increase in the ODA/GNP ratio can be expected again in the next few years, since budgetary and appropriations have been maintained at a level close to 1 per cent of GNP.[1]

Swedish total official flows represent mainly ODA as OOF started only in 1977 and its share is nominal. As in the case of other DAC donors, Swedish ODA is composed of two main parts: bilateral official development assistance and contributions to multilateral institutions. Swedish bilateral ODA reached $675.8m in 1980 compared with $373.2m in 1975 and $63.1m in 1970. Its share in ODA was 73, 66 and 54 per cent respectively. With the exception of 1971, Swedish bilateral ODA was higher than Swedish contributions to multilateral institutions

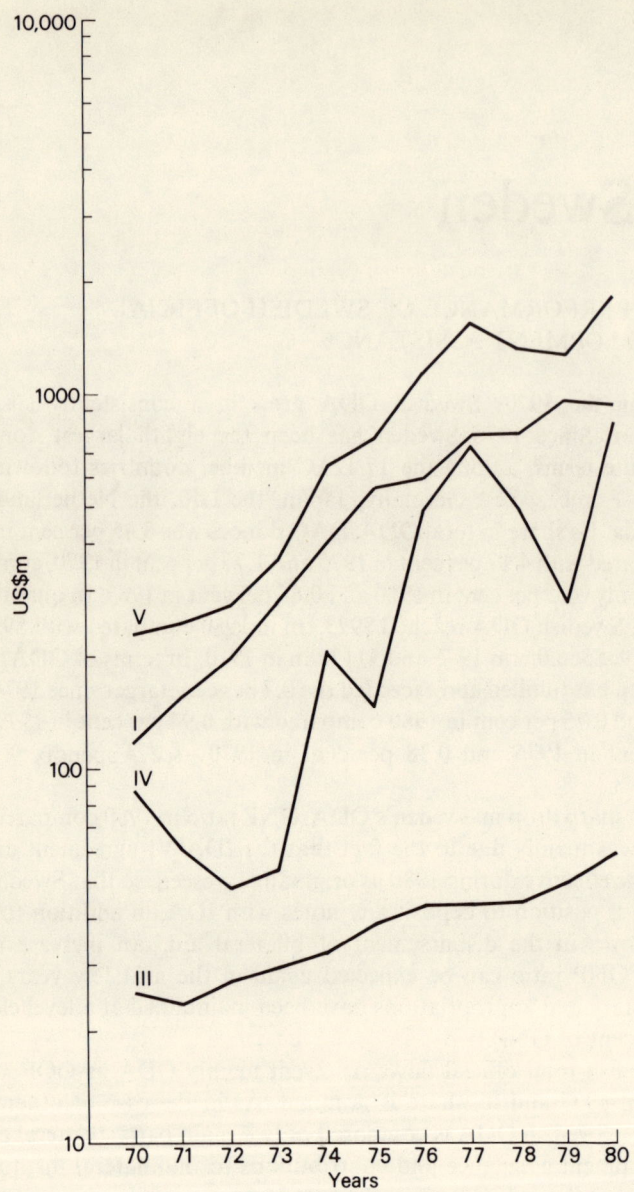

CHART 8 Flow of financial resources to developing countries and multilateral agencies by type: Sweden 1970–80
Source: Appendix 9.1

during the period 1970–80. The latter reached $247.3m in 1980 compared with $192.8m in 1975 and $53.9m in 1970 – see Appendix 9.1.

Swedish total resource flows to developing countries and multilateral agencies are mainly official flows. Table 9.1 shows the percentage share of Swedish official flows compared with private flows at market terms. The table shows no major trend for Swedish official flows compared with Swedish private flows but indicates a higher share of official flows during the period 1970–80. Grants by private voluntary agencies have grown in quantitative terms (but not in percentage) during the second half of the 1970s, reaching $59.0m in 1980 (3 per cent of Swedish total flows), compared with $49.0m in 1979 (4 per cent), $38.8m in 1975 (5 per cent) and $25.2m in 1970 (11 per cent) – see Appendix 9.1.

TABLE 9.1 Swedish Official Flows, Private Flows at Market Terms as a Percentage of Total Swedish Resource Flows (1970–80)

Year	Official flows %	Private flows %
1970	51	38
1971	65	25
1972	72	18
1973	77	15
1974	63	32
1975	75	20
1976	54	43
1977	50	47
1978	60	37
1979	75	21
1980	51	46

Source: Original data from Appendix 9.1.

SWEDISH PRIVATE FLOWS

The main feature of Swedish private investment in developing countries is that it is mainly directed to countries other than those receiving substantial official assistance from Sweden, whereas investment guarantees are restricted to countries receiving Swedish assistance. Swedish private flows at market terms have increased substantially since 1974, reaching $205.8m in that year compared with $54.3m in 1973 and $87.1m in 1970. They declined in 1975 compared with 1974, 1978 compared with 1977, and 1979 compared with 1978, as in 1977 they reached $730.9m compared with $483.4m in 1976 and $147.7m in 1975. In 1979 Swedish private flows at market terms reached $274.0m compared with $490.7m in 1978 – see Appendix 9.1. Table 9.2 shows the major percentage components of Swedish private flows.

TABLE 9.2 Major Components of Swedish Private Flows as a Percentage of Total Private Flows (1970–80)

Year	Direct investment %	Bilateral portfolio investment %	Multilateral portfolio investment %	Private export credits %
1970	42	7	6	35
1971	66	8	(−4)	31
1972	87	9	13	(−8)
1973	40	22	32	6
1974	24	2	5	69
1975	56	1	0.5	43
1976	26	3	(−0.1)	72
1977	17	35	0.01	47
1978	23	36	(−0.08)	41
1979	47	5	(−0.2)	48
1980	11	2	(0.0)	87

Source: Original data from Appendix 9.1.

Multilateral portfolio investment did not represent a significant component in Swedish private flows except for the years 1972 and 1973. On the other hand, private export credit since 1974 and bilateral portfolio investment during 1977/78 were important components. As for direct investment, with few exceptions it declined in its importance in the second half of the 1970s compared with the first. In general, Swedish private flows at market terms are a package of three main components: direct investment, bilateral portfolio investment and private export credits, with no major trends during the period 1970–80.

The Swedish investment guarantee scheme was approved by the Swedish Parliament in 1968.[2] The Swedish Export Credits Guarantee Board (EKN) has been empowered to issue investment guarantees and to define in more detail the questions pertaining to the establishment of the scheme. Guarantees may be issued up to a maximum total amount of Swedish Kr400m. Intended primarily to encourage projects which are of benefit to developing countries, the scheme has strict eligibility criteria as regards the contribution of the project to the economic and social development of the host country, and investors are eligible only if they can demonstrate a 'reasonable connection' between the investment and Swedish production, export or other interest. The availability of investment guarantees is restricted to those countries with which Sweden is carrying out substantial official development co-operation programmes. The geographical coverage of the scheme has been gradually adapted to changes in the geographical distribution of the Swedish Assistance Programme. As for fiscal measures, Sweden applies the same taxes on the net income of foreign branches and domestic operations. Unless a double taxation treaty applies, foreign tax on foreign source income may under certain conditions be deducted from gross profits as a cost, or credited against the Swedish national income tax burden on the foreign source income.

SWEDISH DEVELOPMENT ASSISTANCE POLICY

There is increasing recognition in Sweden that independence is a two-stage process; first political, then economic. SIDA, along with ILO, has helped promote the designing of a 'Strategy for Basic Needs' – water, food, sanitation, clothing, housing, hospitals and schools – to deal with the most urgent problems of the poorest countries, and the more products such as water pipes, paper for textbooks, clothing, etc., these countries can produce for themselves, the better. Another task is to remove tariff barriers, offer better terms of trade, assure access to capital and promote transfer of technology and production capacity, instead of just giving aid and products. It would then no longer be aid, but not quite trade. As Ruth Link indicated:

> It is not charity the developing countries want, but a chance to stand on their own feet – to sell more goods at fairer prices and to have a greater share of the world's capital, technology and industry. So instead of schools and clinics, Sweden's new policy is to give factories and joint-finance industrial projects. Though trade between equals may be far in the future, mere aid will soon belong to the past. Meanwhile, bridging the two is TRAID.[3]

A specific Swedish policy towards the developing countries exists in the sense that the developing countries will be affected by the line

Sweden has adopted towards the demands for a new world economic order. Solidarity with the poor of the Third World provides a sufficient motive for large-scale Swedish assistance, a view endorsed by the Riksdag in 1962, and confirmed by the commission for the Review of Sweden's International Development Co-operation. The goals of Swedish assistance policy are based upon the criteria that Swedish efforts should contribute to growth of resources, economic and social equalisation, economic and political independence, and democratic social development.[4] Swedish policy for overall co-operation with developing countries emphasises the importance of an active and co-ordinated effort, based on mutual interest. In recent years several developing countries have become large purchasers of Swedish industrial equipment, while well-established and good relations with a broad range of developing countries are important for Swedish energy supplies. Assistance to certain programme countries has been terminated and efforts have instead been made to develop co-operation with these countries on a mutual interest basis. The recently established Inter-ministerial High-level Consultative Group for Relations with the Developing Countries has proved to be a valuable forum for exchange of information between representatives of the various government offices. Most of the questions discussed have concerned several ministries, for example those relating to massive transfers of resources, structural changes, environment and development, and the Swedish attitude to the proposal for a global round of negotiations, concerning energy questions. Regarding Swedish policy on bilateral development co-operation, Swedish relations with the developing countries have become increasingly diversified and at the same time more extensive. This applies not only to Swedish traditional co-operation partners, such as Brazil, India and Mexico, with which Sweden has had substantial commercial relations over a long period, but also to many other countries. This trend has been especially noticeable as regards the main recipient countries of Swedish bilateral assistance, the so-called programme countries. Direct Swedish assistance to these countries has often also given rise to other forms of co-operation, not least in the commercial field. For FY1980/81, a total increase of SKr600m or 13.5 per cent was made in the appropriations for international development assistance, which will bring the total appropriations for international development co-operation up to SKr5015m. Like FY1979/80, the appropriations have been estimated to equal somewhat more than 1 per cent of GNP. The proposed increase comes within the appropriation for international development assistance programmes, which receives an additional SKr165m, and the appropriation for bilateral development co-operation, which receives an additional SKr403m. It has been estimated that multilateral and bilateral assistance will receive 29.3 per cent and 64.9 per cent respectively of the total appropriations for FY1980/81.[5]

The financial terms of Swedish ODA are among the most concessional in the DAC with 99 per cent of total commitments in 1978 extended in grant form. Sweden decided in 1978 to write off all outstanding debt from ODA loans extended to the LLDCs and MSAs (Bangladesh, Botswana, Ethiopia, India, Kenya, Pakistan, Sudan and Tanzania). Swedish ODA is largely untied, the share of tied aid corresponding to approximately 17 per cent of 1978/79 ODA appropriations. While the ODA programme is characterised by a high degree of continuity, Sweden has broadened its development and co-operation policy to include elements based on the concept of mutual interest calling for a greater involvement of the private sector. New initiatives have focused especially on a strengthening of industrial co-operation, for which, in addition to increased resources put at the disposal of SIDA for that purpose, a Fund for Industrial Co-operation with Developing countries (SWED-FUND) was set up in 1979 for the promotion of joint ventures between Sweden and developing-country partners.[6] A mixed financing scheme to soften the terms of commercial credits was initiated with an appropriation of $14m in 1980–81. Programmes designed to assist imports from the developing countries are implemented by the Swedish Import Promotion Office for Products from Developing Countries (IMPOD), while research activities are being assisted by the Swedish Agency for Research co-operation (SAREC).[7]

ADMINISTRATION OF THE SWEDISH AID PROGRAMME

The Swedish International Development Authority

Establishment and Organisational Structure

The preparation and implementation of Swedish Programmes for bilateral development co-operation is the responsibility of the Swedish International Development Authority (SIDA) which was established in 1965 as a central government agency. This is in line with the organisational pattern of Swedish public administration, by which policy guidelines are established by the government on the basis of decisions by

Parliament. The SIDA Board of Directors consists of thirteen members, and the Chairman is the Director General, with members of the Board representing political parties and non-governmental organisations. The Management Committee is a group for consultation and information, and is composed of the Director General, his deputy and two assistant Director Generals. The so-called Extended Management Committee also includes the Division Heads. SIDA's operations are conducted by ten Divisions.[8]

(1) *Policy Planning and Programme Review Division*: which administers and co-ordinates investigations primarily in development assistance policies and cross-disciplinary questions, multilateral assistance issues, evaluation studies, women's issues, legal issues.
(2) *Area Division*: which plans, negotiates, and administers the development co-operation mainly with so-called programme countries.
(3) *Industry Division*: which administers development support to industry, transport, power supply, water supply and export promotion.
(4) *Agricultural Division*: which administers development support to agriculture with animal husbandry, forestry, and fisheries as well as general rural development, co-operative and ecological questions.
(5) *Education Division*: which administers development support to general and vocational education as well as public administration.
(6) *Population, Health and Nutrition Division*: which administers matters related to population policies, demography, health and medical care, family planning and nutrition, and research related to these areas.
(7) *Financial Division*: which is in charge of budget and planning, accounting, administrative questions relating to Development Co-operation Offices, organisational development, office supplies and services, printing and related services.
(8) *Personal Assistance Resource Division*: which is in charge of recruitment, training and administration of personnel working for SIDA's recipient countries or on UN assignment to various countries.
(9) *Personnel Division*: which is in charge of all SIDA staff at headquarters and at Development Co-operation Offices.

(10) *Information Division*: which administers issues relating to granting of subsidies to non-governmental organisations, contacts with the mass media, schools, higher education, publications, information service to the general public as well as internal information.

In addition to the above ten divisions, SIDA's organisation includes:

(1) *Development Co-operation Offices*: for the local administration of Swedish assistance there are sections within the Swedish Embassies in twelve of the Swedish programme countries in Africa and Asia as follows:
    Africa: Botswana, Ethiopia, Guinea-Bissau, Kenya, Mozambique, Tanzania, Tunisia and Zambia;
    Asia: Bangladesh, India, Sri Lanka and Vietnam.
(2) *The Swedish Agency for Research Co-operation with Developing Countires (SAREC)*: to advise the government on the programme of research financed from Swedish aid funds and to process research projects and programmes up to the stage of decision by SIDA and the government.

SIDA's Budget Proposals

By 1 September SIDA submits its annual budget proposals to the government for the next fiscal year. The proposals deal with the total Swedish appropriations and with policy guidelines for Swedish Development Co-operation.[9] The proposals are examined by the Ministry for Foreign Affairs where the Minister is assisted by the Office for International Development Co-operation, a separate department within the Ministry for Foreign Affairs. The office prepares the annual development assistance programme in accordance with the guidelines for multilateral and bilateral co-operation drawn up by the government, analyses SIDA's proposals and prepares underlying data for decisions. The government presents its proposals in the Budget Bill put before the Riksdag (Parliament) in January each year, and a special debate is devoted to development assistance issues in April or May each year. Following that debate the Riksdag adopts resolutions on international development co-operation, which are mainly concerned with allocations to individual countries, international organisations, special initiatives, administration, information, etc., and give general guidelines for development co-operation policy. When the Riksdag has finally adopted the Budget Bill, the government sends a Letter of Official Confirmation to SIDA for the fiscal year commencing on 1 July.

SIDA's Programme Cycle

A co-operation programme evolves in nine separate steps which are repeated annually or every other year depending on the period of the agreement. The SIDA Programme Cycle is as shown in Figure 9.1. The needs, activities and requests of the programme country are always to be the focus of programmes. The two-headed arrows demonstrate that the centrality of the recipient country or work on the field steers the dialogue throughout the programming process. SIDA's Development Co-operation Office plays a decisive role in this context. It has regular meetings with ministries and other competent authorities in the recipient country.

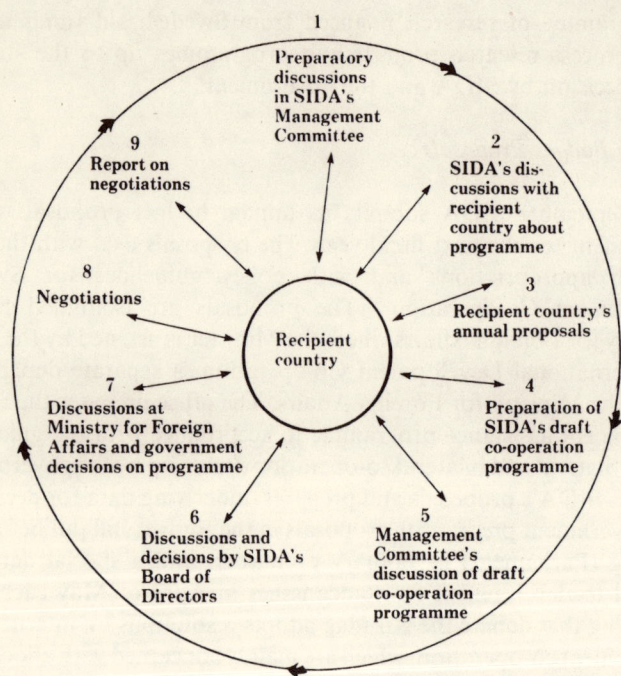

FIGURE 9.1 SIDA's programme cycle

Source: *faKtablad* (fact sheet), SIDA 3A, "SIDA's Role in Decision Making on Development Co-operation with Individual Countries", August 1979.

Aid through SIDA to Developing Countries

According to a statement in Parliament the government, through SIDA, should primarily co-operate with countries which are themselves attempting to improve conditions for the majority of their inhabitants. Co-operation can include countries with different political systems. Approximately 90 per cent of the direct assistance goes to countries which the United Nations has defined as extremely poor. Direct development co-operation takes place with a limited number of countries, in order to ensure that it is effective. The co-operation takes place within the economic framework which is established in Parliament for each financial year, and the assistance is formed in accordance with the recipient country's own wishes. In 1978/79 the government, through SIDA, had programmes for long-term development co-operation with twenty countries. Table 9.3 shows aid through SIDA to developing countries in 1978/79.

The geographical distribution of SIDA's commitments by region during 1978/79–1979/80 has shown that Asia received Skr985m in 1979/80 compared with Skr925m in 1978/79 (47 per cent compared with 48 per cent consequently). Southern Africa and other African countries received Skr1027m in 1979/80 compared with Skr974m in 1978/79 (49 per cent compared with 50 per cent consequently). Other countries received Skr70m in 1978/79 and 1979/80 (4 per cent in 1978/79 compared with 3 per cent in 1979/80). The ratio of disbursements to commitments indicates a good and quick implementation of SIDA: this ratio reached 97 per cent in 1978/79 and 91 per cent in 1979/80. SIDA's aid disbursements by sector (during 1978/79–1979/80), have shown that the import support sector's share reached 39 per cent of total disbursement in 1979/80 compared with 41 per cent in 1978/79: industry 15 per cent compared with 14 per cent, agriculture 11 per cent compared with 12 per cent during the same period. This indicates that these three sectors represented about 65 per cent of total SIDA disbursements in 1979/80, the rest were distributed for education (8 per cent), population (1 per cent), health (5 per cent), transport and communications (2 per cent), water and power (12 per cent), business and finance (4 per cent), and public administration (1 per cent). Table 9.4 shows the geographical distribution of SIDA commitments and disbursements.

SIDA's Aid Through Non-governmental Organisations

Among its activities, SIDA has a programme for support to Swedish non-governmental organisations (NGOs), for information activities on

TABLE 9.3 Aid Through SIDA to Developing Countries 1978/79

Country	Aid (SKrm)
Vietnam	380
Tanzania	310
India	270
Mozambique	115
Bangladesh	115
Zambia	95
Kenya	90
Sri Lanka	80
Ethiopia	70
Angola	60
Botswana	55
Guinea-Bissau	50
Portugal	40
Pakistan	40
Laos	40
Tunisia	30
Cuba	30
Cape Verde	20
Lesotho	12
Swaziland	10
Total	1912

Source: Swedish Development Co-operation – A Summary, 1978/79, SIDA, Information Division, 1978.

TABLE 9.4 Geographical Distribution of SIDA Commitments and Disbursements in 1978/79, 1979/80 (SKrm)

Region	Commitments		Disbursements	
	1978/79	1979/80	1978/79	1979/80
Asia	925	985	851	916
Southern Africa	347	399	344	316
Other Africa	600	628	617	592
Others	70	70	68	69
Total	1942	2082	1880	1893

Source: Information received from SIDA.

developing countries as well as for development projects in the Third World.[10] Humanitarian organisations, the co-operative movement and trade union organisations receive an increasing part of SIDA's NGO funds, most of which are used for activities within the fields of education, health and agriculture. Aid through NGOs is considered a valuable supplement to official aid, since the NGOs are in a special position to promote the general goals of development co-operation by contributing to the growth of NGOs in less developed countries, by supporting neglected groups and by testing inovations and initiating experiments. Further, the development work of the NGOs contributes to an increased interest, knowledge and involvement in regard to the poorest countries within Swedish society. SIDA's contributions to Swedish NGOs are governed by the government's general policy for development assistance to countries receiving official aid from Sweden. SIDA grants can be given to Swedish non-profit NGOs for the following purposes:

(i) well-defined development work in Third World countries, provided SIDA has adequate opportunities to check how SIDA grants are used;
(ii) development work in all sectors receiving Swedish official aid;
(iii) preparatory studies and multiyear projects;
(iv) volunteers;
(v) projects and personnel that are accepted by the pertinent authorities in the country.

To qualify for a grant, the Swedish organisation should be:

(i) non-profit organisation;
(ii) administratively stable;
(iii) contribute substantially (at least 20 per cent of the total costs) to the projects;
(iv) be actively involved in the planning, execution and evaluation of the project;
(v) produce satisfactory reports.

Requests from Swedish NGOs for SIDA grants may be submitted to SIDA twice a year, prior to 1 March and 1 September deadlines. Decisions are made public within four months after the application deadline.

Techniques Applied and Problems of Aid Evaluation

Sweden has for its development co-operation programme adopted the philosophy of recipient orientation and country programming since experience has convinced the Swedish authorities of the advantage of this approach compared with the previously applied techniques. During its first years Swedish development assistance was programmed on a project basis, and this continued to be the case even after the adoption of a policy, dating from the middle of the 1960s, whereby the available resources were to be concentrated on co-operation with a limited number of countries. It was not until after the transfer of resources when these countries acquired greater financial and political significance that it became increasingly important to have a more comprehensive approach to the resource planning for each country. Thus, along with some other donor countries, Sweden began to evolve a system for country programming during the early 1970s. Country programming, as practised by Sweden, has the following characteristics:[11]

(1) The needs and priorities of the recipient country as articulated by its government form the basis for the planning.
(2) The planning is based on the minimum amount to be made available during the three-year period for the country concerned.
(3) The planning aims at an agreement on the composition of the programme and on the terms and modalities of the transfer of resources.

The degree of coverage of the aid programme submitted to evaluation in the future cannot be easily determined since the responsibility rests with the recipient countries, but generally built-in evaluation is preferred by SIDA. SIDA regards evaluation as a management tool aiming at increasing the effectiveness and efficiency of the project by giving the project implementers the information necessary for steering the project towards higher goal fulfilment, and the organisation hopes that more projects and programmes will be evaluated as an integrated component of the project in the future, since responsible authorities in the recipient countries are becoming increasingly aware of the value of a well-run evaluation system. Most evaluations are carried out by outside consultants, often by a team agreed upon by the two parties concerned, and SIDA assists in selecting consultants, writing terms of reference and giving service to the evaluation teams. SIDA tries to engage the host government agency for the evaluation work and does not usually wish to carry out evaluations of its own. If the host country so wishes, however, SIDA is prepared to administer the evaluation work, more or less as a service. As for problems in evaluation, major issues to be considered are identification of the needs that the project should satisfy; formulation of goals and purposes and analysis of goals; identification of conflicts and inter-relationships between goals; analysis of external factors and their influence; identification of side-effects; analysis of goal attainment and means of improving it, etc.[12] Evaluation is mainly considered as a management tool to give steering impulses and a problem of great importance is how to utilise the findings in the most appropriate way, so that findings can be presented to government or project managers in order really to improve ongoing projects.

SIDA comments from field experience stressed the importance of improvements of on-going projects, improved knowledge of crucial factors for the success or failure of projects in the same field, improved design of new projects, better awareness of the importance of good project preparation and goal analysis, and awareness of some of the risks in projects aiming at economic development (such as widened income gaps).

APPENDIX 9.1 The Flow of Financial Resources to Developing Countries and Multilateral Agencies by Type (1970–80)
Country: Sweden

Disbursements Net disbursements	1970	1971	1972	1973	1974	1975	1976	1977	1978	1979	US$m 1980
I Official Development Assistance (a + b)	117.0	158.9	197.7	275.3	401.7	566.0	607.6	779.4	782.6	956.1	923.1
(a) Bilateral ODA	63.1	67.7	106.7	153.1	233.8	373.2	401.3	486.0	473.0	619.2	675.8
(b) Contributions to multilateral institutions	53.9	91.2	91.0	122.2	167.9	192.8	206.3	293.3	309.6	336.8	247.3
II Other Official Flows (a + b)	—	—	—	—	—	—	—	1.5	19.9	2.2	8.0
(a) Bilateral OOF	—	—	—	—	—	—	—	—	18.8	—	8.0
(b) Multilateral institutions	—	—	—	—	—	—	—	1.5	1.1	2.2	0.0
Subtotal (I + II): Total official flows	117.0	158.9	197.7	275.3	401.7	566.0	607.6	780.9	802.5	958.2	931.2
III Grants by private voluntary agencies	25.2	23.6	27.2	29.9	32.9	38.8	43.4	43.5	44.3ᵃ	49.0	59.0
IV Private flows at market terms (1–4)	87.1	61.1	48.2	54.3	205.8	147.7	483.4	730.9	490.7	274.0	846.3
(1) Direct investment	36.5	40.1	41.9	21.9	49.0	82.2	125.0	126.3	115.0	127.4	90.1
(2) Bilateral portfolio investment and other	5.7	5.0	4.1	11.9	3.6	1.1	12.4	258.3	174.3	14.7	19.6
(3) Multilateral portfolio investment	5.0	−2.7	6.1	17.5	11.2	0.8	−0.6	0.1	−0.4	−0.5	0.0
(4) Private export credits	30.9	18.7	−3.9	3.0	142.0	63.6	346.6	346.2	201.4	132.4	736.6
V Total resource flows (I–IV)	229.3	243.5	273.1	359.5	640.4	752.4	1,134.4	1,555.2	1,337.5	1,281.3	1,836.5
ODA as % of GNP	0.38	0.44	0.48	0.56	0.72	0.82	0.82	0.99	0.90	0.94	0.76
Total resource flows as % of GNP	0.74	0.67	0.66	0.73	1.15	1.09	1.53	1.98	1.53	1.26	1.51

Sources: OECD, Development Co-operation, Reviews 1974–81.

10 The Commission of the European Economic Community

THE PERFORMANCE OF EEC[1] OFFICIAL DEVELOPMENT ASSISTANCE

The flow of financial resources to developing countries and multilateral agencies by the EEC is only in the form of official flows. Net ODA by EEC reached $1245.8m in 1980 compared with $1257.3m in 1979, $721.7m in 1975 and $375.3m in 1973. Bilateral official development assistance by the EEC constitutes the major component of ODA while contributions to multilateral institutions, which started in 1974, represent on the average 14 per cent of ODA during the period 1974-78, 11 per cent in 1979 and 19 per cent in 1980. Other official flows are only in the form of bilateral flows which reached $257.2m in 1980 compared with $162.3m in 1979, $26.6m in 1975 and $6.5m in 1973. Thus total official flows by the EEC reached $1503.0m in 1980 compared with $1419.6m in 1979, $748.3m in 1975 and $381.8m in 1973. Total official flows by the EEC increased during the period 1973-75, declined in 1976 but increased again in the following four years – see Appendix 10.1 and Chart 9. Grants and grant-like contributions represented 89 per cent of the bilateral official development assistance provided by the EEC in 1980 compared with 75 per cent in 1979, and 100 per cent in 1973. Food aid grants represented the main contribution by the EEC to multilateral institutions, especially during the period 1977-80, as it reached 87 per cent on the average, whereas food aid in the form of bilateral development assistance represented on the average about 33 per cent during the same period.[2] Most of this aid was granted directly by the EEC; the main recipients in 1978 were Vietnam, Egypt, Bangladesh, Pakistan and India, which together received more than 50 per cent of such direct aid; 33 per cent was channelled into the African, Caribbean

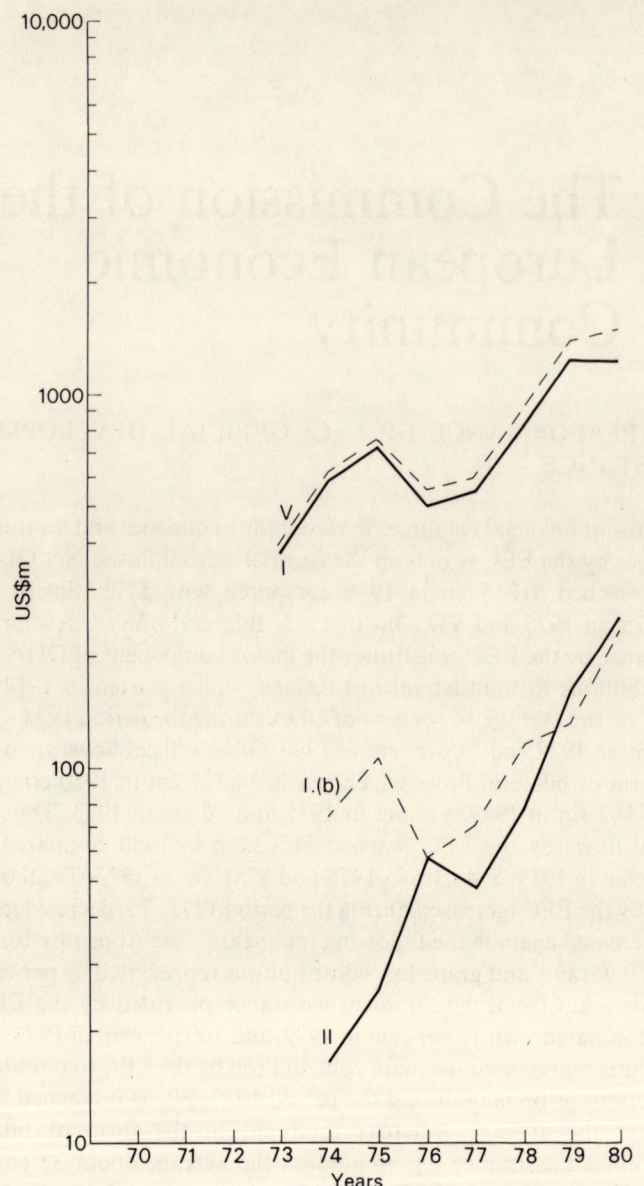

CHART 9 Flow of financial resources to developing countries and multilateral agencies by type: EEC 1973–80

Source: Appendix 10.1

and Pacific (ACP) State signatories of the Lomé Convention. The remaining balance of community food aid is disbursed primarily through the World Food Programme, UNICEF and the United Nations High Commissioner for Refugees who, in 1978, distributed more than 10 per cent of indirect EEC food aid as against 1 per cent in 1977.[3]

Community financial aid to developing countries is governed by three different sets of contractual arrangements:

(1) The Lomé Convention, which establishes full contractual relations between the Community and the developing countries of Africa (South of the Sahara), the Caribbean and the Pacific and encompasses the trade sector and co-operation in the financial, industrial, agricultural, mining, energy and other fields.
(2) Bilateral agreements between the Community and the Southern Mediterranean Countries (Maghreb, Mashreq, Israel – the MMI agreements).
(3) Council decisions providing for Community financial aid to other developing countries (in Latin America and South-East Asia) – known as the 'non-associated' developing countries.

It should be noted that the largest sums are those European Units and Accounts (EUA) provided for in the two Lomé Conventions (3500m EUA in the case of Lomé I, and 5600m EUA under Lomé II).[4] These resources are managed partly by the European Investment Bank but primarily by the Commission (The European Development Fund – EDF): 3000m EUA under Lomé I; 4500m EUA under Lomé II. The volume of resources available under the MMI agreements totals 699m EUA for the period 1977–81, and the non-associated developing countries were allocated financial aid totalling 110m EUA in 1979.

DEVELOPMENT ASSISTANCE POLICY OF THE EEC UNDER THE LOMÉ CONVENTIONS

The first Lomé Convention (Lomé I) covered the period 1975–80, followed by the second Lomé Convention (Lomé II), signed on 31 October 1979, which covers the period 1980–85, between the Community and 58 'ACP States'.[5] Lomé II is the second convention governing trade and other relations between the groups; the first Lomé

Convention expired on 1 March 1980, at the end of the long and tense negotiations summarised below.

A two-day ministerial meeting between the nine Common Market countries, The European Commission and the ACP states opened in Brussels (Belgium) on 13 March 1978 to start preliminary negotiations on the renewal of the Lomé I Convention. The Convention which was signed on 28 February 1975 was a novel contractual arrangement linking the industrialised and developing worlds. In addition to providing for concessionary treatment on trade, development aid and technical co-operation, it embodied the so-called 'Stabex' system for stabilising ACP countries' receipts from exports of more than thirty commodities. Payments from Stabex are made automatically when a country's export receipts from a given commodity in any one year fall below a fixed reference level. In most cases, the EEC guarantees only receipts from exports to the Community and requires that any product covered should account for more than 7.5 per cent of a country's total export earnings. A common complaint among the ACP countries was that Stabex did not compensate them for losses in purchasing power caused by rising production costs and imported inflation. They demanded that the Lomé II Convention should include a mechanism to protect their real earnings, and also wanted Stabex to be applied to additional products, particularly minerals like copper and phosphates. There was also pressure to free at least the very poorest countries from the 7.5 per cent limit and the obligation to refund money to Stabex when commodity prices rose above certain levels. Countries with few natural resources, which are heavily dependent on tourism, showed interest in a suggestion by the Seychelles that the EEC should protect them against sharp falls in tourist receipts. The issue of human rights was raised by Dr David Owen, then the UK Foreign Secretary, who suggested the granting of benefits under Lomé II should be made subject to the respect of human rights in the recipient countries. Most ACP leaders made it clear however that they saw no place for a politically controversial human rights clause in what they regarded as an arrangement for economic and technical co-operation. Some ACP states believed, however, that if the EEC forced the issue it should be met by counter-demands for concessions in the treatment of immigrant workers and stronger measures by European governments against social discrimination.[6]

The European Economic Community made concessions to the ACP countries which had been complaining of lack of progress in negotiations for a new trade and aid pact, at a one-day ministerial meeting in

Brussels on 21 December 1978. The Community agreed to study the effects of inflation on the export earnings of ACP countries, although the EEC was not ready to accept any kind of indexed formula. The EEC also agreed to study, on a case-by-case basis, products, especially minerals such as copper, which were not included in the Stabex export earnings compensation scheme of the Lomé I Convention. The meeting was not intended to reach agreements but to study the possibility of speeding up negotiations which the EEC hoped to conclude before the UNCTAD V meeting in Manila in May 1979. There was agreement on a large number of objectives in May 1979, especially in industrial co-operation, but the EEC resisted the ACP demands for setting up a special fund for industrial co-operation.[7]

During three days of ministerial negotiations in Freeport (Bahamas) in March 1979 the EEC and ACP nations agreed to conclude negotiations on Lomé II, a new trade and aid pact. The most important issue was the size of the aid package to be committed to the ACP countries. The thirty-one poorest countries were given easier terms than those previously given on the Community's Stabex scheme, which covered iron and nineteen agricultural products. They qualified for Stabex payments if earnings from a specific product dropped by more than 2 per cent from average level of the four preceding years, compared with 2.5 per cent under the first convention. This fluctuation threshold dropped to 6.5 from 7.5 per cent for other ACP states. The terms under which Stabex payments must be refunded to the Stabex funds if export earnings rebound were also clarified. Lomé II gave countries seven years to make their repayments, with two years grace for poor countries, and more if bad years intervened. The EEC also announced in the Bahamas meeting that sesame had been added to the list of products covered by the Stabex scheme, with immediate effect. The principal beneficiaries were Sudan and Ethiopia.[8]

A small increase in the EEC's financial offer to the ACP countries, negotiating a successor to the 1976–80 Lomé Convention, led to the reopening of talks in Brussels on 25 June 1979. The ACP group broke off talks in May 1979 when presented with an offer including total funding of 5.1bn European Currency Units ($6.6bn) which the Community insisted was final and non-negotiable. When talks resumed in June 1979, the EEC negotiators agreed to increase this amount by around 300m ECUs to be made available in loans through the European Investment Bank (EIB). They also agreed to transfer the cost of maintaining EEC delegations in ACP countries to the Community's own budget, releasing 180m ECUs within the original 5.1bn offer for development projects.

The main points of the Lomé II Convention are as follows:[9]

(1) *Financial Aid*: the EEC provides aid totalling 5.6bn Units of Account (about $7.5bn) during the five-year period of the new Convention, an increase of 2.2bn Units of Account on aid under the expired Lomé I agreement.
(2) *Trade*: quotas for certain products remaining in the 5 per cent of the total ACP exports still subject to customs duty will be increased. The ACP countries wanted all these remaining goods to be duty-free.
(3) *Stabex*: the stabilisation system applied to export earnings under the first Convention, which applied to nineteen agricultural products and to iron ore, has been extended to take in ten new products.
(4) *Minerals*: the main innovation of the Lomé II Convention is a system aimed at enabling ACP countries to 'maintain their production potential' in the mining sector. This scheme covers copper, cobalt, manganese, phosphates, tin, iron ore, bauxite and alumina and, among African countries, is of interest to Zaire, Zambia, Togo, Senegal, Guinea, Gabon, Mauritania, Liberia and Rwanda. If their production falls by over 10 per cent they can ask for an EEC loan to help keep up production. This would carry an interest rate of 1 per cent per year and be repayable within forty years.
(5) *Industrial Co-operation*: under the Lomé II Convention the EEC will help ACP countries' industrial development, particularly with manufactured products.
(6) *Agricultural Co-operation*: a technical co-operation centre has been set up to ensure the best dissemination of technological inovations.
(7) *Investment Protection*: another innovation is the special attention drawn to the protection of European investments in ACP countries. The Convention indicated that the promotion of private investment in mining and energy sectors may be based on specific investment protection agreements.

The basic fundamentals of the Lomé policy are as follows:[10]

(1) Dependable co-operation relations based on a system of entitlement laid down in a freely negotiated contract between equal partners.
(2) One contract binding two regional groups, excluding any man-

ipulation or discrimination inspired by unilateral assessments of the partners' sovereign choice of economic systems, political regimes and development models. This means non-alignment and respect for national and cultural individuality.
(3) A global approach defining and combining a whole series of instruments of co-operation which provides a well balanced response, in the light of the priorities the ACP countries themselves define, to needs that vary with economic structure and level of development.
(4) Co-operation based on a permanent dialogue ensured by the institutional structure taken over from Lomé I, and in which consultations have been stepped up over much wider scope.

The institutional structure of EEC–ACP co-operation of Lomé II maintains the existing institutional structure but certain measures have been taken to improve the operation of the institutions as follows:[11]

(1) *The EEC–ACP Council of Ministers*: meets once a year and is the top decision- and policy-making body. The new convention should make it possible to work out more detailed arrangements for holding consultations and exchanges of views between meetings.
(2) *The Committee of Ambassadors*: meets at least twice a year. It supervises and stimulates a large number of subcommittees (committees on industrial co-operation, trade co-operation and so on). The Convention makes provision for new specialised committees to be set up, notably one on the administration of financial and technical co-operation.
(3) *The Consultative Assembly*: consisting of delegates from the ACP countries and members of the European Parliament, meets at least once a year. The subjects for discussion are prepared by a Joint Committee, which normally meets twice a year.
(4) *Consultations with the Two Sides of Industry*: can be arranged on the initiative of the Assembly. *Ad hoc* meetings can also be held under the aegis of the EEC–ACP Council 'on clearly defined matters of common interest'.

The EEC's development policy towards the Third World combines two approaches: special contractual agreements on a regional basis, and action at world level.[12] The Community has concluded a wide range of regional agreements: the Lomé Agreements, the agreements with the

Maghreb countries and with Mashreq countries. These kinds of regional agreements combine all types of financial, technical and commercial action, written into international treaties ratified by the parliaments. The Community's global policy for co-operation with the Third World, taking account of the growing interdependence between North and South, needs greater financial resources. But financial aid by itself is only one aspect of the problem. Developing countries must be able to guarantee their export earnings against violent fluctuations, they need to have the best possible access to the industrialised world's markets, to acquire industrial technology and know-how easily and cheaply. Thus the EEC's Co-operation Policy with developing countries could only be recognised as being of marginal importance as long as it consisted of financial aid only. Once it includes guaranteed export earnings (Stabex system), guaranteed selling at fixed prices (ACP sugar-cane agreement), action for industrial redeployment, access to European technology for developing countries (EEC–ACP industrial co-operation), and movement of workers (agreements with Maghreb countries), the very notion of international division of labour is called in question. For it then directly affects the Community's economy and Community industries and workers. For a successful global development policy, the Community has to be ready to assume the economic and political consequences within its own economic zone. Productivity gains, transfers or reductions in activity should be taken into account financially, socially and politically. In return for opening its economic zone to help the Third World Countries' development, the EEC benefits from a new economic zone of considerable size: an area it lacks. In contrast to large continents such as the USA and the USSR, the Community does not have sufficient supplies, markets and natural assets to guarantee its future. Hence the need for co-operation with the Third World is a must.

AID ADMINISTERED BY THE COMMISSION OF THE EUROPEAN COMMUNITIES

The European Development Fund

Resources and Procedures of Financing

The European Development Fund is financed not from the Community budget and its own resources, but by fixed contributions from the member states. The fund is endowed for the whole lifetime of the implementing convention[13] (five years) and is free of the constraints of annual budgeting. The relationship enshrined in the convention is one of co-operation, not assistance and, as a matter of principle, EDF-financed operations are devised and implemented jointly by the donors and recipients of Community funds. Moreover, as the Commission is accountable to the Council and Parliament for the financial management of the EDF and the use made of EDF resources, it has to give an account of its stewardship and must therefore supervise the implementation of projects. One of the main ways in which it does this is through its representatives on the spot, the Commission Delegates. One of the most important innovations contained in the first Lomé Convention and reaffirmed under Lomé II is the greater responsibility of the recipient state for the administration and management of aid. The previous conventions[14] undoubtedly ensured that responsibility was to some extent shared, but the two Lomé Conventions have gone further, providing for active participation by the recipient states at each stage of the project; programming of the aid, project design and appraisal, preparation of the financing decisions, implementation of the project and evaluation of the results.

Aid Programming

Programming takes place in two separate stages:

(1) Pre-programming, which allows co-ordination and exchanges of views at Community level on the performance and aims of Community aid to the various recipient countries.
(2) Programming proper, which involves negotiations with the recipient country's authorities to finalise an indicative aid programme.

In addition to these two stages, there may also be a 'post-programming' stage, if a majority of the Community member states feel, after seeing the indicative programme that there should be an exchange of views on its contents and implications.

Project Design and Appraisal

Each state is responsible for the preparation of the projects and programmes put forward in the jointly-devised Community Aid Programme. If requested, the Community may provide technical assistance for the compilation of project dossiers. The state initiates a request for financing, as was the case under previous conventions, and as soon as Commission officials receive a request for financing, they appraise the project in question, in close collaboration with the country concerned. For the purposes of implementing the EDF, there is a division of labour between the Commission and the European Investment Bank. The Commission is responsible for the appraisal of projects financed by grants or special loans (80 per cent of the total). The EIB, in addition to financing projects from its own resources, appraises interest rate subsidies and risk capital. Appraisal involves the scrutiny of a project from all angles – economic, social, financial, technical and administrative.

Financing the Project

Before a financing proposal is submitted to the Community's decision-making bodies, it goes either to the EDF Committee or to the EIB Committee, depending on the type of financing, for an opinion. Both committees are composed of representatives of the member states' governments. The EDF Commttee returns an opinion on financing proposals for projects to be financed by grant or special loan. The committee takes its decisions by a weighted qualified majority requiring 69 out of 100 votes. The EIB Committee gives its opinion on financing proposals for projects to be financed by subsidised loans or risk capital. Its voting procedures are the same as those of the EDF Committee. Accompanied by the opinion of the appropriate committee, the financing proposal is then submitted to the Commission (grants and special loans) or the EIB's Board of Directors (subsidised loans or risk capital) for a final decision.

Problems of Implementation and Remarks from Field Experience

While the Commission is responsible for the financial administration of the EDF and for ensuring that its resources are used properly, it has never engaged in 'turnkey' projects, preferring to allow the authorities in beneficiary countries to take responsibility for overseeing implementation. Moreover, the Commission has set up a decentralised control system enabling it to see that EDF-financed operations are carried out in accordance with the convention and the regulations based on it. This supervisory function is performed by the Commission Delegates.[15]

In an interview, one of the officials from the Commission indicated that Africa received the highest share of the Community's financing due to colonial historical background and before the UK joined the European Common Market. The influence of France for the former French African Colonies was great and the Commission is trying now to moderate the picture to make it rather more balanced. On the other hand, the belief behind the ACP states is that the financial resources entitled for these countries are their right, and there is a belief that the Commission should adopt its policies according to the demands from ACP states as the key element in this sort of assistance. Moreover, the problems of different information received by different donors from recipient countries are considered to be of great importance, due mainly to the wide discrepancies of figures presented. Thus, co-financing, co-ordination and co-operation among different donors financing the same project in the same country are considered to be of the utmost importance.

Stage Reached in the Lomé II Programming

An initial stock-taking on the basis of an examination of twenty-nine Indicative Programmes (IP) established (as at 7 May 1980) suggests that the priority areas on which the Community's financial aid will focus during the Lomé II conventions are as follows:[16]

		% of the total programmed
(1)	Rural development	40
(2)	Energy and mining	6
(3)	Transport and communications	18
(4)	Housing, town planning, drainage, water supplies	9
(5)	Welfare sector	12
(6)	Technical co-operation	3
(7)	Specific instruments of co-operation (micro projects, trade promotion, industrial co-operation, etc.)	3

According to the advance timetables adopted with each of the ACP states during the programming, the overall face of commitments year by year (which is liable to change) appear to be as follows:

1st Year 13%
2nd Year 23%
3rd Year 28%
4th Year 22%
5th Year 14%

The second Lomé Convention provides for Community financial aid from both European Development Fund (EDF) resources (4542m EUA), comprising Member States' budgetary contributions, and from the EIB's own resources. The finance is to be managed as follows:[17]

	(EUAm)
Commission of the European Communities (from EDF resources)	
Grants	2753
Loans on special conditions	504
Transfers for the stabilisation of export earnings (Stabex)	550
Special financing facility for mineral products (Sysmin)	280
European Investment bank	
Loans from the EIB's own resources	685
Risk capital from EDF resources	280
Interest subsidies from EDF resources	175
In addition, the Community has provided for the possibility of financing from the EIB's own resources for mining and energy projects of mutual interest to the ACP state concerned and the Community, for an amount totalling up to	200

Loans from the bank's own resources (that is, chiefly the proceeds of its borrowings on the capital markets) attract an interest subsidy for which an aggregate amount of EUA 175m has been earmarked from EDF grants. This subsidy is normally 3 per cent, although, where necessary, it will automatically be adjusted so that the interest rate actually borne by the borrower is neither less than 5 per cent nor more than 8 per cent. Moreover, in accordance with a Community declaration annexed to the second Lomé Convention, the EIB may commit up to a further EUA 200m in the form of loans from its own resources for mining and energy projects of mutual interest to the state concerned and the Community. These loans are subject to particular conditions: they are not eligible for interest subsidies and must be approved on a case-by-case basis by the bank's Board of Governors. Parallel to the second Lomé Convention, and in line with previous conventions, a Decision of the Council of Ministers of the European Communities provides for specific aid for Overseas Countries and Territories (OCT) enjoying special ties with certain member countries.

The European Investment Bank[18]

Establishment and Financial Resources

The European Investment Bank (EIB) was created as a non-profit independent public institution by the Treaty of Rome. The members of the European Investment Bank are the nine member states of the Community, who have all subscribed to its capital which stood at EUA 7200m,[19] as at 1 January 1981. The amount paid-in or to be paid-in being EUA 925.71m. Greece, which had become associated to the Community, became the bank's tenth member upon accession to the EEC on 1 January 1981.

For development finance outside the European Economic Community, ceiling amounts over five-year periods are laid down in Financial Protocols (concluded with individual countries or groups of countries). In these countries the bank uses both its own resources collected in the market and budget resources provided by the EEC. The bank raises the bulk of the funds required for financing its lending operations on the capital markets of the Community and non-member countries, and on international markets. Capital is subscribed by member states; the bulk of resources, however, comes from borrowings – principally public or private bond issues on national capital markets inside and outside the Community and on the international market. Table 10.1 shows the capital structure and the borrowings of the bank.

A doubling of the EIB's subscribed capital to 14.4bn ECUs[20] was approved, subject to national budgetary procedures, by the bank's Board of Governors (composed of one Minister from each of the ten EEC Member States) at its annual meeting in Luxembourg on 15 June. The part of the increase to be paid in by the member states is set at 540m ECUs (7.5 per cent), which will bring the total amount of the bank's capital paid-in or to be paid-in to 1,465.715m ECUs. The member states will pay in the 540m ECUs in eight half-yearly instalments, the first on 30 April 1984. The bank's capital structure therefore changes as follows (in million ECUs):

	Subscribed	As from 31.12.1981 Paid-in and to be paid-in	%
Germany	3,150.00	320.625	21.875
France	3,150.00	320.625	21.875
United Kingdom	3,150.00	320.625	21.875
Italy	2,520.00	256.505	17.50
Belgium	829.50	84.43	5.76
Netherlands	829.50	84.43	5.76
Denmark	420.00	42.75	2.925
Greece	225.00	22.90	1.563
Ireland	105.00	10.6875	0.729
Luxembourg	21.00	2.1375	0.146
Total	14,400	1,465.715	100

Source: *Annual Meeting of the Governors of the European Investment Bank*, Press Release, Luxembourg, 15 June 1981.

TABLE 10.1 Capital Structure and Borrowing of the European Investment Bank

Capital structure (as at 1 January 1981)		EUAm[a]		Borrowings 1961-80	
	Subscribed capital[b]	Total paid-in and to be paid-in[b]	%	Year	EUAm
Germany	1,575.00	202.50	21.875	1961-72	1,973.5
France	1,575.00	202.50	21.875	1973	612.3
United Kingdom	1,575.00	202.50	21.875	1974	825.5
Italy	1,260.00	162.00	17.50	1975	830.7
Belgium	414.75	53.325	5.76	1976	748.9
Netherlands	414.75	53.325	5.76	1977	1,161.5
Denmark	210.00	27.00	2.925	1978	1,949.7
Greece	112.50	14.46	1.563	1979	2,481.2
Ireland	52.50	6.75	0.729	1980	2,466.8
Luxembourg	10.50	1.35	0.146	1980	2,466.8
Total	7,200.0	925.71	100.0		13,050.1

[a] The Board of Governors is to examine in 1981 proposals concerning the bank's next capital increase.

[b] The capital set to be paid-in equals approximately 13 per cent of the subscribed capital; all or part of the remainder could be called in by decision of the Board of Directors should the bank's obligations towards lenders' ever require this.

Source: European Investment Bank, *Brochure*, January 1981.

Scope of Activities

The bank's basic function under Article 130 of the Rome Treaty is to contribute, on a non-profit-making basis, to the balanced development of the Community. The EIB grants and guarantees long-term loans to enterprises, public authorities and financial institutions to finance projects contributing to regional development, projects for converting undertakings or creating fresh activities and projects of common interest to several member states or the Community as a whole. Article 18 of the bank's Statute, which forms a Protocol to the Treaty of Rome, provides for financing operations in non-member countries (on special authorisation from the EIB's Board of Governors).

Lending inside the Community to end-1980 totalled almost EUA 15bn (roughly US $19.5bn): half of this sum had been provided since 1978. In 1980 alone, lending in the Community totalled almost EUA 3bn (US $3.9bn). Regional development has always had priority and about 70 per cent of lending has gone to investment in less-favoured regions, where the problems are most serious. The bank intends to play a major role in Community efforts to help recovery of the areas in Southern Italy hit by the November 1980 earthquake.

Finance is provided for almost every sector of industry and for all main branches of infrastructure (water, sewerage, irrigation, transport and telecommunications, improved gas or electricity supplies to serve industry). The EIB gives special emphasis to helping small and medium-sized industrial ventures (particularly important in terms of job creation) by making global loans to regional or national financing bodies which use the funds to support investments chosen in agreement with the EIB: by end-1980 some 90 global loans had been made worth about EUA 1bn (US $1.3bn) from which credits had been provided for 1750 ventures. Action in financing projects of common interest centred recently on limiting Community dependence upon oil imports by:

(i) developing European resources, for example North Sea and Mediterranean oil and gas; hydro, nuclear, coal-burning and geothermal power stations; coal and uranium mining and peat extraction;
(ii) diversifying imports, for example the Algeria–Italy gasline;
(iii) saving energy, for example rationalising consumption in industry, the production of insulation materials.

Energy projects supported by the EIB during 1977–80 were planned when completed to provide extra resources or enable economies equivalent in total to about 50m tons of oil per year (corresponding to ± 12 per cent of Community imports in 1980). Under the same common interest, the EIB finances investment in improved communications between member countries; industrial projects involving co-operation between enterprises from different EEC countries; development of European capacities in advanced technology fields and protection of the environment. Table 10.2 shows a survey of financing provided by the bank.

Table 10.2 Finance Provided by EIB from 1958 to 1980

Location	1980 Amount (EUAm)	%	1973–80 Amount (EUAm)	%	1958–80 Amount (EUAm)	%
Community						
Belgium	153.2	5.2	318.6	2.6	385.8	2.6
Denmark	99.3	3.4	307.1	2.5	307.1	2.1
Germany	14.2	0.5	547.4	4.4	901.0	6.1
France	279.0	9.5	1,739.8	14.0	2,310.2	15.5
Ireland	376.0	12.7	1,076.9	8.7	1,076.9	7.2
Italy	1,290.3	43.7	4,752.7	38.2	6,165.0	41.4
Luxembourg	—	—	—	—	9.0	0.1
Netherlands	—	—	62.3	0.5	105.2	0.7
United Kingdom	688.0	23.3	3,421.3	27.5	3,421.3	23.0
Non-member countries[a]	50.8	1.7	200.8	1.6	200.8	1.3
Subtotal[b]	2,950.8	100.0	12,426.9	100.0	14,882.3	100.0
Outside the Community						
From the bank's own resources	371.4	67.8	1,381.5	69.3	1,537.2	64.6
From budgetary resources	176.3	32.2	613.2	30.7	844.1	35.4
Subtotal	547.7	100.0	1,994.7	100.0	2,381.3[c]	100.0
Total	3,498.5	—	14,421.6	—	17,263.6	—

[a] Loans granted for energy projects in Austria, Norway and Tunisia but of direct importance to the Community.
[b] Including loans from the resources of the New Community Instrument for borrowing and lending (1979: EUA277m of which 105.3m in the United Kingdom, 86.7m in Ireland and 85m in Italy; 1980: EUA197.6m of which 137.8m in Italy, 41.7m in Ireland and 18.2m in Denmark).
[c] Of which EUA351.4m in Greece prior to its accession to the Community (341.4m own resources, 10m budgetary resources).
Source: European Investment Bank, *Brochure*, January 1981.

Operations within the Community

Loans granted for investment projects located in member countries amounted to EUA 2753.2m in 1980 as against 2281.2m in 1979 and 1966.5m in 1978. This rise of 21 per cent in 1980, as against 30 per cent in 1979 and 40 per cent in 1978, was achieved against a background of continuing economic difficulties, meeting the desire expressed by the European Council on 25 and 26 March 1977 for the bank to step up its activity in favour of creating jobs, raising the level of investment and halting divergence in member countries' economic performances. Projects for which the bank provided financing conform to its statutory terms of reference: regional development projects, projects for modernising or converting enterprises, and projects of common interest to several member countries or to the community as a whole. Table 10.3

TABLE 10.3 EIB's Financing Provided within the Community in 1980 and from 1958–80: Breakdown by Economic Policy Objectives

Objective	1980 (EUAm)	%	1958–80 (EUAm)	%
Regional development	1,815.7	100.0	10,366.9	100.0
Belgium	6.2	0.3	90.0	0.9
Denmark	17.5	1.0	152.4	1.5
Germany	—	—	372.6	3.6
France	148.4	8.2	1,436.1	13.8
Ireland	318.7	17.5	925.4	8.9
Italy	825.4	45.5	4,776.5	46.1
Luxembourg	—	—	4.0	—
Netherlands	—	—	70.5	0.7
United Kingdom	499.5	27.5	2,539.4	24.5
Modernisation and conversion of undertakings	31.4	100.0	274.7	100.0
Common European interest	1,213.0	100.0	5,670.8	100.0
Energy	1,102.7	90.9	4,268.5	75.3
Communications	103.5	8.5	954.3	16.8
Other infrastructure	—	—	21.2	0.4
Protection of the environment	5.1	0.4	30.7	0.5
Industrial co-operation	1.7	0.2	366.1	6.5
New technology-research	—	—	30.5	0.5
Deduct to allow for duplication in the case of financing justified on the basis of several objectives.	−306.9		−1,904.7	
Total	2,753.2		14,407.7	

Source: European Investment Bank, Annual Report, 1980.

shows the bank's financing provided within the Community broken down by economic policy objectives.

Operations outside the Community

Since 1963, the bank has assisted in implementing the Community's policy of economic and financial co-operation with an increasing number of developing countries. Operations have been mounted under the various agreements, financial protocols and decisions concerning Greece, Turkey, the African, Caribbean and Pacific states, the overseas countries and territories (of France), Portugal, Yugoslavia and Lebanon. Between 1963 and 1978, these countries received a total of EUA 1320.6m., comprising EUA 744.9m from the bank's own resources and 575.7m from budgetary funds made available to the bank by member states, either directly or through the European Development Fund. 1979 marked a growth in bank financing which rose to EUA 512.9m of which 426.5m was channelled to countries in the Mediterranean region and 86.4m to ACP states. Furthermore, 1980 marked further growth in financing outside the Community, following the sharp upturn record in 1979. Table 10.4 shows the bank's financing provided outside the Community, broken down by region.

Approaches and Techniques Applied

The layout and contents of documents in the project file submitted to the bank are the responsibility of the borrower who may, if necessary, seek outside help with their preparation. During appraisal of a project, the bank keeps in close touch with the ACP country, enterprise or administrative body concerned, in order to obtain any additional information necessary and to discuss the main problems likely to arise before and after commissioning of the project. For industrial, mining or tourism projects, the documentation must cover the following main points.

General and Legal Information. About the enterprise, its principal partners or promoters:

> The enterprise: memorandum and articles of association, shareholders, tax regime, certificate of incorporation, concessions, activities, accounting and administrative structure, balance sheets, trading accounts, profit and loss accounts, movement of funds statement for

TABLE 10.4 EIB Financing Provided Outside the Community in 1980 and Cumulative up to 1980

Region	From EIB own resources	Special section operations	Total
		Amount (EUAm)	
1980			
Northern Mediterranean	215.0	135.0	350.0
Maghreb	25.0	20.0	45.0
Mashreq	7.0	—	7.0
Total	247.0	155.0	402.0
1963–80			
Northern Mediterranean	797.4	561.0	1358.4
Maghreb	75.0	34.0	109.0
Mashreq	118.7	3.8	122.5
Other	3.0	5.0	8.0
Total	994.1	603.8	1597.9
1980			
Africa	95.9	20.46	116.36
Caribbean	10.0	—	10.0
Pacific	11.5	—	11.5
Total ACP	117.4	20.46	137.86

Source: European Investment Bank, *Annual Report*, 1980.

the last three financial years, details of short, medium and long-term liabilities.
Principal partners and promoters: articles of association, shareholders, activities, references, balance sheets and profit and loss accounts for the last three financial years.

Technical data. General purpose, location, factors of production, rated and forecast production capacities.

Technical description: technology, site and site development, buildings, production and storage plant, general services, conveyance systems and equipment, measures to protect the environment.
Study and implementation: organisation, consultants (if any), procedures for awarding orders and contracts, supervision, work schedule.
Detailed estimate of investments, itemising site and plant expenditure, provision for contingencies and price rises, interest on capital

during construction, initial and start-up expenses, together with a cost breakdown in foreign and local currencies.
Operation: raw materials and products, flowcharts, consumption and input levels, managerial staff and workers, management organisation, technical assistance where applicable.

Economic data. Market: statistics showing present and forecast trends in supply, demand and prices.

Production outlets: sales policy and organisation, position of company in relation to main competitors, domestic and export sales.
Jobs created: permanent and seasonal jobs, numbers of expatriates and nationals, professional training, projected replacement of staff (if any).
Part played by the project in the development programme of the country concerned.
Data used for calculating the economic rate of return of the project and assessing its contribution to the economic development of the country concerned. Its impact on the balance of payments and public finance.

Financial data. Breakdown of operating costs, depreciation and overheads.

Projected trading accounts until the project comes fully on stream (with previous trading accounts, if any).
Estimate of working capital needed and changing requirements over the same period: stocks of raw materials, finished products, credits to customers, suppliers' credits.
Projected balance sheets and financial statements for the same period (with previous balance sheets, if any).
Financing plan for the project and schedule of projected expenditure.
Security offered.
Policy concerning return of the capital of the enterprise.

For infrastructure or energy projects, the information to be supplied must be tailored to the precise nature of the enterprise and the project. Additional details must be given on what needs the project is fulfilling, its implementation, potential use, pricing principles and methods, and the social costs and benefits to the Community.

Terms and Conditions

Interest Rate: very low on budget resources provided by EEC.
Subsidised rate for loans on bank resources.
Repayment Period: usually 10–15 years.
Grace Period: in line with the needs of the project.
Guarantee: normally government guarantee from recipient country.

Management and Administration

As a bank with specialised tasks, the EIB was given a legal personality and administrative structure separate from that of other Community institutions. It has its own decision-making bodies.

Board of Governors. One Minister from each member state (usually the Finance Minister): lays down general guidelines on credit policy, approves the balance sheet and annual report, decides on capital increases, appoints Directors, Members of the Management Committee and Audit Committee.

Board of Directors. Nineteen Members (eighteen high-level officials from public credit institutions, finance, economy and industry ministries nominated by member countries and one nominated by the Commission) and eleven alternates (ten nominated by member countries, one by the Commission): assures that the bank is managed according to the provisions of the Treaty of Rome, the bank's Statute, and directives laid down by the Governors; has sole responsibility for deciding on loans and guarantees, raising loans and fixing interest rates.

Management Committee. The full-time 'motor' of the bank: composed of the bank's President and, at present, four Vice-Presidents, the Committee controls all current operations, recommends decisions to the directors and is then responsible for carrying them out. The President presides as Chairman at meetings of the Board of Directors, the Vice-President as Vice-Chairmen.

Audit Committee. Three members chosen on the grounds of their competence (in practice officials responsible for public accounts in member countries) who verify that the operations of the bank have been conducted in a proper manner.

Organisation. Seven Directorates: General Administration, headed by the Secretary-General; Operations in the Community; Operations outside the Community; Finance and Treasury; Research; Legal; Technical Advisory Service.

Future Strategy for Financing

Depending on the conclusion of agreements provided for financial assistance between developing countries and the EEC.

APPENDIX 10.1 The Flow of Financial Resources to Developing Countries and Multilateral Agencies by Type (1970–80)
EEC

US$m

Disbursements Net disbursements	1973	1974	1975	1976	1977	1978	1979	1980
I Official Development Assistance (a+b)	375.3	597.5	721.7	501.1	549.2	804.6	1,257.3	1,245.8
(a) Bilateral ODA	375.3	521.6	613.9	442.9	477.9	684.8	1,124.4	1,013.1
(b) Contributions to multilateral institutions	—	75.9	107.8	58.2	71.3	119.8	132.9	232.7
II Other Official Flows (a+b)	6.5	16.2	26.6	58.2	48.7	78.4	162.3	257.2
(a) Bilateral OOF	6.5	16.2	26.6	58.2	48.7	78.4	162.3	257.2
(b) Multilateral institutions	—	—	—	—	—	—	—	0.0
Subtotal (I+II): Total official flows	381.8	613.7	748.3	559.3	597.9	883.0	1,419.6	1,503.0
III Grants by private voluntary agencies	—	—	—	—	—	—	—	—
IV Private flows at market terms (1–4)	—	—	—	—	—	—	—	—
(1) Direct investment	—	—	—	—	—	—	—	—
(2) Bilateral portfolio investment and other	—	—	—	—	—	—	—	—
(3) Multilateral portfolio investment	—	—	—	—	—	—	—	—
(4) Private export credits	—	—	—	—	—	—	—	—
V Total Resource Flows (I–IV)	381.8	613.7	748.3	559.3	597.9	883.0	1,419.6	1,503.0

Sources: OECD, Development Co-operation, Reviews 1974–81.

Part II

The Performance of OPEC Development Funds, Regional Development Banks and the World Bank Group

Case-studies

OPEC Funds:
Kuwait Fund, Abu Dhabi Fund, Saudi Fund, Arab Fund, Arab Bank for Economic Development in Africa, Islamic Development Bank and the OPEC Fund for International Development

Regional Banks:
African Development Bank, Asian Development Bank, Caribbean Development Bank and Inter-American Development Bank

World Bank Group:
International Bank for Reconstruction and Development, International Development Association and International Finance Corporation

11 The Performance of the Organisation of the Petroleum Exporting Countries

OPEC: A NEW FACTOR IN THE WORLD ECONOMY

The Organisation of Petroleum Exporting Countries, a new factor in the world economy, came into being in Baghdad in September 1960. Its headquarters are in Vienna, Austria. The founding members were Iran, Iraq, Kuwait, Saudi Arabia and Venezuela, which were at that time the most important exporters of oil. Qatar joined shortly afterwards, and Indonesia and Libya became members in 1962. Abu Dhabi followed in 1967, its membership subsequently being transferred to the United Arab Emirates. In 1969, Algeria became the tenth member and Nigeria joined in 1971. Ecuador joined in 1973 and in 1975, Gabon was accepted as a full member of OPEC. The Caribbean state of Trinidad and Tobago has observer status. The seven Arab OPEC states also belong to OAPEC (Organisation of Arab Petroleum Exporting Countries), the other OAPEC members being Bahrain, Egypt and Syria.[1] Egypt was suspended from OAPEC membership following the signature of the Camp David agreement with Israel in 1979. In 1973, two massive price increases were the culmination of a dramatic shift of bargaining power from the consumers to the producers of oil which had begun three years earlier in the summer of 1970. During this short period, which was marked by a succession of price adjustments and a string of takeovers of the operations of western companies in OPEC countries, the previous structure of the world's oil industry had been swept away. In the West this revolution was seen as an outright disaster, in OPEC states it was viewed as the triumphant conclusion of a twenty-year struggle for a fair return on a diminishing natural resource.[2] When Egyptian troops advanced across the Suez Canal in October 1973, they were the spearhead for a force far greater than any of them can have imagined. Their aim was merely to free the Israeli-occupied parts of Egypt in the Sinai Peninsula. Behind them, however, was the solidarity of the Arab Gulf states who for the first time united to use oil as an economic weapon, suspending supplies to the USA and some European countries. For two or three years the major industrial powers had been growing more conscious that resources which had been taken for granted in the supply of their expanding economies were not as inexhaustible as had been assumed in the previous decade when oil was a cheap source of energy. Controversies had developed between pessimists who had proved to their own satisfaction that many of the world's minerals would be exhausted within a single lifetime, and optimists who considered that the ingenuity of man would always produce timely substitutes. On top of the worry about the distant future there was the simple economic fact that a sharp worldwide boom had been raising the demand for and the prices of raw materials of all kinds to record levels.[3] Adjustment to a scarcity of oil imposed either because of price or of availability of supply means much more than a simple reversion to past techniques which use energy in smaller quantities or different forms. The fact that oil consumption has grown during a period of rapid industrialisation, itself based on cheap energy, means that adjustment must involve a much larger industrial base. Even if the growth rate of consumption is reduced, unconventional energy sources will have to be developed. These unconventional sources are of higher cost than current sources, and it follows that to justify investment in them conventional energy prices will have to rise.[4]

Much has been said about the adverse impact of oil price increases on the world economy particularly with respect to the problems of inflation and recession in the first half of the 1970s. A careful reading of the data indicates, however, that both recession and inflation in the international economy are traceable to the economic policies of the developed economies. The International Monetary Fund (IMF) has concluded that the proximate cause of the recession was the unexpectedly high rate of inflation. This unexpected strength of price pressure made it difficult for policy-makers to engage in another round of expansionary policy lest they should worsen inflationary pressures.[5] Thus, the impact of the rise in the price of imported oil on the economies of developing countries cannot be isolated from the other forces of change in the world economy that have influenced the economies of the Third World countries. There is no doubt, however, that a substantial increase in both concessional and non-concessional financial flows is necessary if developing countries are to cope with rising deficits and a mounting debt burden, maintaining at the same time a reasonable rate of growth. The responsibility for such an increase should fall on all donors; DAC as well as OPEC countries. There is growing concern about the ability of developing countries, especially the least developed among them, to cope with their mounting deficits whether due to the increase in the price of oil or the increase in the cost of imported food, fertilisers, machinery and manufactured goods from the industrial countries. The deficit on current account of the developing countries was projected to reach $73bn in 1980 compared with $28.2bn in 1977 and $45.6bn in 1975. Table 11.1 shows the development of current account for industrial, oil-exporting, and non-oil developing countries.

TABLE 11.1   Current Account for Industrial, Oil-exporting and Non-oil Developing Countries 1975–80
(US $bn)

	1975	1976	1977	1978	1979	1980
Industrial countries	16.2	−2.3	−5.6	29.5	−10.5	−30
Oil-exporting countries	35.0	40.0	31.8	5.9	68	100
Non-oil developing countries	−45.6	−32.2	−28.2	−36.7	−52.5	−73

Source: World Economic Outlook, The Current Picture, IMF, ID/80/1, 3 January 1980.

A critique on the impact of oil price increases[6] has pointed out that the picture of the current account of the non-oil developing countries is misleading on the ground that the deficits of the non-oil developing countries are not all due to a heavier oil import bill. They contain a bigger or a smaller part on account of their trade relations with the industrial countries. A major problem remains for most of the non-oil developing countries, but to what extent it is a problem related to oil prices can only be found by a close examination of the situation in each country. Table 11.2 shows the distribution of the oil import bill among the oil-importing developing countries.

The inordinate prominence given to oil price increases and their supposed impact on inflation, deflation and the external balance of the LLDCs seems to imply that OPEC countries are uniquely responsible for a good deal of the problems besetting the world economy. Such an implication, as GATT indicated, is both wrong and dangerous. It is dangerous since it shifts the responsibility to where it does not belong.[7]

TABLE 11.2 Net Oil Imports by Non-OPEC Developing Countries – 1978–79

Group	Number of countries	Net oil imports as % of total
Less than $50m[a]	30	2.0
Between $50m and $100m[b]	15	3.6
Between $100m and $250m[c]	13	6.4
Between $250m and $500m[d]	11	10.1
Between $500m and $1bn[e]	2	3.5
Above $1bn[f]	10	74.3
Total	81	100.0

[a] Countries in each of which the cost of oil imports is less than $20m per annum: Niger, Mauritania, Mali, Cape Verde, Laos, Belize, Benin, Chad, Nepal, Upper Volta, Rwanda, Central African Republic, Gambia, Burundi, Comoros, Western Samoa, Guinea-Bissau.
Between $20m and $50m per annum: Mauritius, Somalia, Barbados, Fiji, Madagascar, Uganda, Guinea, Afghanistan, Guadeloupe, Sierra Leone, Haiti, Togo, Malawi.
[b] Zimbabwe, Tanzania, Paraguay, Papua New Guinea, Honduras, Mozambique, Senegal, Mongolia, Surinam, Liberia, Guyana, Malta, Ethiopia, Cameroon, Yemen Arab Republic.
[c] Sri Lanka, Dominican Republic, Jordan, North Korea, Guatemala, Ghana, Viet Nam, Nicaragua, Costa Rica, Yemen Democratic Republic, El Salvador, Cyprus, Zambia.
[d] Jamaica, Chile, Sudan, Panama, Kenya, Bangladesh, Uruguay, Argentina, Colombia, Ivory Coast, Lebanon.
[e] Pakistan, Morocco.
[f] Brazil, South Korea, Turkey, Taiwan, India, Yugoslavia, Philippines, Thailand, Cuba, Singapore.

Source: Said El-Naggar, *The Impact of Oil Price Increase: A Critique*, The World Bank, unpublished document, 12 February 1980.

At the time of the 1973 oil price increase there were many who feared that the international monetary system would be unable to cope with the resulting massive financial flows. They were wrong, as the system successfully relent large OPEC surpluses to deficit countries. A massive increase in commercial bank lending was particularly important to this success.[8] The OPEC current account surplus for 1981 is likely to be around $87bn, a surplus that represents major money-making opportunities for international banks. The Arab oil exporters seem determined to see their own institutions play a bigger role but the bulk of their surplus is still likely to be deposited with the major western institutions, as it was after 1973 when the Arab institutions failed to profit after the first oil price raise of 1973–74 from the intermediation of funds between surplus and deficit countries. The big American, European and Japanese banks took the bulk of the business. Yet the emphasis amongst the Arab oil exporters is not so much on diverting deposits into their own institutions, though inevitably that trend must strengthen, rather it is on having sufficient institutions with enough capital and expertise to attract deposits in the inter-bank market and to stamp an Arab mark on international lending.[9]

Oil exporters argue that they require a special understanding as their present and future economic well-being is based upon depletion of a non-renewable asset. The foreign receipts from oil exports are not cumulative in this sense and, therefore, should not be considered as ordinary reserves. These countries generally have no self-sustaining economies from within and their international reserves will eventually show a sharp decline under the needs of financing their own economic development. They are at present participating in the increment of international liquidity for other developing countries through the extension of loans from their foreign reserves and through investment. As has been shown (in Part I) the traditional sources for development financing for the Third World, the industrialised nations, are not showing expansion on a large scale. Oil money is therefore a promising and important source of development finance for the Third World. The monetary reserves of the major oil exporters are also financing an important part of the flows of Euro-currency money to developing countries with joint Arab-European financial institutions playing an active role in many of these transactions. This suggests the importance of the financial resources available from oil-exporting countries and is an indicator of the growth in investment which can be expected to derive from these countries, directed both regionally and internationally.[10]

OPEC FINANCIAL ASSISTANCE TO DEVELOPING COUNTRIES

The most important development in the pattern of relationships between OPEC and non-OPEC developing countries is in the field of finance. OPEC member countries have, in response to the increase in oil revenues, individually and collectively created national, regional and multilateral funds for the purpose of channelling financial resources to other Third World countries. Such financial flows have been channelled either directly to individual countries or indirectly through international organisations. OPEC financial flows have also been provided jointly with international institutions to individual developing countries. The objectives of these financial flows were either to alleviate balance of payments adjustment problems or to provide development finance for particular projects. Three major observations regarding OPEC financial flows have been indicated and can be summarised as follows:[1]

(1) The magnitude of the flow of funds to non-OPEC developing countries is significant relative to OPEC countries' GNP. Regardless of the type of financial flow used – commitments versus disbursements or concessional versus non-concessional – the ratio of these flows to GNP far exceeded anything that has been attempted by the developed countries.
(2) OPEC assistance to other Third World countries has been targeted to those countries with a low per capita income.
(3) National savings of major oil-exporting countries have displaced those of the industrialised countries as the ultimate net source of funds flowing in the various forms to other developing countries.

The OPEC ODA:GNP ratio, as applied to ten OPEC donor countries,[2] stood at 1.42 per cent in 1973, reached its highest point, 2.94 per cent, in 1975 and was 1.48 per cent in 1979 and 1.35 in 1980. The average OPEC ODA:GNP ratio for the entire 1973–80 period was thus 1.88 per cent. In addition, most OPEC aid has been given in quick disbursing loans for general balance of payments support. OPEC member countries have as a result achieved unusually high disbursement: commitment ratios, exceeding 90 per cent in some years. If OPEC aid is to be judged by the standard target optimistically proclaimed by the UN more than a decade ago and recently recommended by the Brandt Commission as the level to be reached by 1985 (0.7 per cent of the GNP of the donor country) then the major OPEC donors have by far exceeded that level since 1973. In fact, the target was exceeded in 1975 by more than 22 times by Qatar, 20 times by UAE, 11 times by Kuwait and 6 times by Saudi Arabia. Table 11.3 shows OPEC/ODA net disbursements in absolute amount and as a percentage of GNP.

The volume of OPEC aid is still far below the financial needs of the developing countries. OPEC aid flows did not match the increased costs of oil imports by the developing countries in the two exceptional years which saw high jumps in oil prices, 1973/74 and 1978/79. This was not the case, however, for some of the poorest recipients, which received more OPEC aid than their incremental oil bills, or in some cases than their total oil bills. For example, the LLDCs' receipts from OPEC as a share of increase in net oil imports in the year 1974 was 277.3 per cent compared with 142.5 per cent in the same year for MSA countries. In

TABLE 11.3 OPEC[a] ODA Net Disbursements in US $m and as a Percentage of GNP (1973–80)

Year:	1973	1974	1975	1976	1977	1978	1979	1980
OPEC ODA US $m	1308	3447	5517	5593	5853	4338	6101	6950
OPEC ODA/GNP %	1.42	1.96	2.94	2.43	2.12	1.38	1.48	1.35

[a] Ten OPEC members excluding Ecuador, Gabon and Indonesia.
Sources: 1973–78, OPEC and OPEC Aid Institutions, a Profile, *The OPEC Fund*, Vienna, Austria, 1980.
1979–80, OECD, *Development Co-operation*, Review, 1981.

1975 these two ratios reached 251.9 per cent and 132.3 per cent.[13] It has also been indicated that OPEC aid continued in the years when no significant increase in oil prices took place. From Table 11.3 it can be seen that OPEC aid reached a high level in 1975, a year which actually witnessed a decline in oil prices. OPEC aid has therefore not been given as compensation to those who import oil, according to the volume of their oil imports. There is no linkage between OPEC aid and the cost of oil imports, and such a linkage, if applied, would work to the disadvantage of the poorest countries.[14]

Non-concessional flows from OPEC member countries are channelled largely through multilateral institutions. This is a reflection of the fact that non-concessional flows to multilateral agencies are almost exclusively in the form of bonds or subscriptions, which carry a low risk element for the donor and permit shifting detailed planning as to the ultimate utilisation of the resources to the multilateral institution actually administering the resources. In contrast to the situation with respect to concessional flows, the outflow of non-concessional flows from OPEC to multilateral institutions largely financed by non-OPEC sources, such as the World Bank, has been of considerable importance. The geographical distribution of flows from multilateral institutions largely financed by OPEC has been heavily influenced by the predominant position occupied by the IMF Oil Facility in these flows, particularly during 1974 and 1975, when this facility accounted for 93 per cent of commitments and 96 per cent of disbursements of such flows during this period.[15]

TERMS AND MEANS OF OPEC AID INSTITUTIONS IN TRANSFERRING FINANCIAL RESOURCES TO DEVELOPING COUNTRIES[16]

The various OPEC aid institutions have thus far had relatively little experience in extending development assistance to developing countries, compared to that of development aid institutions in the industrialised countries, and those of international organisations. OPEC institutions can be divided into two types. First are the national funds, including the Kuwait Fund for Arab Economic Development, the Abu Dhabi Fund for Arab Economic Development, the Saudi Fund for Development, the Iraqi Fund for External Development, the Libyan Bank for Foreign Assistance and the Venezuelan Fund. The second type are multilateral in nature, including the Arab Fund for Economic and Social Development, the Islamic Development Bank, the Arab Bank for Economic Development in Africa, the Arab Monetary Fund, the Arab Authority for Agricultural Investment and Development (AAAID), and the OPEC Fund for International Development. All members of these institutions are themselves developing countries, with most of them still dependent mainly on their oil revenues to finance their economic development. The relations between these OPEC aid institutions and the developing countries are concerned primarily with the provision of financial aid for development, given mainly in the form of finance for development projects and technical assistance. With the exception of the Kuwait Fund for Arab Economic Development, founded in 1961, the Arab Fund for Economic and Social Development, launched in 1971, and the Abu Dhabi Fund for Arab Economic Development, established in the same year, all other funds and agencies were established after the increases in oil prices in 1973, with the specific objective of directing surplus oil revenues, either directly or indirectly, through regional and international organisations, to the Third World. Most aid provided by these institutions has been directed towards the LLDCs.

Although the authorised capital of the various OPEC funds differs substantially, the conditions attached to loans made by them, however, are relatively the same in terms of interest rates, repayment periods, grace period, and methods of repayment. For example, the Kuwait Fund generally fixes a repayment period of between 10 and 25 years, which can, however, be extended to 49 years for the least developed countries. The Abu Dhabi Fund generally allows between 10 and 15 years, and the Saudi Fund between 20 and 30 years. Interest rates for the

Kuwait Fund vary, depending on the type of project and which economic sector it falls into. In the agricultural sector, the rate is 2.5 per cent per annum, and 3.5 per cent per annum for the industrial sector. There is an additional 0.5 per cent per annum as an administration fee. The Abu Dhabi Fund's interest rates range between 3.5 per cent and 5.5 per cent per annum, plus 0.5 per cent per annum administrative fee. In the case of the Saudi Fund, the rate is an average of 4 per cent per annum, as an administrative fee. There is also similarity in methods of repayment. All of the funds require semi-annual payments, although grace periods differ. In the case of the Kuwaiti Fund, it is the period for completion of the project, plus 7 years, with a maximum grace period of 10 years. For the Abu Dhabi Fund, it varies from project to project, with an average period of 5 years, while for the Saudi Fund, it varies between 5 and 10 years.

A comparison between the regulations of these three national funds, those of Kuwait, Abu Dhabi, and Saudi Arabia, reveals a further similarity between the limit of a loan as a percentage of the capital of the fund. In the case of the Kuwaiti Fund, no loan should exceed more than 10 per cent of the capital, with the same applying to the Abu Dhabi Fund, although in the case of the Saudi Fund, the limit is restricted to 5 per cent. The Kuwait Fund also is not permitted to provide more than half of the total cost of a project, although this percentage can be increased in exceptional cases, provided that two-thirds of the Board of Directors concur. As far as the provision of finance in local currency is concerned, this varies from country to country, with the conditions of the Kuwait and Abu Dhabi Funds being similar. The Saudi Fund has one special condition not to be found in the regulations of the other two funds, namely that no country may receive loans that in total exceed more than 10 per cent of the Fund's authorised capital. These terms and conditions indicate that the loans offered by the three national funds are 'soft' in nature. This is due primarily to the fact that the aim of these funds is not to seek financial benefit, but rather, as a prior concern, to aid the Third World countries in their development. Moreover, the loans provided by these three funds are without conditions or strings, while the choice of contractors and consultants is a matter for international tenders.

As far as OPEC regional and multilateral funds are concerned there is also considerable variation in their capital. A comparison of the status of the Arab Fund for Economic and Social Development, the Islamic Development Bank, and the Arab Bank for Economic Development in Africa reveals several interesting facts. The repayment period for the

Arab Fund is between 15 and 25 years, for the Arab Bank in Africa (ABEDA) 25 years, and for the Islamic Development Bank 10 years for commercial projects, and up to 50 years for infrastructural projects in least developed countries. The interest rate charged by the Arab Fund is 4 per cent for those Arab countries which fall into the category of 'least developed', namely Mauritania, Sudan, Somalia and the two Yemens, and 6 per cent for other Arab countries. ABEDA has an interest rate of between 1 and 6 per cent per annum, while the Islamic Development Bank, in accordance with the principles of the Islamic Sharia Law, charges no interest although it does charge administrative expenses at a rate of between 2–3 per cent a year. The other two charge no administrative expenses. Repayment is made in semi-annual instalments for loans from the Arab Fund and ABEDA. In the case of the Islamic Development Bank, it varies according to country and project. The grace period for the Arab Fund is between 4 to 6 years, and for ABEDA 5 years. This bank provides loans mainly to least developed countries in Africa.

There is no limit on loans from the Arab Fund, although approval from the government of the recipient country and a letter of guarantee is required before financing the project. In the case of private sector projects, other guarantees are required. ABEDA's Board of Governors determines the maximum amount for loans and the necessary guarantees, while the Islamic Development Bank finances projects with a guaranteed economic viability, provided that two-thirds of the Bank's members are in favour. Tenders follow normal rules of international competition.

As in the case of the three national funds, these three multilateral regional institutions aim to provide development assistance to the developing countries, rather than seeking to make a profit from dealing with them. Their purposes, and their conditions for loans are similar, although there are some minor differences in their scope of activities. The Kuwaiti Fund finances projects in the fields of energy, agriculture and industry, as well as infrastructure. The Abu Dhabi Fund, besides these sectors, may engage in equity participation, while the Saudi Fund extends loans also to the public service sector. On the other hand, the Arab Fund finances projects that foster economic integration among its member countries while ABEDA mainly finances infrastructural and agricultural projects, as well as some projects in the fields of energy and industry, also providing technical assistance through the financing studies. The Islamic Development Bank provides loans for all types of projects, though mainly in the sectors of industry, agriculture, infrastructure and public services, throughout the Islamic world, and pays special attention to projects that will increase the volume of trade between these countries – see Table 11.4.

The approaches taken by OPEC development institutions are mainly based upon sending delegations to developing countries to study particular projects, both to appraise them prior to financing, and to pursue their implementation. The governments of the developing countries approach these institutions in a similar manner, by sending missions to seek assistance. Evaluation missions sent to study projects are, on occasion, made up of members of more than one of the funds. The funds, with the agreement of the recipient countries, hire international consultants, while advice from specialised organisations of the United Nations in evaluating proposed project is also accepted. The funds also engage in co-financing with other national and international development aid organisations. On the completion of feasibility studies, the proposed project for financing is submitted to the Boards of the funds for approval.

All committed to development in the Third World, the OPEC Funds have different strategies that are evident from their choice of projects. Recently, however, they have tended to concentrate on aid to the LLDCs, especially through the financing of infrastructural and agricultural projects. It is now time that a clear and well-defined strategy be drawn up for these OPEC development institutions to ensure that aid continues to be extended to the developing countries of the Third World. Such aid can help in the restoration of political and economic stability and can enable them to develop and progress. In the future such aid can lead to co-operation between the OPEC donors and the recipients in the field of investment. It is also important that the LLDCs should receive priority in the provision of concessionary assistance. OPEC Development Funds should also finance projects that will contribute to the promotion of international trade among developing countries (including OPEC countries themselves), as well as for paying special attention in the future to public service projects, which are of such importance for any development programme. There is always a need for further co-ordination between the various OPEC development institutions, so that they can together finance big projects that have consequently major effects on the recipient countries. This can best be achieved through the drawing up of a general strategy for OPEC aid agencies.

TABLE 11.4 Loans and Grants by Arab OPEC Development Institutions in 1980 (US $m)

Name of institution	Loans and grants	Sectoral distribution						Regional distribution			
		Transport	Power	Agriculture	Industries	Financing of foreign trade	Others	Arab world	Asia	Africa	Other regions
Kuwait Fund	267.80	87.62	49.45	35.22	77.22	—	18.29	97.88	61.58	99.02	9.32
Abu Dhabi Fund	202.69	121.96	30.37	17.69	32.67	—	—	169.56	27.00	6.13	—
Saudi Fund	331.24	180.24	120.93	16.78	—	—	13.29	55.31	150.41	125.52	—
Iraqi Fund	253.01	87.62	—	—	—	161.95	3.44	95.76	137.66	19.59	—
Arab Fund	106.94	39.53	11.27	43.75	—	—	12.39	106.94	—	—	—
Arab Bank for Africa	81.02	43.92	11.20	10.90	15.00	—	—	—	—	81.02	—
Islamic Dev. Bank	429.08	10.93	18.00	11.00	32.64	337.16	19.35	194.07	145.36	89.65	—
OPEC Fund	250.77	31.02	97.50	5.50	17.00	92.75	7.00	30.20	85.32	101.00	34.25
All institutions											
Loans	1911.74	598.09	338.43	139.47	174.53	591.86	69.36	746.98	602.40	518.79	43.57
Grants	10.81	4.75	0.29	1.37	—	—	4.40	2.74	4.93	3.14	—
Grand total	1922.55	602.84	338.72	140.84	174.53	591.86	73.76	749.72	607.33	521.93	43.57

Source: Co-ordination Secretariat at the Arab Fund for Economic and Social Development.

12 The Kuwait Fund for Arab Economic Development

Establishment and Capital

The Kuwait Fund was established in 1961 as a public corporation with an independent legal personality. Its initial authorised capital was KD50m, increased to KD200m in 1966, and further increased to KD1bn in 1974. KFAED's paid-up capital reached KD618m as of 31 December 1979. The purpose of the fund is to assist Arab States and other developing states in developing their economies and, in particular, to provide such states with loans for the implementation of their development programmes, in accordance with the provisions of a charter to be made by order of the Prime Minister.[1]

Resources and Capacity for Financing

KFAED's capital is paid in an amount of KD400m out of government reserves by transfers made from time to time according to need. The remaining part of the fund's capital, amounting to KD600m, is paid out of the public revenues of the state by annual appropriation of a percentage of the revenues.[2] The Kuwait Fund may borrow and issue bonds subject to the limit of twice the amount of its capital and reserves. Also, it may not finance by means of a loan more than 50 per cent of the total costs of any project or programme. However, the Board of Directors may, by a majority of two-thirds of the members present, approve loans in amounts exceeding this limit in exceptional cases.

Scope of Activities

Since 1974 the Kuwait Fund has extended its mandate to provide foreign assistance to all developing countries in the world. The share of non-Arab beneficiary countries increased from 1 per cent in 1974 to 36 per cent in 1975, and to 62 per cent for the first half of 1976. In FY1975-76, the fund granted 34 loans amounting to KD159.35m; 20 were to Arab countries (84.3 per cent of the total amounts). In FY1976 the fund provided 9 loans (KD59.3m) in Asia, and 5 loans (KD15.75m) in Africa.[3] During FY1977-78, the KFAED pursued its activities in the service of the economic development of the less developed countries in general and that of the Arab countries in particular. Loans amounting to a total of KD57.52m were granted during this year, 8 to Arab countries, 4 to African countries, and 1 loan each to Thailand and Malta.[4] FY1978-79 witnessed a noticeable expansion in the fund's activities, when 25 loans amounting to a total of KD100.35m were extended, of which the share of Arab countries was 60 per cent, while the Asian and African countries received 27 and 11 per cent respectively. In addition during 1978-79, the fund commenced its operations in Oceania with a loan to Papua New Guinea.[5]

During its eighteenth year (the financial year 1979/80) of continued development assistance activity, the Kuwait Fund investigated several projects submitted for consideration by developing countries with the result that 24 projects were approved as technically sound and economically feasible. In the course of the years under review, of the approved 24 loans, the Kuwait Fund concluded 20 new loans with a total value of KD71.93 m, while 4 loans with a total value of KD7.2m still remained unsigned. By the end of the year 22 projects under consideration were also listed in 21 countries. Of the total value of signed loans extended to 20 countries, 7 Arab countries received 41.5 per cent, 5 African countries 21 per cent, 7 Asian countries 34.0 per cent, and Cyprus 3.5 per cent.

By the end of its financial year (1979/80) and during its entire eighteen years of life, KFAED's total loan commitments reached KD662.11m for 162 loans covering 52 countries. The share of these countries in these commitments were: 16 Arab countries received 64.9 per cent, 20 African countries 11.9 per cent, 13 Asian countries 22.3 per cent and 3 other countries 0.9 per cent. As far as sectoral distribution is concerned, the highest share went to transport, communications and storage (30.5 per cent), followed by power (26.9 per cent), industry and services (23.8 per cent) and agriculture and primary sectors (18.8 per cent). However, the apparent low share of agriculture in this distribution does not in effect contain what positive contribution the other sectors such as transport and communications, for example, make to the development of agriculture. The fund has also extended credit lines to national development banks and continued during the year 1979/80 to extend technical assistance grants in order to assist countries to identify, study and prepare projects in a sound manner, by using the services of qualified consultants, for their proper implementation. During the year 9 countries (3 Arab, 5 African and 1 Asian) received technical assistance grants totalling KD1.6m. This brings the total number of grants extended from the establishment of KFAED up to 30 June 1980 to 51 grants (benefiting 27 countries: 10 Arab, 12 African, 4 Asian in addition to Malta) with a total value of KD6.83m. The increase in the number and value of these technical assistance grants highlights the fund's support and encouragement of this field of development activity for the vital role they play in the proper implementation of projects.[6] Table 12.1 shows the sectoral and geographical distribution of KFAED loans.

TABLE 12.1 Sectoral and Geographical Distribution of Fund Loans
1.1.1962–30.6.1980
(KDm)

Countries \ Sectors	Agriculture and primary sector	Transport communications and storage	Electricity	Industry and Services	Total	(%)
Arab countries	85.715	148.033	64.902	131.085	429.735	64.9
African countries	14.910	33.600	20.870	9.500	79.880	11.9
Asian countries	20.100	18.300	92.350	16.915	147.665	22.3
Other countries	3.700	2.130	—	—	5.830	0.9
Total	124.42	202.063	178.122	157.500	662.110	100.0
Percentage	18.8	30.5	26.9	23.8	100.0	

Source: Kuwait Fund for Arab Economic Development, *Annual Report* 1979–80.

Terms and Conditions

Interest rate: ½–7 per cent.
Repayment period: 10–50 years.
Grace period: Under 1 year–10 years.
Guarantee: The government of the recipient country.

Management and Administration

KFAED derives its power from a six-man Board of Directors, chaired by the Prime Minister of Kuwait and including representatives of the business community as well as government officials. Directors are appointed by the Prime Minister for two-year terms. The Board's function is to decide general policy and to give final approval to loans and to the fund's own accounts. The day-to-day operation of the fund is the responsibility of the Director-General, who is appointed by the Chairman, attends Board meetings, but does not vote. The internal operations of the fund are informal rather than structured and official meetings are kept to a minimum.[7]

Approaches and Techniques Applied

The Kuwait Fund's assistance may be directed to any field of economic development of a country to bring about a high developmental impact. Although no sectoral limitations restrict the fund's activities, the focal points for project financing strongly support physical infrastructure projects. The fund gives clear priority to projects such as land reclamation, irrigation, power generation and transport. It has refrained from financing social infrastructure projects except in cases where they constitute elements of other projects. This concept is backed by the philosophy that social projects are politically sensitive, and therefore these services should be provided directly by the governments concerned, possibly with the concurrence of other financing aid sources. The emphasis on physical infrastructure may be explained not only by the consideration that infrastructural projects are prerequisites of economic development, but also that these capital-intensive ventures require concessional finance which cannot be provided from other sources. Since the Kuwait Fund aims simultaneously at assisting regional projects, a bias towards infrastructure could well be reinforced.[8]

The procedures in identifying projects are based upon the preference that the fund waits for governments to submit them rather than acting as a catalyst. Once it gets involved, however, the fund sometimes uses its influence to encourage a certain development that it thinks would benefit the borrower. KFAED's appraisal procedures are flexible as the fund's appraisal mission has the authority to negotiate all the issues. A representative of the borrower could come to the fund to sign the loan agreement, and ratification and other steps for making the agreement effective then follow in the normal way. The fund also helps the poorest countries through the application stage with technical assistance grants for hiring consultants and undertaking other preparatory work. Normally, the fund determines what the interest rates and maturity periods for a given loan will be. Its approach is, however, flexible. If, during negotiations, a borrower indicates that the interest rate is too high, the fund might agree to lower the rate provided the maturity is shortened. In some recent cases, however, the borrower was told what the grant element would be and then given the choice of deciding on the length of the repayment period and the rate of interest, provided that the combination of the two added up to the approved grant element of the loan.[9]

Problems of Implementation and Remarks from Field Experience

The officials of the Kuwait Fund indicate (based upon answers to the questionnaire) that problems are mainly related to delays in ratification, appointments of consultants, issue of tenders, and analysis of bids. Moreover, problems related to submission of withdrawal applications and progress reports have also occurred. In addition to the above, other problems based upon the experience of co-financing and meetings can be identified, summarised as follows:

(1) Inability of some developing countries (especially the least developed ones) in following up and managing projects.
(2) Lack of efficiency in project management due mainly to lack of proper supervision in some recipient governments.
(3) Delays in withdrawal procedures and incomplete procedures in some cases.
(4) Lack of well-prepared feasibility studies for projects (especially in some LLDCs).
(5) Problems of security and stability in some areas.
(6) Delays in the implementation of projects and their impact on cost escalation.
(7) Delays in repayment loan instalments and interest rates in some cases in LLDCs.
(8) Problems related to the efficiency of local consultants and contractors especially those in LLDCs.

Strategy for Financing and Technical Assistance

The Kuwait Fund does not follow a medium- or long-term strategy for financing and technical assistance. However, the fund is following a one-year programme to finance approximately 20–25 projects amounting to KD80–100m. The fund participates in technical assistance in some

LLDCs (Comoro Islands, South Yemen, Djibouti) through its regional offices abroad for the purpose of assisting these countries in preparing development programmes.

Reviewing the experience of the Kuwait Fund, it appears that it will raise the share of its assistance to non-Arab developing countries, especially in Africa, Asia and in some Latin American countries. It is also expected that the fund will continue extending loans to development banks and institutions in these countries. It has been indicated that KFAED is concentrating on financing infrastructure projects, and it is likely to continue in the future with its good impact on regional projects. Although it was not indicated in its law and regulation, the Kuwait Fund appears to have all the capabilities for fostering regional development in some areas of developing countries and all that it needs is a defined strategy for fulfilling this target. The fund is also likely to increase its technical assistance facilities in non-Arab developing countries, especially the least developed ones. If this is geographically planned to meet the requirements of infrastructure projects in the least developed countries, KFAED could play a leading role in regional development in these countries.

13 The Abu Dhabi Fund for Arab Economic Development[1]

In this chapter, the experience of the Abu Dhabi Fund for Arab Economic Development in the aid process as a rapidly growing corporation with a promising future is examined. ADFAED acts not only as a developmental lending agency but also as a consultant and data source for the Abu Dhabi Government and the Government of the Federation of the United Arab Emirates on both economic and financial matters on the international level. Advice is given to the government which assists in the decisions concerning financial aid from the state reserves. Moreover, the fund has participated effectively in technical assistance to some developing countries and is considered to be an investment promotion centre for the United Arab Emirates through its daily contacts with international financial markets, which provide a sound background for information on the money and capital markets worldwide. ADFAED stands as concrete evidence of the growing trend for investment of capital surplus funds and the increase in its capitalisation reflects both its success and Abu Dhabi's commitment to continuing and expanding its international financing.

Legal Status, Purpose and Power of ADFAED

The Abu Dhabi Fund for Arab Economic Development was established in July 1971 (a few months before Britain's withdrawal from the Gulf) as a general corporation with an independent legal personality. Based in Abu Dhabi, the fund's purpose was to offer economic aid to Arab countries in support of their economic development, either in the form of loans or participation in share-holding. The fund can also guarantee projects or grant other forms of aid as defined by its regulations. The capital of the fund was authorised at Bahrain D50m or $120m at its inception, paid by the Abu Dhabi Government.[2] In June 1974 (when the currency changed) the fund's capitalisation was raised to 2000m dirhams, equal to BD200m or $500m and its scope of activities enlarged to include not only Arab countries but also African and Asian countries. ADFAED, like KFAED and AFESD, is permitted to issue bonds to an amount not exceeding twice its capital plus reserves. According to an amendment approved in 1974, one-half of the capital is due to be paid in four equal annual instalments starting from 1974 and the other half is subject to call by the Board of Directors. The fund's Board of Directors, at their meeting on 25 September 1979, agreed to double the fund's authorised capital to Dh4bn. The fund's Law of Establishment is in the process of amendment to take account of this decision on the increase of its capital.[3]

Scope of Activities

ADFAED makes no distinction between developing countries in the provision of financial assistance. Special commitments towards developing countries most seriously affected by crisis or towards the least developed among the developing countries were felt to be the responsibility of the government as well as of the fund. Reviewing the last seven years (1974–80) of the fund's operations showed that it concluded cumulative loan agreements amounting to Dh3210.6m. In 1980 the fund signed loan agreements amounting to Dh375.70m compared with Dh402.80m in 1979, Dh840m in 1978, Dh539.00m in 1977, Dh662.14m in 1976, D183.64m in 1975 and Dh199.2m in 1974. The following presentation is the yearly operation of the fund loan agreements.[4]

In 1974, ADFAED concluded 9 project agreements in 6 Arab countries, the biggest of which was Dh51.483m for part of the Banias Electrical Co-ordination Centre in Syria. In 1975 the number of loan agreements concluded was reduced. The fund signed 4 project agreements covering 3 Arab countries only, the biggest of which was Dh130m million for part of the Abu Qir Electric Power Plant in Egypt. The year 1976 witnessed major advances as the fund concluded 18 project agreements in 13 developing countries, of which the biggest was Dh100m for the second stage of Sitra Power and Water Station in Bahrain. Amongst these 13 countries, 6 were Asian, and 2 were African countries. In 1977, the fund concluded 13 loan agreements to Arab, African and Asian countries (8 loan agreements for Arab countries, 3 for African countries and 2 for Asian countries). In 1978, the fund concluded 9 loan agreements (3 to Arab countries, 3 to African countries, 2 to Asian countries and 1 for Malta). In 1979, the fund concluded 6 loan agreements (3 for Arab countries and 3 for African countries). No loan agreements were concluded in this year for Asian countries. In 1980 the fund concluded 10 loan agreements (5 for Arab Countries, 4 for African countries, and 1 for Turkey). As in 1979, no loan agreements were concluded in 1980 for Asian countries. Table 13.1 shows the cumulative geographical distribution of the fund loans.

TABLE 13.1 Geographical Distribution of the Fund's Loans 1974–80 (Dhm)

Arab countries	
Jordan	145.5
Bahrain	220.0
Tunisia	429.9
Sudan	140.5
Syria	107.5
Oman	723.0
Lebanon	67.8
Egypt	266.4
Morocco	150.4
Mauritania	160.0
Yemen AR	126.5
PDR Yemen	208.2
Total	2745.3

African countries	
Burundi	4
Mali	16
Gambia	7.9
Tanzania	24
Guinea	16
Uganda	25
Lesotho	7
Madagascar	16
Senegal	4
Seychelles	4
Comoro Islands	4
Cape Verde	4
Guinea Bissau	12
Total	143.9

(*continued overleaf*)

TABLE 13.1(contd.)

Asian countries	
Bangladesh	100
India	68
Maldives	8
Malaysia	33
Sri Lanka	20
Indonesia	57
Afghanistan	30
Total	316

Other countries	
Malta	28
Turkey	100
Total	128

Source: Abu Dhabi Fund for Arab Economic Development *Annual Report*, 1980.

The distribution of ADFAED's loans and equity participation by sector during 1974–80, which reached Dh3334.31m, shows that manufacturing industries received 26.4 per cent, extractive industries 25.3, water and electricity 23.6, transport, communications and storages 11.1, agriculture, fisheries and rural development 10.6, and hotels and tourism 3. In 1980, more emphasis was given to the agricultural sector (32.5 per cent) and water and electricity (29.2 per cent). The scope of the fund's activities has been increased to include the provision of technical advice to the government of UAE and representing the government in the management of a number of special foreign aid projects in several Arab and African countries. By the end of 1980, these cumulative loans and grants reached Dh2308.2m compared with Dh1477.2m in 1979 and Dh1212.2m in 1978.

Management, Terms and Conditions

ADFAED is administered by an appointed Board of seven headed by H. H. Sheikh Khalifa bin Zayed as Chairman of the Board of Directors, and Sheikh Surour bin Mohammed al Nahayan, Chief of Cabinet of H. H. the Ruler of Abu Dhabi, as Deputy Chairman. Members of the Board of Directors of the fund are appointed by Decree for a period of five years, subject to renewal. The standard loan terms could be described as 'soft' compared with commercial rates. Repayment periods are likely to be over 10 to 15 years at interest ranging from 3.5 to 5.5 per cent, with half of 1 per cent as a service charge for administrative expenses. ADFAED may require guarantees by any co-financing international or regional organisation, according to the nature and circumstances of each operation supported. The fund has the freedom to participate in projects in almost any form it chooses. Participation in any project may not exceed 10 per cent of the fund's capital and participation in the form of direct loans may not exceed 50 per cent of the total cost of the supported project unless it is deemed an exceptional case by the majority of two-thirds of the present members of the Board. All transactions are paid and collected in UAE Dirhams.

Approaches and Techniques Applied

In carrying out its policy, ADFAED selects development projects from those presented to it officially, either by delegations visiting the fund, or missions from the fund visiting countries. In selecting these projects, to be co-financed with other aid agencies and financial institutions, the fund's policy is to eliminate social projects and cash credit, as its aim is to offer economic aid based upon project financing in support of the countries' economic development. Thus the responsibility of financing social projects is felt to be that of the government rather than the fund. Most ADFAED projects are infrastructure, manufacturing and agricultural projects, with agricultural projects receiving great priority, similar to infrastructure projects. This policy is self-justifiable since infrastructures are essentially a prerequisite for the economic development of any developing country, especially the LLDCs. Moreover, the agricultural sector in Africa deserves special attention as Africa (amongst the least developed countries) is rich in natural resources and fertile land but requires a sound policy for financing agricultural development, especially those projects related to food needs. Africa could contribute significantly to solving the international food crisis but a pragmatic programme is needed, based upon comparative advantages and economies of scale. Thus infrastructure and agricultural sectors go hand in hand in Africa, a policy that ADFAED believes to be the optimum one. The fund's policy is unbiased in terms of loan distribution among different countries; based upon the idea of balanced financing among different projects in different countries. Thus there has been no concentrating policy on a few projects and a few countries. This policy is aimed at filling in the gap in financing projects, thus overcoming the bottlenecks of financing.

ADFAED carries out its technical appraisal studies on three levels: (a) macro (national); (b) sectoral; (c) micro (project). At macro level, the fund carries out country surveys, analysing the economic and financial structures of different developing countries on the basis of time-series data of national accounts. The purpose is to test the absorptive capacity and ability to repay of each recipient country and a programme of lending for different groups of countries. For that purpose, standard country sheets are prepared as data background for the macro study. Country survey includes points like major problems and specific problems, economic and financial characteristics, economic potentialities, economic sectors, the balance of payments situation and external debt, as well as a review of the plan (if any) covering main targets, policies, resource allocation, sectoral planning, etc. The study also includes (based upon macro appraisal) recommendations for the best direction of financing in the future in specific sectors and subsectors.

Sectorally, development of the different sectors is analysed showing their shares in Gross National Product, the inter-relationship among sectors, capital output ratios and investment for each sector according to the plan. Sectoral studies are included in the macro appraisal studies and their data are also included in the country sheet.

At project (micro level) the fund measures the economic as well as the commercial rates of return of a proposed project by using the flow of funds analysis and certain parameters. Sensitivity analysis is also included in the study. The fund benefits from feasibility studies done by well-sounded consultants as a guideline but carries out parallel studies, based upon consultations with officials in the countries concerned and their terms of reference. This micro level analysis should, of course, fulfil the guidelines of the fund's lending policy. At this stage, the fund gives the economic criterion more emphasis.

Problems of Implementation and Remarks from Field Experience

Problems of project implementation are similar, in general, to the problems of other Arab funds and, in particular, to problems indicated by the Kuwait Fund. As for remarks from field experience, the following are a set of problems in developing countries which, the author believes, from his experience in the field with the fund, should be given the utmost consideration.

1 Problem of Project Selection and Appraisal

To select projects on a rational basis is rather a difficult task, but a well-defined strategy of which planning is the key can ease this task in LLDCs. Planning by itself cannot do miracles to make such projects productive or valuable, but planning as a tool of public purpose can aid in the easy implementation of such a task. Moreover, the institutional set-up and the machinery for project appraisal provide additional hindrances to wise selection and appraisal. The lack of economic and social criteria based upon well defined and sound parameters is again one of the main problems facing these countries in the field of project appraisal and implementation.

2 Problem of Priority Areas

Priority areas from which a policy-maker or planner could select the best projects on a rational basis constitute another important problem which has to be solved before any decision can be taken, a matter which might lead to economic and social reactions. The history of many LLDCs is rich in such matters and the trauma of bad projects could be avoided well before implementation or even before the decision-making. It is the policy-maker who will have the main responsibility for zone areas and their priorities, and he in turn should be well informed on different sections of the economy, their needs and capacities, based upon a well-defined programme or plan for each sector. This inter-relationship between different sectors of the economy is the key element for solving problems of priority areas.

3 Problems of Implementation and Decision-Making

This is the problem of the utmost importance: the implementation of decision-making. Is it the problem of the policy-maker, the manager, the economist or of all of them? Naturally it is the problem of all, but not to the same extent. The decision which the policy-maker is going to take should be implemented by his staff who, amongst them the economist and the manager, should advise him whether or not to take such a decision. The time gap between taking the decision and the implementation of that decision should be an important concern in these countries.

4 A Need for an Effective Machinery

This does not mean that LLDCs have reached deadlock in this field. It only pinpoints the circumstances of the main problems that impede progress in this important field of project appraisal and implementation. A well-defined and effective machinery for project selection and appraisal could be the main solution in this respect. The operation of the whole economy would work better if every project in each sector were functioning well. The role of such machinery for project selection and implementation should be equipped with better and efficient factors such as:

(i) well-trained staff;
(ii) balance between duties and responsibilities;
(iii) a well-defined public purpose for each project;
(iv) a leading role for the project in the sector concerned not only economically but also socially as well.

Although many of these countries understand such problems and try to find their own solutions, they all lack the machinery for follow-up based upon gradual and efficient implementation.

14 The Saudi Fund for Development

Establishment and Capital

The Saudi Fund for Development, established in 1974, started its operations in mid-1975. The fund is an agent of the Saudi Arabian Government, with authorised capital of Saudi riyals (SR) 10bn ($2.860bn), and by the end of 1977 it had received SR8bn ($2.3bn), with its authorised capital increasing to SR15bn in 1980. SFD has no borrowing power as any additional capital must be authorised from the government and capital can only be increased by a decision of the Council of Ministers. The purpose of the fund is to provide financing of development projects in Arab, Islamic and friendly developing countries by the provision of concessionary loans. It is the only one of the three Arab national funds which attempts to reach all the developing world. The fund provides its assistance to governments only for projects in the public sector. The amount of lending to any one country should not exceed more than 10 per cent of the authorised capital, and lending to any project should not exceed 5 per cent of the authorised capital. In addition, the fund provides no more than 50 per cent of the total costs of a project. Loans are normally extended and repaid in Saudi riyals. The fund does not guarantee the loans of other Saudi institutions, although equity participation is possible under its charter. As a general rule the fund does not make technical assistance grants.

Scope of Activities

By the end of the financial year 1977/78 the activities of SFD covered more than 50 countries in Asia, Africa and Latin America. To these countries the fund had extended 130 loans amounting to SR10.3bn. During the financial year 1977/78, the fund signed 26 loan agreements which amounted to about SR2.36bn compared with 20 loan agreements amounting to SR1724m in the fiscal year 1976/77. During the two fiscal years 1974/75 and 1975/76, the fund provided loan agreements amounting to SR483m and SR1477m respectively.[1] The fund's loans are mainly extended in the fields of infrastructure such as power stations, water supply, sewerage, mining, mineral resources, education, sanitary and housing projects. Transportation projects are the fund's top priority as it has allocated more than 39 per cent of its total loans extended through the period 1974/75–1977/78 to this sector.[2] This priority is based upon SFD's philosophy that the meagre share of the Third World countries in international trade represents a huge obstacle for economic development of these countries. Developing countries are badly in need of transportation of capital goods to use in implementing their development plans but the lack of foreign exchange funds is an obstacle to those plans. It is in this field that the Saudi Fund exerts its efforts to finance ports, canals, highways and airport projects in these countries. Industrial projects that SFD finances are regarded essentially as infrastructure. In addition, many of the loans that go for agricultural projects are for rural development rather than the outright production of food. The geographical distribution of the fund's activities does not treat Arab countries as a separate group but rather treats them among African and Asian countries according to their geographical locations. Reviewing the fund's operations during the period 1974/75–1977/78, it provided financing to 76 projects in African countries which amounted to SR5038.3m (49 per cent of total signed and committed loans); 52 projects in Asian countries amounted to SR5007.7 (49 per cent); and only 2 projects in other countries amounted to SR264.6m (2.5 per cent). This indicates that the fund is pursuing a balanced lending policy among African and Asian countries, and that its operations in Latin American countries are very limited. However, the fund is working with the Inter-American Development Bank in seeking sound projects in Latin America and it has identified projects in Ecuador and extended a loan to a project in Brazil. The balanced operations policy carried out by the fund was the result of a summit conference of Arab and African countries in Cairo in March 1977 when the Saudi Arabian Government announced that it was committing $1bn of Saudi Government funds for aid to African countries over what had been given before. About $850m of it was to be disbursed through SFD. Before this summit Asia was far ahead of Africa in terms of the fund's operations. This was based upon the belief that Asian nations have much larger populations than African nations and thus have correspondingly larger projects.[3]

During the period 1975–May 1979, SFD allocated SR12,276m with contributions benefiting 152 different projects in 51 developing countries – an average of SR80.76m per project or SR240.71m per country. During the same period, SFD signed 83 loan agreements totalling SR7427m. This was in addition to 11 loan and grant agreements administered by SFD on behalf of the Ministry of Finance and National Economy, totalling SR2566m. SFD allocated funds according to each country's priorities, which are supported by feasibility studies. The size of the borrowing country and its absorptive capacity are also taken into consideration. Roads and railways, a total of 34 projects, were allocated SR2966.6m. Electricity projects, a total of 25, received SR2824.1m, and a total of 39 agricultural projects were allocated SR2267.0m Overall, Asian countries were allocated SR6376.9m for 63 projects and African countries received SR5634.3m for 87 projects. The remaining two projects were in Latin America and Malta.

By the end of 1980, SFD-extended loans amounted to SR1005.13m compared with SR871.16m in 1979 and SR1266.75m in 1978. The share of Arab countries in total SFD loans declined from 64 per cent in 1978 to 38 per cent in 1979 and 18 per cent in 1980. On the other hand, the share of total SFD loans to African countries increased from 27 per cent in 1978 to 47 per cent in 1980, and in the case of Asian countries the share was also consequently increased from 8 to 35 per cent. There was a sharp decline in loans extended to African countries in 1979 as they reached only 3 per cent while there was a sharp increase in loans extended to Asian countries during the same year, reaching 58 per cent. Table 14.1 shows the loans extended by the Saudi Fund by country and region.

Terms and Conditions

In replying to the questionnaire sheet, SFD staff indicated that terms and conditions depend upon the economic situation of each recipient country, its classification as a 'most seriously affected', or as a 'least developed' one. Repayment periods range between 15 and 25 years, grace periods between 3 and 5 years. Interest rates vary between concessionary rates and less than the market rate and usually between 2 and 4 per cent, the latter being the rate applied to most of the fund's operations. The borrower pays an additional service charge at the rate of half 1 per cent per annum. The fund, at the request, and acting as an agent, of the borrower, purchases with Saudi riyals withdrawn from the Loan Account such currencies as are required to meet payments to be financed out of the proceeds of the loan, provided that such currencies

TABLE 14.1 Loans Extended by the Saudi Fund by Country and Region 1978–80
(SRm)

	1978	1979	1980
Arab countries			
Syrian Arab Republic	160.0	—	—
Yemen Arab Republic	655.0	—	90.45
Federal Islamic Republic of Comoro Islands	—	48.00	—
Islamic Republic of Mauritania	—	166.50	—
Democratic Republic of Sudan	—	120.16	20.10
Hashemite Kingdom of Jordan	—	—	38.50
Democratic Republic of Somalia	—	—	35.30
Total of Arab countries	815.00	334.66	184.35
(percentage of total)	(64)	(38)	(18)
African countries			
Republic of Mali	46.80	—	33.60
Republic of Gabon	70.60	—	9.00
Republic of Guinea Bissau	15.90	—	—
Republic of Kenya	87.25	—	66.10
Republic of Liberia	70.60	—	—
Republic of Madagascar	42.40	—	—
Republic of Senegal	13.20	—	—
Republic of Togo	—	16.60	35.18
United Republic of Cameroon	—	12.30	—
Republic of Gambia	—	—	26.88
Republic of Zaire	—	—	230.50
Republic of Guinea	—	—	100.00
Kingdom of Lesotho	—	—	15.12
Republic of Burundi	—	—	8.70
Republic of Botswana	—	—	36.50
Republic of Cape Verde	—	—	8.70
Total of African countries	346.75	29.90	471.28
(percentage of total)	(27)	(3)	(47)
Asian countries			
Republic of China	105.0	—	149.40
People's Democratic Republic of Bangladesh	—	106.00	—
Malaysia	—	94.90	—
Islamic Republic of Pakistan	—	306.70	200.10
Total of Asian countries	105.00	507.60	349.50
(percentage of total)	(8)	(58)	(35)
Grand Total	1266.75	871.6	1,005.13

Sources: Co-ordination Secretariat at the Arab Fund for Economic and Social Development 1978–80.

are used by the Saudi Arabian Monetary Agency in its transactions. The principal of the loan and loan charge and other charges are payable in Saudi riyals.[4]

Management and Administration

Like the other two national Arab funds, the Saudi Fund has a Board of Directors, Chairman of the Board, Vice-Chairman and Managing Director. It is the Board which has the final decision on loan commitments. Besides the Chairman, there are five members, holding renewable three-year terms. The fund's Managing Director, who is also Deputy Chairman, sits on the Board and casts a deciding ballot in the event of a tie vote. The organisational structure of the fund is based mainly upon capital and loan administration, documents and information, legal advice, evaluation and follow-up.[5]

Approaches Applied

The fund carries out its operations in a simple approach. Projects usually submitted by host governments should have high economic or social priority. The government encourages regional projects and supports them through SFD. The fund adopts a co-ordination policy with other experienced aid institutions and is willing to co-finance projects recommended to it by organisations such as the World Bank, Asian Development Bank, African Bank, Kuwait Fund, Abu-Dhabi Fund, etc. This has served to help its aid operation move smoothly.

Problems of Implementation and Follow-up

As in the case of the other two national Arab funds the Saudi Fund faces similar problems regarding delays in ratification, tenders and bids, withdrawal applications, progress reports, problems of security, management, etc. On the other hand, the Saudi Fund's officials have also indicated in several meetings the existence of problems related to the selection of foreign consultants and their preference, agreements between host governments and contractors, cost duties and rights and the problems of relying on sub-contractors, contractors' agreements between Third World countries and European contractors who take unfair advantage of the position of the developing countries. Problems of local taxes, availability of local materials, local components, currency fluctuations, cost escalations and fulfilling of the host government's obligations regarding employment and financing have also been identified.

Strategy for Financing and Technical Assistance

The Saudi Fund does not follow a medium- or long-term strategy regarding the amount of aid to be disbursed in the next three to five years not does it provide technical assistance. Its policy is mainly based upon year-to-year operations in the field of project lending, and, as indicated before, is based upon balanced amounts of loans to be provided between Asian and African countries. The fund should perhaps give more attention in future operations to the most seriously affected and least developed countries among the Third World. If it follows a programme of lending for the transportation sector as a key sector for development with its good impact upon foreign trade among those countries the fund could implement and follow a strategy for aid and development in the future. The fund could also gain great experience in feasibility studies of these projects and could play a leading role in this sector, and it could then provide technical assistance in this field.

A Proposal for Establishing a Joint Technical Resource Centre

During a conference of the presidents of Arab Development Funds in Riyadh in June 1976, the Saudi Fund was invited to study the establishment of an Inter-Arab consultative agency–Joint Technical Resource Centre. The conclusions of the study[6] revealed that the size of the centre is not beyond the absorptive limit of the seven Arab funding institutions (Abu Dhabi Fund, Arab Bank, Arab Fund, Islamic Development Bank, Kuwait Fund, Iraq Fund and Saudi Fund). It produces a net chargeout saving of about 18 per cent per staff member for 49 man-years of contract work, which would result in annual savings of $1.3m. The study also concluded that if professional staff functions were to be performed by those funding institutions, and if only five of these institutions were each to develop its own minimum staff code of 10 members each, a saving of nearly 25 man-years would result. Most fundamentally, the centre would resolve a critical shortage of services and personnel which it would not be reasonable to expect could otherwise be overcome. Table 14.2 compares the main activities within the project cycle identified in the course of fact-finding visits by the consultants to the institutions.

The study was, in general, acceptable, but comments were made in the

TABLE 14.2 Project Cycle Identified in Six Arab Funds

	Abu Dhabi Fund	Arab Bank (BADEA)	Arab Fund	Islamic Development Bank	Kuwait Fund	Saudi Fund
Project Identification	Reliance on applications by borrowers related to 'mature projects' confirmed by internal analysis. Use is also made of macroeconomic reviews and summaries by research department	Mainly application by borrowers with some from co-lenders and others are identified by BADEA	Mainly direct requests from borrowers plus co-lenders and some on own initiative	Relies heavily on co-financiers to compensate for lack of data supporting applications. Arranges identification missions in minority of cases	Uses studies of international agencies and mounts own missions for project identification in addition to considering direct applications	Reliance on borrowers. Where possible, identification missions are sent
Feasibility studies	Preferred responsibility of borrower	May be omitted altogether or may be carried out either by BADEA or borrower	May be omitted especially in public utilities where need is clear. Or borrower may be asked to make study using own or consultant resources. Otherwise undertaken by fund or commissioned consultants	Generally expected to be submitted by applicant in support of request	Normally required from borrower but KFD may assist with cost and in preparing terms of reference	Responsibility of borrower in most cases

(continued overleaf)

TABLE 14.2 (Contd.)

	Abu Dhabi Fund	Arab Bank (BADEA)	Arab Fund	Islamic Development Bank	Kuwait Fund	Saudi Fund
Appraisal	Team of four from fund's own staff with occasional involvement of individual external experts. Study includes visit to applicant and country	Preferably team of two to three of bank's own staff plus, possibly, freelance consultant in certain cases requiring particular specialist input	Team of three from fund's own staff plus short-term external specialist if required. Externals usually from Arab sources average 10% of man-power used on appraisals	Internal staff supplemented by external engineering specialists in some cases	Internal staff with negligible outside support. Appraisal includes general economic review of country plus visiting mission	Internal staff of fund in all but few instances. Appraisal comprises study of documents and site visit
Funding negotiation	Internal staff only					
Implementation and follow-up	Internal staff of funds but recipients of finances in most cases employ consultants for design and supervision					

Source: Feasibility of Joint Technical Resource Centre (A Study) by the Urwick Group, March 1978.

meeting that too much theoretical thinking should be avoided and a pragmatic approach based upon the different experiences of the development funds should be adopted. The starting point in the correct channel was recommended as the one which would influence the performance of the centre. Government participation in the centre, through equity financing, was also considered while it was proposed that the scope of activities of the centre should be enlarged to include co-ordination and co-operation efforts among the participant funds as this could be a target of the centre in its own right instead of it just acting as a clearing house among the funds. The following concepts in the plan for the centre should be defined and elaborated further:[7]

(1) Definition and scope of technical resources.
(2) Definition and nature of technical services.
(3) Elaboration of co-ordination policies in the field of financing development projects.
(4) Follow-up and implementation should be within the authority of each development institution.
(5) As most of these institutions are newcomers in the field of foreign aid, it would be appropriate to evaluate their lending policies.
(6) It is important to find the optimum linkage between the centre and those institutions by avoiding duplications and contradictions.
(7) Each institution should determine its capital needs for its future operations without any interference by the centre.
(8) Programmes for financing and technical assistance in the Arab Development Funds should be co-ordinated among these institutions as a prerequisite stage.
(9) The importance of gaining experience from other development funds in Europe, Africa, Asia and Latin America as well as the experiences of UN agencies.

15 The Arab Fund for Economic and Social Development

Establishment and Financial Resources

The Arab Fund for Economic and Social Development is an Arab regional financial institution with an independent legal personality based in Kuwait. It was established in July 1968 for the purpose of financing development and social projects in Arab countries. The members of the fund are the members of the Arab League. The Board of Governors of the fund may decide to admit both Arab public and private financial organisations for participation in the capital of the fund. According to the Agreement establishing the fund, its capital was 100m Kuwaiti Dinars exchangeable into convertible currencies. The capital of the fund was divided into 10,000 shares each having a value of KD10,000. The founding members subscribed their share of the capital of the fund as shown in Table 15.1.

According to the Agreement establishing the fund, the purposes of the fund are the financing of economic projects, of an investment character, by means of loans granted on easy terms to governments, and to public or private organisations and institutions, giving preference to economic projects that are vital to the Arab entity and to joint Arab projects. AFESD also encourages, directly or indirectly, the investment of public and private capital in such a manner as to ensure the development and growth of the Arab economy. Moreover, the fund provides technical expertise and assistance in various fields of economic development.[1]

AFESD's resources consist of the capital subscribed, the reserves, and the loans raised by the fund through the issuing of bonds or the obtaining of credits from public and private Arab institutions or from individuals or international institutions. The value of the bonds issued by the fund may not at any time exceed twice the amount of the capital,

TABLE 15.1 Subscribed Shares of the Capital of AFESD by Country

State	Number of shares
The Hashimite Kingdom of Jordan	200
The Republic of Tunisia	50
The Algerian Democratic and People's Republic	400
The Democratic Republic of the Sudan	150
The Republic of Iraq	750
The Kingdom of Saudi Arabia	
The Syrian Arab Republic	300
The Libyan Arab Republic	1200
The Arab Republic of Egypt	1050
The Yemen Arab Republic	50
The State of Kuwait	3000
The Republic of Lebanon	100
The Kingdom of Morocco	200
The People's Democratic Republic of Yemen	1
The State of The United Arab Emirates	500
The State of Bahrain	50
The State of Qatar	100

Source: Agreement establishing the Arab Fund for Economic and Social Development.

unless by special resolution of the fund's Board of Governors to be adopted by a two-thirds majority of votes.[2] Total paid-up capital reached KD260.667m by the end of 1980 compared with total subscribed capital amounting to KD395.110m, and authorised capital of KD400.00m. The cumulative total income of the fund at the end of 1980 reached KD72.570m while cumulative total expenditures reached KD12.322m, with excess income reaching KD60.248m. The value of total cumulative loans at the end of 1980 reached KD342.884m, with an average loan value of KD5.531m. Cumulative technical assistance, by the end of 1980, reached KD2.713m, and disbursements reached KD1.681m. Table 15.2 summarises the financial position of the fund.

The summary of the financial position of AFESD in Table 15.2 shows that the share of loan disbursements to commitments reached 53 per cent during the period 1974–80. As for technical assistance, this ratio reached 62 per cent during the same period, a good indication of high disbursements of loans and technical assistance. The ratio of loan disbursements to paid-up capital reached 69 per cent, an indication of the speed of implementation of projects. The share of paid-up capital to authorised capital reached 65 per cent. The share loan commitments to paid-up capital had reached 132 per cent, indicating the necessity of raising the paid-up capital to cope with the high commitments of loans

TABLE 15.2 Summary of the Financial Position of AFESD (1974–80) (KDm)

	1974	1975	1976	1977	1978	1979	1980	Cumulative as at 31-12-1980
Authorised capital	102.500	400.000	—	—	—	—	—	400.000
Subscribed capital	18.850	2.190	87.460	180.930	—	14.700	9.970	395.110
Paid-up capital	14.219	16.079	47.618	32.227	33.001	37.775	58.017	260.667
Total income	2.924	3.706	5.929	10.227	11.331	14.696	22.130	72.570
Total expenditures	0.831	0.928	1.449	2.107	2.199	1.997	2.204	12.322
Excess income	2.093	2.778	4.480	8.170	9.132	12.700	19.926	60.248
Loans	33.700	56.100	98.200	103.900	—	26.200	24.800	342.884
Disbursements of loans	1.809	11.753	18.285	24.681	61.822	36.967	25.458	180.755
Technical assistance	0.125	0.115	0.628	0.805	0.366	0.200	0.474	2.713
Disbursements of technical assistance	0.125	0.112	0.159	0.623	0.278	0.169	0.215	1.681

Source: Arab Fund for Economic and Social Development, *Annual Reports*, 1979–80 (in Arabic).

as well as to give the fund enough financial resources for its future activities.

Scope of Activities

By the end of 1980 AFESD had extended 62 loans, amounting to KD342.884m, to many Arab countries.[3] 1976 saw substantial growth in the fund's activities, in both nature and quantity. During this year it intensified its lending operations and devoted increased attention to technical assistance activities and inter-Arab projects. In 1976, the number of loans concluded with member countries reached 14 compared with 11 loans in 1975 and 8 loans in 1974. The value of loans increased to reach KD98.200m in 1976, compared with KD56.100m in 1975 and KD33.700m in 1974. During 1976, the fund's lending operations concentrated on development projects aimed at removing constraints which impede economic and social development in member countries. Loans to infrastructural projects amounted to about 66 per cent of the total value of loans for this year, with industrial and agricultural projects accounting for the remainder. Abour 43 per cent of the total loans committed in 1976 were for the least developed countries in the Arab region, where infrastructural projects accounted for 80 per cent of the gross value of loans to these countries.[4]

During 1977, the efforts designed to identify and study joint Arab projects entered a new phase. Technical assistance projects were given more attention and particular efforts were made to study the development of human resources and of qualified technical cadres in a selected number of specialisations, the exploitation of natural resources, and the main obstacles hindering development in the least developed Arab countries and the means of overcoming such obstacles. In lending operations, the number of loans extended by the fund in this year reached 15 loans at a value of KD103.900m. AFESD's contribution to the financing of projects in 1977 represented about 12 per cent of their total costs and was instrumental in attracting the additional funds required for the financing of these projects from other sources. In this year, the fund continued to direct most of its loans to infrastructure projects, believing that such projects are the vital base required for any economic or social progress. Thus, of the total value of loans extended in 1977, about 76 per cent went to infrastructure projects such as roads, electricity, water and telecommunications while about 24 per cent went to industrial and agricultural productive projects. The least developed member countries of the Arab region received about 26 per cent of the total value of loans extended in 1977, all of which was directed to finance infrastructure projects in these countries. In this year, the fund also provided technical assistance to 13 national and regional projects and to one project in the field of studies and scientific research of which the fund's total commitment amounted to KD805,000, or 30 per cent of its total costs. The fund also took measures concerning 'The Basic Programme for Agricultural Development in the Democratic Republic of Sudan'. These measures culminated in the establishment of 'The Arab Authority for Agricultural Investment and Development', which aims at the development of agricultural resources in the Arab countries with a view to meeting their food requirements and increasing the volume of agricultural products exchanged among them. The authority was actually established in March 1977 when the agreement establishing it was declared effective. In relation to long-term planning for the Arab region the fund looked into the question of studying aspects relating to the preparation of a Regional Development Model for the Arab area suitable for use as a basis for regulating patterns of Arab co-operation and integration and joint Arab investments on the one hand, and the relationship between the Arab region and the international economic system on the other hand.[5]

In 1978, the fund's activities centred on three main elements: ways and means to expand financial resources; appraisal of projects and follow-up of their implementation; and identification of inter-country projects and the formulation of special programmes geared to specific and critical development problems, especially in the Arab LLDCs. AFESD's concern with these aspects followed resolutions of the Board of Governors of the fund regarding the expansion of the absorption capacity of Arab member countries and the strengthening of Arab economic integration efforts. The fund made no new loan commitments during this year, due mainly to the fact that it was giving special attention to the supervision of ongoing projects. In the same year, under its programme of technical assistance, however, it allocated a total of KD0.366m in support of six regional and country projects that aimed at strengthening the technical and administrative capabilities of development organisations and the rationalisation of the use of natural resources.[6]

AFESD resumed its loan commitments in 1979, when it committed KD26.200m for six loans to finance projects in the sectors of road, electricity, water, mining and agriculture. Four least developed Arab countries – Mauritania, Yemen Democratic Republic, Somalia and Sudan – received about 79 per cent of these loans.[7]

During 1980, the fund committed KD24.8m to finance new projects in agriculture, transport and telecommunications, water and drainage, and power sectors. Two Arab least developed countries, the Yemen Arab Republic and the Democratic Republic of Yemen, received about 20 per cent of these loans. As for technical assistance, the fund provided KD0.474m for supporting development activities in the fields of agricultural, power, training and development finance research works.[8] Table 15.3 shows the cumulative distribution of the loans of the fund.

TABLE 15.3   AFESD Cumulative Loans by Country and their Percentages (1974–80)

Country	Loans (KDm)	Percentages
Arab Republic of Egypt	67.9	19.8
Democratic Republic of Sudan	38.4	11.2
Morocco	33.0	9.6
Yemen Arab Republic	30.8	9.0
Syria, Arab Republic	24.7	7.2
Jordan	22.7	6.6
Mauritania	22.2	6.5
Yemen Democratic Republic	22.1	6.4
Algeria, Democratic Republic of	20.3	5.9
Tunisia	19.8	5.8
Somalia, Democratic Republic of	16.0	4.7
Lebanon	11.0	3.2
Sultanate of Oman	9.0	2.6
Bahrain	5.0	1.5
Total	342.9	100

Source: Arab Fund for Economic and Social Development, *Annual Report* 1980 (in Arabic).

Table 15.3 shows that Arab LLDCs received KD129.5m (37.8 per cent) and other Arab countries received KD214.7m (62.2 per cent) of the total loans committed by AFESD during 1974–80. The distribution of these loans by economic sector, during the same period, shows that infrastructural projects received the majority of these loans, amounting to KD213.8m (62.3 per cent), manufacturing projects KD57.9m (16.9 per cent), agricultural projects KD42.4m (12.3 per cent), and projects in the service sector received KD7.00m (2 per cent). Arab joint projects (namely communications, and telecommunications, airports and roads) received KD22.0m (6.4 per cent).

Terms and Conditions

Interest rate: 4 per cent in least developed Arab countries (Mauritania, Somalia, Yemen Arab Republic, and Yemen Democratic Republic), 6 per cent in other Arab countries. There is no service charge.
Repayment period: Semi-annual instalments, maturity 15–25 years.
Grace period: 4–6 years.
Guarantee: Government guarantees for all loans are required. Additional special guarantees are needed for projects in the private sector.

According to Article 16 of the Agreement establishing the fund, it may modify the terms of the loan contract at the borrower's request. It may also modify the conditions of repayment of the loan without prejudice to the interest of the fund or other members and subject to the approval of the guaranteeing government.

Management and Organisation

AFESD is managed by a Board of Governors, the Director General as a Chairman of the Board of Directors, the Board of Directors, the Loan Committees and the staff. The Board of Governors consists of governors and their deputies, each appointed by a member country of the fund for a period of five years. Every year the Board elects one of the governors as its Chairman. The Board of Governors is considered as the General Assembly of the Fund and has all powers. However, it may delegate to the Board of Directors any of its powers, except the following:

(i) admittance of new members;
(ii) increasing the capital;
(iii) suspending a member;
(iv) settling disputes over the interpretation of the provisions of the Agreement establishing the fund;
(v) concluding agreements for the purpose of co-operating with other international organisations;
(vi) terminating the operations of the fund and liquidating its assets;
(vii) determining the distribution of the net income of the fund.

Each member country has 200 votes, regardless of the number of shares it holds, plus one additional vote for each share held. All matters before the Board of Governors are decided by an absolute majority of votes. The Board of Governors appoints the Director General of the fund, who presides at the meetings of the Board of Directors with no vote except in the event of an equal division of votes, in which case he has a casting vote. The Board of Directors is charged with all the activities of the fund in a general manner, and exercises the powers delegated to it by the Board of Governors. Loan Committees are formed to submit the necessary reports on the projects and the adequacy of loans requested. Each committee includes an expert selected by the governor representing the member in whose territory the project is located, and one or more members of the technical staff of the fund appointed by the Chairman of the Board of Directors.[9] The staff of the fund are organised into two main areas: operational units and service units. In the operational area, the main task of the Projects Department is field missions, appraisal work, implementation and follow-up, and the Programme Department is mainly concerned with country studies and sectoral policies. As for the service area, there is a Finance Department for portfolio management, a Legal Department for legal documentation and legal matters, and an Administration Department for recruitment and public relations.

Approaches and Techniques Applied

Arab member countries submit loan requests to the fund which, according to the inter-sectoral priorities within a country identified by the Programme Department, studies the request with the Projects Department and submits a country programme paper. An appraisal mission is then sent to appraise the project in the field, submitting the result to the management of the fund. An Appraisal Draft Report is prepared and finalised incorporating the comments of loan committees: the Statutory Loan Committee where representatives of the recipient country concerned are informed of the project; and the Operational Loan Committee, chaired by the President of the fund, discusses crucial issues of the report. Negotiation and approval of the loan is conducted by the Board of Directors. The fund generally complies with the urgent socio-economic needs of each recipient country but it is neither the mandate nor the role of the fund to change the targets established by various Arab national plans. The evaluation process of the fund is to improve the development impact in the recipient country, and although the applications for project assistance are often generated by the interested governments, the fund has adopted an activist policy to identify and prepare projects.[10] It can advance funds to conduct feasibility studies on project proposals, with expenditures being repaid as part of the loans.

AFESD applies its own appraisal of projects on the basis of pre-investment study in the form of appraisal reports. Projects should be technically sound and economically viable for the country, and must be able to stand on their own feet financially. The fund therefore attaches great importance to the country approach in project appraisal. Moreover, it acts as a financial catalyst by stimulating co-financing by other development funds and private Arab capital. Like other Arab development funds, AFESD adopts withdrawal procedures based upon conditions to be met prior to commencement of withdrawals on proceeds of a loan. Loan proceeds are only disbursed to meet or cover actual approved expenditures or payments due on the project, supported by full documentation, in accordance with the provisions of the Loan Agreement.

Strategy for Financing and Technical Assistance

As the fund is a regional development organisation, it adopts a regional integration approach for inter-Arab and regional project identification and promotion. It carried out a programme for the identification and preparation of inter-country projects and related feasibility studies jointly with UNDP during 1975–80. The programme aimed at providing technical assistance to Arab countries in identifying viable inter-Arab projects and preparing their feasibility studies. This programme has prepared feasibility studies for a number of inter-Arab projects in the fields of infrastructure and natural resources development.[11] The programme also prepared feasibility studies for linking the telecommunication networks of some Arab countries in Western Asia and between them and Egypt. Other activities included a survey of the prospects of manufacturing agricultural machinery and equipment in the Arab region, and pre-investment study for the preparation of a programme on pre-school education.[12] AFESD also adopted a 'Basic Programme for Development of the Agricultural Sector in Sudan', 1976–81–86. The programme led to the establishment of the 'Arab Authority for Agricultural Investment and Development'. This authority is an embodiment of joint Arab economic efforts aimed at an optimal utilisation of Arab agricultural resources, enhancing the agricultural production capabilities of the region, meeting a greater proportion of the food security requirements of the Arab World, and promoting economic integration between its various parts. The authority was entrusted with the implementation of the First Investment Plan, prepared within the framework of the Basic Programme, in consultation with the Government of Sudan and in co-operation with AFESD. The authority is entitled by decision of the Board of Shareholders to undertake, in consultation with the countries concerned, the formulation and implementation of similar agricultural development programmes in any of the contracting countries.[13]

As part of its strategy, AFESD extends international credit lines to Arab members' institutions for the purpose of distributing institutionalised credits to medium- and small-size enterprises where the allocation of credit lines follows the specialisation of the recipient institutions. The fund also regularly studies aspects relating to the preparation of a Regional Development Model for the Arab region suitable for use as a basis for regulating patterns of Arab economic co-operation and integration and joint Arab investments, on the one hand, and the relationship between the Arab region and the international economic system on the other. Moreover, the fund plays a role as co-ordinator of the activities and operations of Arab development funds, in preparing and calling for periodic meetings by such funds.[14] A key principle of the fund is to channel its resources, whenever possible, into the least developed countries of the Arab members, such as Sudan, Somalia, the Yemen Arab Republic, the Democratic Republic of Yemen and Mauritania. However, the absorptive capacity of these countries, with the exception of Sudan, is a problem facing the fund in implementing such a strategy. As for sectoral priorities, the fund, as indicated before, is giving a high priority to the financing of 'inter-Arab projects' involving two or more countries especially in the infrastructural sector with the most emphasis on electric power (19 per cent 1974–80) and road projects (15.6 per cent 1974–80).[15]

Problems of Implementation and Remarks from Field Experience

AFESD shares with other development funds in the field of financing projects the common problems from the recipient countries outlined in the previous chapters. However, the Arab Fund, as a regional organisation, faces more problems than the national funds, due mainly to the fact that it concentrates on a country approach and regional projects rather than a project approach and national projects. As a co-ordinator among other Arab funds AFESD has a difficult task, especially with relation to the procedure for the withdrawal of loans and procedures for implementation. It also places emphasis on the financing of infrastructural projects which are complex and huge, requiring close supervision and updated information on the country and sectoral levels, as well as on the project level. Technical aspects for these types of projects are considered to be of vital importance, which has led the fund to choose the best sort of technology suitable for implementation and supervision. Moreover, as the fund's future strategy seems to be concentrated on least developed Arab countries, it has to cope with the need to provide these countries with technical assistance. As the fund's most important future role is to act as a financial catalyst, it has to equip itself with the most recent information gathered from the financial markets regionally as well as internationally. It also has to carry out regular studies and surveys on recent economic developments in the Arab countries and to appraise the viability of huge regional projects with their future effects and the economies of scale that could foster the process of Arab economic co-operation and integration. The fund is actually making considerable efforts to achieve this target especially in 1981. The new Arab development decade is evidence of this trend. To prepare for the new era of Arab economic and social development, the fund has published several important studies. A study on Arab economic development in the 1970s and prospects in the 1980s has been carried out by the fund as a guideline for its future activities and for encouraging utilisation of public and private capital and technical assistance for Arab economic development in the 1980s.[16] AFESD has also published a study on the flow of Arab private capital to evaluate its pattern, size and characteristics for the purpose of encouraging Arab capital to play an active effective role in Arab economic and social developments as an important tool for achieving Arab economic co-operation and integration.[17] The fund has also, in co-operation with the Arab Monetary Fund, published its first Annual Economic Report, for 1980. The Report aims to provide basic information on Arab economic and social developments and the main economic issues facing the Arab countries.[18] Moreover, the fund has published a study on development problems in the least developed Arab countries, related to the economic and social situations of these countries, their infrastructural problems and productive sectors, and their procedures, recommendations, needs and finance.[19] Another publication was a study on the development of human resources and labour forces in the Arab region. The study focused on the problems facing the development of human resources and the labour force in Arab countries and the institutional mechanism suitable for carrying out this development.[20]

AFESD has a still larger role to play in fostering Arab regional projects in different sectors and in different Arab countries, as well as in Arab joint co-ordination policies, foreign aid policies and financial policies. It should become more active in playing a pioneer role for suggesting an Arab aid development strategy and in establishing Arab machinery for follow-up and implementation for development financing. One way to achieve these targets would be through direct contact with the Arab governments and their financial institutions, to play an active important role in fostering regional economic co-operation among Arab countries. This could be implemented through the opening up of viable economic sector channels for economic co-operation not only for the infrastructural sector but also for other sectors, mainly agriculture, industry, tourism and finance. In addition, the fund has not yet proved to be active in the field of Arab social development, an important area that will be of great importance in the years to come. Such a wide scope of activities, however, would require substantial new sources of funds.

16 The Arab Bank for Economic Development in Africa

Establishment and Financial Resources

The Arab Bank for Economic Development in Africa[1] is an independent regional development institution established and financed by member countries of the Arab League for the purpose of participating in the economic development of non-Arab African countries, in order to strengthen the economic and friendly co-operation between the two groups. The bank was established in accordance with a resolution of the Arab Head of States Meeting in Algeria on 28 November 1973. It began operations effectively from March 1975, based in Khartoum, Sudan. According to the Agreement establishing the Bank, it is to participate in financing economic development of the African countries, encourage the participation of Arab capitals in African developments, and participate in providing technical assistance for Africa.[2] The initial subscribed capital of the bank was US $100,000 for each share. These should be paid for by each subscribing member country in four equal instalments. The minimum number of shares for each member should not be less than ten shares, to be paid in American dollars. The bank may increase its capital if three-quarters of the votes in the Board of Governors agree. At a special meeting of the Board of Governors held in Cairo on 15 December 1976, it was agreed that the capital subscription of the Special Arab Aid Fund for Africa (SAAFA)[3] be merged with the bank's capital. Table 16.1 shows the original subscription to the bank by Arab member countries.

The amount of the initial capital subscription and the 1977 replenishment brought the subscribed capital of ABEDA to US $738.25m by the end of 1980. The 1977 capital replenishment represented US $507.25m. The paid-up capital of the bank at the end of 1980 reached

TABLE 16.1 Original Subscription to ABEDA by Arab Member Countries (US$m)

Country	Original subscription
Algeria	20.0
Bahrain	1.0
Egypt	1.0
Iraq	30.0
Jordan	1.0
Kuwait	20.0
Lebanon	5.0
Libya	40.0
Mauritania	1.0
Morocco	10.0
Oman	4.0
PLO	1.0
Qatar	20.0
Saudi Arabia	50.0
Sudan	1.0
Syria	1.0
Tunisia	5.0
UAE	20.0
Total	231.0

Source: John Law, *Arab-Aid: Who Gets it, For What, and How*, Chase World Information Corporation, 1978.

US $718.652m, with the difference between subscribed capital and paid-up capital being US $19.598m. This difference is mainly accounted for by the sums due from six Arab countries, namely UAE (US $10.00m), Libya (US $6.66m), Oman (US $2.00m), Mauritania (US $0.432m), Egypt (US $0.333m) and Sudan (US $0.166m).[4] These due amounts were not urgently required to enable the bank to meet its loan commitments as the total amount of loans and grants committed by the bank reached only US $383.63m by the end of 1980. Disbursements reached only US $165.2m during the same period. The ratio of total disbursement to total commitments reached 43 per cent, and the ratio of total commitments to paid-up capital reached 52 per cent, indicating the availability of capital resources to be utilised. Table 16.2 shows the situation of the capital subscription of the Arab member countries to the bank as it stood at the end of 1980 and the distribution of voting powers.

TABLE 16.2 Capital Subscription by Arab Member Countries to ABEDA and Their Voting Powers (31 December, 1980)

Country	Subscriptions			Voting powers	
	Value (US $m)	Number of shares	Percentage	Number of votes	Percentage
Algeria	30.000	300	4.07	500	4.55
Bahrain	1.500	15	0.20	215	1.96
Egypt	1.500	15	0.20	215	1.96
Iraq	105.000	1050	14.23	1250	11.38
Jordan	1.500	15	0.20	215	1.96
Kuwait	110.000	1100	14.90	1300	11.84
Lebanon	5.000	50	0.67	250	2.28
Libya	120.000	1200	16.26	1400	12.75
Mauritania	1.500	15	0.20	215	1.96
Morocco	11.000	110	1.49	310	2.82
Oman	11.000	110	1.49	310	2.82
PLO	1.500	15	0.20	215	1.96
Qatar	60.000	600	8.13	800	7.28
Saudi Arabia	180.000	1800	24.38	2000	18.21
Sudan	1.500	15	0.20	215	1.96
Syria	1.00	10	0.14	210	1.96
Tunisia	6.250	62.5	0.85	262.5	2.39
UAE	90.000	900	12.19	1100	10.01
Total	738.250	7382.5	100.00	10982.5	100.00

Source: Arab Bank for Economic Development in Africa, Annual Report, 1980 (in Arabic).

To increase its resources, the bank is authorised to borrow money (through credits, long- and medium-term deposits, and issuance of bonds in the Arab and international financial markets), up to twice the amount of its paid-up capital and reserves, unless the Board of Governors decides otherwise. The 200 per cent condition is not applicable to deposits.[5] By the end of 1980, the bank had not exercised its right in this sort of borrowing activities, as its paid-up capital far exceeded total commitments, as indicated before. However, it is probable that future additions to the authorised capital of the bank will come from borrowing. Indications are that future operations of the bank will require this sort of financing as a supplementary source for additional funds, with all the merits of gaining experience in this field.

Scope of Activities

ABEDA is the only Arab development institution that operates entirely in Africa. It finances projects only in non-Arab African countries, which are members of the Organisation for African Unity (OAU), but not members of the Arab League. This makes the bank the only Arab institution that does no lending to Arab countries. From the date of its commencement of operations in 1975 until the end of 1980, the bank had reached agreements on 53 loans and 4 grants, with the cumulative volumes of loans and grants reaching US $383.63m by the end of 1980. Table 16.3 gives a summary of the bank's operations.

TABLE 16.3 Summary of ABEDA's Operations 1975–80 [a]

	1975	1976	1977	1978	1979	1980	Total
Number of agreed loans	10	9	9	9	7	9	53
Number of agreed grants	—	1	—	3	—	—	4
Number of credit facilities	—	—	—	1	1	—	2
Number of emergency relief operations	—	—	—	14	—	—	14
Number of loans signed	—	12	11	10	4	13	50
Number of loans implemented	—	5	8	15	6	5	39
Value of loans and grants (US $m)	71.6	61.9	66.24	67.87	44.07	71.95	383.63
Disbursements (US $m)	—	2.1	7.6	55.7	52.0	47.8	165.2

[a] The operations of the Special Arab Aid Fund for Africa (SAAFA) are not included.
Source: Arab Bank for Economic Development in Africa, *Annual Report*, 1980 (in Arabic).

By the end of 1980, ABEDA had completed six years of its operations in African non-Arab countries, with average yearly commitments reaching US $64m. If loans attended by SAAFA, which amounted to about $214m, are included, the average rises to US $100m. The bank's participation in financing projects in Africa represents 10–15 per cent, on average, of the total Arab aid commitments for African non-Arab countries. The share of the bank's financing of the total costs of projects represents, on average, about 12 per cent during the period 1975–80. With the exception of 1979, the bank's commitments of loans and grants have steadily grown, reaching US $71.95m in 1980 compared with US $67.87m in 1978, and US $61.9m in 1976. The number of African countries which have benefited from the bank's assistance increased from 12 in 1975 to 20 in 1976, 22 in 1977, 30 in 1978, 31 in 1979, and 33 in 1980. As for subregional loan distribution, the West African countries received a greater share of assistance compared with East African countries. However, the bank operated in 15 East African countries, out of the total number of 18, and reached a coverage ratio, in terms of number of countries, of 84 per cent compared with 18 West African countries, out of a total of 23, with a coverage ratio of 78.2 per cent. The bank financed 30 loans in West African countries compared with 25 loans for East African countries, with the average size of loan being similar, reaching US $6.7m for West African countries compared with US $6.5m for East African countries. However, in 1980, the bank started to give more emphasis to its activities in East African countries to establish a pattern of equilibrium between the two regions in the near future. Table 16.4 shows the geographical distribution of the bank's committtments between Eastern and Western Africa.

TABLE 16.4 ABEDA's Geographical Distribution of Commitments between Eastern and Western African Countries 1975–80 (in US $m and %)

Distribution	1975	1976	1977	1978	1979	1980	Total
West Africa	51.60 (72.1%)	27.80 (44.9%)	40.24 (60.7%)	40.463 (59.6%)	33.60 (76.2%)	27.5 (38.2%)	221.203 (57.7%)
East Africa	20.00 (27.9%)	34.00 (54.9%)	26.00 (39.3%)	25.898 (38.2%)	10.47 (23.8%)	44.45 (61.8%)	160.818 (41.9%)
Others	—	—	—	—	—	—	1.609[a] (0.4%)
Grand total	71.60	61.90	66.24	67.87	44.07	71.95	383.630

[a] For regional organisations concerned with Africa as a whole.
Source: Arab Bank for Economic Development in Africa, *Annual Report*, 1980 (in Arabic).

ABEDA gave great attention to the financing of infrastructural projects (44.5 per cent) followed by agricultural and manufacturing projects (20.1 and 20.2 per cent respectively) while energy projects received about 11.3 per cent of the bank's total commitments during the period 1975–80. The bank's emphasis on infrastructural projects, similar to that of other Arab aid agencies, is based upon the belief that most African countries are in great need of development in this sector, which includes transport, communication and telecommunications, dams, bridges, water and drainage. This trend of the bank's sectoral priorities will continue in future years. Table 16.5 shows the bank's sectoral distribution of commitments.

TABLE 16.5 ABEDA's Sectoral Distribution of Commitments 1975–80 (in US $m and %)

Sector	1975	1976	1977	1978	1979	1980	Total
Infrastructure	42.0 (58.7%)	29.1 (47.0%)	13.20 (19.9%)	17.60 (25.9%)	36.67 (83.2%)	32.25 (44.8%)	170.82 (44.5%)
Agriculture	11.6 (16.2%)	17.8 (28.8%)	12.20 (18.4%)	14.65 (21.6%)	2.40 (5.5%)	18.50 (25.7%)	77.15 (20.1%)
Manufacture	18.0 (25.1%)	— (—)	24.84 (37.5%)	9.70 (14.3%)	5.00 (11.3%)	20.00 (27.8%)	77.54 (20.2%)
Energy	— (—)	15.0 (24.2%)	16.00 (24.2%)	10.92 (16.1%)	— (—)	1.20 (1.7%)	43.12 (11.3%)
Special programme	— (—)	— (—)	— (—)	15.00 (22.1%)	— (—)	— (—)	15.00 (3.9%)

Source: Arab Bank for Economic Development in Africa, *Annual Report*, 1980 (in Arabic).

During 1978, ABEDA complied with the appeal from the Organisation for African Unity regarding the serious economic situation which faced several African countries, mainly because of drought, and implemented an emergency special aid programme especially for the Sahel countries, whose purpose was to extend loans to these countries for protection of the environment, crops, rural irrigation, development of rice farms, water, energy and livestock.[6] This programme was of value, but not in itself sufficient, as these problems in the Sahel require a substantial amount of loans and grants on a regular basis for the purpose of making structural changes in the use of water resources.

Terms and Conditions

Interest Rates

These range from 1 to 6 per cent depending upon the economic condition of the recipient country, the kind of project to be financed and the economic sector in which the project is located. The lower interest rates are for the poorest countries and agricultural projects also benefit from lower interest rates. There is no administrative fee. For countries in which annual per capita income is less than US $200, rates of interest on projects are close to the minimum rate of 1 per cent, especially if the project to be financed has long-term impacts on the economy of the recipient country, or has a social contribution. For other countries interest rates are close to the maximum rate of 6 per cent, taking into consideration the viability of the project. Thus the bank adopts a flexible approach for determining interest rates, or what is called a 'Central Rate of Interest'[7] rather than rigid rates.

Repayment Periods

Semi-annual instalments, maturity 20 years as a standard repayment period, but in some cases maturities could be lower than 20 years depending upon the type of project and the economic condition of the recipient country.

Grace Period

The standard period is five years.

Guarantee

Government guarantee is required. In the case of financing projects in two or more countries each country should provide the bank with separate guarantees, according to the size of financing for each country. In addition the bank requires additional guarantees in the case of private projects.

The bank does not participate with more than US $10m for any project. In special circumstances, however, it may waive this condition with the approval of its Board of Directors. Moreover, the bank finances only the foreign exchange components of the project. The American dollar is the operating standard currency for its operations.[8] ABEDA does not engage in local currency financing for projects unless it is deemed necessary under the conditions determined in the loan agreement.

Management and Organisational Structure

The bank is managed by the Board of Governors, the Board of Directors, the President and the staff. The Board of Governors represents the highest authority of the bank, Governors and Deputy Governors are appointed by each member country. The Board of Governors instruct the Board of Directors regarding the general bank policy and could delegate it to carry out some of its responsibilities with the exception of the following:

The Arab Bank

(1) Incrementation of the capital of the bank.
(2) Appointment of the Chairman of the Board of Directors who is also the Managing Director of the bank.
(3) Approval of the financial system of the bank.
(4) Appointment of the external auditors.
(5) Approval of the balance sheet and the financial situation of the bank after reviewing the report submitted by the Board of Directors and the report of the external auditors.
(6) Allocation of net income of the bank.
(7) Amendment of the Agreement establishing the bank.
(8) Termination of the membership of a country.
(9) Termination of the bank's operation.

The Board of Governors meets once every year. It may also meet at any other time if it is considered important, or if the Board of Directors calls for such a meeting. Each member country in the Board of Governors has 200 votes plus one vote for each share in the capital of the bank. Decisions in the Board of Governors are taken by the majority of the voting powers.[9] Any member country having 200 shares in the bank automatically gets a seat on the Board of Directors. The other Directors – except for the Chairman, who sits *ex officio* and votes when there is a tie – are elected jointly for four-year terms by the governors who represent the remaining member countries. The President of the bank is elected for a five-year term with a renewable mandate. To help keep contact with potential borrowers and co-financiers, the bank has set up representative offices in both Washington and Paris.[10] The operational units of the bank are composed of the Operations Department, the Technical Department and the Financial and Disbursement Department. Service units comprise the Administration, Legal and Information Departments.

Approaches and Techniques applied

Like the other Arab funds, ABEDA begins to consider a project when a loan request comes from the government of the country where the project is located. The government should provide the bank with the necessary guarantee required, according to the bank's procedures. The viability of the project and its contribution to economic development in the recipient country must also be studied before the bank starts to finance the project. The bank also pays great attention to projects that have positive impacts on other projects and on the economic and social environment of the country concerned. As the bank has imposed a ceiling limit for financing any project of US$10m, it has to look seriously at co-financing with other Arab aid agencies, the African Development Bank, and the World Bank. As a new agency, the bank needs some time to study the present economic situation in Africa and to investigate the economic plans in countries in which it operates or plans to operate. Consequently, the bank at the present time depends to some extent on the experience of other organisations in this field and makes use of outside consultants. As for the techniques for project appraisal, the bank makes use of outside consultants who should obtain the following information.[11]

(1) A recent report on the economic development of the recipient country.
(2) Economic plans or programmes for the country concerned, both medium- and long-term, as well as the economic potential.
(3) A complete feasibility study on the project from the economic, financial, technical and social aspects.
(4) Economic and financial information about the African and non-African organisations with whom the bank is planning to co-finance the project.
(5) All information and guarantees regarding the management of the project or the organisations with whom the bank participates.

Thus ABEDA's project appraisal procedures are established in co-operation with other Arab, African and international finance institutions for the purpose of quick commitments at this early stage and for avoiding lengthy appraisals. However, the bank has started recently to prepare complete and lengthy feasibility studies on different projects in the region.

Strategy for Financing and Technical Assistance

ABEDA follows a strategy based upon encouraging potential economic activities which have priorities for development in Africa. For implementing this strategy, the bank gives priorities to the following sectors:[12]

(i) agriculture, agro-industries and food industries;
(ii) utilisation of natural resources;
(iii) infrastructure;
(iv) manufacturing industries which contribute to African productivity;

(v) human resource developments;
(vi) development in the service sector related mainly to the development of transport and tourism.

The bank believes in co-operation among Arab development funds in financing projects in Africa. It also believes in technical co-operation between Arab and African countries as this directly leads to enhancement of the investment's absorptive capacities for development. For that purpose the bank follows a strategy based upon what has been agreed in international development meetings and tries to adopt their recommendations within its scope of activities. Thus the bank gives special emphasis to least developed African countries, most seriously affected African countries, and Sahel countries. ABEDA's prospective development activities in the future will place more emphasis on financing development projects in Sub-Saharan African countries that have a regional impact, and on credit lines to national development banks operating in the same countries. Moreover, the bank is adopting a regional integration approach by promoting and assisting development projects in Africa within the frame of the global strategy of Arab-African co-operation. As the bank's main strategy is based upon the objective of enhancing Arab-African co-operation, the main principles of this co-operation are based upon the following:[13]

(i) no tied aid;
(ii) co-operation within the frame of international development and trilateral co-operation;
(iii) co-operation as a means of achieving development in both African and Arab countries.

The implementation of this strategy requires a substantial amount of financial resources to be directed to African economic development. Moreover, it requires a complete survey on African resources and needs in the medium- and long-run and also information about the flow of funds from developed countries and aid agencies to these countries. The Arab-African strategy should therefore be considered not in isolation from other development efforts in Africa but as part of an overall effort.

Problems of Implementation and Remarks from Field Experience

Like other development agencies financing projects in Africa, the ABEDA faces different problems ranging from one country to another, depending upon the stage of development and economic management of each particular country. The series of problems that the bank faces in the stage of implementation and follow-up of projects includes the lack of local currencies, delay in disbursements, bad management, lack of direct communication, problems of productivity of labour, lack of stability in economic systems in some countries, and a rise of the total costs of the projects during implementation, as well as fluctuations in the value of foreign currencies required to import tools and machinery. There are also problems with contractors and consultants, different estimates of total costs and components for the project submitted to different donors. Many projects have been delayed in implementation not because of foreign exchange financing but because of an inadequate supply of local currency. This is mainly related to the internal economic and financial situation of the recipient African country. Thus, as the bank has similar problems to other agencies in the stage of project implementation, it faces chronic problems especially in the case of least developed African countries, namely the Sahel countries.

Following a joint meeting in Kuwait in November 1980 between the Heads of Arab development funds and the Ministers of the Permanent Committee of Sahel Countries, the bank has been asked to prepare a study on the role of Arab aid in these countries within a framework of their development strategy. The bank sent missions to these countries for that purpose, and a summary of the preliminary study was circulated at the Arab Funds' Co-ordination meeting in Kuwait in April 1981.[14] The main feature of the strategy for Arab aid in Sahel countries presented by the bank is based upon basic alternatives with emphasis upon mining projects and road projects. The strategy is also based upon an integrated approach for development assistance to these countries. Moreover, the strategy emphasises the importance of joint studies related to agriculture and energy, which are directed towards economic structural changes in these countries.

Any sort of development strategy adopted by aid agencies in this part of the world should be mainly based upon solving the chronic problems facing these countries: in irrigation, water supplies and dams as well as human resource development. ABEDA, as stated before, is already active in these fields but to implement the new strategy it has diverted its activities to other aspects of development which are not considered to be top priority for a strategy to be implemented in Sahel countries.

17 The Islamic Development Bank

Establishment and Financial Resources

IsDB is an international financial institution established in pursuance of the Declaration of Intent issued by a Conference of Finance Ministers of Muslim Countries held in Jeddah in December 1973. The inaugural meeting of the Board of Governors took place in July 1975, and the bank formally opened on 20 October 1975. The bank's headquarters are in Jeddah, Saudi Arabia, and it is authorised to establish agencies or branch offices elsewhere. The purpose of the bank is to foster the economic development and social progress of member countries and Muslim communities individually as well as jointly in accordance with the principles of the Shariah (Muslim code of Law). The authorised capital stock of the bank is 2bn Islamic Dinars (ID), divided into 200,000 shares having a par value of ID10,000 each. The value of the Islamic Dinar, which is a unit of account in the bank, is equivalent to one SDR (Special Drawing Right of the International Monetary Fund). The subscribed capital of the bank is ID790m payable in freely convertible currency acceptable to the bank.[1] Table 17.1 shows a list of the bank's members and their voting power.

Among numerous economic resolutions passed at the Islamic Summit Conference in Taif in January 1981, was one to increase the subscribed capital of IsDB by another ID1210m so that the subscribed capital of the bank would reach the authorised amount of ID2000m. The bulk of this increase was pledged by Saudi Arabia. This decision was taken due to the need to consider mobilising additional financial resources for development in the Muslim developing countries.[2] The bank has no borrowing power due to the fact that it cannot pay interest rates, but it is authorised to accept deposits and to raise funds in any other manner. Deposits are to be used for equity investments, in which the member governments will take a share of profits. The bank turns over its

TABLE 17.1 Islamic Development Bank's Member Countries' Subscription and Voting Power

Member	Total subscription Amount (IDm)	% of total	Voting power No. of votes	% of total
Republic of Afghanistan	2.5	0.32	750	0.76
Democratic and Popular Republic of Algeria	25.0	3.16	3,000	3.03
State of Bahrain	5.0	0.63	1,000	1.01
People's Republic of Bangladesh	10.0	1.26	1,500	1.51
United Republic of Cameroon	2.5	0.32	750	0.76
Republic of Chad	2.5	0.32	750	0.76
Federal Islamic Republic of Comoro Islands	2.5	0.32	750	0.76
Republic of Djibouti	2.5	0.32	750	0.76
Arab Republic of Egypt	25.0	3.16	3,000	3.03
Republic of Gambia	2.5	0.32	750	0.76
Republic of Guinea	2.5	0.32	750	0.76
Republic of Guinea Bissau	2.5	0.32	750	0.76
Republic of Indonesia	25.0	3.16	3,000	3.03
Republic of Iraq	10.0	1.26	1,500	1.51
Hashemite Kingdom of Jordan	4.0	0.50	900	0.90
State of Kuwait	100.0	12.65	10,500	10.60
Republic of Lebanon	2.5	0.32	750	0.76
Socialist People's Libyan Arab Jamahiriyah	125.0	15.82	13,000	13.13
Malaysia	16.0	2.02	2,100	2.12
Republic of Maldives	2.5	0.32	750	0.76
Republic of Mali	2.5	0.32	750	0.76
Islamic Republic of Mauritania	2.5	0.32	750	0.76
Kingdom of Morocco	5.0	0.63	1,000	1.01
Republic of Niger	2.5	0.32	750	0.76
Sultanate of Oman	5.0	0.63	1,000	1.01
Islamic Republic of Pakistan	25.0	3.16	3,000	3.03
Palestine	2.5	0.32	750	0.76
State of Qatar	25.0	3.16	3,000	3.03
Kingdom of Saudi Arabia	200.0	25.32	20,500	20.70
Republic of Senegal	2.5	0.32	750	0.76
Somali Democratic Republic	2.5	0.32	750	0.76
Democratic Republic of Sudan	10.0	1.26	1,500	1.51
Syrian Arab Republic	2.5	0.32	750	0.76
Republic of Tunisia	2.5	0.32	750	0.76
Republic of Turkey	10.0	1.26	1,500	1.51
Republic of Uganda	2.5	0.32	750	0.76
United Arab Emirates	110.0	13.92	11,500	11.61
Republic of Upper Volta	2.5	0.32	750	0.76
Yemen Arab Republic	2.5	0.32	750	0.76
People's Democratic Republic of Yemen	2.5	0.32	750	0.76
Total 40 members	790.0	100.00	99,000	100.00

Source: Islamic Development Bank, Annual Report, 1979/1980.

undisbursed funds to the Saudi-Arabian Monetary Agency (SAMA) for investment. At 8 November 1980, these deposits reached ID503.2m and those with commercial banks ID20.5m.[3] The bank also holds deposits from the Islamic Solidarity Fund (ISF).

Scope of Activities

The functions of the bank are to participate in equity capital and making loans for productive projects and enterprises, as well as providing financial assistance to member countries in other forms for economic and social development. The bank is also required to establish and operate special funds for specific purposes including a fund for assistance to Muslim communities in non-member countries, in addition to setting up trust funds. The bank is also charged with the responsibility of assisting in the promotion of foreign trade, especially in capital goods, among member countries, providing technical assistance to member countries, extending training facilities for personnel engaged in development activities and undertaking research for enabling the economic, financial and banking activities in Muslim countries to conform to the Shariah.[4] With five years of lending behind it, the bank is gaining experience that should enable it to lend faster still. Total operations approved since its inception amount to ID1243.68m (US $1575.28m) in 36 of its 40 member countries. The operations of the bank include project financing, equity participation, leasing, profit-sharing, and foreign trade financing. Project financing covers the financing of projects and technical assistance. The total amount approved for project financing since the inception of the bank and until 1979/1980 totalled ID445.43m (US $554.86m). Foreign trade financing totalled ID798.24m (US $1020.42m) which represented 64 per cent of the total operations of the bank during the same period. From its inception up to 1979/80 IsDB had financed 80 foreign trade operations of which 64, amounting to ID610.69m (US $783.63m), were conducted among the member countries. The commodities financed included crude oil, refined petroleum products, urea fertiliser, cement and clinker, raw cotton and cotton yarn, jute, vegetable oil and palm oil, intermediate industrial goods, electricity generators, etc. Table 17.2 shows the bank's operations.

The sectoral allocations of the bank's project financing during the five years of its operation (1976-80) have shown substantial improvement in financing in the agriculture and agro-industries sector, whose share in total financing increased to 14.9 per cent in 1980 compared to 7.9 per cent in 1979. The allocations in other sectors in 1980 showed a more

TABLE 17.2 IsDB's Operations over Five Years (1976–80) (IDm)

Type of operation	1976 No	1976 Amount	1976 %	1977 No	1977 Amount	1977 %	1978 No	1978 Amount	1978 %	1979 No	1979 Amount	1979 %	1980 No	1980 Amount	1980 %	Total No	Total Amount	Total %
Loan	1	6.00	44.60	11	55.41	55.6	6	31.96	39.3	6	33.74	28.3	9	52.677	40.0	33	179.785	40.36
Equity	1	7.45	55.40	8	38.23	38.3	6	34.36	42.2	9	44.78	37.6	8	38.939	29.6	32	163.769	36.77
Leasing	—	—	—	1	5.22	5.2	1	10.00	12.3	5	39.05	32.8	5	36.473	27.7	12	90.743	20.37
Profit-sharing	—	—	—	—	—	—	1	4.27	5.3	—	—	—	—	—	—	1	4.270	0.96
Technical assistance	—	—	—	4	0.88	0.9	3	0.82[a]	1.0	6	1.68	1.4	4	3.492	2.7	17	6.867	1.54
Total Projects	2	13.45	100	24	99.74	100	17	81.41	100	26	119.25	100	26	131.581	100	95	445.434	100
Foreign trade Financing	—	—	—	5	43.61	30.4	15	127.14[a]	61.0	24	262.43	68.8	36	365.064	73.5	80	798.244	64.18
Total operations	2	13.45	100	29	143.35	100	32	208.55	100	50	381.68	100	62	496.645	100	175	1243.678	100

[a] These amounts are less than that published in the Third Annual Report due to cancellation of one technical assistance project amounting to ID0.120m and one foreign trade financing operation amounting to ID12.50m approved during 1398H which appeared in the Third Annual Report.

Source: Islamic Development Bank, *Annual Report*, 1979/1980.

balanced distribution as compared to 1979. However, the cumulative project financing, from the inception of the bank until 1980, shows that the bank gives most emphasis to industry and mining projects (43 per cent) followed by transport and communication projects (27 per cent). Table 17.3 shows the cumulative sectoral distribution of the bank's project financing.

TABLE 17.3 The Cumulative Sectoral Distribution IsDB's Project Financing (1976–80) (IDm)

Sectors	Total from 1976 to end of 1980	
	Amount	%
Agriculture	52.050	11.69
Industry and mining	189.558	42.56
Transport and communication	115.699	26.96
Utilities	57.464	12.90
Social services	23.343	5.24
Others	7.320	1.64
Total	445.434	100[a]

[a] Due to rounding of figures totals may not correspond to individual figures in the column.
Source: Islamic Development Bank, *Annual Report*, 1979/1980.

The lending programme for 1980/81 puts commitments at $825m, with $500m for foreign trade financing, $275m for project financing and $50m for technical assistance. Foreign trade operations in the programme approved have included supplies of crude oil for member countries such as Niger and Morocco, supplies of petroleum products for Guinea Bissau and urea-based fertilisers for Sudan.[5] The share of financing devoted to the LLDCs amounted to 46 per cent of the bank's operations as of 1979/80, and the bank is devising a series of policy measures which constitute an action programme to assist the development of these members. The special operations of the bank commenced following a Resolution passed by the Board of Governors at the Third Annual Meeting of the bank held in Kampala in 1979 to utilise the net proceeds accruing from its deposits in foreign banks after writing off the losses in the value of deposits due to currency fluctuations. They were to be used for the purpose of the promotion of training and research in Islamic banking, the provision of relief in the form of appropriate goods and services to member countries and Islamic communities afflicted by natural disasters and calamities, and for the promotion of financial assistance to member countries for the furtherance of Islamic causes. During 1979/80 the bank approved special operations amounting to ID7.89m (US $10.35m) for four countries, namely Cameroon, Pakistan, Palestine and Somalia.[6] The average ratio of disbursements to commitments from the period of the bank's inception to 8 November 1980 reached 55 per cent. The foreign trade financing ratio was higher than this average, reaching 68 per cent, while the ratio for project financing reached an average of 31 per cent. The components of the project financing: disbursement ratio are of particular interest since they show a high ratio of disbursements for profit-sharing operations (98 per cent), and a low ratio for technical assistance operations (9 per cent), 21 per cent for loans, 19 per cent for leasing and 48 per cent for equity participations. This wide difference in the status of authorised disbursements by the bank for ordinary operations indicates the need for more efforts to avoid delays in the implementation of three types of operations, loans, technical assistance, and leasing. Table 17.4 shows the status of authorised disbursement by the bank.

TABLE 17.4 Status of Authorised Disbursement of the Bank (1976–80) (ID)

A Ordinary operations	Amount disbursed	Percentage of amount approved
Loans	37,780,237.06	21.01
Technical assistance	635,014.01	9.25
Profit-sharing	4,166,001.17	97.60
Leasing	15,400,665.92	18.94
Equity	78,621,429.36	48.08
Subtotal	136,603,347.52	31.33
B Foreign trade financing operations	545,247,044.59	68.27
Grand total	681,850,392.11	55.23

Source: Islamic Development Bank, *Annual Report*, 1979/1980.

Terms and Conditions

Interest Rates

Loans are interest-free, as IsDB applies the Sharia Law which prohibits the taking of interest. However, it imposes loan charges to enable it to cover the costs of its non-interest loans. These service charges range from 2–3 per cent per annum, and should be paid in an agreed convertible currency.

Repayment Periods

Repayment of loans can be in any freely convertible currency determined by or acceptable to the bank. As indicated in the Agreement establishing the bank, the unit of account of the bank is the Islamic dinar, and all loan amounts are denominated in Islamic dinars, unless otherwise determined by the Board of Executive Directors.[7] Repayment conditions are determined according to the economic situation of the country and the project. In general cases, maturity of loans is based upon long-term periods from 10 years for commercial ventures up to 50 years for infrastructure projects in least developed member countries.[8]

Guarantee

The bank does not require a government guarantee for equity investments, which can be made in either public or private enterprises and in common or preferred stock. However, the bank requires an assurance from the government of the country where the project is taking place that it is acceptable and in accordance with its development priorities. If the borrower of loans is another entity than a member government, there must be a guarantee from the government or from another agency acceptable to the bank, either a central bank or a commercial bank of repute.[9]

The IsDB does not provide loan assistance to a project in which it has equity participation, except in special cases, after special authorisation endorsed by two-thirds of the voting powers of the Board of Executive Directors. The bank provides loans mainly for foreign exchange components. In special circumstances, however, it may provide the local cost component, especially in the LLDCs.[10]

Management and Organisational Structure

Like many other multinational aid organisations, the organisational structure of the IsDB is composed of the Board of Governors, the Board of Executive Directors, the President of the bank, the Vice-President, the Secretary and the staff. The bank derives its authority from the member countries, which are represented by their Finance Ministers on the

Board of Governors. The Board, in turn, appoints a ten-man Board of Executive Directors to take over responsibility for the running of the bank. Four of the members of the Board of Executive Directors are appointed, one by each of the governors representing countries having the largest number of shares, and the rest are elected by other governors. The directors hold office for a period of three years and may be re-elected.[11] The Board of Governors holds its annual meeting at Jeddah (during the month of Rabia Al-Thani) every year or at such other time and place as the Board determines. Special meetings of the Board can be called whenever requested by at least one-third of its members or upon the request of the Board of Executive Directors. The President of the bank is elected by the Board of Governors for a period of five years and may be re-elected for another five years subject to the approval of the governors by the majority of two-thirds of the number of votes. The President or, in his absence, the Vice-President, serves as Chairman of the Board of Executive Directors, but does not vote except in the case of a tie. The Secretary of the bank acts as Secretary of the two Boards who are, under the direction of the President, responsible for the preparation of a summary record of the proceedings of the meetings of the Board of Executive Directors. The Board may establish committees to facilitate the conduct of the general operations of the bank.[12] The daily working operations of the bank are carried out through operations units (including the Operations and Project Department), and servicing units (including the Economic and Policy Planning Department, the Treasurer's Department, the Audit Office, the Administration Department, the Office of the Secretary, and the General Council Office).[13]

Approaches and Techniques Applied

The bank sends its own mission to the field in the recipient country, but in most cases, it appraises the project jointly with other aid agencies. As the bank places emphasis on co-financing with other development finance institutions, techniques of project appraisal are carried out in co-operation with these lending institutions. The resources of the bank are, however, used in accordance with the decisions of the Board of Executive Directors, taken in conformity with the decisions and general directives of the Board of Governors. The bank's resources are separated into three main categories, namely the Ordinary Capital Resources, the Special Fund Resources, and the Trust Fund Resources. These resources are used and accounted for entirely separately from each other.[14] By 1979/80, as a result of the increased number of professional staff and their growing experience and expertise in project appraisal, the IsDB was able to streamline its operations and undertake independent appraisal of a number of projects, in line with its policy of evolving into an independent international financial institution capable of providing development assistance. The bank is determined to continue its efforts in building up the organisational strength which enables it to play an increasingly active role in project identification, appraisal, financing and follow-up in accordance with its own priorities and principles. In this direction, it has prepared a document, *Foreign Trade Financing Guidelines*, which contains the rules, regulations and procedures governing foreign trade financing operations.[15] In all of its operations the bank applies principles and procedures to cope with the purpose of its establishment. In this regard it adopts the following main principles.[16]

(1) It requests guarantees for its loan operations.
(2) It needs assurance that the borrower is in a good financial situation.
(3) It fulfils the financial needs of its least developed member countries.
(4) It strengthens economic integration among its member countries.
(5) It participates in raising the standards of living among its member countries through participation in economic and social development and fostering labour opportunities.
(6) It adopts a flexible appropriate ratio between equity participation and loan financing.
(7) Priority is given to joint projects that help to strengthen economic co-operation among its member countries.

Strategy for Financing and Technical Assistance

As the aim of the bank, as stated by its Agreement, is to foster economic and social development of the Muslim communities throughout the world, its strategy is to operate effectively within its all member countries and other Muslim communities. The bank's strategy is based upon giving top priority to the most needy and least developed Muslim countries, with industry and agro-business projects being given the most emphasis in case of equity participation. Infrastructural projects receive the top priority in project lending, while regional and complementary projects among Muslim countries are also likely to receive a high priority. Moreover, assistance to the national development banks of its member countries is also important in the bank's strategy for channelling funds into productive investment projects. The bank's prospective development activities are direct investment in its member countries and other Muslim communities. The IsDB has not indicated in quantitative terms its programme of lending, investment, and technical assistance for future years although it has spelled out its policy targets according to its mandate. In doing this, the bank decided to become operational in the shortest possible time, with the aim of developing as an independent Islamic international development financing institution, operating entirely in conformity with the principles of Shariah. Co-operation with local Islamic banks, national development banks, and other institutions represents an important aspect of this policy. In conformity with these guidelines, the bank has provided assistance in the implementation of the recommendations of the meetings of Governors of Islamic central banks, and in establishing a Research and Training Institute. The bank also provides financing for technical assistance either in the form of loans or grants or a combination of both, mainly to cover feasibility studies. In the period from its commencement up to 1980 the bank has approved US $8.68m for 17 technical assistance projects in 10 member countries.[17] More is to be done in this field in future years.

Problems of Implementation and Remarks from Field Experience

The bank's experience in the field of implementation and follow-up of projects is similar to that of other aid agencies, especially those problems related to LLDCs, many of which are Muslim. The bank's experience in its early years of operations was of course, limited, which obliged it to depend, at the beginning, upon other experienced aid agencies in identification and appraisal, with all the shortcomings that derive from the divergence between its mandate and that of the others. The bank was, however, aware of this problem and has started effectively to build up its own approach and technique. Until now, however, it has not established its own guidelines on project identification and appraisal, although several attempts have been made, with most emphasis upon foreign trade financing. The bank is more concerned with the stage of project implementation and follow-up, leaving the early stage of the project cycle to well-tried consultants and aid agencies. At the last co-ordination meeting of the Arab Funds in Vienna in June 1981 IsDB presented a paper relating to cost overrun financing based upon its own experience.[18] The paper covered the bank's experience in identifying the most common causes for cost overrun, and suggested possible measures to deal with such situations. The bank believes that inadequate co-ordination in the various stages of project management is a major cause of cost overruns and recommended that much greater importance be given in the project planning stage to the needs of such co-ordination under various categories of technical, managerial and financial co-operation. The bank believes that each aid institution should review the issue in accordance with its rules and regulations, so that with the progress of time and closer co-ordination and exchange of views and opinions it may be feasible to evolve a system that may contribute to the alleviation of the difficulties encountered due to cost overruns. It also recommended that efforts be made to explore the ways in which the increasingly strong pressures tending towards cost overrun be mini-mised as far as possible.

A review of IsDB's operations from the limited amount of material available over its short period of operations suggests that it has made a promising start towards achieving its objectives, and should continue to progress towards those goals, provided that more financial resources are committed. Given the increase in the membership of the bank and in the number of recipient countries, cost escalation, rising price levels, and the increase in the number of joint and regional projects, substantial new financial resources are required. The Taif conference in January 1981 was an essential step but its recommendations must be implemented effectively and much more effort is also needed in the field of technical assistance and investment promotion. Given that the bank's financial resources needs are met, efforts should be undertaken to draw up a strategy for the future which will require preparation of a detailed manual for the bank's operations, taking into consideration the economic and social impacts of its activities on the global Muslim community.

18 The OPEC Fund for International Development

Establishment and Objective

The OPEC Fund for International Development, formerly called the OPEC Special Fund, was established by virtue of an agreement signed by all OPEC member countries in Paris on 28 January 1976. Signatories to the agreement are Algeria, Ecuador, Gabon, Indonesia, Iran, Iraq, Kuwait, the SP Libyan AJ, Nigeria, Qatar, Saudi Arabia, the United Arab Emirates and Venezuela. The fund is not endowed with a capital structure, and its resources consist of contributions by member countries, and monies received from operations or accruing to the fund. They amount to US $2.4bn, of which US $800m was approved in 1979 and finalised in January 1980, of which about US $1.2bn is committed.[1] Table 18.1 shows the initial contributions of each member country.

The endowments of the fund have been replenished three times and the resources committed to it as of July 1980 were in the order of US $4bn.[2] The OPEC Fund was originally created as an international account for providing financial assistance from OPEC member countries to other developing countries. Since early 1980, the fund has evolved into an international agency for financial co-operation and assistance. Its objective remains the same, but it is now endowed with an international legal personality and a stronger institutional structure. According to its Constituent Agreement, the objective of the fund is broadly defined as reinforcing financial co-operation between OPEC member countries and other developing countries by providing financial support on appropriate terms to assist the latter countries in their economic and social development efforts. The fund was created to complement, and not to substitute for, the other existing bilateral and multilateral channels through which OPEC member countries have

TABLE 18.1 Initial Contributions of OPEC Members to the OPEC Fund

Country	Contributions (US $m)
Algeria	20.00
Ecuador	—
Gabon	1.00
Indonesia	2.00
Iran	200.00
Iraq	40.00
Kuwait	72.00
SP Libyan AJ	40.00
Nigeria	52.00
Qatar	18.00
Saudi Arabia	200.00
United Arab Emirates	33.00
Venezuela	112.00

Source: The OPEC Special Fund, *Agreement of Establishment* (in Arabic).

individually extended financial support to the rest of the developing world. Like other initiatives of OPEC member countries in the field of financial co-operation with other developing nations, the fund is designed to assist in promoting the economic development of developing countries and to embrace solidarity among them. It was conceived as an operational instrument to promote the establishment of the New International Economic Order.[3]

Scope of Activities

The fund operates in all developing countries, other than OPEC member countries, with special emphasis on assisting the least developed countries. It finances all types of development projects with most emphasis on projects that can make LLDCs self-sufficient in energy and food. The fund also participates in financing infrastructure projects and some projects in the productive sectors and extends lines of credit to small-scale enterprises. It does not operate in equity participations, short-term or medium-term loans. All its loans are soft long-term loans, generally interest-free, and carrying maturities of up to 20 years. Both in collaboration with UNDP and other UN affiliated agencies and directly the fund provides technical assistance to some developing countries.[4] Its first lending programme began in December 1976, in the form of a balance of payments (BOP) support operation, involving an allocation of US $200m to assist the most seriously affected countries in the world (as defined by the United Nations). All the recipients were countries with a low per capita income and largely agricultural economies. They were characterised by low labour productivity, high mortality rates, and populations living at the margin of subsistence. The urgent provision of aid to these countries was considered a matter of high priority to the fund. In March 1977, the fund embarked upon its second lending programme, which concentrated on project financing, following the allocation by its Governing Committee of US $142.3m for this purpose. There were 38 countries which benefited from the programme, were spread over a vast geographical area encompassing the continents of Africa, Asia and Latin America. The third lending programme was initiated with an allotment of US $400m, and its implementation began in July 1978. All the loans advanced in 1979 were part of this programme, which reached 62 developing countries – out of the 65 originally targeted – in the form of 36 BOP support loans and 46 project loans.[5] The implementation of the fourth lending programme began in 1980. The fund's volume of direct lending during this year totalled US $250.8m, an increase of about 18 per cent over 1979. The fund's cumulative lending reached US $904.3m as of the end of December 1980. A fifth lending programme to cover operations started on 1 January 1981 was submitted to the fund's Governing Board. The fund's direct lending activities are supplemented by contributions to other international financial institutions. After adding these contributions, the fund's total commitments as of the end of 1980 stood at about US $1.5bn and disbursements at over US $800m, resulting in a disbursements to commitments ratio of 54.2 per cent.[6] Table 18.2 shows the fund's total commitments and disbursements.

Terms and Conditions

Pursuant to the Agreement establishing the OPEC Fund, long-term and interest-free loans constitute an important form of the fund's assistance. It applies three types of lending terms: BOP support loans, programme loans and project loans as follows:

(1) *BOP Support Loans*
   Interest rate: no interest on loans to the low-income developing countries. A service charge of 0.5 per cent per annum on amounts disbursed and outstanding.

TABLE 18.2 OPEC Fund Commitments and Disbursements, as of 31 December 1980 (US $m)

	Commitments	Disbursements
1. Lending operations		
Project	494.54	128.71
Programme	10.50	—
BOP[a]	399.25	351.40
Subtotal	904.29	480.11
2. Technical assistance grants[b]	38.00	14.37
3. Other grants	0.38	0.28
4. IFAD	435.50	201.71[c]
5. IMF Trust Fund	110.72	110.72
Total	1,488.89	807.19

[a] Balance of payments support loans.
[b] Programmes under which technical assistance is provided are carried out in co-operation with UNDP and other international agencies.
[c] Not including promissory notes amounting to US$150.62m already 'paid' to IFAD.
Source: The OPEC Fund for International Development, *Annual Report*, 1980.

Repayment period: of 7 years after the grace period. The repayment period is subject to reduction to 5 years if no agreement is reached on the financing of a development project or programme from the equivalent amount in the currency of the borrower, which the borrower deposits against withdrawal from the fund's loan for balance of payments support purposes.

Grace period: a grace period of 3 years.

(2) *Programme Loans*

Interest rate: no interest on loans to the low-income developing countries. A service charge of 0.75 per cent per annum on the amounts withdrawn and outstanding.

Repayment period: of 10 years, after the grace period. The repayment period is subject to reduction to 7 years if no agreement is reached on the financing of a development project or programme from the equivalent amount in the currency of the borrower, which the borrower deposits against withdrawal from the fund's loan.

Grace period: A period of 5 years grace.

(3) *Project Loans*

Interest rate: no interest on loans to the low-income developing countries. A service charge of 0.75 per cent per annum on the

amounts withdrawn and outstanding. The interest rate applied on loans to the relatively higher-income countries has so far been 4 per cent per annum and in some cases 5 per cent per annum. A higher rate is envisaged for loans to high-income developing countries when such loans are concluded.
Repayment period: of 15 years, after a grace period.
Grace period: a period of 5 years grace.

In all of the above types of loan, the US$ is the Unit of Account of the fund and the means of payment of its loans. However, the borrower may repay the principal of the loans in any other freely useable currency acceptable to the fund management equivalent to the dollar amount due, according to the market exchange rate prevailing at the time and place of repayment.[7]

Management and Administration

Unlike the usual multilateral lending organisation, the OPEC Fund does not have a two-tiered management structure composed of a Board of Governors and a Board of Directors; instead, it has a Ministerial Council and Governing Board on which all contributing countries are represented. The Governing Board sets the general policies and its chairman signs the loan agreements as agent of the contributing countries, who are, legally, the creditors of the fund's loans. The Board also appoints the Director General of the fund who manages its activities and is responsible for the work of the Governing Board and the implementation of its decisions.

Approaches and Techniques Applied

The general procedure for obtaining a loan from the OPEC Fund is, based upon government requests, to address a letter to the Director General through the minister in charge of mobilising foreign assistance, usually the Finance Minister. In order to expedite the process the letter should be accompanied by appropriate documents, such as evidence of the need for BOP support or a project report. After an official loan request accompanied by sufficient data has been received by the fund management and favourably reviewed, it is submitted to the Governing Board for approval. The Governing Board may then authorise signature of the loan agreement. The fund does not engage in the appraisal of new projects, instead it has co-financed projects already appraised and approved by other institutions. This enables the fund to achieve a high disbursement to commitment ratio and actually to transfer resources to its recipients in a short time. Similarly, the administration of the fund loans has generally been left to an appropriate co-financing agency. More recently, however, the amendments of the Agreement establishing the fund included a clause enabling the fund to appraise projects and to administer its project loans, if it so determines.[8] The fund plans gradually to strengthen its appraising capacity, especially in the energy sector.

Strategy for Financing and Technical Assistance

Since its inception, the OPEC Fund has allocated a large share of its aid to the LLDCs, and has treated these countries on a priority basis. During 1979, it provided 11 balance of payments loans representing US $32.15m, and 9 development project loans, to the amount of US $54.25m, were extended to 19 LLDCs. The total amount of aid extended to the LLDCs (US$86.4m) constituted about 41 per cent of the resources provided by the fund during 1979, for direct lending purposes. As of the end of 1979, the fund's cumulative direct aid to the LLDCs took the form of 45 BOP support loans totalling approximately US$137m and 24 project loans to the amount of about US$104m.[9] These loans benefited 29 LLDCs, with a total population of 250m people and GNP per capita of US$195 in 1977. The fund also gives priority to the MSACs. These countries are most in need of increased concessional financial assistance, as they face serious difficulties in their efforts to implement essential development programmes. By the end of 1980, the Fund had devoted 76 per cent of its direct loans to both LLDCs and MSACs. Table 18.3 shows the fund cumulative loan commitments to these countries.

The OPEC Fund places growing importance on the energy and food needs of the developing countries, as it puts high priority in its project lending activities on projects related to these two sectors. The emphasis is put on the development of indigenous energy resources so as not only to help the beneficiary countries reduce their dependence on energy imports, but also to meet their growing requirements. To assist these countries in meeting such needs is a task the fund considers of key importance. The other priority is assigned to the food production sector and is indicated by the significance of that sector in developing countries from which an overwhelming majority of people earn their livelihood. These priorities, however, are not totally exclusive of the fund's

Table 18.3 OPEC Fund Loan Commitments to LLDCs and MSAs, as of 31 December 1980

	Amount (US $m)	As % of fund's total loan commitments for each type of assistance
Project loans	354.00	71.8
Programme loans	10.50	100.0
BOP support loans	324.25	81.2
Total	688.75	76.2

Source: The OPEC Fund for International Development, *Annual Report*, 1980.

involvement in other sectors where the governments of the borrowing countries have set other justified priorities in their national development plans. Table 18.4 shows the fund's cumulative project lending operations by sector.

Table 18.4 OPEC Fund's Cumulative Project Lending Operations as of the end of 1980
(Loan distribution by sector – in %)

Sector	Loan distribution %
Energy	44.4
Agriculture and Agro-industry	14.0
Transportation	20.6
Industry including development banks	14.8
Public utilities	5.6
Communications	0.6

Source: The OPEC Fund for International Development, *Annual Report*, 1980.

The technical assistance provided through the fund is conducted, by and large, in collaboration with the UNDP. In 1979 the fund allocated, on a grant basis, US$20m to finance technical assistance projects. This was the second allocation of its kind, being preceded by an equivalent one in 1977. In both instances, it was agreed that the projects financed would be regional or inter-regional in character and would have a direct impact on an economy's productive capacities, such as those projects related to the development of natural and human resources.[10] In 1980, the fund was among the first donors to announce its support for the

UNDP initiative to establish an Energy Fund for Exploration and Pre-investment Surveys. It pledged a grant of US$6m, representing 10 per cent of the resources required as voluntary contributions over the first three years. The Energy Fund's objective is to help finance pre-investment surveys as well as exploration and demonstration projects in the energy sector. This scheme comprises two components: one consists of petroleum surveys with concentration on low-income countries with a per capita GNP of less than US $500; the second deals with the financing of pre-investment assessments of non-petroleum energy resources.[11] The cumulative amounts extended for technical assistance by the fund reached US $38.0m at the end of 1980, used in the financing of 20 projects of which US$14.37m had been disbursed. Table 18.5 shows the Fund's cumulative technical assistance projects.

TABLE 18.5 OPEC Fund: Technical Assistance Projects, as of 31 December 1980 (US $000s)

	Allocations	Amounts utilised
UNDP-assisted projects	28,481	9,621[a]
Consultative Group on International Agricultural Research (CGIAR)	2,000	650
United Nations Relief and Works Agency (UNRWA)	2,471	930
Latin American Energy Organisation (OLADE)	5,000	1,866
Refinery orientation programme	50	—
Total	38,002	13,068[a]

[a] Excluding US $1297,000 transferred to UNDP but not yet utilised.
Source: The OPEC Fund for International Development, *Annual Report*, 1980.

The performance of the fund's operation reveals that it is likely to continue in its future strategy for financing towards the least developing countries as the first priority. Energy and agriculture sectors will be the two priority sectors. Concerning general policy, balance of payments support loans will continue as a major operation of the fund. As for future strategy for technical assistance it seems likely to be the same as at present with more emphasis in areas related to development of the energy resources of LLDCs.

19 The African Development Bank

Establishment and Capacity for Financing

The African Development Bank, like the Asian, Caribbean and Inter-American Banks, was shaped largely by the historical circumstances which led to its creation. However, the AfDB is unique among the regional banks in that throughout its early history, it was a purely regional institution without financial support from outside. The AfDB was shaped almost exclusively by the way in which Africans themselves perceived their needs and their place in the broader global environment. The idea of establishment of the bank goes back to January 1960, when the 'All-African People's Conference' held in Tunis proposed that a special development fund might be set up for Africa. A resolution was adopted in favour of the setting up of an African investment bank to promote development projects. The proposal was taken up again at the third session of the Economic Commission for Africa (ECA), in February 1961. The ECA unanimously adopted a resolution requesting its executive secretary to undertake a thorough study of the possibilities of establishing an African Development Bank and to report to the Commission at its next session.[1] At the first OAU summit held in Addis Ababa in May 1963, the African Heads of State and Government decided to establish a regional development bank and instructed their Finance Ministers to take all the steps needed for the immediate establishment of the bank. On 10 September 1964, the Agreement establishing the African Development Bank entered into force and the bank commenced its operations on 1 July 1966.

The purpose of the AfDB is 'to contribute to the economic development and social progress of its regional members individually and jointly'.[2] The bank accords priority to projects which contribute to regional co-operation and the integration of the economies of these countries. It promotes public and private capital investment in Africa and provides technical assistance needed for the appraisal, preparation, financing and implementation of development projects and programmes. The authorised capital stock of the bank was initially fixed at 250m Units of Account (UA), US $250m in 1964, divided into 25,000 shares of a par value of 10,000 Units of Account each share. The value of the Unit of Account was set up at 0.88867088 grammes of fine gold. The authorised capital stock is divided into paid-up shares and callable shares. The equivalent of 125,000,000 Units of Account is paid-up, and the equivalent of 125,000,000 Units of Account is callable in gold, convertible currency or in the currency required to discharge the obligation of the bank for the purpose for which the call is made.[3] At 31 December 1979, the authorised capital increased to UA1,220m or US $1,607m (at a rate of 1UA = US $1.31733). The capital stock is made up of a paid-up portion (25 per cent) and a callable portion (75 per cent) which serves as guarantee for borrowings, that is for the mobilisation of resources on the capital markets. This new authorised capital stock is allocated for subscription to regional and non-regional members in such proportions that the number of shares would, if fully subscribed, result in regional members holding two-thirds of the total voting power and non-regional members one-third of the total voting power. Non-regional countries which are, or become, members of the African Development Fund, or which have made, or are making, contributions to the African Development Fund under terms and conditions similar to the terms and conditions of the Agreement establishing the African Development Fund,[4] may also be admitted to the bank, at such times and under such general rules as the Board of Governors shall have established. The bank's resources are made up of the subscriptions to its capital stock, reserves, borrowing and interest income.

Scope of Activities

To implement its purpose, the bank has the following activities:[5]

(1) To use the resources at its disposal for the financing of investment projects and programmes relating to the economic and social development of its regional members, giving special priority to:
   (i) projects or programmes which by their nature or scope concern several members; and
   (ii) projects or programmes designed to make the economies of

its members increasingly complementary and to bring about an orderly expansion of their foreign trade.
(2) To undertake, or participate in, the selection, study and preparation of projects, enterprises and activities contributing to such development.
(3) To mobilise and increase in Africa, and outside Africa, resources for the financing of such investment projects and programmes.
(4) Generally, to promote investment in Africa of public and private capital in projects or programmes designed to contribute to the economic development or social progress of its regional members.
(5) To provide such technical assistance as may be needed in Africa for the study, preparation, financing and execution of development projects or programmes.
(6) To undertake such other activities and provide such other services as may advance its purpose.

The bank may also establish, or be entrusted with the administration of, special funds which are designed to serve its purpose and come within its functions. The resources of such special funds are kept separate and apart from the ordinary capital resources of the bank.

From the date of its inception the bank tried to respond to the economic and financial difficulties of its member countries. However, it was able to play only a very minor economic role in its early years due to its lack of resources which continued until 1973 when the African Development Fund was set up with 50 per cent of the stock being under AfDB control and the rest held by non-regional countries. Because of the small scale of its resources compared with other development regional lending institutions, the bank in its early years engaged to complete the financing of small- to medium-scale development projects and increasingly finds itself in the position of the junior partner with other regional banks or with the World Bank in its larger loans, though it remains an independent lender in the case of a large number of small loans. As the bank was aware of the insufficiency of its own resources to meet the immense needs of its member countries, it made considerable efforts to mobilise external resources. These efforts have culminated in the creation of institutions managed by the bank which concentrate together with the bank in what has come to be known as the Group of the African Development Bank or the Bank Group (African Development Bank, AfDB, African Development Fund, AfDF, and Nigerian Trust Fund, NTF).[6]

The cumulative lending commitments by the AfDB during 1977–80 amounted to UA1062.71m in respect of 263 loans compared with UA830.39m for 235 loans as at the end of 1979. In terms of sectoral distribution, excluding cancellations, the public utilities sector, comprising projects in telecommunications, electricity and water supply and sewerage, accounted for the largest share of cumulative bank lending, amounting to UA361.28m or 34.0 per cent of the total at 1980. The transport sector came second with UA261.56m or 24.61 per cent. A notable development in the sectoral allocation relates to the agricultural sector, whose relative position rose from UA85.77m (13.78 per cent) at the end of 1978 to UA166.23m (15.64 per cent) at the end of 1980. This reflects a long-term policy to allocate a larger proportion of bank resources to agricultural development in member countries. Commitments to industry and development banks maintained a constant average of about 20 per cent up to 1979 but increased in values and percentage to reach UA255.64m or 24 per cent at the end of 1980. The relative positions of the region, on a cumulative basis as at the end of 1979, showed that countries in Eastern Africa accounted for UA238.18m, or 29 per cent of cumulative commitments, representing an increase of 4 percentage points over 1978, while West Africa accounted for about UA260.82m, or 31 per cent, compared with 27 per cent in 1978. Both North and Central Africa maintained their relative share of 21 and 19 per cent respectively.[7] Table 19.1 shows the cumulative bank lending operations by sector.

Terms and Conditions[8]

> Interest rate: 8 per cent.
> Repayment period: usually over 10 years.
> Grace period: AfDB projects provide a grace period ranging from 2–7 years.
> Guarantee: government.

According to Article 18 of the Agreement establishing the bank (paragraph 3.c), the bank states the currency in which all payments to it under the contract concerned shall be made. At the option of the borrower, however, such payments may be made in gold or convertible currency or, subject to the agreement of the bank, in any other currency. The bank also may attach such other terms or conditions as it deems appropriate, taking into account both the interest of the member directly concerned in the project and the interests of the members as a whole (Article 18, paragraph 3.d).

TABLE 19.1 AfDB Cumulative Loan Approvals by Sector 1977–80[a] (UAm)

Sector	1977	%	1978	%	1979	%	1980	%
Agriculture	50.37 (21)	10.84	85.77 (28)	13.78	142.42 (37)	17.15	166.23 (47)	15.64
Transport	136.11 (46)	29.28	160.28 (53)	25.75	206.58 (62)	24.88	261.56 (68)	24.61
Public utilities	182.79 (60)	39.33	245.80 (74)	39.49	303.25 (83)	36.52	361.28 (90)	34.00
Industry and development banks	95.54 (37)	20.55	128.64 (44)	20.66	168.14 (51)	20.25	255.64 (61)	24.06
Education and health	—	—	2.00 (1)	0.32	10.00 (2)	1.20	18.00 (3)	1.69
Total	464.81 (164)	100.00	622.49 (200)	100.00	830.39 (235)	100.00	1,062.71[b] (263)	100.00

[a] The figures exclude cancellations and have been revised. Thus this year's figures may be somewhat different from those of previous Annual Reports. The numbers in brackets show the number of loans and do not include the five loans cancelled between 1967 and 1977.
[b] Excluding capitalised interests amounting to UA 0.21m for 2 loans. A change adjustment amounting to UA 0.34m for a non-convertible loan is not deducted.

Source: African Development Bank, Annual Report, 1980.

Management and Administration

According to Article (4) of the Agreement establishing the bank, 'the Bank has a Board of Governors, a Board of Directors, a President, at least one Vice-President and such other officers and staff to perform such duties as the Bank may determine'. Each member state is represented on the Board of Governors by a governor and a deputy governor. Each governor and his deputy serves for five years subject to termination of appointment at any time at the pleasure of the appointing member. The Board of Governors is the supreme organ of the bank. All the powers of the bank are vested in the Board of Governors. The Board issues general directions concerning the credit policy of the bank. The Board of Governors may delegate to the Board of Directors all its powers except the power to decrease the authorised capital stock of the bank, to establish or accept the administration of Special Funds, or to authorise the conclusion of general arrangements for co-operation with the authorities of African countries which have not yet attained independent status. The Board of Directors is composed of nine members who are not governors or deputy governors. They are elected by the Board of Governors for a term of three years and may be re-elected. Each director appoints a deputy who cannot be of the same nationality as himself. Directors and their deputies are nationals of member states. The Board of Directors is responsible for the conduct of the general operations of the bank. The Board of Directors exercises, in addition to the powers conferred on it expressly in the Agreement, all the powers delegated to it by the Board of Governors. It determines the rates of interest for direct loans and of commission for guarantees, submits the accounts for each financial year and an annual report for approval to the Board of Governors at each annual meeting, furthermore it determines the general structure of the services of the bank.

Non-Regional States in the African Development Bank

The Board of Governors of the African Development Bank in its resolution 02–78 taken at its Annual Meeting in Libreville on 4 May 1978 concerning the mobilisation of resources for the bank, invited non-regional states interested in becoming members to join. The President of the bank contacted those non-regional states to discuss the matter in four multilateral meetings, held in Washington DC on 30 September 1978, in Rabat 27–29 November 1978, in Abidjan 11–12 January 1979, and in London 13–14 February 1979. At these meetings, the principles and conditions for the admission of non-regional states were discussed in detail. The discussions were based on extensive documentation prepared by the bank and forwarded to the non-regional states. After consultations with the President and discussions among themselves, the non-regional states submitted their position about the proposals for the opening of the bank's capital stock for the final negotiations. The non-regional states were prepared to accept the ratio of 66 2/3 per cent regional to 33 1/3 per cent non-regional participation. They unanimously agreed that representation on the Board of Directors should be proportional to participation. The non-regional states felt strongly that they should be represented by six executive directors in order to give members with smaller participation an equal opportunity to be represented on the Board from time to time. This would result in a proportional increase of the number of regional directors. Decisions on the policies of the bank should be made, in general, subject to a majority of 51 per cent of votes. The delegates of the non-regional states had taken note of the bank's intention to make available for subscription capital stock to the equivalent of US $6,300m in connection with the admission of non-regional members. While delegations were not yet in a position to commit their countries, the majority of the non-regional states had indicated their willingness to support a target of US $2100m for non-regional participation. The maximum participation of 40,000 shares proposed by the bank (each share at a par value of UA10,000, that is UA400m − equivalent to about US $480m) corresponding to 22.86 per cent of the total participation of US $2100m offered to the non-regional states was acceptable.[9] A scheme for the share allocation to the non-regional states is shown in Table 19.2.

While these negotiations have been very rapid in terms of accomplishment, they have nevertheless been carried out in a most careful and thorough manner which permitted mature consideration of the issues and very careful documentation on the basis of which decisions could be made. Given these factors, it proved possible to obtain a quick response from the non-regional states to the invitation extended to them by the Board of Governors. The result of these negotiations was a package of two sets of interdependent proposals, one of which represented those proposals put forward by the African Development Bank which have been largely accepted by the non-regional states without alteration; while the other set contained those proposals which the non-regional states had amended, and new proposals raised on the basis of additional points emanating from the non-regional states. The sets of proposals were interdependent, and carefully balanced so that benefits accrued to

TABLE 19.2 Initial Subscriptions of Non-regional States (%)

Member	%
Belgium	1.64
Canada	9.70
Denmark	3.00
Finland	1.26
France	9.40
Germany	10.90
Italy	6.37
Japan	14.21
Kuwait	1.14
Netherlands	1.95
Norway	3.00
Spain	1.50
Sweden	4.00
Switzerland	3.80
United Kingdom	6.37
United States of America	17.20
Austria	1.14
Unallocated	3.42[a]
Total	100.00

[a] Reserved for three minimum participations each of 1.14 per cent.
Source: See note 9.

both sides. Acceptance of the bank's proposals by the non-regional states was conditional upon acceptance by the bank of the recommendations made by non-regional countries.

By far the most important result of these negotiations has been the acceptance by the non-regional states of a sharply increased lending programme by the bank for the 1982–86 period. Despite some scepticism on the part of non-regional states that this was overambitious, the bank's negotiators were able to overcome their doubts and to convince them of the bank's seriousness of purpose. Thus it was possible to agree on a considerable increase of capital, bringing the authorised capital stock of the bank to $6.3bn, of which the non-regional states are prepared to subscribe $2.1bn. These are additional resources, not substitutions, because the bank insisted on maintaining the integrity and separation of the African Development Fund from the bank. In this manner, the bank's negotiators achieved their principal objective, that is additional resources through partnership with non-African members without lessening the African character of the institution.[10]

Approaches and Techniques Applied

In considering an application for a loan or guarantee, the AfDB pays due regard to the ability of the borrower to obtain financing elsewhere on terms and conditions that the bank considers reasonable. For projects limited to one country, the bank normally requires a guarantee from the national government, except where the loan is made to the government itself. In the case of loans extended to finance multinational projects, it is the bank's policy to request guarantees from all governments concerned. As a general rule, the bank provides financing to cover the foreign exchange expenditures incurred in a project. In special cases, the bank also finances expenditures in national currencies to a limited extent. Loans are normally only granted for projects approximately 50 per cent of the cost of which has been or is expected to be funded from sources other than the bank. However, in considering loans to governments or government agencies and in determining the proportion of the bank's participation in the financing of projects, account is taken of the country's overall development effort. The bank also undertakes co-financing of projects together with other international and national development banks and other institutions. Once the loan is granted, the bank supervises its disbursement to ensure that the proceeds are applied only against project expenditures as incurred and are used by the borrower only for the procurement of goods and services required for the project being financed. In some instances, loans are disbursed by way of letters of credit in favour of suppliers specified by the borrowers. The bank also maintains a continuous relationship with borrowers after loans are made and requires that borrowers submit progress reports on a regular basis.[11]

Unlike the World Bank and the International Monetary Fund, the bank does not appraise member-states' macroeconomic policies. However, it has recently launched a policy planning department to identify sectors that would benefit from its involvement. The bank has also been prepared in the past to support projects that would not normally receive World Bank approval, and has awarded loans to airport facilities in landlocked countries such as Botswana, an example of the African Development Bank's individual approach compared with that of institutions such as the World Bank.[12] Management and administration of projects financed by the bank is mainly the responsibility of the host government, although the bank sometimes provides technical assistance. Projects with inadequate information on price and production which need marketing studies are usually undertaken by the host government, although the bank may also support them as part of a feasibility study. Its techniques for project appraisal vary from country to country and also depend on the nature of the project. However, labour-intensive techniques for countries with high unemployment rates have been emphasised by the bank.[13]

Strategy for Financing and Technical Assistance

The bank has based its strategy on financing specific projects which clearly contribute to the economic development of its member states, particularly those included within regional or national development programmes. A special preference is accorded to all projects which benefit two or more member states and thus stimulate intra-African co-operation. Such projects include transportation links, telecommunication links, irrigation and flood control, joint production and/or distribution of electric power and other forms of energy, industrial, agricultural, and educational and vocational training projects. A high priority is also accorded to loans for those development projects which demonstrate clear efforts at self-help, to mobilise local resources or assist member states to attract additional capital from non-African sources. In response to regional needs and the specific circumstances of the member states, the bank intends to increase the proportion of its lending devoted to agriculture and related agricultural infrastructure projects and to endeavour to achieve a more balanced regional distribution of its financing. These were among the main objectives of the bank's five-year lending programme (1977–81).[14] As for technical assistance programmes, the bank provides technical assistance for the study, preparation, financing, implementation and administration of development projects and programmes in its member states. Project identification and preparatory technical assistance to member countries is provided by the bank in the framework of its co-operative agreements with FAO, WHO and UNESCO. The World Bank Group has maintained active co-operation with the bank especially in co-financing several development projects in the member countries, and also offers training facilities to AfDB's staff both in Washington and at the Bank Training Centre in Abidjan. In addition the bank was appointed an executive agency for UNDP-assisted projects.[15] The future strategy for financing and technical assistance by the bank is planned to give more emphasis to the following sectors: agriculture, economic infrastructure, education and health, and agro-industry. Projects in all these sectors will receive great attention but more emphasis will be placed on agricultural projects. The future general policy of the bank is to augment its financial resources by opening the capital stock to non-regional members.[16] The bank's future strategy for technical assistance is parallel to its financial strategy with the aim of equipping recipient countries with the necessary expertise required for successful project implementation.

Problems of Implementation and Remarks from Field Experience

Meeting the obligations from the host governments necessary for completing the project on schedule as well as the delays in the receipt of progress reports are considered to be the main problems of implementation facing the bank which require action to be taken. While AfDB is doing all it can to help its member countries in their economic development efforts, experience indicates that it needs to strengthen its resource base substantially, which will enhance its contribution in both financial and technical terms.[17] In this connection there has been long discussion by the Finance Committee of questions on the resource mobilisation requirements of the bank. As a result, the Board of Directors has developed a policy which is based on requirements in terms of the bank's commitment capacity, on the one hand, and on the need to maintain a judicious liquidity, on the other. This policy provides for strategies and market approaches aimed at getting the bank into new, more varied and appropriate markets, whilst attempting to limit the financial burden arising out of its borrowing. The bank has no manual or guidelines for project appraisal techniques, a handicap for its standard performance which must be overcome before, and not after, the invitation for non-regional states to participate in its membership. If the bank intends to emphasise its African character, it ought to be aware of African techniques and procedures. This issue has recently been brought to the attention of the bank's management, and in a recent statement,[18] the Acting President indicated that two comprehensive manuals, one on operating procedures and the other on administrative procedures, had been issued to staff for use on a trial basis. The informal meetings of the Operations Committee have had the effect of bringing about new decisions and policy guidelines which were then adopted by the Board of Directors. Special attention paid to project implementation has led to a number of recommendations concerning ways and means of improving project implementation and loan disbursement as well as provisions for granting technical assistance to the bank's member states.

20 The Asian Development Bank

Establishment and Financial Resources

The Asian Development Bank, a younger institution than the Inter-American Development Bank (IDB), started operations on 19 December 1966. In size it falls between the IDB and AfDB and the Caribbean Development Bank (CDB). AsDB is an international development finance institution owned by its member governments, with headquarters in Manila, Philippines. The bank was established mainly for the purpose of lending funds and providing technical assistance to developing member countries in the region of Asia and the Far East, including the South Pacific, and for promoting investment and generally fostering economic growth in the region. Article 1 of the Agreement establishing the Asian Development Bank stated that 'the purpose of the bank shall be to foster economic growth and co-operation in the region of Asia and the Far East and to contribute to the acceleration of the process of economic development of the developing member countries in the region, collectively and individually'.[1] The background of the establishment of the bank goes back to the first Ministerial Conference on Asian Economic Co-operation, held in Manila in December 1963 under the auspices of the Economic and Social Commission for Asia and the Pacific (ESCAP) – then known as the Economic Commission for Asia and the Far East (ECAFE) – which passed a resolution endorsing a proposal to establish a regional development bank for Asia. ESCAP in turn set up a Working Group of Experts to report on the resolution and the report submitted by the Group was circulated to ESCAP member governments. At its twenty-first session in Wellington in March 1965, ESCAP set up a Consultative Committee which visited various member countries of ESCAP and other interested nations in order to elicit their views on the establishment of the bank. The Committee also prepared a draft of an Agreement establishing the Asian Development Bank which was adopted at ESCAP's Second Ministerial Conference on Asian Economic Co-operation held in Manila in November/December 1965. At this conference a Committee on Preparatory Arrangements for the Establishment of the Asian Development Bank was formed and entrusted with the task of undertaking the necessary initial steps for action by the Board of Governors at its Inaugural Meeting. The Preparatory Committee functioned until the Inaugural Meeting of the Board of Governors in Tokyo on 24 November 1966.[2] The meeting was chaired by Japan's then Finance Minister, Takeo Fukuda, who had long been a supporter of the establishment of the bank. Unanimously elected as the bank's first President was Takeshi Watonabe, who set the standards of economic and social development allied with sound banking practice which have been followed ever since; he pledged the exertion of 'every effort towards establishing a high credit standing and proving the worthiness of this institution.[3] When AsDB opened its doors for business, it faced an enormous challenge to act as stimulator and catalyst to economic and social development in a region that is home to a third of the world's population.

The financial resources of the bank consist of:

(1) Ordinary capital resources consisting of subscribed capital, funds raised through borrowings and reserves.
(2) Special funds resources comprising contributions made by developed member countries and capital set aside by the bank for concessional lending to the poorest member countries.
(3) Technical assistance special fund consisting of contributions made by both developed and developing member countries for technical assistance activities.

According to Article 4, the authorised capital stock of the bank is US $1bn, in terms of US $ of the weight and fineness of gold in effect on 31 January 1966, divided into 100,000 shares having a par value of $10,000 each which are available for subscription only by members in accordance with the bank's Agreement.[4] The original authorised capital stock is divided into paid-in shares and callable shares, each having an aggregate par value of $500m. The authorised capital stock of the bank may be increased by the Board of Governors, at such time and under such terms and conditions as it may deem advisable, by a vote of two-thirds of the total number of Governors, representing not less than three-fourths of the total voting power of the members. Subscriptions to the second general capital increase as of 31 December 1978 amounted to $4795.4m. During 1979, three member countries subscribed to their full entitlements in the following amounts: Belgium $22.2m, Cook Islands $0.2m, and Western Samoa $0.4m; thus total subscriptions as of 31 December 1979 amounted to $4818.2m.[5] Membership of the bank is open to members and associate members of ESCAP and other regional and non-regional developed countries which are members of the UN or any of its specialised agencies. Admission to membership of the bank requires the affirmative vote of two-thirds of the total number of governors, representing not less than three-fourths of the total voting power of the member countries. The membership of AsDB reflects the intention of the founders that, while its operations should be limited to the region, it should also incorporate the active participation and financial resources of developed nations outside the region. The bank up to 31 December 1980 had 29 regional members who provided 64.759 per cent of its capital, and 14 non-regional members providing 35.241 per cent. Table 20.1 shows the subscriptions to capital stock and voting power.

TABLE 20.1 Subscriptions to the Capital Stock and Voting Power of the Asian Development Bank as of 31 December 1980

Country	Subscriptions par value expressed in US $000s	Per cent of total	Per cent of total voting power
Regional			
Afghanistan	15,241	0.173	0.603
Australia	636,901	7.215	6.237
Bangladesh	112,389	1.273	1.484
Burma	59,944	0.679	1.008
Cambodia	11,160	0.126	0.566
China, Republic of	119,889	1.358	1.552
Cook Islands	293	0.003	0.468
Fiji	7,487	0.085	0.533
Hong Kong	59,944	0.679	1.008
India	696,846	7.894	6.780
Indonesia	599,443	6.790	5.897
Japan	1,498,607	16.975	14.046
Kiribati	446	0.005	0.469
Korea, Republic of	554,484	6.281	5.490
Laos	3,138	0.036	0.494
Malaysia	299,721	3.395	3.181
Maldives	446	0.005	0.469
Nepal	16,185	0.183	0.612

(*continued overleaf*)

TABLE 20.1 (Contd.)

Country	Subscriptions par value expressed in US $000s	Per cent of total	Per cent of total voting power
New Zealand	169,043	1.915	1.997
Pakistan	239,777	2.716	2.638
Papua New Guinea	10,331	0.117	0.559
Philippines	262,250	2.971	2.842
Singapore	37,459	0.424	0.804
Solomon Islands	740	0.008	0.472
Sri Lanka	63,834	0.723	1.044
Thailand	149,861	1.698	1.823
Tonga	446	0.005	0.469
Viet Nam	89,916	1.019	1.280
Western Samoa	740	0.008	0.472
Total regional	5,716,961	64.759	65.297
Non-regional			
Austria	37,459	0.424	0.804
Belgium	37,459	0.424	0.804
Canada	575,758	6.522	5.683
Denmark	37,459	0.424	0.804
Finland	14,986	0.170	0.601
France	187,320	2.122	2.163
Germany, Fed. Rep. of	476,161	5.394	4.780
Italy	149,861	1.698	1.823
Netherlands	82,417	0.934	1.212
Norway	37,459	0.424	0.804
Sweden	14,986	0.170	0.601
Switzerland	51,488	0.583	0.932
United Kingdom	224,791	2.546	2.502
United States	1,183,491	13.406	11.190
Total non-regional	3,111,095	35.241	34.703
Grand total	8,828,056	100.000	100.000

Source: Asian Development Bank, *Annual Report*, 1980.

Scope of Activities

The region in which AsDB operates extends from Afghanistan, in the high knot of mountains where the spines of Europe and Asia meet, to the Cook Islands, deep in the southern Pacific Ocean. It is an area of mass and high growth of population. The regional member countries are varied in size, life-style, needs and potentials. The economic patterns of the bank's regional members vary from the heavily urbanised city-states of Hong Kong and Singapore to the predominantly rural countries, from small islands with an extremely limited range of products to the broad potential in minerals and agriculture of an archipelago like Indonesia, or a compact area like the main river basin of Thailand. Parts of the bank's working region are modernised, and enjoy a fully developed and efficient infrastructure – transport, communications, financial institutions and education – and parts are still relatively unmapped forest. This gives some idea of the width and depth of the economic challenge facing the bank.[6]

Lending operations of the bank are mainly based on two kinds of loans – ordinary loans to the somewhat better-off developing member countries (DMCs) and concessional loans to its poorest member countries. By the end of 1980, the bank cumulative lending had reached $8,093m for 455 projects in 24 developing member countries. Of these, loans totalling $5,653m (70 per cent) were from ordinary capital resources (OCR) and $2,440m (30 per cent) from special funds (SF). In addition to financing the foreign exchange costs of goods and services needed for these projects, the bank has also financed, in specific circumstances, interest and other charges during construction as well as a portion of the local currency expenditures of some projects. Table 20.2 shows the bank's cumulative loan approvals by country and by source of funds.

The bank has financed a variety of development activities: irrigation and rural development, fisheries development, agricultural credit, livestock, seed production, fertiliser plants, forestry, agro-procession industries, power generation and distribution, industries (both directly and through national development finance institutions), highways and feeder roads, ports and harbours, airports, railways, telecommunications, water supply and sewerage, urban development, health, education, etc. At the end of December 1980 the cumulative distribution of the bank's loans (1967–80) to major economic sectors was: agriculture and agro-industry 28.0%; energy 24.2%; industry and non-fuel minerals and development banks 18.2%; transport and communications and multiprojects 15.9%; water supply 8.7%; urban development, education and health 5.0%.[7] Under its charter, AsDB, subject to specific authorisation by the Board of Governors, can undertake equity investment. It has, however, not sought to activate this provision so far, as it was believed that the bank should first concentrate on gaining more operational experience in the various aspects of socio-economic development. The bank has made credit lines to National Development

TABLE 20.2 AsDB's Cumulative Loan Approvals by Country and by Source of Funds 1967–80
(US $m)

Country	OCR	SF	Total	%
Afghanistan	—	95.10	95.10	1.18
Bangladesh	11.40	619.93	631.33	7.80
Burma	6.60	283.96	290.56	3.59
Cambodia	—	1.67	1.67	0.02
China, Rep. of	100.39	—	100.39	1.24
Cook Islands	—	1.00	1.00	0.01
Fiji	29.90	—	29.90	0.37
Hong Kong	101.50	—	101.50	1.25
Indonesia	1,068.98	162.28	1,231.26	15.21
Kiribati	—	1.75	1.75	0.02
Korea, Rep. of	1,168.33	3.70	1,172.03	14.48
Lao People's Dem. Rep.	—	36.84	36.84	0.46
Malaysia	589.95	3.30	593.25	7.33
Nepal	2.00	217.72	219.72	2.71
Pakistan	479.37	525.95	1,005.32	12.42
Papua New Guinea	35.95	61.94	97.89	1.21
Philippines	1,067.05	64.30	1,131.35	14.00
Singapore	178.08	3.00	181.08	2.24
Solomon Islands	—	14.85	14.85	0.18
Sri Lanka	14.13	210.11	224.24	2.77
Thailand	795.18	57.10	852.28	10.53
Tonga	—	4.37	4.37	0.05
Viet Nam, Soc. Rep. of	3.93	40.67	44.60	0.55
Western Samoa	—	31.03	31.03	0.38
Total	5,652.74	2,440.57	8,093.31	100.00

Source: Asian Development Bank, *Annual Report*, 1980.

Finance Institutions (DFIs) which in turn made funds available to a larger number of enterprises in the private sector. As of the end of 1980, the bank had approved 58 credit lines for a total of $1,106m to 25 development banks in 17 DMCs, representing 13.7 per cent of total bank lending.[8]

An important element of the bank's developmental role is the provision of technical assistance to DMCs to improve their capabilities of making use of external project financing, both from the bank and other sources. Technical assistance grants are financed mainly from the Technical Assistance Special Fund of the bank. In addition it administers technical assistance projects financed from other sources such as UNDP and EEC. It also co-operates with FAO on a cost-sharing basis in providing project preparatory technical assistance in the agricultural sector. Although mainly focused on project preparation, the bank's technical assistance activities are also directed towards implementation of development projects in DMCs, and to improving the technical, managerial and organisational capabilities of DMCs, as well as helping to establish and strengthen the various development institutions in those countries and assisting in the formulation of national and/or sectoral development strategies and plans. Table 20.3 shows the bank's cumulative technical assistance by country.

TABLE 20.3 AsDB Cumulative Technical Assistance by Country 1967–80 (US $000)

Country	No.	Total amount	%
Afghanistan	15	2,465.70	2.86
Bangladesh	44	12,659.94	14.71
Burma	22	3,941.00	4.58
Cambodia	2	111.00	0.13
China, Republic of	1	100.0	0.12
Cook Islands	2	161.00	0.19
Fiji	4	389.00	0.45
Indonesia	58	11,320.52	13.15
Kiribati	2	148.00	0.17
Korea, Republic of	16	2,827.30	3.29
Lao People's Democratic Republic	17	4,334.08	5.04
Malaysia	9	1,487.00	1.73
Maldives	2	268.00	0.31
Nepal	38	12,485.70	14.51
Pakistan	16	2,904.00	3.37
Papua New Guinea	11	1,335.60	1.55
Philippines	33	5,912.00	6.87
Singapore	1	34.70	0.04
Solomon Islands	10	1,246.34	1.45
Sri Lanka	26	3,772.50	4.38
Thailand	15	3,763.10	4.37
Tonga	6	830.00	0.96
Viet Nam	11	1,110.60	1.29
Western Samoa	15	1,632.50	1.90
Subtotal	376	75,239.58	87.42
Regional	75	10,825.23	12.58
Total	451	86,064.81	100.00

Source: Asian Development Bank, *Annual Report*, 1980.

Terms and Conditions

Interest Rate

The bank's lending rate on loans from its ordinary capital resources is 7.40 per cent per annum (for the year 1979). Project loans from the special funds resources bear only a service charge of 1 per cent per annum. The principal is repayable at the rate of 2 per cent a year for 10 years after the grace period and 4 per cent a year thereafter. Programme loans carry the providing interest rate or service charge applicable to the particular source of bank financing.

Repayment Period

This is 10–30 years for loans from the bank's ordinary capital resources. However, for higher-income developing member countries whose per capita GNP exceeded US $850 at the end of 1972, the maturity period of loans approved on or after 1 January 1977 would be subject to a limit of 15 years, inclusive of a grace period of 3 years. Project loans from the special funds resources are repayable over 40 years, including a 10-year grace period. All programme loans from the bank's ordinary capital resources are amortised over 15 years including a 3-year grace period.[9]

Grace Period

Is 2–7 years for loans from the bank's ordinary capital resources.

Guarantee

In cases where the recipient of loans or guarantees of loans is not itself a member government, the bank may, where necessary, require the guarantee of the member government or another acceptable entity.

Organisational Structure

The organisational structure of the bank consists of a Board of Governors, a Board of Directors, a President, two Vice-Presidents and other officers and staff. Each country nominates one governor and one deputy governor. The governor or deputy governor exercises the voting power to which the member is entitled. The Board of Governors is the bank's highest policy-making body. All the powers of the bank are vested in the Board of Governors which may delegate its power to the Board of Directors except on certain matters such as the admission of new members, change in the authorised capital stock of the bank, the election of Directors and the President, and amendment of the charter. The Board of Governors holds regular annual meetings. The Board of Directors, which is elected by the Board of Governors, consists of twelve members, eight representing regional members and four representing non-regional members. The directors hold office for a term of two years and may be re-elected. The Board of Directors normally meets once a week. The President of the bank is elected by the Board of Governors for a term of office of five years, after which he may- be re-elected. The President is the Chairman of the Board of Directors, but has no vote except a deciding vote in case of an equal division. The Vice-Presidents of the bank are appointed by the Board of Directors or by the recommendation of the President. They are deputies of the President in the management and operation of the bank; one is responsible for the operational functions while the other deals with finance and administration. The bank has sixteen departments and offices.[10] It reorganised its operational functions with effect from 1 April 1978, with the purpose of dealing more effectively with its expanding activities in line with the projected growth in the volume and scope of its lending and technical assistance programmes, its increasing involvement in inter-agency cooperation, and the need for more attention to be given to expediting the implementation and completion of projects. The reorganisation was also intended to provide more effective policy formulation and future review.

Approaches and Techniques Applied

The bank has no set application form for loans. In processing an application for a loan, it deals only with the applicant or his authorised representative. Prospective borrowers are expected to address preliminary inquiries to the bank. On receipt of these inquiries, the bank decides what additional information is required. Since only projects of high national priority and having governmental support will be considered, applications are normally submitted through the governments concerned. Basic information which the bank needs in order to study loan applications includes:

(i) a brief history of the business and principal activities of the proposed borrowers;

(ii) a general description of the project;
   (iii) a plan of operations for the activity;
   (iv) feasibility studies or pre-investment surveys;
   (v) detailed cost estimates;
   (vi) details of the loan required from the bank;
   (vii) the results of efforts, if any, made to obtain financing or facilities elsewhere;
   (viii) financial reports;
   (ix) estimates of financial results and cash flow;
   (x) estimates of the volume and value of sales for each year until the project is expected to be in normal operation.

A general review of a country's economic development, with emphasis on the national and sectoral development programmes and prospects, is a prerequisite to the identification of projects for AsDB financing. Project identification missions are sent regularly to DMCs for discussions with the authorities concerned and to select suitable projects for bank assistance. Since the level of economic growth and the development priorities vary from one country to another, particular attention is paid to selection of projects which will most effectively contribute to the economic and social development of the country concerned. In several instances, especially in the bank's smaller and less developed member countries, the very process of project identification may call for external help. In such cases, the bank provides technical assistance to help them identify and prepare projects. Bank missions to DMCs keep in touch with the activities of bilateral aid agencies through contracts with the offices of such agencies and with the aid co-ordination departments of member governments. The bank's Executive Directors also serve as a useful source of information about the activities of the bilateral agencies concerned.[11]

In appraising projects, the bank pays specific attention to such aspects as their economic, technical and financial feasibility, their effects on the general development activity of the country concerned, their contribution to economic bottlenecks, the capacity of the borrowing country to service additional external debt, the introduction of new technologies to raise productivity, and expansion of employment opportunities, and other social considerations.[12] Following the completion of the review of the guidelines on the use of consultants in 1978, revised guidelines were adopted in 1979. The new guidelines encourage to a large extent the use of domestic consultants and consultants from other developing countries through, among others, collaboration arrangements with consultants from developed member countries. Borrowers may, if they prefer to invite price proposals together with technical proposals, adopt a two-envelope system for inviting consultant's proposals and expeditious recruitment of consultants. The Post-Evaluation Office (PEO), which was established in 1978, concentrates on the formulation of standards and procedures governing the preparation of Project Performance Audit Reports (PPARs) which evaluate, verify and audit the findings of Project Completion Reports (PCRs), prepared by the respective Project Departments of the bank. The purpose of PPARs is to assess completed projects independently in terms of their design, implementation and intended objectives. Findings and recommendations of PPARs are examined by the bank with a view to improving its future operations.[13]

Strategy for Financing and Technical Assistance

AsDB's charter provides that while assisting all the developing member countries of the region, it should pay special attention to the needs of the smaller and less developed member countries. Borrowing DMCs have been classified into three groups.

Group A consists of DMCs that will have full access to AsDB loans and includes the least developed countries and those most seriously affected by world economic developments. DMCs in this group will be given priority in the allocation of AsDB resources and will receive at least 85 per cent of total allocations. Given the limited availability of the bank's resources, ordinary loans for certain Group A DMCs may also be provided in exceptional cases, having regard to their repayment capacity and their development potential. Group A DMCs are Afghanistan, Bangladesh, Burma, Cambodia, the Cook Islands, Laos, the Maldives, Nepal, Pakistan, the Solomon Islands, Sri Lanka, Tonga, Viet Nam and Western Samoa.

Group B consists of four DMCs (namely: Indonesia, Papua New Guinea, the Philippines and Thailand) that will have modest access to AsDB loans, in that not more than 15 per cent of total AsDB lending during 1979–82 may be provided to them. The rest of the countries, comprising *Group C*, will not have access to the limited resources of AsDB. Group C DMCs are the Republic of China, Fiji, Hong Kong, the Republic of Korea, Malaysia and Singapore.

A developing member country fully eligible for concessional loans may also receive ordinary loans on a case-by-case basis if the size of the bank's operational programme in the country is larger than can reasonably be financed from Special Funds, and if the country has the capacity to absorb the harder terms of ordinary loans. In lending, priority in allocating Special Funds Resources is to be given to projects with a high social and economic value but a low financial return, a low foreign exchange earning capacity, or a long gestation period.[14] The banks efforts to help the poor have been reflected in the selection of projects for financing. Thus, the main thrust of the bank's operational strategy has been its assistance to agriculture and rural development. This strategy aimed not only to bring the benefits of the bank assistance to the poor in the low-income DMCs, but also to reduce relative poverty in DMCs with higher income, like the Philippines and Thailand. In 1979, after a review of its role in the agriculture and rural development sector, the bank decided to aim at increasing the level of its lending to this sector by 20 per cent each year during the following three years. It was also decided that within the basic framework of bank policy, programme lending for this sector would be made more flexible to meet its special requirements. Project financing by the bank in the fisheries and livestock subsectors benefits poor fishermen and farmers by increasing their production capacity (and hence their incomes) through larger fish catches and better breeds of livestock as well as improving their nutritional standards and those of other poor people through the supply of cheap animal proteins. Bank lending to other sectors like rural electrification projects, small-scale and cottage industries, fertiliser projects, and coal development projects is also receiving great attention as part of the bank's strategy. Moreover, increasing attention has been directed by the bank to the needs of the urban poor, especially since the establishment of a Social Infrastructure Division in the bank in 1978. Labour-intensive and light-capital technologies have been adopted, where appropriate, as the bank's favourite strategy to create additional employment opportunities and promote more even income distribution.[15] The future strategy of AsDB financing will highlight the efforts made by the bank in the past to benefit the poor. In the coming years, the bank will redouble its efforts to ensure that the benefits of its assistance reach the poor.

The strategy of technical assistance provided by the bank covers three broad areas: project preparation, project implementation and advisory services. Technical assistance for project preparation is provided to assist or review the formulation of a project, comprising a study of the technical, economic and financial feasibility of the project, sometimes including a more general preliminary sectoral survey or the preparation of a master plan. Project implementation technical assistance is usually provided to assist executive agencies – including development financing institutions – in the implementation of bank-financed projects. Advisory technical assistance need not be directly related to a project financed by a bank loan. It may help to establish or strengthen an institution, to carry out studies on sectoral policies and strategies, or to formulate national development plans. According to the bank's strategy, technical assistance for regional activities may be provided for project preparation, project implementation, or advisory purposes. The bank's technical assistance to member countries has covered all the principal sectors and subsectors of economic and social development, but the main focus has been on agriculture and agro-industry. This emphasis reflects the bank's belief in the urgent need of DMCs to build up this sector for expanded food production and employment. Projects in this field, particularly for integrated rural development, are usually complex and technical assistance is often required for project preparation. In its efforts to tailor its technical assistance to the needs of its smaller and less developed DMCs, the bank has given special attention to its member countries in South Pacific and has assisted Tonga and Western Samoa to prepare five-year development plans and to identify priority projects. It has been engaged in helping to establish and/or strengthen development finance institutions, or other suitable intermediaries, in the Cook Islands, Fiji, Papua New Guinea, Western Samoa, Tonga and the Solomon Islands. The future strategy of the bank's technical assistance is based upon the new policy guidelines which were accepted by the Board of Directors in May 1977.[16] The new policy aims at improving the capacity of the DMCs to absorb external assistance and furthering their economic development. Special attention will be given to meeting the technical assistance needs of the smaller and least-developed DMCs, where constraints on project development and the lack of capacity to implement projects may be of a very pronounced nature.

Problems of Implementation and Remarks from Field Experience

Since AsDB's loans are in most cases made to meet the foreign exchange cost of the project, significant disbursements under a loan can take place only when all the preliminary steps enumerated earlier, right up to the placing of orders, are completed. Even then, depending on the nature of the capital equipment ordered and the time-scheduling of various segments of the project, it may take quite some time for completion of delivery of the items ordered. Thus, where a project takes about five years for completion, disbursements do not usually start until it is well into the second year, and they may not reach any sizable proportion until the fourth or fifth year. Some of the bank's borrowers have not had much experience of the procedures followed by international financial institutions. There are also problems arising from the fact that certain countries are situated beyond easy physical access. Project implementation in these countries is naturally somewhat slower than in others. In order to help to solve these problems, the bank has been conducting seminars on loan administration, particularly on procurement and disbursement.[17] As its future strategy for financing will place more emphasis on small and least developed member countries, it will naturally face problems of implementation in depth with their consequent impact upon the performance and quick effectiveness of its operations. To avoid these problems the bank will clearly have to provide more technical assistance for these countries which will be more costly but with long-term benefits. Fortunately the bank has already done so and has wisely reorganised the ways of tackling such problems. However, the availability of funds needed to solve these problems in the greater part of the world will remain an open question.

The bank's experience in the field of its operations has revealed some interesting points, which could be summarised as follows:[18]

(1) In most of AsDB's developing member countries, agricultural development has become an urgent necessity for survival – with the need to produce enough food to meet the demands of fast-growing populations. With the technological break-throughs of recent years there is now optimism that the battle will be won. But food production is only part of what is at stake. Also vital to Asian development planners is the predominant role of agriculture in the region's overall economic growth. Agriculture will have to provide not only enough food for Asia's rapidly growing populations, but also the increasing employment that will be needed to absorb the region's expanding labour supply for many years to come. In facing up to this challenge one of the bank's first operational tasks was to commission a regional agricultural survey which was undertaken in 1967, a year after AsDB was founded.

(2) Infrastructure financing is channelled to development fields recognised as basic to the economic growth of the bank's DMCs in Asia and the South Pacific. Since many of these infrastructure projects are capital-intensive, most of the bank's largest individual loans have been approved in this field.

(3) Although the economies of most developing countries in Asia rely heavily on agriculture, national planners in the region accord high priority to industrialisation as an important means of accelerating economic growth. DMCs of the bank see in the process of industrialisation at least a partial answer to their chronic problems of poverty, unemployment and adverse balance of trade. Industrialisation also brings in its wake an overall improvement of the human infrastructure for economic growth through training and acquisition of technical skills. In line with the specific needs and priorities of DMCs, the bank has been playing an active role in promoting industrialisation in the region.

(4) Spurred in large measure by the need to increase industrial employment opportunities, many Asian developing countries are establishing new programmes or upgrading existing programmes for the promotion of small-scale industries. The bank is aware of the many advantages, social as well as economic, which derive from a healthy small-scale industries subsector. It is also aware of the many difficulties a member country faces in attempting to implement a small-scale industries promotion programme.

(5) Most DMCs of the bank with generally unfavourable export performance have showed great instability in their export earnings. Many of these DMCs are highly dependent on exports of limited numbers of agricultural commodities. Agricultural export growth of such DMCs has also been constrained by the inadequate domestic supply capacity. Foreign investments and improving export competitiveness are relatively important factors for growth of DMCs manufactured exports.

(6) The Asian Development Bank has been increasingly concerned with the need to ensure that the technological input in projects assisted by it is appropriate to the individual circumstances of each country and project. The various international and bilateral aid agencies could organise a system of mutual exchange of information on this subject on a periodic basis, the results of such an exchange being made available in sufficient detail to all developing countries.

(7) The seeds of economic and social development in some of the poorest member nations of the bank are often planted through its technical assistance operations, designed to help assess, prepare and implement economically viable projects. Fulfilling one of the basic functions of the bank, technical assistance works two ways. It is attractive to DMCs, since, in appropriate cases, bank

involvement can lead to follow-up investment. On the other hand, from the bank's point of view, technical assistance improves the capacity of recipient countries to absorb external assistance.

Based upon the above presentation of the performance of the Asian Development Bank, we have to indicate that it is beyond the capacity of the bank and even of all the multilateral and bilateral development assistance programmes which channel resources into the region, to provide all the funds needed to cope with the huge economic problems of Asia. The aim of the bank can only be to help each developing member country to find its own solutions. The solution of the Asian drama of poverty is far beyond the capacity of such institutions as AsDB, but the more strong and powerful the bank is, the more effective the impact of its operations will be.

21 The Caribbean Development Bank

Establishment and Financial Resources

The historical background of the establishment of the CDB goes back to the 1960s when, following the demise of the West Indies Federation and the subsequent failure of the attempt at forming a federation of the Little Eight (comprising Barbados, the four Windward Islands and the three Leeward Islands), the United Kingdom, Canada and the United States of America, in January 1966, set up a team of experts to make an economic survey of Barbados and the Windward and Leeward Islands with a view to formulating plans for their achieving economic viability. Among the recommendations of this team was the establishment of a Regional Development Agency including a Development Bank Division to serve the territories. In November 1966 it was agreed that consideration should be given to the establishment of an institution to serve all the Commonwealth Caribbean Countries and Territories. The Draft Agreement establishing the Caribbean Development Bank was submitted in 1968, and adopted after three meetings at the ministerial level. The Agreement was signed at Kingston, Jamaica, on 18 October 1969 and entered into force on 26 January, 1970.[1]

Article 1 of CDB's charter states that the purpose of the bank is 'to contribute to the harmonious economic growth and development of the member countries of the Caribbean (the region) and to promote economic co-operation and integration among them, having special and urgent regard to the needs of the less developed members of the region'. Article 2 of the bank's charter specifies the functions which CDB should perform in order to achieve its purpose. These are:

(1) To assist regional members in the co-ordination of their development programmes with a view to achieving better utilisation of their resources, making their economies more complementary,

and promoting orderly expansion of their international trade, in particular intra-regional trade.
(2) To mobilise within and outside the region additional financial resources for the development of the region.
(3) To finance projects and programmes contributing to the development of the region or any of the regional members.
(4) To provide appropriate technical assistance to its regional members, particularly by undertaking or commissioning pre-investment surveys and by assisting in the identification and preparation of project proposals.
(5) To promote public and private investment in development projects by, among other means, aiding financial institutions in the region and supporting the establishment of consortia.
(6) To co-operate and assist in other regional efforts designed to promote regional and locally controlled financial institutions and a regional market for credit and savings.
(7) To stimulate and encourage the development of capital markets within the region.
(8) To undertake or promote such other activities as may advance its purpose.

The bank's charter allows for the membership of the following states and territories:

(i) states and territories of the region; and
(ii) non-regional states which are members of the UN or any of its specialised agencies or of the International Atomic Energy Agency.

The following states and territories are founding members of the bank, that is those states and territories which signed the Agreement establishing the bank in 1969.

(1) *Regional Members*: Antigua, Bahamas, Belize, British Virgin Islands, Cayman Islands, Dominica, Grenada, Guyana, Jamaica, Montserrat, St Kitts–Nevis–Anguilla, St Lucia, St Vincent, Trinidad and Tobago, and the Turks and Caicos Islands.
(2) *Non-regional Members*: Canada and the United Kingdom.

In addition, Venezuela and Colombia have been admitted as regional members, the former in April 1973 and the latter in November 1974.[2]

The financial resources, of the bank consist of:

(i) ordinary capital resources, comprised mainly of subscribed capital and borrowing; and
(ii) special funds resources which consist of the resources of the Special Development Fund established by Article 8 of CDB's charter and resources accepted by the bank for inclusion in other special funds established or administered by it.

The original authorised capital stock of the bank was US $50m (US $25m paid up and US $25m callable). Over the ten years of its operations (1970–80), the growth in the bank's membership and increases in subscribed capital have resulted in significant increases in the volume of shares and a slight shift in the distribution of shares between regional and non-regional bank members. Total share holdings increased from 10,000 in 1970 to 39,316 in 1979, with the percentage held by regional members increasing from 60 in 1970 to 64.7 in 1979. The authorised capital of the bank (as of September 1980) reached US $218.6m, ordinary capital resources US $116.7m and special funds resources US $235.8m.[3] Total resources of the bank as at the end of 1980 reached US $402.576m compared with US $374.861m at the end of 1979, an increase of $27.715m over the year. The components of the bank's total resources (in 1980 compared with 1979) are shown in Table 21.1.

Non-regional members may hold not more than 40 per cent of the total shares of the bank and regional members not less than 60 per cent.[4] The callable shares are subject to call only as and when required by the bank to meet its obligations incurred on borrowings or on guarantees chargeable to the ordinary operations of the bank.

Scope of Activities

Projects financed by CDB from both ordinary capital and special funds resources cover a wide range of development activities including ports, agriculture, livestock, processing of agricultural products and marketing facilities, industrial estates, roads and bridges, water and electricity, sea and air transport equipment, airport building, hotels and tourist facilities, agricultural credit, small and medium industries, residential mortgages and student loans. The bank has financed projects in the countries and territories of the Commonwealth Caribbean Region which are members of the bank, namely Antigua, Bahamas, Barbados,

TABLE 21.1 CDB's Total Resources, 1980 and 1979
($000s)

	1980	1979
I. Ordinary capital resources	132,385	116,731
(a) Paid-up capital and ordinary reserves	50,603	44,169
(b) Borrowings	81,782	72,562
II. Venezuelan Trust Fund	25,022	25,022
III. Special funds resources	245,169	233,108
(a) Special Development Fund	106,387	97,127
(b) Other Special Funds Resources by contributors[a]		
Country contributions/loans		
(i) Canada contributions	9,117	9,362
(ii) Nigeria loan	5,000	5,000
(iii) Trinidad and Tobago loan	4,167	4,167
(iv) USA (through USAID) loans	72,800	72,800
Institutional contributions/loans		
(i) IDB	12,424	12,500
(ii) IDA[b]	7,964	8,000
Non-reimbursible contributions[c]		
USAID grant programmes	22,329	22,216
Other grant funds	4,981	1,936
Grand total	402,576	374,861

[a] Does not include UK Special Trust Fund amounting to $5,338,000 earmarked for LIAT's acquisition of an additional carrier and EDF's provision of $8,260,000 for on-lending to WISCO to finance its fleet expansion programme.
[b] Includes an amount of $1m from the EEC Special Action Credit with IDA.
[c] Excludes $3,247,000 in respect of USAID grant to CARICOM, previously included in 1979 totals.
Source: Caribbean Development Bank, *Annual Report*, 1980.

Belize, British Virgin Islands, Cayman Islands, Dominica, Grenada, Guyana, Jamaica, Montserrat, St Kitts/Nevis/Anguilla, St Lucia, St Vincent, Trinidad and Tobago, and the Turks and Caicos Islands. This indicates that of CDB's membership of twenty, only the sixteen Commonwealth Caribbean countries have borrowed. These countries have a combined population of 5.1m. During the ten-year period (1970–79), the bank's total financing approvals amounted to $269.0m of which 56.7 per cent or $152.5m was to the LLDCs. Loans accounted for 94.6

per cent of total approvals, grants which totalled $11.77m in 1979 alone have assured increased significance in the bank's portfolio, accounting for 4.6 per cent of total financing approvals at the end of 1979 compared to a modest 0.3 per cent up to 1978. The distribution of soft funds resources shows that of a total of $175.2m approved during 1970–79, the LLDCs were the recipients of $129.6m or 74 per cent. The bank's soft funds approvals to the LLDCs represented 85 per cent of total financing approvals to these countries. An examination of disbursements for the period shows that disbursements for the first five years of the bank's operations totalled $6.4m compared with $122.7m in the latter five-year period. Cumulative disbursements as a percentage of cumulative approvals peaked at 53.8 per cent in 1978 from 10.3 per cent in 1974 but declined to 50.0 per cent in 1979.[5] This decline was related to the rapid increase in loan approvals in 1979. By the end of 1980, the Bank's cumulative total financing approvals since 1970 amounted to $309.613m of which 28.4 per cent came from ordinary capital resources, 29.8 per cent from the Special Development Fund, and 24.8 per cent from other special funds. Table 21.2 shows the bank's approvals of loans by country and by Fund.

The distribution of CDB's total financing by sector during 1970–80 has shown that three sectors – agriculture (25.8 per cent), infrastructure including ports (43.5 per cent), and industry and tourism (19.6 per cent) – accounted for 88.9 per cent of total financing approvals.[6] Since its establishment in 1970, the bank has provided increasing amounts of technical assistance to borrowing member states, particularly the LLDCs. This has been felt necessary as it is recognised that a major obstacle to the timely and effective utilisation of the increased flow of resources to the region is the shortage of middle and higher level management, administrative and technical personnel which imposes a severe limitation on the capacity of borrowing member states. In 1978, in co-operation with other donors active in the region (Canada, Trinidad and Tobago, the UK, the USA and Venezuela), the bank established a Technical Assistance Fund in the sum of $4m. At least 70 per cent of the resources of the fund are to be directed to the LLDCs and the balance to the MDCs and regional institutions. The fund's resources are to be allocated to four areas of technical assistance: general development, pre-investment and project preparation, project implementation and bank development. The resources of the fund can be utilised on a grant, loan or contingency recoverable basis. In addition, the bank has negotiated resources for technical assistance purposes from the IDB and the EEC. A portion of the contribution of some of the

TABLE 21.2 Approvals of Loans, Contingent Loans, Equity and Grants (Net) by Country and by Fund 1970–80 ($000s)

Country	Ordinary capital resources	Venezuelan Trust Fund	Special Development Fund	Agricultural fund	Housing funds	Counterpart contribution fund	Other special funds	Total	%
Antigua	2,800	366	7,075	1,504	642	109	3,957	16,451	5.3
Bahamas	5,300	3,248	700	—	—	—	—	9,248	3.0
Barbados	5,508	3,646	4,996	—	—	—	6,558	20,708	6.7
Belize	6,690	—	23,786	7,402	1,624	550	2,145	42,197	13.6
British Virgin Islands	349	—	1,923	1,008	—	—	1	3,281	1.1
Cayman Islands	804	—	3,012	500	515	—	2	4,833	1.6
Dominica	892	—	10,403	3,579	1,664	1,040	2,757	20,335	6.5
Grenada	107	—	3,480	2,876	975	620	2,027	10,085	3.3
Guyana	28,330	1,590	1,073	—	—	—	10,504	41,497	13.4
Jamaica	26,889	4,396	3,800	—	962	—	21,100	57,147	18.5
Montserrat	679	—	1,132	867	86	33	517	3,314	1.1
St Kitts/Nevis	1,474	259	4,839	59	285	219	4,087	11,222	3.6
St Lucia	2,979	677	8,356	3,422	—	370	3,192	19,036	6.1
St Vincent	488	1,598	8,910	3,843	931	502	2,759	19,031	6.1
Trinidad and Tobago	1,850	—	—	—	—	—	—	1,850	0.6
Turks and Caicos Islands	368	—	711	—	—	—	1	1,080	0.3
Regional Projects									
LDC Focus	—	—	6,869	658	—	—	15,531	23,058	7.5
MDC Focus	2,358	—	1,074	—	—	—	—	3,432	1.1
LCD/MDC Focus	—	—	25	194	—	—	1,587	1,806	0.6
Total	87,865	15,780	92,204	25,913	7,684	3,443	76,725	309,613	100.0
%	28.4	5.1	29.8	8.3	2.5	1.1	24.8	100.0	

Source: Caribbean Development Bank, *Annual Report*, 1980.

donors to CDB's Special Development Fund can also be used for such purposes. All these resources can be used to finance project preparation and pre-investment studies. The bank has also established a Technology Information Unit to assist in ensuring that the design of projects takes into account the appropriate technology needs of the bank's borrowing member countries and also to disseminate information on appropriate technology having due regard to the balance surplus situation in the region.[7]

Terms and Conditions

Interest Rates

The bank's terms for lending vary from time to time in accordance with decisions taken by the Board of Directors. The interest rates (inclusive of the commission of 1 per cent) on loans financed from its ordinary capital resources are as follows:

	% per annum
Government financial intermediaries	$8\frac{1}{2}$
Government (infrastructure and public utilities)	9
Productive enterprises (agriculture)	$9\frac{1}{2}$
Productive enterprises (industry and tourism)	$10\frac{1}{2}$

The interest rate on loans financed from special funds resources is 4 per cent per annum which includes, in the case of projects financed from the Special Development Fund, a service charge of 1 per cent.

Repayment Periods

Loans financed from the bank's ordinary capital resources are repayable over a period of 10–15 years except in the case of loans for industry and tourism which are repayable over a period of 10–18 years. Loans financed from special funds resources are repayable over a period of 15–20 years.

Grace Periods

Loans financed from the bank's ordinary capital resources have an appropriate grace period depending on the project being financed. Loans financed from special funds resources have a grace period which is usually up to 5 years.

General Policy

In its ordinary operations, the bank lends to a government for a project an amount in the currency of that government not exceeding 20 per cent of the cost of the project together with further amounts in other currencies, not exceeding 70 per cent of the cost of the project in the case of its more developed member countries, and 80 per cent in the case of its less developed member countries. In its special operations, or in projects mixing ordinary capital and special funds resources, the bank lends to a government up to 90 per cent of the cost of the project. The bank may also make loans or guarantee loans for financing enterprises in the private sector. It may not finance a project if the government of the territory in which the project is located indicates an objection to it. In appropriate cases the bank may also require a government undertaking to permit the borrower to convert local currency into the foreign currencies needed for serving the bank's loan. The CDB levies a commitment fee of $\frac{3}{4}$ of 1 per cent per annum on the undisbursed portion of a loan from ordinary capital resources from a date 60 days after the loan agreement has been concluded. The bank may guarantee loans raised by public or private borrowers from other parties, and charges a commission for such guarantees. The charge is 1.5 per cent per annum on the outstanding balance of the repayment guaranteed comprising 0.5 per cent guarantee fee plus 1 per cent service charge.[8]

Organisational Structure

The bank has a Board of Governors, a Board of Directors, a President, a Vice-President and other officers and staff. The Board of Governors is the highest policy-making body of the bank. Each member country nominates one governor and one deputy governor. For this purpose, the member territories of Montserrat, the British Virgin Islands, the Cayman Islands and the Turks and Caicos Islands are regarded as one member. Each governor casts the votes of the member territory or territories which he represents. Voting power is roughly proportional to shares subscribed, with a slight weighting in favour of the smaller member territories. At a special meeting of the Board of Governors held in 1971, the Board decided that Commonwealth Caribbean members should always have a majority of the voting power in the bank and a majority of the number of directors. All the powers of the bank are vested in the Board of Governors which may delegate its powers to the Board of Directors except on certain matters, such as admission of new members, change in capital stock of the bank, election of directors and the President, amendment of the Charter, and termination of the operations of the bank. The Board of Directors comprises eleven directors, nine representing the regional members of the bank and two representing the non-regional members. Directors hold office for a term of two years and are eligible for re-election for a further term or terms of office. Each director appoints a deputy with full power to act for him when he is not present. The Board of Directors is responsible for the general policy and direction of the operations of the bank. The Board exercises all powers delegated to it by the Board of Governors and, in conformity with the Charter, takes decisions concerning loans, guarantees and other investments by the bank, borrowing programmes, technical assistance and other operations. It also approves the administrative budget of the bank and submits accounts pertaining to each financial year for approval by the Board of Governors. The President, under the direction of the Board of Directors of which he is Chairman, is responsible for the organisation and operation of the bank, including appointments of staff and investigation of loan proposals. He serves for a five-year term and may be re-elected. The Vice-President exercises the authority and performs the functions of the President in the absence or incapacity of the President or while that office is vacant. The President is advised by the directors of the following five departments: Secretary and Administration, Projects, Economics and Programming, Finance and Legal.[9]

Twenty-seven of the professional staff are financed (wholly or partially) under Technical Assistance Programmes with UNDP, USAID, CFTC, EEC, ITC, IDB and the governments of West Germany and New Zealand.[10] From 1 January 1979 a new organisational structure came into effect. Under this new structure the divisions formerly responsible for activities in agriculture, industry, tourism and infrastructure were placed under the umbrella of a newly created Projects Department, and the functions of financial and economic analysis were made the responsibility of a new Project Design and Analysis Division within the Projects Department. The Projects Department was also given responsibility for administering the Loan Supervision Unit, which works closely with project supervisors to monitor project implementation and supervision. The need for greater attention to the needs and problems of the financial intermediaries led to the establishment of a special section within the Projects Department to deal with this matter. An Energy and Technology Unit was also established in the bank in 1979 within the administration of the Projects

Department.[11] The reorganised Economics and Programming Department was given the responsibility for quality control in project analysis works jointly with the Projects Dpartment in the bank's project identification activities. This department also has responsibility for programming the bank's overall lending operations. This considerably enlarged working group in the Projects Department underwent the experience of adjustment to new procedures and new premises while still maintaining a full impetus on an increased pipeline of projects.

Approaches and Techniques Applied

Prospective borrowers address preliminary inquiries to the bank which then decides what additional information is required and provides the prospective borrower with an appropriate loan application form. In processing an application for a loan or guarantee, the CDB deals only with the applicant or an authorised representative, not with intermediaries. However, in practice, many projects for bank financing are identified when it sends missions to its member countries, or when the bank staff visit these countries in their normal course of duty. The bank's project staff are in constant contact with their counterparts and there is, therefore, a continuous process of project identification.[12] In appraising the projects that it proposes to finance, the bank appraises these projects with regard to their technical, commercial, financial, legal, organisational and managerial, environmental and social aspects, their effects on the general development of the beneficiary country, their contribution to the removal of economic bottlenecks, the capacity of the borrowing country to service additional external debt, the introduction of appropriate technologies and the expansion of employment opportunities.[13]

In replying to the author's questionnaire sheet, the bank staff indicated that the CDB uses normal project appraisal techniques, primarily the Little–Mirrlees methodology.[14] Prospective borrowers are required to submit full details, including the results of market surveys, estimates of cost, feasibility studies, projections of sales and of cash flows, and any other information bearing on the expected profitability of the project including development incentives and other concessions from the government. The bank also examines title deeds, engineering drawings and construction and insurance contracts to assure the soundness of the assets or securities which are offered as backing for its financial participation.

The bank employs consultants in connection with technical assistance programmes that it finances with studies for which the bank is the executive agency and where it finds it necessary to supplement its own staff whether at the stage of project appraisal or of scrutiny of project execution. In all these cases, the consultants are selected by the bank. After termination of their employment such consultants are required to abstain from any subsequent work on the same project, except as agreed by the bank. On the other hand, borrowers may find it desirable to employ individual consultants as advisers where expertise not otherwise available is needed, or to employ consulting firms to facilitate the satisfactory implementation of the project for which a loan is made by the bank. The need for the employment of consultants is considered by the bank at the time of making the appraisal of the loan application and the bank may, where necessary, require that consultants be engaged by the borrower. Where borrowers employ consultants, they are responsible for their selection but, before such selection is made, the bank has to be satisfied of the competence and functions of the consultants to be engaged. After a consulting firm has been chosen, the bank's primary interest is to see that the responsibilities of the firm are clearly set out in its contract with the borrower and carried out by that firm alone. To achieve this, the bank reviews the draft contract prepared by the consultant and may, if necessary, seek clarification from the borrower and from the consultant of any specific issues in the contract to ensure that the consultant is aware of the terms and conditions of employment and that the borrower fully appreciates the responsibilities and authority which the consulting firm bears. During the review of the contract the bank makes clear any requirements which it may have in regard to the work.[15]

The CDB is required by its Articles of Agreement (Article 15) to use the proceeds of financing from ordinary operations for the procurement in members' territories of goods and services produced in those areas. In support of this Article, the bank pays due regard to the need to develop and strengthen the undertakings, entities and skills of individuals belonging to the region. In special cases the Board of Directors may, however, determine the circumstances in which the procurement of goods and services may be permitted elsewhere, giving particular consideration whenever practicable to the procurement of goods and services produced in the territory of countries which have contributed substantially to the resources of the bank. Non-member countries in which procurement of goods and services is permitted pursuant to a determination made by the Board of Directors are the USA, West Germany, IBRD member countries and Switzerland (in respect of procurement from the proceeds of an IBRD Loan). The arrangements between the bank and the borrower regarding the use of the proceeds of the particular loan or credit, the procurement contracts which are to be financed, the currency or currencies in which the contracts are to be executed, the extent to which procurement documents are subject to bank review, are set forth in each case in the contractual document for the loan or credit.[16]

Strategy for Financing and Technical Assistance

The Charter of the CDB requires it to promote economic co-operation and integration among its regional member countries, and for this purpose one of the functions of the bank is to assist regional members in the co-ordination of their development programmes, with a view to achieving better utilisation of their resources, making their economies more complementary, and promoting the orderly expansion of their international trade, in particular intra-regional trade. The bank has based its strategy upon the promotion of projects which have a direct integration aspect in three sectors: agriculture, transport and industry. In agriculture, the bank has initiated the process of promoting and financing regional agricultural projects (including fisheries and livestock) as part of the Regional Food Plan accepted by the Conference of Heads of Governments of the Caribbean Community in December 1975. In the area of intra-regional transportation facilities, the bank has made loans to regional projects in shipping and air transport. Within the limits of its financial and technical resources, the bank promotes and explores the possibilities of financing regional projects in the industrial sector with a view to making industrial development in the various countries of the region more complementary. From its inception the bank has provided technical assistance to its member states, especially in the field of project preparation and implementation, general studies and direct support for work undertaken by government departments particularly in statistics, national income accounting and planning. The bank estimates that about 30 per cent of its staffs' time is devoted to technical assistance. Growing demands for this have persuaded the bank to establish a Technical Assistance Fund to the sum of US $4m. The fund is financed through resources obtained from the Inter-American Development Bank, the USA, the UK, Canada, Venezuela, Trinidad and Tobago, and the bank itself. This fund enables the bank to react to requests for assistance not only for project-oriented purposes but also for other areas related to the general development field.[17]

In replying to the questionnaire, the bank's staff indicated that the future regional strategy for financing will cover all borrowing member countries with one exception; that is Trinidad and Tobago, where only the private sector will be covered as that government is not requesting loans. The future sectoral strategy for financing will cover agriculture, industry, tourism, infrastructure (ports, roads, power, sea and air transport, equipment, water and sewerage, housing), and education (student loans). Sources of financing will be mainly directed to projects in the region but also some programme loans. The future strategy for technical assistance will mainly be related to projects financed by the bank plus some general development technical assistance.

From a comparison between what the staff of the bank have stated in the questionnaire and what has been indicated in the bank's documents, it is clear that the CDB, if it follows what has been stated by its staff, will not be able to cope in the short term with the terms in its Charter relating to economic integration. The bank's Annual Report of 1979 indicated that the year did not see any significant progress towards deepening integration but it was rather a period of review and consolidation.[18] Regional economic developments during 1979 reflected to a great extent the conditions prevailing on the international scene. Higher oil prices, rising international inflation, and weakening demand have had marked repercussions on the economies of the region. Moreover, domestic problems such as natural disaster and labour unrest have contributed to a depressed level of economic activity.

Problems of Implementation and Remarks from Field Experience

The CDB's staff indicated in their answers to the questionnaire that the main problems of implementation and follow-up of projects are the frequent delays in implementation, due largely to the lack of expertise in borrowing countries, and legal and administrative hold-ups in decisions to satisfy conditions of precedent. They also indicated that all projects are monitored by the bank's staff. The experience of the bank and the challenges of its operations in the future can be understood from the statement by the President to the Board of Governors at the Tenth Annual Meeting in May 1980.[18] He indicated that economic performance and the problems of the national economies during the 1970s showed that most of the countries of the region faced reduced rates of economic growth, and serious fiscal, balance of payments and debt service problems. In some cases the smaller countries with good economic management and with growing tourism receipts, and the only oil exporter, escaped many of these difficulties. But few have been able to cope successfully with the inherited structural problems of high unemployment, heavy imports of food and lack of linkages in their national economies. The President indicated the five challenges facing the borrowing member countries in the 1980s as follows:

(1) Improvement of the balance of payments and determining urgent sectoral priorities in production.
(2) Improvement and better utilisation of the member countries' human resources.
(3) Definition of the role and functioning of the state, of small-scale enterprise and of the private sector.
(4) The deepening of the regional integration movement.
(5) Improvement of the quality of national economic management.

The President also indicated five challenges facing the CDB in its policies and operations as follows:

(1) Determination of the role of the bank as a development agency.
(2) Re-definition of the financing priorities of the bank.
(3) Improvement of the structure and functioning of the national DFCs.
(4) Determination of the levels of the bank's lending programmes and the terms and conditions of raising funds.
(5) Consolidation and rationalisation of relationships with other aid donors.

The above indicates that the bank has many problems to face in the 1980s so long as its member countries continue to face serious economic difficulties. The bank should, however, be able to ease these problems gradually over the decade if it chooses to adopt for itself a leading role in economic co-operation and integration among its member states. As with the other two regional banks (AfDB and AsDB), the problem of the limited financial resources of the bank will be a harsh handicap to its ambitions and development, and it should therefore raise its capital substantially by further expanding its membership to non-regional countries and organisations, while keeping its Caribbean character.

22 The Inter-American Development Bank

Establishment and Financial Resources

The historical background to the establishment of the IDB lies in the political climate which prevailed in Latin America in May 1958, when Richard Nixon undertook his Vice-Presidential tour. It was a climate of growing consciousness of Latin American identity, equipped with an institutional framework within which long-standing political suspicion of the USA had been translated into specifically focused economic resentment, not only against the USA, but also against the existing institutions of international economic relations, a resentment which contained within itself, among other features, a demand for a more imaginative, a more political, and above all a more social approach to the challenge of development. A few months before Mr Nixon's visit, the Latin American nations had made a determined effort to initiate the preparatory steps towards the setting up of an Inter-American bank. In August and September 1957, the Economic Conference of the Organisation of American States, meeting in Buenos Aires, had recommended that the Inter-American Economic and Social Council should set up a special committee to study the possibilities of establishing the bank. On 12 August 1958, however, the US representative announced, at a special session of the Council, that his government was ready to consider the establishment of such a bank. A month later, at an informal meeting of North, Central and South American foreign ministers in Washington, the recommendation made a year previously in Buenos Aires was given more concrete shape, in the form of a recommendation that the Council should set up an inter-governmental committee to negotiate and draft a charter. This Committee, on which all nations that were members of the Inter-American system were represented, met in Washington from 9 January to 8 April 1959, at the end of which an agreement was signed. The necessary instruments of ratification having been deposited, the agreement came into effect on 30 December 1959, and six weeks later the Board of Governors held its first meeting.[1]

The agreement establishing the Inter-American Development Bank stated that 'the purpose of the bank is to contribute to the acceleration of the process of economic and social development of the regional developing member countries, individually and collectively.'[2] To implement its purpose, the functions of the bank are as follows:[3]

(1) To promote the investment of public and private capital for development purposes.
(2) To utilise its own capital, funds raised by it in financial markets, and other available resources, for financing the development of member countries, giving priority to those loans and guarantees that will contribute most effectively to their economic growth.
(3) To encourage private investment in projects, enterprises and activities contributing to economic development and to supplement private investment when private capital is not available on reasonable terms and conditions.
(4) To co-operate with member countries to orient their development policies toward a better utilisation of their resources, in a manner consistent with the objectives of making their economies more complementary and of fostering the orderly growth of their foreign trade.
(5) To provide technical assistance for the preparation, financing and implementation of development plans and projects, including the study of priorities and the formulation of specific project proposals.

The resources of the bank consist of the ordinary capital resources, the inter-regional capital resources, and the resources of the Fund for Special Operations. The authorised ordinary capital stock of the bank was originally US $850m of the weight and fineness of gold in effect on 1 January 1959 divided into 85,000 shares having a par value of $10,000 each. The original authorised inter-regional capital stock was US $420m of the weight and fineness in effect of 1 January 1959 divided into 42,000 shares having a par value of US $10,000 each. As for the Fund for Special Operations, it was established with the original resources of US $150m of the weight and fineness of gold in effect on 1 January 1959 contributed by the original members of the bank in accordance with the quotas specified in the bank's Agreement. Each member could pay 50 per cent of its quota at any time and the remaining 50 per cent was to be paid at any time subsequent to the year after the bank had begun operations, in such amounts and at such times as determined by the bank; provided, however, that the total amount of all quotas was made due and payable not later than the date fixed for payment of the third instalment of the subscriptions to the paid-in capital stock of the bank. It should be indicated that the 'inter-regional capital resources' of the bank include the following:

(i) amortised inter-regional capital, including both paid-in and callable shares;
(ii) all funds raised by borrowings;
(iii) all funds received in repayment of loans;
(iv) all income derived from loans made from the above mentioned funds or from guarantees;
(v) all other income derived from any of the resources mentioned above.

The Fund for Special Operations was established for the making of loans on terms and conditions appropriate for dealing with special circumstances arising in specific countries or with respect to specific projects. Table 22.1 shows the original subscriptions to the authorised capital stock of the bank and contribution quotas for the Fund for Special Operations.

The development of the total resources of the bank during the period 1961–80 showed that its ordinary capital subscriptions reached US $11,773m at the end of 1980 compared with US $5965m in 1975, US $2763m in 1970, US $1770m in 1965 and US $813m in 1961. Subscriptions for inter-regional capital reached US $3371m at the end of 1980 compared with US $558m in 1976 (as in the first year of subscriptions). Funds for special operations reached US $7669m at the end of 1980 compared with US $4395m in 1975, US $2328m in 1970, US $1119m in 1965, and US $146m in 1961.[4] The bank's capital resources and its Fund for Special Operations represent the backbone of its resources. From its earliest years, however, the bank has been given responsibility for administering other special funds provided for Latin America's development by various countries. These funds totalled US $1176m by the end of 1980, the two largest being the US $525m Social Progress Trust Fund placed under the bank's administration in 1961 by the United States and the US $500m Venezuelan Trust Fund established by the latter country in 1979.[5] The IDB has also administered special funds provided by Argentina, Canada, Germany, Norway, Sweden, Switzerland, the United Kingdom and the Vatican. These last funds were established before the donor countries became

TABLE 22.1 Subscriptions to Authorised Capital Stock of the Bank and Contribution Quotas for the Fund for Special Operations

Country	Paid-in capital shares	Callable shares	Total subscription	Quota (US$000s)
	(in shares of US$10,000 each)			
Argentina	5,157	5,157	10,314	10,314
Bolivia	414	414	828	828
Brazil	5,157	5,157	10,314	10,314
Chile	1,416	1,416	2,832	2,832
Colombia	1,415	1,415	2,830	2,830
Costa Rica	207	207	414	414
Cuba	1,842	1,842	3,684	3,684
Dominican Republic	276	276	552	552
Ecuador	276	276	552	552
El Salvador	207	207	414	414
Guatemala	276	276	552	552
Haiti	207	207	414	414
Honduras	207	207	414	414
Mexico	3,315	3,315	6,630	6,630
Nicaragua	207	207	414	414
Panama	207	207	414	414
Paraguay	207	207	414	414
Peru	691	691	1,382	1,382
United States of America	15,000	20,000	35,000	100,000
Uruguay	553	553	1,106	1,106
Venezuela	2,763	2,763	5,526	5,526
Total	40,000	45,000	85,000	150,000

Source: *Agreement Establishing the Inter-American Development Bank*, amended 1977.

members of the bank. Table 22.2 shows the development of total resources of the bank.

As of 31 December 1980, the capital of the bank was as follows:[6]

	(US $m)		
	Payable in cash	Callable	Total
Ordinary capital (OC)	1,198	10,575	11,773
Intra-regional capital (IC)	467	2,904	3,371
Fund for Special Operations (FSO)	6,589	1,080	7,669
Total	8,254	14,559	22,813

TABLE 22.2 Development of Total Resources of the Bank 1961–80 (US $m)

Year	Ordinary capital	Inter-regional capital	Subscriptions (end of year) Fund for Special Operations	Other funds	Total
1961	813	—	146	394	1,353
1962	813	—	146	394	1,353
1963	813	—	146	394	1,353
1964	1,285	—	291	534	2,038
1965	1,770	—	1,119	544	3,433
1966	1,770	—	1,119	570	3,459
1967	1,779	—	2,321	577	4,677
1968	2,260	—	2,321	595	5,176
1969	2,282	—	2,328	595	5,205
1970	2,763	—	2,328	610	5,701
1971	3,466	—	2,328	631	6,425
1972	4,373	—	3,987	639	8,999
1973	5,710	—	4,394	650	10,754
1974	5,954	—	4,394	655	11,003
1975	5,965	—	4,395	1,159	11,519
1976	6,906	558	5,743	1,179	14,386
1977	7,861	1,163	5,905	1,173	16,102
1978	9,651	1,916	5,906	1,173	18,646
1979	9,651	1,933	5,907	1,173	18,664
1980	11,773	3,371	7,669	1,176	23,989

Sources: Inter-American Development Bank, *Annual Reports*, 1979, 1980.

In replying to the questionnaire sheet the staff of the bank indicated that the IDB's lendable resources are generally calculated at the sum of its capital payments received, its usable callable capital and loan repayments received, less cumulative approvals. It is clear that the Inter-American Development Bank, compared to both the African Development Bank and the Asian Development Bank, has the greater volume of resources at its disposal. It was shown in the previous two chapters that financial constraints, in addition to limiting the scale of operations, had an impact on AfDB's and AsDB's policies. The IDB, in contrast, has succeeded in attracting additional resources as it needs them.

Scope of Activities

The IDB's scope of activities covers the area of the western hemisphere in the Latin American and Caribbean regions. The projects that the bank finances include participating in projects that foster the economic and social development of the member countries. These projects cover all major sectors; some are in areas that involve several economic sectors such as the case of integrated rural development, where physical infrastructure, productive and social programmes form a precisely targeted package. The bank has also participated and continues to participate in projects in agricultural credit, agricultural expansion, irrigation, rural development, fisheries, forestry, industry and tourism, energy exploration, transport, transmission, production and generation, roads, ports, environmental control, sanitation, health, education, technology, transfer and pre-investment activities such as project preparation and design. Table 22.3 shows the bank's distribution of authorised cumulative loans by sector.

TABLE 22.3   IDB's Distribution of Cumulative Loans by Sector (1961–80)

Sector	1961–80 (US $m)	%
Productive sectors		
Agriculture and fisheries	4,159	23
Industry and mining	2,751	15
Tourism	170	1
Physical infrastructure		
Energy	4,372	24
Transport and communications	2,686	15
Social infrastructure		
Urban development	556	3
Education, science and technology	806	5
Environmental and public health	1,696	10
Other		
Export financing	346	2
Pre-investment	208	1
Other	90	1
Total	17,840	100

Source: Inter-American Development Bank, *Annual Report*, 1980.

The bank was the first regional institution to venture into the financing of rural development projects on a large scale. During the early period 1961–67, bank financing in this sector focused on agrarian reform, land settlement, drinking-water supply and rural roads. In the second stage, 1968–74, these efforts were expanded to include support for productive activities of small-scale farmers through irrigation and farm credit, marketing programmes and research and extension services. More recently, the bank has focused its efforts on financing integrated rural development programmes, including the provision of social services in the field. One of the bank's continuing major concerns has been to help provide better living conditions for the people of Latin America through the financing of projects in environmental and public health and urban development. Consistent with Latin America's growing demand for energy to meet its development requirements, the bank sharply increased its lending to that sector in its second decade of operations. In 1961–69, support for the energy sector represented about 14 per cent of the bank's total lending; during 1970–79, it rose to 25 per cent. The bank also supported the manufacturing sector through loans which finance individual industrial projects, as well as through loans channelled to small- and medium-sized borrowers through the region's development banking institutions. Moreover, the use of Latin American financing institutions as intermediaries has enabled the bank to reach thousands of small industrial enterprises and farmers. About one-third of the loans made by the bank in agriculture, industry and mining have been channelled through such institutions.

Since 1971, the bank has followed a policy of giving preferential treatment in its lending to its least developed member countries and to those with a limited market. For example, in 1979 the bank extended $839m in loans to the two groups of countries – ten classified as least developed and seven classified as having limited markets. Of that amount, $678m went to the least developed group and $161m to the limited market countries. The comparable figures in 1978 were $657m for the least developed and $135m for the limited market countries. The bank also concentrated its concessional lending in freely convertible currencies in the least developed group. Some 76 per cent of the freely convertible currencies extended from the Fund for Special Operations went to that group. When countries with limited markets are added to the group, that figure rises to 90 per cent.[7] During 1980 the bank continued its policy of providing preference in the use of its concessional resources to its least developed member countries. Under its goals for the Fifth Replenishment, it planned to lend at least an average of $351m each year in 1979 and 1980, in convertible currencies, to the least developed countries of the region from the Fund for Special Operations. That amount represented 75 per cent of total convertible currency lending from those resources for those two years. This goal was exceeded. The bank lent $366m in 1979 and $432m in 1980 to that group of countries. Nevertheless, they also had to resort to the bank's conventional resources to meet their external financing needs, because of the limitations on the availability of concessional resources.[8] Table 22.4 shows the bank's cumulative lending by country.

TABLE 22.4 IDB's Cumulative Lending by Country 1961–80[a]
(Net of cancellations and exchange Adjustments, US $m)

Country	Total Amount	Ordinary capital	Inter-regional capital	Fund for Special Operations	Funds in administration
Argentina	2,106.3	1,142.1	549.5	359.9	54.8
Bahamas	5.4	—	3.3	—	2.1
Barbados	55.5	20.6	—	32.9	2.0
Bolivia	653.6	71.9	46.7	465.0	70.0
Brazil	3,594.8	1,693.0	861.1	900.0	140.7
Chile	581.4	291.7	41.4	204.3	44.0
Colombia	1,446.6	467.6	312.8	601.2	65.0
Costa Rica	559.9	93.1	132.1	286.4	48.3
Dominican Republic	581.3	31.6	22.3	461.0	66.4
Ecuador	832.9	122.3	164.6	453.6	92.4
El Salvador	416.8	39.0	—	303.1	74.7
Guatemala	473.8	51.1	—	353.4	69.3
Guyana	97.9	12.7	—	79.2	6.0
Haiti	165.1	—	—	164.1	1.0
Honduras	492.4	0.5	18.0	418.8	55.1
Jamaica	183.7	15.7	8.0	138.9	21.1
Mexico	2,395.0	1,218.8	655.1	486.1	35.0
Nicaragua	396.9	23.6	—	311.7	61.6
Panama	428.7	101.5	67.9	216.4	42.9
Paraguay	334.2	26.5	42.8	251.1	13.8
Peru	776.3	265.7	83.9	341.6	85.1
Trinidad and Tobago	19.2	0.4	—	18.8	—
Uruguay	294.3	138.0	65.1	58.3	32.9
Venezuela	319.8	145.5	—	101.4	72.9
Regional	628.2	407.7	17.7	180.0	22.8
TOTAL	17,840.0	6,380.6	3,092.3	7,187.2	1,179.9

[a] Adjusted for exchange rate fluctuations which in 1980 consisted of net decreases of $103.7 million in the ordinary capital and $24.3 million in the inter-regional capital and net increases of $0.2 million in funds in administration.
Source: Inter-American Development Bank, *Annual Report*, 1980.

By the end of 1980, IDB had approved loans which brought the annual lending total to more than $2bn, raising its cumulative loan total to nearly $18bn. These loans were for projects whose total costs were more than $61bn. The bank collaborated in financing these projects with such international agencies as the European Economic Community, the OPEC Fund for International Development and the International Fund for Agricultural Development. It has also carried out parallel financing operations with such public sources of external financing as the Venezuelan Investment Fund and the Saudi Fund for Development. The development of the two decades of the bank's operations, 1961–80, shows that its annual authorised loans reached $2309m in 1980 compared with $1375m in 1975, $645m in 1970, $374m in 1965, and $294m in 1961. Annual loans from the Fund for Special Operations reached $824m in 1980 (36 per cent of total annual loans), compared with $634m in 1975 (46 per cent), $443m in 1970 (69 per cent), $197m in 1965 (53 per cent), and $48m in 1961 (16 per cent). Table 22.5 shows the development of the bank's annual loans from their origins, and reveals that annual loans extended by the bank from ordinary capital were higher (during 1961–64) than loans extended from the Fund for Special Operations. Since 1965 and until 1971, the situation was reversed, from 1972 and until 1975, loans from ordinary capital were higher again than those from the Fund for Special Operations, and since 1976 loans from ordinary capital have been lower than those from the Fund for Special Operations, with one exception, in 1979. The major trend of the two main components of the bank's loans has, therefore, not been consistent or budgeted according to previous plans. The bank's future strategy for financing may reveal the reasons behind these trends.

The IDB does not participate in loans or equity investments made by others, but has, however, sold participations in early maturities of its own fixed rate long-term loans and, more recently, sold all maturities in specific medium-term loans approved under commercial terms, including floating interest rates, under its Complementary Financing Programme. This programme is a mechanism designed to increase the flow of private capital for Latin American development. The external financing necessary to maintain a sustained growth of the Latin American economies, at the rates achieved in the last two decades, has far exceeded the resources available from international development institutions and other public sources of funds. The bank's resources, however, are still far from sufficient to meet the financial requirements of the development programmes submitted by the borrowing member countries. In response to these needs the bank introduced, in mid-1975, a

TABLE 22.5 Development of the Bank's Authorised Annual Loans by Origin 1961–80
(US $m)

Year	Ordinary capital	Inter-regional capital	Fund for Special Operations	Other funds	Total
1961	130	—	48	116	294
1962	83	—	41	205	329
1963	179	—	33	47	259
1964	164	—	49	86	299
1965	122	—	197	55	374
1966	101	—	291	4	396
1967	171	—	313	12	496
1968	194	—	210	27	431
1969	209	—	413	10	632
1970	195	—	443	7	645
1971	236	—	400	16	652
1972	443	—	344	20	807
1973	453	—	427	4	884
1974	636	—	475	—	1111
1975	646	—	634	95	1375
1976	536	236	662	94	1528
1977	385	749	577	125	1809
1978	339	767	683	81	1870
1979	648	601	620	182	2051
1980	519	905	824	61	2309

Source: Inter-American Development Bank, *Annual Reports*, 1979, 1980.

new financial programme designed to complement its lending ability, beyond the resources available through its various loan windows, by fostering greater and closer co-operation with private sources of funds for the financing of development projects. The new mechanism, known as complementary financing, consists of structuring the bank's financing for specific projects to include loans extended on terms and conditions suitable for funding, under a participation agreement, by the various segments of the international capital markets, such as commercial banks operating in the Euro-currency market or banks and institutional investors in a particular market. The formula closely resembles loan participation, sold without recourse, except that the terms and conditions of the complementary loan are pre-negotiated with the potential lenders. Under the participation arrangement the bank is responsible for disbursing and collecting loans. A large number of banks from Canada,

Europe, Japan and the United States have participated in the operations of the programme, and a much larger number of banks have presented bids for participation in it. Although, for practical reasons, the bank must limit the number of banks invited in each case to bid on the underwriting of a complementary loan, once an offer is selected, the underwriters are usually encouraged by both the bank and the borrower to syndicate the complementary loans in order to allow for as wide a participation as possible. In addition, the bank has pursued a practice of inviting bids from different financial institutions from the major international centres for each project. This practice is limited only by the number of institutions known to the bank to be interested in such operations and that number has been growing rapidly. As of 30 June 1979, the bank had completed eleven complementary financing operations, worth a total of $293m, which were extended in conjunction with loans funded with its own resources to the amount of $763m. The bank's loans contributed to the financing of projects which had a total cost estimated at $3208m, while the borrower's own contribution and other sources of financing provided the remaining funds required to undertake these investments.[9] Table 22.6 shows the bank's complementary financing operations.

Terms and Conditions

The bank sets the following terms and conditions:

	OC/IC	FSO
Interest rate	8.25%[10]	1.00–4.00%
Repayment period	25 years[11]	15–40 years
Grace period	—	5–10 years
Guarantee	Government	Government
Insurance	None	None

Moreover, according to the Agreement establishing the bank, there is a special commission on all loans, participations or guarantees, or guarantees made out of or by commitment of the ordinary capital resources of the bank. The special commission is payable periodically and computed on the amount outstanding on each loan, participation or guarantee at a rate of 1 per cent per annum, unless the bank, by a two-thirds majority of the total voting power of the member countries, decides to reduce the rate of commission. The amount of commission

TABLE 22.6 IDB Complementary Financing Operations as of 30 June 1979 (US$m)

Project	Total loan	Bank funds	Complimentary financing	Total cost
1976				
CHIXOY – Guatemala (hydroelectric)	105	90	15	340
ACINDAR – Argentina (private steel mill)	70	55	15	179
1977				
ALTO PARANA – Argentina (private pulp & paper Co.)	83	51	32	349.5
LA FORTUNA – Panama (hydroelectric)	98	70	28	259.9
SAN LORENZO – El Salvador (hydroelectric)	90.4	75.4	15	200.3
BAHIA BLANCA – Argentina (petrochemical industry)	105	65	40	338
1978				
ENDE – Bolivia (hydroelectric)	52	37	15	74.5
PAUTE – Ecuador (hydroelectric)	125	75	50	573
JAGUAS – Columbia (hydroelectric)	99.5	69.5	30	177.2
CEMIG – Brazil (hydroelectric)	88.3	68.3	20	194.3
EL CAJON – Honduras (hydroelectric)	95	77	18	462.1
1979				
CFN – Ecuador (global ind. credit programme)	45	30	15	60.0
Total	1,056.2	763.2	293	3,207.8

Source: Inter-American Development Bank, *The Complementary Financing Program of the Inter-American Development Bank*, Finance Department, 1979.

received by the bank is set aside as a special reserve for meeting its liabilities. Loans made from the Fund for Special Operations may be partially or wholly repayable in the currency of the member in whose territory the project is being financed, with the part of the loan not repayable in the currency of the member being paid in the currency or currencies in which the loan was made. The currency of any member held by the bank in its ordinary capital resources, inter-regional capital resources, or in the resources of the Fund for Special Operations may be used by the bank and by any recipient from the bank without restriction by the member country. A valuation of any currency in terms of another currency, or in terms of gold, is determined by the bank after consultation with the International Monetary Fund.[12] Complementary loans are made for maturities based on prevailing conditions in the credit markets, which in the operations made in 1979 ranged from 10–10½ year maturities, with adjustable interest rates determined by a fixed spread over a reference rate such as the London Inter-Bank Offered Rate (LIBOR).[13]

Organisational Structure of the Bank

As in the case of the African Development Bank and the Asian Development Bank, the organisational structure of the IDB is formed by the Board of Governors, Board of Executive Directors, President, Vice-President, managers of departments, and the staff. They include: Board of Governors (1 governor, 1 deputy appointed by each member country), Board of Executive Directors (12, with 12 alternates); President (elected by the Board of Governors for a five-year term); Executive Vice-President; managers of departments (8), Controller (1), advisers.

Similar to AfDB and AsDB, all the powers of IDB are vested in the Board of Governors. Each member appoints one governor and one deputy, who serve for five years, subject to termination of appointment at any time, or to reappointment. The Board selects one of the governors as Chairman, who holds office until the next regular meeting of the Board. The Board of Governors may delegate to the Board of Executive Directors all its powers except the power to:[14]

(i) admit new members and determine the conditions of their admission;
(ii) increase or decrease the authorised ordinary capital stock and inter-regional capital stock of the bank and the contributions to the fund;
(iii) elect the President of the bank and determine his remuneration;
(iv) suspend a member;
(v) determine the remuneration of the executive directors and their alternates;
(vi) hear and decide any appeals from interpretations of the Agreement given by the Board of Executive Directors;

(vii) authorise and conclude general agreements for co-operation with other international organisations;
(viii) approve, after reviewing the auditors report's, the general balance sheets and the statements of profit and loss of the institution;
(ix) determine the reserves and the distribution of the net profits of the ordinary capital resources and of the inter-regional capital resources and of the Fund;
(x) select outside auditors to certify to the general balance sheets and the statements of profit and loss of the institution;
(xi) amend the agreement; and
(xii) decide to terminate the operations of the bank and to distribute its assets.

The Board of Executive Directors is responsible for the conduct of the operations of the bank, and for this purpose may exercise all the powers delegated to it by the Board of Governors. The governors of the regional developing member countries elect eight executive directors while the governors for the non-regional countries elect two executive directors in accordance with specific provisions.[15] The Board of Executive Directors makes all major decisions affecting the authorisation of bank expenditures, including those for lending and technical co-operation programmes. For example, the Board approves the detailed budget of the bank's administrative expenses, its organisation, the size and compensation of staff, the basic operational policies, the lending and technical co-operation programme levels, the borrowing of money and basic loan conditions as well as each individual loan and technical co-operation authorisation.[16] Each member country has 135 votes plus one vote for each share of ordinary capital stock and for each share of inter-regional capital stock of the bank held by that country. On the Board of Governors, each governor is entitled to cast the votes of the member country which he represents. Except as otherwise specifically provided in the Agreement, all matters before the Board of Governors are decided by a majority of the total voting power of the member countries, and likewise with the Board of Executive Directors.

The bank was created with an original membership of twenty countries: The United States and nineteen Latin American countries. Six other western hemisphere nations subsequently joined, bringing the regional membership to twenty-six countries, including Canada and the new nations of the Caribbean. In July 1976, a change in the charter of the bank brought about a far-reaching transformation in its structure by allowing industrialised nations from outside the western hemisphere to join the bank, and as a result, membership had increased to forty-three countries by the end of 1980. Table 22.7 shows regional and non-regional members of the bank and their voting power.

TABLE 22.7 Regional and Non-regional Members of IDB and their Voting Power, 31 December 1980

Members	Number of votes	Percentage of total number of votes[a]
Regional developing members		
Argentina	149,873	11.88
Bahamas	2,364	0.19
Barbados	1,926	0.15
Bolivia	12,155	0.96
Brazil	149,873	11.88
Chile	41,251	3.27
Colombia	41,218	3.27
Costa Rica	6,143	0.49
Dominican Republic	8,157	0.65
Ecuador	8,157	0.65
El Salvador	6,143	0.49
Guatemala	8,157	0.65
Guyana	2,364	0.19
Haiti	6,143	0.49
Honduras	6,143	0.49
Jamaica	8,157	0.65
Mexico	96,390	7.64
Nicaragua	6,143	0.49
Panama	6,143	0.49
Paraguay	6,143	0.49
Peru	20,201	1.60
Suriname	1,379	0.11
Trinidad and Tobago	6,143	0.49
Uruguay	16,190	1.28
Venezuela	80,360	6.37
Total regional developing members	697,316	55.29
United States	435,746	34.55
Canada	57,539	4.56
Non-regional members		
Austria	810	0.06
Belgium	2,101	0.17

(*continued overleaf*)

TABLE 22.7 (*Contd.*)

Members	Number of votes	Percentage of total number of votes[a]
Denmark	1,039	0.08
Finland	810	0.06
France	8,363	0.66
Germany	10,713	0.85
Israel	802	0.06
Italy	8,363	0.66
Japan	11,657	0.92
Netherlands	911	0.07
Portugal	238	0.02
Spain	9,827	0.78
Sweden	1,237	0.10
Switzerland	2,441	0.19
United Kingdom	10,464	0.83
Yugoslavia	810	0.06
Total non-regional members	70,586	5.60
Grand total	1,261,187	100.00

[a] Data are rounded to the nearest one-hundredth of 1 per cent; detail may not add to subtotals and grand total because of rounding.
Source: Inter-American Development Bank, Annual Report, 1980.

Approaches and Techniques Applied

The usual approach taken is that borrowing member countries' external financing requirements and potential projects for the bank's financing are discussed during annual country programming missions dispatched by the bank. Project-financing proposals are also submitted through the IDB's representatives in each of the borrowing member countries, or directly to its headquarters in Washington. The bank's Project Analysis Department has published a series of Guidelines for the Preparation of Loan Applications, in different sectors,[17] which were prepared for the purpose of providing guidance to interested institutions of the bank's member countries concerning information to be furnished in loan applications. The contents are adjusted and adapted according to the specific characteristics of each project. These guidelines indicate how the data should be furnished in the loan application, and offer a general guide to information required by the bank for multidisciplinary analysis of projects. After approval and assignment of priority by competent authorities of the central government concerned, the loan applications, together with the information requested in the guidelines, are sent to the President of the bank through the field office in the member country. After receiving the application, the bank may request further information deemed pertinent for analysis and evaluation, while the field office in the country concerned may be contacted to provide additional clarifications about contents of the document, or presentation and processing of loan applications. In general the stages or phases which make up investment projects are as follows:

   (i) project identification;
   (ii) pre-feasibility study;
   (iii) feasibility study;
   (iv) preparation and organisation of project execution;
   (v) execution;
   (vi) initiation and operation;
   (vii) impact evaluation.

The bank carries out its own project appraisal based on standard criteria for technical, financial, socio-economic, legal and institutional evaluation. For this task, an interdisciplinary team travels to the field, to gather all pertinent infomation, and then a project appraisal report is drafted. This document passes through middle management and higher management committee reviews, and after all issues have been resolved a loan proposal and the project appraisal report are sent to the Board of Directors for review and approvals. Project appraisal, in more detail, uses the following techniques.

Technical Evaluation

An analysis and evaluation of the project is made, reviewing the appropriateness of the technology being used, the optimal design of the project as well as its implementation schedule. The cost of equipment and services is reviewed in order to ascertain the cost of the project at the time of analysis.

Financial Evaluation

Involves the use of standard practices aimed at determining the financial rate of return of the project, the financial viability of the executing agencies and the financial projections of the institution, as well as the availability of local counterpart funds required.

Economic Evaluation

Entails the use of standard cost-benefit analysis techniques centred on the calculation of an economic rate of return. 'State of the art' appraisal follows the methods of Little and Mirrlees and Squire and Van der Talk. Special analysis is made to determine the distribution of project benefits to the low-income segments of the population during the entire economic life of the project.

Legal Evaluation

Means review and establishment of the required legal ordinances to assure project execution and project life. Contractual arrangements are made, and negotiations on these matters are carried out with the borrower.

As for loan portfolio analysis, the bank has prepared a methodology,[18] based upon its own experience and the exchange of ideas with the borrowing institutions, which provides the techniques that are necessary for the overall analysis of a loan portfolio. The objectives of this methodology are:

(1) To make available to the management levels of the Development Finance Institutions (DFI) the necessary criteria for making decisions and implementing preventive and/or corrective measures to improve the administration, control and application of policies that are sound for the institution.
(2) To judge the status of the portfolio and the degree of efficiency with which a loan portfolio is being administered.
(3) To provide the necessary criteria for evaluation of the financial situation and lending policy that the DFI has been applying.

This methodology is comprehensive, providing information on accounts in arrears and also considering other aspects relevant to the problem such as sectors financed, use of the loan, geographic location of the borrower, etc.

Strategy for Financing and Technical Assistance

IDB staff indicated, in replying to the questionnaire sheet, that the operational policies of the bank are currently guided by the targets set by the Fifth Replenishment agreement, which calls for a total investment in Latin America in the period 1979-82 of US $8170m. Furthermore, of this total volume, 50 per cent should be allocated to projects that directly benefit low-income individuals. In regard to the sectoral composition, the agreement also allocates the funds as follows:

(i) 30-35 per cent of the resources towards rural development schemes;
(ii) 10-15 per cent to urban development projects, including in this concept support for small urban industries;
(iii) 25 per cent to finance energy projects;
(iv) 20-25 per cent to finance the external sector, mainly for projects that directly increase, or substitute imports; and
(v) finally, the 10 per cent that remains is devoted to projects in sectors that, while representing a lower priority from a regional point of view, are still essential for eliminating existing bottlenecks in certain countries (transportation, communications, pre-investment).

The bank grants to its members project-related and non-project-related technical assistance in the neighbourhood of US $45m per year. Non-project-related technical assistance is given to strengthen and develop public institutions, especially in the areas of economic planning, public finance and public administration, while project-related technical co-operation is mainly used to develop investment opportunities in the country. This includes activities within the project cycle such as sector studies, project identification, pre-feasibility, feasibility and engineering design. Technical assistance for all the member countries is granted according to financial conditions which depend on the relative development of the country, and on the nature of the assistance. Assistance extended for the purpose of project preparation in productive activities is generally approved on a contingent repayment basis. Assistance for studies that become loans is generally repaid as part of the loan for the project while assistance for studies that indicate non-feasible projects becomes a technical assistance grant. The Fifth Replenishment of the bank's resources has a broad significance not only for the bank but also for its developing member countries since it will enable the bank to continue to offer an increasing level of public external financing to its member countries, including concessional resources to those most in need of them. In approving the increase, the bank's Board of Governors provided guidelines which govern the bank's strategy at the start of the 1980s. It will:

(1) Continue and intensify its efforts to ensure that its lending contributes to the improvement of the economic and social well-being of the low-income sectors of its member countries and to the acceleration of the progress of the relatively less advanced countries of the region.
(2) Co-operate with its member countries in implementing strategies to achieve an integrated development of their natural resources, including energy resources.
(3) Join in the efforts being made by Latin American countries to improve the efficiency of their productive systems, making them more competitive in international markets and increasing their exports both within the region and to the rest of the world.

At the twenty-first Annual Meeting of IDB in Rio de Janeiro 14–16 April 1980, the President, Mr Antoni Ortiz Mena, said that the bank must diversify its operating techniques during the 1980s while adhering to the multilateral philosophy upon which it was founded. While continuing to finance its traditional activities, it must expand its function of recycling international liquidity, finance Latin American enterprises and projects with a high social content and, through increased technical co-operation, both promote the preparation of projects and determine the most suitable modes of financing them.[19] In his address to the National Press Club on 26 February in Washington, the President also described the 1980s as 'a decade of trial' for Latin America. He said that the coming decade 'will test many of our basic concepts . . . and our resolve to meet head-on the consequences of the profound changes which are taking place in our world'.[20]

Problems of Implementation and Remarks from Field Experience

The staff of the bank indicated in the questionnaire sheet that project implementation and follow-up is monitored by the appropriate sectoral specialists and the bank's representatives in the borrowing countries, and by the Operations Department at headquarters. Problems that may arise during implementation are normally resolved with the bank's representative or the Operations Department except when it is necessary for other departments, the Controller, the top management and, ultimately, the Board of Executive Directors to become involved. *Ex-post* review, appraisals and evaluations are conducted by independent auditors, the bank's Controller and the office of External Review and Evaluation which reports directly to the Board of Executive Directors. In addition, borrowers are required to perform economic *ex-post* evaluation.

IDB has realised that, in providing development loans, it cannot substitute its management or its technical capabilities for those of borrowers, and has instead designed systems to obtain the same degree of assurance regarding each project as if the bank were managing or carrying out the work itself. Thus, it has developed an integrated loan control programme consisting of: separation of functions; pre-lending analysis; contractual requirements; on-site inspection and surveillance; approval of selection of contractors, consultants and suppliers; approval of disbursements and requirements for supporting documentation, together with various types of audits and evaluations. Audit reports supply information that the bank needs, such as:

(1) The financial situation of borrowers and/or executing agencies and the projects; the borrower's capacity to handle debt servicing.
(2) Use of loan resources and local contributions.
(3) Availability of local contributions; financial capacity of the institutions involved to continue punctual payment of local contributions.
(4) Evidence of compliance with clauses of an accounting and financial nature set forth in the loan contract.
(5) Measures recommended by the auditors to correct any shortcomings found in the administrative and accounting controls of institutions and of projects.

As a rule, the bank requires that the borrower evaluate the results and impact of the project partially financed by it. Through participating in a process of measuring project results, the borrowers obtain direct feedback which can contribute to future project selection, preparation and analysis in the same sectors, whether or not the future projects are financed by the bank. The process also assists the borrowing country to develop its own evaluation tools and capabilities through the process of 'learning by doing'. The data and information are also useful to the bank for its own in-depth, analytical *ex-post* project evaluations.[21]

The staff also indicated that the bank utilises its field experience to study the absorptive capacity, the external debt structure and investment priorities of the developing countries on a continuing basis. Partial results of these studies are published annually in 'Economic and Social Progress in Latin America',[22] and are reflected in the bank's lending and technical co-operation programmes. The bank also attempts to assist the borrowing countries in the solutions to their economic development, financial and institutional funding requirements through periodic consultations, provision of technical co-operation, assistance for institution strengthening and, ultimately, through its lending operations directed to high-priority development projects and aimed at the resolution of bottlenecks to economic and social progress.

Based on the above presentation of the experience of the Inter-American Development Bank, it is interesting to note that the bank has followed a concrete pattern of lending policy. Its strategy for financing and its future prospects regarding extending more aid to its least developed member countries is however, questionable. The bank has recently followed approaches and techniques which are more than satisfactory for project appraisal and implementation, while efforts have been made to increase its capital substantially. However, experience of meeting the 'basic needs' by adopting a strategy of lending for this growing demand in the least developed countries among its members is still lacking and more effort has to be made in this direction. Its social programme of lending is another aspect to which the bank has to give more attention in the near future. Moreover, the bank should extend its operations to cover more programme and sector loans as well as project loans, emphasising more on 'soft' loans for its least developed member countries. The bank appears securely established as a strong major development agency operating in Latin America, and in the course of its two decades of operations it has developed its own particular style in response to the particular environment of the continent that it serves. However, for the future it should develop a character markedly different from that of its first two decades in order to cope with the new environment and changes that have taken place in recent years. It will, of course, be argued that whatever sacrifice is entailed by the policy, changes required by the programme aid will have more impact on economic and social development in its member countries than in the case of project and package aid. Finally, it is important to note that as the establishment of the bank has coincided with the period of greatest activity in the formation of groups of countries in process of integration, it should be more active as a forum in which significant aspects of its activities are developed, so that it can participate more effectively in the process of Latin American economic integration.

23 The International Bank for Reconstruction and Development

Establishment and Financial Resources

The delegates who assembled at Bretton Woods in July 1944 encountered great difficulty in finding a name for their institution. The representatives of the United Kingdom thought it should be called 'the International Corporation for Reconstruction and Development' or be given some other title omitting the word 'Bank'. El Salvador proposed 'the International Financial Institution for Reconstruction and Development'. And as Lord Keynes remarked, 'the Bank should be called the Fund and the Fund the Bank'. Not only its name but even its coming into being were in doubt until almost the last minute. In his letter to forty-four governments inviting them to send representatives to a Conference at Bretton Woods, the US Secretary of State described this as being 'for the purpose of formulating definite proposals for an International Monetary Fund, and possibly a Bank for Reconstruction and Development'. Almost all the preliminary work on the proposed bank had been done within the US Government, and until the meeting in Atlantic City of the Committee that was to shape the agenda for Bretton Woods, the participation of other countries had been perfunctory. The draft presented to the delegates at Bretton Woods was, in its general outline, very similar to the Articles of Agreement that emerged from the Conference. The substance of each article, however, was presented in different versions – the US version, the UK version, new material, and material taken from the draft of the Monetary Fund proposal. Delegates were asked to submit new suggestions and proposals. The first week's discussion at Bretton Woods was devoted entirely to the fund. The delegates from many of the less developed countries, however, were much more interested in the bank than in the fund, and so were a number of European countries whose economies had been damaged by the war. As a result, a group was designated to work on the bank, and four committees and a number of subcommittees organised under Commission II were useful in collecting additional proposals. But the actual redrafting of what became the Articles of Agreement was undertaken by a smaller group. The agreements negotiated at Bretton Woods did not bind governments, and there remained the task of ratification by potential members having the requisite number of votes. Most of the governments represented at Bretton Woods waited for the United States to act. In January 1945, President Roosevelt sent to Congress the Articles of Agreement of the bank and the fund, with a request for their approval. In the debate in Congress which produced the Bretton Woods Agreement Act, signed by President Truman on 31 July 1945, the opposition focused on the fund and there was very little discussion of the bank, which had become almost non-controversial.[1]

The main purposes of the IBRD, according to its Articles of Agreement,[2] are:

(1) To assist in the reconstruction and development of territories of members by facilitating the investment of capital for productive purposes, . . . and the encouragement of the development of productive facilities and resources in less developed countries.
(2) To promote private foreign investment by means of guarantees or participations in loans and other investments made by private investors, . . .
(3) To promote the long-range balanced growth of international trade and the maintenance of equilibrium in balances of payments by encouraging international investment for the development of productive resources of members, . . .
(4) To arrange the loans made or guaranteed by it in relation to international loans through other channels so that the more useful and urgent projects, large and small alike, will be dealt with first.
(5) To conduct its operations with due regard to the effect of international investment on business conditions in the territories of members and, in the immediate post-war years, to assist in bringing about a smooth transition from a wartime to a peacetime economy.

The original members of the bank were those members of the fund which accepted membership in the bank before 31 December 1945. The bank began its operations on 25 June 1946 with an authorised capital of

$10bn in terms of US $ of the weight and fineness of gold in effect on 1 July 1944. The capital stock was divided into 100,000 shares with a par value of $100,000 each, which was available for subscription only by members. However (according to Article II), the capital stock may be increased when the bank deems it advisable by a three-fourths majority of the total voting power. Each member subscribed for shares of the capital stock of the bank with the minimum number subscribed by the original members set forth as shown in Table 23.1.

TABLE 23.1 IBRD Original Subscriptions

	(Millions of dollars)		(Millions of dollars)
Australia	200	India	400
Belgium	225	Iran	24
Bolivia	7	Iraq	6
Brazil	105	Liberia	0.5
Canada	325	Luxembourg	10
Chile	35	Mexico	65
China	600	Netherlands	275
Colombia	35	New Zealand	50
Costa Rica	2	Nicaragua	0.8
Cuba	35	Norway	50
Czechoslovakia	125	Panama	0.2
Denmark[a]	—	Paraguay	0.8
Dominican Republic	2	Peru	17.5
Ecuador	3.2	Philippine Commonwealth	15
Egypt	40	Poland	125
El Salvador	1	Union of South Africa	100
Ethiopia	3	Union of Soviet Socialist Republics	1200
France	450	United Kingdom	1300
Greece	25	United States	3175
Guatemala	2	Uruguay	10.5
Haiti	2	Venezuela	10.5
Honduras	1	Yugoslavia	40
Iceland	1	Total	9100

[a] The quota of Denmark shall be determined by the Bank after Denmark accepts membership in accordance with these Articles of Agreement.
Source: *Articles of Agreement* of the International Bank for Reconstruction and Development.

The bank's staff indicated (in replies to the author's questionnaire) that its capital has reached $37.4bn, and also that in January 1980, the bank's Board of Governors approved an increase of the equivalent of $40bn in the authorised capital stock. As of 30 June 1980, the number of shares subscribed by member countries had reached 301,718 compared with 289,902 on 30 June 1979, subscription to capital stock had reached SDR 30,171,800 compared with SDR 28,990,200 and the number of votes was 335,468 compared with 323,402. Total membership of the bank in June 1980 reached 135 countries.[3] In addition to its capital, borrowing through international sale of bonds and notes, net income, sales of loans and repayments on loans are considered as subsidiary financial resources. Table 23.2 shows the development of the bank's subscribed capital and subsidiary resources.

Scope of Activities

The Scope of Operations in the 1950s

The bank's annual lending commitments during the 1950s increased about four times, reaching $703m in 1959 compared with $166m in 1950. The first two years of the bank's operations were dominated by the four reconstruction loans to Europe. Then after a temporary decline in its total commitments, the bank loaned at an annual rate of $300m to $400m until the fiscal year 1958. The geographical distribution of IBRD loans was determined by the ability of member countries to borrow on their own credit in the capital markets of the world, by their access to other sources of funds, by considerations of creditworthiness, by the rate at which feasible projects are brought to the attention of the bank, and by the bank's judgement of the economic performance of member countries. Table 23.3 shows the bank's commitments during the 1950s.

The Scope of Operations in the 1960s[4]

During this decade, the IBRD provided loans only at the normal rates prevailing on the capital market. Repayment periods were adjusted in accordance with the category of the industrial projects financed. In 1970, the total number of loans offered by the bank reached 70 with a total amount of $1580.4m compared with 29 with a total amount of $665.1m in 1962. The bank offered loans to member countries for high-priority development purposes to promote economic growth, international trade and investment and improvement of standards of living. Its range of activities was wide, covering infrastructure, industry, agriculture, education, etc. For example, in 1969 total bank assistance amounted to $1362.8m (compared with $838.4m in 1968) of which $186.8m was for the agricultural sector, $234.5m for industry, $516.3m for transpor-

TABLE 23.2 IBRD's Subscribed Capital, New Borrowing and Net Income 1971–80 (US $m)

Year:	1971	1972	1973	1974	1975	1976	1977	1978	1979	1980
Subscribed capital	23,871	26,607	30,397	30,431	30,821	30,861	30,869	33,045	37,429	39,959
Borrowings: net	819	1,136	955	990	2,483	2,530	3,258	2,171	3,235	2,382
Net income	212	183	186	216	275	220	209	238	407	588

Source: World Bank, *Annual Report*, 1980.

TABLE 23.3 IBRD Gross Commitments in US $m (1950–60)

Fiscal year	Number of loans	Amount of loans
1950	12	166.3
1951	21	297.1
1952	19	298.6
1953	10	178.6
1954	26	323.7
1955	20	409.6
1956	26	396.0
1957	20	387.9
1958	34	710.8
1959	30	703.1
1960	31	658.7

Source: Edward S. Mason and Robert E. Asher, *The World Bank Since Bretton Woods* (The Brookings Institution, Washington DC, 1973).

tation, and $502.1m for electric power. 1969 was a year of considerable expansion for the bank (as well as for the IDA and the IFC). New commitments made by the bank (and its affiliates) to member countries rose to a level substantially higher than in any previous year in the World Bank Group's history. The bank's borrowing in FY1970 amounted to $735m compared with $271m in 1962, and with the 1969 fiscal year's record level of $1224m. The principal supplier of the new borrowed funds in 1970 was the Bank of Japan, the World Bank's first yen borrowings. A review of the bank's activities by sector during 1964–70 indicates that transportation, electric power and industry, as a single group, comprised its main activities, reaching an average of 81.6 per cent of total bank loans for all purposes. Bank loans to the agricultural sector reached an average of about 12 per cent, with a rapid expansion in the last three years of the period. Loans for other purposes, such as telecommunications, project preparation, water supply, family planning and general development, represented only a minor proportion of the total with the telecommunications sector the main recipient in this group. A review of the geographical distribution of the loans offered by the bank during 1962–70 shows that Latin American countries were the main recipients, comprising an average of 43 per cent of total assistance by the bank. The Near East and South Asia took second place with an average of 19 per cent followed by East Asia, Africa and Europe, which reached an average of 15 per cent, 14 per cent and 9 per cent respectively during the same period. The development of the bank's activities during 1962–70 did not indicate a clear major trend in any of these regions. Table 23.4 shows the geographical distribution of assistance from IBRD during this period.

The bank had practically ceased to lend to developed countries by 1968, and its last loan to Japan was in 1966. In general, the developed countries were considered to be capable of borrowing in the capital markets on their own credit. However, there were a number of countries which, although they were able to borrow on their own credit in the capital markets, were considered unable to borrow in sufficient volume to meet their needs. Thus, IBRD has continued to lend (since 1967) in small volume to such countries as Iceland, Ireland, Finland and New Zealand, which were judged to be in this position.[5]

The Scope of Operations in the 1970s

The bank entered the 1970s with a reputation for considerable competence, earned during its first quarter-century of operations since 1946. The 1970s were marked by a series of economic shocks: a notable slowdown in the growth of the developed countries, coupled with high rates of inflation, a rise in the price of crude oil, increases in the costs of imported capital goods and food, a massive build-up of liquidity in the international capital markets, and unusually large fluctuations in commodity prices. During the 1970s, therefore, the bank adjusted its lending operations and its role in providing technical assistance to meet the evolving needs of its developing member countries. Bank funds and technical assistance in general were increasingly channelled to the poorer segments of society in the borrowing countries through changes in sectoral priorities. At the end of the 1960s, nearly 60 per cent of IBRD lending went to the development of infrastructure, but by the end of the 1970s, such lending had fallen to one-third of the total, with nearly half of bank lending directed to sectors such as agriculture and rural development, education, population and nutrition, urbanisation, and small-scale industries. Even infrastructure lending has changed, with, for example, emphasis on highway maintenance and construction of rural roads and with the beginning of lending for oil and gas exploration and production. Table 23.5 shows the distribution of the bank's lending by sector.

IBRD has shown a substantial increase in the amount of loans provided to member countries during the 1970s, reaching $7644m in 1980 compared with $6989m in 1979, $4320m in 1975 and $1921m in

TABLE 23.4 IBRD Geographical Distribution by Region (US $m) (1962–70)

Regions	US fiscal year: 1962	1963	1964	1965	1966	1967	1968	1969	1970
Near East and South Asia (Average 18.9%)	161.2 (24.2)	106.5 (26.8)	78.6 (13.9)	158.4 (22.0)	59.8 (8.5)	121.3 (19.9)	138.5 (16.5)	345.9 (26.0)	201.2 (12.7)
Latin America (Average 42.9%)	408.1 (61.3)	122.8 (30.9)	252.5 (44.8)	207.8 (28.9)	374.7 (53.5)	271.1 (44.5)	372.4 (44.4)	457.7 (33.5)	703.0 (44.4)
East Asia (Average 14.6%)	40.8 (6.1)	69.6 (17.5)	67.7 (12.0)	93.5 (13.0)	86.0 (12.2)	120.2 (19.7)	145.0 (17.2)	236.5 (17.3)	254.5 (16.1)
Africa (Average 14.3%)	54.9 (8.2)	32.7 (8.2)	91.2 (16.1)	123.0 (17.1)	139.1 (19.8)	86.2 (14.1)	65.1 (7.7)	267.6 (19.6)	281.7 (17.8)
Europe (Average 8.9%)	— (—)	65.0 (16.3)	73.2 (12.9)	135.0 (18.8)	40.0 (5.7)	10.0 (1.6)	110.5 (13.1)	46.0 (3.3)	135.5 (8.5)

(—) Percentage of total activities to developing countries.
Source: Hassan Selim, *External Sources of Financing Economic Development*, 'Case-studies on Selected Sources in East–West Developed Countries and International Organisations, UNIDO/IPPD, 60. December 1971.

TABLE 23.5 The Distribution of the Bank's Lending by Sector
US $m and Percentages, Fiscal Years 1978–81

Fiscal years Sectors	1978 (US $m)	%	1979 (US $m)	%	1980 (US $m)	%	1981 (US $m)	%
Agriculture and rural development	1929.0	32	1568.1	22	1700.4	22	2406.0	27
Development finance companies	782.5	13	559.0	8	743.0	10	1042.0	12
Education	268.9	4	245.5	4	360.1	5	374.6	4
Energy								
Gas, oil and coal	—	—	82.4	1	328.5	4	564.0	6
Power	900.0	15	872.5	13	1584.5	21	1282.5	15
Industry	360.0	6	721.0	10	393.5	5	475.8	5
Non-project	80.0	1	301.5	4	280.0	4	789.0	9
Population, health and nutrition	25.0	—	17.0	—	65.0	—	12.5	—
Small-scale enterprises	51.8	1	69.6	1	222.0	3	157.5	2
Technical assistance	11.0	—	—	—	—	—	49.5	1
Telecommunications	153.6	2	110.0	2	66.0	1	—	—
Tourism	50.0	1	66.7	1	—	—	—	—
Transportation	918.1	15	1430.9	21	1205.0	16	763.0	9
Urbanisation	222.4	4	297.5	4	249.8	3	459.0	5
Water supply and sewerage	345.4	6	647.3	9	446.4	6	433.5	5
Total	6097.7	100	6989.0	100	7644.2	100	8,808.9	100

Source: World Bank, *Annual Reports*, 1980, 1981.

1971. Loan disbursements were, however, much lower as compared with loan commitments with an average ratio (disbursements: commitments ratio), reaching 51 per cent in 1971–80. Table 23.6 shows the bank's loan commitments and disbursements.

A review of IBRD lending by region during 1971–80 shows that the bank in 1980 provided $150.5m for Eastern Africa, $439.2m for Western Africa, $2160.5m for East Asia and the Pacific area, $125.0m for South Asia, $2174.0m for Europe, the Middle East and North Africa, and $2595.0m for Latin America and the Caribbean. For all of these regions, lending for agriculture, rural development and energy received major and increasing attention. As in the 1960s, Latin America and the Caribbean received the largest amount of lending by IBRD. On the other hand, South Asia and East Africa received only small amounts, compensated for by a substantial amount of lending through IDA. Table 23.7 shows the bank's lending by region.

TABLE 23.6 IBRD Loan Commitments and Disburscments in US $m and in percentage ratios
Fiscal years 1971–81

Fiscal year	Loan commitments 1	Loan disbursements 2	Ratio 2−1 × 100 (%)
1971	1921	915	48
1972	1966	1182	60
1973	2051	1180	58
1974	3218	1533	48
1975	4320	1995	46
1976	4977	2470	50
1977	5759	2636	46
1978	6098	2787	46
1979	6989	3602	52
1980	7644	4363	57
1981	8809	5063	57

Source: Loan Commitments and Loan Disbursements, World Bank, *Annual Reports*, 1980, 1981.

TABLE 23.7 IBRD Lending by Region (FY1971–81)
(US $m)

Region	Annual Average 1971–75	1976	1977	1978	1979	1980	1981
Eastern Africa	176.8	216.0	311.7	162.4	266.0	150.5	304.0
Western Africa	167.4	291.8	259.1	303.4	317.1	439.2	554.8
East Asia and Pacific	475.1	1458.5	1452.0	1586.9	1791.6	2160.5	2227.9
South Asia	102.2	260.0	394.0	330.0	300.0	125.0	430.0
Europe, Middle East and North Africa	912.4	1341.9	1474.3	1660.5	2081.5	2174.0	2173.2
Latin America and the Caribbean	861.4	1408.9	1868.2	2054.5	2232.8	2595.0	3119.0

Source: World Bank, *Annual Reports*, 1980, 1981.

Technical assistance, an integral part of the bank's operations, grew in both volume and scope through the years of its operations, resulting in an increase in committed and disbursed funds. Technical assistance components included in loans and credits in all sectors reached $534m for 197 operations in 1980 compared with $359m and 181 operations in

1979. If supervision implementation engineering services are included as part of the technical assistance component, the allocation totalled $807m for fiscal year 1980. In 1975, the bank created a Project Preparation Facility (PPF) to help overcome weaknesses in borrowers' capacities to complete project preparation and to support the entities responsible for preparing or carrying out projects. The bank also acts as executive agency for a number of projects financed by UNDP. Growing demand for planning assistance has become a well-established trend for the bank. There is considerable variety among the specific objectives of planning projects, ranging from assistance for the rehabilitation of a country's economy to improvement of project management or development of planning capabilities in key ministries. Each project has, as its overall goal, help to the country concerned in becoming self-sufficient in trained manpower and in developing efficient planning mechanisms. Each project has therefore emphasised promotion of national expertise in planning and in implementation of plans. The bank also provides an array of technical assistance outside of conventional banking operations. Examples include short-term training, secondment of advisers, transfers of technology such as computer expertise, serving on evaluation and monitoring panels, and providing demographic, financial and economic advice for project preparation. Moreover, the bank has been able to contribute to its borrowers' needs for capital transfers beyond its own lending by securing co-financing for its projects, particularly in the later 1970s. The principal agencies active in co-financing IBRD projects were the Kuwait Fund for Arab Economic Development, the Arab Fund for Economic and Social Development, the Kreditanstalt für Wiederanfbau, and a number of commercial banks. Also the bank's role in convening consultative groups for different developing countries contributed to aid flows to these countries. The Economic Development Institute (EDI) was established in 1955 to provide mid-career training in economic management techniques and policies for senior officials of developing countries. Since then, the scope of EDI training has been expanded to cover problems and methods of identifying, preparing, appraising, executing and managing development projects. The institute has enlarged its training capability not only in English, but also in French and Spanish, and it has expanded its activities in developing countries, mostly in collaboration with other institutions.[6]

Terms and Conditions of Loans

The staff of the bank indicated in replies to the author's questionnaire the following terms:

Interest rate: During the calendar year 1979, the interest rate ranged from 7.0 to 7.95 per cent. A new policy took effect on 1 January 1980, when the rate was set at 8.25 per cent. At least once a year, and more often if necessary, a lending rate is suggested so as to achieve a spread of approximately 0.50 per cent above IBRD's cost of borrowing. This cost (weighted by amount and maturity) is estimated for a 12-month period, using the actual cost of borrowing during the preceding 6 months and the estimated cost of borrowing for the succeeding 6 months.

Repayment period: 15–20 years.

Grace period: 3–5 years.

Guarantee: A guarantee by the member government is required.

Management and Organisational Structure

The staff also indicated that all the bank's powers are vested in a Board of Governors, which delegates its powers for the conduct of the general operation of the bank to a Board of Executive Directors that performs its duties on a full-time basis at the bank's headquarters. The President of the Bank is the Chairman of the Board of Executive Directors.

As is indicated in the Articles of Agreement, the Board of Governors consists of one governor and one deputy governor appointed by each member country. Each governor and each deputy serves for five years and may be reappointed. The Board of Governors may delegate to the Executive Directors the authority to exercise any powers of the Board, except the power to:

(1) Admit new members and determine the conditions of their admission.
(2) Increase or decrease the capital stock.
(3) Suspend a member.
(4) Decide appeals from interpretations of the Articles of Agreement given by the Executive Directors.
(5) Make arrangements to co-operate with other international organisations (other than informal arrangements of a temporary and administrative character).
(6) Decide to suspend permanently the operations of the bank and to distribute its assets.
(7) Determine the distribution of the net income of the bank.

The Board of Governors holds an annual meeting and such other meetings as may be provided for by the Board or called by the executive directors. Meetings of the Board are called by the directors, whenever requested by five members or by members having one-quarter of the total voting power. A quorum for any meeting of the Board of Governors is determined by a majority of the governors, exercising not less than two-thirds of the total voting power. As for voting power, each member country has 250 votes plus one additional vote for each share of stock held. Except as otherwise specifically provided, all matters before the bank are decided by a majority of the votes cast.[7] As of the fiscal year 1980, there were twenty executive directors,[8] and as provided for in the Articles of Agreement, five are appointed by the five members having the largest number of shares, and the rest are elected by the other members. The executive directors fulfil dual responsibilities, representing their constituents' interests and concerns to the Board and management when determining policy or considering individual projects. They also represent the bank's interests and concerns to the country or countries that appointed or elected them. The executive directors, therefore, act as a two-way channel of communication between the bank and the member countries. Since the bank operates on the basis of a philosophy of consensus (formal votes are rare), this dual role is a demanding one, involving constant communication and consultations with governments and careful preparation to reflect their views in Board discussions. The executive directors select a President who is not a governor or an executive director or a deputy for either. The President has no vote except a deciding vote in the case of an equal division. He may participate in meetings of the Board of Governors, but does not vote at such meetings, and he ceases to hold office when the executive directors so decide. The President is the Chief of the operating staff of the bank, and conducts, under the direction of the executive directors, the ordinary business of the bank. Subject to the general control of the executive directors, he is responsible for the organisation, appointment and dismissal of the officers and staff.[9]

Approaches and Techniques Applied

The bank's staff indicated in the questionnaire sheet that priorities of IBRD's lending for economic development are determined on the basis of member countries' economic review, with suitable projects then being selected for the bank's lending programme. They also indicated that the bank applies up-to-date economic and financial techniques and to some extent social factors in assessing the viability of a project. The bank does not prepare market studies, but focuses on the marketing aspect during project appraisal. Before project selection is discussed, it must first be considered whether a member country is eligible to borrow from the IBRD or IDA. If the country is able to obtain the proposed loan on reasonable terms in the private capital market, it should not resort to the bank. Japan, for example, which had been a heavy borrower from the bank up to 1967, now has ample excess to private capital markets. On the other hand, since the bank expects to be paid back, the borrower must be creditworthy for borrowing on its terms. Even if a country is judged to be creditworthy on bank terms, it may become ineligible to borrow if it is pursuing policies likely to endanger its future creditworthiness or its contribution to the financing of bank-supported projects.[10]

In its evaluation of projects, the bank undertakes both an economic and a financial analysis.[11] Each yields an expected rate of return. In some cases both the economic and the financial returns are judged to be adequate, and in some cases both are judged to be inadequate. When the calculated economic return diverges from the calculated financial return, which is not uncommon, it is either because the economic analysis uses shadow prices while the financial analysis does not, or because a significant fraction of the expected benefits or of the anticipated costs to the economy cannot be captured by, or are not incurred by, the project itself. Since governments in many developing countries frequently encounter great difficulties in raising revenue for investment, financial analysis may well have to be concerned with how the project entity may be enabled to generate funds for its own expansion. A large proportion of bank-financed projects are revenue-producing but, increasingly, the bank (and IDA) finance non-revenue-producing projects in fields such as road transportation, education and family planning. The bank's staff recognise the fact that the external influence of a sizable investment project in a developing country may extend far beyond changes in the pattern of current economic activities, and in view of these possible influences that are external to the project itself, Hirschman has made an effort to evaluate the bank's techniques of project appraisal. While finding the indirect or side-effects of project lending to be of great importance, he considers that these effects are so varied as to escape detection by one or even several criteria uniformly applied to all projects. It is Hirschman's view, based on a study of some eleven World Bank project loans, that upon inspection, each project turns out to represent a unique constellation of experiences and consequences, of direct and indirect effects. This uniqueness in turn results from the varied inter-play between the structural characteristics of projects, on the one hand, and the social and political environment, on the other.[12]

From the above it is clear that the IBRD does not apply a standard or a manual for project appraisal but rather uses different up-to-date techniques based upon financial and economic factors. The bank is required by its Articles of Agreement to use objective economic criteria in all its judgements, and this has been the subject of most of its research work. World Bank Staff Occasional Papers deal (amongst other subjects) with methods and techniques of project analysis, risk analysis and project appraisal under uncertainty. *Methods of Project Analysis: A Review*,[13] was published in 1976 for the purpose of comparing and critically evaluating various alternative project-selection procedures for its application in developing countries and to show how the different methods fit in with economic theory as well as their own immediate practical preoccupations. *Risk Analysis in Project Appraisal*,[14] is another research paper by bank staff published in 1970 as part of a continuing effort in the bank to find ways to tackle the problem of uncertainty, and relates primarily to work in the Transportation and Public Utilities Projects Departments. The purpose of this paper was to describe three case-studies in the use of risk analysis in project appraisal which served to illustrate different aspects of the practical problem. It illustrated a number of methodological problems and presented some general observations on the usefulness of the approach. *Techniques for Project Appraisal under Uncertainty*, published in 1970,[15] is a research paper concerned with the appraisal of events which have uncertain outcomes and recommended that the best available judgements about the various factors underlying the cost and benefit estimates of the project be recorded in terms of probability distributions and that these distributions be aggregated in a mathematically correct manner to yield a probability distribution of the rate of return, or net present worth, of the project. Project-related decisions could be made more easily and more intelligently if returns on projects were reported not in terms of a single rate, or of a wide range of possible returns with undefined likelihoods of occurrence, but in terms of a probability distribution. The bank also publishes a series of progress reports dealing with different aspects of development projects not only from the economic and financial aspects but also from organisations' and human factors' aspects.[16]

Strategy for Financing and Technical Assistance

In replying to the questionnaire the IBRD staff gave increased emphasis to investments that can improve the productivity and well-being of the mass of poor people in developing countries. As for general policy for technical assistance, they emphasised the need to enhance the economic development of member countries in general, with additional direct technical assistance to some countries in the Middle East, Latin America and Africa as an important part of the bank-financed projects. In his address to the Board of Governors on 30 September 1980,[17] Robert McNamara, then President of the World Bank, indicated that the assistance the developing countries will need in the 1980s – both to alleviate their burden of absolute poverty, and to facilitate the structural changes in their economies required by the changes in the external environment – is much greater than was projected before. He also emphasised the fact that developing countries need to devise policies and investment programmes to assist the poor in their societies to become more productive, and to ensure an equitable distribution of basic services to them. The World Bank Group's Lending Programme for FY1981–85 reflects the bank's assessment of the future financial requirements of the developing countries as they appeared early in 1977, when the plan was prepared. In the light of that assessment, the President of the World Bank believed that the planned level of lending would permit the bank to increase its new commitments each year by 5 per cent in real terms, and that this projected growth would allow the bank to make an adequate contribution to its member countries' priority development needs. That assessment is no longer tenable due to the unexpected rate of inflation. As a result, the real value of the lending programme planned for 1981–85 will fall 10.5 per cent below what was projected, by over $5.6bn. Table 23.8 shows the Working Plan of the World Bank Group.

The Development Committee,[18] in its meeting in Belgrade at the end of September 1979, called on the World Bank to increase its programme of lending as a way of accelerating the flow of financial resources to developing countries.

The programme of lending is in the form of loans which are not related to a specific project but are of the nature of balance of payments support. This programme has been very restricted, comprising not more

TABLE 23.8 World Bank Group: Working Plan FY1981–85 (US $bn)

	Working Plan[a]				
	FY81	FY82	FY83	FY84	FY85
New loans					
IBRD	8.6	9.6	10.7	11.9	13.2
IDA	3.6	4.1	4.7	5.0	5.3
IFC	0.6	0.7	0.8	0.9	1.1
Total – Current $	12.8	14.4	16.2	17.8	19.6
– Constant FY80 $	11.9	12.6	13.3	13.8	14.3
Disbursements					
IBRD	5.2	6.3	7.4	8.3	9.2
IDA	1.8	2.2	2.7	3.5	4.1
IFC	0.3	0.5	0.7	0.8	0.9
Total – Current $	7.3	9.0	10.8	12.6	14.2
– Constant FY80 $	6.7	7.6	8.6	9.4	9.9

[a] The Working Plan is subject to annual review by the executive directors and is based on the assumption that necessary legislative action on the General Capital Increase and IDA VI replenishment will be completed according to schedule.

Source: *Address to the Board of Governors* by Robert McNamara, President, World Bank, 30 September 1980.

than 2–3 per cent of total IBRD lending. In order to avoid this constraint and to respond positively to the request of the Development Committee, the bank's management proposed a new type of programme called 'structural adjustment lending'. The basic idea was to extend the programme of loans to countries which suffer from structural imbalances, provided that these countries undertake a well-defined adjustment programme in agreement with the World Bank. This type of non-project lending has the specific objective of helping developing countries to reduce their current account deficit to more manageable proportions over the medium term by supporting programmes of adjustment that encompass specific policy, industrial and other changes designed to strengthen their balance of payments, while maintaining their growth and developmental momentum. Lending for structural adjustment is a new form of bank assistance which is considered to be an evolution of the traditional programme assistance that has always been a part of the bank's lending operations designed to meet the immediate consequences of crisis. However, investment in long-term development projects will continue to absorb the greatest part of the bank's technical assistance and lending resources.

Problems of Implementation and Remarks from Field Experience

Bank staff replied to the questionnaire sheet with regard to problems of implementation and follow-up by indicating that the World Bank conducts strict supervision of projects. Problems are brought to the attention of borrowers and corrective action is recommended, pinpointing the nature of the problems of implementation without going into detailed presentation. As a result, the bank's staff have a difficult task in covering the scope of these problems. The country studies prepared by staff, based upon their findings in missions, indicate that it is not possible to generalise on problems as each recipient country is unique, but some major problems are common to all as indicated in the previous chapters. An approach of dealing with regional groups regarding these problems was considered, but tended to lead to the problems of development in each region related mainly to field experience. By reviewing World Bank documents on this issue, however, it is clear that the problems of project implementation are related to physical implementation and construction, costs and financial matters, and operational issues. It is interesting to note that the staff of the bank believe that political problems as such, and other exogenous factors, are behind some other problems, for example, financial difficulties due to political constraints on tariffs. Projects in transport and public utilities became problem projects mainly because of difficulties related to financial matters and costs, or of physical implementation; projects in agriculture and education had problems because of staffing and management inadequacies and difficulties with project execution. A review of the courses of action followed by the bank in each of these problem projects, and of the solution adopted, does not reveal a general pattern. This is only to be expected, since the solutions were adapted in each case to the particular circumstances. Supervision missions visited the projects for discussion with senior management, and strong representations were made to the agency in charge and the government concerned to help achieve a solution.

As for the bank's experience from field operations, there were no comments by the staff. The bank has tremendous experience which it is difficult to generalise about, but earlier material in this chapter could shed some light on it. Moreover, the sector working papers published by the World Bank are useful in revealing more experience in different fields of operations. For example, problems of urbanisation are mainly problems of urban poverty and unemployment, a problem of inadequacy of housing and urban infrastructure. The severity of the problems reflects primarily on the rapidity of overall population growth and the acute shortage of resources with which to equip additions to the urban population. The proliferation of squatter settlements and slums, and the rising backlog in urban services, have been accompanied by a growing recognition that development implies much more than just expansion of output. Yet, with few exceptions, measures so far undertaken have signally failed to reverse these trends or produce more efficient patterns of urban growth. In recognition of the importance of these issues, the World Bank has decided to supplement its activities in individual sectors with a more direct focus on problems of urbanisation.[19] Land reform is another sector to which the bank is giving important consideration as it is concerned with changing the institutional structure governing man's relationship with the landlord as one of the basic factors of production for food and other agricultural products. With food production rising in the developing countries at about the same rate as population, there is growing pressure on land resources to increase output. Much of this increase will have to come from higher output per hectare. Thus changing the pattern of land ownership and redistributing land can contribute to increases in output in some countries but will make little difference in others. The World Bank's policy in this sector is to give priority in agricultural lending to those member countries that pursue broad-based agricultural strategies directed toward the promotion of adequate new employment opportunities, with special attention to the needs of the poorest groups. Thus the bank supports policies of land reform designed to further these objectives.[20] The training and visit system of agricultural extension has helped increase agricultural productivity impressively in several areas. In the Seyhan project in Turkey, farmers increased cotton yields from 1.7 tons to over 3 tons per hectare in three years. In Chambal, Rajastan (India), farmers increased paddy yields from about 2.1 tons to over 3 tons per hectare in two years. Combined irrigated and non-irrigated wheat yields in Chambal, Madhya Pradesh (India), rose from 1.3 tons to nearly 2 tons per hectare after one season and have since risen higher. The area under high-yielding paddy and wheat varieties in the entire state of West Bengal increased its yield substantially in a single year. This system has been put into operation in areas where the need is to improve the level of agricultural production by large numbers of farmers cultivating mostly small farms using low-level technology and usually traditional methods.[21] International technology transfer to developing countries has been agreed in relation to the costs of the transfer, the appropriateness of products and techniques which are transferred, the effects of transfer on learning and technological development in LLDCs, and the effects on independence. It has been argued that the appropriate policies will vary according to the stage of development of each country, its technological capacity and its own objectives. However, in general the bank believes that an active technology policy is desirable if the costs associated with technology transfer are reduced and the benefits increased.[22]

The performance of the World Bank has shown that it has done much for developing countries in the 1970s. However, it could have done better had it adjusted its activities more rapidly in more constructive directions. The bank must be ready to face the challenging problems of development in the 1980s, and without increasing its financial resources substantially it will be handicapped in solving the serious financial problems that will face its developing member countries. This requires a structural change in its Articles of Agreement and in its membership and voting powers. As an international institution it should amend its charter to include the centrally planned economies as potential members. However, it is now considering the admission of the People's Republic of China, which should be a first step to admitting other countries in the communist world to the bank as active and responsible members. As the bank has already increased its capital from $45bn to $85bn, its status should be amended to change its 1:1 gearing ratio to a 2:1 ratio as recommended by the Brandt Commission. This would enable the bank to raise its borrowing capacity to $160bn, a proposal supported by Robert McNamara in his last address as President on 30 September 1980. What is needed is to implement this proposal in a gradual manner without affecting the bank's market standing. The need for more World Bank co-financing with the private sector is going to be a major issue in the 1980s. A. W. Clausen, nominated as President of the World Bank from June 1981, in one of his interviews,[23] has indicated a strong belief in seeking more ways in which additional funds can be obtained from the private sector through co-financing and co-operation between the private sector and the World Bank. Unless these three big issues – membership and voting power, gearing ratio, and co-financing with the private sector – are implemented during the 1980s, the World Bank will be unable to meet its obligations as a world development institution.

24 The International Development Association

Establishment and Financial Resources

The International Development Association, the soft loan affiliate of the World Bank, came into being in 1960, and can be viewed as a significant indirect result of the vigorous campaign of the less developed countries for a sizable fund to provide long-term, low-interest loans for economic and social development. The Western Europeans and the Australians were becoming too creditworthy to borrow from the World Bank. The Japanese were still large borrowers but obviously not destined to remain so. Among the less developed countries, on the other hand, India, Pakistan and some other major borrowers were piling up external debt so rapidly as to call into question their continued creditworthiness for loans on World Bank terms. The creditworthiness of newly independent countries in Africa for interest-bearing loans was also questionable. Thus, IDA had to be created to keep the World Bank pre-eminent, or at least eminent, in the growing complex of multilateral agencies attempting to facilitate international development. The executive directors of the bank were in reality waiting for the instructions issued by their Board of Governors in October 1959. The IDA concept had by then been debated for ten years. In May 1959, the US executive director had sent to other directors a memorandum outlining his government's current thinking on the major points of substance to be considered in establishing an IDA – size, purpose, structure, voting rights, replenishment arrangements, currencies to be subscribed, use of currencies subscribed, and so forth. The executive directors already had the experience of negotiating articles of agreement for the International Finance Corporation. Eugene Black chaired the negotiation sessions, and by late January 1960 a highly flexible charter was distributed to governments for approval. By 24 September 1960, enough governments had accepted membership to bring the IDA into being.[1]

According to its Articles of Agreement, the purposes of IDA are to promote economic development, increase productivity and thus raise standards of living in the less developed areas of the world included within its membership, in particular by providing finance to meet their important developmental requirements on terms which are more flexible and bear less heavily on the balance of payments than those of conventional loans, thereby furthering the developmental objectives of the IBRD and supplementing its activities.[2] The initial subscription assigned to each original member was in the amount set forth opposite its name in Table 24.1.

Of the initial subscription of each original member 10 per cent had to be payable in gold or freely convertible currency, and the remaining 90 per cent in gold or freely convertible currency in the case of members listed in Part I, and in the currency of the subscribing members in the case of members listed in Part II. IDA was empowered at such time as it deemed appropriate in the light of the schedule for completion of payments on initial subscriptions of original members, and at intervals of approximately five years thereafter, to review the adequacy of its resources and, if it deemed desirable, to authorise a general increase in subscriptions. When any additional subscription is authorised, each member is given an opportunity to subscribe, under such conditions as determined by IDA, an amount which enables it to maintain its relative voting power, but no member is obliged to subscribe. All decisions related to additional subscriptions are made by a two-thirds majority of the total voting power.[3]

IDA authorised capital stock, according to a questionnaire sheet filled in by World Bank staff, reached $16.50bn at FY1979. Membership in IDA is open to all members of the World Bank, and by September 1980 121 had joined. The funds used by IDA, called credits to distinguish them from Word Bank loans, have come mostly in the form of subscriptions, general replenishments from IDA's more industrialised and developed members, special contributions by IDA's richer members, and transfers from the net earnings of the World Bank. The agreement on IDA's Sixth Replenishment, which the executive directors approved in January 1980, for the three-year period, FY1981–83, calls for funding in an amount totalling the equivalent of $12,000m. It provides that the twenty-six governments that contributed to the funding of IDA's Fifth Replenishment, which amounted to the equivalent of $8700m, will be joined by seven first-time donors in the

Table 24.1 IDA Initial Subscriptions (US $m)[a]

Part I

Australia	20.18	France	52.96	Norway	6.72
Austria	5.04	Germany	52.96	Sweden	10.09
Belgium	22.70	Italy	18.16	Union of South Africa	10.09
Canada	37.83	Japan	33.59	United Kingdom	131.14
Denmark	8.74	Luxembourg	1.01	United States	320.29
Finland	3.83	Netherlands	27.74		
					763.07

Part II

Afghanistan	1.01	Haiti	0.76	Panama	0.02
Argentina	18.83	Honduras	0.30	Paraguay	0.30
Bolivia	1.06	Iceland	0.10	Peru	1.77
Brazil	18.83	India	40.35	Philippines	5.04
Burma	2.02	Indonesia	11.10	Saudi Arabia	3.70
Ceylon	3.03	Iran	4.54	Spain	10.09
Chile	3.53	Iraq	0.76	Sudan	1.01
China	30.26	Ireland	3.03	Thailand	3.03
Colombia	3.53	Israel	1.68	Tunisia	1.51
Costa Rica	0.20	Jordan	0.30	Turkey	5.80
Cuba	4.71	Korea	1.26	United Arab Republic	6.03
Dominican Republic	0.40	Lebanon	0.45	Uruguay	1.06
Ecuador	0.65	Libya	1.01	Venezuela	7.06
El Salvador	0.30	Malaya	2.52	Vietnam	1.51
Ethiopia	0.50	Mexico	8.74	Yugoslavia	4.04
Ghana	2.36	Morocco	3.53		
Greece	2.52	Nicaragua	0.30		236.93
Guatemala	0.40	Pakistan	10.09		
				Total	1000.00

[a] In terms of US $ of the weight and fineness in effect on 1 January 1960.

Source: *Articles of Agreement* of the International Development Association, 24 September 1960.

funding of the Sixth Replenishment. Table 24.2 shows the development of IDA Replenishments.

The agreement calling for a real increase in IDA resources was based on the belief of the thirty-three governments involved that sustained

TABLE 24.2 The Development of IDA Replenishments

Country	First Replenishment[a] ($m)	(% total)	Second Replenishment[a] ($m)	(% total)	Third Replenishment[a] ($m)	(% total)	Fourth Replenishment[b] ($m)	(% total)	Fifth Replenishment[c] ($m)	(% total)	US$m equivalent	SDRm equivalent	Percentage of total proposed contribution
Argentina	—	—	—	—	—	—	—	—	—	—	—	—	0.21
Australia	19.80	2.66	24.00	2.00	48.00	1.97	90.00	2.00	146.90	1.91	25.00	19.07	1.91
Austria	5.04	.68	8.16	0.68	16.32	0.67	30.00	0.68	49.70	0.65	229.20	174.83	0.68
Belgium[d]	8.25	1.11	20.40	1.70	40.80	1.67	76.50	1.70	124.60	1.62	81.60	62.25	1.68
Brazil[e]	—	—	—	—	—	—	—	—	—	—	201.60	153.78	0.42
Canada	41.70	5.60	75.00	6.25	150.00	6.15	274.50	6.10	447.90	5.83	50.00	38.14	4.30
Denmark	7.50	1.01	13.20	1.10	26.40	1.08	54.00	1.20	87.80	1.14	516.00	393.61	1.20
Finland	2.30	.31	4.08	0.34	12.24	0.50	25.20	0.56	41.00	0.53	144.00	109.85	0.60
France	61.87	8.31	97.20	8.10	150.00	6.15	253.55	5.63	413.30	5.38	72.00	54.92	5.38
Germany[f]	72.60	9.75	117.00	9.75	234.00	9.59	514.50	11.43	838.80	10.91	645.60	492.47	12.50
Greece	—	—	—	—	—	—	—	—	—	—	1500.00	1144.23	0.05
Iceland[g]	—	—	—	—	0.45	0.02	1.35	0.03	2.20	0.03	6.00	4.58	0.03
Ireland[h]	—	—	—	—	4.00	0.16	7.50	0.17	8.59	0.11	3.60	2.75	0.11
Israel	—	—	—	—	—	—	1.00	0.02	—	—	13.20	10.07	—
Italy	30.00	4.03	48.36	4.03	96.72	3.96	181.35	4.03	295.90	3.85	—	—	3.85
Japan[m]	41.25	5.54	66.48	5.54	144.00	5.90	495.00	11.00	792.00[i]	10.30[i]	462.00	352.42	14.65
Korea	—	—	—	—	—	—	—	—	1.00	0.01	1757.54	1340.68	0.03
Kuwait	3.36	0.45	5.40	0.45	10.80	0.44	27.00	0.60	180.00[i]	2.34[i]	3.00	2.29	1.67
Luxembourg	0.37	0.05	0.60	0.05	1.20	0.05	2.25	0.05	3.60	0.05	200.00	152.56	0.05
Mexico	—	—	—	—	—	—	—	—	—	—	6.00	4.58	0.17
Netherlands	16.50	2.22	29.28	2.44	67.56	2.77	132.75	2.95	216.70	2.82	20.00	15.26	3.00
New Zealand[j]	—	—	—	—	—	—	11.74	0.26	7.65	0.10	360.00	274.61	0.08
Norway	6.60	0.89	10.68	0.89	24.00	0.98	49.50	1.10	80.60	1.05	10.02	7.65	1.20
Portugal[g,k]	—	—	—	—	—	—	—	—	—	—	144.00	109.85	0.06
Romania[l]	—	—	—	—	—	—	—	—	—	—	7.00	5.33	—
Saudi Arabia	—	—	—	—	—	—	—	—	—	—	—	—	3.25
South Africa	3.99	0.54	3.00	0.25	3.00	0.12	9.00	0.20	350.00	4.56	390.00	297.50	3.25
Spain	—	—	—	—	2.50	0.10	13.33	0.30	10.00	0.13	10.00	7.63	0.08
Sweden	15.00	2.01	29.64	2.47	102.00	4.18	180.00	4.00	21.00	0.27	50.00	38.14	0.42
Switzerland	—	—	12.10	1.01	31.80	1.30	(66.18)[n]	(1.47)	293.80	3.82	360.00	274.61	3.00
											—	—	—

International Development Association

United Arab Emirates[*l*]	—	—	—	—	—	—	—	—	—	—	—	—	—	—	0.66	0.66
United Kingdom	96.60	12.97	155.52	12.96	311.04	12.74	499.50	11.10	—	—	50.75	814.30	10.60	60.42	924.58	10.10
United States	312.00	41.89	480.00	40.00	960.00	39.33	1500.00	33.32	—	—	2400.00	31.22	3240.00	27.00
Venezuela	—	—	—	—	—	0.17	—	—	—	—	20.00	0.17	15.26	0.17
Yugoslavia	—	—	—	—	4.04	0.17	5.00	0.11	—	8.10	0.11	20.00	15.26	0.17
Unallocated	—												161.44	123.15	1.32
TOTAL	744.73	100.00	1200.10	100.00	2440.87	100.00	4501.30	100.00	7686.19	100.00	12000.00	100.00	9153.86	100.00

[a] Contributions are shown in 1960 US$

[b] Contributions are expressed in US$ equivalents as of 27 September 1973.

[c] Amounts are shown in US$ equivalents as of 14 March 1977. Including Saudi Arabia's increased contribution from $250m at Vienna to $350m in April 1978.

[d] Belgium and Luxembourg joined IDA in 1964. At that time, it was agreed that their contributions would be divided equally between an initial subscription and a contribution to the First Replenishment.

[e] Brazil intends to pay $20.44m equivalent of its contribution to the Sixth Replenishment through release in usable form of the 90 per cent portion of its initial subscription in the Association.

[f] Germany is proposed contribution in US$ equivalent (ordinary) = 1,098.46, per cent of total contribution (ordinary = 12.00) (Extra) = 60.00 (Extra = 0.50)

[g] Tentative figures, since as of 12 December 1979, Iceland and Portugal were not in a position to make a decision on these amounts: Iceland was a part II member of IDA from 1961 to 1971, and became a Part I member thereafter.

[h] Ireland was a Part II member of IDA from 1960 to 1974, and became a Part I member thereafter.

[i] Includes 'extra' contributions of Japan and Kuwait to the Fifth Replenishment of $144m (1.87 per cent of the total) and $136.1m (1.77 per cent of the total) respectively.

[j] New Zealand became a Part I member of IDA in 1975.

[k] Portugal, Romania, the United Arab Emirates and Venezuela are not yet members of IDA, but are considering membership in connection with the Sixth Replenishment.

[m] Japan's proposed contribution in US$ equivalent (ordinary = 1,440.00), SDR equivalent (ordinary = 1,098.46) per cent of total contribution (ordinary = 12.00) (Extra = 317.54). (Extra = 242.22) (Extra = 2.65)

[n] The intended loan from Switzerland under the Fourth Replenishment was rejected in a referendum in June 1976.

[l] United Arab Emirates is not yet a member of IDA but is expected to become a Part I member.

Source: IDA RPL/79–2 and World Bank Annual Report, 1980.

progress in reducing poverty in the poorest countries would be impossible without an acceleration in their growth rates, and that external assistance on appropriate terms could play a critical supporting role in efforts by the poorest countries to mobilise domestic resources to achieve faster growth. The replenishment becomes effective when 'Instruments of Commitment' and 'Qualified Instruments of Commitment' are deposited for about 80 per cent of the total replenishment. The former is a formal notification to IDA that the donor country will pay the full amount of its contribution. The latter is a formal notification that the donor will pay part of its contribution without qualification, but that payment of the remainder is subject to obtaining necessary legislative appropriations. In June 1980, the Executive Directors of the IDA authorised IDA Commitments, as well as the repayment obligations of IDA borrowers, to be expressed in special drawing rights (SDRS), beginning with the Sixth Replenishment. The action was taken so as to reduce the impact of fluctuations in exchange rates on IDA's commitment authority, to allow for more accurate planning of the timing of the proposed credits, and to reduce the possibility of a shortfall in the resources needed to meet disbursements of commitments.[4]

Scope of Activities

The Scope of Operations in the 1960s[5]

During the period 1961–70, IDA made 221 commitments, totalling $2773.1m net in 55 countries for agriculture, education, transportation, electric power, water supply, telecommunications, industry, project preparation and technical assistance. As in the case of the IBRD, transportation, electric power and industry were the main important sectors that benefited from the IDA facilities, especially during 1964–68. The average share of the above three sectors in the total activities of IDA to developing countries reached a level of 58 per cent during the period 1963/64–1969/70, while agriculture's share in the total reached an average of 19.7 per cent during the same period. During the two years (1968/69, 1969/70), however, there was an expansion of IDA credit facilities for agriculture. In 1968/69 the share of agriculture in total IDA facilities reached 23.1 per cent compared to 24.2 per cent in transportation, electric power and industry, and in 1969/70 reached 37.3 per cent compared to 39.2 per cent (Table 24.3). The fiscal year 1970 has marked a substantial increase of IDA credits to the agriculture sector, which

TABLE 24.3 IDA Credits by Economic Sector
(US $m, 1964–70)

Activities by purpose	_____ Fiscal years _____						
	1964	1965	1966	1967	1968	1969	1970
Agriculture	15.60	88.34	31.70	25.60	27.20	89.10	226.08
Education	17.60[a]	23.50	31.20	36.20	13.60	24.50	27.60
Telecommunications	—	33.00	—	—	—	44.30	16.70
Transportation	106.50	110.25	72.10	33.40	51.20	86.02	144.50
Electric power	—	39.00	23.00	—	14.00	7.40	35.15
Industry	90.00	15.00	125.00	255.00	—	—	58.00
Project preparation	—	—	—	1.49	0.55	8.68	8.58
Water supply and sewerage systems	53.50	—	1.10	1.75	—	—	14.00
Family planning	—	—	—	—	—	—	—
General development and industrial imports	—	—	—	—	—	125.00	75.00
Totals	283.20	309.09	284.10	353.54	106.55	385.00	605.61
The share of transportation, electric power and industry in the total (%) Average (58.0%)	(69.3)	(53.1)	(77.4)	(81.5)	(61.1)	(24.2)	(39.2)
The share of agriculture (%) Average (19.7%)	(5.5)	(28.5)	(11.1)	(7.2)	(25.5)	(23.1)	(37.3)

[a] Education projects.
Sources: World Bank and IDA, *Annual Reports*, 1963/64, 1964/65, 1965/66, 1966/67, 1968, 1969, 1970.

received $226.08m compared to $89.10m in 1969 and $15.60m in 1964. This sharp increase was in response to the recommendations of the Pearson Commission Report.[6]

IDA has offered credit facilities in a wider range of countries. The Near East and South Asia were the main recipient regions of IDA credit facilities with an average of 66.2 per cent during the period 1962–70 (compared to 18.9 per cent of the IBRD). Africa was the second most important recipient region with an average of 20.5 per cent (compared to 14.3 per cent of the IBRD) during the same period, followed by East Asia and Latin America with an average of 6.7 and 6.2 per cent respectively, and with no assistance to European developing countries. Table 24.4 shows the geographical distribution of assistance from IDA during 1962–70.

TABLE 24.4 IDA, Geographical Distribution by Region (US $m) (1962–70)

Regions	Fiscal years								
	1962	1963	1964	1965	1966	1967	1968	1969	1970
Near East and South Asia	78.6	213.9	216.3	228.1	248.2	260.6	12.0	222.4	354.5
(Average 66.2%)	(63.1)	(83.0)	(87.2)	(73.8)	(87.3)	(73.8)	(11.2)	(57.7)	(58.5)
Latin America	30.0	11.3	11.6	18.5	7.5	2.0	9.1	14.6	11.0
(Average 6.2%)	(24.0)	(4.3)	(4.6)	(5.9)	(2.6)	(0.5)	(8.5)	(3.7)	(1.8)
East Asia	13.1	14.0	(—)	(—)	(—)	(—)	11.0	69.3	95.5
(Average 6.7%)	(10.5)	(5.4)					(10.3)	(18.0)	(15.7)
Africa	2.8	18.4	20.1	62.3	28.4	90.3	74.4	77.2	135.2
(Average 20.5%)	(2.2)	(7.1)	(8.1)	(20.1)	(9.9)	(25.5)	(67.7)	(20.0)	(22.3)
Europe	—	—	—	—	—	—	—	—	—

(—) Percentage of total activities to developing countries.

Sources: US Overseas Loans and Grants and Assistance from International Organisations, Special Report Prepared for the House Foreign Affairs Committee, 1971.

The Scope of Operations in the 1970s

IDA commitments in FY1980 totalled $3838m, 103 projects were assisted in 40 countries compared with $3022m, 105 projects in 43 developing countries in FY1979, and $584m, 51 projects in 34 countries in FY1971. In FY1980, most IDA commitments (87 per cent) were to the poorest of developing countries, those with annual per capita GNP of $360 or less. Table 24.5 shows the development of IDA's credits and disbursements.

TABLE 24.5 IDA Credits and Disbursements (1971–81) (US $m)

	Fiscal year										
	1971	1972	1973	1974	1975	1976	1977	1978	1979	1980	1981
Credit amounts	584	1000	1357	1095	1576	1655	1308	2313	3022	3838	3482
Disbursements	235	261	493	711	1026	1252	1298	1062	1222	1411	1,878
	Number										
Operations approved[a]	51	68	75	69	68	73	67	99	105	103	106
Borrowing countries	34	38	43	41	39	39	36	42	43	40	40
Member countries	107	108	112	113	114	116	117	120	121	121	125

[a] Joint bank/IDA operations are counted only once as bank operations.
Source: World Bank Annual Reports, 1980, 1981.

The composition of IDA lending by sector shows that agriculture is the dominant sector, as it was in the 1960s, reaching 46 per cent of IDA total lending in FY1980 compared with 32 per cent in FY1979 and 58 per cent FY1978. The energy sector has received growing attention in recent years, reaching 21 per cent of total IDA lending in FY1980 compared with 16 per cent in FY1979 and 11 per cent in FY1978. The transportation sector is the third most important sector of IDA total lending, reaching 6 per cent in FY1980 compared with 16 per cent in FY1979 and 8 per cent in FY1978. Table 24.6 shows IDA trends in lending by sector.

A review of IDA lending by region shows that in 1980 it provided $664.5m for Eastern Africa, $292.4m for Western Africa, $208.4m for East Asia and Pacific, $2311.5m for South Asia, $271.7m for Europe, Middle East and North Africa, and $89.0m for Latin America and the

TABLE 24.6 IDA Trends in Lending by Sector in US $m and Percentages (FY1978–81)

Sectors \ Fiscal years	1978 (US$m)	(%)	1979 (US$m)	(%)	1980 (US$m)	(%)	1981 (US$m)	(%)
Agriculture and rural development	1340.7	58	953.7	32	1758.0	46	1357.0	39
Development finance companies	18.4	1	32.2	1	74.5	2	70.5	2
Education	83.0	4	250.5	8	80.0	2	360.7	10
Energy								
Oil, gas, and coal	—	—	30.0	1	128.5	3	95.5	3
Power	246.2	11	482.4	16	807.8	21	40.5	1
Industry	27.0	1	121.5	4	29.0	1	409.7	12
Non-project	75.0	3	105.0	3	242.5	6	223.0	6
Population, health and nutrition	33.1	1	97.0	3	78.0	2	—	—
Small-scale enterprises	62.0	3	16.0	1	38.0	1	71.5	2
Technical assistance	9.3	—	29.7	1	13.0	—	81.6	2
Telecommunications	67.5	3	—	—	65.0	2	329.2	9
Tourism	—	—	46.5	2	—	—	—	—
Transportation	174.8	8	473.5	16	239.5	6	299.8	9
Urbanisation	146.2	6	12.0	—	99.0	3	42.0	1
Water supply and sewerage	29.8	1	371.5	12	184.7	5	101.1	3
Total	2313.0	100	3021.5	100	3837.5	100	3482.1	100

Source: World Bank *Annual Reports*, 1980, 1981

Caribbean. As in the 1960s, the 1970s have shown Asia receiving the largest amount of lending by IDA followed by Africa, while Latin America received the lowest amount. This, of course, is compensated for by a high level of IBRD loans to Latin America and the Caribbean and small amounts to Asia and Africa. Table 24.7 shows IDA amount of lending by region.

Terms and Conditions

According to replies to the questionnaire sheet the terms and conditions adopted by IDA are as follows:

Interest rate: interest-free. No interest is charged on IDA credits, although there is a service charge of $\frac{3}{4}$ of 1 per cent.

TABLE 24.7 IDA Lending by Region (FY 1971–81)
(US $m)

Region	Fiscal years Annual average 1971–75	1976	1977	1978	1979	1980	1981
Eastern Africa	189.4	224.6	260.5	397.9	379.8	664.5	570.1
Western Africa	90.3	158.3	133.0	205.9	239.2	292.4	383.5
East Asia and Pacific	113.1	—	23.0	139.3	338.4	208.4	130.5
South Asia	583.5	1089.2	770.2	1318.9	1777.0	2311.5	2101.2
Europe, Middle East and North Africa	113.9	143.7	95.8	195.4	255.1	271.7	262.6
Latin America and the Caribbean	35.3	39.5	25.0	55.6	32.0	89.0	34.2

Source: World Bank *Annual Reports*, 1980, 1981.

Repayment period: 50 years.
Grace period: 10 years.
Guarantee: member government guarantee is required.

The IDA may, when and to the extent it deems appropriate in the light of all relevant circumstances, including the financial and economic situation and prospects of the member concerned, and on such conditions as it may determine, agree to a relaxation or other modification of the terms on which any of its financing shall have been provided.[7]

Management and Organisational Structure

IDA has a Board of Governors, executive directors, a President and staff to perform the duties of the association. All the powers of the association are vested in the Board of Governors. Each governor and deputy governor of the World Bank appointed by a member country of the bank which is also a member of the association is *ex officio* a governor or deputy governor, respectively, of the association. No deputy governor may vote except in the absence of his principal. The Chairman of the Board of Governors of the World Bank is *ex officio* Chairman of the Board of Governors of the association except that if the Chairman of the Board of Governors of the World Bank represents a state which is not a member of the association, then the Board of

Governors select one of the governors as Chairman of the Board of Governors. The Board of Governors may delegate to the executive directors authority to exercise any of its powers, except the power to:

(1) Admit new members and determine the conditions of their admission.
(2) Authorise additional subscriptions and determine the terms and conditions relating thereto.
(3) Suspend a member.
(4) Decide appeals from interpretations of the Articles of Agreement given by the executive directors.
(5) Make arrangements to co-operate with other international organisations (other than informal arrangements of a temporary and administrative character).
(6) Decide to suspend permanently the operations of the association and to distribute its assets.
(7) Determine the distribution of the association's net income.
(8) Approve proposed amendments to the Articles of Agreement.

Except as otherwise specifically provided, all matters before the association are decided by a majority of the votes cast. The executive directors are responsible for the conduct of the general operations of the association and exercise all the powers given to them by the Articles of Agreement or delegated to them by the Board of Governors. A quorum for any meeting of the executive directors is a majority of the directors, exercising not less than one-half of the total voting power. The President of the World Bank is the President of IDA, and is Chairman of the executive directors of the association, but has no vote except as a deciding vote in case of an equal division. He may also participate in meetings of the Board of Governors but without a vote. The association is an entity separate and distinct from the World Bank and the funds of the association are kept separate and apart from those of the bank. The Association does not borrow from or lend to the World Bank, although this does not preclude it from investing funds not needed in its financing operations in obligations of the bank. The association may, however, make arrangements with the bank regarding facilities, personnel and services and arrangements for reimbursement of administrative expenses paid in the first instance by either organisation on behalf of the other.[8]

The voting structure of the association incorporates the two-tier membership system. The number of votes for Part I member countries

(21 countries), as of 30 June 1980, reached 2,267,244 votes, representing 63.36 per cent of the total voting power of all member countries. The number of votes for Part II member countries (100 countries) was 1,311,022 votes, representing 36.64 per cent of the total voting power. Comparing the voting power of the association with the IBRD's voting power, the bank's number of votes reached 335,468 as of 30 June 1980. While there is no classification of the bank membership similar to the association, the 21 countries in Part I in the case of IDA represent 200,366 votes, or 59.73 per cent of the total number of votes (335,468). Thus 21 industralised countries dominate the voting power of the World Bank and the association, with more power in the hands of the USA, the UK, West Germany, France and Japan, the big five donors. Table 24.8

TABLE 24.8 IDA Part I Member Countries with Corresponding Numbers in the World Bank Voting Power
30 June 1980

Members	IDA Number of votes	Per cent of total	IBRD Number of votes	Per cent of total
Australia	56,652	1.47	6,700	2.00
Austria	21,822	.61	2,946	.88
Belgium	42,397	1.18	7,518	2.24
Canada	137,025	3.83	11,372	3.39
Denmark	34,353	.96	2,774	.83
Finland	18,404	.51	2,217	.66
France	138,669	3.88	17,817	5.31
Germany, Federal Republic of	236,831	6.62	17,862	5.32
Iceland	7,802	.22	472	.14
Ireland	10,393	.29	1,516	.45
Italy	69,910	1.95	8,775	2.62
Japan	201,476	5.63	17,789	5.30
Kuwait	37,613	1.05	944	.28
Luxembourg	8,363	.23	547	.16
Netherlands	70,182	1.96	7,929	2.36
New Zealand	10,413	.29	2,097	.63
Norway	30,464	.85	2,660	.79
South Africa	12,445	.35	3,713	1.11
Sweden	93,315	2.61	3,926	1.17
United Kingdom	263,576	7.37	26,250	7.82
United States	769,139	21.49	70,833	21.11
Totals	2,267,244	63.36	216,657	64.54

Source: World Bank Annual Report, 1980.

shows the comparison between Part I member countries of the association voting power with the corresponding numbers in the World Bank.

Most of the low-income countries are likely to be more and more insistent on what they call their right to run their own affairs in their own way. It is possible that many of them may even decide that to give up foreign aid is for them a lesser evil than to accept foreign aid at the price of constant outside interference in their affairs. It is therefore vital that the rich member countries of the World Bank Group make it easier for the low-income member countries to distinguish clearly between 'foreign aid' and aid from the Bank Group, and between 'outside interference' and the Bank Group's contribution to dialogue between partners. A principal obstacle to their making this distinction is the heavy majority of votes held by the rich countries in the governing bodies of the Bank Group, which is so great as to make it difficult for the poorer countries to believe that the Bank Group is in any real sense a proper partnership between the rich countries and themselves.[9]

Approaches and Techniques Applied

The projects for which IDA gives financial assistance constitute the main vehicle by which the association transfers financial and technical resources to the poorest countries of the world. The professional staff undertake extensive economic and sector analyses within each borrowing country, thus providing the framework for formulating an appropriate long-term development strategy for the country's economy and its major sectors, including policy and institutional changes. As has been indicated, the lending terms of IDA credits are much more concessional than for World Bank loans, but, aside from lending terms, the procedures applying in IDA projects are identical to those used for bank projects and the same standards in assessing the soundness of projects are applied. The decision as to whether a project will receive World Bank or IDA financing is decided on country eligibility grounds, not in relation to project characteristics. Eligibility for IDA financing is determined by country-specific criteria, with factors taken into consideration including a country's relative poverty, its lack of creditworthiness for conventional lending, and its ability to use IDA resources effectively. The selection and preparation of projects, the tests of economic and financial viability, the eligible uses for loan proceeds, procurement standards, and the close supervision projects during execution are all exactly the same as for World Bank-financed projects. IDA, though legally a separate and distinct entity, has the same management and staff as the bank, and its policies are set, and its operations controlled by, the same Board of Executive Directors, who report to the same Board of Governors. Every IDA project must be approved by IDA's Board of Directors, based upon staff documentation assessing the project's feasibility, its expected developmental impact, and the required institutional and financial arrangements needed to ensure efficient implementation at a cost commensurate with the project's expected benefits. The cycle of a typical IDA project usually consists of six sequential stages: identification, preparation, appraisal, negotiation and approval, supervision, and *ex-post* evaluation, with IDA typically being involved with a project for approximately eleven years from inception to complete fruition. Priority and suitability of projects are normally established through various tests of project acceptability. First the proposed project must fall in a sector of high economic and social priority for development as interpreted by the government's development plans, and agreed by the association. Thereafter, it must be established whether a project has sound technical and economic prospects. In this process, greater stress is being placed on local capabilities in generating projects. Project preparation and appraisal are, however, more than simply a process of satisfying particular requirements for approval of a lending operation. Project preparation involves careful consideration of the full range of technical, institutional, economic and financial conditions necessary to achieve the project's objectives. It covers the procedures necessary to establish unequivocally the feasibility of the proposed technical design and operations of the project and prove the proposed project to be the best economic solution; in some cases, it must satisfy financial accounting and economic rate of return requirements, and conclude definite arrangements for management and implementation of the project. The ultimate goal is to ensure that the benefits of IDA investments are as high as IDA and borrower ability in project design can achieve.[10] The process of project supervision includes those activities after a loan or credit has been approved by the executive directors, and is designed to ensure the sound execution and operation of projects and the carrying out of obligations relating to projects contained in the loan documents. It is carried out principally through the review of periodic progress reports and regular missions by staff to visit borrowers and project sites. Missions normally include engineers, agriculturists, economists or financial analysts, but may include other disciplines, such as lawyers or disbursement officers, whenever necessary. Because of the importance of having project experience fully available, consultants are only used on supervision missions where special expertise not possessed by available project staff is required. A full report is prepared within 30 calendar days after the mission's return.[11] In 1968 a system of *ex-post* evaluation of World Bank and IDA projects was established, and since then this has been steadily expanded and improved. Evaluation of projects at the end of the disbursement period, comparing actual experience with previously expected results, has become an essential element of IDA procedures. Such evaluation reports have contributed significantly to the improvement of on-going projects and have provided valuable insights into the major constraints to development. To ensure that the evaluation process is functioning properly, and that an independent assessment is made of IDA operations, a separate operations evaluation department, working since 1974 solely under the responsibility of the Director General, Operations Evaluation, conducts independent reviews, on a selective basis, and reports annually to the Board of Executive Directors.[12]

Strategy for Financing and Technical Assistance

IDA assistance is concentrated on the poorest countries where people are living in absolute poverty, for whom malnutrition, illiteracy, disease, low life expectancy and squalor are the normal conditions of life. IDA takes four main criteria into consideration in distributing its resources:[13]

(1) The poverty level in member countries.
(2) The creditworthiness of prospective IDA borrowers.
(3) The economic performance of prospective borrowers.
(4) The availability of projects suitable for IDA financing.

As the association concentrates on the very poor countries – mainly those with an annual per capita gross national product of less than $625 (in 1978 dollars), more than 50 countries are eligible under this criterion.[14] However, the dimensions of poverty can be seen in a range of indicators in addition to the level of per capita income. For example, the median life expectancy in the primarily rural agricultural countries is only 41 years and in the dualistic and better resource base groups it is about 50 years, compared with the median for industrialised countries of 70 years. It is estimated that one-third to one-half of the people in the IDA countries suffer from hunger or malnutrition in terms of both total calorie intake and protein deficiency. As a result, malnutrition is a major cause of death in children under 5 years of age, and millions of those who do not die lead impeded lives. Thus, in general, measures to alleviate poverty in IDA countries will require major efforts in the rural areas. Paralleling the concentration on the poorest countries, there has been a conscious effort during the 1970s to develop IDA projects that benefit the lowest income groups within eligible countries. Since 1977, most IDA investments are in projects carefully designed to share certain features, as follows:

(1) An effort to increase the productivity of large numbers of poor people, thus at the same time earning a good economic rate of return on the total investment.
(2) The incorporation of simple technical standards so that production techniques can eventually be afforded by persons in the lower income categories, and project costs will not be inflated because expensive, hard-to-maintain equipment has been bought.
(3) A low cost per beneficiary so that successful projects can readily be extended to other areas when additional resources become available.
(4) The inclusion of a comprehensive package of inputs (such as improved seed strains, fertilisers, access to credit, and technical assistance in the case of agricultural projects) in order to maximise the increase in productivity and income and to achieve economies of scale.

The IDA strategy in the 1970s has meant (contrary to its strategy in the 1960s) that the percentage of commitments for agriculture has increased greatly, while the percentage of commitments in the transportation sector has decreased substantially.[15] The strategy has attempted to overcome the difficulties of directing the benefits of development projects primarily toward the 'target groups' of the rural poor by continuing the financing of capital expenditure mostly for irrigation and on-farm improvements, with the provision of extension services, rural water supplies, and health and education facilities. The combination of the various components differed from project to project, but its primary objective was always the same: to raise the productivity, and with it the living conditions, of the 'target groups', which were defined in terms of per capita (and family) income appropriate for the rural poor in the recipient country. As a simple device to monitor the success in implementing the policy of directing lending in the agricultural sector primarily toward the low-income target groups, only projects with more than one-half of all direct beneficiaries in the absolute poverty groups were considered and designated as 'rural development projects', although other projects in the agricultural sector also provide financial resources and services to a large number of rural poor.[16] Reflecting the importance of the agricultural sector, nearly one-half of IDA lending (FY1978–80) was for agricultural and rural development. Investments in infrastructure (such as roads and telecommunications) are also essential for growth, including the growth in incomes of the poorest elements of the community. Credits for this purpose have continued to be an important part of IDA lending. Table 24.9 shows IDA lending by sector as percentages of total lending and operations.

TABLE 24.9 IDA Lending by Sector
(as % of total lending and operations)
(FY1978–80)

Sector	% of lending	% of operations
Agricultural and rural development	46	45
Basic infrastructure[a]	24	19
Industry and urbanisation	10	12
Other	17	22
Non-project	3	2
Total	100	100

[a] Power, telecommunications and transportation.
Source: *Additions to IDA Resources: Sixth Replenishment*, IDA/R79-145, 20 December 1979.

The need of the poorest countries for greatly expanded external assistance on concessionary terms was described in the World Bank's first World Development Report.[17] The analysis contained in that report made clear that substantial and sustained progress in reducing poverty in these countries will be impossible without acceleration of their growth rates. The mobilisation of domestic resources to achieve faster growth will require a major effort on their part, but external assistance on appropriate terms can play a critical supporting role. The bank's second World Development Report[18] pointed to a deterioration in the prospects for developing countries since the first report was prepared. The Sixth Replenishment of IDA can be seen against this general background which, it was recommended, should be taken into account in the international development strategy for the 1980s. Against this background, deputies were provided with illustrative estimates of how the economies of the countries that contribute to IDA might evolve over the medium- to long-term future in order to place the scale of the Sixth Replenishment within the context of the budgetary possibilities and resource transfer policies of contributors. It was also recommended that a larger term perspective was necessary because while contributors will be providing IDA with renewed commitment authority in the early 1980s, the actual cash impact on contributors is spread out over the decade as a whole, as IDA draws on the contributions to meet disbursements. Table 24.10 illustrates how the pattern of disbursements arising from Sixth Replenishment credits is projected, with two-thirds of disbursements occurring in the mid-1980s.

TABLE 24.10 Per cent Drawings on Commitments to IDA 6 (1981–90)

Fiscal years	Drawings %
1981	1
1982	5
1983	13
1984	20
1985	20
1986	15
1987	10
1988	7
1989	5
1990	4
—	100

Source: *Additions to IDA Resources*: Sixth Replenishment, IDA/R79-145, 20 December 1979.

The illustrative estimate made by World Bank staff for the deputies showed the Gross Domestic Product (GDP) for the group of 26 countries that contributed to the Fifth Replenishment rising in nominal terms at about 10 per cent per annum in the 1980s. According to this assumption a level of IDA 6 of $12bn would maintain the ratio of commitments by contributors to IDA at the same ratio to GDP as in IDA 5. Table 24.11 shows commitments to IDA and GDP of contributors in IDA 5 and IDA 6.

TABLE 24.11 Commitments to IDA and GDP of Contributors[a] in IDA 5 and IDA 6, FY1978–80 and FY1981–83

	IDA 5 FY1978–80	IDA 6 FY1981–83
Commitments to IDA ($bn)	8.7	12.0
GDP of contributors ($bn)	18,900.0	26,000.0
Commitments of GDP, %	0.046	0.046

[a] GDP is for the total three-year replenishment period.
Source: *Additions to IDA Resources*: Sixth Replenishment, IDA/R79-145, 20 December 1979.

Each donor country agreed to provide the IDA Sixth Replenishment in three instalments as follows: a first instalment equal to at least 29 per cent of its contribution to be notified to IDA by 8 October 1980, a second instalment equal to at least 33 per cent of its contribution to be notified to IDA by 8 October 1981, and a third instalment equal to 38 per cent of its contribution (or the balance remaining) to be notified to IDA by 8 October 1982.[19]

Problems of Implementation and Remarks from Field Experience

The experience of IDA operations has revealed a need for more emphasis on promoting the growth of institutions which can effectively administer development projects and programmes in key sectors. The inclusion of training components in an increasing number of projects, technical assistance for establishing planning units and greater emphasis on policy dialogue with member governments are also needed. Another problem area, which requires considerable attention, both during the course of supervision and *ex-post* evaluation, is the monitoring and analysis of delays in project implementation. There are no uniform standards that can be applied in judging whether a project, or particular elements of a project, should have been completed faster than was actually the case. Most measurement is done against earlier expectations which might have been unrealistic. It is essential, therefore, to ensure that project preparation and appraisal take into account all the circumstances that might affect project implementation. Identification of the problems along with the experience gained in prior projects in various countries and sectors has resulted in better prepared projects executed on a more timely basis.[20] The critical issue arising from IDA's experience is the fact that if IDA's resources remain inadequate, many high-priority development projects will have to be shelved and millions of people will be left out of the development process, with their search for productive work and a better life delayed. In the world's poorest countries, there is no shortage of projects that can be shaped to make economic and financial sense. There is, however, a shortage of resources, and in the case of IDA, this could have serious consequences, both economic and political. Domestic savings in the poorest countries are low and can be raised only gradually. Foreign sources of finance capable of providing loans on terms as favourable as those of IDA are few. IDA's effectiveness depends upon the willingness of the governments in the rich countries to contribute more resources for its replenishments, but on a politically neutral basis, in order to help build a better future for more than a billion people in desperately poor countries. The worst aspects of absolute poverty in these countries include not only low income, but also malnutrition, a high rate of child mortality, disease and ignorance. All of which can be improved by human development programmes, an area to which IDA needs to give greater attention in the coming years.

25 International Finance Corporation

Establishment and Financial Resources

Although the first suggestions for an International Finance Corporation date back to 1948, the IFC did not come into being until 1956, this long gestation period being evidence of hesitation among those officials and private groups whose co-operation was necessary. The governments of industrialised countries for some time did not see a clear need for the IFC, and when it was finally created, it was considerably weaker than its initiators had intended. Not until 1970 did it finally begin to operate with the resources and the powers originally envisaged.[1] The corporation was established as an affiliate of the World Bank, its aim being to encourage the flow of domestic and foreign capital into productive private investments in developing countries. It supplements the economic development efforts of the IBRD and IDA by filling two gaps:

(i) it supplies capital in any form, as long-term loans, equity subscriptions, or a combination of both; and
(ii) it invests without government guarantee of repayment.

When the IFC was set up, the World Bank was ten years-old and had already made efforts to help the less-developed countries build the infrastructure to support industrial growth. However, the World Bank is a lending institution, not an investment institution, and cannot supply risk capital or invest in equities. It lends only to governments or on a government guarantee, so that there was a serious gap in the World Bank structure with respect to the support of private enterprise. The IFC was established to fill this gap. According to its Articles of Agreement, 'the purpose of the Corporation is to further economic development by encouraging the growth of productive private enterprise in member countries, particularly in the less-developed areas, thus supplementing the activities of the International Bank for Reconstruction and Development'. In carrying out this purpose, the corporation shall:[2]

(1) In association with private investors, assist in financing the establishment, improvement and expansion of productive private enterprises which would contribute to the development of its member countries by making investments, without guarantee of repayment by the member government concerned, in cases where sufficient private capital is not available on reasonable terms.
(2) Seek to bring together investment opportunities, domestic and foreign private capital, and experienced management.
(3) Seek to stimulate, and to help create conditions conducive to, the flow of private capital, domestic and foreign, into productive investment in member countries.

The IFC also engages in a number of other activities designed to promote the growth of private investment. These include:

(1) Project identification and promotion.
(2) Helping to establish, finance and improve privately owned development finance companies and other institutions which are themselves engaged in promoting and financing private enterprise.
(3) Encouraging the growth of capital markets in the developing countries.
(4) Creating in the capital-exporting countries interest in portfolio investments in enterprises located in the developing countries.
(5) Giving advice and counsel to less-developed member countries on measures that will create a climate conducive to the growth of private investment.

Although intended to be an investment institution, IFC came into existence without the power to invest in equities. Accordingly, in 1960 at the Fourth Annual Meeting of the Board of Governors, a proposal to change the charter of IFC to enable investment in capital stock was favourably received. The amendment includes a provision that:

the Corporation shall not assume responsibility for managing any enterprise in which it has invested and shall not exercise rights for such purpose or for any other purpose which, in its opinion, properly is within the scope of the managerial control.

IFC was thus able to play a full part in providing and mobilising risk capital for investment in the less developed countries, able to promote projects itself and to reinforce projects in which it invested, and also able to work with sponsors in shaping and setting up investments in a way that would render them attractive to other private investors. It also became possible for IFC, through underwriting or standby commitments, to help in spreading share ownership in the developing countries. As the President of the Corporation indicated in 1961:

> One of the most important activities made possible by this charter change will be IFC's ability to assist in spreading share ownership in the developing countries. By underwriting or providing standby commitments it can provide facilities, often lacking, for the growth of capital markets.

The increase in IFC's equity operations created a new problem. The World Bank Group became aware that there was a demand for loan capital not guaranteed by member governments, and in larger amounts than IFC could supply. The problem was resolved by an amendment of the Articles of the World Bank and of IFC in FY1966/67 which enabled IFC to borrow from the World Bank up to a limit of four times its own unimpaired subscribed capital and surplus.

Originally the authorised capital stock of the IFC was $100,000,000 in terms of US$. On 3 September 1963, the authorised capital stock was increased to $110,000,000 divided into 110,000 shares of $1000 each. Table 25.1 shows the original subscriptions to capital stock of the corporation.

In replies to the author's questionnaire, IFC staff indicated that as of 30 June 1979, paid-up share capital of the corporation reached $228.6m and general reserves reached $119.0m. The staff also indicated that in addition to capital, the IFC can borrow from the IBRD up to four times its capital and unrestricted reserves, that is approximately a total of $2.0bn as of 30 June 1979. Also as of 30 June 1980, the corporation's paid-up capital reached $307m, with its capital resources provided by 113 member countries, 92 of which were developing, who collectively determined its policies and activities. Table 25.2 shows the IFC's resources and income.

TABLE 25.1 Subscriptions to Capital Stock of the International Finance Corporation

Country	Number of shares	Amount (US$)	Country	Number of shares	Amount (US$)
Australia	2,215	2,215,000	Iran	372	372,000
Austria	554	554,000	Iraq	67	67,000
Belgium	2,492	2,492,000	Israel	50	50,000
Bolivia	78	78,000	Italy	1,994	1,994,000
Brazil	1,163	1,163,000	Japan	2,769	2,769,000
Burma	166	166,000	Jordan	33	33,000
Canada	3,600	3,600,000	Lebanon	50	50,000
Ceylon	166	166,000	Luxembourg	111	111,000
Chile	388	388,000	Mexico	720	720,000
China	6,646	6,646,000	Netherlands	3,046	3,046,000
Colombia	388	388,000	Nicaragua	9	9,000
Costa Rica	22	22,000	Norway	554	554,000
Cuba	388	388,000	Pakistan	1,108	1,108,000
Denmark	753	753,000	Panama	2	2,000
Dominican Republic	22	22,000	Paraguay	16	16,000

(continued overleaf)

TABLE 25.1 (Contd.)

Country	Number of shares	Amount (US$)	Country	Number of shares	Amount (US$)
Ecuador	35	35,000	Peru	194	194,000
Egypt	590	590,000	Philippines	166	166,000
El Salvador	11	11,000	Sweden	1,108	1,108,000
Ethiopia	33	33,000	Syria	72	72,000
Finland	421	421,000	Thailand	139	139,000
France	5,815	5,815,000	Turkey	476	476,000
Germany	3,655	3,655,000	Union of South Africa	1,108	1,108,000
Greece	277	277,000	United Kingdom	14,400	14,400,000
Guatemala	22	22,000	United States	35,168	35,168,000
Haiti	22	22,000	Uruguay	116	116,000
Honduras	11	11,000	Venezuela	116	116,000
Iceland	11	11,000	Yugoslavia	443	443,000
India	4,431	4,431,000			
Indonesia	1,218	1,218,000	Total	100,000	100,000,000

Source: Articles of Agreement of the *International Finance Corporation*, 20 July 1956.

TABLE 25.2   IFC's Resources and Income
FY1976–FY81
(US $m)

	1976	1977	1978	1979	1980	1981
Capitalisation, borrowings	327	445	462	455	438	509
Paid-in capital, accumulated earnings	108	108	144	229	307	392
	78	87	100	119	140	159
Earnings, net income	7.7	8.9	12.5	19.2	20.7	19.5

Source: International Finance Corporation, *Annual Reports*, 1980, 1981.

Scope of Activities

The Scope of Operations in the 1960s [3]

IFC investments in developing countries amounted to $111.1m in 1970 compared to $15.2m in 1962 and $24.9m in 1965. Its average share in the total assistance of the World Bank Group to developing countries reached a level of 3.5 per cent during 1962–70 compared to 25.9 per cent for IDA and 70.4 per cent for IBRD during the same period. By 30 June 1971, the cumulative gross total of the IFC's investments in business enterprises amounted to $577.8m, invested in 172 enterprises in 47 developing countries. Other investors had provided $2465m for those enterprises, making a total investment in them of $3043m. This means that for every dollar invested by IFC others have concurrently invested over four dollars. The ratio of cumulative gross commitments: cumulative total project costs was subject to yearly fluctuations during the period 1961–67, but showed a steady increase in the last three years of the decade, 1968–70. The equity:loan ratio expanded rapidly during 1961–67, but did not show a continuation of the trend during 1968–70. Thus IFC did not exercise any kind of policy to fix the share of its contributions or to design a desired form of its portfolio. The actual proportion of equity to loan in any given investment varied depending on the needs of the enterprise being financed and on the relationship between the risk and the overall return to IFC as an investor. Table 25.3 shows IFC total commitments and portfolio (cumulative) during the period 1961–70.

In its earlier operations IFC concentrated on finance for the manufacturing industry, but at the end of the 1960s, the corporation was in a position to provide broader investment, for example in tourism and

TABLE 25.3 IFC Total Commitments and Portfolio (Cumulative) during the Period 1961–70 (US $m)

Activities	Fiscal years									
	1961	1962	1963	1964	1965	1966	1967	1968	1969	1970
Gross commitments,[a] cumulative	51.2	72.2	90.6	111.4	137.0	172.4	221.4	271.8	364.7	476.5
Total projects[b] costs, cumulative	230.5	373.9	529.8	768.1	927.5	1062.1	1397.9	1632.0	2116.4	2609.2
The ratio (1:2) %	22.2	19.3	17.1	14.5	14.7	16.2	15.8	16.6	17.2	18.2
Portfolio held[c] by IFC										
Loans	35.4	48.4	46.1	46.0	49.6	60.8	84.1	105.2	125.9	180.7
Equity	—	5.1	13.2	21.3	24.0	35.0	49.7	55.6	72.5	98.4
Equity Loan ratio (%)	—	10.5	28.6	46.3	48.3	57.5	59.0	52.8	57.1	54.4

[a] Included commitments made from 1956.
[b] Total new investment, by IFC and others, in assisted enterprises.
[c] Included commitments which have been signed but on which funds may not be withdrawn until certain legal formalities have been completed and other conditions fulfilled.

Source: Original data from IFC *Annual Report*, 1970.

utilities. There was also more substantial involvement in pulp and paper and in fertilisers. The cumulative total of IFC commitments by type of business is listed in Table 25.4 by order. The percentage distribution indicates that cement and other construction materials, pulp and paper products, and textiles and fibres formed about one-third of IFC total commitments. Fertilisers, iron and steel, developing finance companies and mining formed another third and the rest was with the other activities listed in the table.

TABLE 25.4 IFC Commitments by Type of Business Cumulative Totals (1957–71) (US $m)

Type of business	US $m	Percentage of the total
Cement and other construction materials	71.52	12.3
Pulp and paper products	69.78	12.0
Textiles and fibres	60.05	10.3
Fertilisers	56.60	9.7
Iron and steel	54.62	9.4
Development finance companies	53.17	9.1
Mining	36.74	6.3
Other manufacturing	36.50	6.3
Chemical and petro-chemical products	35.75	6.3
Machinery	34.45	5.9
Food and food processing	24.16	4.1
Utilities, printing and publishing	23.50	4.0
Tourism	20.50	3.5
Money and capital markets	0.70	0.1
Total	578.04	100

Source: Commitments in US $m from International Finance Corporation, *Annual Report*, 1971.

The IFC geographical distribution of its investments by region during the period 1962–70 indicates that Latin America was the main recipient of its assistance (as in the case of the World Bank) with an average of 40.2 per cent compared to 6.2 per cent of IDA. The Near East and Asia were the second most important recipients (also as in the case of the World Bank) with an average of 23.1 per cent compared to 66.2 per cent of IDA, while Africa received 20.2 per cent of total IFC investments (compared to 20.5 per cent of IDA), East Asia 12.7 per cent and Europe 3.6 per cent during the same period. Table 25.5 shows the

TABLE 25.5 Geographical Distribution of IFC's Investment to Developing Countries (US $m) (1962/63–1970/71)

Regions	1962	1963	1964	1965	1966	1967	1968	1969	1970
Near East and South Asia	4.4	1.3	6.6	8.3	5.7	14.9	a	26.1	29.6
(Average 23.1%)	(28.9)	(6.1)	(34.0)	(33.3)	(16.1)	(32.4)	—	(30.1)	(26.6)
Latin America	7.7	10.0	6.8	10.2	23.9	11.6	17.2	26.6	33.7
(Average 40.2%)	(50.6)	(47.6)	(35.0)	(40.9)	(67.7)	(25.2)	(34.0)	(30.6)	(30.3)
East Asia	—	4.4	1.5	—	1.6	12.0	4.2	24.0	21.1
(Average 12.7%)	—	(20.9)	(7.7)	—	(4.5)	(26.1)	(8.3)	(27.6)	(18.9)
Africa	—	5.0	4.5	5.9	4.1	7.2	29.2	9.9	16.7
(Average 20.2%)	—	(23.8)	(23.1)	(23.6)	(11.6)	(15.6)	(57.8)	(11.4)	(15.0)
Europe	3.0	0.3	a	0.5	a	0.2	—	—	10.0
(Average 3.6%)	(19.7)	(1.4)	—	(2.0)	—	(0.4)	—	—	(9.0)

(—) Percentage of total activities to developing countries,
a Less than $50,000
Source: US Overseas Loans and Grants and Assistance from International Organisations, Special Report Prepared for the House Foreign Affairs Committee, 1971.

geographical distribution of IFC's investments to developing countries during this period.

The Scope of Operations in the 1970s

During the fiscal year 1973, 28 investments in 18 countries were made, The IFC's new commitments, in loan and equity, and in underwriting agreements, totalled $146.7m. During this year the corporation for the first time made investments in Afghanistan, Bolivia and Cyprus. The cumulative total of its commitments, $848.1m, represents the gross amount invested by IFC in the seventeen years since 1956. Of this total, $334 (39 per cent) was invested in Latin America and the Caribbean, $232.2m (27 per cent) in Asia, $145m (17 per cent) in Africa and the Middle East, and $135.9m (16 per cent) in Europe.[4] The IFC's investments in FY 1974 totalled a record $203.4m. During this year, it made 32 investments, in loan and equity, in 19 developing countries and for the first time made investments in the Dominican Republic, Israel and Jordan. The cumulative gross total of the corporation's investments since 1956 reached in FY1974 $1049.1m, in 225 enterprises in 54 developing countries. Of this cumulative total, $465m (44.3 per cent) was in Latin America and the Caribbean, $251.5m (24 per cent) in Asia, $173.6m (16.5 per cent) in Europe, $108m (10.3 per cent) in Africa and $50m (4.8 per cent) in the Middle East.[5] The consequences of recession, inflation and the contraction of the international capital market were increasingly felt in the sphere of private direct investment during FY 1975. In this year 33 investments in loan and equity, totalling $211.7m, were made by the IFC. These commitments were made to 32 enterprises in 20 developing countries. In 1975 the IFC also for the first time made investments in Cameroon, Nepal and Paraguay. Its operations in FY1975 brought the cumulative gross total of the corporation's investments, since its establishment, to $1262m in 249 enterprises in 57 developing countries, in which others had concurrently invested approximately $5131m. Of this cumulative total of IFC investments, $545m (43 per cent) was committed in Latin America and the Caribbean, $307m (24 per cent) in Asia, $238m (19 per cent) in Europe, $113m (9 per cent) in Africa and $59m (5 per cent) in the Middle East.[6] FY1976 marked the twentieth anniversary of the establishment of the IFC. In this year it invested a greater total amount in more developing countries than in any previous year: 33 investments, in loan and equity $245.3m, were made, in 33 enterprises in 23 developing countries, three more than in FY 1975. In FY 1976 IFC also for the first time made investments in

Egypt, Malawi, Rwanda and Uruguay. The IFC's operations in FY1976 brought the cumulative gross total of the corporation's investments, since it was established, to $1505m in 271 enterprises in 61 developing countries, in which others had concurrently invested approximately $6300m. Of the cumulative total of the IFC commitments, $582m (39 per cent) was invested in Latin America and the Caribbean, $382m (25 per cent) in Asia, $329m (22 per cent) in Europe, $147m (10 per cent) in Africa, and $65m (4 per cent) in the Middle East.[7] In FY1977, the Board of Governors agreed on a resolution to make the first capital increase in the history of the corporation to member countries, with a total of $480m allocated for subscription. It had become clear that the original capitalisation of approximately $100m was increasingly inadequate for the IFC to carry out effectively its function as a catalytic factor to attract other sources of capital, domestic and private, into productive investment in the private and mixed sectors of its developing country membership. In the context of the capital increase, the directors in January 1977 reviewed the future activities and directions of the IFC. Strong emphasis was given to its role as a development institution, whose fundamental concern was the economic development of its member countries through assistance to private enterprise, including the 'mixed' sector. The objective of the capital increase was to permit a considerable expansion in the number and volume of operations, and also a wider range of activity. In particular, there was a clear endorsement of the objective of substantially expanding activities in the poorer countries. The IFC hoped substantially to increase the number of its operations in the smaller and economically least developed among its members in Latin America, Asia and Africa, particularly the latter. The subject of resource development, especially of energy resources and of non-fuel minerals, also received considerable attention as a result of the shortages of the early 1970s and of the increases in energy prices. Based upon this background, IFC continued its efforts in FY1977 to encourage productive private enterprise in the developing countries by itself investing in projects that either established new business or expanded, modernised or diversified existing business. IFC played a major role in bringing together foreign investors and companies in developing countries; in assisting purely domestic enterprises which needed finance, either equity or loan finance or both; and in technical assistance of the type which IFC can provide as a result of its international investment experience. In FY1977, the Board of Directors of the IFC approved loan and equity investments totalling $258.9m in 34 enterprises in 20 developing countries. Commitments of $206.7m were made to 33 enterprises during that period, and during this year the first investment was made in Madagascar. The cumulative gross total of the IFC's commitments, since it was established, reached $1712m. Of this cumulative total, $663m (39 per cent) was invested in Latin America and the Caribbean, $411m (24 per cent) in Asia, $392m (23 per cent) in Europe, $180m (10 per cent) in Africa, and $65m (4 per cent) in the Middle East.[8]

During FY 1978, the IFC significantly expanded both the volume and scope of its activities and at the same time reoriented its operations to prepare for the capital increase approved by the Board of Governors. In this year, the Board of Directors approved $338.4m in loan and equity investments for 41 projects in 31 countries throughout the developing world, and investments were undertaken for the first time in Mali, Lesotho, Swaziland, the Yemen Arab Republic and Trinidad and Tobago. In FY1978, IFC-approved investments were broadly distributed geographically with 16 in Latin America and the Caribbean (of which 8 were in South America), 12 in Africa, 6 in Asia, 4 in Europe, and 3 in the Middle East. Of the cumulative total of IFC investments since 1956, $604m (29 per cent) was invested in Europe and the Middle East, $587m (28 per cent) in LAC II, $423m (20 per cent) in Asia, $248m (12 per cent) in LAC I,[9] and $241m (11 per cent) in Africa. During this year, a large number of approved projects were in the least advanced of the IFC's member countries. About half were in countries with a per capita gross national product of less than $520 per annum and about 70 per cent of the projects were in countries whose per capita GNP was less than $1075 per annum.

The action taken by IFC's Board of Governors in November 1977 to increase IFC's authorised capital from $110m to $650m was an important milestone in its history. In response to its changed circumstances, the IFC developed a Five-year Programme not only to achieve an orderly expansion, but also to direct its activities in such a way as to maximise their contribution to economic development. The programme was considered and approved by IFC's Board of Directors in April 1978.[10] FY1979 was the IFC's first year of operations following the Board of Directors' approval of the five-year programme to significantly expand and reorient IFC's activities. With the additional resources of its capital increase, the IFC increased its investment activities, as called for in the programme. It also moved ahead rapidly towards a long-term reorientation of its operations – especially with respect to increasing its activities in the least developed regions and developing natural resources, particularly energy resources. In this year, the Board approved

$425.4m in loan and equity investments for 48 projects in 33 developing countries with particular attention to its lower income member countries. Of these, 52 per cent were in countries with per capita GNP of less than $581 per year compared with 42 per cent in FY1978. IFC's approved investments in FY1979 were broadly distributed geographically with 14 projects in Latin America, 12 in Africa, 14 in Asia, 5 in Europe and 3 in the Middle East.[11] As for FY1980, the IFC was expanding and reorienting its operations in line with previously established priorities. Supported by the increase in its capital, it continued to expand the volume of its investment activities in real terms. Both the number of projects and the number of investments approved by the Board of Directors expanded rapidly during FY1980. The total dollar volume of equity and loan investments reached $681m, about $45m of which was for equity investments. The number of projects undertaken in the least developed and smaller member countries continued to increase: 28 projects, or roughly half of the total, were in countries with a per capita GNP of less than $625 per year. These efforts were particularly related to the poorest countries, with less than $361 per capita GNP, where 15 investments were approved during FY1980. In this year, IFC's approved investments were broadly distributed geographically with 15 projects in Africa, 17 in Asia, 7 in Europe and the Middle East and 16 in Latin America and the Caribbean. By dollar volume, Africa accounted for 16 per cent of the total investments in FY1980, Asia 15 per cent, Europe and the Middle East 13 per cent and Latin America and the Caribbean 56 per cent.[12] Table 25.6 shows IFC's operations during the period 1975–81.

Terms and Conditions

In replies to the author's questionnaire sheet, the staff of the corporation indicated the following:

Interest Rate: based on commercial rates ($11\frac{1}{4}$ and $11\frac{1}{2}$ fixed rate – at the time the questionnaire sheet was filled in 25 January 1980).
Repayment Period: any but most commonly between 7–12 years.
Grace Period: based on construction time for project, generally about 2–3 years.
Guarantee: No government guarantees required or asked for.

According to Article III, section 3-v, the IFC undertakes its financing

TABLE 25.6 IFC's Operations FY1975–FY1981
(US $m)

	1975	1976	1977	1978	1979	1980	1981
Approved investments							
Number of projects	29	33	34	41	48	55	56
Number of countries	20	22	21	31	33	30	34
Amount (gross $s)	232	236	259	338	425	681	811
Total project costs	1,526	1,383	1,228	1,872	1,714	2,377	3,340
Cumulative approvals							
Number of projects	324	357	391	432	480	535	588
Amount (gross $s)	1,270	1,506	1,765	2,103	2,528	3,209	4,063
Total project costs	6,421	7,804	9,032	10,904	12,618	14,995	18,493
Syndications	360	440	548	688	890	1,157	1,559
Investments held							
Number of firms	—	187	200	225	253	288	314
Loans	517	627	704	799	889	1,159	1,374
Equity	142	152	160	184	223	245	273
Total	659	779	864	983	1,112	1,404	1,647

Sources: IFC Operations in 1975: International Finance Corporation, *Annual Report*, 1979. IFC Operations in 1976–81: International Finance Corporation, *Annual Report*, 1981.

on terms and conditions which it considers appropriate, taking into account the requirements of the enterprise, the risks being undertaken by the corporation and the terms and conditions normally obtained by private investors for similar financing.[13] According to its 'Operational Guideline', the IFC before entering into an investment must be satisfied that the project is to the economic benefit of the host country, and at the same time, it must be potentially profitable. The IFC always invests with others and, in line with its objectives of encouraging private sector development, in conjunction with local interest. It provides its financing on commercial terms but is flexible with regard to the type or manner of financing. It lends or makes equity investments in any combination depending upon the financing needs of the project. It normally lends at fixed rates for periods ranging from seven to twelve years but is, however, willing to lend for longer terms if necessary for prudent and successful project implementation. Its financing is not limited to the foreign exchange portion of the project nor to specific purchases, but may be used for any legitimate business purpose related to the project. The only requirement is that it be spent in one of the member countries of the World Bank or in Switzerland.[14]

Management and Organisational Structure

The ultimate authority of the IFC is lodged with the Board of Governors of member countries. Operations are carried out under the authority of the Board of Directors appointed by member countries. Day-to-day operations are under the supervision of the Executive Vice-President, who is appointed by the directors. All the powers of the corporation are vested in the Board of Governors. Each governor or deputy governor of the World Bank appointed by a member of the World Bank which is also a member of the corporation, is *ex officio* a governor or deputy governor, respectively, of the corporation. The Board of Governors may delegate to the Board of Directors authority to exercise any of its powers, except the power to:

(1) Admit new members and determine the conditions of their admission.
(2) Increase or decrease the capital stock.
(3) Suspend a member.
(4) Decide appeals from interpretations of the Articles of Agreement given by the Board of Directors.
(5) Make arrangements to co-operate with other international organisations (other than informal arrangements of a temporary and administrative character).
(6) Decide to suspend permanently the operations of the corporation and to distribute its assets.
(7) Declare dividends.
(8) Amend the Articles of Agreement.

The Board of Directors is composed, *ex officio*, of all executive Directors of the World Bank. Each director who is an appointed executive director of the bank is entitled to cast the number of votes which the member by which he was so appointed is entitled to cast in the IFC. The Board of Directors meet as often as the business of the corporation may require. The President of the World Bank is, *ex officio*, the Chairman of the Board of Directors of the corporation, but has no vote except a deciding vote in case of an equal division. He may also participate in meetings of the Board of Governors, but without a vote at such meetings. In the affairs of the corporation, each member country has 250 votes plus one additional vote for each share of stock held, with all matters decided by a majority of the votes cast.

Approaches and Techniques Applied

The purpose of the IFC is to further economic development by encouraging the growth of productive private enterprise in member countries. Thus the corporation assists in financing the establishment, improvement and expansion of productive private enterprises, seeks to bring together investment opportunities, domestic and foreign private capital and experienced management, and seeks to stimulate and create conditions conducive to the flow of private capital. Although the above, taken from questionnaire answers, is not directly related to the main issue of the techniques of project appraisal conducted by the corporation, it can nevertheless be considered as a background for the approaches and techniques adopted by the IFC.

The Articles of Agreement of the IFC related to financing operations state:

> The Corporation may make investments of its funds in productive private enterprises in the territories of its members. The existence of government or other public interest in such an enterprise shall not necessarily preclude the Corporation from making an investment therein.[15]

Prior to the formation of the Corporation, World Bank financing of relatively small-scale private enterprise was undertaken through loans to commercial and investment banks and development finance companies. The bank soon discovered, however, that, apart from well-established investment banks in the developed countries there was a lack of institutions prepared to undertake long- and medium-term financing of private enterprise. If this kind of lending were to be undertaken in most of the less developed world, therefore the bank would have to participate in bringing such institutions into being. This situation changed rapidly, beginning in the early 1960s. Before 1962 most of the World Bank's promotional work on development finance companies (DFCs) had been carried out by special consultants. The appraisal of such companies in preparation for loans and credits was done by the staff of the Industry Division of the Technical Operations Department, and no-one in that division devoted full time to DFCs, though two or three had specialised in the area. In January 1962, the work was transferred to a Development Finance Company Division of the IFC, and the staff were put on a full-time basis.[16] An appraisal of the contribution of DFCs to economic development takes into account the following:

(i) their relative success in channelling investment and entrepreneurship into financially viable enterprises;
(ii) their success in mobilising savings and contributing to the creation of functioning capital markets; and
(iii) the social costs and benefits of DFC investments as compared to possible alternatives.

Based upon the above the IFC's special role is to mobilise private resources on commercial terms for development projects where a market-oriented approach is not only applicable but economically preferable and where the projects would not be undertaken in a timely or appropriate way without the corporation's participation. It also promotes investments by facilitating the process by which the investors, and often the host governments, can arrive at mutually satisfactory agreements. In this matter, the IFC recognises that the degree to which private sector resources can contribute to economic development depends upon the needs and circumstances of each member country. Thus it supports projects varying from purely private to mixed public/private ventures and even wholly-owned government enterprises where they act as channels for assistance to the private sector.[17] In addition, since it recognises that the Euro-currency market offers scope for mobilising additional private capital for the developing countries, the IFC offers the developing countries the opportunity of obtaining financing jointly from the corporation and from the Euro-currency market, aiming at enabling them to improve the terms and conditions of their overall investment financing. Much of the current Euro-lending is being done on the basis of broad syndication, with the accent on risk-distribution rather than on an analysis of the creditworthiness of the borrower. The appraisal which is an integral part of all the IFC's investments aims at reducing the risk of potential lenders, and improving the terms and conditions of the credit for borrowers. The corporation provides its own financing on terms which make the total financial package more suited to the requirements of the borrower.[18] IFC gives increasing attention to project development, with the object of identifying situations in which private enterprise, local and foreign, could make a contribution to local economic development. To expand those initiatives undertaken in the course of normal operations, and by special missions, the Department of Investment Promotion and Special Projects was created in 1973, with the specific responsibility for promoting projects from their conception, particularly in the corporation's least developed member countries. Such countries include those where, because of the absence of a sufficiently developed indigenous private entrepreneurial class and of local capital resources, or because public sector initiative has been predominant, local and foreign private industrial investment has not made a significant contribution to development. As is known, the task of developing projects requires exceptional efforts to bring together knowledge of relevant government policies, local and external markets, appropriate technology, and available financial and human resources.[19] The IFC continues to give attention to this task and to broadening its co-operation with the private sector, host governments and interested international institutions, but it is not clear what sort of criteria and alternative approaches it follows. The corporation does not adopt a manual for project appraisal and implementation, because it operates in close contact with the World Bank, using its facilities and research work on developing countries.

As a financial institution, IFC performance must also be measured against financial criteria. The ventures it assists must therefore be financially sound and potentially profitable. By maintaining and applying these investment criteria the corporation can attract business and financial partners to its investment, turn over its capital by selling its investments, and do its best to ensure that the projects it supports do not become economic liabilities to its member countries. In addition, the earnings from its investments defray administrative costs, support project promotion and technical assistance programmes, and are an important source of funds for expanding the volume of business.[20] These criteria of course apply to any financial institution seeking maximisation of its profits, but are not necessarily independent criteria for a development financial institution seeking to contribute to economic and financial development in developing countries. The paucity of capital markets in developing countries, and their non-existence in the least developed countries, impedes the application of the general rule that the corporation should not tie itself down but should enlarge its techniques and approaches to reach the least developed countries. In doing this, the IFC should seek to be a unique developmental financial institution with its own approach and criteria for the benefit of developing countries in general and least developed countries in particular.

Strategy for Financing and Technical Assistance

In April 1978, the Board approved a five-year programme (FY1979–83) which set forth new operational priorities and objectives for the IFC, following the emergence of a situation where for various external and internal reasons, it was essential for its operations to be undertaken within a better defined strategy and programme framework. The programme reflected the corporation's efforts to ensure that the capital increase approved by its member countries is deployed most effectively. It focuses on four primary targets.[21]

(1) Broadening country coverage, including a greater emphasis on the least developed regions.
(2) Setting country programme objectives responsive to the development priorities and circumstances of its member countries.
(3) Using the corporation's enhanced ability to play an increasingly important role as an intermediary in international investment flows.
(4) Increasing non-project-related policy assistance aimed at improving the environment for private enterprise and enhancing its contribution to economic and social development.

In contrast with the IFC's operations in FY1973–77, the proposed operational programme for FY1979–83 called for a substantial real increase. The aggregate number of investments approved by the corporation's Board was planned to rise from a level of 159 between FY1973–77 to 275 between FY1979–83. The aggregate volume of the corporation's approvals (including amounts syndicated) was planned nearly to double from an actual level US$1.11bn between FY1973–77 to around US$2.1bn, in constant 1978 dollars, for the five-year period FY1979–83. The annual volume of approvals was planned to rise from around US$306m in FY1978 to around US$510m by FY1983, or at an annual rate of real growth of around 11 per cent in the dollar volume over the period. In current terms, the dollar volume over the five years was planned to amount to about US$2.6bn. Table 25.7 shows the corporation's indicative operational programme for FY1979–83. The programme represented a major relative shift in the focus of the IFC's efforts towards lesser developed regions and towards lesser developed countries within regions. It called for increases in the relative shares of Africa and LAC I at the expense of declining relative shares in Asia and Europe and the Middle East. The share of operations in LAC II was

TABLE 25.7 IFC's 'Indicative' Operational Programme for FY1979–83[a] (US $m)

	FY73–77	FY78	FY79	FY80	FY81	FY82	FY83	FY79–83	Increase[b] %
Board Approvals									
No. of investments	159	40	45	51	56	60	63	275	73
Annual growth rate %			13	13	10	7	5	9	
Programme in constant 1978 dollars									
IFC's own account		206	226	249	286	323	358	1,442	102
of which equity		(20)	(30)	(41)	(55)	(66)	(76)	(268)	195
Participations		100	113	124	135	142	149	663	67
Gross approvals		306	339	373	421	465	507	2,105	90

[a] The figures for FY73–77 are actuals in current dollars – the figures for FY78 are based on actuals for the first half of the fiscal year and projected for the second half. All figures for FY79 onwards are projected.
[b] FY79–83 over FY73–77; gross increase for the five-year period.
Source: International Finance Corporation, *Five-year Programme FY79–83*, March, 1978.

expected to increase only marginally. In absolute terms, however, there was an across-the-board increase in all regions.[22] Table 25.8 shows the corporation's indicative regional distribution of investment for 1979-83 compared with FY1973-77.

Over the programme period, an increasing proportion of the IFC's investments was planned to be directed to natural resource development, particularly energy resources. The corporation felt that it could effectively contribute to an international effort aimed at developing the substantial potential resources of fuel and non-fuel minerals which exist in the developing countries, feeling that it could do so by operating as an equity investor working to create a more stable investment environment and helping to raise the large amounts of funds needed for these projects.

As for future strategy for financing and technical assistance, the staff of the IFC indicated in the questionnaire sheet that the IFC's future financing strategy would be directed to the least developed regions and within countries into the least developed parts. They also indicated that although most investments are in the area of manufacturing, the corporation is giving increased attention to the development of renewable and non-renewable natural resources. Technical assistance is worldwide among member countries mainly in the financial sector in various financial institutions, provided at the request of member governments on the basis of resource availability.

Problems of Implementation and Remarks from Field Experience

The staff of the IFC indicated in the questionnaire sheet that implementation responsibility remains in the hands of the project sponsor. Regular follow-up and supervision is part of the corporation assistance to the firms it finances, but although it takes equity in firms, it does not participate in active management of these firms. This leads to different problems at the stage of implementation in different firms, but not at the same levels, and suggests that some consideration should be given to this issue in the near future, perhaps by amending the corporation's Articles of Agreement to give it more role to play in the management of the firms in which it has equity participation. However, as part of the corporation's programme (FY1979-83), and in anticipation of accelerated lending operations, it has introduced new systems to strengthen the internal review and evaluation of its activities. In addition, the IFC has strengthened its regular project supervision reviews. The new process includes a requirement that upon physical

TABLE 25.8 'Indicative' Regional Distribution of IFC Investments (FY1973–77 and FY1979–83)

Regions[a]	FY73–77		FY78		FY79–83		Increase in	
	No.	Share %	No.	Share %	No.	Share %	No.	Share %
Africa	31	19.5	10	25.0	75	27.3	+142	+ 7.8
Asia	46	28.9	7	17.5	51	18.5	+ 11	−10.4
Europe/M.E.	38	23.9	8	20.0	53	19.3	+ 39	− 4.6
Central America (LAC I)	20	12.6	8	20.0	51	18.5	+155	+ 5.9
South America (LAC II)	24	15.1	7	17.5	45	16.4	+ 88	+ 1.3
Total	159	100.0	40	100.0	275	100.0	+ 73	—

[a] This regional breakdown corresponds to IFC's Investment Departments. In this connection, it is important to note that Egypt is included in the Middle East; Mexico, Colombia, Guyana, Venezuela, and the Caribbean countries are included in LAC I; while LAC II includes Ecuador, Peru, Chile, Bolivia, Brazil, Argentina, Paraguay and Uruguay.

Source: International Finance Corporation, Five-year Programme FY79–83, March, 1978.

completion, the future prospects of each investment project be assessed against its original objectives.[23]

The staff of the IFC indicated that the most difficult area is in project definition and preparation, although here the corporation provides extensive assistance to project sponsors. Whether or not this is a sufficient solution to the problems facing the corporation in the stage of follow-up projects, remains an open question for the future management of the corporation. They should give great attention in the near future to policies for project identification, definition, appraisal and follow-up and implementation, that is, policies related to the project cycle based upon a concrete manual for project appraisal, taking into consideration all the management problems that the corporation has faced in the field. In addition, the corporation should carry out an international investment strategy by devising new methods to allow its member countries to assess and compare across national borders various opportunities, taking into consideration the different political, economic and market contexts as well as the respective accounting methods that should be used. This would obviously add a new dimension to the IFC's activities.

Appendix I A Profile Summary of Selected Aid Agencies

DAC Development Agencies

Name and address of agency	Establishment and financial resources	Scope of activities	Terms and conditions
1. **Agency for International Development (AID)** 320, 21st Street NW Washington DC 20523 Telephone: (202) 632-1850 Telex: 440001 AIDWNDC USA	Established in 1961 under the Foreign Assistance Act. Acting as an Agency for the US Government's foreign economic aid activities.	Extending development loans repayable in dollars and tied to US Commodities and Services. Grants and technical assistance for emergencies and certain contributions to international development organisations. AID's development assistance programme consists of integrated project assistance in the sectors of food and nutrition (including agricultural production and rural development), health and population, education and human resource development.	Loans and grants at concessional terms.

Management	Approaches and techniques applied	Strategy for financing and technical assistance	Problems of implementation and remarks from field experience
Aid programme to be administered by an officer to be appointed by the President in a unit within the State Department.	AID missions and bureaux evaluate each of their operational non-capital assistance projects annually. Special evaluations of projects, subsector and sector, country programmes and assistance problems and techniques. A manual and work sheets are provided.	To encourage the recipient country to assume the leadership in planning, managing and evaluating development projects and programmes which are financially assisted by AID. To assist developing countries in pursuing basic human needs.	Experience confirms the need for complete and periodic coverage for most AID activities to measure progress and to reassess relevance. AID has found that the effective management of project level assistance requires a system of complete and periodic coverage with simplified but vigorous evaluation.

Name and address of agency	Establishment and financial resources	Scope of activities	Terms and Conditions
2. Overseas Development Administration Eland House, Stag Place London SW1 5DH Telephone: 01 213 4900 Telex: 263907-ODM LDN UK	A semi-autonomous unit within the Foreign and Commonwealth Office. Financial resources and administration costs are financed directly from the British budget.	Extending soft loans to developing countries (mainly Commonwealth countries) in the form of project aid and programme aid. Areas of concern are mainly water supply, roads, communications, education and power stations.	Countries with low per capita incomes, who form the bulk of the recipients, usually receive interest-free loans. Assistance to Asia, Latin American countries and Turkey is generally wholly tied to procurement from the UK.

Management	Approaches and techniques applied	Strategy for financing and technical assistance	Problems of implementation and remarks from field experience
One of the junior ministers under the Secretary of State for Foreign and Commonwealth Affairs has the title Minister for Overseas Development. All powers legally belonging not to the Minister but to the Foreign Secretary under the Conservative government, the Ministry of Overseas Development transferred into a part of the Foreign and Commonwealth office under the title Overseas Development Administration.	The Ministry of Overseas Development has prepared a *Guide to the Economic Appraisal of Projects in Developing Countries*. The Overseas Development Administration has prepared a series of 'Project Data Handbooks', covering different projects based upon their experience in different sectors in developing countries.	Greatest possible increase in the standard of living of the population of developing countries over a period of time and the optimisation of income flows.	Aid has been concentrated on individual projects and in most countries it did not provide a sufficient number of projects in any one sector to justify the sectoral approach. Statistics on technical assistance have not been well organised and there is little data on how technical assistance was distributed between sectors.

Name and address of agency	Establishment and financial resources	Scope of activities	Terms and conditions
3. **Commonwealth Development Corporation (CDC)** 33 Hill St. London W1A3AR Telephone: 01-629 8484 Telex: 21431 UK	A public corporation established by Act of Parliament in 1948 as the Colonial Development Corporation originally to assist the economic development of the then British-dependent territories. The Minister may, by order made with the consent of the Treasury, increase the long- and medium-term borrowing powers to £570m, of which not more than £550m comes from exchequer funds.	CDC operates on broadly commercial lines and it does not make grants, but offers investment in the development of resources in countries in which it is empowered to operate in development projects. It is empowered to undertake, either alone or in association with others, projects for the promotion or expansion of economic development enterprises covering basic development, primary production and processing and industry and commerce.	CDC does not normally make short-term loans. Its investments are not tied to UK procurement or British sponsors.

Profile Summary of Selected Aid Agencies 407

Management	Approaches and techniques applied	Strategy for financing and technical assistance	Problems of implementation and remarks from field experience
CDC operates through a decentralised structure with regional offices (Caribbean, Asia, Pacific Islands, East and Central, Southern and West Africa) and a number of country representatives. Investment and policy guidelines are made by the CDC Board whose members are appointed by the Minister for Overseas Development.	Approaches to CDC should usually be to the Regional Controller or have his support. The investigations department appraises projects in consultation with other specialist departments. Financial analysis of projects is usually followed by an economic cost-benefit analysis.	Gradual expansion in countries where CDC is already operational and into new developing countries. Priority is given primarily to RNR projects but also to public utilities and industry.	Usually centre around cost escalations and financial control. CDC attaches utmost importance to sound management of projects. Developing countries, and particularly the least developed of them, need help from effective and experienced management to ensure that projects are carried out as planned.

Name and address of agency	Establishment and financial resources	Scope of activities	Terms and conditions
4. **Caisse Central de Coopération Economique (CCCE)** 233 Boulevard Saint-Germain Paris viie Telephone: 551-62-83 Telex: CAISCOP Paris 20-750 France	A public corporation with independent legal personality with a capital of Ffr 200m since 1978. Capacity for financing is Ffr1bn, mainly from long-term borrowing by issuing bonds.	Operates on a project basis, with an emphasis on project-type production projects, mainly agricultural and industrial. Long-term loans are the main principal form of its assistance. It is the executive agent of the Fund of Aid and Co-operation in Tropical Africa, of the Ministry of Foreign Affairs technical assistance programme and of government loans from Treasury Funds.	Interest Rate: first window; average rate 5.8%. Favourable conditions can be applied for poorest countries (1.5% for the first ten years, 2% afterwards). Second window; market rate. Repayment 10–20 years. Grace period up to 10 years. Government guarantee always required.

Profile Summary of Selected Aid Agencies

Management	Approaches and techniques applied	Strategy for financing and technical assistance	Problems of implementation and remarks from field experience
CCCE is subject to ministerial supervision jointly exercised by the Ministry of Finance (Treasury) and the minister responsible for the country under consideration. CCCE is led by a managing director appointed to a supervisory board 'Conseil de Surveillance'. The Chairman of the Board is designated by the Minister of Finance. As from 1 March 1981, the organisational structure of CCCE has been based on geographical distribution: Western Africa, Central Africa and Eastern and Indian Ocean. For each department there are two units: economic and financial, and technical.	CCCE takes no initiative in launching projects; it can only deal with applications submitted by states or their national institutions. Applications are studied both by the local agency and by the Paris Foreign Financing Department, with the technical support of the experts of the Development Department. If the dossier is accepted, it is then submitted to the Board for a decision.	Solving the crop problem (the food problems) and raising productivity in the agricultural sector. CCCE intends to organise its strategy for financing on the basis of 30% for the infrastructural projects sector and 70% for the productive projects sector. Financing technical assistance provided by CCCE is mainly related to solving the problems of management, financial experts, education, and promotion of development banks.	Problems related to the quality of technical leadership in rural development, the standing and competence of industry, strict management of public utility companies, and to the balanced operation of public utility services. Developing countries, and those most underdeveloped, should help the 'Aid Agencies' in proceeding accurately along the stages of project appraisal. Co-operation between both sides is a must.

Name and address of agency	Establishment and financial resources	Scope of activities	Terms and conditions
5. Deutsche Entwicklungsgesellschaft (DEG) German Development Company Belvederestrasse 40 D-5000 Köln 41 (Cologne) Telephone: (02 21) 49861 Telex: 8881949 8883470 Federal Republic of Germany	Set up by the Federal German Government in 1962 for the purpose of encouraging and supporting private investment activities in developing countries. A non-profit-making institution, but it operates on normal business principles to the extent that this is compatible with its general objectives.	DEG invests in private enterprises in developing countries by participating in their equity capital, granting loans and advising enterprises interested in investments in developing countries. It endeavours to bring together prospective investment partners in joint ventures. DEG concentrates its activities on the establishment or expansion of small and medium-sized enterprises in the form of joint ventures in the industrial, agricultural and tourist sectors.	DEG does not normally provide more than half of the total finance required, and projects must eventually be capable of self-financing. In general, DEG charges 1.5% of its commitments (capital participation and/or loan with equity features) as a contribution to the appraisal costs and advisory services rendered in connection with the project.

Profile Summary of Selected Aid Agencies 411

Management	Approaches and techniques applied	Strategy for financing and technical assistance	Problems of implementation and remarks from field experience
Supervising Board, General Management and Executive Management Board; Chief Executive and staff. Geographical units: Central and South America, South West Europe, Africa, Asia, and the Middle East and Mediteranean countries, South East Europe.	Once a common concept for a co-operation and partnership has been developed, DEG appraises the project. The appraisal is based on the documentation provided by the West German technical partner. As a result of the appraisal, forecasts are prepared on production, financial structure, costs and earnings as well as on the liquidity of the project company for at least five years of operation.	DEG's general strategy is to assist the founding of new enterprises on a partnership basis by German firms in developing countries by providing capital and know-how. It has become an important partner to the German raw material supply industry, particularly as regards investment to safeguard raw materials supplies.	DEG emphasised obstacles to investment in raw materials in developing countries as circumstances are increasingly against more investment by the German raw materials industry in producer countries, particularly in Third World countries rich in raw materials. Other problems include the smaller metal content of new deposits, less favourable sites and thus increased infrastructure costs, longer running-in periods of projects and higher capital and political risks.

Name and address of agency	Establishment and financial resources	Scope of activities	Terms and conditions
6. **Kreditanstalt für Wiederaufbau (KfW)** Palmengartenstrasse 5-9 6000 Frankfurt am Main 1. Telephone: (0611) 7431-1 Telex: 411352 Federal Republic of Germany	A corporation under public law. It has no branch offices. Its capital amounts to DM 1 bn, with the Federal Republic providing DM 800m, and the individual states DM 200m. It can issue bonds, and take loans from the Federal Government, from Deutsche Bundesbank, and from foreign countries.	Granting loans for projects serving the reconstruction or promotion of the West German economy, granting loans in connection with export transactions of domestic enterprises issuing guarantees, and granting loans for financing projects in developing countries. It provides soft loans and technical assistance to developing countries with no tied conditions. It has no limitation by region.	Loans to LLDCs and MSACs are granted at an interest rate of 0.75% and for a 50-year term including a 10-year grace period. Loans to developing countries at an intermediate stage of development 2% for a 30-year term including a 10-year grace period. Loans to countries at an advanced stage of development or having high foreign exchange proceeds of their own 4.5% for a 20-year term including a 5-year grace period. All private projects should be guaranteed by the government concerned.

Management	Approaches and techniques applied	Strategy for financing and technical assistance	Problems of implementation and remarks from field experience
Board of Directors, Board of Management and staff. The Board of Management conducts the business and administers the assets of the corporation in conformity with the law, the by-laws, and any rules that the Board of Directors may issue.	No special form is required for loan application. The government of the developing country addresses its application to the Government of the Federal Republic of Germany, usually through the West German Embassy. The requested capital aid loan is granted on the basis of a government agreement. All standard techniques of appraisal are applied. Distinctions are being made between investment opportunity studies, pre-feasibility studies, and feasibility studies.	To support the underemployed in the rural areas, the small holders, tenant farmers and landless workers in such a way as to raise productivity, to maintain and expand employment facilities and to exploit better the available soil. This promotion is supplemented by development of small crafts and trades in rural areas and in suburban areas in developing countries. Terms and conditions of financing have to correspond both to the development level of the individual country and to the relevant kind of project.	Many capital-aid projects involve investment costs per job exceeding by far the average figures. This mainly applies to infrastructure projects. Possibilities of implementing adapted technological procedures have been found to be very limited. Some developing countries lack a correct assessment of project evaluation.

Name and address of agency	Establishment and financial resources	Scope of activities	Terms and conditions
7. **Overseas Economic Co-operation Fund (OECF)** Takebashi Godo Building 4-1, Ohtemachi 1-Chome. Chiyoda-Ku Tokyo, 100 Telephone: (03) 215-1311 Telex: Call Number J 28360, J 28430, J 28790 Answer Back Code: COOPFUND Japan	Established on 16 March 1961 in accordance with The Overseas Economic Co-operation Fund Law of 27 December 1960. It was established for the purpose of promoting overseas economic co-operation. It is considered as Japan's principal organ for extending ODA to developing countries. Financial needs of OECF are met primarily by an annual subscription from the General Account of the government, borrowing from the Trust Fund Bureau, and the OECF's own funds.	Contributing to the industrial development and economic stability of South East Asia and other overseas developing regions. It may, however, finance projects in the fields of agriculture, forestry, fisheries and mining (limited to prospecting), pre-investment studies and experimental projects, which are deemed to be conducive to the economic development of the recipient countries, when it is difficult for the Export-Import Bank of Japan to make the loan.	The softest loan bears an interest of 1.75% per annum with a 30-year maturity, including a 10-year grace period. The hardest bears 5.75% interest and matures in 15 years, including a 5-year grace period. Interest rates and repayment terms have varied according to the situation of the country and the nature of the project involved.

Profile Summary of Selected Aid Agencies 415

Management	Approaches and techniques applied	Strategy for financing and technical assistance	Problems of implementation and remarks from field experience
Advisory Council consists of 8 vice-ministers of the ministries and agency concerned. President, 4 Executive Directors, Auditor, 3 loan Departments, Economic Research and Technical Appraisal Department, Co-ordination Department, secretariat, Controller's office, Overseas Investment Consulting office and Overseas Representative offices (Bangkok, Seoul, Manila, Jakarta, New Delhi, Cairo, Nairobi and Lima).	Negotiations are in most cases undertaken in the recipient country by the Japanese mission. Cabinet approval of the exchange of notes follows, after which a loan agreement is concluded between the recipient government and OECF. Project preparation and payment of loan carried out in accordance with provision of the agreement.	Intending to extend its activities to other sectors (e.g. educational and medical sectors) to meet the requirements of developing countries. Close historical, geographical, cultural and economic ties with the rest of Asia have led OECF to extend the majority of its commitments to the economic and social development of the region.	Loans performances are hampered by delays at project sites, cost overrun, low disbursement, delayed projects, fall in commodity disbursement.

Name and address of agency	Establishment and financial resources	Scope of activities	Terms and conditions
8. Export-Import Bank of Japan (EXIM Bank) 4-1 Ohtemachi, 1-Chome, Chiyodaku, Tokyo 100 Telephone: Tokyo 287-1221 Telex: 2223728 (AAB) 2223728 YUGINJ Japan	Established in December 1950 under the name of Export Bank of Japan, renamed in April 1952 as the Export-Import Bank of Japan. It is an independent governmental financial institution designed to supplement or encourage commercial banks in financing exports, imports and overseas investments in the field of trade between Japan and foreign countries. Operational funds consist of paid-up capital, borrowings and internal resources.	With the rapid expansion of the Japanese economy and trade in the 1950s and 1960s, the bank expanded the scope of its operations to include loans to domestic corporations, refinancing and guaranteeing of obligations.	The bank makes loans when it is difficult for commercial banks and other private institutions to provide funds on ordinary terms.

Management	Approaches and techniques applied	Strategy for financing and technical assistance	Problems of implementation and remarks from field experience
President, Deputy President, Executive Directors, Auditors, 4 Loan Departments, Legal Department, Budget Department, Administration Department, 14 Overseas Offices.	The bank provides technical services credits to domestic suppliers for surveying, feasibility studies, design of plants and supervision of activities of various types overseas. It makes financial resources available for exports to suppliers among domestic corporations, through the extension of credits, together with co-financing institutions.	To participate in the development of oil resources and its alternatives, to export technology to developing countries, promotion of imports entering Japan, for the restoration of a balanced pattern of trade.	Although the bank's operating rules do not restrict it to one particular currency, it funds itself primarily in yen and all export suppliers' credits are denominated in yen.

Name and address of agency	Establishment and financial resources	Scope of activities	Terms and conditions
9. **Japan International Co-operation Agency (JICA)** P. O. Box 216 Shinjuku Mitsui Building 2-1, Nishi-Shinjuku, Shinjuku-ku Tokyo Telephone: 03-346-5311 Telex: 22271 JICAHDQ J Japan	Established in August 1974, under the Japan International Co-operation Agency Law (Law No. 62, 1974) as an executive organ of Japan's international Co-operation Services for the socio-economic progress of developing countries. The funds required by the agency for carrying out its operational activities are budgeted by the Japanese Government under its Official Development Assistance (ODA).	Grant Aid Co-operation promotion programme, Development Co-operation Programme (investment and financing of development projects), technical and training co-operation.	JICA provides developing countries with soft loans which are difficult to obtain from the Export-Import Bank of Japan or OECF for reasons of risk, profitability or technical difficulties involved in the projects.

Management	Approaches and techniques applied	Strategy for financing and technical assistance	Problems of implementation and remarks from field experience
President, Vice-President, Advisory Committee, Executive Directors, Auditors, 11 Departments for sectoral activities and training, Finance, Planning, Personnel and General Affairs Departments. Branch offices, representative in Brazil, and overseas offices (16 offices).	Preliminary survey and basic survey to prepare the master plan of the project. Feasibility studies conducted to map out the facilities construction plan and the implementation plan for the project. Surveys for detailed design aimed at providing various data, detailed designs, specifications, etc., required for construction work involved in the project.	The agency aims at broadening its overseas co-operation activities in developing countries in development projects in industry, natural resources and foreign trade. Infrastructural improvement for agriculture and welfare. Social development, covering education and medical care, etc.	Because different types of surveys are needed at successive stages of a project, completing one project could require three or four surveys, often through different agencies. The geographical distribution of surveys carried out reflected more generally the spread of aid itself and their funds.

Name and address of agency	Establishment and financial resources	Scope of activities	Terms and conditions
10. **The Netherlands Investment Bank for Developing Countries** 4, Carnegieplein P. O. Box 380 2501 BH The Hague Telephone: (070) 469464 Telex: 31368 INVES NL The Netherlands	The bank acts as the agent of the government in the matter of aid. Its function lies within the framework of the bilateral development aid provided by the government. Its financial resources are obtained, under government guarantee, by issuing loans in the public and private sectors of the capital market.	Provides loans and grants in its own name and with a guarantee from the government. In principle, the loans are partially untied, so that the proceeds may be used in the Netherlands or in developing countries, including the recipient country. The role of the bank may be described as one of a trustee with somewhat extended powers.	Terms of loans vary according to the degree of developments of the country concerned. 3.75% interest, 30-year life including an 8-year period of grace, 2.5%. 30-year life including an 8-year period of grace, 0.75% 50-year life including a 10-year period of grace. Grants are in principle subject to the provision that they are spent on goods or services of Dutch origin.

Management	Approaches and techniques applied	Strategy for financing and technical assistance	Problems of implementation and remarks from field experience
Supervisory Board, Board of Management, President, Assistant Managing Director, Secretary, Foreign Loans Department (developing countries).	The government determines which countries receive aid. The bank, at the request of the government, then provides loans and grants to selected countries, or to bodies nominated by them, and makes payments to suppliers of goods and or services as well as taking steps to ensure that the monies are used for the purposes agreed between the Netherlands Government and the receiving country.	The least developed countries receive aid solely in the form of grants. The others, who are assisted wholly or partly with loans, are divided into three groups for the purpose of interest which (as stated under Terms and Conditions) ranges from 0.75% to 3.75%. Loans are partially untied under an agreement between a number of member states of the DAC.	The present shortage of food in developing countries demands intensification of efforts to increase agricultural production. This requires, among other things, the simultaneous implementation of a coherent package of measures aimed at eliminating the factors which stand in the way of higher production and better distribution of food. Encouragement of greater mechanisation is desirable. Particular attention must be paid to the matter of employment. Efforts must be made to develop and apply technologies matched to the economic and social situations in various developing countries.

Name and address of agency	Establishment and financial resources	Scope of activities	Terms and conditions
11. **Netherlands Finance Company for Developing Countries (FMO)** Nassaulaan 25 The Hague P. O. Box 85899 2508 CN, The Hague Telephone: 070-614201 Telex: 33042 NEFMO Netherlands	Formed in 1970 from co-operation between Dutch private business and industry and the State of the Netherlands for the purpose of stimulating economic and social progress in developing countries by promoting local business and industry. Funds for investment are obtained from state-guaranteed borrowings on the Dutch capital market and from state contributions in the form of interest-free loans and interest subsidies.	FMO provides finance and technical assistance in developing countries. It contributes to the equity of firms in these countries by participating in their share capital. Most of the finance made available by FMO, however, is in the form of loans. In exceptional cases the provision of grants is not entirely ruled out.	Interest charged generally corresponds to that payable on similar loans in the country where the financed enterprise is established. The company charges a commission on the total amount that may be borrowed under the loan agreement. Loans are granted as a rule for periods varying from 5–15 years, depending on the nature of the financed activities. FMO requires security in the form of collateral on appropriate assets. No obligation to spend in the Netherlands for the funds which the company invests in a project, but it claims the right to appoint a director to the Board of firms which it finances.

Profile Summary of Selected Aid Agencies 423

Management	Approaches and techniques applied	Strategy for financing and technical assistance	Problems of implementation and remarks from field experience
Supervisory Board, Management Board, Projects Committee, Secretary.	The party taking the initiative to submit a written application accompanied by a completed short questionnaire. Projects financed by FMO are expected to contribute to the economic development of the beneficiary countries and should be economically viable, guided both by the Dutch Government's policy on development co-operation and by the development aspirations of the authorities in the countries themselves.	The emphasis is on productive activities capable of contributing significantly to the economic and social development in developing countries and which are at the same time economically viable.	The increased number of projects that have reached the stage of implementation have resulted in a heavier work load for the projects management and delays in their implementation. Some enterprises were faced with marketing problems. There are difficulties between the partners in joint ventures financed by the company.

Name and address of agency	Establishment and financial resources	Scope of activities	Terms and conditions
12. **Swedish International Development Authority (SIDA)** S-105-25 Stockholm Office: Birger Jarlsgatan 61 Telephone: 08-150100 Telex: 11450 SIDA STHLM Sweden	Established in 1965 as a central government agency for the preparation and implementation of Swedish programmes for bilateral development co-operation. Policy guidelines are established by the government on the basis of decisions by Parliament. SIDA submits its annual budget proposals to the government.	The Swedish programme for bilateral development co-operation is the responsibility of SIDA. It has a programme for support to Swedish non-governmental organisations for information activities on developing countries as well as for development projects in the Third World.	The majority of bilateral assistance took the form of grants. Other sorts of financing are mostly interest-free with a 50-year maturity, including a 10-year grace-period. Tied aid is defined as grant aid tied to procurement in Sweden of goods and services, its use is decided by the recipient countries themselves within a given financial frame.

Management	Approaches and techniques applied	Strategy for financing and technical assistance	Problems of implementation and remarks from field experience
Board of Directors (13 members), and the Chairman is the Director General, with members of the Board representing political parties and non-governmental organisations. The Management Committee is a group for consultation and information. SIDA's operations are conducted by ten divisions and development co-operations offices, 8 in Africa and 4 in Asia.	SIDA's development co-operation programme adopted the philosophy of recipient orientation and country programming. Most evaluations are carried out by outside consultants, and SIDA assists in selecting consultants, writing terms of reference and giving service to evaluation teams. It tries to engage the host government agency for the evaluation work and does not usually wish to carry out evaluations of its own.	To co-operate with countries which are, themselves, attempting to improve the conditions for the majority of their inhabitants. Co-operation can include countries with different political systems. Approximately 90% of direct assistance goes to countries which the UN has defined as extremely poor. Direct development co-operation takes place with a limited number of countries, in order to ensure that it is effective.	Evaluation is mainly considered as a management tool. A problem of great importance is how to utilise the findings in the most appropriate way. SIDA comments from field experience stress the importance of improvements of on-going projects, improved design of new projects, better awareness of the importance of good project preparation and goal analysis, awareness of some of the risks in projects aiming at economic development, e.g. widened income gaps.

Name and address of agency	Establishment and financial resources	Scope of activities	Terms and conditions
13. **European Development Fund (EDF)** The Commission of the European Communities Rue de la loi 200 B-1049 Brussels Telephone: 7350040, 7358040 Telex: 21877 'COMEUB' Belgium	The first EDF was established in 1959 as an implementing convention of the Treaty of Rome which governed the special relations between EEC and dependent overseas countries and territories. The fund is endowed for the whole lifetime of the convention (5 years). It is financed by fixed contributions from the member states.	EDF-financed operations are devised and implemented jointly by the donors and recipients of Community funds. The Commission is accountable to the Council and Parliament for the financial management of the EDF and the use made of its resources.	For each project the conclusions of the appraisal are summarised in a financing proposal prepared by the community and submitted to the ACP state. The proposal is backed by the opinion of the relevant committee, is submitted for a decision to the Commission (grants or special loans) or the EIB's Board of Directors (subsidised loans or risk capital).

Profile Summary of Selected Aid Agencies

Management	Approaches and techniques applied	Strategy for financing and technical assistance	Problems of implementation and remarks from field experience
EDF Committee composed of representatives of the member states' governments. The Commission is responsible for the financial administration of the EDF.	The state initiates a request for financing, Commission officials appraise the project in close collaboration with the country concerned. Appraisal involves the scrutiny of a project from all angles – economic, social, financial, technical and administrative.	Programming in two separate stages. Pre-programming for co-ordination and exchanges of views at community level on the performance and aims of Community aid to various recipient countries. Programming proper for negotiations with the recipient country's authorities to finalise an indicative aid programme. In addition, there may also be a post-programming stage, if the majority of the Community member states feel that there should be an exchange of views on the contents of the indicative programme and its implications.	Problems of different information received by different donors from recipient countries are considered to be of great importance due mainly to wide discrepancies of the figures presented. Co-financing and co-ordination among different donors financing the same project in the same country are of great importance. Former French African colonies received the highest share of the Community's financing due to historical background, and before Britain joined the European Common Market.

Name and address of agency	Establishment and financial resources	Scope of activities	Terms and conditions
14. **European Investment Bank (EIB)** Boîte Postale 2005 Luxembourg Telephone: 435011 Telex: 8530 BANKEU LU Luxembourg	Created as a non-profit independent public institution by the Treaty of Rome, which came into force on 1 January 1958, establishing the European Economic Community. Members of the bank are the member states of the Community. For development finance outside the Community, the bank uses both its own resources collected in the market and budget resources provided by EEC. The bulk of resources comes from borrowings, principally public or private bond issues in national capital markets inside and outside the Community and on the international market.	The bank's basic function is to contribute, on a non-profit-making basis, to the balanced development of the Community. It grants and guarantees long-term loans to enterprises, public authorities and financial institutions to finance projects contributing to regional development. The bank also finances operations in non-member countries (on special authorisation from the Board of Governors). Since 1963, the bank has assisted in implementing the Community's policy of economic and financial co-operation with an increasing number of developing countries.	Interest rates: very low on budget resources provided by EEC. Subsidised rate for loans on bank's resources. Repayment period: usually 10–15 years. Grace period is in line with the need of the project. The bank usually requires guarantees from the recipient country.

Management	Approaches and techniques applied	Strategy for financing and technical assistance	Problems of implementation and remarks from field experience
Board of Governors, Board of Directors, Management Committee, Audit Committee, 7 directorates and representative offices.	The layout and contents of documents in the project file submitted to the bank are the responsibility of the borrower. However, during appraisal of the project, the bank keeps in close touch with the ACP country, enterprise or administrative body concerned. For industrial, mining or tourism projects, the documentation must cover legal information, technical, economic and financial data. For infrastructure or energy projects, information must be tailored to the precise nature of the enterprise and the project.	Finance is provided for almost every sector of industry and for all main branches of infrastructure (water, sewerage, irrigation, transport and telecommunications, improved gas or electricity supplies to serve industry). The bank gives special emphasis to helping small and medium-sized industrial ventures by making global loans to regional or national financing bodies which use the funds to support investments chosen in agreement with the EIB. Action in financing projects of common interest centres on limiting Community dependence upon oil imports.	The same as for the European Development Fund (EDF).

OPEC Development Agencies

Name and address of agency	Establishment and financial resources	Scope of activities	Terms and conditions
National Arab/OPEC Development Funds **15. Kuwait Fund for Arab Economic Development (KFAED)** P. O. Box. 2921 Telephone: 439078 Telex: 22025 ALSUNDUK KT 22613 KFAED KT Kuwait	Established in 1961 as a public corporation with an independent legal personality. The fund's authorised capital (1974) reached KD1bn. The purpose of the fund is to assist Arab States and other developing countries in developing their economies by providing loans for the implementation of their development programmes. The fund may borrow and issue bonds subject to the limit of twice the amount of its capital and reserves.	Since 1974, the fund has extended its mandate to provide foreign assistance to all developing countries in the world. Activities in transport, communications and storage, power, industry and services and agriculture and primary sectors. The fund also provides technical assistance to developing countries in terms of grants to identify, study, and prepare projects in a sound manner.	Interest rate: $\frac{1}{2}$–7%. Repayment period: 10–50 years. Grace period: Under a year–10 years. Guarantee by the government of the recipient country is required. The fund does not participate in equity financing. It may not finance by means of a loan more than 50% of the total costs of any project or programme.

Profile Summary of Selected Aid Agencies

Management	Approaches and techniques applied	Strategy for financing and technical assistance	Problems of implementation and remarks from field experience
Board of Directors chaired by the Prime Minister of Kuwait and including representatives of the business community as well as government officials. Director General is appointed by the Chairman, attends Board meetings, but does not vote.	Based upon the preference that the fund waits for governments to submit projects rather than acting as a catalyst. The fund's appraisal procedures are flexible as its appraisal mission has the authority to negotiate all the issues. If, during negotiations, a borrower indicates that the interest rate is too high, the fund might agree to lower the rate provided the maturity is shortened.	The fund does not follow a medium- or long-term strategy for financing and technical assistance. However, it is following a one-year programme to finance approximately 20–25 projects amounting to KD 80–100 m.	Problems are mainly related to delays in ratification, appointments of consultants, issue of tenders, and analysis of bids. Moreover, there are problems related to submission of withdrawal application and progress reports.

Name and address of agency	Establishment and financial resources	Scope of activities	Terms and conditions
16. **Abu Dhabi Fund for Arab Economic Development (ADFAED)** P. O. Box 814 Abu Dhabi UAE Telephone: 822865 Telex: 22287 FUND EM Abu Dhabi	Established in July 1971 as a general corporation with an independent legal personality for the purpose of offering economic aid to Arab, African, Asian and other countries, either in the form of loans or participation in share-holding. The fund's capital in 1974 was Dh2000m. In September 1979, the Board of Directors took the decision to double the fund's authorised capital to Dh4bn. The fund is permitted to issue bonds to an amount not exceeding twice its capital plus reserves.	Loans, equity participations and technical assistance in manufacturing and extractive industries, water and electricity, transport, communication and storage, agriculture, fisheries and rural development, and tourism sectors. The fund's activities have increased to include the provision of technical advice to the government of UAE and representing the government in the management of a number of special foreign aid projects in several Arab and African countries.	Repayment periods are likely to be over 10–15 years at interest rates ranging from 3.5–5.5%. The fund may require guarantees by any co-financing international or regional organisation. Participation in any project may not exceed 10% of the fund's capital and may not exceed 50% of the total cost of the supported project.

Profile Summary of Selected Aid Agencies

Management	Approaches and techniques applied	Strategy for financing and technical assistance	Problems of implementation and remarks from field experience
Appointed Board of Directors, Chairman of the Board, Vice-Chairman. Members of the Board are appointed by Decree for a period of 5 years, subject to renewal, Director General and two Assistants for Operations and Financial Affairs.	The fund selects development projects from those presented to it officially, either by delegations visiting the fund, or missions from the fund visiting countries. The fund carries out technical appraisal studies on three levels: macro (national), sectoral, and micro (project). The fund also benefits from feasibility studies done by well-sounded consultants as guidelines but carries out parallel studies based upon consultations in developing countries and field missions. The fund is giving the economic criterion more emphasis.	The fund makes no distinction between developing countries in the provision of financial assistance. Special commitments towards developing countries most seriously affected by crisis or towards least developed countries are felt to be the responsibility of both the government and the fund.	Problems of implementation of projects are most likely the same problems as in the case of KFAED. The fund's field experience with developing countries is mainly related to problems of project selection and appraisal, of priority areas, of implementation and decision-making, and of a need for an effective machinery for project implementation.

Name and address of agency	Establishment and financial resources	Scope of activities	Terms and conditions
17. **Saudi Fund for Development (SFD)** P. O. Box 1887, Riyadh Saudi Arabia Telephone: 4640292 Telex: 20145 SUNDOQ SJ Saudi Arabia	Established in 1974 as an agent of the government with authorised capital of SR10bn, increased to SR15bn in 1980. The fund's purpose is to provide financing of development projects in Arab, Islamic and friendly developing countries by the provision of concessionary loans. It has no borrowing power as any additional capital must be authorised by the government and capital can only be increased by a decision of the Council of Ministers.	The fund's loans are mainly extended in the fields of infrastructure, such as power stations, water supply, sewerage, mining, mineral resources, education, sanitary and housing projects. Transportation projects are the fund's top priority. Industrial projects are regarded essentially as infrastructure. Agricultural projects are for rural development rather than the outright production of food. Geographical distribution of the fund's activities does not treat Arab countries as a separate group but rather treats them among African and Asian countries according to their geographical locations.	Repayment periods range between 15–25 years. Grace period between 3–5 years. Interest rates usually between 2%–4%. The fund provides its assistance only to governments for projects in the public sector. The amount of lending to any one country should not exceed more than 10% of the authorised capital, and lending to any project should not exceed 5% of the authorised capital. In addition, the fund provides no more than 50% of the total costs of a project. It does not guarantee loans by other Saudi institutions, although equity participation is possible. The fund does not make technical assistance grants.

Management	Aproaches and techniques applied	Strategy for financing and technical assistance	Problems of implementation and remarks from field experience
Board of Directors, Chairman of the Board, Vice-Chairman and Managing Director. Managing Director sits on the Board and casts a deciding ballot in the event of a tie vote.	Projects, usually submitted by host governments, should have high economic or social priority. The fund is adopting a co-ordination policy with other experienced aid institutions and is willing to co-finance projects recommended to it by them.	The fund does not follow a medium- or long-term strategy regarding the amount of aid disbursed in the following 3–5 years, nor does it provide technical assistance. Its policy is mainly based upon year-to-year operations and balanced amounts of loans to be provided to Asian and African countries.	Similar problems of implementation as for in KFAED and ADFAED. These are particular problems related to the selection of foreign consultants and their preference, and to agreements between host governments and contractors. The fund considers most contractors' agreements between Third World countries and European contractors unfair in that advantage is taken of the position of the developing countries.

Multinational Arab/OPEC Development Agencies

Name and address of agency	Establishment and financial resources	Scope of activities	Terms and conditions
18. **Arab Fund for Economic and Social Development (AFESD)** P. O. Box 21923-Safat Kuwait Telephone: 431870 Telex: INMARABI 22153 KT Kuwait.	Established in July 1968 as an Arab regional financial institution with an independent legal personality. The purpose of the fund is financing development and social projects in Arab countries. Authorised capital (1975) KD400m. The fund can issue bonds or obtain credits from public and private Arab institutions or from individuals or international institutions.	Infrastructural projects receive the majority of loans followed by manufacturing projects, agricultural projects, Arab joint projects (communications and telecommunications, airports and roads), and projects in the service sector. The fund participates in technical assistance projects, particularly in human resources and exploitation of natural resources in the least developed Arab countries. It encourages, directly or indirectly, the investment of public and private capital in the Arab economy.	Repayment periods 15–25 years, interest rate 4% for least developed countries and 6% for other Arab countries. Grace period 4–6 years. The fund requires the recipient government's guarantee for all loans and special guarantees for projects in the private sector. It may modify the terms of the loan contract at the borrower's request without prejudice to its interest or that of other members.

Profile Summary of Selected Aid Agencies

Management	Aproaches and techniques applied	Strategy for financing and technical assistance	Problems of implementation and remarks from field experience
Board of Governors, Director General as Chairman of the Board of Directors, Board of Directors, and Loan Committees. Staff of the Fund is organised into two main areas; Operational and Service units.	Member countries submit loan requests to the fund, which, according to the intersectoral priorities within a country identified by the Programme Department, studies the request with the Project Department and submits a country programme paper. An appraisal mission is sent to appraise the project in the field, submitting the result to the management of the fund. The fund applies its own appraisal of projects on the basis of pre-investment study in the form of appraisal reports. Projects should be technically sound and economically viable for the country, and must be able to stand on their own feet financially. The fund attaches great importance to the country approach in project appraisal.	The fund adopts a regional integration approach for inter-Arab and regional project identification and promotion. A key principle of the fund's strategy is to channel its resources, wherever possible, into the least developed countries of the Arab members.	The fund shares with other Arab/OPEC funds the common problems of implementation. As a co-ordinator among other Arab funds, it has a difficult task, especially with relation to the procedure for the withdrawal of loans and procedures for implementation.

Name and address of agency	Establishment and financial resources	Scope of activities	Terms and conditions
19. **Arab Bank for Economic Development in Africa (ABEDA)** French abbreviation (BADEA) Sharea El Baladia P. O. Box 2640 Khartoum Sudan Telephone: 73646 Telex: 248 KM Sudan	Established in 1973 as an independent regional financial institution, financed by member countries of the Arab League for the purpose of participating in the economic development of non-Arab African countries, encouraging the participation of Arab capitals in African developments, and participating in providing technical assistance for Africa. The initial subscribed capital of the bank (US$231m) and the 1977 replenishment brought the subscribed capital to US$738.25m (by the end of 1980). The bank is authorised to borrow money (through credits, long- and medium-term deposits, and issuance of bonds in the Arab and international financial markets) up to twice the amount of its paid-up capital and reserves.	Great attention to the financing of infrastructural projects followed by agricultural and manufacturing projects, energy projects and a special programme for the Sahel countries. Participation mainly in West and East African countries.	Maturity 20 years as a standard repayment period. Grace period 5 years as a standard period. Interest rates range from 1%–6% depending upon the economic condition of the recipient country, the kind of project and the economic sector. Government guarantee is required and additional guarantees in the case of private projects. The bank does not participate with more than US$10m for any project. It finances only foreign exchange components of the project.

Profile Summary of Selected Aid Agencies

Management	Approaches and techniques applied	Strategy for financing and technical assistance	Problems of implementation and remarks from field experience
Board of Governors, Board of Directors, and the President (Chairman of the Board of Directors) who is elected for a 5-year term with a renewable mandate. The bank works through operational and service units, and has representative offices in both Washington and Paris.	Loan requests come from the government of the country where a project is located. The government should provide the bank with the necessary guarantee required. The viability of the project and its contribution to economic development in the recipient country is studied before the bank starts to finance the project. The bank pays great attention to projects that have a positive impact on other projects and on the economic and social environment of the country. The bank makes use of outside consultants for the techniques of project appraisal.	The bank follows a strategy based upon encouraging potential economic activities which have priorities for development in Africa. It gives special emphasis to least developed African countries, most seriously affected African countries, and Sahel countries. It places most emphasis on financing development projects in Sub-Saharan African countries that have a regional impact, and on credit lines to National Development Banks operating in the same countries. It adopts a regional integration approach by promoting and assisting development projects in Africa within the frame of the global strategy of Arab-African co-operation.	Lack of local currencies, delay in disbursements, bad management, lack of direct communication, problems of productivity of labour, lack of stability in economic systems in some countries, increase of total costs of projects during implementation, fluctuations in the value of foreign currencies required to import tools and machinery, and problems with contractors and consultants as well as different estimates of total costs and components for a project submitted to different donors. The bank faces chronic problems in the case of least developed African countries, namely the Sahel countries.

Name and address of agency	Establishment and financial resources	Scope of activities	Terms and conditions
20. **Islamic Development Bank (IsDB)** P. O. Box 5925, Jeddah Saudi Arabia Telephone: 31120 Telex: 401137 BISLAM SJ Saudi Arabia	Established in 1975 as an international financial institution to foster the economic development and social progress of member countries and Muslim communities individually as well as jointly in accordance with the principles of the Shariah (Muslim code of law). Authorised capital of the bank is ID2bn (equivalent to 2bn SDR of IMF). The bank has no borrowing power, but it is authorised to accept deposits, to be used for equity investments, and to raise funds in any other manner. It turns over its undisbursed funds to the Saudi-Arabian Monetary Agency (SAMA) for investment.	The activities of the bank include project financing and technical assistance, equity participation, leasing, profit-sharing, and foreign trade financing. The bank's project financing is in industry and mining, transport and communication, utilities, agriculture, social services, and other sectors. The bank is also required to establish and operate special funds for specific purposes including a fund for assistance to Muslim communities in non-member countries, in addition to setting up trust funds. The bank undertakes research for enabling the economic, financial and banking activities in Muslim countries to conform to the Shariah.	Loans are interest-free as the Bank applies the Sharia Law which prohibits the taking of interest. However, it imposes service charges of from 2–3% per annum. Repayment periods range from 10 years for commercial ventures up to 50 years for infrastructure projects in least developed member countries. The bank does not require a government guarantee for equity investments. If the borrower is another entity than a member government, there must be a guarantee from the government or from another agency acceptable to the bank. The bank does not provide loan assistance to a project in which it has equity participation except in special cases.

Management	Approaches and techniques applied	Strategy for financing and technical assistance	Problems of implementation and remarks from field experience
Board of Governors, Board of Executive Directors, President, Vice-President, and Secretary General. The President serves as Chairman of the Board of Executive Directors, but does not vote except in the case of a tie. He is elected by the Board of Governors for a period of 5 years and may be re-elected for another term. The Secretary of the bank acts as Secretary of the two Boards. The Board of Executive Directors may establish committees to facilitate the conduct of the operations of the bank, which are carried out through operations and servicing units.	The bank sends its own mission to the field in the recipient country but in most cases it appraises the project jointly with other aid agencies. Techniques of project appraisal are carried out in co-operation with other lending institutions. The bank has prepared a document, *Foreign Trade Financing Guidelines*, which contains the rules, regulations and procedures governing foreign trade financing.	The bank's strategy is based upon giving top priority to the most needy and least developed Muslim countries, with industry and agro-business projects being given the most emphasis in the case of equity participation. Infrastructural projects receive the top priority in project lending, while regional and complementary projects among Muslim countries are also likely to receive a high priority. Assistance to the national development banks of its member countries is also important.	The bank's experience in the field of implementation and follow-up of projects is similar to that of other aid agencies, especially those problems related to least developed countries. The bank believes that inadequate co-ordination in the various stages of project management is the major cause of cost overruns and recommends that much greater importance be given in the project planning stage to the needs of such co-ordination under various categories of technical, managerial and financial co-ordination.

Name and address of agency	Establishment and financial resources	Scope of activities	Terms and conditions
21. **The OPEC Fund for International Development** P. O. Box 995, 1011 Vienna, Austria Telephone: 315536/0 Telex: 131734 FUND A 134831 FUND A Austria	Established by virtue of an agreement signed by all OPEC member countries in Paris in January 1976. The fund is not endowed with a capital structure, and its resources consist of contributions by member countries, and funds received from operations or accruing to the fund. Resources committed to the fund (1980) have reached US$4bn. The objective of the fund is broadly defined as reinforcing financial co-operation between OPEC member countries and other developing countries by providing financial support on appropriate terms to assist them in their economic and social development efforts.	The fund operates in all developing countries, other than OPEC member countries, with special emphasis on assisting least developed countries. It extends three types of loan: balance of payment support loans, programme loans and project loans. The fund also, in co-operation with international agencies, provides technical assistance grants. Project-lending loans are in energy, agriculture and agro-industry, transportation, industry (including development banks), public utilities and communications sectors.	BOP support loans: no interest on loans to low-income developing countries. A service charge of 0.5% per annum. Repayment period of 7 years after a grace period of 3 years. Programme loans: no interest on loans to low-income developing countries. A service charge of 0.75% per annum. Repayment period of 10 years after a grace period of 5 years. Project loans: no interest on loans to low-income developing countries. A service charge of 0.75% per annum. For relatively higher income countries 4% interest rate, and a higher rate to high-income developing countries. Repayment period of 15 years after a grace period of 5 years.

Profile Summary of Selected Aid Agencies

Management	Approaches and techniques applied	Strategy for financing and technical assistance	Problems of implementation and remarks from field experience
A Ministerial Council and Governing Board on which all contributing countries are represented. The Governing Board sets the general policies and its Chairman signs the loan agreements as agent of the contributing countries. The Board appoints the Director General of the fund who manages the activities of the fund and is responsible for the work of the Governing Board and the implementation of its decisions.	The general procedures for obtaining a loan from the fund are based upon government requests, by addressing a letter to the Director General through the minister in charge of mobilising foreign assistance, usually the Finance Minister. After an official loan request accompanied by sufficient data has been received and favourably reviewed, it is submitted to the Governing Board for approval. The fund does not engage in the appraisal of new projects, instead it co-finances projects already appraised and approved by other institutions.	Since its inception, the fund has allocated a large share of its aid to the least developed countries, and has treated these countries on a priority basis. It places growing importance on the energy and food needs of the developing countries, as it places high priority in its project lending activities on projects related to these two sectors. Technical assistance provided through the fund is conducted, by and large, in collaboration with the UNDP.	The administration of the fund loans has generally been left to an appropriate co-financing agency. More recently, however, the amendments of the Agreement establishing the fund included a clause enabling it to appraise projects and to administer its own project loans, if it so determines. The fund plans gradually to strengthen its appraising capacity, especially in the energy sector.

Regional Development Banks

Name and address of agency	Establishment and financial resources	Scope of activities	Terms and conditions
22. **African Development Bank (AfDB)** 01 BP 1387 Abidjan 01 Ivory Coast Telephone: 32-07-11 Telex: 3717/3498/3263 Ivory Coast	The Agreement establishing the bank entered into force on 10 September 1964 and the bank commenced its operations on 1 July 1966. The purpose of the bank is to contribute to the economic development and social progress of its regional members, both individually and jointly. The authorised capital stock of the bank was initially fixed at UA250m	The financing of investment projects and programmes relating to the economic and social development of its regional members, promoting investment in Africa of public and private capital in projects or programmes and providing technical assistance. The bank may also establish special funds which are designed to serve its purpose. It initiated the African	Interest rate 8%, repayment period usually over 10 years, grace period ranges from 2–7 years. A government guarantee is required. The bank may also attach such other terms and conditions as it deems appropriate, taking into account both the interest of the member directly concerned in the project and the interest of the members as a whole.

(US$250m) in 1964. At 31 December 1979, the authorised capital increased to UA1220m (US$1607m). Capital stock is made up of a paid-up portion (25%) and a callable portion (75%). The new authorised capital stock is allocated for subscription to regional and non-regional members in such proportions that they result in regional members holding two-thirds of the total voting power and non-regional members one-third. The bank's resources are made up of the subscriptions to its capital stock, reserves, borrowing and interest income.

Development Fund (AfDF) in 1972 and the Nigerian Trust Fund (NTF) in 1976 as two subsidiaries. The bank's loan activities are in public utilities, transport, industry and development banks, agriculture, and the education and health sectors.

Management	Approaches and techniques applied	Strategy for financing and technical assistance	Problems of implementation and remarks from field experience
Board of Governors, Board of Directors, a President of the Board of Directors (Chairman of the Board of Directors), Vice-President, and Secretary General. The Board of Governors is the supreme organ of the bank. The Board of Directors are elected by the Board of Governors for a term of 3 years and may be re-elected. The Board of Directors is responsible for the conduct of the bank.	In considering an application for a loan or guarantee, the bank pays due regard to the ability of the borrower to obtain financing elsewhere on terms and conditions that the bank considers reasonable. For projects limited to one country, the bank normally requires a guarantee of the national government. In the case of loans extended to finance multinational projects the bank requests	The bank bases its strategy on financing specific projects which clearly contribute to the economic development of its member states, particularly those included within regional or national development programmes. Special preference is accorded to projects which benefit two or more member states and thus stimulate intra-African co-operation. A high priority is also accorded to loans for	Meeting the obligations from the host governments necessary for completing the project on schedule as well as the delays in the receipt of progress reports are considered to be the main problems of implementation facing the bank.

guarantees from all governments concerned. Once the loan is granted, the bank supervises its disbursement. It does not appraise member states' macroeconomic policies. The bank's techniques for project appraisal vary from country to country and also depend on the nature of the project. However, labour-intensive techniques for countries with high unemployment rates have been emphasised.

those development projects which demonstrate clear efforts to self-help, to mobilise local resources or assist member states to attract additional capital from non-African sources. The bank intends to increase the proportion of its lending devoted to agriculture and related agricultural infrastructural projects and to endeavour to achieve a more balanced regional distribution of its financing.

Appendix I

Name and address of agency	Establishment and financial resources	Scope of activities	Terms and conditions
23. **Asian Development Bank (AsDB)** P. O. Box 798 Manila Philippines 2800 Telephone: 80-26-31 Telex: 0571 ASIANBK PM. Philippines.	AsDB started operations on 19 December 1966 as an international regional development finance institution owned by its member governments. The purpose of the bank is for lending funds and providing technical assistance to developing member countries in the region of Asia and the Far East, including the South Pacific, and for promoting investment and generally fostering economic growth in the region. Membership of the bank is open to members and associate members of ESCAP and other regional and non-regional developed countries which are members of the UN or any of its specialised agencies. The bank (on 31 December 1980) has 29 regional members providing 65% of its capital and 14 non-regional members providing 35%. Subscriptions to capital stock (par value) reached	Lending operations of the bank are mainly based on two kinds of loans – ordinary loans to the somewhat better off developing member countries (DMCs) and concessional loans to its poorest member countries. Bank loans are for major economic sectors such as agriculture and agro-industry, energy, industry and non-fuel minerals and development banks, transport and communications and multiprojects, water supply, urban development, and education and health sectors. The bank can undertake equity investment but, however, it has not as yet sought to activate this provision. It offers credit lines to national development finance institutions and provides technical assistance to DMCs to improve their capabilities to make use of external project financing. Technical assistance grants	The bank's lending rate on loans from the ordinary capital resources is 7.40% per annum. Project loans from the special funds resources bear only a service charge of 1% per annum. The repayment period is 10–30 years for loans from the bank's ordinary capital resources, with a grace period of 2–7 years. However, for higher income developing member countries, the maturity period of loans would be subject to a limit of 15 years, inclusive of a grace period of 3 years. Project loans from the special funds resources are repayable over 40 years, including a 10-year grace period. In cases where the recipient of loans or guarantees of loans is not itself a member government, the bank may require the guarantee of the member government or another acceptable entity.

US$8.8bn (31 December 1980). The financial resources of the bank are of ordinary capital resources consisting of subscribed capital and funds raised through borrowing and reserves, and special funds resources, comprising contributions made by developed member countries and capital set aside by the bank for concessional lending to the poorest member countries. There is a technical assistance special fund consisting of contributions made by both developed and developing member countries for technical assistance activities.

are financed mainly from the Technical Assistance Special Fund. In addition the bank administers technical assistance projects financed from other sources such as UNDP and EEC.

Management	Approaches and techniques applied	Strategy for financing and technical assistance	Problems of implementation and remarks from field experience
Board of Governors, Board of Directors, a President (Chairman of the Board of Directors) and 2 Vice-Presidents, one for operations and the other for finance and administration. The Board of Governors is the bank's highest policy-making body. The Board of Directors, which is elected by the Board of Governors, consists of 12 members, 8 representing regional members and 4 representing non-regional members. The directors hold office for a	The bank has no set application form for loans. Applications are normally submitted through the governments concerned. A general review of a country's economic development is a prerequisite to the identification of projects for bank financing. Project identification missions are sent regularly to DMCs for discussions with the authorities concerned and the selection of suitable projects for bank assistance. In appraising projects, the bank pays specific attention to such	The bank's efforts to help the poor have been reflected in the selection of projects for financing. The main thrust of the bank's operational strategy has been its assistance to agriculture and rural development. This strategy aimed not only to bring the benefits of the bank assistance to the poor in the low-income DMCs, but also to reduce relative poverty in DMCs with higher income. Bank lending to other sectors like rural electrification projects, small-scale and cottage	Since the bank's loans are in most cases made to meet the foreign exchange cost of the project, significant disbursements under a loan can take place only when all the preliminary steps enumerated earlier right up to the placing of orders are completed. Even then, it may take quite some time for completion of delivery of the items ordered. Some of the bank's borrowers have not had much experience of the procedures followed by international financial insti-

term of 2 years and may be re-elected. The President is elected by the Board of Governors, his term of office is 5 years and he may be re-elected.

aspects as their economic, technical and financial feasibility, their effects on the general development activity of the country concerned, their contribution to overcoming economic bottlenecks, the capacity of the borrowing country to service additional debt, the introduction of new technologies to raise productivity, the expansion of employment opportunities, and other special considerations.

industries, fertiliser projects, and coal development projects are also receiving great attention. The strategy of the technical assistance provided by the bank covers three broad areas: project preparation, project implementation, and advisory services.

tutions. There are also problems arising from the fact that certain countries are situated beyond easy physical access. Project implementation in these countries is somewhat slower than in others.

Name and address of agency	Establishment and financial resources	Scope of activities	Terms and conditions
24. **Caribbean Development Bank (CDB)** P. O. Box 408 Wildey, St. Michael Barbados, West Indies Telephone: 61152 Telex: WB 2287 West Indies	The bank was established as a regional development organisation on 26 January 1970 to contribute to the harmonious economic growth and development of the member countries of the Caribbean (the region) and to promote economic co-operation and integration among them with special regard to the needs of the less developed members of the region. Authorised capital of the bank (September 1980) reached US $281.6m. Financial resources consist of ordinary capital resources, comprised mainly of subscribed capital and borrowing, special funds resources of the Special Development Fund, and resources accep-	Projects financed by both ordinary capital and special funds resources cover a wide range of development activities. The distribution of the bank's total financing by sector (during 1970–80) has shown that three sectors – agriculture, infrastructure (including ports) and industry and tourism – accounted for 89% of the total financing approvals. The bank provides technical assistance to borrowing member states, particularly the LLDCs. In 1978 it established (in co-operation with other donors active in the region) a Technical Assistance Fund. The bank has also established a Technology Information Unit.	Interest rates (inclusive of the commission of 1%) on loan financed from its ordinary capital resources are: $8\frac{1}{2}$% for government financial intermediaries, 9% for government infrastructure and public utilities, $9\frac{1}{2}$% for productive enterprises (agriculture), $10\frac{1}{2}$% for productive enterprises (industry and tourism). Interest rate on loans financed from special fund resources is 4% per annum. Repayment periods for loans financed from the bank's ordinary capital resources 10–15 years except loans for industry and tourism which are 10–18 years. Loans financed from special funds resources are repayable

Profile Summary of Selected Aid Agencies 453

ted by the bank for inclusion in other special funds established or administered by it. By the end of 1980 total financial resources of the bank reached $402.576m. Membership of the bank is allowed for the states and territories of the region and non-regional states which are members of the UN or any of its specialised agencies or of the International Atomic Energy Agency. Non-regional members may hold not more than 40% of the total shares of the bank and regional members not less than 60%.

over a period of 15–20 years. Grace periods for loans financed from the bank's ordinary capital resources depend on the project being financed. Loans financed from special funds resources have a grace period usually up to 5 years.

Management	Approaches and techniques applied	Strategy for financing and technical assistance	Problems of implementation and remarks from field experience
Board of Governors, Board of Directors, a President (Chairman of the Board of Directors), a Vice-President. The Board of Governors is the highest policy-making body of the bank. Voting power is roughly proportional to shares subscribed, with a slight weighting in favour of the smaller member territories. The Board of Directors comprises 11 Directors, 9 representing the regional members and 2 non-regional members. The Board is responsible for the general policy and direction of operations of the bank. The President serves for a 5-year term and may be re-elected: He is advised by 5 Directors of Departments: Secretary and Administration, Projects, Economics and Programming, Finance and Legal.	Prospective borrowers address preliminary inquiries to the bank which decides what additional information is required and provides the prospective borrower with an appropriate loan application form. In examining the projects that it proposes to finance, the bank appraises them with regard to their technical, commercial, financial, legal, organisational and managerial environmental and social aspects, their effects on the general development of the beneficiary country, their contribution to the removal of economic bottlenecks, the capacity of the borrowing country to service additional external debt, the introduction of appropriate technologies and the expansion of employment opportunities. The bank uses normal project ap-	The bank has based its strategy upon the promotion of projects which have a direct integration aspect in three sectors: agriculture, transportation and industry. In agriculture, the bank has initiated the process of promoting and financing regional agricultural projects (including fisheries and livestock) as part of the Regional Food Plan, accepted by the conference of Heads of Governments of the Caribbean Community in December 1975. In the area of intra-regional transportation facilities, the bank has made loans to regional projects in shipping and air transport. Within the limits of its financial and technical resources, the bank promotes and explores the possibilities of financing regional projects in the industrial sector with	Major problems are frequent delays in implementation, due largely to the lack of expertise in borrowing countries, and legal and administrative hold-ups in decisions to satisfy conditions of precedent.

praisal techniques, primarily the Little–Mirrlees methodology. Prospective borrowers are required to submit full details, including the result of market surveys, estimates of cost, feasibility studies, projections of sales and of cash flows, and any other information bearing on the expected profitability of the project, including development incentives and other concessions from the government.

a view to making industrial development in the various countries of the region more complementary.

Name and address of agency	Establishment and financial resources	Scope of activities	Terms and conditions
25. **Inter-American Development Bank (IDB)** 808 17th Street NW Washington D.C. 20577 USA Telephone: 256-0382 Telex: 650052 ITAMDEV USA	Established on 30 December 1959 as a regional development organisation, the purpose of the bank is to contribute to the acceleration of the process of economic and social development of the regional developing member countries, individually and collectively. The resources of the bank consist of the ordinary capital resources, the inter-regional capital resources, and the resources of the Fund for Special Operations. As of 31 December 1980, ordinary capital reached US$11,773m, intra-regional capital $3371m, and the	The bank's scope of activities covers the area of the western hemisphere in the Latin American and Caribbean regions. The types of projects that the bank finances cover all major sectors: agriculture and fisheries, industry and mining, tourism, energy, transport and communications, urban development, education service and technology, environmental and public health, export financing, and pre-investment. The bank's Complementary Financing Programme is a mechanism designed to in-	Projects financed from ordinary capital and intra-regional capital resources: Interest rate 8.25%. Repayment period 25 years. Projects financed from Fund for Special Operations: Interest rate 1%–4%, Repayment period 15–40 years, Grace period 5–10 years. In all cases, guarantee by government is required. There is special commission on all loans, participations, or guarantees, or guarantees made out of or by commitment of the ordinary capital resources of the bank. Complementary loans are made for

Fund for Special Operations $7669m. The Fund for Special Operations was established for the making of loans on terms and conditions appropriate for dealing with special circumstances arising in specific countries or with respect to specific projects. The bank has been given responsibility for administering other special funds totalling US $1176m (31 December 1980), the two largest being the US $525m Social Progress Trust Fund placed under the bank's administration in 1961 by the United States and the US $500m Venezuelan Trust Fund established by the latter country in 1979. The bank has also administered special funds provided by Argentina, Canada, Germany, Norway, Sweden, Switzerland, the UK and the Vatican. These last funds were established before the donor countries became members of the bank.

crease the flow of private capital for Latin American development. In mid-1975, a new financial programme was designed to complement its lending ability beyond the resources available through its various loan windows, by fostering greater and closer co-operation with private sources of funds for the financing of development projects.

maturities based on prevailing conditions in the credit markets which in 1979 operations made in 1979 ranged from 10–$10\frac{1}{2}$-year maturities, with adjustable interest rates determined by a fixed spread over a reference rate such as the London Inter-Bank Offered Rate (LIBOR).

Management	Approaches and techniques applied	Strategy for financing and technical assistance	Problems of implementation and remarks from field experience
Board of Governors (1 Governor, 1 deputy appointed by each member country). Board of Executive Directors (12, with 12 deputies), President (elected by the Board of Governors for 5-year term), Executive Vice-President, Managers of Department (8) Controller (1) advisors and staff. The governors of the regional developing member countries elect 8 executive directors while the governors for the non-regional countries elect 2 executive directors in accordance with specific provisions. The Board of Executive Directors makes all major decisions affecting the authorisation of bank ex-	Borrowing member countries' external financing requirements and potential projects for the bank's financing are discussed during annual country programming missions despatched by the bank. Project-financing proposals are also submitted through the bank's representatives in each of the borrowing member countries, or directly to the bank's headquarters. The bank's Project Analysis Department has published 'Guidelines for the Preparation of Loan Applications', in different sectors, which were prepared for the purpose of providing guidance to interested insti-	The bank's Board of Governors provided the following guidelines governing the bank's strategy at the start of the 1980s: (1) To intensify and continue its efforts to ensure that its lending contributes to the improvement of the economic and social well-being of the low-income sectors of its member countries and to the acceleration of the progress of the relatively less advanced countries of the region. (2) To co-operate with its member countries in implementing strategies to achieve an integrated development of their natural resources, including energy resources.	Problems that may arise during the implementation are normally resolved with the bank's representative or the Operations Department except that when necessary other departments, the Controller, the top management and ultimately the Board of Executive Directors may become involved. *Ex-post* review, appraisals and evaluations are conducted by independent auditors, the bank Controller and the office of External Review and Evaluation which reports directly to the Board of Executive Directors. In addition, borrowers are required to perform economic *ex-post* evaluation.

penditures, including those for lending and technical cooperation programmes.

Each member country has 135 votes plus one vote for each share of ordinary capital stock and for each share of inter-regional capital stock of the bank held by that country.

As of 31 December 1980 the bank's membership (regional and non-regional members) reached 43 countries.

tutions of the Bank's member countries concerning information to be furnished in loan applications. Project appraisal is based on standard criteria for technical, financial, socio-economic, legal and institutional evaluation. A multidisciplinary team travels to the field, to gather all pertinent information, and then a project appraisal report is drafted. This document passes through middle management, and higher management committee reviews, and after all issues are resolved a loan proposal plus the project appraisal report are sent to the Board of Directors for review and approvals.

(3) To join in the efforts being made by Latin American countries to improve the efficiency of their productive systems, making them more competitive in international markets and increasing their exports both within the region and to the rest of the world.

The bank has realised that, in providing development loans, it cannot substitute its management or its technical capabilities for those of borrowers, and has instead designed systems to obtain the same degree of assurance regarding each project as if the bank were managing or carrying out the work itself.

Appendix I

World Bank Group

Name and address of agency	Establishment and financial resources	Scope of activities	Terms and conditions
26. **International Bank for Reconstruction and Development (IBRD)** 1818 H Street, NW Washington, DC 20433 USA Telephone: (202) 477-1234 Cable: INTBAFRAD Washington DC	IBRD was established at Bretton Woods in July 1944, and commenced operations in June 1946. The main purpose of the bank is to assist in the reconstruction and development of territories of members by facilitating the investment of capital for productive purposes, and encouragement of the development of productive facilities and resources in less developed countries. It began its operations with an authorised capital of US $10bn. By 1980, the capital had reached US $40bn. Total member-	The bank operates in the following sectors: agriculture and rural development, development finance companies, education, energy, industry, non-project, population, health and nutrition, small-scale enterprises, technical assistance, telecommunications, tourism, transportation, urbanisation, and water supply and sewerage. Its lending by region covers East Africa, Western Africa, East Asia and Pacific, South Asia, Europe, the Middle East and North Africa, and Latin America and the Caribbean.	Interest rate (effective on 1 January 1980) 8.25%. At least once a year, and more often if necessary, a lending rate is suggested so as to achieve a spread of approximately 0.50% above IBRD's cost of borrowing. Repayment period 15–20 years; Grace period 3–5 years. A guarantee by member country government is required.

ship of the bank (in June 1980) was 135 countries. In addition to its capital, borrowing through the international sale of bonds and notes, net income, sales of loans and repayments on loans are considered subsidiary financial resources.

Technical assistance is an integral part of the bank's operations. Its components are included in loans and credits in all sectors. The bank (in 1975) credited a project preparation facility (PPF) to help overcome weaknesses in borrowers' capacities to complete project preparation and to support the entities responsible for preparing or carrying out projects. It also acts as the executive agency for a number of projects financed by UNDP. Growing demand for planning assistance has become a well-established trend for the bank. The Economic Development Institute (EDI) was established in 1955 to provide mid-career training in economic management techniques and policies for senior officials of developing countries.

Management	Approaches and techniques applied	Strategy for financing and technical assistance	Problems of implementation and remarks from field experience
Board of Governors, Board of Executive Directors, the President (Chairman of the Board of Executive Directors). All powers of the bank are vested in the Board of Governors, which delegates its power for the conduct of general operations to the Board of Executive Directors that performs its duties on a full-time basis at the bank's headquarters. The Board of Governors consists of one governor and one deputy governor appointed by each member country. Each mem-	Priorities of the bank's lending are determined on the basis of member countries' economic reviews, with suitable projects then being selected for the bank's lending programme. Before project selection is discussed, the eligibility of a member country's borrowing from the bank or from IDA is considered. If the country is able to obtain the proposed loan on reasonable terms from the private capital market, it should not resort to the bank. IBRD applies up-to date economic	Increased emphasis is given to investments that can improve the productivity and well-being of the mass of poor people in developing countries. As for general policy for technical assistance, emphasis is on the need to enhance the economic development of member countries in general, with additional direct technical assistance to some countries in the Middle East, Latin America and Africa as an important part of the bank's financial projects.	Country studies prepared by IBRD staff, based upon their findings in missions, indicate that it is not possible to generalise on problems as each recipient country is unique: however, major problems are common. An approach of dealing with regional groups regarding these problems was considered, but tended to lead to the problems of development in each region related mainly to field experience.

ber country has 250 votes plus one additional vote for each share of stock held. All matters, except as otherwise specifically provided, are decided by the majority of the votes cast. 5 Executive directors are appointed by the 5 members having the largest number of shares, and the rest are elected by the other members. The President should not be a governor or an executive director and has no vote except a deciding vote in case of an equal division. The bank has two offices abroad: the European office in Paris ard the Tokyo office.

and financial techniques and to some extent social factors in assessing the viability of a project. It does not prepare market studies, but focuses on the marketing aspect during project appraisal. The bank is required by its Articles of Agreement to use objective economic criteria in all its judgements. This in fact has been the subject of most of the bank's research work. It does not apply a standard or a manual for project appraisal but rather employs different techniques based upon financial and economic factors. Financial analysis is concerned with how the project entity may be enabled to generate funds for its own expansion.

Lending for structural adjustment is a new form of IBRD assistance which is considered to be an evaluation in the traditional programme assistance that has always been (and continues to be) a part of the bank's lending operations designed to meet the immediate consequences of crisis. The basic idea was to extend the programme of loans to countries which suffer from structural imbalances, provided that these countries undertake a well-defined adjustment programme in agreement with the bank. This type of non-project lending has the specific objective of helping developing countries to reduce their current account deficit to more manageable proportions over the medium term by supporting programmes of adjustment that encompass specific policy, industrial and other changes designed to strengthen their balance of payments, while maintaining their growth and developmental momentum.

Problems of project implementation are related to physical implementation and construction, costs and financial matters, and operational issues. Political problems as such and other exogenous factors are behind some other problems, for example, financial difficulties due to political constraints on tariffs. Projects in transport and public utilities become problem projects mainly because of difficulties related to financial matters and costs, or of physical implementation; projects in agriculture and education become problems because of staffing and management problems and difficulties with project execution. These problems are brought to the attention of borrowers and corrective action is recommended.

Name and address of agency	Establishment and financial resources	Scope of activities	Terms and conditions
27. **International Development Association (IDA)** 1818 H Street, NW Washington, DC 20433 USA Telephone: (202) 477-1234 Cable: INTBAFRAD Washington DC	Established in 1960 as a soft-loan affiliate of the World Bank, the purposes of IDA are to promote economic development, increase productivity and raise the standards of living in the less developed areas of the world included within IDA's membership by providing finance to meet their important developmental requirements on terms which are more flexible and bear less heavily on the balance of payments than those of conventional loans, thereby furthering the developmental objectives of IBRD and supplementing its activities. The initial subscription of capital, in January 1960, reached US$1.00bn, US$763.07m, from Part I countries and US$236.93m from Part II countries, of which 10% of the initial subscription of each original member had to be payable in	Similarly to IBRD's classification, IDA extends credits to the following sectors; agriculture and rural development, development finance companies, education, energy, industry, non-project, population, health and nutrition, small-scale enterprises, technical assistance telecommunications, tourism, transportation, urbanisation and water supply and sewerage. The agricultural sector is the dominant sector of IDA total lending. The energy sector has received growing attention in recent years, followed by the transportation sector. It also operates in the following regions: Eastern Africa, Western Africa, East Asia and Pacific, South Asia, Europe, the Middle East and North Africa, and Latin America and the Caribbean. Asia receives the largest amount of lending from IDA, followed by Africa,	No interest is charged on IDA credits, although there is a service charge of $\frac{3}{4}$ of 1%. Repayment period 50 years, grace period 10 years. Member government guarantee is required. IDA may, when and to the extent it deems appropriate, agree to a relaxation or other modification of its terms.

gold or free convertible currency, and 90% in gold or free convertible currency in the case of Part I members, and in currency of the subscribing member in case of Part II countries. Authorised capital stock reached US$16.50bn at fiscal year 1979. Membership of IDA is open to all members of the World Bank, and by September 1980, 121 countries had joined IDA. Funds used by IDA are called credits to distinguish them from World Bank loans, and come mostly in the form of subscriptions of capital, general replenishments from IDA's more industrialised and developed members, special contributions by IDA's richer members, and transfers from net earnings of the World Bank. IDA's Sixth Replenishment, which the executive directors approved in January 1980, for the 3-year period, FY 1981–83, calls the funding in an amount totalling the equivalent of US$12.00bn.

while Latin America receives the lowest amount. This is compensated for by a high level of IBRD loans to Latin America and the Caribbean and small amounts to Asia and Africa.

Management	Approaches and techniques applied	Strategy for financing and technical assistance	Problems of implementation and remarks from field experience
Board of Governors, Board of Executive Directors. The President of the World Bank is the President of IDA, and is Chairman of the Executive Directors of the association. Each governor and deputy governor of the World Bank appointed by a member country of the bank which is also a member of the Association, is *ex officio* a governor and deputy governor, respectively, of IDA. The Chairman of the Board of Governors of the bank is *ex officio* Chairman of the Board of Governors of the association. All matters before the association are decided by a majority of the votes cast. The voting structure of IDA incorporates a two-tier membership system. As of 30 June 1980, Part I member countries' votes (21 countries) represented 63.36% of the total voting	Procedures applying in IDA projects are identical to those used for World Bank projects and the same standards in assessing the soundness of projects are applied. The decision as to whether a project will receive World Bank or IDA financing is decided on country eligibility grounds, not in relation to project characteristic. Eligibility for IDA financing is determined by country-specific criteria, with factors taken into consideration including a country's relative poverty, its lack of creditworthiness for conventional lending and its ability to use IDA resources effectively. The selection and preparation of projects, the tests of economic and financial viability, the eligible uses for loan proceeds, procurement standards, and close supervision of projects during ex-	IDA assistance is concentrated on the very poor countries – mainly those with an annual per capita GNP of less than $625 (in 1978 dollars): more than 50 countries are eligible under this criterion. IDA strategy in the 1970s has meant (contrary to the 1960s) that the percentage of commitments for agriculture has increased greatly, while the percentage of commitments in the transportation sector has decreased substantially. The strategy attempts to overcome the difficulties of directing the benefits of development projects primarily toward the 'target groups' of the rural population. IDA strategy for the 1980s is based upon the needs of the poorest countries for greatly expanded external assistance on concessionary	Problems of project implementation are the same problems as faced by the World Bank. Special attention has been given to the problem of monitoring and analysis of delays in project implementation. There is no uniform standard that can be applied in judging whether a project, or particular elements of a project, should have been completed faster than was actually the case. Most measurement is done against earlier expectations which might have been unrealistic. It is essential, therefore, to ensure that project preparation and appraisal take into account all the circumstances that might affect project implementation. Identification of the problems along with the experience gained in prior projects in various countries and sectors have resulted in better

power of all member countries, while Part II member countries' votes (100 countries) represented 36.64% of the total voting power.

The IDA is an entity separate and distinct from the World Bank and the funds of the association are kept separate and apart from those of the bank.

ecution are all exactly the same as for bank-financed projects. Every IDA project must be approved by IDA's Board of Directors, based upon staff documentation assessing the project's feasibility, its expected developmental impact, and the required institutional and financial arrangements needed to ensure efficient implementation at a cost commensurate with the project's expected benefits. The cycle of a typical IDA project usually consists of six sequential stages: identification, preparation, appraisal, negotiation and approval, supervision, and *ex-post* evaluation. A system of *ex-post* evaluation of World Bank and IDA projects was established in 1969, and since then has been steadily expanded and improved. This system of comparing actual experience with previously expected results has become an essential element of IDA procedures.

terms. The Sixth Replenishment of IDA has taken into account the international development strategy for the 1980s to fulfil these needs.

prepared projects executed on a more timely basis.

Name and address of agency	Establishment and financial resources	Scope of activities	Terms and conditions
28. **International Finance Corporation (IFC)** 1818 H Street, NW Washington DC, 20433, USA Telephone: (202) 477-1234 Telex: ITT 440098 Cable: CORINTFIN	Established in 1956 as an affiliate of the World Bank. Its aim is to encourage the flow of domestic and foreign capital into productive investments in developing countries. The IFC supplements the economic development efforts of the IBRD and IDA by filling two gaps: (1) It supplies capital in any form, as long-term loans, equity subscriptions, or a combination of both. (2) It invests without government guarantee of repayment.	The IFC operates in its member countries in Africa, Asia, Europe and the Middle East, and Latin America and the Caribbean. Latin America and the Caribbean region represent the highest share in the total investment of the corporation. Investments by business sector are: cement and steel, wood, pulp and paper, fertilisers and petrochemicals, energy and minerals, agro-industry, light industry and tourism.	Interest rate is based on commercial rates. The repayment period varies, however, most commonly between 7–12 years. The grace period is based on construction time for the project generally about 2–3 years. No government guarantee is required. IFC's financing is not limited to the foreign exchange portion of the project nor to specific purchases, but may be used for any legitimate business purpose related to the project. The only

ment. Originally the authorised capital stock of IFC was US$100m. As of 30 June 1980, the paid-up capital reached US$307m, with capital resources provided by 113 member countries, 92 of which were developing.

In addition to capital and reserves the IFC can borrow from the IBRD up to four times its capital and unrestricted reserves. Repayments and sales of investment, income from loans and equities are also considered to be important financial resources of the corporation.

The IFC also engages in project identification and promotion helping to establish, finance and improve privately owned development finance companies and other institutions which are engaged in promoting and financing private enterprises, creating in the capital-exporting countries interest in portfolio investments in enterprises located in developing countries, and giving advice to developing member countries on measures that create a climate conducive to the growth of private investment.

requirement is that it be spent in one of the member countries of the World Bank or in Switzerland.

Management	Approaches and techniques applied	Strategy for financing and technical assistance	Problems of implementation and remarks from field experience
Board of Governors, Board of Executive Directors. Day-to-day operations are under the supervision of the Executive Vice-President, who is appointed by the directors. Each governor or deputy governor of the World Bank appointed by a member of the bank, which is also a member of the IFC, is *ex-officio* governor or deputy governor, respectively, of the corporation. Each director who is an appointed executive director of the World Bank is entitled to cast the number of votes which the member by which	The IFC does not adopt a manual for project appraisal and implementation, because it operates in close contact with the World Bank, using its facilities and research work on developing countries. The appraisal which is an integral part of all IFC's investments aims at reducing the risk to potential lenders, and improving the terms and conditions of the credit for borrowers. The corporation gives increasing attention to project development, with the object of identifying situations in which private	An increasing proportion of IFC's investments was planned to be directed to natural resource development, particularly energy resources. The corporation felt that it could effectively contribute to an international effort aimed at developing the substantial potential resources of fuel and non-fuel minerals which exist in the developing countries by operating as an equity investor working to create a more stable investment environment and helping to raise the large amounts of funds needed for these projects.	The most difficult area is in project definition and preparation, although here the IFC provides extensive assistance to project sponsors. Implementation responsibility remains in the hands of the project sponsor. Regular follow-up and supervision is part of the corporation assistance to the firms it finances. Although the IFC takes equity in firms, it does not participate in active management of these firms.

he was so appointed is entitled to cast in the corporation. The President of the World Bank is, *ex officio* the Chairman of the Board of Directors of the corporation.

Each member country has 250 votes plus one additional vote for each share held, with all matters decided by a majority of the votes cast.

enterprise, local and foreign, could make a contribution to local economic development. To expand those initiatives undertaken in the course of normal operations, and by special missions, the Department of Investment Promotion and Special Projects was created in 1973, with specific responsibility for promoting projects from their conception, particularly in the IFC's least developed member countries. Appraisal of the contribution of DFCs to economic development takes into account their relative success in channelling investment and entrepreneurship into financially viable enterprises, their success in mobilising saving and contributing to the creation of functioning capital markets, and the special costs and benefits of DFC investments as compared to possible alternatives.

The IFC's future financing strategy will be directed to the least developed regions and within countries into the least developed parts.

Technical assistance is worldwide among member countries, mainly in the financial institutions, provided at the request of member governments on the basis of resource availability.

Appendix II Survey of International Development Strategy

UN SECOND DEVELOPMENT DECADE

The fundamental goals of the international development strategy for the Second United Nations Development Decade, adopted by the General Assembly on 24 October 1970, were to raise rates of growth and standards of living in developing countries, recognising the crucial role of financial resources from abroad in supplementing domestic resources in the financing of development. The international development strategy called upon each economically advanced country to provide annually to developing countries financial resource transfers of a minimum net amount of 1 per cent of its GNP at market prices in terms of actual disbursements. The strategy further stated that those developed countries which were unable to achieve this target by 1972 would endeavour to attain it not later than 1975. It also stated that each developed country should progressively increase its official development assistance to developing countries and exert its best efforts to reach a minimum net amount of 0.7 per cent of its GNP at market prices by 1975 or very soon thereafter, but in no case later than 1980.[1] The 1 per cent has been widely accepted as a matter of principle, but a majority of DAC member countries (including the USA) have not accepted the target date. The 0.7 per cent official development assistance target to which developing countries have attached particular importance has been accepted by only a minority of DAC member governments. The socialist countries of Eastern Europe did not consider the targets for financial flows applicable to them. The official development assistance target therefore failed to be implemented by the developed countries taken as a group and a number of issues have been raised by developing countries and some developed countries regarding the appropriateness of certain features of the targets. An important task for the international development strategy was to forge a new consensus in the international community regarding the way in which financial flows may best be targeted in support of the objectives of international development strategy.

The chief target was that developing countries as a whole should achieve, during the decade, an average annual rate of growth in their GDP of at least 6 per cent. Six subsidiary targets were derived from this main goal. They were: an overall average annual increase in the developing countries of 3.5 per cent in GDP per capita; annual growth rates of 8 per cent in manufacturing, 4 per cent in agricultural production, and 7 per cent in export volume; a domestic savings rate that would reach 20 per cent of GDP by 1980; and annual ODA from the developed countries reaching 0.7 per cent of thier GNP by 1975. In his address to the Board of Governors of the World Bank in October 1979, Robert McNamara stated that the performance figures from 1970–78 could project, with reasonable accuracy, the results for the remaining two years of the decade. The chief target – the 6 per cent growth rate in the combined GDP of all the developing countries – had not been achieved. At best, their growth had not exceeded 5.2 per cent per year. This reflected the gradual slowing of growth throughout the world in the second half of the 1970s. Further, there were major shortfalls in each of four subsidiary goals. Of particular importance were the deficiencies in agricultural production, with a growth rate of only 2.8 per cent, rather than the targeted 4 per cent; and official development assistance from the developed countries, which averaged less than half the target.[2] These results were due mainly to the fact that there was no united international determination or pressure to support these targets.

PREPARATION FOR UN THIRD DEVELOPMENT DECADE

Preparation for an international development strategy for the Third United Nations Development Decade has been taking place according to the terms of Resolution 33/193 of the United Nations General Assembly passed on 29 January 1979. The resolution affirmed that the new international development strategy should be designed to promote the development of the developing countries and should be formulated within the framework of the New International Economic Order and be directed towards the achievements of its objectives. The resolution further emphasised that the new international development strategy should give particular attention to the most pressing problems and the deteriorating situation of the least developed countries and should contain special and effective measures aimed at the elimination of the basic constraints facing these countries to ensure their accelerated development.

The LLDCs as a group recorded declines between 1970 and 1977 in each of the following key areas: agricultural production, manufacturing output, gross domestic investment, export purchasing power and import volume. They were moving backwards and had weaker per capita indicators of overall performance in the 1970s than the already distressing ones of the 1960s. If average growth rates for the period 1960–77 are projected until 1990, the per capita performance of the LLDCs for all key indicators would be little changed from their present low levels. In spite of a growing awareness of the shortcomings of aid, it is clear that larger flows of assistance to least developed countries are necessary, if not sufficient, for accelerated economic development. There will be an acute need to expand import capacities in order to overcome the past record of decline and stagnation as well as to improve basic living conditions. Resolution 122 (v) of UNCTAD V outlines a comprehensive new programme of action for the LLDCs for the 1980s.

After having played a pioneering role in developing the least developed category and in placing the issue before the international community in the 1970s, UNCTAD itself hoped to fulfil a key role in continued efforts. The first step involved the preparatory work leading to a UN Conference in 1981. A number of key policy issues regarding external assistance were certain to arise in the course of discussions about a comprehensive new action programme; amongst them were:[3]

(1) How serious are donors about helping to create fundamental change in the least developed countries?
(2) What are the appropriate terms of financing?
(3) What sectors need to receive priority attention during the 1980s?
(4) What is the degree of common purpose in political and economic fields of the developing countries?
(5) What is the correct institutional response?

A crucial and essential challenge of the Third Development Decade is not necessarily to ensure the graduation of any member from the least developed category, but rather to ensure acceptable levels of basic services to the vast majority of populations in the poorest countries by 1990.

Survey of International Development Strategy 475

THE NORTH-SOUTH DIALOGUE

The North-South dialogue reached a critical stage in 1979 with UNCTAD V in May and other UN-sponsored meetings included one on science and technology and one on rural development. Throughout the year there were preparations for the Special Session of the United Nations General Assembly which was planned to take place in mid-1980 to consider a strategy for the Third Development Decade. In December 1978 a symposium was jointly organised by the Parliamentary Assembly of the Council of Europe and OECD so that development problems could be discussed by the Parliamentarians whose views were so important in determining the final results of the dialogue. Seven principal conclusions emerged from the Overseas Development Council's analysis on the central issues in the North-South dialogue as follows:[4]

(1) The international economic system is no longer working well for either the North or the South. In its judgement, unless there are major structural changes, the industrial democracies face the prospect through the 1980s and 1990s of persistent high inflation and slower growth.
(2) There is a consensus emerging that a return to satisfactory economic progress with lower inflation in the industrial democracies depends on far greater co-operation with – and involvement of – the developing countries of the South than is currently the case.
(3) The most basic human needs of some 800 million people are not being met. It is worth remembering that this number is actually considerably larger than the number of people in absolute poverty twenty years ago.
(4) If the worst aspects of absolute poverty could be overcome worldwide by the year 2000, this would mean 10 million fewer people dying each year and some 15–20 million fewer people born each year.
(5) The OECD area can generally be put into the category of not yet having made up its mind on exactly what to do on North–South and development co-operation issues.
(6) It is very unlikely that there will be sustained progress on either the economic set of issues or the basic human needs set of issues unless the two go together.
(7) There is need for a new 'Statecraft' in the last decades of this century analogous to that which emerged in the late 1940s and

early 1950s when the OECD countries were suddenly confronted with a new set of major political and economic realities. This new foreign policy must accommodate the new forces on the world scene.

The key question is what is going to be done on North–South issues. Thus far the general feeling is that there is, among the leadership both in the North and the South, a vision of the potential of mutually beneficial co-operation. The issue being therefore how to translate this vision into action. The world's rich and poor countries have failed to achieve their targets set at the twenty-seven-nation talks in Paris in June 1977 – the so called North–South Dialogue. Two of the main issues were commodity price support schemes and debt relief for some of the less developed countries (LDCs).[5]

The developing countries were particularly concerned that no agreements has been reached on the issue of debt relief. The West has said it is prepared to accept new procedures for helping developing countries before they reach the brink of bankruptcy. The nineteen developing countries, however, were insisting that any new rules should apply automatically to all countries while the West maintained that each case should be treated separately. The West's offer of $1bn in emergency aid was intended to help to provide immediate relief for the poorest countries (developing countries' debts exceeded $200bn according to OECD figures at that time), while the second part of the West's offer was a more favourable approach to the Geneva negotiations on the proposed common fund for commodities. The developing countries wanted as much as $6bn to be allocated to the common fund to finance a new series of eighteen commodity agreements, in particular to finance buffer stocks to be bought and sold to stop prices fluctuating too much. The West believed that no more than five to seven Commodity Agreements, covering such products as coffee, tin, rubber and cocoa made economic sense and did not want to put up any money until the agreements were actually negotiated and the financial requirements had become clear. They were also opposed to any suggestion that the fund should be used to raise the price of raw materials against market trends.

NEW INTERNATIONAL ECONOMIC ORDER

In April 1974, the General Assembly held its Sixth Special Session, the sole item on the agenda being 'Study of the Problems of Raw Materials and Development'. At the close of this session, the Assembly adopted by consensus the 'Declaration on the Establishment of a New International Economic Order'. The declaration was based on the view that the current economic order, which was established when most of the developing countries had not achieved independence, tended to perpetuate the inequalities of that era. The declaration stressed the interdependence of all nations, the interrelationship between the prosperity of the developed countries and the growth and development of the developing countries. It proposed various principles such as the full participation on a basis of equality of all countries in the solving of world economic problems; the full sovereignty of every country over its natural resources and all economic activities and an equitable relationship between the prices of raw materials exported by developing countries and the price of manufactured goods imported by them. The Assembly also adopted a 'Programme of Action on the Establishment of a New Economic Order.'[6]

The General Assembly, in its Resolution 32/174 of 19 December 1977, affirmed that all negotiation of a global nature relating to the establishment of the New International Economic Order should take place within the framework of the United Nations system. The UN decided to convene a special session of the Assembly in 1980 at a high level in order to assess the progress made in the various forums of the United Nations system in the establishment of the New International Economic Order and, on the basis of that assessment, to take appropriate action for the promotion of the development of developing countries and international economic co-operation, including the adoption of the new international development strategy for the 1980s. The committee established under General Assembly Resolution 32/174 held two organisational plenary meetings at UN headquarters on 14 and 17 February 1978. The committee also held informal consultations during that period.[7] In October 1978 the Parliamentary Assembly of the Council of Europe adopted a resolution on a New International Economic Order and took a position on the various elements based upon the following order.[8]

(1) A significant improvement in the terms of trade of the developing countries and easier access for their exports to the markets of the industrialised countries.
(2) Attainment of the Official Development Aid objective of 0.7 per cent of GNP.
(3) Alleviation of the debt burden of developing countries.

(4) The establishment of an international agreement on commodities assuring equitable and remunerative prices for developing countries' exports.
(5) Facilitation of the transfer of technological expertise.
(6) The recognition of the right of the developing countries to play their proper role in all international negotiations.

The Council of Europe has often adopted a forward looking position which unfortunately has not always been followed by the governments of its member states.

BRANDT COMMISSION

The idea of establishing an international development commission under the Chairmanship of Mr Willy Brandt, the ex-Chancellor of West Germany, was first hinted at by Mr McNamara in the Manila Annual Meeting of the World Bank in October 1976 and was further elaborated in his Boston speech in the spring of 1977. At that time, the North–South dialogue was still under way. Mr Perez-Guerrero, the Co-Chairman of the Paris Conference on International Economic Co-operation (CIEC) expressed some doubts about the wisdom of establishing such a commission while the North–South dialogue was in progress. Accordingly, both Mr Brandt and Mr McNamara decided to postpone action on the establishment of the commission pending the conclusion of the Paris conference. CIEC concluded its deliberations and negotiations in May 1977 when the results of the North–South dialogue were adopted by universal consensus. From the viewpoint of developing countries CIEC could be categorised as almost a total failure. It was agreed, however, that the unresolved issues that were before CIEC should be taken up by the various international organisations each within its field of competence. In view of the poor results achieved by CIEC, the idea of establishing a new body such as the Brandt Commission was revived with the main objective being to identify politically feasible areas of action which could command public and legislative support in rich and poor countries alike. Such actions should in a mid-term perspective of five to ten years speed up the development process in the Third World and thus contribute effectively towards the common goal of more human dignity for the absolute poor and more equality of opportunity

Survey of International Development Strategy

among nations. The Commission endeavoured to make suggestions on the following issues:[9]

(1) The policy, aid and trade support that the industrialised countries should supply.
(2) The policy and structural changes that the developing countries need to undertake to make additional assistance contribute fully to development.
(3) How to apply these mutually supporting efforts effectively to meet the basic human needs of every citizen in the world community.

In 1980 a Report on International Development Issues, under the Chairmanship of Willy Brandt, was published.[10] It dealt with some of the world's needs of the 1980s and discussed North–South relations as a great social challenge. Over a period of two years, the Commission discussed and debated a great number of issues. Regarding a new approach to development finance, it recommended that the flow of official development finance should be enlarged by:

(1) An international system of universal revenue mobilisation, based on a sliding scale related to national income, in which East European and developing countries – except the poorest countries – would participate.
(2) The adoption of timetables to increase Official Development Assistance from industrialised countries to the level of 0.7 per cent of GNP by 1985, and to 1 per cent before the end of the century.
(3) The introduction of automatic revenue transfers through international levies on some of the following: international trade, arms production or exports; international travel; the global commons, especially sea-bed minerals.

Lending through international financial institutions should be improved through:

(1) Effective utilisation of the increased borrowing capacity of the World Bank resulting from the recent decision to double its capital to $80bn.
(2) Doubling the borrowing:capital ratio of the World Bank from its present gearing of 1:1 to 2:1, and similar action by Regional Development Banks.

(3) Abstaining from the imposition of political conditions on the operations of multilateral financial institutions.
(4) Channelling an increasing share of development finance through regional institutions.
(5) A substantial increase in programme lending.
(6) The use of IMF gold reserves either for further sales, whose profits would subsidise interest on development lending, or as collateral to borrow for on-lending to developing countries.
(7) Giving borrowing countries a greater role in decision-making and management.

The report also recommended that consideration should be given to the creation of a new international financial institution – a World Development Fund – with universal membership, and in which decision-making was more evenly shared between lenders and borrowers, to supplement existing institutions and diversify lending policies and practices. The World Development Fund would seek to satisfy the unmet needs of the financing structure, in particular that of programme lending.[11]

THE WORLD DEVELOPMENT REPORTS

The World Bank's *World Development Report* of 1978[12] was the first in a series of Annual Reports providing a comprehensive assessment of the global development issues. The first report dealt with a number of fundamental problems confronting the developing countries, and explored their relationship to the underlying trends in the international economy. According to this report, absolute poverty on so massive a scale was already a cruel anachronism. But unless economic growth in the developing countries could be substantially accelerated, the inevitable increases in population would mean that the numbers of the absolute poor would remain unacceptably high even at the end of the century. The twin objectives of development, according to the report, were to accelerate economic growth and to reduce poverty. Greater progress toward these goals required an immense effort by the developing countries matched by a more realistic level of support from the industrialised nations. As the international economy is growing more interdependent, that evaluation can benefit developing and developed countries alike. If it is to do so there must be adjustments in the global patterns of trade to reflect shifts in comparative advantage.

The resources available to the developing countries must be supplemented by an adequate inflow of external capital. In this area, there are uncertainties as they relate to the increased availability of ODA, the rate of growth of private lending, and the expansion of the lending capacity of the multilateral financial institutions. Additional concessional resources would permit both a higher rate of growth and greater progress in dealing with poverty. The large investments necessary to accelerate growth in agriculture and expand public services require an increased flow of concessional capital to the low-income countries and to the poorer of the middle-income countries. The net flow of capital at market terms is of special importance to the middle-income countries. Much of the recent growth in private lending to developing countries may be limited by the growth of the banks' own capital and by internal considerations of appropriate balance in their portfolios. International lending institutions are the principal source of long-term capital for developing countries. Their declining share in the total supply of capital is reflected in the deteriorating maturity profile of the debt of middle-income countries. The achievement of a better balance between medium-term lending from private sources and long-term lending from the international institutions crucially depends on the capacity of the latter to increase their lending. This requires early agreement to expand the capital of these institutions. Action to do this is now under consideration. Increased lending by the international financial institutions not only helps to improve the maturity structure of debt but also provides assurance to private lenders – either through co-financing activities or indirectly – about the quality of investment programmes and debt management in the developing countries.

The *World Development Report* of 1979[13] examined a number of attractive growth scenarios to illustrate the range of policy choices that needed to be considered in the effort to accelerate the current pace of development. The report concluded that the low-income countries and some of the poorer middle-income nations would continue to rely primarily on ODA for their external capital needs. In addition to increasing the flow of official resources, the share of such resources going to low-income countries needs to be raised to have a substantial impact on absolute poverty. On the other hand, in devising policies to encourage foreign investment and to increase the flow of net benefits to the host country, a developing nation's overall economic policies are of crucial importance. These, together with a country's economic structure and stage of development, are much more important in attracting foreign investment than are special incentives. The size of the flow from the industrialised countries will depend on the growth of trade and, more generally, on the nature of international relations. The World Bank's initial assumption of real growth for the non-concessional capital flows seems modest, but more important are the institutional and financial conditions that must be created to permit a balanced growth of aggregate flows.

The third *World Development Report*, in 1980,[14] was published at a time of difficulty and uncertainty for the world economy – particularly for the developing countries. It emphasised that the direct attack on poverty, if it was ultimately to be successful, must be combined with measures to ensure that the economies of the developing countries continued to expand. The active support of the richer nations would be required to assist this process through the provision of capital and technical knowledge and through the opening of their markets to developing-country exports. The report emphasised that there was a serious risk that reluctance or inability to finance large external deficits in developing countries would lead to lower levels of trade, investment and economic efficiency, hence to lower growth. Even in the later years of the 1980s, when the severity of payments imbalances is expected to diminish, the growth of developing countries will continue to depend on inflows of foreign capital. For the low-income countries which can borrow little commercially, this means more aid. There is a real danger that the modest aid increases projected will not be achieved. In their own long-term interests, as well as those of the developing countries, both OECD and OPEC donors should make every effort to expand their aid relative to GNP, even in periods of domestic stringency. And they should concentrate their aid even more on low-income countries. Commercial capital, mainly from banks but also from the bond market, private direct investment and official sources, will be available to help the middle-income countries. But not all countries will be well placed to borrow much more from private commercial sources and without additional financial assistance from other sources, their growth will slow down. In particular there is not enough long-term programme (non-project) finance to support the structural changes required in many countries. Some will benefit from the structural adjustment lending of the World Bank and assistance from the IMF; enlarged official flows of this sort, particularly from multilateral agencies, could and should play a larger role.

The fourth *World Development Report*, in 1981,[15] focused on the international context of development. It examined both past trends and future prospects for international trade, energy and capital flows as well as their effects on developing countries, followed by an analysis of national adjustments to the international economy. According to the report, concessional finance has stagnated; and there are signs of uncertainty in the commercial capital markets. Even under the relatively optimistic assumptions of the report's high-case projections, the income gap between the richest and the poorest countries will continue to increase; under the low case, even the number of individuals living in absolute poverty will rise.

The projections in the report indicate the continuing need for substantial external finance – commercial loans for the better-off countries, and (mainly) concessional loans and grants for the poorer countries. There will be a need for national governments and international financial institutions to bear a larger share of the overall flow of recycled funds. The latter in particular can assist in lengthening maturities, in co-ordination capital flows with adjustment needs and in co-operating with commercial capital markets. For the low-income countries, the adjustment problem described in the report has no short-term solution. Apart from immediate balance-of-payments needs, the longer-term tasks of investment and restructuring will require a decade or more of increased support with concessional funds. The time-scale is even longer for the very poorest countries, where the essential foundations of economic development – infrastructure, human capital, commercial networks, and effective administrative capacity at all levels – are not yet in place.

OECD RESEARCH PROJECT ON FACING THE FUTURE

The OECD Research Project on *The Future Development of Advanced Industrial Societies in Harmony with That of Developing Countries*[16] has shown that there is a real danger that distribution of income over the Third World as a whole may become even more inegalitarian. The next twenty-five years (according to the OECD Project) will probably see an increased concentration of the poor population in South Asia (including Indonesia) and in Sub-Saharan Africa. In these circumstances, the project recommended that aid policy might therefore be based on the following principles:

(1) Aid should be redefined in the whole context of exchanges (financial, trade, industrial, cultural, political) between industrialised and developing countries.

(2) Aid cannot be confined to a commitment in general terms, but must refer to precise development targets which can be used as criteria and standards. Among these, priority must be given to income-redistribution efforts by the governments of Third World countries.

(3) Aid must be concentrated on the poorest population. Hence, two sets of consequences:
  (a) A gradual reorientation towards the two huge poorest regions (Sub-Saharan African and South Asia) with, at the same time, a levelling off and then a decline in aid to Latin America and the other regions of the developing world (with the exception of certain very poor countries in these regions). This geographical redistribution of aid has to take account of the absorptive capacities of the countries concerned.
  (b) An endeavour to select action which has an effective impact on the poorest groups and therefore on sectors such as agriculture and the infrastructure, the criteria of 'basic needs'.

(4) Even though the actual concept of a volume aid target is being increasingly disputed, it is still desirable, in order to speed the development of the poorest third of mankind, to increase the volume of aid to an initial minimum of 0.5 per cent of GNP for each industrial country.

(5) It might be well to reflect on institutional forms of aid; clubs, like the Club du Sahel, might be formed to get plans for regional assistance going; the rate of non-governmental organisations might be strengthened; an international foundation might even be envisaged to distribute part of governmental aid, since in its negotiations with the developing countries (for example on basic needs), a foundation of this kind would not be a political spokesman for the developed countries.

THE ROLE OF AGRICULTURE

The agricultural sector in developing countries and in particular in Africa deserves special attention, as Africa, amongst the least developed regions, is the richest in natural resources and fertile land, requiring only a sound international co-operation policy for financing agricultural development, especially those projects which are related primarily to food needs. Africa could contribute significantly to solving the international food crisis facing the world today, but a world pragmatic programme is needed, based upon comparative advantages and economies of scales.[17] As for the development of small farms, we should deal with the problem of defining the optimum size of farm according to agro-economics and agro-business indicators, the law of diminishing returns (or law of increasing costs), stages of development, production function and others. However, we should not ignore the fact that the problems of the small farmers are that social, economic and political forces run counter to their interests. In approaching a development programme for small farmers, we should illustrate the major issues and present different specific solutions according to different specific cases. The incorporation of small farmers' development in national plans, the development of appropriate institutions, reallocation of resources to small farmers, institutions to improve productivity and technology are all healthy solutions, but we should look for different approaches to deal with different cases by region and by country. In this regard, a package approach including credit, seeds, fertiliser and pesticides could be the correct one for each developing country.

The optimum solution for small farmers' development should be subjected to an appraisal of each farm in each country, with an adequate incentive system. Co-operative societies could play a much more important role as well as specialised agricultural financial institutions for mobilising domestic savings in favour of small farmers' development. Agricultural price policy could also play an important role to provide more resources in favour of small farmers, but this policy should be flexibly based upon conditions of supply and demand, elasticity of demand for each form of commodity, stability and instability in each farm product and marketing studies. In other words, the more the problem is measured in quantitative terms, the more practical solutions are obtained and small farmers in developing countries are badly in need of these solutions.[18]

A comprehensive programme for reducing post-harvest food losses requires substantial financial resources whether for building storage structural or processing facilities or for providing recurrent costs in the controlling of losses. In this respect, we should separate agricultural projects submitted by governments to donors from those related to such a programme. FAO could also act as a third party in preparing feasibility studies and a guarantee machinery or insurance system for the benefit of donors could be created through FAO. The very low cost per project in an action programme leads us to be cautious about their effectiveness, especially if the governments submit projects for financing based upon complementary activities. On the other hand, as infrastructure is usually poor in developing countries, these countries may not be in a position to provide, for example, facilities to improve farm grain storage. Any suggested programme for reducing post-harvest food losses should take into consideration the external economies and economies of scale to be implemented through such a programme.[19]

FAO's recognition of the need to start action for the reduction of post-harvest food losses began in 1947. Since that time, however, emphasis on increasing production yields has received a much higher priority. The basic concept of increasing world food supplies by preventing post-harvest (and post-catch) losses has received worldwide attention since 1968 when the 'War on Waste' was launched. The impetus for action in this area was further stressed at the World Food Conference (Rome, 1974) while the growing international awareness of need for reducing post-harvest food losses culminated on 19 September 1975 in a resolution adopted at the Seventh Special Session of the United Nations General Assembly. Resolution 3362 (S-VII) on 'Development and International Economic Co-operation' stated that 'the further reduction of post-harvest food losses in developing countries should be undertaken as a matter of priority, with a view to reaching at least 50 per cent reduction in 1985'.[20] This resolution has shown a new consciousness of the need for the prevention of food losses as a means to economic progress, self-reliance and nutritional self-sufficiency. There is, however, no agreed methodology of post-harvest assessment. Therefore, for each important food crop in each country studies will be required in several communities over a minimum period of several years, once methodology is agreed upon.

THE CLUB du SAHEL

The Club du Sahel was set up in March 1976 in Dakar, Senegal, as an informal association of aid donors and the eight nations of the CILSS, the Permanent Inter-state Committee on Drought Control in the Sahel: Chad, Gambia, Mali, Mauritania, Niger, Senegal, Upper Volta and the Cape Verde Islands. The Club du Sahel seeks to reinforce the efforts of the CILSS and other international bodies and to help mobilise resources for the development of the Sahel.

Representatives of the eight West African nations, aid donor countries and international organisations have adopted a long-term economic development strategy for the drought-prone Sahel region, one of the world's poorest areas, whose main objective, which also included an action programme for 1978–82, was to ensure self-sufficiency in food for the Sahel. It was approved by the Club du Sahel meeting held from 30 May to 2 June 1977 in Ottawa, at the invitation of the Canadian Government. The strategy provided for a first general development programme (1978–82) estimated to cost at least $3bn. The programme sought specifically to develop water resources, protect crops, combat desertification through reafforestation, improve fisheries, livestock and agricultural productivity, and strengthen regional training and research programmes. Many donors and institutions informed the Ottawa Conference of planned increases in their financial contributions.[21] One of the current activities of the Club du Sahel is to standardise the initial step in the project cycle; the project identification documents. A meeting held at the OECD in May 1979 reached a consensus among donors on a draft project identification document.

LEAST DEVELOPED COUNTRIES

In April 1975, the UN Committee for Development Planning decided to concentrate on two related topics at its 1976 session.[22] The first was the condition and problems of transfers to developing countries, and the second was the plight of the poorest countries, which are largely gathered in two principal depressed regions of the world. Accordingly, in the latter part of 1975, working groups of the committee, together with the secretariat and consultants, prepared materials on these subjects for the 1976 session. The committee brought up to date its broad assessment of the current position of the developing countries and of international efforts on their behalf. Circumstances were such that, once this current position is considered, it is not difficult to assess prospects for the rest of the decade relative to the goals of the Second Development Decade.

In a general sense, performance has been disappointing. Further, the performance of the international community in contributing to the development process has been the most disappointing of all. During the first three years of the 1970s, the dialogue on relations between developed and developing countries was radically transformed under the rubric of the New International Economic Order, and that was promising. As the committee discussed in its report in 1975, there were major and, in many respects, hopeful developments, but they had not really begun to reverse a development-promoting performance by the international community that, measured against the aspirations of 1970, could only be called quite dismal. Hence the focus on the phenomenon of transfers, broadly conceived, was in favour of developing countries. Moreover, unless there was literally a revolution in the political will of the world's more favoured countries by 1980, the international contribution to the new Development Decade would be grossly deficient and almost sure to fail.

A long-standing feature of international resource transfers is that the amounts received vary widely from country to country, even between countries with broadly similar needs. What has emerged more clearly is that the lower-income countries, considered as a group of least developed among developing countries, have attracted a disproportionately small share of such resources in relation to their population and needs. What is even more striking is that these countries (all but a few of the smaller among them) are located contiguously in two areas, which can be appropriately characterised as the depressed regions of the world. One such region extends across the middle of Africa, stretching from the Sahara in the north to Lake Nyasa in the south, and includes all countries within the area, with the exception of some West African Coastal States. The other, beginning with Afghanistan and Pakistan in the west, stretches eastward across South Asia and some South-East Asian countries (hereafter, for brevity, referred to as 'Southern Asia'). While these two depressed regions resemble each other in that acute poverty and slow growth are their common fate, they have major differences, which invite different policy responses. Most of the countries located in the depressed region of Africa are characterised by the small size of their markets. Generally the density of population is low, with the mainly rural population being widely scattered. Although, on the average, these countries have small populations, factors that do more to limit the size of their domestic markets are the low level of income and the uneven manner in which income is distributed. Another factor limiting development is the low level of infrastructural investment in these countries. Investment in transport, communications and social services is inadequate to support high rates of development. Increased investment in the provision of these services is a precondition for the development of agriculture and industry. Generally speaking, the natural resource base of the depressed region of Africa is not unfavourable. While it is true that some of the countries suffer from a shortage of water and pockets of overpopulation, the ratio of land to labour is still favourable to increased agricultural production. As to industrialisation, given the low present levels and the favourable natural resource base, in principle there are both export-promotion and import-substitution possibilities. The success of import substitution, however, will be largely contingent on effective economic co-operation arrangements that greatly enlarge the scale of individual national markets. The success of export promotion will depend on the efficiency of production of exportable goods, on economic co-operation arrangements and on the willingness of developed market economies and centrally planned economics to give freer access to processed products from these countries.

The problems of Southern Asia are different in some respects. This region is characterised by high population density and, consequently, by very considerable pressure of population on land. A large part of the rural population is 'landless'. For this reason, rapid agricultural development may be held back in Southern Asia in the absence of far-reaching institutional and organisational changes that would make possible the fuller utilisation of manpower and more intensive use of land. Several countries of the region, however, have made greater progress in industrialisation as well as in building up some of the overheads of development, than the countries of the depressed African region. The mobilisation of idle labour, particularly of those who have little or no land, requires large supplies of food. Fluctuations in agricultural output make this problem a very serious one in most of these countries.

International efforts – for example, through a system of world grain reserves or through food aid programmes – can help to minimise the impact of such fluctuations and make available assured supplies of food in adequate quantity. It is feasible for such efforts to avoid adverse effects on indigenous agricultural production, and if that caution is observed such programmes can be of great value. Their impact on poverty and unemployment will be both direct and immediate.

The process of industrialisation can be given impetus to the extent that markets can be opened up in the advanced countries for manufactured products in which the developing countries of Southern Asia have a comparative advantage. Thus far the beneficiaries of preferred treatment in regard to imports of manufactured products have been confined largely to the countries of Africa that were previously colonies of countries in Western Europe. The countries of Southern Asia have not received any help of this kind and have also been faced with numerous obstacles to the movement of their manufactured products to the markets of the developed countries. This matter deserves pointed further attention from the international community.

The United Nations Conference on Trade and Development has played a pioneering role in efforts to provide for special measures in favour of the least developed among the developing countries, and geographically disadvantaged developing countries. Work on the least developed countries and the land-locked developing countries began with the first conference. The third conference launched a study of the special problems of developing island countries, and this work has since been refined to stress measures for the more geographically disadvantaged developing island countries. In the Fourth Session of the United Nations Conference on Trade and Development held in Nairobi in May 1976,[23] special measures in favour of these countries were recommended. For financial and technical assistance measures, the conference recommended seeking the following measures:

(1) Far larger flows of technical and financial assistance, applied under far more flexible norms than in the past, should be made available to the least developed countries.
(2) These flows, wherever possible, should be in the form of grants with outstanding bilateral official development assistance loans being converted to grants.
(3) Effective steps should be taken to provide at least an adequate minimum flow to each of the least developed countries.
(4) Effective steps should be taken to seek agreement between donor agencies and the least developed countries on a global plan for a much more rapid increase in growth and welfare in these countries, based on longer-term assurance of far larger assistance flows.

Paragraph 35 of Resolution 98 (IV) adopted by the Fourth Session of the conference in Nairobi in May 1976 stated:

The Secretary-General of UNCTAD should convene as soon as possible a special meeting at which multilateral and bilateral financial and technical assistance institutions can carry out, together with representatives of the least developed countries themselves, a general review and assessment of their requirements and progress and of the problems arising in the co-ordination and implementation of assistance programmes on both the donor and the recipient sides, with the aim of agreeing on specific proposals for the more rapid increase in growth and welfare in the least developed countries.[24]

The meeting was scheduled to take place in Geneva at the Palais des Nations 14–22 March 1977. The major purpose was to discuss the aid process in the hope that it could be made simpler, more effective and more responsive to the needs of the least developed countries. The meeting was intended to provide the occasion for a practical, technical discussion of major problems among senior officials from both the donor and the recipient sides who dealt on a day-to-day basis with policies, negotiations or management of aid for these countries. For various reasons the meeting took the form of an unofficial round table and the official meeting was scheduled to take place at the end of October 1977.

Notes

PREFACE

1. Hassan M. Selim, *External Sources of Financing Economic Development*, Case-Studies on Selected Sources in East–West Developed Countries and International Organisations, UNIDO/IPPD, 60, December 1971.
2. Hassan M. Selim, *Financing and Project Appraisal in Developing Countries*, Case-Studies on Caisse Central de Coopération Economique (CCCE), Kreditanstalt für Wiederaufbau (KfW), and the Commonwealth Development Corporation (CDC), unpublished report, February 1977.

CHAPTER 1 : INTRODUCTION

1. Jan Tinbergen (co-ordinator), *Reshaping the International Order*, a report to the Club of Rome (Dutton, New York, 1976).
2. Speech at the 15th World Conference, Society for International Development, Amsterdam, by Jan Tinbergen, *Reshaping the International Order (RIO)*, 28 November–3 December 1976, Doc. SID. XV/17.

CHAPTER 2 : THE PERFORMANCE OF THE DEVELOPMENT ASSISTANCE COMMITTEE

1. George Cunningham, *The Management of Aid Agencies* (The Overseas Development Institute, London, 1974).
2. 'Billion' throughout the book refers to US billions (thousand million).
3. *World Development Report 1979* (World Bank, Washington DC, August 1979).
4. *Partners in Development*, Report of the Commission on International Development (Pearson Report) 1969.
5. Bruce Dinwiddy (ed.), *Aid Performance and Development Policies of Western Countries*, Overseas Development Institute (Praeger, 1973).
6. OECD, *Development Co-operation*, Reviews 1974–80.

CHAPTER 3 : THE UNITED STATES OF AMERICA

1. Hassan M. Selim, *External Sources of Financing Economic Development*, UNIDO/IPPD6O, December 1971. See also Appendix 3.1.

2. Appendix 3.1 and OECD, *Development Co-operation*, Review 1974.
3. See Appendix 3.1 and OECD, *Development Co-operation*, Review 1974.
4. Selim, op. cit., p. 14.
5. Ervin Laszlo (Gen. ed.), *Goals for Mankind*, A report to the Club of Rome (Hutchinson, London, 1977).
6. Robert A. Asher, *Development Assistance in the Seventies* (Brookings Institution, Washington DC, 1970).
7. *The United States and the Third World*, A Discussion Paper, Department of State Publication, General Foreign Policy Series 301, 1976.
8. Selim, op.cit., pp. 20–2.
9. *Implementation of The 'New Directions' in Development Assistance*. Report to the Committee on International Relations on Implementation of Legislative Reforms in the Foreign Assistance Act of 1973–22 July 1976.
10. *Meeting Basic Human Needs: The US Stake in a New Development Strategy*, A Report of the 25th Anniversary, International Development Conference, 7–9 February 1978, Washington DC.
11. Ibid., p. 20.
12. Ibid., p. 22.
13. *US Science and Technology for Development*: A contribution to the 1979 UN Conference on Science and Technology for Development, Vienna, 1979 (printed by the US Department of State).
14. George Cunningham, *The Management of Aid Agencies* (Overseas Development Institute, London, 1974).
15. Bruce Dinwiddy, (ed.) *Aid Performance and Development Policies of Western Countries* (Praeger, New York, 1973).
16. Selim, op. cit. p. 18.
17. Selim, op. cit, p. 19.
18. *Agency for International Development, Congressional Presentation*, Fiscal Year, 1980, Main volume, Dept. of State, AID, Washington DC, 1 February 1979.
19. OECD, *Aid Evaluation*, The Experience of Members of the Development Assistance Committee and of International Organisations, Paris, 1979. (A report on the exchanges of views which took place under the auspices of DAC between aid evaluation experts at Amsterdam on 27, 28, 29 June 1973. This meeting was the follow-up to a meeting on the same subject held at Wassenaar in 1970. A DAC Meeting of Experts on Project Appraisal was also held in Copenhagen on 8–10 October 1975.)
20. Ibid., pp. 93–5.

CHAPTER 4 : THE UNITED KINGDOM

1. OECD, *Development Co-operation*, Reviews 1979 and 1980.
2. OECD, *Resources for Developing Countries 1980 and Recent Trends*, Press Release, Press/A(81)26, Paris, 15 June 1981.
3. OECD, *Development Co-operation*, Review 1979.
4. Hassan M. Selim, *External Sources of Financing Economic Development*, UNIDO/IPPD.60, December 1971.
5. Ibid., p. 26.

Notes to Chapter 4

6. OECD, *Development Co-operation*, Review 1974.
7. OECD, *Development Co-operation*, Review 1978.
8. OECD, *Development Co-operation*, Review 1979, op. cit.
9. OECD, *Development Co-operation*, Review, 1980.
10. OECD, *Development Co-operation*, Review, 1974, op. cit.
11. Selim, op. cit., p. 28.
12. The decision in 1979 by the Conservative Government to abolish exchange control is too recent to be assessed.
13. OECD, *Investing in Developing Countries*, Chapter XVI (Paris, 1975).
14. *The Development Assistance Policy of the United Kingdom*, a speech by Reginald Prentice, Minister of Overseas Development, UK at the Vienna Institute for Development, 24 September 1969.
15. Selim, *External Sources of Financing Economic Development*, op. cit., pp. 29–31.
16. OECD, *Development Co-operation*, Review, 1975.
17. OECD, *Development Co-operation*, Review, 1977.
18. OECD, *Development Co-operation*, Review, 1979.
19. *United Kingdom Memorandum to the Development Aid Committee of the OECD*, Overseas Development Administration, 1979.
20. *The Mexican Summit and the Brandt Commission Report – The British Government's Role*, Foreign and Commonwealth Office, 2 October 1981.
21. George Cunningham, *The Management of Aid Agencies* (The Overseas Development Institute, London, 1974).
22. Bruce Dinwiddy (ed.), *Aid Performance and Development Policies of Western Countries*, Overseas Development Institute (Praeger, London, 1973).
23. Selim, op. cit., p. 29.
24. Cunningham, op. cit., p. 101.
25. Dinwiddy, op. cit., p. 31.
26. Ministry of Overseas Development, *A Guide to the Economic Appraisal of Projects in Developing Countries* (HMSO, London, revised edn 1977).
27. Ministry of Overseas Development, Economic Planning Staff, *Appraising Investment Proposals*, Vols. I and II (HMSO, London, 1978).
28. See for example: Overseas Development Administration, Project Data Handbooks on *Public Water Supplies, Ports, Tourism*, all in March 1972, *Buildings* (hospitals, schools, etc.), April 1972. See also Ministry of Overseas Development, Project Data Handbook, Section 7 on *Forestry and Wood-using Industries*.
29. See for example, Overseas Development Administration, Sector Appraisal Manuals: *Rural Development*, July 1980; *Beef*, June 1980; *Power Sector Planning*, June 1979.
30. OECD, *Aid Evaluation*, The experience of members of the Development Assistance Committee and of International Organisations (Paris, 1975).
31. This section is an abstract taken from an unpublished paper written by the author in 1977, *Financing and Project Appraisal in Developing Countries*; case-studies on Caisse Centrale de Coopération Economique, Kreditanstalt für Wiederaufbau, and the Commonwealth Development Corporation, updated and modified on the basis of information and comments received from CDC for which the author is most grateful.

CHAPTER 5 : FRANCE

1. OECD, *Development Co-operation*, Review, 1979.
2. OECD, *Development Co-operation*, Review, 1979.
3. In June 1978 the following countries belonged to the franc area: France, the French Overseas Departments (Guadeloupe, Guyana, Martinique, Réunion), the French Overseas Territories (Comoro Islands, New Caledonia, Wallis and Futuna, St. Pierre and Miquelon, French Polynesia), Cameroon, the Central African Empire, Chad, Congo (People's Republic of), Benin, Gabon, Ivory Coast, Mali, Niger, Senegal, Togo and the Upper Volta.
4. OECD, *Investing in Developing Countries* (Paris, 1978).
5. Ibid., p. 40.
6. Hassan M. Selim, *External Sources of Financing Economic Development*, UNIDO/IPPD.60, December 1971.
7. OECD, *Development Co-operation*, Review, 1974.
8. OECD, *Development Co-operation*, Review, 1975.
9. OECD, *Development Co-operation*, Review, 1976.
10. OECD, *Development Co-operation*, Review, 1977.
11. OECD, *Development Co-operation*, Review, 1978.
12. OECD, *Development Co-operation*, Review, 1980.
13. OECD, *Development Co-operation*, Review, 1981.
14. George Cunningham, *The Management of Aid Agencies* (The Overseas Development Institute, London, 1974).
15. This section is an abstract taken from an unpublished paper written by Hassan Selim in 1977, *Financing and Project Appraisal in Developing Countries*, case-studies on Caisse Centrale de Co-opération Economique, Kreditanstalt für Wiederaufbau, and the Commonwealth Development Corporation. Updated and modified on the basis of comments received from CCCE, for which the author is most grateful.

CHAPTER 6 : WEST GERMANY

1. Hassan M. Selim, *External Sources of Financing Economic Development*, UNIDO/IPPD.60, December 1971.
2. OECD, *Development Co-operation*, Review, 1979.
3. OECD, *Investing in Developing Countries* (Paris, 1978).
4. German Development Assistance Policies in 1972.
5. OECD, *Development Co-operation*, Review, 1975.
6. OECD, *Development Co-operation*, Review, 1978.
7. OECD, *Development Co-operation*, Review, 1979, p. 124.
8. *The Federal Republic of Germany and the Third World*, Co-operation in Development; translation published by the Press and Information Office of the Federal Government, Bonn, 30 May 1979.
9. OECD, *Development Co-operation*, Review, 1981.
10. Selim, *External Sources of Financing Economic Development*, op. cit.
11. DEG, *Annual Report*, 1980.
12. OECD, *Investing in Developing Countries*, op. cit., p. 57.

13. DEG, *Annual Report*, 1980, op. cit., p. 19.
14. DEG, *Investing in Developing Countries*, 4th edition, January 1979.
15. DEG, *Investing in Developing countries*, op. cit., pp. 16–17.
16. DEG, *Annual Report* 1979, op. cit., p. 15.
17. DEG, *Annual Report* 1979, op. cit., p. 13.
18. This section is an abstract taken from an unpublished paper written by the author in 1977, *Financing and Project Appraisal in, Developing Countries*, case-studies on Caisse Centrale de Coopération Economique, Kreditanstalt für Wiederaufbau, and Commonwealth Development Corporation updated and modified on the basis of comments received from KfW, for which the author is most grateful.

CHAPTER 7 : JAPAN

1. OECD, *Resources for Developing countries 1980 and Recent Trends*, Press Release, Press/A(81)26 (Paris, 15 June 1981).
2. OECD, *Investing in Developing Countries*, Fourth revised edition (Paris, 1978).
3. Ibid., pp. 62–3.
4. *Japan's Economic Cooperation*, Ministry of Foreign Affairs Japan, 1976.
5. *The Developing Countries and Japan*, Ministry of Foreign Affairs, Japan, 1979.
6. *New Economic and Social Seven-Year Plan*, Economic Planning Agency, Government of Japan, August 1979.
7. *Japan's Economic Co-operation*, Ministry of Foreign Affairs, Japan, 1976.
8. *The Overseas Economic Co-operation Fund, Japan, Its Role and Activities, 1979*. Information received by OECF Co-ordination Department in March 1981.
9. The Export-Import Bank of Japan, *Annual Report* 1976/77; *Role and Function*, 1976/77; *Annual Report*, Fiscal Year 1978 (year ended 31 March 1979); *Annual Report*, Fiscal Year 1979 (year ended 31 March 1980). Information received from the Export-Import Bank of Japan.
10. Japan International Co-operation Agency *Annual Report*, 1978.
11. Ibid., 1980.
12. Information received from JICA.
13. Japan International Co-operation Agency, *Annual Report*, 1980.
14. Japan International Co-operation Agency, *Annual Report*, 1978.
15. Japan International Co-operation Agency, *Annual Report*, 1979.
16. Japan International Co-operation Agency, *Annual Report*, 1980.

CHAPTER 8 : THE NETHERLANDS

1. OECD, *Investing in Developing Countries*, Fourth revised edition (Paris, 1978).
2. Ibid., pp. 66–7.
3. George Cunningham, *The Management of Aid Agencies* (The Overseas Development Institute, London, 1974).

4. OECD, *Development Co-operation*, Review, 1979.
5. *Bilateral Development Co-operation Concerning the Quality of Netherlands Aid*, 'Note presented to Parliament in September 1976 by the Netherlands Minister for Development Co-operation, Mr J. P. Pronk', Netherlands Co-operation with Developing Countries 12 (Development Co-operation Information Department of the Ministry of Foreign Affairs, The Hague).
6. *Development Co-operation and the World Economy*, Co-operation between the Netherlands and Developing Countries 16 (Development Co-operation Information Department of the Ministry of Foreign Affairs, The Hague).
7. *Netherlands' Development Co-operation Policy 1980*, Co-operation between the Netherlands and Developing Countries 17, (Development Co-operation Information Department of the Ministry of Foreign Affairs, the Hague).
8. Cunnigham, *The Management of Aid Agencies*, op. cit.
9. Netherlands Development Co-operation Policy 1980, op. cit.
10. The Netherlands Investment Bank for Developing Countries, *Annual Reports*, 1976, 1977, 1978, 1979, 1980 and information received from the bank.
11. Information received from Netherlands Investment Bank.
12. Netherlands Finance Company for Developing Countries, FMO *Brochure*, November 1979; FMO *Annual Reports* 1978, 1980. OECD, *Investing in Developing Countries*, Third revised edition (Paris, 1975); *Investing in Developing Countries*, Fourth revised edition (Paris, 1978). Information received from FMO.

CHAPTER 9 : SWEDEN

1. OECD, *Resources for Developing Countries, 1980 and Recent Trends*, Press Release, Press/A(81)26, (Paris, 15 June 1981).
2. OECD, *Investing in Developing Countries*, Fourth revised edition, (Paris, 1978).
3. Ruth Link, *TRAID*, reprint, Sweden, 1 November 1978.
4. *Guidelines for International Development Co-operation*, Statement by Mr Ola Ullsten, Minister for International Development Co-operation, in the Government Bill on International Development Co-operation, presented in Parliament on 30 March 1978, Stockholm.
5. Sweden's policy for International Development Co-operation, extracts from the Budget and Finance Bill for Fiscal year 1980/81, Stockholm 1980.
6. OECD, *Development Co-operation*, Review, 1979.
7. OECD, *Development Co-operation*, Review, 1981.
8. *Faktablad* (fact sheet), SIDA 1A, 'SIDA's Organisation', February 1977.
9. *Faktablad* (fact sheet), SIDA 3A, 'SIDA's Role in Decision Making on Development Co-operation with Individual Countries', August 1979.
10. Ernst Michanek (Director of SIDA), *Role of Swedish Non-governmental Organisations in International Development Co-operation*, a paper for UNITAR, April 1977.
11. Lars Ekengren and Lennart Wohlgemuth, SIDA, *Policy and Institutional Aspects of Project Appraisal – Swedish Experience*, Meeting of Experts on Project Appraisal, Copenhagen 8–10 October 1975 (OECD Working Document, Paris, 18 September, 1975).

12. OECD, *Aid Evaluation*, The Experience of Members of the Development Assistance Committee and of International Organisations (Paris, 1975).

CHAPTER 10 : THE COMMISSION OF THE EUROPEAN ECONOMIC COMMUNITY

1. Members of the European Community are Belgium, Denmark, France, West Germany, Ireland, Italy, Luxembourg, Netherlands, the United Kingdom and Greece (1 January 1981).
2. OECD, *Development Co-operation*, Review, 1981.
3. OECD, *Development Co-operation*, Review, 1979.
4. On 2 May 1980, 1 EUA = $1.384.
5. As of January–February 1981, ACP States included sixty members, they are: Bahamas, Barbados, Benin, Botswana, Burundi, Cameroon, Cape Verde, The Central African Republic, Chad, Comoros, Congo, Djibouti, Dominica, Equatorial Guinea, Ethiopia, Fiji, Gabon, Gambia, Ghana, Grenada, Guinea, Guinea Bissau, Guyana, Ivory Coast, Jamaica, Kenya, Kiribati, Lesotho, Liberia, Madagascar, Malảwi, Mali, Mauritania, Mauritius, Niger, Nigeria, Papua New Guinea, Rwanda, St Lucia, St Vincent and the Grenadines, Sao Tome Principe, Senegal, Seychelles, Sierra Leone, Solomon Islands, Somalia, Sudan, Suriname, Swaziland, Tanzania, Togo, Tonga, Trinidad and Tobago, Tuvalu, Uganda, Upper Volta, Western Samoa, Zaire, Zambia, Zimbabwe. *The Courier*, No. 65, January–February, 1981.
6. *Africa Research Bulletin*, 15, No. 2, 31 March 1978 (edited and published monthly by Africa Research Ltd).
7. *Africa Research Bulletin*, 15, No. 12, 31 January 1979.
8. *African Research Bulletin*, 16, No. 3, 30 April 1979.
9. *African Research Bulletin*, 16, No. 6, 31 July 1979.
10. ACP–EEC Convention of Lomé II, *The Courier*, No. 58, Special Issue, November 1979.
11. Ibid., p. 35.
12. *The European Community and The Third World*, Office for Official Publications of the European Communities, Luxembourg, November 1977.
13. An implementing Convention of the Treaty of Rome governed the special relations between the EEC and dependent overseas countries and territories; the first European Development Fund was established in 1959.
14. The attainment of independence, between 1960 and 1962, by eighteen African countries and Madagascar led to the signing of the first Yaoundé Convention, which came into effect on 1 June 1964 for a five-year period. It primarily contained trade arrangements involving reciprocal preferences and established the second EDF. It was followed by the second convention (launching the third EDF), which was signed in Yaoundé on 29 July 1969, came into effect on 1 January 1971, and expired on 31 January 1975. An Association Agreement with the three East African States (Kenya, Uganda and Tanzania) was signed in Arusha on 24 September 1969 to cover the same period as Yaoundé II and also expired on 31 January 1975. This agreement was, however, more limited in scope, and dealt mainly with trade

arrangements. It did not include provisions on financial and technical co-operation. Commission of the European Communities, *Information Memo*, Brussels, October 1979.
15. *EDF Procedures*, X/77/80-EN, Brussels, 3 January 1980.
16. Commission of the European Communities, Memo on *Stage reached in the Lomé II Programming*, VIII/617/80-EN, Brussels, 5 May 1980.
17. European Investment Bank, *Financing under the Second Lomé Convention*, May 1980.
18. This section is based upon a questionnaire sheet on financing and project appraisal prepared by the author and partially completed by the bank staff. It is also based upon the following reports and booklets provided by EIB: *Financing under the Second Lomé Convention*, January 1981; *Annual Report 1980*, May 1981; *Annual Report, 1979*, May 1980; *20 Years, 1958–78*, March 1978; *Annual Report, 1978*, May 1979; *Annual Report, 1977*, April 1978; *Operations under the Lomé; Convention, 1979; Financing outside the Community: Mediterranean Countries*, October 1978; *A memo on the Role of the European Investment Bank under the New EEC–ACP Convention*, 1979; *General Background on European Investment Bank*, 1977, 1978.
19. The EIB borrows and lends in many currencies. It keeps its accounts and statistics in units of account (EUA) which are the same in value as the European Currency Unit (ECU), composed of the sum of fixed amounts of the first nine member states' currencies DM0.828, £0.0885, Ffrs1.15, Lira109, Gld0.286, Bfr3.66, Lfr0.14, Dkr0.217, IR£0.00759. The conversion rates used for this leaflet are those of 31 December 1980, when 1 unit of account was equal to DM2.57, £0.55, Ffr5.94, Lira1217, Gld2.79, Bfrs41.34, Lfrs41.34, Dkr7.89, Dr61.26, IR£0.69, US$1.31.
20. On 12 June 1981, 1 ECU = DM 2.53, £0.54, Ffr6.03, Lira1261, Gld2.81, Bfrs41.33, Lfrs41.33, Dkr7.95, Dr61.26, Ir£0.69, US$1.31.

CHAPTER 11 : THE PERFORMANCE OF THE ORGANISATION OF THE PETROLEUM EXPORTING COUNTRIES

1. *OPEC, Facts, Figures and Analysis*, Deutsche Bank, May 1975.
2. Michael Field, *A Hundred Million Dollars a Day* (Sidgwick & Jackson, London, 1975).
3. Nicholas Fallon, *Middle East Oil Money and its Future Expenditure* (Graham & Trotman, London, 1975).
4. Philip Connelly and Robert Perlman, *The Politics of Scarcity, Resource Conflicts in International Relations* (Oxford University Press, London, 1975).
5. International Monetary Fund, *Annual Reports*, 1974–78.
6. Said El-Naggar, *The Impact of Oil Price Increase: A Critique*, The World Bank, unpublished document, 12 February 1980.
7. Ibid., p. 25.
8. Overseas Development Institute, 'OPEC Aid', *Briefing Paper*, No. 4, August 1980.
9. 'Arab Banks: recycling the OPEC surplus', *Middle East Review*, 1981.
10. Hassan M. Selim, 'Surplus Funds and Regional Development', *Energy and*

Development, Chapter II, Proceedings of the International Conference on the Economics of Energy and Development, (Ragaei El-Mallakh and Carl Mc Quire (eds), University of Colorado, Boulder, USA. A publication of the International Research Center for Energy and Economic Development, 1974.
11. Ibrahim F. I. Shihata and Robert Mabro, *The OPEC Aid Record*, The OPEC Special Fund, Vienna, January 1978.
12. Ecuador, Gabon and Indonesia are not included.
13. 'The OPEC Special Fund', *The UNCTAD Report on OPEC Aid*; A summary, July 1979.
14. Ibrahim F. I. Shihata, *OPEC as a Donor Group*, The OPEC Fund for International Development, December 1980.
15. *The UNCTAD Report on OPEC Aid*, op. cit., pp. 13, 16.
16. This section is mainly based upon information in the following chapters outlining the detailed performance of different OPEC institutions.

CHAPTER 12 : THE KUWAIT FUND FOR ARAB ECONOMIC DEVELOPMENT

1. Law No. 25, 1974, Articles 1 and 2.
2. Law No. 25, 1974, Article 3.
3. Traute Scharf, *Trilateral Co-operation*, Vol. 1. *Arab Development Funds and Banks: Approaches to Trilateral Co-operation* (Development Centre, OECD, Paris 1978).
4. Kuwait Fund for Arab Economic Development, *Sixteenth Annual Report*, 1977–78.
5. Kuwait Fund for Arab Economic Development, *Seventeenth Annual Report*, 1978–79.
6. Kuwait Fund for Arab Economic Development, *Annual Report* 1979–80.
7. John Law, *Arab Aid: Who Gets It, For What, and How* (Chase World Information Corporation, 1978).
8. Scharf, op. cit., p. 59.
9. Law, op. cit., pp. 56–7.

CHAPTER 13 : THE ABU DHABI FUND FOR ARAB ECONOMIC DEVELOPMENT

1. This chapter is based upon a paper submitted by the author to the *UNCTAD Meeting on Bilateral and Multilateral Financial and Technical Assistance Institutions and Representatives of the Least Developed Countries* (Geneva 14–22 March 1977 and 31 October–8 November, 1977) updated from the fund's Annual Reports and Documents.
2. When ADFAED was established, one Bahraini Dinar (BD) was equivalent to US $2.10. At the end of 1973, the exchange rate was BD1.00 = US $2.53. In mid-1973, a new currency was introduced, Dirham (Dh) with a gold content of 0.186621 gram of fine gold, thus set to be equal to SDR 0.21 and US $0.253.

3. ADFAED, *Annual Reports* 1978, 1979.
4. ADFAED, *Annual Reports* 1974–80.

CHAPTER 14 : THE SAUDI FUND FOR DEVELOPMENT

1. Saudi Fund for Development, *Annual Reports*, 1976/77, 1977/78.
2. Saudi Fund, *Annual Report*, 1977/78.
3. John Law, *Arab Aid: Who Gets It, For What, and How* (Chase World Information Corporation, 1978).
4. Article IV, Sections 4.01 and 4.02a, *General Conditions Applicable to Loan Agreements*, 26 July 1976.
5. Law, op. cit., p. 80.
6. The Saudi Fund for Development, *Feasibility of Joint Technical Resource Centre* (A Study) submitted by Urwick International Ltd, March 1978.
7. Comments by the author, *Meeting of the Delegates from Arab Funds and Banks* held on 28 and 29 June 1977 at the Saudi Fund for Development to discuss the Study on Joint Technical Resource Centre, Preliminary Report, Stage I, Urwick International.

CHAPTER 15 : THE ARAB FUND FOR ECONOMIC AND SOCIAL DEVELOPMENT

1. Article 2 of *Agreement Establishing the Arab Fund for Economic and Social Development*.
2. Article 10 of *Agreement Establishing the Arab Fund for Economic and Social Development*.
3. Arab Fund for Economic and Social Development, *Annual Report*, 1980 (in Arabic).
4. Arab Fund for Economic and Social Development, *Annual Reports*, 1974, 1975, 1976.
5. Arab Fund for Economic and Social Development, *Annual Report*, 1977.
6. Arab Fund for Economic and Social Development, *Annual Report*, 1978.
7. Arab Fund for Economic and Social Development, *Annual Report*, 1979 (in Arabic).
8. Arab Fund for Economic and Social Development, *Annual Report*, 1980.
9. AFESD, Agreement establishing the fund, op. cit., pp. 20–5.
10. Traute Scharf, *Trilateral Co-operation*, Vol. I, *Arab Development Funds and Banks: Approaches to Trilateral Co-operation* (OECD, Paris, 1978).
11. AFESD, *Annual Report* 1976, para. 6 of the Summary.
12. AFESD, *Annual Report* 1978, para. 7 of the Summary.
13. AFESD, *Annual Report*, 1976, para. 5 of the Summary.
14. AFESD, *Annual Report*, 1977, para. 11 of the Summary.
15. AFESD, *Annual Report*, 1977, (in Arabic) p. 80.
16. *Arab Economic Development in the Seventies and their Prospects in the Eighties*, Arab Fund for Economic and Social Development, April 1980 (in Arabic).
17. *Study on Arab Private Investment Flows in the Arab World*, A preliminary

report, Arab Fund for Economic and Social Development, March 1981 (in Arabic).
18. *Arab Economic Report 1980*, Arab Monetary Fund and Arab Fund for Economic and Social Development, August 1980 (in Arabic).
19. *Study on Economic Problems in the Least Developed Arab Countries*, Arab Fund for Economic and Social Development, March 1978 (in Arabic).
20. *Study on Human Resources and Labour Force Development in the Arab Region*, Arab Fund for Economic and Social Development, March 1978 (in Arabic).

CHAPTER 16 : THE ARAB BANK FOR ECONOMIC DEVELOPMENT IN AFRICA

1. ABEDA but French abbreviation BADEA.
2. *Agreement Establishing the Arab Bank for Economic Development in Africa*, Article 4 (in Arabic).
3. SAAFA was created to provide emergency balance-of-payment support after the 1973 oil price increase.
4. Arab Bank for Economic Development in Africa, *Annual Report*, 1980 (in Arabic).
5. Article 9 of the Agreement establishing the bank.
6. Arab Bank for Economic Development in Africa, *Annual Report*, 1978 (in Arabic).
7. Arab Bank for Economic Development in Africa, *Practical Procedures for the Bank's Financial Policy* (in Arabic).
8. Due to the problems of fluctuations in the value of the American dollar the management is studying alternative approaches including SDR and units of account.
9. *Agreement Establishing the Arab Bank for Economic Development in Africa* (in Arabic), Articles 17–20.
10. John Law, *Arab Aid: Who Gets it, For What, and How* (Chase World Information Corporation, 1978).
11. Arab Bank for Economic Development in Africa, op. cit., p. 10.
12. Arab Bank for Economic Development in Africa, op. cit., p. 9.
13. Arab Bank for Economic Development in Africa, *Arab-African Co-operation, Present and Future*, by Chedly El-Ayari, President of the Bank, November 1975 (in Arabic).
14. Arab Bank for Economic Development in Africa, *Arab Aid to African Sahel Countries*, Working Paper, April 1981 (in Arabic).

CHAPTER 17 : THE ISLAMIC DEVELOPMENT BANK

1. Islamic Development Bank, *Annual Report*, 1979/1980.
2. 'Arabia', *The Islamic World Review*, February 1981.
3. Islamic Development Bank, *Annual Report* 1979/1980, p. 99 (The Balance Sheet).
4. Islamic Development Bank, *Annual Report* 1979/80, p. 4.
5. Arabia, *The Islamic World Review*, op. cit., p. 50.

6. Islamic Development Bank, *Annual Report*, 1979/80, pp. 72–4.
7. Islamic Development Bank, *Regulations and By-Laws*, 1977.
8. Traute Scharf, *Trilateral Co-operation*, Vol. I, *Arab Development Funds and Banks: Approaches to Trilateral Co-operation* (OECD, Development Centre Studies, Paris, 1978).
9. John Law, *Arab Aid: Who Gets it, For What, and How* (Chase World Information Corporation, 1978).
10. Islamic Development Bank, *Agreement Establishing the Bank*, 1977 (in Arabic).
11. Law, op. cit., p. 140.
12. Islamic Development Bank, Regulations and By-Laws, pp. 5, 21–5.
13. Traute Scharf, op. cit., p. 198.
14. Islamic Development Bank, Regulations and By-laws, p. 30.
15. Islamic Development Bank, *Annual Report* 1979/1980, p. 67.
16. Islamic Development Bank, Agreement establishing the bank, op. cit., p. 12.
17. Islamic Development Bank, *Annual Report*, 1979/80, p. 52.
18. Islamic Development Bank, *Issues Relating to Cost Overrun Financing*, 12th Co-ordination Meeting of the Islamic Development Bank and the Arab Funds, Vienna, June 1981.

CHAPTER 18 : THE OPEC FUND FOR INTERNATIONAL DEVELOPMENT

1. Questionnaire on the orientation of OPEC Fund assistance prepared by the author and completed by the staff of the OPEC Fund, February 1980.
2. The OPEC Fund for International Development, *Basic Information*, July 1980.
3. Ibid., p. 4.
4. Questionnaire sheet.
5. The OPEC Fund, *Annual Report*, 1979.
6. The OPEC Fund, *Annual Report*, 1980.
7. The OPEC Fund for International Development, *Basic Information*, July 1980, pp. 7–9.
8. The OPEC Fund for International Development, *Questions and Answers*, July 1980.
9. The OPEC Fund, *Annual Report*, 1979.
10. The OPEC Fund, *Annual Report*, 1979.
11. The OPEC Fund, *Annual Report*, 1980, p. 26.

CHAPTER 19 : THE AFRICAN DEVELOPMENT BANK

1. John White, *Regional Development Banks* (Overseas Development Institute Ltd, London, 1970).
2. *Agreement Establishing the African Development Bank*, Article 1.
3. Ibid., Article 5.
4. The African Development Fund (AfDF) was established in July 1972 on the initiative of the African Development Bank as a multinational institution to

which 22 non-African capital-exporting countries agreed to subscribe. These participants (as at 31 December 1979) are: Argentina, West Germany, Saudi Arabia, Belgium, Brazil, Canada, Denmark, Spain, the United States of America, Finland, France, Italy, Japan, Norway, the Netherlands, the United Kingdom, Sweden, Switzerland, Yugoslavia, Kuwait, the United Arab Emirates.

AfDF has increased its capital stock substantially. The total contributions made since its inception currently amount to US $1,157.55m in respect of already ratified subscriptions and US $221.43m in respect of amounts that are yet to be ratified. *African Development Bank News*, March 1980.
5. *Agreement Establishing the African Development Bank*, Article 2.
6. The agreement establishing the Nigerian Trust Fund was signed on 26 February 1976 by the AfDB and the Federal Government of Nigeria. This Agreement entered into force on 25 April 1976. The Nigerian Trust Fund grants loans for a period of up to 25 years, with a grace period of up to 5 years. These loans carry an interest rate of 4 per cent per annum on the disbursed and outstanding amount and 0.75 per cent on the undisbursed portion. The resources of NTF are made up of funds contributed by the Federal Government of Nigeria. The NTF's initial resources amounted to 50m Naira or US $80m. *African Development Bank News*, op. cit., p. 37.
7. African Development Bank, *Annual Report*, 1979.
8. AfDF/NTF provide a grace period of about 10 and 5 years respectively. AfDF charges no interest but imposes service charges. NTF interest amounts to 3 per cent. Questionnaire sheet.
9. Letter from Dr Horst Moltrecht, The Co-ordinator of the Non-regional States, transmitting the Position Paper of the Non-regional States invited to participate in the African Development Bank. ADB/BG/XV/05 D. London, 14 February 1979.
10. African Development Bank, *Report on consultations held between the African Development Bank and non-regional states concerning their possible membership in the Bank*, Abidjan, Ivory Coast, February 1979.
11. African Development Bank, *Basic Information*, Abidjan, Ivory Coast, 30 June 1978.
12. 'African Development Bank Attracts International Interest', *African Economic Digest*, 30 May 1980.
13. Questionnaire sheet.
14. African Development Bank, *Basic Information*, op. cit., p. 8.
15. African Development Bank, *Annual Report*, 1979, p. 38.
16. Substantial additions to the resources of the AfDF are expected.
17. Questionnaire sheet.
18. Statement by Mr G. E. Gondwe, Acting President of the Bank and Fund, African Development Bank, Board of Governors, *Sixteenth Annual Meeting*, Abidjan, 23–27 June 1980.

CHAPTER 20 : ASIAN DEVELOPMENT BANK

1. Asian Development Bank, *Agreement Establishing the Asian Development Bank*, Chapter 1, Article 1.

Notes to Chapters 20–21

2. Asian Development Bank, *Questions and Answers*, April 1979.
3. Asian Development Bank, *A Decade of Progress*, Alan Chalkley, April 1977.
4. Asian Development Bank, *Agreement Establishing the Asian Development Bank*, Chapter II, Article 4 – Authorised Capital.
5. Asian Development Bank, *Annual Report*, 1979.
6. Asian Development Bank, *A Decade of Progress*, op. cit., p. 6.
7. Asian Development Bank, *Annual Report*, 1980.
8. Ibid., p. 39.
9. All programme loans from AsDB resources are amortised over 25 years including an 8-year grace period. Asian Development Bank, *Basic Information*, 1979.
10. Ibid., pp. 19–20.
11. Asian Development Bank, *Questions And Answers*, op. cit., pp. 17–19.
12. Asian Development Bank, *Basic Information*, op. cit., pp. 11–12.
13. Asian Development Bank, *Annual Report* 1979, pp. 39, 50.
14. Asian Development Bank, *What it is; What it does; How it works*, 1979.
15. Asian Development Bank, *Annual Report* 1979, pp. 25–27.
16. Asian Development Bank, *Technical Assistance Activities*, 1978.
17. Asian Development Bank, *Questions and Answers*, op. cit., p. 44.
18. *Asian Development Bank In Action*, a series of four feature articles, Asian Development Bank, 1977; Asian Development Bank, *Export Expansion and Economic Growth in the Developing Member Countries (DMCs) of AsDB*, occasional papers, No 10, May 1977; Asian Development Bank, *Appropriate Technology and its Application in the Activities of the Asian Development Bank*, Occasional papers, No 7, April 1977; Asian Development Bank, *Promoting Small-scale Industries: The Role of the Asian Development Bank*, occasional papers, No 9, June 1977.

CHAPTER 21 : CARIBBEAN DEVELOPMENT BANK

1. Caribbean Development Bank, *The First Ten Years 1970–1980*.
2. Caribbean Development Bank, *Its Purpose, Role and Functions, Twenty Questions and Answers*, May 1980.
3. Questionnaire sheet, 5 September 1980.
4. Caribbean Development Bank, *Its Purpose, Role and Functions*, op. cit., p. 9.
5. Caribbean Development Bank, *The First Ten Years*, op. cit., pp. 21–4.
6. Caribbean Development Bank, *Annual Report*, 1980.
7. Caribbean Development Bank, *The First Ten Years*, op. cit., p. 27.
8. Caribbean Development Bank, *Financial Policies*, Revised September 1979.
9. Caribbean Development Bank, *Its Purpose, Role and Functions*, op. cit., pp. 6–8.
10. Caribbean Development Bank, *Annual Report*, 1980, p. 60.
11. Caribbean Development Bank, *Annual Report*, 1979.
12. Caribbean Development Bank, *Its Purpose, Role and Functions*, op. cit., p. 14.

13. Caribbean Development Bank, *The First Ten Years*, op. cit., p. 14.
14. According to the Little–Mirrlees methodology, projects are considered and evaluated at all levels from a junior engineer to the Planning Commission or the World Bank. They are also analysed at all depths, from the back of an envelope to many volumes of erudite programming and scientific guesswork or prediction. Project decisions are taken at all levels: the process of design consists of rejecting and accepting alternatives, many of which are projects in the L–M sense of the term. L–M methodology deals with the economic rationale of social cost-benefit analysis in developing countries, and develops practicable procedures for evaluating investment projects. Many important issues in development economics are discussed, such as government objectives, income distribution, employment and shadow wage rates, the balance of payments, the role of planning agencies, and the treatment of the private sector. The chief purpose is to provide detailed procedures (and short cuts) that can be used by those who develop projects, prepare reports on them, or take decisions about them, and to explain the economic arguments for these procedures. See I. M. D. Little and J. A. Mirrlees, *Project Appraisal and Planning for Developing Countries* (Heinemann Educational, London, first published 1974).
15. Caribbean Development Bank, *Guidelines for Choice of Consultants*, revised, December 1978.
16. For procedures for procurement see Caribbean Development Bank, *Guidelines for Procurement*, September 1979.
17. Caribbean Development Bank, *Its Purpose, Role and Functions*, op. cit., pp. 17–19.
18. Caribbean Development Bank, *Annual Report* 1979, p. 25.
19. Caribbean Development Bank, *The Challenges of the Nineteen-Eighties*, Statement by President Mr William G. Demas to the Board of Governors at the Tenth Annual Meeting held at the Ambassador Beach Hotel, Nassau, Bahamas, 5–6 May 1980.

CHAPTER 22 : INTER-AMERICAN DEVELOPMENT BANK

1. John White, *Regional Development Banks* (Overseas Development Institute, London, 1970).
2. *Agreement Establishing the Inter-American Development Bank*, amended, 1977, Article I, Section 1.
3. Ibid., Article I, Section 2, p. 1.
4. Inter-American Development Bank, *Annual Report*, 1979, twenty years of activities.
5. Inter-American Development Bank, *Annual Report*, 1980.
6. Inter-American Development Bank, *Annual Report* 1980, p. 16.
7. Inter-American Development Bank, *Annual Report*, 1979, p. 35.
8. Inter-American Development Bank, *Annual Report*, 1980, p. 4.
9. Inter-American Development Bank, *The Complementary Financing Program of the Inter-American Development Bank* (Finance Department, Washington, DC 1979).

10. Rate valid for 1980. Also, loans to a member in its own currency at 4.0 per cent.
11. Includes grace period.
12. *Agreement Establishing the Inter-American Development Bank*, op. cit., p. 41.
13. IDB, *Annual Report*, 1979, p. 41.
14. *Agreement Establishing the Inter-American Development Bank*, op. cit., pp. 18–19.
15. Inter-American Development Bank, *By-Laws of the Bank and other Regulations Pertaining to the Board of Governors*, Washington DC, 1979.
16. Inter-American Development Bank, *Audit, Evaluation and other Control Systems*, 1980.
17. Inter-American Development Bank, Project Analysis Department, Guidelines for the Preparation of Loan Applications, *Agriculture: Integrated Agricultural and/or Rural Development*, May 1978; *Agriculture: Agricultural Research and Extension*, August 1978; *Fishery*, November 1978; *Water Supply*, June 1978; *Sewerage*, July 1978; *Industry*, June 1979; *Industry – Global Credit to Development Finance Institutions*, August, 1979; *Industrial Parks*, June, 1978; *Mining*, May 1978; *Tourism*, March, 1979; and *Education*, June 1977.
18. Inter-American Development Bank, Project Analysis Department, *Loan Portfolio Analysis: Methodology and Interpretation*, March, 1979.
19. *IDB News*, May 1980, 7, Number 3.
20. *IDB News*, April 1980, 7, Number 2.
21. IDB, *Audit, Evaluation and Other Control Systems*, op. cit., pp. 12, 14.
22. Annual series published by the bank since 1961. The purpose of these reports is to present a detailed review of development in Latin America in two principal aspects, economic and social. Each report is divided in two parts: the first one comprises a regional description of general and sectoral trends; the second one consists of such an analysis on a country-by-country basis. The preparation of these reports is the responsibility of the Economic and Social Studies Sub-Department in the Bank's Economic and Social Development Department. See, for example, *Inter-American Development Bank, Economic and Social Progress in Latin America*, 1979 Report, Washington DC.

CHAPTER 23 : THE INTERNATIONAL BANK FOR RECONSTRUCTION AND DEVELOPMENT

1. Edward S. Mason and Robert E. Asher, *The World Bank Since Bretton Woods* (The Brookings Institution, Washington DC, 1973).
2. International Bank for Reconstruction and Development, *Articles of Agreement* (as amended effective 17 December 1965), Article I.
3. World Bank, *Annual Report*, 1980.
4. This section is mainly from a paper submitted by Hassan Selim. *External Sources of Financing Economic Development*, Case-studies on Selected Sources in East-West Developed Countries and International

Organisations', Part III: 'Sources in International Organisations', UNIDO/IPPD.60. December 1971.
5. Mason and Asher, *The World Bank Since Bretton Woods*, op. cit., p. 193.
6. World Bank, *Annual Report*, 1980, pp. 57, 74–6.
7. IBRD, *Articles of Agreement*, op. cit., p. 9.
8. World Bank, *Annual Report*, 1980, p. 95.
9. IBRD, *Articles of Agreement*, op. cit., p. 10.
10. Mason and Asher, *The World Bank since Bretton Woods*, op. cit., p. 233.
11. The emphasis of financial analysis is on the cash flow of private and public sector funds related to a project and its effect on resource use, especially on investment in future periods.
12. Hirschman, 'Development Projects Observed', in Mason and Asher, *The World Bank since Bretton Woods*, op. cit., pp. 247–50.
13. Deepak Lal, *Methods of Project Analysis: A Review*, World Bank Staff Occasional Papers, No. 16 (Johns Hopkins University Press, Baltimore and London, 1976).
14. Louis Y. Pouliquen, *Risk Analysis in Project Appraisal*, World Bank Staff Occasional Papers, No. 11 (Johns Hopkins University Press, Baltimore and London, 1970).
15. Shlomo Rentlinger, *Techniques for Project Appraisal Under Uncertainty*, World Bank Staff Occasional Papers, No. 10 (Johns Hopkins University Press, Baltimore and London, 1970).
16. See, for example, *The design of Organizations for Rural Development Projects* – A Progress Report, World Bank Staff Paper, No. 375, March 1980. Also *Human Factors in Project Work*, World Bank Staff Working Paper No. 397, June 1980.
17. Robert S. McNamara, President, World Bank, *Address to the Board of Governors*, Washington, DC 30 September 1980.
18. Formally, the Joint Ministerial Committee of the Boards of Governors of the World Bank and the International Monetary Fund (IMF) on the Transfer of Real Resources to Developing Countries. Established in October 1974, the Committee consists of twenty members, generally Ministers of Finance, appointed in turn for successive periods of two years by one of the countries or groups of countries that designates a member of the bank's or IMF's Board of Executive Directors as the case may be. The Committee is required to advise and report to the Boards of Governors of the bank and the IMF on all aspects of the broad questions of the transfer of real resources to developing countries, and to make suggestions for consideration by those concerned regarding the implementation of its conclusions.
19. World Bank, *Urbanisation*, Sector Working Paper, June 1972.
20. World Bank, *Land Reform*, Sector Policy Paper, May 1975.
21. World Bank, *Agricultural Extension, the Training and Visit System*, by Daniel Benoi and James G. Harrison, May 1977.
22. *International Technology Transfer: Issues and Policy Operations*, prepared by Frances Stewart, Policy Planning Division, World Bank Staff Working Paper No. 344, July 1979.
23. 'Third World Needs are Immense', *Newsweek*, 24 November 1980.

CHAPTER 24 : THE INTERNATIONAL DEVELOPMENT ASSOCIATION

1. Edward S. Mason and Robert E. Asher, *The World Bank Since Bretton Woods* (The Brookings Institution, Washington DC, 1973).
2. International Development Association, *Articles of Agreement*, Article I.
3. *IDA Articles of Agreement*, Articles II and III.
4. World Bank, *Annual Report*, 1980.
5. This section is mainly from a paper submitted Hassan Selim, *External Sources of Financing Economic Development*, 'Case-studies on Selected Sources in East-West Developed Countries and International Organisations', Part III: *Sources in International Organisations*, UNIDO/IPPD.60. December 1971.
6. The Report of the Commission on International Development sponsored by but independent of the World Bank, was presented to the President of the bank on 15 September 1969, by the Commission's Chairman, Mr Lester B. Pearson, former Prime Minister of Canada. The Report, *Partners in Development*, surveyed in detail the past performance and the future prospects of the world development assistance effort. The report contained a large number of specific recommendations for policy actions by both donors and recipients of assistance. The President of the bank has submitted to the executive directors analytical memoranda on the recommendations directly affecting the World Bank Group's policies and operations. The directors' decisions related mainly to policies for the diversification of production activity in the primary producing countries, for strengthening the competitive position of primary products, and for assistance to appropriate international commodity arrangements. World Bank and IDA *Annual Report*, 1970.
7. IDA *Articles of Agreement*, Article 5, Section 3.
8. IDA *Articles of Agreement*, Article 6, Sections 1, 2, 3, 4, 5 and 6.
9. Escott Reid, *Strengthening the World Bank* (The Adlai Stevenson Institute, Chicago, Illinois, 1973).
10. *IDA Project Work*, IDA/RPL/79-6, 15 February 1979, a paper prepared for the information of the deputies.
11. *The Supervision and Evaluation of IDA Projects*, IDA/RPL/79-10, 11 May 1979, a paper prepared for the information of the deputies.
12. IDA *Project Work*, op. cit., p. 9.
13. IDA, *International Development Association*, World Bank, April 1977.
14. World Bank, *Annual Report*, 1980, p. 3.
15. IDA, International Development Association, April 1977, op. cit., p. 13.
16. *International Development Association, Resources and Operations*, The World Bank, May 1977.
17. *World Development Report, 1978*, The World Bank, Washington DC, August 1978.
18. *World Development Report, 1979*, The World Bank, Washington DC, August 1979.
19. *Additions to IDA Resources*: Sixth Replenishment, IDA/R76-145-20 December, 1979.
20. *IDA Project Work*, op. cit., p. 10.

CHAPTER 25 : THE INTERNATIONAL FINANCE CORPORATION

1. Edward S. Mason and Robert E. Asher, *The World Bank since Bretton Woods* (The Brookings Institution, Washington DC, 1973).
2. *Articles of Agreement of the International Finance Corporation*, 20 July 1956 (as amended by resolutions effective 21 September 1961 and 1 September 1965), Article I.
3. This section is mainly from a paper submitted by Hassan Selim, *External Sources of Financing Economic Development*, 'Case-studies on Selected Sources in East–West Developed Countries and International Organisations', Part III: *Sources in International Organisations*, UNIDO/IPPD.60, December 1971.
4. International Finance Corporation, *Annual Report*, 1973.
5. International Finance Corporation, *Annual Report*, 1974.
6. International Finance Corporation, *Annual Report*, 1975.
7. International Finance Corporation, *Annual Report*, 1976.
8. International Finance Corporation, *Annual Report*, 1977.
9. LAC I countries include Mexico, Colombia, Venezuela, Guyana, Central America and the Caribbean; LAC II includes all other Latin American countries.
10. International Finance Corporation, *Annual Report*, 1978.
11. International Finance Corporation, *Annual Report*, 1979.
12. International Finance Corporation, *Annual Report*, 1980.
13. *Articles of Agreement of the International Finance Corporation*, op. cit., p. 3.
14. IFC, *Annual Report*, 1979, p. 11.
15. IFC, *Articles of Agreement*, op. cit., Article III, Section 1, p. 2.
16. Mason and Asher, *The World Bank since Bretton Woods*, op. cit., pp. 359–60.
17. IFC, *Annual Report*, 1979, p. 10.
18. IFC *Annual Report*, 1973, p. 5.
19. IFC *Annual Report*, 1975, p. 8.
20. IFC *Annual Report*, 1978, p. 11.
21. IFC *Annual Report*, 1979, p. 10.
22. International Finance Corporation, *Five-year Programme FY79–83*, March, 1978.
23. IFC *Annual Report*, 1979, p. 11.

APPENDIX II : SURVEY OF INTERNATIONAL DEVELOPMENT STRATEGY

1. UN, *The Concepts of the Present Aid and Flow Targets*, Report by the Secretary-General of UNCTAD, New York, 1975.
2. Robert S. McNamara, President of the World Bank, *Address to the Board of Governors*, Belgrade, Yugoslavia, 2 October 1979.
3. Thomas G. Weiss, 'The Least Developed Countries during the 1980s', *Transnational Perspectives*, 5, No. 3, 1979.
4. James Grant, President – Overseas Development Council, 'Central Issues in the North–South Dialogue', *OECD Observer*, No. 96, January 1979. (The Overseas Development Council is a private, non-profit body concerned with

development research and public information and located in Washington.)
5. 'Disappointing End to Paris Talks', *Financial Times*, 3 June 1977.
6. Henry C. Beerits, *The United Nations and Human Survival* (American Friends Service Committee, Philadelphia, Pennsylvania, 1976).
7. Report of the committee established under General Assembly *Resolution 32/174* United Nations General Assembly, Thirty-third Session, A/33/34 (Part I), 1 March 1978.
8. Hans de Koster, the Netherlands, President of the Parliamentary Assembly of the Council of Europe, 'Elements of a New International Economic Order', *The OECD Observer*, No. 96/January 1979.
9. Draft *Terms of Reference* for the Brandt Commission.
10. *North–South: A Programme for Survival*, the Report of the Independent Commission on International Development Issues under the Chairmanship of Willy Brandt (Pan Books, London, 1980).
11. Ibid., pp. 290–2.
12. *World Development Report*, the World Bank, August 1978.
13. *World Development Report*, the World Bank, August 1979.
14. *World Development Report*, the World Bank, August 1980.
15. *World Development Report*, the World Bank, August 1981.
16. *Interfutures, Facing the Future: Mastering the Probable and Managing the Unpredictable* (OECD, Paris, 1979).
17. Comments by Hassan Selim on *Medium and Long Term Outlook for Food and Agricultural Development*, FAO, COAG/77/4, *Committee on Agriculture*, Fourth Session, Rome, 20–28 April 1977.
18. Comments by Hassan Selim on *Small Farmers' Development*, FAO, COAG/77/7, *Committee on Agriculture*, Fourth Session, Rome, 20–28 April 1977.
19. Comments by Hassan Selim on *Reducing Post-Harvest Food Losses*, FAO, COAG/77/6, *Committee on Agriculture*, Fourth Session, Rome, 20–28 April 1977.
20. A. Aten, *The World Needs More Food: Some Aspects of the World Food Problem*, Annex to the 65th Annual Report (1975) of the Royal Tropical Institute, Amsterdam.
21. 'Sahel Development Strategy Adopted', *The OECD Observer*, No. 87, July 1977.
22. *International Finance, Depressed Regions and Needed Progress*, Views and Recommendations of the Committee for Development Policy, United Nations, Department of Economic and Social Affairs, New York, 1976.
23. UNCTAD IV, *Least Developed Among Developing Countries, Developing Island Countries and Developing Land-Locked Countries*, TD/191/1976.
24. UNCTAD, Fourth Session, *Resolution Adopted by the Conference*, 98 (IV) TD/RES/21 June 1976.

References

Abu Dhabi Fund for Arab Economic Development, *Annual Reports*, 1974–80.
African Development Bank, *Basic Information*, Abidjan, Ivory Coast, 30 June, 1978.
—— *Report on Consultations held between the African Development Bank and Non-regional States concerning their Possible Membership of the Bank*, February 1979.
—— *African Development Bank News*, March 1980.
—— *Agreement Establishing the African Development Bank*, 10 September 1964.
African Economic Digest, 'African Development Bank Attracts International Interest', 30 May 1080.
Africa Research Bulletin, 15, Nos. 2 and 12, 31 January 1979; 16, No. 3, April 1979; 16, No. 6, 31 July 1979 (edited and published monthly by Africa Research Ltd).
Agency for International Development, *Congressional Presentation, Fiscal Year 1980*, Main Volume, Department of State Aid, Washington DC, 1 February 1979.
Arab Bank for Economic Development in Africa, *Annual Reports*, 1978–80 (in Arabic).
—— *Agreement Establishing the Arab Bank for Economic Development in Africa*, March 1975 (in Arabic).
—— *Arab Aid to African Sahel Countries*, Working Paper, April 1981 (in Arabic).
—— *Practical Procedures for the Bank's Financial Policy* (in Arabic).
Arab Economic Report 1980, Arab Monetary Fund and Arab Fund for Economic and Social Development, August 1980 (in Arabic).
Arab Fund for Economic and Social Development, *Agreement Establishing the Arab Fund for Economic and Social Development*, July, 1968.
—— *Study on Economic Problems in the Least Developed Arab Countries*, March 1978 (in Arabic).
Arab Fund for Economic and Social Development, *Annual Reports*, 1974–80.
—— *Arab Economic Development in the Seventies and their Prospects in the Eighties*, April 1980 (in Arabic).
—— *Study on Arab Private Investment Flows in the Arab World*, A preliminary report, March 1981 (in Arabic).
—— *Study on Human Resources and Labour Force Development in the Arab Region*, March 1978 (in Arabic).
Arabia, the Islamic World Review, February 1981.

Asher, Robert A. *Development Assistance in the Seventies* (Brookings Institution, Washington DC, 1970).
Asian Development Bank, *Agreement Establishing the Asian Development Bank*, December 1966.
—— *Annual Reports*, 1979, 1980.
—— *Appropriate Technology and its Application in the Activities of the Asian Development Bank*, occasional papers, No. 7 April 1977.
—— *Basic Information*, 1979.
—— *Export Expansion and Economic Growth in the Developing Member Countries (DMCs of AsDB)*, occasional papers, No. 10, May 1977.
—— *Promoting Small-scale Industries: The Role of the Asian Development Bank*, occasional papers, No. 9, June 1977.
—— *Questions and Answers*, April 1979.
—— *Asian Development Bank in Action*, a series of four feature articles, 1977.
Asian Development Bank, *Technical Assistance Activities*, 1978.
—— *What it Is; What it Does; How it Works*, 1979.
Beerits, Henry C., *The United Nations and Human Survival* (American Friends Service Committee, Philadelphia, Pennsylvania, 1976).
Benoi, Daniel and Harrison, James G. *Agricultural Extension, the Training and Visit System*, World Bank.
Brandt Commission, Draft, *Terms and Reference* for the Brandt Commission, 1977.
Caisse Centrale de Coopération Economique, *Annual Reports*, 1977–80.
—— *Aperçu des Opérations dans les Pays d'Afrique et de l'ocean Indien en 1980*.
Caribbean Development Bank, *Annual Reports* 1979, 1980.
—— *The Challenges of the Nineteen Eighties*, Statement by President Mr William G. Demas to the Board of Governors at the Tenth Annual Meeting, Nassau, Bahamas, 5–6 May 1980.
—— *Financial Policies*, revised, September 1979.
—— *The First Ten Years*, 1979–80.
—— *Guideline for Choice of Consultants*, revised, December 1978.
—— *Guideline for Procurement*, September 1979.
—— *Its Purpose, Role and Functions, Twenty Questions and Answers*, May 1980.
Chalkley, Alan, *A Decade of Progress*, Asian Development Bank, April 1977.
Commission of the European Communities, *Information Memo*, Brussels, October 1979.
—— Memo on: *Stage Reached in the Lomé II Programming*, VIII/617/80-EN, Brussels, 5 May 1980.
Connelly, Philip and Perlman, Robert, *The Politics of Scarcity, Resource Conflicts in International Relations* (Oxford University Press, London, 1975).
The Courier, 'ACP-EEC Convention of Lomé', No. 58, special issue, November 1979.
Cunningham, George, *The Management of Aid Agencies* (Overseas Development Institute, London, 1974).
DEG, *Investing in Developing Countries*, 4th edition, January 1979.
Dinwiddy, Bruce (ed.), *Aid Performance and Development Policies of Western Countries*, Overseas Development Institute (Praeger, 1973).
Department of State Publication, *The United States and the Third World*, A Discussion Paper, General Foreign Policy Series 301, 1976.

Deutsche Bank, *OPEC: Facts, Figures and Analysis*, May 1975.
EDF Procedures, X/77/80-EN, Brussels, 3 January 1980.
Ekengren, Lars and Wohlgemuth, Lennart, SIDA, *Policy and Institutional Aspects of Project Appraisal*, Copenhagen, 8–10 October 1975, OECD Working Document, Paris, 18 September 1975.
El-Ayari Chedly, *Arab-African Co-operation, Present and the Future*, Arab Bank for Economic Development in Africa. November 1975 (in Arabic).
El-Nagar, Said, *The Impact of Oil Price Increase: A Critique*, The World Bank, unpublished document, 12 February 1980.
The European Community and the Third World (Office for Official Publications of the European Communities, Luxembourg, November 1977).
European Investment Bank, *Brochure*, January 1981.
—— *Annual Meeting of the Governors of the European Investment Bank*, Press Release, Luxembourg, 15 June 1981.
—— *Annual Reports* 1977–80.
—— *20 Years, 1958–1978*, March 1978.
—— *Financing Outside the Community: Mediterranean Countries*, October 1978.
—— *Financing under the Second Lomé Convention*, May 1980.
—— *General Background on European Investment Bank*, 1977, 1978.
—— *A Memo on the Role of the European Investment Bank under the New EEC-ACP Convention*, 1979.
—— *Operations under the Lomé Convention*, 1979.
The Export-Import Bank of Japan, *Annual Reports* 1976/77–1979/80.
—— *Role and Functions*, 1976/77.
Fallon, Nicholas. *Middle East Oil Money and its Future Expenditure* (Graham & Trotman, London, 1975).
The Federal Republic of Germany and the Third World, Co-operation in Development (Press and Information Office of the Federal Government, Bonn, 30 May 1979).
Field, Michael, *A Hundred Million Dollars a Day* (Sidgwick & Jackson, London, 1975).
Financial Times, 'Disappointing End to Paris Talks', 3 June 1977.
FMO, Netherlands Finance Company for Developing Countries, *FMO Brochure*, November 1979.
—— *Annual Reports*, 1978, 1980.
Foreign and Commonwealth Office, *The Mexican Summit and the Brandt Commission Report – The British Government's Role*, 2 October 1981.
'German Development Assistance Policies in 1972', memorandum submitted by the Federal Republic of Germany for the Annual Aid Review 1973 of the Development Assistance Committee of OECD.
The German Development Company (DEG), *Annual Report*, 1978, 1979, 1980.
Gondwe, G. E. (Statement), Acting President of the Bank and Fund, African Development Bank, Board of Governors, *Sixteenth Annual Meeting*, Abidjan, 23–27 June 1980.
Government of Japan, *New Economic and Social Seven-Year Plan*, Economic Planning Agency, August 1979.
Grant, James, President, Overseas Development Council, 'Central Issues in the North–South Dialogue', *OECD Observer*, No. 96, January 1979.

Inter-American Development Bank, *IDB News*, May 1980, 7, No. 3 and April 1980, 7, No. 2.
—— *Agreement Establishing the Inter-American Development Bank*, Amended, 1977.
—— *Annual Report* 1979, twenty years of activities, and *Annual Report*, 1980.
—— *Audit, Evaluation and other Control Systems*, 1980.
—— *By-Laws of the Bank and other Regulations Pertaining to the Board of Governors* (Washington DC, 1979).
—— *The Complementary Financing Program of the Inter-American Development Bank* (Finance Department, Washington DC, 1979).
—— *Economic and Social Progress in Latin America*, 1979 Report (Washington DC).
Inter-American Development Bank, Project Analysis Department, Guidelines for the Preparation of Loan Applications. Agriculture: *Integrated Agricultural and/or Rural Development*, May 1978; *Agriculture: Agricultural Research and Extension*, August 1978; *Fishery*, November 1978; *Water Supply*, June 1978, *Sewerage*, July, 1979; *Industry*, June 1979, *Industry – Global Credit to Development Finance Institutions*, August, 1979, *Industrial Parks*, June 1978; *Mining*, May 1978; *Tourism*, March 1979; *Education*, June 1977.
—— Project Analysis Department, *Loan Portfolio Analysis*: *Methodology and Interpretation*, March 1979.
International Bank for Reconstruction and Development, *Articles of Agreement* (as amended effective 17 December 1965).
International Development Association, *Articles of Agreement*.
—— *Resources and Operations*, The World Bank, May 1977.
—— Additions to IDA Resources: Sixth Replenishment, IDA/R79-145, 20 December 1979.
—— *IDA*, World Bank, April 1977.
—— *IDA Project Work*, IDA/RPL/79–6, 15 February 1979, a paper prepared for the information of the deputies.
—— *The Supervision and Evaluation of IDA Projects*, IDA/RPL/79–10, 11 May 1979, a paper prepared for the information of the deputies.
International Development Conference, *Meeting Basic Human Needs: The U.S. Stake in a New Development Strategy*, a report of the 25th Anniversary.
International Finance Corporation, *Annual Reports*, 1970–81.
—— *Articles of Agreement*, 20 July 1956 (as amended by resolutions effective 21 September 1961 and 1 September 1965).
—— *Five Year Programme FY79–83*, March 1978.
International Monetary Fund, *Annual Reports*, 1974–78.
Islamic Development Bank, *Agreement Establishing the Bank*, 1977 (in Arabic).
—— *Annual Report*, 1979/80.
—— *Issues Relating to Cost Overrun Financing*, 12th Co-ordination Meeting of the Islamic Development Bank and the Arab Funds, Vienna, June 1981.
—— *Regulations and By-Laws*, 1977.
Japan's Economic Co-operation, Ministry of Foreign Affairs, Japan, 1976.
Japan International Co-operation Agency (JICA), *Annual Reports*, 1978–80.
Koster, Hans (The Netherlands), President of the Parliamentary Assembly of the Council of Europe, 'Elements of a New International Economic Order', *The OECD Observer*, No. 96/January 1979.

Kuwait Fund for Arab Economic Development, *Sixteenth Annual Report* 1977–78; *Seventeenth Annual Report* 1978–79, *Eighteenth Annual Report*, 1979–80.

Lal Deepak, *Methods of Project Analysis: A Review*, World Bank Staff Occasional Papers, No. 11 (Johns Hopkins University Press, Baltimore and London, 1976).

Laszlo, Irvin (general ed.), *Goals for Mankind, A Report to the Club of Rome* (Hutchinson, London, 1977).

Law, John, *Arab Aid: Who Gets It, For What and How* (Chase World Information Corporation, 1978).

Link, Ruth, *Traid*, reprint, Sweden, 1 November 1978.

Little, I. M. D. and Mirrlees, J. A., *Project Appraisal and Planning for Developing Countries* (Heinemann Educational, London, first published 1974).

Mason, Edward S. and Asher, Robert E., *The World Bank Since Bretton Woods* (The Brookings Institution, Washington DC, 1973).

McNamara, Robert S., President of the World Bank, *Address to the Board of Governors*, Belgrade, Yugoslavia, 2 October 1979.

—— *Address to the Board of Governors*, Washington DC, 30 September 1980.

Michanek, Ernst (Director of SIDA) *Role of Swedish Non-Governmental Organisations in International Development Co-operation*, a paper for UNITAR, April 1977.

Middle East Review, 'Arab Banks: Recycling the OPEC Surplus', 1981.

Ministry of Foreign Affairs (Japan), *The Developing Countries and Japan*, Tokyo, 1979.

Ministry of Overseas Development, Economic Planning Staff, *Appraising Investment Proposals*, Vols. I and II (HMSO, London, 1978).

—— *A Guide to the Economic Appraisal of Projects in Developing Countries* (HMSO, London, revised edn 1977).

Moltrecht, Horst, the co-ordinator of the non-regional states transmitting the position paper of the non-regional states invited to participate in the African Development Bank. ADB/BG/XV/05 D. London, 14 February 1979.

Netherlands Co-operation with Developing Countries 12, *Bilateral Development Co-operation concerning the Quality of Netherlands Aid*, Note presented to Parliament in September 1976 by the Netherlands Minister for Development Co-operation, Mr J. P. Pronk (The Hague).

Netherlands Ministry of Foreign Affairs, *Development Co-operation and the World Economy*, Co-operation between the Netherlands and Developing Countries 16, published by the Development Co-operation Information Department (The Hague).

—— *Netherlands' Development Co-operation Policy 1980*, Co-operation between the Netherlands and Developing Countries 17 (The Hague).

Netherlands Investment Bank for Developing Countries, *Annual Reports*, 1976–80.

Newsweek, 'Third World Needs are Immense', interview, A. W. Clausan, 24 November 1980.

North–South: A Programme for Survival, The Report of the Independent Commission on International Development Issues under the Chairmanship of Willy Brandt (Pan Books, London, 1980).

OECD, *Aid Evaluation*, The experience of Members of the Development Assistance Committee and of international organisations (Paris, 1979).

—— *Development Co-operation*, 1974–81 Reviews.
—— *Interfutures, facing the Future: Mastering the Probable and Managing the Unpredictable*, (Paris, 1979).
—— *Investing in Developing Countries* (Paris, 1975, 1978).
—— *Resources for Developing Countries 1980 and Recent Trends*, Press Release, Press/A(81)26, Paris, 15 June 1981.
The OPEC Fund, *OPEC and OPEC Aid Institutions, a Profile* (Vienna, Austria, 1980).
—— *Annual Reports* 1979, 1980.
—— *Basic Information*, July 1980.
—— *Questions and Answers*, July 1980.
The OPEC Special Fund, *The UNCTAD Report on OPEC Aid: A Summary*, July 1979.
Overseas Development Administration, Project Data Handbooks on *Public Water Supplies, Ports*, Tourism, all in March 1972, Buildings (Hospitals, Schools etc.), April 1972. Ministry of Overseas Development. Project Data Handbook, Section 7 on *Forestry and Wood–using industries*.
—— *United Kingdom Memorandum to the Development Aid Committee of the OECD*, 1979.
Overseas Development Institute, 'OPEC Aid', *Briefing Paper*, No. 4, August 1980.
Overseas Development Minister, *The Development Assistance Policy of the United Kingdom*, a speech by Reginald Prentice, Minister of Overseas Development, UK, at the Vienna Institute for Development, 24 September 1969.
The Overseas Economic Co-operation Fund, Japan, Its Role and Activities (Tokyo, 1979).
Partners in Development, Report of the Commission on International Development (Pearson Report) 1969.
Pauliquen, Louis Y., *Risk Analysis in Project Appraisal*, World Bank Staff Occasional Papers, No. 11 (Johns Hopkins University Press, Baltimore and London, 1970).
Reid, Escott, *Strengthening the World Bank* (Adlai Stevenson Institute, Chicago, Illinois, 1973).
Rentlinger, Shlomo, *Techniques for Project Appraisal Under Uncertainty*, World Bank Staff Occasional Papers, No. 10 (Johns Hopkins University Press, Baltimore and London, 1970).
Royal Tropical Institute, Amsterdam, *The World Needs More Food*, by A. Aten, some aspects of the world food problem, Annex to the 65th Annual Report (1975).
The Saudi Fund for Development, *Feasibility of Joint Technical Resource Centre* (A Study), submitted by Urwick International Ltd, March 1978.
Scharf, Traute, *Trilateral Co-operation*, Vol. 1. *Arab Development Funds and Banks: Approaches to Trilateral Co-operation* (Development Centre OECD, Parsis, 1978).
Selim, Hassan, *External Sources of Financing Economic Development*, Case-studies on Selected Sources in East-West Developed Countries and International Organisations, UNIDO/IPPD.60, December 1971.
—— *Financing and Project Appraisal in Developing Countries*, Case-studies on

Caisse Central de Coopération Economique (CCCE), Kreditanstalt für Wiederaufbau (KfW), and the Commonwealth Development Corporation (CDC), unpublished Report, February 1977.

—— *Medium and Long Term Outlook for Food and Agricultural Development*, FAO, COAG/77/4, *Committee on Agriculture*, Fourth Session, Rome, 20–28 April 1977.

—— *Comments: Meeting of the Delegates from Arab Funds and Banks* held on 28 and 29 June 1977 at the Saudi Fund for Development to discuss the 'Study on Joint Technical Resource Centre', Preliminary Report, State I, Urwick International.

—— *Reducing Post-Harvest Food Losses*, FAO, COAG/77/6, Committee on Agriculture, Fourth Session, Rome, 20–28 April 1977.

—— *Small Farmers' Development* FAO, COAG/77/7, *Committee on Agriculture*, Fourth Session, Rome, 20–28 April 1977.

—— 'Surplus Funds and Regional Development', *Energy and Development*, Chapter 11, Proceedings of the International Conference on the Economics of Energy and Development, Ragaei El-Mallakh and Carl McQuine (eds), University of Colorado, Boulder, USA (International Research Centre for Energy and Economic Development, 1974).

Shihata, Ibrahim, and Mabro, Robert, *The OPEC Aid Record* (The OPEC Special Fund, Vienna, January 1978).

SIDA, *faktablad* (fact sheet) SIDA 1A, 'SIDA's Organisation', February 1977.

—— *faktablad* (fact sheet), SIDA 3A, 'SIDA's Role in Decision Making on Development Co-operation with Individual Countries', August 1979.

Stewart, Francis, *International Technology Transfer: Issues and Policy Operations*, Policy Planning Division, World Bank Staff Working Paper No. 344, July 1979.

Swedish Development Co-operation – A Summary 1978/79, SIDA, Information Division, 1978.

Tinbergen, Jan (Co-ordinator) *Reshaping the International Order*, a report to the Club of Rome (Dutton, New York, 1976).

Ullesten, Ola (Statement) *Guidelines for International Development Co-operation*, Statement by Minister for International Development Co-operation, in the Government Bill on International Development Co-operation, presented in Parliament on 30 March 1978 (Stockhoolm, 1978).

United Nations. *The Concept of the Present Aid and Flow Targets*, Report by the Secretary-General of UNCTAD, (New York, 1975).

—— *International Finance, Depressed Regions and Needed Progress*, Views and Recommendations of the Committee for Development Policy, United Nations, Department of Economic and Social Affairs (New York, 1976).

—— Report of the Committee Established Under General Assembly *Resolution 32/174* UN General Assembly, Thirty-Third Session, A/33/34 (Part I), 1 March 1978.

UNCTAD IV, *Least Developed Among Developing Countries, Developing Island Countries and Developing Land-Locked Countries*, TD/191/1976.

UNCTAD, Fourth Session, *Resolution Adopted by the Conference, 98 (IV)* TD/RES/21 June 1976.

US Department of State, *U.S. Science and Technology for Development*: a

contribution to the 1979 UN Conference on Science and Technology for Development, Vienna, 1979.
US Overseas Loans and Grants and Assistance from International Organisations, Special Report prepared for the House Foreign Affairs Committee, 1971.
Weiss, Thomas G., 'The Least Developed Countries during the 1980s' *Transnational Perspectives*, 5, No. 3, 1979.
White, John, *Regional Development Banks* (Overseas Development Institute, London, 1970).
World Bank, *Annual Reports*, 1963/1964–1966/67, 1968–81.
—— *The Design of Organisations for Rural Development Projects, A Progress Report*, World Bank Staff Paper, No. 375, March 1980. Also *Human Factors in Project Work*, World Bank Staff Working Paper No. 397, June 1980.
—— *Land Reform*, Sector Policy Paper, May 1975.
—— *World Development Reports* 1978–81, Washington DC, August 1978, 1979, 1980 and 1981.
—— *Urbanisation*, Sector Working Paper, June 1972.

Questionnaire on Financing and Project Appraisal in Developing Countries

Prepared by Dr Hassan M. Selim

1. Name and address of organisation:

2. Capital:

3. Resources and capacity for financing:

4. Scope of activities:
   4.1 Area:
   4.2 Region:
   4.3 Sub-region:
5. Project type:
   5.1 Development project:
   5.2 Infrastructure project:
   5.3 Productive project:
   5.4 Others:
6. Participation:
   6.1 Shareholding:
   6.2 Short-term loan:
   6.3 Medium-term loan:
   6.4 Long-term loan:
   6.5 Soft loan:
   6.6 Tied aid:
   6.7 Supplementary financing:

6.8 Concessionary aid:
6.9 Technical assistance:
6.10 Others:
7. Terms and conditions of:
   7.1 Interest rate:
   7.2 Repayment period:
   7.3 Grace period:
   7.4 Guarantee:
   7.5 Insurance:
8. Management and administration:

9. Marketing studies:

10. Approaches to be taken:

11. Techniques to be applied:

12. Problems of implementation and follow-up:

13. Strategy for financing and technical assistance:
    13.1 Area (region):
    13.2 Sector:
    13.3 Project
    13.4 General policy:
14. Future strategy for financing and technical assistance:
    14.1 Area (region):
    14.2 Sector:

14.3 Project:
14.4 General policy:
15. Remarks from field experience:

Index

Abu Dhabi 199
Abu Dhabi Fund for Arab Economic Development (ADFAED) xx, 14, 15, 206, 207, 217–24, 432
  approaches and techniques applied 221–2
  field experience 224–4
  legal status, purpose and power of 217–18
  management of 220–1
  problems of implementation 222–4
  scope of activities 218–20
  terms and conditions 220–1
Abu Qir Electric Power Plant 218
Accounting Rate of Interest (ARI) 68
ACP states 174–80
Afghanistan 290, 297, 389, 488
Africa 58, 75, 103, 135, 147, 173, 190, 216, 218, 225, 347, 389–92, 484, 488
African Development Bank 19, 77, 254, 276–86, 444
  approaches and techniques applied 284–5
  establishment of 276–7
  field experience 286
  financial resources 276–7
  management and administration 281
  non-regional states 281–4
  problems of implementation 286
  scope of activities 277–9
  strategy for financing and technical assistance 285–6
  terms and conditions 279

African Development Fund 86
African Solidarity Fund 86
Agency for International Development (AID) 6, 44–7, 52–3, 403
Agricultural sector in developing countries 484–6
Agricultural Trade Development and Assistance Act 49
Algeria 83–5, 199, 268
Antigua 304, 305
Antilles 84
Appraising Investment Proposals 68
Arab Authority for Agricultural Investment and Development (AAAID) 14, 206
Arab Bank for Economic Development in Africa (ABEDA) 14, 16, 206, 207, 208, 246–56, 438
  approaches and techniques applied 253–4
  establishment of 246–8
  field experience 255–6
  financial resources 246–8
  management and organisational structure 252–3
  problems and implementation 255–6
  scope of activities 249–51
  strategy for financing and technical assistance 254–5
  terms and conditions 251–2
Arab Fund for Economic and Social Development (AFESD) 14, 16, 206, 207, 234–45, 436
  approaches and techniques applied 241–2
  establishment of 234–7
  field experience 243–5

AFESD – *continued*
  financial resources 234–7
  management and organisation 240–1
  problems of implementation 243–5
  scope of activities 237–9
  strategy for financing and technical assistance 242–3
  terms and conditions 240
Arab Monetary Fund (AMF) 14, 206
Argentina 84
Asia 48, 66, 75, 87, 103, 135, 147, 216, 218, 225, 347, 389–92
Asian Development Bank (AsDB) 19, 27, 287–302, 448
  approaches and techniques applied 295–7
  establishment of 287–8
  field experience 299–302
  financial resources 288–9
  organisational structure 294–5
  problems of implementation 299–302
  scope of activities 290–3
  strategy for financing and technical assistance 297–9
  terms and conditions 294
Australia 35
Austria 35

Bahamas 83, 304, 305
Bahrain 83
Bangladesh 58, 64, 143, 163, 173, 297
Bank of International Settlements (BIS) 145
Barbados 303, 305
Belize 304, 306
Bergsten, C. Fred 45, 46
Bolivia 389
Botswana 163
Brandt Commission 14, 478–80
Brazil 43, 83, 85, 162
British Council 64
British Virgin Islands 304, 306
Burma 297

Caicos Islands 304, 306
Caisse Central de Coopération Economique (CCCE) xxi, 8, 77, 84, 87, 88–95, 408
  approaches and techniques applied 93–4
  establishment of 88–9
  field experience 95
  financial resources 88–9
  management and administration 93
  problems of implementation 95
  scope of activities 89–92
  strategy for financing and technical assistance 94
  terms and conditions 92
Cambodia 84, 297
Cameroon 70, 141, 389
Caribbean 64, 75, 173, 190, 347, 389, 390–2
Caribbean Development Bank 20, 303–16, 452
  approaches and techniques applied 312–14
  establishment of 303–4
  field experience 315–16
  financial resources 303–5
  organisational structure 310–12
  problems of implementation 315–16
  scope of activities 304
  strategy for financing and technical assistance 314–15
  terms and conditions 309–10
Castle, Barbara 66
Cayman Islands 304, 306
Central Bank of the Central African States 84
Central Office of Programme Methods and Evaluation 52
China 297
Clausen, A. W. 358
Club de Sahel 484, 486–7
Commonwealth Development Corporation (CDC) xxi, 7, 69–78, 406
  approaches and techniques applied 76
  establishment of 69–70

field experience 77–8
financial resources 69–70
management and administration 75–6
marketing department 76
participation 70
problems of implementation 77–8
strategy for financing and technical assistance 76–7
technical assistance 73–4
term loans 74–5
Comoro Islands 216
Conference on International Economic Co-operation (CIEC) 478
Cook Islands 297, 299
Costa Rica 70
Cyprus 49, 389

Denmark 35
Départements d'Outre-mer 87
Department of Technical Co-operation 65
Deutsche Entwicklungsgesellschaft (DEG) 9, 104–9, 410
 approaches and techniques applied 107–8
 establishment of 104
 field experience 108–9
 objectives of 104
 problems of implementation 108–9
 scope of activities 104–7
 strategy for financing and technical assistance 108
 terms and conditions 107
Development Assistance Committee 3, 24–6
 contributions to multilateral institutions 34–5
 establishment of 31–2
 financial resources 32
 history of 31
 performance of 31–8
 see also under specific countries
Development Assistance Group 31
Development Assistance Policies 4–5

Development Co-ordination Committee 52
Development industriel à l'etranger 84
Discount rate 68
Djibouti 216
Dominica 304, 306

Economic Commission for Asia and the Far East (ECAFE) 287
Economic Development Institute 349
Economic and Social Commission for Asia and the Pacific (ESCAP) 287
Ecuador 70, 268
Egypt 49, 135, 141, 173, 199, 200, 218, 390
Energy Fund for Exploration and Pre-investment Surveys 275
Ethiopia 70, 163
Europe 347, 389–92
European Development Fund 87, 180–5, 426
 aid programming 181
 financing the project 182
 problems of implementation 182–3
 project design and appraisal 181–2
 remarks from field experience 182–3
 resources and procedures of financing 180
European Economic Community 3, 12–13, 35, 173–95
 aid administered by 180–94
 bilateral agreements 175
 Development Assistance Policy 175–80
 financial resources 174
 Official Development Assistance 173–5
European Investment Bank (EIB) 177, 182, 184, 185–94, 428
 approaches and techniques applied 190
 economic data 192
 establishment of 185

EIB – *continued*
   financial data   192
   financial resources   185, 195
   general and legal information   190–1
   management and administration   193
   operations outside the Community   190
   operations within the Community   189
   scope of activities   187–8
   technical data   191
   terms and conditions   193
Export Credits Guarantee Board (EKN)   160
Export Credits Guarantee Department (ECGD)   60, 62
Export-Import Bank of Japan (EXIM Bank)   10, 125, 127–31, 416
   establishment of   127–8
   financial resources   127–8
   scope of activities   128–31
   strategy for financing and technical assistance   131

Fiji   297, 299
Finland   35
Food and Agricultural Organisation   485–6
Food for Peace Grant Programmes   53
Foreign and Commonwealth Office   58–9, 63, 65
France   7, 34–7, 64, 80–96
   Development Assistance Policy   85–8
   financial flows   88
   financial resources   81
   official development assistance   80–2
   private flows   82–5
Fund for Aid and Co-operation (FAC)   84
Future Development of Advanced Industrial Societies in Harmony with that of Developing Countries   483–4

Gabon   268
GDP   377
Geneva Conference   103
German Agency for Technical Co-operation (GTZ)   102
German Appropriate Technology Exchange (GATE)   102
German Development Company. *See* Deutsche Entwicklungsgesellschaft
German Foundation for International Development (DSE)   101
Gilligan, John J.   45
GNP   3, 7, 11, 14, 32, 34, 55, 63, 65, 80, 86, 87, 138, 142, 157, 162, 204, 222, 472, 473, 482, 484
Grenada   304, 306
Greece   43, 190
Guide to the Economic Appraisal of Projects in Developing Countries   67, 68, 69
Guidelines for Bilateral German Capital Aid   110
Guinea   84
Guyana   304, 306

Hallway Hotels Overseas Limited   74
Honduras   70
Hong Kong   291, 297

India   57, 58, 64, 85, 162, 163, 173
Indonesia   64, 70, 135, 141, 199, 268, 297
Industrial Project Appraisal in Developing Countries   67
Inter-American Development Bank   21, 86, 226, 317–38, 456
   approaches and techniques applied   332–4
   establishment of   317–18
   field experience   336–8
   financial resources   318–21
   organisational structure   329–31
   problems of implementation   336–8
   scope of activities   321–7
   strategy for financing and technical assistance   335–6
   terms and conditions   327–9

Index

Inter-ministerial High-level Consultative Group for Relations with the Developing Countries 162
International Bank for Reconstruction and Development (IBRD) 21, 64, 339–58, 460
  approaches and techniques applied 351–4
  establishment of 339–40
  field experience 356–8
  financial resources 340–2
  management and organisational structure 350–1
  problems of implementation 356–8
  scope of activities 342–9
  strategy for financing and technical assistance 354–6
  terms and conditions of loans 349–50
International Development Association (IDA) 22–3, 148, 359–79, 464
  approaches and techniques applied 372–4
  establishment of 359
  field experience 378–9
  financial resources 360–4
  management and organisational structure 369–72
  problems of implementation 378–9
  scope of activities 364–8
  strategy for financing and technical assistance 374–8
  terms and conditions 368–9
International Development Bank 27, 43
International Development Corporation 44
International Development Council 43
International Development and Humanitarian Assistance Act 44
International Development Institute 43, 44
International development strategy 24–7, 472–91

International Export Credit Guarantee Facility 145
International Finance Corporation 23–4, 380–402, 468
  approaches and techniques applied 395–7
  establishment of 380
  field experience 400–2
  financial resources 382
  management and organisational structure 394
  problems of implementation 400–2
  scope of activities 385–92
  strategy for financing and technical assistance 398–400
  terms and conditions 392–3
International Monetary Fund (IMF) 145, 200, 329, 480
International Security Assistance Act 44
Iran 85, 199, 268
Iraq 199, 268
Iraqi Fund for External Development 14, 206
Islamic Development Bank 14, 17, 206–8, 257–67, 440
  approaches and techniques applied 264–5
  establishment of 257–9
  field experience 266
  financial resources 257–9
  management and organisational structure 263–4
  problems of implementation 266
  scope of activities 259–62
  strategy for financing and technical assistance 265–6
  terms and conditions 262
Islamic Sharia Law 208
Israel 49, 85, 175, 199, 200
Ivory Coast 70, 141

Jamaica 58, 304, 306
Japan 9, 34, 35, 118–37
  Development Assistance Policy 122–4
  financial flows 124–37
  financial resources 119, 137

Japan – *continued*
  Official Development Assistance 118
  private flows 118–21
  strategy for financing and technical assistance 127
Japan Emigration Service Co-operation 135
Japan International Co-operation Agency (JICA) 10, 131–7, 418
  development co-operation programme 135
  development survey programme 133–5
  establishment of 131
  financial resources 131
  scope of activities 131–3
  training programme 133

Kasungu Flue-cured Tobacco Authority 74
Kenya 57, 58, 141, 163
Kenya Tea Development Authority 74
Korea 141, 297
Kreditanstalt für Wiederaufban (KfW) 9, 109–16, 412
  approaches taken 112–13
  establishment of 109
  field experience 116
  financial resources 109
  management and administration 112
  marketing studies 112
  problems of implementation 116
  scope of activities 109–11
  strategy for financing and technical assistance 114–16
  technical assistance 110
  techniques applied 113–14
  terms and conditions 111
Kuwait 199, 268
Kuwait Fund for Arab Economic Development (KFAED) 14, 15, 206, 211–16, 430
  approaches and techniques applied 214–15
  capital 211
  establishment of 211
  management and administration 213–14
  problems of implementation 215
  remarks from field experience 215
  resources and capacity for financing 211
  scope of activities 211–13
  strategy for financing and technical assistance 215–16
  terms and conditions 213

Labour costing 67
Laos 84, 297
Latin America 48, 66, 135, 147, 175, 216, 225, 226, 317, 347, 389–92
Least developed countries (LLDCs) 15, 17, 18, 20, 25, 65, 86, 87, 102, 103, 105, 110, 143, 148, 163, 201, 204, 206, 209, 215, 216, 221, 224, 238, 239, 261, 263, 266, 269, 273, 275, 306, 307, 358, 474, 487–91
Lebanon 85, 190
Leeward Islands 303
Lesotho 391
Less developed countries 476
Liberia 70
Libya 199, 268
Libyan Bank for Foreign Assistance 14, 206
Little, I. M. D. 67
Lomé Conventions 175–81

McNamara, Robert 473
Madagascar 84, 93
Maghreb 175
Malagasy 85
Malawi 58, 390
Malaysia 73, 85, 135, 141, 297
Maldives 297
Mali 391
Malta 57, 212
Mananga Agricultural Management Centre 73
Mashreq 175
Mauritania 238, 240
Methods of Project Analysis: a Review 353
Mexico 43, 84, 162
Middle East 135, 347, 389–92

Ministry of Overseas Development (ODM) 66
Mirrlees, J. A. 67
Montserrat 304, 306
More Help for the Poorest (White Paper) 63
Morocco 141
Most seriously affected countries (MSA) 103

National Development Finance Institutions (DFIs) 291–2
Nepal 64, 297, 389
Net Present Value (NPV) 68
Netherlands 10–11, 32, 34, 84, 138–56
   administration of aid programme 146–55
   Development Assistance Policy 142–6
   financial resources 139, 156
   Official Development Assistance 138–46
   private flows 140–2
Netherlands Finance Company for Developing Countries (FMO) 11, 149–55, 422
   approaches taken and techniques applied 153–4
   establishment of 149–51
   field experience 154
   financial resources 149–51
   management of 153
   problems of implementation 154
   scope of activities 151
   terms and conditions 151–2
Netherlands Investment Bank for Developing Countries 11, 147–9, 420
New International Economic Order 2, 25, 269, 473, 476–8, 487
Nigeria 73, 84, 268
North Africa 87, 89
North-South dialogue 475–6
Norway 35

OAPEC (Organisation of Arab Petroleum Exporting Countries) 199

Official Development Assistance (ODA) 3, 25, 32–4, 39–40
OPEC 3, 8, 24–6, 77, 145, 199–210, 482, 487
   aid institutions 206–9
   development assistance to developing countries 206
   Development Assistance Committee 26
   development funds 13–19
   financial assistance to developing countries 203–5
   new factor in world economy 199–203
OPEC Fund for International Development 14, 18, 206, 268–75, 442
   approaches and techniques applied 272
   establishment and objective 268–9
   management and administration 272
   scope of activities 269–70
   strategy for financing and technical assistance 273
   terms and conditions 270–2
Organisation for Economic Co-operation and Development 67, 142, 145, 148, 482, 487, 483–4
   Research Project 483–4
Organisation for European Economic Co-operation (OEEC) 31
Overseas Departments and Territories 86
Overseas Development Administration 7, 59, 63–9, 404
Overseas Economic Co-operation Fund (OECF) 10, 124, 136, 414
   establishment of 124
   financial resources 124
   scope of activities 125–6
   terms and conditions 126
Overseas Private Investment Corporation (OPIC) 43
Overseas Technical Co-operation Agency 135

Pacific Islands 75

Pakistan   58, 85, 163, 173, 297, 488
Papua New Guinea   297, 299
Paraguay   389
Philippines   49, 70, 85, 135, 297
Policy Paper on Co-operation with Developing Countries   103
Portugal   190
Prices, international   67
Private flows   35–7
  see also under specific countries
Project Data Handbooks   68
Project Evaluation Guidelines   52
Project Evaluation Workbook   52
Project Performance Audit Reports   297
Project Preparation Facility   349
Public Law 480 Programme   49

Qatar   199, 268

Reddaway Report   61
Regional Development Banks   3, 19, 25
Reshaping the International Order   1
Risk Analysis in Project Appraisal   353
Ruth Link   161
Rwanda   70, 390

Sahel   87
Sahel Development Programme   47, 48
St Kitts-Nevis-Anguilla   304, 306
St Lucia   304, 306
St Vincent   304, 306
Saudi Arabia   199, 268
Saudi Arabian Monetary Agency   229
Saudi Fund for Development (SFD)   14, 15, 206, 207, 225–33, 434
  approaches applied   229
  authorised capital   225
  establishment of   225
  financial resources   225
  Joint Technical Resource Centre   230–3
  management and administration   229
  problems of implementation and follow-up   229
  scope of activities   225
  strategy for financing and technical assistance   230
  terms and conditions   227–9
Savannah Sugar Company   73
Scandinavia   32, 34
Security Supporting Assistance Programme   48
Select Committee on Overseas Development   64
Senegal   141
SHELTER-AFRIQUE   77
Sinai Support Mission   49
Singapore   85, 297
Society for International Development   xxi
Solomon Islands   297, 299
Somalia   238, 240
South-East Asia   175
South Yemen   216
Southern Asia   58, 488, 489
Spain   49, 84
Special Arab Aid Fund for Africa (SAAFA)   246
Sri Lanka   64, 297
Sudan   70, 141, 143, 163, 238
Swaziland   73, 391
Swaziland Irrigation Scheme   74
Sweden   11–12, 157–72
  administration of aid programme   163–71
  Development Assistance Policy   161–3
  financial resources   158, 172
  multilateral investment   160
  Official Development Assistance   157–9
  private flows   159–61
Swedish International Development Authority (SIDA)   12, 161, 163–71, 424
  aid through non-governmental organisations   167–9
  aid to developing countries   167
  budget proposals   165
  divisions of   164
  establishment of   163–5
  organisational structure   163–5
  problems of aid evaluation and techniques applied   170–1

programme cycle 166
Switzerland 36, 37
Syria 199

Taiwan 43
Tanzania 141, 143, 163
Task Force on International Development 44
Techniques for Project Appraisal under Uncertainty 353
Technology Information Unit 309
Territoires d'Outre-mer (TOM) 87
Thailand 70, 135, 212, 297
Title I Programme 50
Title II Programme 50, 51, 53
Title III Programme 50
Tobacco Board of Zambia 74
Tonga 297, 299
TRAID 161
Trinidad and Tobago 199, 304, 306, 391
Trust Fund Bureau 125
Tunisia 70, 84, 141
Turkey 49, 66, 190
Turks Islands 304, 306

Uganda 141
Union pour le financement et l'expansion du commerce international (UFINEX) 84
United Arab Emirates 199, 217, 268
United Kingdom 6, 34, 36, 37, 55–79
  Development Assistance Policy 61–5
  financial flows 65–79
  financial resources 57, 79
  management of aid programme 65–7
  Official Development Assistance 55–9
  private flows 59–61
  project appraisal in developing countries 67
United Nations Conference on Trade and Development (UNCTAD) 490–1
United Nations Industrial Development Organisation (UNIDO) xx

United Nations Second Development Decade 472
United Nations Seventh Special Session 1
United Nations Third Development Decade 473
United States 6, 34, 36, 37, 39–53
  development assistance programme 42–8
  foreign aid programme 43
  official development assistance 39–40
  private flow 40–2
Upper Volta 143
Uruguay 390

Venezuela 199, 268
Venezuelan Fund 14, 206
Vietnam 84, 173, 297

West Germany 8, 31, 34–7, 64, 97–117
  Development Assistance Policy 101–3
  financial flows 104–17
  financial resources 98, 117
  Official Development Assistance 97–9
  private flows 99–101
Western Samoa 297, 299
Windward Islands 303
World Bank Group xx, 3, 21–5, 27, 39, 66, 254, 285, 356–8, 369, 372, 376, 377, 380, 394, 395, 479, 480
World Development Fund 480
World Development Report
  1978 376, 480
  1979 481
  1980 482
  1981 482–3
World Food Programme 50

Yemen Arab Republic 240, 391
Yemen Democratic Republic 238, 240
Yugoslavia 141, 190

Zaire 70
Zambia 58

DATE DUE			

PRINTED IN U.S.A.